ALABAMA

A Guide to the Deep South

ALABAMA
A Guide to the Deep South

NEW REVISED EDITION
ALYCE BILLINGS WALKER, *Editor*

Originally Compiled by the Federal Writers Project
of the Works Progress Administration
in the State of Alabama, later called
the Writers Program

ILLUSTRATED

AMERICAN GUIDE SERIES
HARRY HANSEN, *General Editor*

HASTINGS HOUSE ● *Publishers* ● New York

Copyright © 1975 by Hastings House, Publishers, Inc. New York

Copyright © 1941 by The Alabama State Planning Commission

Library of Congress Cataloging in Publication Data

Walker, Alyce Billings, 1907-
  Alabama.

  (American guide series)
  "Originally compiled by the Federal Writers Project
of the Works Progress Administration in the State of
Alabama."
    Bibliography: p.
    Includes index.
    1. Alabama—Description and travel—1951-
Guide-books. 2. Alabama. I. Writers' Program.
Alabama. Alabama; a guide to the deep South.
II. Title. III. Series.
F324.3.W34   1975   917.61'04'6   75-16314

ISBN 0-8038-0391-5

Published simultaneously in Canada by
Saunders of Toronto, Ltd., Don Mills, Ontario

Printed in the United States of America

A Note About the New Revised Edition

In presenting this, the first revised edition of *Alabama, A Guide to the Deep South,* since its original issue, the publisher offers an updated version of an important unit of the American Guide Series. This pioneer collection of books, covering the states and major cities of the Union, began "as part of a nation-wide plan to give employment to professionally trained writers, journalists, and research workers," during the depression years. Called the Federal Writers Project, it was a part of the Works Progress Administration authorized by the United States Congress. Henry G. Alsberg was director of the Project, 1935-39, and set the pattern for the series. In Alabama Myrtle Miles was State supervisor.

The new Federal policy of providing sustenance for artists was the beginning of relief measures on a national scale and stirred up considerable opposition among conservatives. By 1939 this was strong enough in Congress to force curtailment of appropriations for the arts. A new act stipulated that 25 percent of the cost of any State Guide must be provided by non-Federal agencies. In less than two years later all Government help ended. In its final phase the enterprise underwent a change of organization and nomenclature. The Alabama State Planning Commission stood sponsor until completion. The Project became the Writers' Program, and the WPA became the Works Projects Administration. William H. Bunce became State supervisor and Jack Kytle and Luther Clark were the editors when the *Alabama Guide* appeared in May, 1941. The record of the extraordinary labors that produced the American Guide Series is now an indelible part of our literary history; it is described in detail by Jerry Mangione in *The Dream and the Deal.*

Since publication of the original *Guide* Alabama has passed through a period of vast social and political change. It has exchanged an empire of cotton for the steel supremacy of the South; has become the laboratory for a huge Federal regional experiment, and the arsenal for the conquest of air space. To record the postwar changes in cities and countryside and yet retain the basic accomplishments of the Federal writers, is the aim of the present revised edition.

v

Contents

Part I. Alabama Yesterday and Today

Part II. Cities

Part III. Tours

Appendix

Illustrations

Gorgas House, on campus of University of Alabama, Tuscaloosa, home of Dr. William Crawford Gorgas
State Bureau of Publicity & Information
Contemporary Collegiate Architecture: Hugh Merrill Business Administration at Jacksonville State University, built 1970
Jacksonville State University
The Towers—Not Apartment Buildings but Student Dormitories, Florence State University, 1967
Florence State University

Maps

General Information

Alabama, the key state of the Deep South, has 51,609 square miles and is the 29th State in area. In 1970 it had 3,444,165 population, as compared with 3,266,740 in 1960, an increase of 5.4 percent, and was 20th in size of population among the States of the Union.

Of the 3,444,165 population, 2,528,983 were white, 908,247 black, and 6,935 of other races. Among both whites and blacks females exceeded males in number.

Alonso Pineda, Spanish explorer, was the first man to enter Mobile Bay in 1519. Hernando de Soto crossed the upper central part in 1540. The French built a fort in 1702 and started a settlement at Mobile in 1711. Alabama was part of the U. S. Territory of Mississippi in 1798, became Alabama Territory March 3, 1817. Alabama became a State December 14, 1819. Alabama is believed to be a rendering of the name of an Indian tribe.

The original *Great Seal* of the State was altered by the Reconstruction legislature of 1878 and restored to use in 1939. It bears a Latin motto meaning "We dare defend our rights."

The *State Flag,* adopted in 1895, consists of a crimson cross of St. Andrew on a field of white.

The *State Flower* is the red camellia, adopted 1959, supplanting the 1927 choice of the goldenrod.

The *State Tree* is the Southern Pine, specifically the long leaf pine.

The *State Bird* is the yellowhammer. Originally Confederate troops from Alabama acquired the nickname, Yellowhammers.

The *State Song,* Alabama, was written by Miss Julia S. Tutwiler, famous educator, and has music composed by Mrs. Edna Gockel Gussen of Birmingham, in 1931.

Alabama was long called the Cotton State. In recent years it often has been called Heart of Dixie.

Airlines: Delta, Eastern, National, Southern, United. Taxi service: Air South, Cherokee, Dixie Air.

Highways: 5 Interstate, 207 State. Highway Patrol controls all Federal, State, and County roads. Gasoline tax averages 12.62¢ per gallon, including 7¢ per gallon State tax plus a 1¢ per gallon Federal tax, and local taxes ranging from 1¢ to 3¢ per gallon in 249 Alabama cities and 12 counties.

Bus Lines: Greyhound Lines, Continental Trailways, intrastate lines.

Steamship: The Port of Mobile is served by more than 100 steamship lines, with connections to the major ports of Latin America, United Kingdom, Europe, Mediterranean, Africa, Asia and the Pacific. Limited passenger service is available.

Recreational Areas: There are 21 State parks, 8 State forests, 5 national forests, 21 public lakes, 49 campgrounds, and many privately operated resort and recreation areas. Tourists are governed in State and national areas by regulations of the State Department of Conservation and Natural Resources; copies may be obtained from the department in Montgomery or from any ranger. Fires caused by negligence draw heavy fines.

Motor Vehicle Regulations: Alabama asks drivers to observe "a careful and prudent speed not greater than is reasonable and proper," safeguarding persons and property. When a driver's view is obstructed he cuts speed to 15 mph. on approaching curves or grade crossings; also when passing a school during recess or when children are entering or leaving. Traffic in a business district moves at 20 mph, in residence areas and public parks at 25 mph. Trucks, semi-trailer trucks and cars carrying property must observe a 40 mph. limit outside cities. Minimum age for drivers is 16 years; non-resident license is not required of visitors. A driver's manual is obtainable at highway patrol stations.

Fishing Laws: Fresh-water game fish are defined as large- and small-mouthed bass, catfish, pickerel, walleyed pike, shellcracker (red ear sunfish), yellow bass, bluegill, white lake bass, sauger, spotted bass and crappie. Salt-water fish are tarpon, channel bass (redfish), sailfish, red snapper, speckled trout, dolphin, flounder, saltwater striped bass, grouper, cobia (ling), bonita, bluefish, mackerel.

Open Season: Open throughout year.

Licenses: Required of all persons over 16 using rod and reel or artificial lure or bait in public streams and bodies of water in which fresh-water fish appear. Resident: $2.15. Non-resident: $5.00. Annual; $2.00, good for seven consecutive days.

Limits (daily): walleyed pike (jack salmon), 15; pickerel (jack), 15; black bass (trout or green trout), 15; yellow bass, 30; white lake bass (striped bass), 30; crappie or white perch, 50; bream (bluegill, shellcracker, redbreast, warmouth, rock bass and other species) in aggregate of all kinds, 50; saltwater striped bass, 5; yellow perch, 50; rainbow trout, 3. No size limitations.

Prohibited: Sale of all game fish taken from public waters; transporting of more than one day's catch of game fish beyond State borders; failure to carry or transport openly all game fish taken; use of devices other than ordinary hook and line, fly, troll, or spinner for catching game fish; use of game fish for bait.

Hunting Laws: Game birds are defined as bobwhite quail, ruffed grouse, wild turkey, wild duck, wild goose, brant, rail, sora, coot (*Poule d'Eaux or Mud Hen*), jacksnipe (Wilson snipe), woodcock, dove, gallinule and merganser. Game animals are defined as alligator, bear, beaver, deer (antlered bucks only), opossum, rabbit, raccoon, squirrel, nutria and fox.

Open Season: Deer, Nov.13-Jan. 11; turkey (gobblers only) Nov. 13-Jan. 11, Mar. 20-Apr. 26; bobwhite quail, Nov. 20-Feb. 27; squirrel, Oct. 15-Jan. 11; rabbit (hunted with guns), Oct. 15-Feb. 27; raccoon & opossum, Oct. 15-Feb. 27; beaver, nutria & fox, no closed season; startlings & blackbirds, no closed season; bear & alligator, no open season; dove, Sept. 21-Nov. 9, Dec. 19-Jan. 7; rail, Nov. 7-Jan. 15; gallinule, Nov. 7-Jan. 15; woodcock, Dec. 13-Feb. 15; Wilson's snipe & jacksnipe, Dec. 13-Feb. 15; duck, Nov. 23-Jan. 16; coot, Nov. 23-Jan. 16; merganser, Nov. 23-Jan. 16; goose, Nov. 14-Jan. 22; teal season sunrise to sunset (except Baldwin & Mobile Counties), Sept. 22-Sept. 30.

Licenses: Required for all hunters over 16. Issued by probate judges and other authorized persons in counties. Resident: state, $3.00; county, $1.00; over 65, 25¢. Non-resident: annual all game, $25.15; annual small game, $10.15; 7-day trip all game, $10.15; 7-day trip small game, $7.15.

Limits: Deer, 1 per day; turkey (gobblers only), 1 a day, 5 during combined fall and spring season; bobwhite quail, 10 a day-10 in possession; squirrel, 8 a day-8 in possession; rabbit, 8 a day-8 in possession; raccoon & opossum, no bag limit; beaver, nutria & fox (daylight hours only), no bag limit; startlings & blackbirds, no bag limit; dove (12 noon to sunset), 18 a day-18 in possession; rail (sunrise to sunset), 15 a day-15 in possession; gallinule (half hour before sunrise to sunset), woodcock, (half hour before sunrise to sunset), 5 a day-5 in possession; Wilson's snipe and jacksnipe, 8 a day, 8 in possession; duck, 6 a day, 12 in possession (daily bag limit may not include more than 2 mallard, 2 wood ducks, 1 redhead or 1 canvasback. Possession limit may not include more than 4 mallards, 4 wood ducks, 1 canvasback or 1 redhead); coot, 15 a day, 30 in possession; merganser, 5 a day, 10 in possession; goose, 5 a day, 5 in possession; special teal season 4 a day, 8 in possession. Migratory birds: State regulations conform to Federal regulations.

Prohibited: Sale of all game. Possession of fur, skin or pelt by fur catcher, dealer, or buyer longer than 20 days after close of season. Baiting of game birds or animals. Hunting on private lands without owner's written permission. Use of live decoys in hunting waterfowl. Possession of more than one day's bag limit of any game bird, game or fur-bearing animal, at any time except where the bag limit of two days is permitted as provided by regulation. Shooting dove between sunset and 12:00 p.m. Any electrically amplified bird calls or sounds whether real or imitation (except crow calls). Any crossbow. Any live decoys, except when hunting unprotected birds or animals. Any dog when hunting turkeys. Deer from water. Failure to carry or transport all game birds or animals openly. Destroying sex of deer or wild turkey (regulation not intended to prevent dressing, for consumption).

Hunting and trapping in State parks, forests & sanctuaries. Possession of firearms in any Wildlife Management Area, refuge or sanctuary. Hunting with shotgun larger than 10-gauge or holding more than three shells at one loading. Hunting or exploding firearm within a distance of 100 yards of any public road, highway or railroad (logging railroad excepted).

Tourists are advised to secure the latest digest of hunting & fishing laws. Hunting limits and open seasons vary in certain counties and/or sections of the State. Digest may be obtained from the Department of Conservation and Natural Resources, Game & Fish Division, Montgomery, Alabama, 36104.

Aboriginal Mounds and Diggings: Indian mounds, burial sites, and fossiliferous strata are numerous in Alabama. Ownership of these and other prehistoric objects is vested in the State. Unauthorized exploration of sites and shipping of prehistoric remains is unlawful and heavy fines are imposed for violations.

Climate and Equipment: Weather usually warm but not uncomfortable, April through September; light weight clothing suitable for season. Moderate temperatures prevail in spring and fall; top coats advisable. Severe winters are rare; snow is unusual. Highway traffic might be interrupted by weather conditions during the months of December, January and February, but such occurrences are rare.

Poisonous Insects, Snakes and Plants: Watch for rattlesnakes and moccasins in heavy undergrowth. Be careful of poison oak, which has a three part leaf, resembling that of an oak. Remember the old adage, "Leaves three, let it be." "Fire ants" are found in this area, watch for mounds, which are easily recognizable, usually the mound has a reddish tint.

Drinking Water: Water from wells in use and free flowing springs may be used safely. Avoid drinking stream water.

Trespass: State laws prohibit wanton picking and digging of wild shrubs and flowers. These laws are strictly enforced.

Calendar of Annual Events

Events, festivals, and exhibitions are listed under the months in which they open. When no specific date is given consult newspapers and public offices of information.

JANUARY

Flower Show, Bellingrath Gardens, Theodore. Camellias in full bloom in the Gardens and Camellia Arboretum.
Art Exhibit, Bellingrath Gardens, Theodore. Exhibit continues through February).
Flea Market, Fayette. Every first Saturday of the month, year around. Fayette Art Museum sponsors at National Guard Armory.
Barter Day, Scottsboro. First Monday of each month. Natives from the surrounding mountains flock to the Court House Square. Coon dogs, antiques and junk are swapped and sold, accompanied by strumming banjos, voices exchanging news and gossip, and the occasional thump of a domino.
Southern Regional Angus Cattle Show & Sale, Montgomery. Sponsored by Alabama Angus Association, at Garrett Coliseum.
Senior Bowl Football Game, Mobile.
Azalea Trail Queen Coronation, Mobile, at Senior Bowl Football Game. The queen is chosen from over 50 local high school seniors. Scholarships awarded.
Annual Camellia Show and Art Exhibit, Tuscaloosa. Art Exhibit sponsored by West Alabama Artists' Association. Tuscaloosa High School Auditorium.

FEBRUARY

Art Guild Annual Show, Montgomery Museum of Fine Arts, Montgomery.
Southeastern Handicrafts, Montgomery Museum of Fine Arts, Montgomery.
National Shooting Dog Championship, Sedgefields Plantation, Union Springs. Usually takes a full week to complete the annual field trials for bird dogs. Any registered pointer or setter is eligible to run. Dogs must be handled by amateurs only. Handlers ride horseback. Dogs must be shot over at least once with a shotgun of 410 gauge or larger. Auspices of the National Shooting Dogs Championship Association.
Mardi Gras Day, Mobile. Gala parades and balls ten days prior to Ash Wednesday. Krewe de Bienville Ball is held for visitors to the City.
Deep South Rattlesnake Rodeo. Opp. The roundup climaxes two months of rattlesnake hunting. Prizes for the most rattlers, with many other categories and prizes. Many special events at end of Rodeo, one of which is a rattlesnake race in downtown Opp on the last day of Rodeo. Beauty contest selects Rodeo Queen. There is also a Rattler Barbeque in front of the Parkmore Restaurant.
Azalea Trail Festival, Mobile. Observance of blossoming of Mobile azaleas. A 35-mile floral extravaganza. Continues into March.
Azalea Trail Festival Square & Round Dance, Mobile. Mobile Municipal Auditorium, Feb. 26-27. For additional information, write to: Mobile Square Dance Association. P.O. Box 6082, Mobile, Alabama 36606.

MARCH

Flower Show, Bellingrath Gardens, Theodore. Spectacular display of flowering azaleas. Mobile Azalea Trail Maids in antebellum costumes in Gardens on weekends.

Annual South Baldwin Trailriders American Quarter Horse Show, Foley. Trailrider Arena, Highway 59 in Foley.

Mobile's Iron Lace & Classic Columns Tour. Mobile, Mar. 15-April 5. Historic southern homes, buildings, and churches. For tickets and additional information contact Tour Headquarters, lobby of Mobile Housing Board, 151 S. Clairborne, Mobile.

Alabama State Junior Steer Show, Garrett Coliseum, Montgomery. Sponsored by Alabama Department of Agriculture & Industries, Alabama State Steer Show Association and Montgomery Area Chamber of Commerce.

Southeastern Livestock Exposition & Rodeo, Montgomery. Also complete week of livestock show activities made up of steer shows. Sponsored by Alabama Cattlemen's Association.

Antiques Show & Sale, Mobile. Dealers from several states stock booths with treasures benefit YMCA, 1060 Government Street, Mobile.

Candelight Tour, Mobile. Tour of Oakleigh Historic House Museum and private homes. Sponsored by Oakleigh Garden Club.

Birmingham Festival of Arts, Birmingham. Founded in 1951, the Festival includes Symphony concerts by the Birmingham Symphony Orchestra, International Fair. Ambassador's Weekend, plus special events sponsored by local civic organizations.

Dogwood Trail Queen Selection & Coronation, Fairhope. Local high school seniors vie for selection as Queen and Court to preside over activities related to 14-mile long route of rural beauty where dogwoods bloom profusely. Trail goes from Spanish Fort through towns of Daphne, Montrose and Fairhope.

Arts & Crafts Week, Fairhope.

Lowndesboro Pilgrimage, Lowndesboro. Annual pilgrimage of antebellum homes, sponsored by Lowndesboro Garden Club.

APRIL

Eufaula Pilgrimage, Eufaula. Opening of impressive antebellum homes during the Spring. Trained hostesses and Southern Belles in hoop skirts will conduct tours of the historic houses.

Eufaula Pilgrimage Antique Show and Sale, Eufaula. Approximately 20 antique dealers from several states exhibit rare items.

Easter Sunrise Services, Mound State Park, Moundville. 19 miles Southeast of Tuscaloosa on Highway 69.

Alabama Jubilee Walking Horse Show, Garrett Coliseum, Montgomery. Sponsored by Alabama Walking Horse Association.

Mobile—Dauphin Island Yacht Race, Fairhope to Dauphin Island. 150 yachts and 500 crewman race.

Open House, Ave Maria Grotto, St. Bernard College, Cullman. The intricate replicas are the lifetime work of Brother Joseph Zoettl, a Benedictine monk of St. Bernard Abbey and College.

Pilgrimage of Homes, Tuscaloosa. Both antebellum mansions and contemporary homes with antiques. Sponsored by the Tuscaloosa County Preservation Society.

House and Garden Tour, Montgomery.

Spring Art, Crafts, & Hobby Fair, Camp Grandview, Millbrook, April 17. Hiking, fishing, swimming, group singing and square dancing; puppet shows.

Chilton County Singing Convention, Chilton County Courthouse, Clanton.

Camera Day, Bellingrath Gardens, Theodore. Junior Misses representing all 50 states.

Fishing Rodeo, Centre. Sponsored by Centre Jaycees and held on Weiss Lake.

Art on the Lake Show, Guntersville. Open to all having original art to display. Contact Guntersville Chamber of Commerce. 20th Century Club.

America's Junior Miss Pageant, Mobile. High School senior girls from 50 states compete in a week-long pageant for the title of America's Junior Miss, as well as thousands of dollars in educational scholarships. Nationally televised.

Annual Tea and Tour, Oakleigh, Mobile. Contact Historic Mobile Preservation Society, 350 Oakleigh Place, Mobile, Alabama 36604, for additional information.

MAY

Art League Clothesline Show, Huntsville. Spring show, first week.

Mountain Laurel Festival, Rock Bridge Canyon, Hodges, first two weeks.

America's Junior Miss Pageant, Mobile—Finals.

Civitan Horse Show, Guntersville.

Annual Bellingrath Art Exhibit, Bellingrath Gardens, Theodore, all month.

Winston 500, Alabama International Motor Speedway, Talladega—NASCAR. Grand National Stock Car Race over the 2.66 mile, high-banked trioval.

Fishing Rodeo, Centre. Sponsored by Centre Jaycees and held on Weiss Lake.

Alabama Fresh Water Fishing Rodeo, Lake Eufaula, Eufaula. Children's Rodeo, also. For information, write Eufaula Chamber of Commerce, P.O. Box 347, Eufaula, Alabama.

JUNE

North South Limited Hydro Plane Races, Braham Spring Park, Huntsville.

Annual Pasture Fence Art Show, Center City Park, Centre.

Tennessee Valley Art Association's Annual Art Show, Tuscumbia, held at birthplace of Helen Keller, "Ivy Green."

Annual Windcreek Rock Swap, Alexander City. Sponsored jointly by the Alabama Mineral and Lapidary Society and Martin Lake Rock and Gem Club.

Northeast Alabama Potato Festival, Fort Payne. Beauty Pageant.

JWA Horse Show, Tuscaloosa.

Pilgrimage of Homes, Fort Payne.

Randolph County Horse Show, Wedowee. Third Saturday.

Chilton County Peach Festival, Clanton. Festival includes selection of Peach Queen.

Boat Races. Guntersville. Contact Guntersville Junior Chamber of Commerce for dates and details. Last days of June.

JULY

Boat Races, Guntersville.

Photo Exhibit, Bellingrath Gardens, Theodore. All month.

Independence Day Barbeque, Clanton.

Independence Day, Fairhope. Sponsored by Eastern Shore Jaycees, P.O. Box 726, Fairhope.

"The Miracle Worker", Ivy Green, Tuscumbia. William Gibson's powerful drama portraying Helen Keller's heroic struggle with the dual handicaps, deafness and blindness. Sponsored by the Helen Keller Property Board and the American Association of University Women. Staged at the birthplace of Helen Keller. Performances given every Friday evening at 8:15 p.m. throughout July and August. Adults, $1.50; students, $.75.

AUGUST

Future Masters Golf Tournament, Dothan. Boys from the age of 7 to 18 competing for trophies in their own age groups, at Dothan Country Club.
"The Miracle Worker", Ivy Green. Tuscumbia. Continues during August.
Photo Exhibit, Bellingrath Gardens, Theodore. All month.
Talladega 500, Alabama International Motor Speedway, Talladega. NASCAR Grand National Stock Car Race over the 2.66-mile, high-banked trioval track.
Annual Lake Eufaula Festival, Eufaula. National Championship Boat Races sanctioned by the National Outboard Association. Sidewalk Art Show including professional, non-professional and children's divisions, Western exhibition dances, Miss Lake Eufaula Beauty Pageant, band concerts, barbeque, ski show. Under the sponsorship of the Eufaula Chamber of Commerce.
Chilton County Fair, Gragg Field, Clanton, last week in August. Agricultural and industrial exhibits. Prize stock awards.

SEPTEMBER

Talladega 200, Alabama International Motor Speedway, Talladega. American Motorcycle Association Championship Race.
Labor Day Barbeque, Clanton, auspices Masonic Lodge.
Madison County Fair, Huntsville.
Manitou Cave Art Show, Fort Payne, Held on Sunday after Labor Day. 9:00 a.m. until sunset. Open to all artists.
Arlington Country Fair, Birmingham. On the Lawn of Arlington, Birmingham's antebellum home. Clowns, games and contests, tally-ho and carousel rides, antiques, art treasures.
West Alabama Fair, Tuscaloosa, sponsored by Tuscaloosa Jaycees, Inc., Jaycee Park.

OCTOBER

Annual Tennessee Valley Old Time Fiddlers Convention, Athens College. Early American rural music revived by competition. Impromptu music making, exhibits of antique rural music instruments and anvil shoots. Sometimes called the "poor man's cannon" the anvil shoot, like old time fiddling, is from America's pioneer past.
Chilton County Singing Convention, Chilton County Courthouse, Clanton.
Annual Shades Mountain Arts and Crafts Show, Birmingham. Bluff Park Community Center atop Shades Mountain. For information contact the Bluff Park Art Association, P.O. Box 26012, Birmingham, Alabama 35216.
Dekalb County VFW Agricultural Fair, Fort Payne, 2nd week. VFW Fairgrounds. North Fort Payne. Tents House Agricultural Exhibits; school, club and educational exhibits from all parts of the county.
Alabama State Fair, Brimingham. Alabama's showcase of industry, space achievements, education, agriculture and livestock. Cash prizes to winning exhibitors. Free Grandstand show. Fair Park has mile long carnival with 30 rides and entertainment devices. Fireworks provide the finale for each night's Grandstand performance.
Flower Show, Bellingrath Gardens, Theodore. Display of chrysanthemums all month.
Fall Sailing Festival, Fairhope. Southeast area small sail craft gather for two days of racing and entertainment.
October Folk Festival and Arts and Crafts Show, Horses Pens 40, Steele. Featuring Arts and Crafts from the Southern United States, along with folk singing, folk drama and folk foods.
National Peanut Festival, Dothan. A full week of festivities; national celebrities and beauties, parades, carnival and fair, soap box derby, dancing

and a beauty pageant. A parade climaxes the week's events and is usually viewed by an estimated 150,000 people.

South Alabama State Fair, Garret Coliseum, Montgomery. Agricultral, educational, livestock, homemaking, community and commercial exhibits. Sponsored by the Kiwanis Club of Montgomery.

Annual Greater Gulf State Fair, Hartwell Field Fair Grounds, Mobile. Staged by the Mobile Junior Chamber of Commerce. Livestock and agricultural exhibits. Individual exhibits in homemaking, art, ceramics, hobbies and flowers with prizes, medals and ribbons to winners.

West Alabama Fair, Tuscaloosa. Sponsored by Tuscaloosa Jaycees, Inc., Jaycee Park.

NOVEMBER

Rock and Gem Show, Fairhope. Regional hobbyists and professionals convene for showing, swapping and selling semi-precious and novelty stones. Sponsored by the Eastern Shore Tourist and Adult Recreation Club.

World's Largest Display of Chrysanthemums, Bellingrath Gardens, Theodore, all month. Literally millions of blooms of every variety and almost every color.

Southern Championship Charity Walking and Gaited Horse Show, Garrett Coliseum, Montgomery. Sponsored by Southern Championship Charity Horse Show Association.

Festival of Sacred Music, Municipal Auditorium, Birmingham. Wed., Thurs. & Fri. During Thanksgiving Week, features Symphony Orchestra and entertainers, with audience participation in sacred hymns.

Junk and Jewels Sale, Mobile. World Fellowship International Tasting Bee in Conjunction.

Sturdivant Museum Antiques Show, Selma Armory, Selma.

Annual Speckled Trout Rodeo, Gulf Shores, for visitors only. Separate contest for local fishermen. A Beauty Queen is chosen. Sponsored by the Foley-Gulf Shores Jaycees. Contact Gulf Shores Information Center. Telephone 968-7134.

DECEMBER

Christmas Parade, Clanton. Ceremony lighting street decorations.

Night Christmas Parade, Fairhope. 60 to 70 units, ranging from bands to decorated aircrafts.

Holiday Flower Show, Bellingrath Gardens, Theodore. Mass blooming of poinsettias and other seasonal plants and flowers.

Hanging of the Greens ceremony, Mobile. Christmas musical program.

Carols Sing-A-Long. YWCA, 1060 Government Street, Mobile.

Christmas at Arlington, antebellum home, Birmingham, Dec. 11-12.

Blue-Gray Football Classic, Cramton Bowl, Montgomery.

PART I

Alabama Yesterday and Today

Alabama Old and New

U NTIL THE mid-Twentieth Century, Alabama was vaguely
thought of as a land of cotton, of white-pillared mansions and
blacks singing spirituals in the fields.

While vestiges of this image still exist in a few places, particularly
in South Alabama, good and bad events have wrought dramatic
changes in the State. A one-crop agrarian economy has been diversified
and supplemented by a landswell of new industries. Black "hoe hands,"
replaced by machinery, have fled the farms for cities. Stately ante
bellum mansions are today as often historic shrines as they are dwellings.
And a two-party political system is flowering where formerly there were
just Democrats.

There may still be some to whom Alabama is a vague "some place
down South," but its three-time governor, George Corley Wallace,
has been in the national and international consciousness since 1963.

That year, racial turmoil put Alabama and its segregationist governor into sharp focus worldwide.

A year-long bus boycott in Montgomery led by a young black
Baptist minister, Martin Luther King, Jr.; Wallace's "stand in the
schoolhouse door" to prevent integration of the University of Alabama;
mass demonstrations in Birmingham and the Selma-to-Montgomery
march, both also led by King, attracted national attention and were step-
ping stones to the Civil Rights Acts of 1964 and 1965.

Espousing opposition to Federal interference with states rights,
Wallace twice, in 1968 and 1972, made determined but unsuccessful
bids for the presidency of the United States. Again in 1974, Wallace
ran for an unprecedented third gubernatorial term and prepared to influence the nomination for the presidency in 1976.

As Alabamians made the difficult adjustments to the Federally-
imposed Civil Rights decisions, fast changing economic conditions began
drawing them into a closer-knit group. The conflicting interests of
agriculture and industry began to lose their former bitterness. Accelerated activities in both fields proved the value of cooperation. Resulting higher incomes, better education, better roads, diversified agriculture and new industries are the catalysts that have made today's
Alabamians a more homogeneous people, with a vibrant State pride.

Previously, the life of the Appalachian mountaineers had nothing
in common with the cosmopolitan culture of the Gulf Coast, and the
Alabamians of industrial Birmingham were totally different from those

3

of the agrarian Black Belt. And while in some sections, Alabamians still cling to the pattern of tradition, the majority now are not so much concerned about where a person was born and what his great-grand-father did at Shiloh and Gettysburg, as about his political opinions and what he himself is accomplishing.

Influx of new industries and a shift in population, especially the exodus of blacks from farms and from the State, have been the most compelling factors in developing a new Alabamian. The shift in population since World War II illustrates the growth of the cities. According to U. S. Census reports, the State in 1940 was 30.2 percent urban and 69.8 rural. In 1950 it was 40.1 percent urban 59.9 percent rural. In 1960 more than half the people were in cities; the State was 51.9 percent urban, 48.1 percent rural. Finally, in the Census of 1970, Alabama had 3,444,163 population, an increase of 177,425, with 58.4 percent urban and 41.6 percent rural.

Twenty-five of the State's 67 counties had fewer people in 1970 than in 1900, all of them rural. Nine counties—Jefferson, Mobile, Montgomery, Madison, Calhoun, Etowah, Morgan, Lauderdale—had over one-half the State's population, and more than 40 percent lived in the first five, according to the U. S. Census.

Blacks composed only 26 percent of the State's population in 1970. Most of them were concentrated in urban centers where they out-numbered whites 62 percent to 57 percent. On the other hand, in 10 rural Black Belt Counties where the ratio of blacks to whites used to be four to one, they now make up little more than half of the population.

This population shift has been accompanied by a steadily increasing inequity of representation in the lawmaking process at both state and national levels. Only until the Federal courts intervened to make the Legislature reapportion itself did the stranglehold exercised by the rural counties begin to lessen.

The upturn in industrialization of Alabama is reflected in the fact that more than 15 firms operating in the State are listed among the leading corporations by *Fortune,* and 15 foreign-based companies have come into the State within the last decade. During 1973, capital investment for new manufacturing plants and expansion of existing facilities reached $1,652,726,535.

These industries are scattered all over the State with only a few counties not sharing in them. For instance, Degussa, a West German industrial giant, is building a $200 million chemical complex, and the American-German Dow Badische Corp. is erecting a $100 million facility in the Mobile area. Sweden's Soderhamm Machine Manufacturing Co. is making forestry machinery at Talladega. Freese Chemical Co., a Japanese joint venture, is making para-cresol at Tuscaloosa.

New industries have meant new and different kinds of jobs for Alabamians, and at the same time have brought new people into the State. The result is a statewide meld of different backgrounds, a merger of old and new, that is giving Alabama a fascinating dual personality. It is not unusual that there will be a symphony concert and a fiddlers' convention in the same locale on the same day, or that a scholarly scientist will say "ya'll", for you all, with a German accent.

However, despite surface changes and a deceptive informal friendliness, it still isn't easy for "outsiders" to crash the bastions of old established Black Belt society. It is in this amazingly fertile central area of the State where the planter class ruled a kingdom founded on cotton and slaves, that the image of the Old South persists most. Many of the families still live on ancestral plantations, but the large servant staffs are missing. Even Selma, on the Alabama River, important transportation point in the steamboat days and arsenal of the Confederacy, is now a mixture of old and new. The same can be said of Tusculoosa, at the fall line of the Black Warrior River, home of the main campus of the University of Alabama and state capital from 1825 to 1846. Many of its beautiful homes were built during this period, when cotton barges and steamboats made regular trips to Mobile. Today, the Druid City—so-called because of the ancient water oaks that line its streets—is crowded the year around with thousands of students while on its outskirts manufacturing plants have replaced cotton fields.

Cotton and rivers were the foundation upon which Old South cities were built. Montgomery, capital of the state and often called Cradle of the Confederacy, has had its downtown spruced up through Urban Renewal. But it is still flanked by cotton fields, and the Alabama River—formed by the confluence of the Coosa and Tallapoosa six miles away—flows past the business district. The white-domed capitol on Goat Hill looks down on beloved landmarks of earlier times, on the impressive buildings that house present-day government activities, and also on textile mills, tile plants and other industries.

On the other hand, a blend of people and life styles has existed in Birmingham since two railroads met there in 1870 and a city was born. Its early tales of land auctions and meteoric business careers have a western boom town flavor. People were drawn from all parts of the nation and from foreign countries by the discovery of rich deposits of iron, coal and limestone, the ingredients for making steel. Still the State's industrial hub and its largest city, Birmingham also continues to be a sophisticated metropolis with many small town attributes.

A mixing of old and new has been underway in the northern part of the State ever since the Tennessee Valley Authority began harnessing the Tennessee River. It was enhanced with the arrival in Huntsville of Wernher Von Braun and his team of more than a thousand German scientists, and swelled by the advent of thousands of other newcomers to man industries supporting the nation's space program.

New arrivals in that section of Alabama found stately, old public buildings and handsome private mansions, relics of the days when rich, slave-holding North Alabama planters lived as lavishly as did their fellow citizens in the Black Belt. Fortunately, these reminders of a glamorous past have not been sacrificed to present-day architecture.

The current impact of new industry, however, is to be seen and felt most in the Mobile area. In addition to the aforementioned new industries, a multi-million dollar expansion of the State Docks and a projected off-shore superport to handle supertankers hauling crude oil, will further point Mobile toward national greatness and diversify its population. It is doubtful, however, that any amount of industry will greatly alter the character of Mobile, which is markedly different from the rest of Alabama.

Though it likes to call itself the City of Five Flags—French, Spanish, English, Confederate and United States—Mobile shows surprisingly few traces of its French and Spanish past. The city was already firmly established when the rest of Alabama was a wilderness. As the State developed, its cotton and other products came to Mobile, Alabama's only port, by water and rail for shipment to foreign lands. The city's long maritime contact with the outside world give it an indefinable cosmopolitan atmosphere that sets it apart from Alabama's other cities. Old customs survive and social lines are still closely drawn —not so much from snobbishness but because of deep-rooted traditions that modern ideas find hard to overcome. Mobile is proud of its new industrial status, but at the same time it preserves its old homes and churches, its moss-draped live oaks and its famous azaleas. It celebrates Mardi Gras with pomp and pageantry, and with an eye on the tourist trade.

Textiles were the first industry to take up the employment slack in Alabama's economy when mechanization reduced the number of needed farm workers. Such giant companies as Dan River Mills, Monsanto Textiles, Westpoint Pepperell, Crumpton Company, Vanity Fair and others as large joined the already Alabama-owned Avondale Mills and Russell Corp. to make textiles Alabama's "Golden Needle," and to turn many sleepy villages into bustling towns. The industry employed some 150,000 persons and generated about $560 million in payrolls during 1973.

Paralleling Alabama's industrial growth and its accompanying changes in Alabamians' life style, has been the improved status of "the man of the land." The State's gross agriculture income in 1973 was $1.6 billion. The chicken walked off with honors as source of the largest agriculture income, accounting for $470 million in 1973. And, despite consumer boycotts, federal controls and other problems, 1973 was one of the best years in the relatively new history of cattle raising. Sales, holdings and investments approached the billion dollar mark. Yet another money tree for Alabama is its forestry industries that employ more than 80,000 and contribute around $2 billion each year to the economy.

With such widespread agricultural-industrial activity rampant, it isn't so easy anymore to sectionalize the State. However, the newcomer or the visitor will sooner or later realize that the Alabamians who fit least into the Deep South concept are the natives in the northern part of the State where the spurs of the Appalachians jut down from Tennessee and Georgia. To this region came hardy pioneers who built their pine-pole cabins and scratched small crops from the narrow clearings. They held the rich planters in contempt because they would do no manual labor. The mountaineer's lot is greatly improved today, but he is still strongly independent, reserving the right to be guided by his "self-made notions." His language also differs from that of other Alabamians. It has its sources in Shakespeare's England and flows with the rhythm of the Bible. It still isn't unusual to hear help pronounced holp, wrop for wrap, the past tense of climb, as clumb, and the minister preaching a sarment on Sunday mornings.

To a lesser extent a similar independence and pioneer tradition still prevails in the Red Hills country northwest of Birmingham and south of the Tennessee Valley. Before and during the War Between the States, this section held to its right to choose between the North and the South. Here is the rugged country of "Free Winston," that once threatened to secede from Confederate Alabama and form the independent state of Nickajack. Like the mountaineers, most of the Red Hill Alabamians are descendants of small farmers who had a deep distrust of the aristocratic planter class. Recent industrial development has greatly changed these distinctive characteristics.

The wiregrass lands in the southern corner of the State are almost entirely free of old Alabama tradition. The people here never had the mountaineers' prejudice against the planters, and they were never involved in the agrarian-industrial political struggle. This flat area, dotted with stands of pine, was thought to be of little value in the days when agriculture meant cotton, for it was comparatively poor land for that purpose. Diversified crops and industries dependent upon them were introduced, such as the making of peanut oil and peanut butter processing. The pine stands have been enlarged and improved and are used for lumber and turpentine.

Perhaps the least changed Alabamians are the Cajuns and the Indians. The Cajuns, a group of mixed and undetermined racial origin living in the piney woods north and west of Mobile, also carry on turpentining and lumbering. Entirely unrelated to the Louisiana Cajuns, who are descended from the Acadians of Canada, the Alabama Cajuns claim descent from early French, English and Spanish settlers who intermarried with the Indians. Cherokee Indians still in Alabama are largely settled in Escambia County.

On the east side of Mobile Bay is the "Province of Baldwin," the largest county east of the Mississippi River. A rich agricultural section, practically free of industry, it has always invited and nourished experiments in ideas as well as in business and agriculture. At Fairhope is America's pioneer single tax colony, founded by Iowans, Ohioans, and Pennsylvanians who came here to put into practice the teachings of Henry George. Here also is the School of Organic Education, an institution that has greatly influenced progressive education throughout the country. Germans, Swedes, Russians, Italians, Greeks and Creoles all live in Baldwin County, lovingly preserving many of the traditions of their homelands, while enjoying benefits from agriculture, cattle raising and increased tourist revenue since opening in 1974 of the handsome, mammoth Gulf State Park at Gulf Shores. Gone, however, except for Bon Secour, are the enchanting little fishing villages reminiscent of the southern coasts of Italy and France that used to dot Baldwin's coastline.

Although the sharp lines between old and new Alabama are shadowy today, each part enhances the other as the State shakes off its leisurely-paced past and builds a strong competitive economy.

Alabama Earth; Its Flora and Fauna

NATURAL SETTING

IN the heart of the deep South is Alabama, a roughly rectangular area of 51,998 square miles between 84° 51' and 88° 31' longitude and 30° 13' and 35° north latitude. It is bounded on the north by Tennessee, on the east by Georgia, on the south by Florida and the Gulf of Mexico, and on the west by the State of Mississippi.

The State is mountainous in the northeast, where spurs of the Appalachians penetrate its boundary. From this off-center elevation of approximately 1,800 feet, the land drops sharply northwest to the Tennessee Valley and slopes more gradually toward the south until it reaches sea level. Westward, the land shelves in a gradually diminishing range of hills which divides Alabama into its two principal drainage systems—the basin of the Tennessee River to the north and the great basin of the Alabama and Tombigbee river systems, known as the Mobile Drainage Basin, which covers almost the remainder of the State.

Alabama's variety of natural regions is closely connected with its geology and soil. The Tennessee Valley in the north is a comparatively level section of about 4,900 square miles on both sides of the Tennessee River. The soil is naturally productive, and successful reclamation in recent years has made it the chief row-crop section of the State, as well as the primary cotton producing area.

To the south of the Tennessee Valley is the Coal Region, a plateau and hilly uplands known as the mineral belt, which covers 6,400 square miles in the northern half of the State. Here the Appalachian sandstone rocks, overlain with sandy soils, contain vast deposits of coal, iron ore, and other minerals.

Paralleling the plateau on the southeast is the Coosa Valley Region, a series of ridges and valleys with fairly fertile soils derived from limestone and shale. Caves, natural bridges, and limestone springs are numerous in both this region and the plateau country. The Coosa Valley is more rugged and less suited to agriculture than the Tennessee Valley. Its narrow ridges, a continuation of the Appalachian chain, rise to heights of several hundred feet. Mount Cheaha, the highest peak in the State (2,407 feet), rises from the northern tip of one of the ridges.

The Piedmont Region, southeast of the Coosa Valley, is an area of small hills. The soil, where not badly eroded, is sandy loam, and is red clay where erosion has removed the top soil. If properly cultivated, the reddish soil is fairly productive. Pine trees grow rapidly here and old fields become reforested in a few years.

South of the Piedmont Region is the Central Pine Belt, a moderately hilly area that extends in a broadening arc from the Georgia line to the northwest corner of the State. The soil is sandy with large patches of gravel and marks the northern edge of the Coastal Plain. It takes its name from the shortleaf pines that formerly thrived there.

The Black Belt, a strip of rolling prairie land with a sticky black, calcareous clay soil, formerly the chief cotton-growing area, is now given over almost entirely to cattle and timber. It crosses Alabama south of the pine country and comprises an area of 4,300 square miles. An elevated section of the country, called Chunnennuggee Ridge, stretches in a southwesterly direction from the eastern edge of the Black Belt and forms a watershed for the southeastern portion of the State.

South of the Black Belt and Chunnennuggee Ridge extends the Coastal Plain, largest agricultural region in Alabama, covering an area of about 9,000 square miles. The northern half of this section is called the Red Hills because of the rolling pine-covered hills of red sandy clay. Approaching the coast, the hills become less prominent and slash pine prevails. From here to the coast the soil, a reddish sandy clay, is uniform. The surface is rolling and hilly to the Florida border, flattening out gradually to sandy dunes and hummocks on the coast.

In the southwestern corner of the Coastal Plain is the Mobile Delta, a swamp about five miles wide and 60 miles long. With this exception, there is little swampy land in Alabama and no section in the entire Coastal Plain that corresponds to the pine barrens of the South Atlantic States.

The State has two principal basins—the Escambia and Mobile. The Escambia includes the southeastern Coastal Plain section and extends through Florida to the coast. It takes its name from the Escambia River which flows through Florida into Pensacola Bay. The principal streams in the basin are the Perdido, forming the Florida-Alabama boundary line; the Conecuh, largest tributary of the Escambia, flowing southwestward through Alabama; and the Choctawhatchee in the east. The basin last named is frequently classed as an independent basin, although for convenience it is sometimes included in the Escambia. None of these streams is much over a hundred miles in length, but their drainage basins have a combined area of 21,930 square miles in Alabama and Florida.

Forests of longleaf and slash pine originally covered practically all of the basin and large stands still remain. Gullying has been eliminated by reforestation and soil reclamation. The high rainfall and slow removal due to low elevation provide an abundant supply of surface water throughout the basin.

The Mobile Basin drains all the remainder of the State with the exception of the Tennessee Valley in the extreme northern portion. A vast network of streams constitute this basin—the Mobile, Alabama,

Tombigbee, Black Warrior, Cahaba, Coosa, and Tallapoosa Rivers with their tributaries. The Tombigbee from the north and the Alabama from the northeast unite about 45 miles above Mobile Bay to form the Mobile River, which flows southward into the bay. The Tombigbee is joined at Demopolis, 185 miles above its mouth, by its principal tributary, the Black Warrior. The basin of the Tombigbee is generally rolling or level country with pine forests and swamps in its lower reaches. The Alabama River is formed by the confluence of the Coosa and Tallapoosa Rivers in central Alabama, near Montgomery. The Coosa, which drains nearly half of the Alabama system, is formed at Rome, Georgia, and flows southward through the Appalachian ridges into the Coastal Plain at Wetumpka, about 11 miles above its junction with the Alabama. The Tallapoosa River drains the eastern Plateau Region, dropping sharply into the Coastal Plain. The Cahaba has its source in the uplands near Birmingham, and flows south into the Alabama about 17 miles below Selma.

The largest lakes in Alabama are man-made, by dams on the Tennessee River: Wheeler Lake, with Wheeler Dam in Lauderdale County, covers 104.8 *sq. m.*, has a shoreline of 1,063 *m.* and is 58 ft. deep; Guntersville Lake, in Jackson and Marshall Counties, covers 108 *sq., m.*, has a shoreline of 963 *m.* and is 60 ft. deep.

GEOLOGY AND PALEONTOLOGY

In 1969 excavation for an expressway through Birmingham's Red Mountain exposed 440 million years of geologic time within a quarter mile. This caused great excitement among geologists world wide, and stirred Alabamians into new awareness of the natural wonders of their State.

The "cut," part of a highway exchange system connecting Interstate 280 (southeast of Birmingham) to I-20, I-65 and I-59 (east, northwest and northeast of Birmingham), is 1,850 feet long, 210 feet deep and 150 feet wide. Its revelation of a myriad of fossils and a great variety of mineral and rock types has swelled the already large number of geology students and visitors from all over the United States who come to see the "Big Seam" iron ore that has been exposed for many years on another part of Red Mountain.

Alabama lies within two geologic provinces—the Appalachian Province and the Coastal Plain, which are separated by a continuation of the irregular boundary line known to geologists as the Fall Line of the Atlantic States. It enters Alabama near Columbus, Georgia, passes by Wetumpka and Tuscaloosa and swings to the northwest corner of the State near which it is indented by the valley of the Tennessee River.

The Appalachian Province has three major divisions. Southernmost is the Piedmont Upland in east central Alabama; north of this are the Appalachian Valley and Appalachian Plateau. The Piedmont Upland is underlain by very ancient igneous rock and crystalline schists, mainly of Archean and Algonkian ages. The Appalachian Valley is characterized by long mountain ridges and valleys running northeast and southwest. The stratified rocks are generally highly inclined, due to the folding and faulting of the rock of the Paleozoic or Old Life era, that very long time marked at the beginning by the appearance of sea shells, which have left fossilized remains, and at the end by the completion of the first great period of coal formation. The Appalachian Plateau, stretching from central Alabama toward the northeast is composed of Paleozoic rocks that are, for the most part, nearly horizontal.

The Coastal Plain is not as old as the northern part of the State. Here the Cenozoic or Recent Life era is represented by formations of all its epochs—the Eocene, Oligocene, Miocene, Pliocene, Pleistocene, and Recent Epoch. It occupies an area of more than 17,000 square miles between the southern boundary of the State and the outcrop of the Upper Cretaceous series. Most of the Cenozoic deposits were laid down on the sea bottom as sand, clay, mud, and calcareous ooze, and many contain marine fossils. Others apparently were formed in swamps or on flood plains. These Cenozoic formations dip toward the south or southwest at rates generally less than 40 feet to the mile. They flatten out from the margin of the Upper Cretaceous rocks upon which they rest and are almost horizontal along the coast. Exceptions to this prevailing dip occur in the Hatchetigbee anticline, a gentile uplift in Choctaw, Washington, and Clarke counties in southwestern Alabama. Here the dip is reversed on its northeastern side and steepened on its southwestern side.

The first dry land in Alabama appeared in pre-Cambrian times, the ancient era when simple life forms were first beginning to stir in earth's warm shallow seas. Granite, gneiss, and marble were pushed up in the east central portion, to form what are now the highest mountains in the State. As the early periods of the Paleozoic era passed, the mainland (known geologically as Old Appalachia) began to rise and the primordial sea that covered northern Alabama receded. The Devonian period, known as the Age of Fishes, passed, and the Carboniferous period began; more land appeared—strata composed of sandstone, limestone, and slate —and dense swampy jungles began to grow.

All the great coal fields of Alabama are found in the Pennsylvanian strata, the formation laid down during the middle epoch of the Mesozoic or Intermediate Life period. In the great swamps or marshes, peat beds were formed through the accumulation of vegetable matter covered by shallow seas. Gradually the swamps were covered with water in which was deposited sand, clay, and gravel, washed in from adjoining lands. Thus sealed, the peat was preserved from decay and compressed by the weight of sediment into a coal bed. As millions of years passed the subsidence ceased; more swamps and more peat bogs were formed and in turn buried in shallow sea water like the first. Through the pressure of overlying rock and through other causes, the water and gases from the vegetable matter were forced out, and the ash and carbon remained to form the coal beds as they exist at the present time. These beds extend from near the center of the State northward to the Tennessee Valley and along the spurs of the Appalachians.

Bituminous coal is found in northern and northeastern Alabama and lignites lies 200 miles south of Birmingham in the Nanafalia formation, which stretches across south Alabama in a wide curve. The bituminous fields are, in order of their importance, the Warrior, Cahaba, Plateau, and Coosa.

Nearly all geologic ages left their rocks in Alabama. Crystalline or metamorphic rocks extend eastward from the center of the State and cover an area of 5,000 square miles. These rocks are mostly pre-Cambrian and contain gold, graphite, mica, pyrite, and a few less important minerals.

LEGACY OF PALEOZOIC ERA

During the Paleozoic era a great succession of phyllite, slate, shale, sandstone, conglomerate, dolomite, and limestone formations were accumulated. The oldest of these Paleozoic rock formations is Talladega slate, which occupies a belt 6 to 10 miles wide extending northeastward from Chilton and Shelby counties to the Georgia Line in Cleburne County. The Talladega mass includes sandstone, limestone, marble, dolomite, chert, graphitic phyllite, and quartz schist. Lying within it is the formation known as Sylacauga marble, a fine-grained white or cream-tinted translucent rock, more or less clouded with green from thin layers of green phyllite within the limestone. This beautiful marble outcrop extends from a point north-northeast of Marble Valley in Coosa County to approximately 4 miles southeast of the city of Talladega.

Extending northwestward from the crystalline area and reaching beyond the boundaries of the State, are Paleozoic rocks of various ages. Along the borders of the crystallines the strata are much folded and faulted, but elsewhere they are nearly horizontal and undisturbed. The strata of the Silurian period forms the most important source of iron ore. The rocks of the Mississippian, first of the Carboniferous epoch, are mostly limestone. Less important minerals such as bauxite, clay, and sandstone are present in the Paleozoic area.

Flanking the older rocks from the northwest corner of Alabama to a little south of the middle portion and extending to the Georgia Line and beyond, are the Cretaceous strata, a belt about 50 miles wide. It is composed mostly of layers of sand, clay, and argillaceous limestone, with important gravel deposits near the larger rivers. Brick and pottery are made from the clays of this area, and some of the limestone is used in the manufacture of cement.

Selma chalk, a marine Cretaceous stratum, crosses the State south of the median line. This stratum contains very fertile soils, as well as sandy loam, and forms the Black Belt region of today, so-called because of the rick black soil. In the southern part of Alabama are Tertiary and Quaternary strata, laid down during the Recent Life era, and consisting of sand, clay, limestone, marl, and sandstone. These strata extend from the Cretaceous belt to the Gulf coast and are overlain with sandy soils of more recent age. Mineral resources of these formations consist of clay, fuller's earth, bauxite, chimney rock, limestone, yellow ochre, lignite, sand, and gravel.

In the late Paleozoic era the earth folded along the eastern part of the United States from Central Alabama to Labrador, forming a newer Appalachian Range. Soft limestone, shale and sandstone, turned under the earth, were eaten out by seepage, subterranean streams, and eventually by surface erosion. In this way the Tennessee and Jones Valleys were carved.

During the Silurian period, when shell-forming sea animals were dominant, beds of sedimentary iron ore were created by the chemical action of decaying marine organisms and sea water, and the ore was later folded into the Appalachian Mountains. The upturned edges of these rocks now wall the entrance to the mines of the Birmingham district, which has a radius of about 75 miles and includes the cities of Bessemer, Tuscaloosa, Anniston, Gadsden, and Jasper. It embraces most of the coal-bearing area of the State, all of the red iron ore territory, and the chief lime-producing district. Ranking second in iron-ore production in the United States, the Birmingham district may prove, according to geologists' estimates, to be the longest-lived iron-ore mining region in the country. A convenient place to view and study a seam of iron ore is in Birmingham at the Twentieth Street crossing on Red Mountain. Here the seam is exposed in almost its full thickness. The "Big Seam," a thin stratum of pebbles and portions of a smaller seam, and finally a layer of shale may be seen. Red sandstone is visible above the large seam.

The only forms of life discovered in Alabama's early Paleozoic rocks are fossils of shell-forming sea animals and insect-like crustaceans. The rocks of the Cambrian period contain the fossils of sea shells such as trilobites and brachiopods, and various coral and plant forms. As the Paleozoic Era passed and the rise of amphibians and land plants began, amphibians left footprints in Alabama mud of the Mississippian epoch.

Throughout the millions of years of the Mesozoic era, the Cretaceous sea advanced over the Appalachian Mountains and laid down sands, gravels, and clays in which many fossils, especially crustaceans and nautilus-like shells, have been preserved. A few fossil remains of the reptiles of that period have been found.

The sea slowly withdrew toward the close of the Mesozoic era, but came back in the Cenozoic or Recent Life Era and deposited sandy materials teeming with shellfish life. Mammals had taken the place of the giant lizards on land, in the Gulf waters, and in the great swamps that fringed the sea. Immense whale-like zeuglodons were abundant and their fossilized remains have been found in the Eocene rocks of Clarke County. The rise and development of the highest orders of plants occurred during this period.

The last section of land to form was in the southern portion of the State, a part of the Coastal Plain bordering the Atlantic Coast States. Much of Alabama's geologic history lies beneath these younger beds of Coastal Plain deposits, which began with the Cretaceous period. Marine deposits, representing the final invasions of the Mississippi Valley by the Gulf of Mexico, extend in fairly even lines across the State.

During the last, or Pliocene Epoch of the Tertiary period, beds of sand and gravel were deposited in the marine waters and along stream courses. While the great glaciers of the Pleistocene or Glacial, the first epoch in Recent Life, were covering the northern half of the continent, Alabama was swept with flood plain material—loam, clay, sand, and gravel—carried southward by torrential summer floods from the glaciers.

PLANT LIFE

Vast primeval forests of pine and hardwoods that once covered Alabama, except in the rolling prairie land of the Black Belt, constituted one of the world's greatest timber regions. Despite intensive lumbering, almost 67 percent of the State is still covered with woodlands. Every county has some forest land, the proportion ranging from 87.5 percent in Clarke County to 28.1 in Limestone County.

Of the State's total 32.7 million acres, some 22 million acres are classified as commercial forest land—land in private and government ownership which is growing crops to be harvested to bolster the economy. Another 28,000 forest acres are non-commercial—in parks and other areas from which timber crops may not be expected.

Of the commercial forest land, foresters have classified 34.4 percent as bearing hardwood types of trees; 22.2 percent, bearing oak and pine, and 43.4 percent softwood types.

The rate of timber growth is constantly increasing through the application of sound forest management practices to more land each year. For example, all of Alabama's forest land is now under organized protection from forest fires, and nearly 1.5 million acres have been planted or seeded to forest trees. More timber is now growing in Alabama than is removed in the annual harvest, plus losses to natural causes. Alabama is one of the top 10 states in reforestation of idle and understocked lands.

Pine still forms the largest proportion of forest growth. In addition to an impressive amount of lumber produced each year, the State is now a major supplier of pine for plywood and produces enough pulpwood to sustain 14 pulp mills making 8,000 tons of pulp daily.

However, most pine sites on non-industrial private forests which make up 75 percent of the ownership are now heavily invaded with undesirable upland hardwood growth due to good fire protection programs, lack of grazing and partial cutting.

Pines include the longleaf, loblolly, slash, Virginia, spruce, pond and sand pine. These coniferous species are included in the group which produces what is known as "southern yellow pine" lumber. Longleaf originally covered much of the central portion of the State, but now there are more shortleaf and loblolly pines. The shortleaf, however, is being greatly endangered by the socalled shortleaf disease.

In addition to pine, there is also in the State an abundance of poplar, cypress, gum and hickory. Red cedar grows throughout the State, but is most common on the slopes of the Tennessee Valley and in the Black Belt, where it sometimes occurs in pure stands. Southern white cedar is found in southwestern Alabama, and hemlock only on the northern Coal Region, its southernmost range on the continent. Along the rivers and in the ponds and swamps of southern Alabama there are fairly large growths of bald cypress, which is extensively used for lumber and poles.

Mixed stands of pines and hardwoods are rapidly becoming things of the past and pure stands of pine, or in some instances other species of trees, are being planted and maintained by large timbering interests, whether they own the land in fee or on a leased basis.

Mixed with the pines, and also in pure stands especially along the river bottoms subject to overflow, are the hardwoods. Oaks are abundant and thrive in all sorts of soil. There are 22 species or varieties of this tree in the State and, along with sweet gum and yellow poplar (tulip), which are used in the veneer industry, are of significant economic value to the State. Together with the pines, these trees form the second-growth forests of the Coal Region, two-thirds of which is wooded, and also cover about half of the Coosa Valley area. There was formerly considerable chestnut, but it is now dead or dying from the blight. There are 20 varieties of the white-blooming haw tree; catalpa, and redbud are widely distributed. The magnificent evergreen tree, *magnolia grandiflora,* is the most common of the magnolias found in Alabama. Other members of this family are the large leaved variety, growing in northern ravines and far down upon the Coastal Plain, and the rare yellow-blooming magnolia, limited to a small area in the Sipsey Fork Valley. Sassafras is common in most localities. The native pecan tree is now cultivated commercially throughout the southern and central portions of Alabama.

Tung trees were imported from China in 1906 and, for several years, it was hoped would open a new tung oil industry. Many of the orchards did not survive severe freezes, which the State occasionally has, and now there are only small scatterings of these trees. Flowering dogwood grows profusely throughout the State. It is no longer cut for shuttles used in cotton mills as it was in the past.

Other native trees of Alabama include hackberry, ash, holly, persimmon, black locust, beech, sycamore, pawpaw, ironwood, and hornbeam. The Gulf coast region has several small species of palmetto, and varieties of palms have been introduced for ornamental purposes.

There are over 150 species of shrubs, some of which are of economic importance. Rhododendron, an evergreen shrub that approaches tree size, is common in the mountainous northern region. Mountain laurel, with its showy pink blossom, grows in hilly sections, especially near streams.

New quality varieties of huckleberries, such as Homebelle and Tifblue, are replacing the old rabbit eye varieties and are an important commercial product. There are still large quantities of blackberries to be found in certain areas.

Cultivated plants typical of the deep South, such as wistaria, camellia,—the State flower, roses, crape myrtle, pomegranate and mock orange, are favorites for decorating purposes, particularly in the older cities. The dahlia, gladiolus, iris, tulips and jonquils are also popular. The azalea, which makes southern gardens famous, was first introduced in Mobile in 1754 from the gardens of the King of France.

Garden clubs are numerous and active in preserving native wild flowers, shrubs and trees and in developing beautiful gardens, parks and bird and plant sanctuaries. The Garden Club of Chunnennuggee, founded in 1847, is the oldest society of its kind in the South, and the old Chunnennuggee Garden has been restored. There are many other magnificent public and private gardens, most famous of which is the Bellingrath Gardens near Mobile. Annual flower shows are held by garden clubs and the Camellia Show in Birmingham during early spring is considered the nation's largest. There are also garden pilgramages, the Dogwood Trail in Birmingham and the Azalea Trail in Mobile attracting nationwide visitors each spring. *See Calendar of Events.*

ANIMAL LIFE

Before the days of white settlement in Alabama, herds of bison and elk grazed the prairies of the Black Belt and Wiregrass sections, and black bear and deer ranged the upland forests and river-bottom canebrakes. Due to well-planned conservation measures the Virginia whitetail deer are again to be found in every county of the State in varying numbers. The black bear, largest game animal in Alabama, is found in only a few counties, but seems to be holding its own and quite often is seen on protected reservations during deer and turkey hunts.

The cougar or panther, the largest predatory animal of the Alabama wilderness, has disappeared, and the bay lynx or bobcat is the largest remaining representative of the cat family. Wolves are now extinct. Beaver colonies, greatly diminished until a few years ago, are now so rampant they have come to be labeled a pest because of the damage they are doing to timber along river and lake banks. Following a highly successful restoration program, they are now found in all 67 counties, with the greatest numbers in the Central section below the fall line. Several counties in this area contain an estimated 5,000 or more beavers.

Although Alabama contains nearly all members of the weasel family, excepting the wolverine and ermine, probably the most familiar is the mink. This small but viscious animal is found over the entire state in lowlands where there is a permanent body of water. Because the demand for mink fur has been great, the Department of Conservation keeps a watchful eye on the trapping of these aquatic animals, attempting to keep a reasonable balance between them and their environment.

Muskrats, prolific as are all rats, are found in abundance throughout the State. Nutria, also a member of the rat family which was brought to this country a relatively few years ago, is increasing in numbers in Alabama. It is found in the same habitats as the muskrat along the coast, but moving farther north with the passing of years. Nutria is nocturnal in habits though it may be seen on dark, cloudy days. Its fur is much desired for apparel.

Another relatively new animal in Alabama is the armadillo, always considered a native of Texas and Mexico. In recent years, this strange mammal has migrated across the Mississippi River and is now found in the coastal counties of the State. Indeed, its numbers have been increasing rapidly enough to raise some concern among farmers and biologists.

Foxes, both red and gray, are fairly common in Alabama, as are raccoons and 'possums. Hunting 'possum, the only marsupial or pouched animal in North America, is a favorite sport among rural folk. Because these two will eat anything and everything, they have been able to hold their own numerically, even in settled areas.

Woodlands and brushy fields afford shelter for rabbits—the eastern cottontail in the northern part of the state, the Florida cottontail in the south. The marsh or swamp rabbit takes the place of the cottontail on the lowlands.

The flying squirrel, rarely seen because of its nocturnal habits, is well distributed throughout the hardwood sections. The grey squirrel commonly called the cat squirrel, is one—if not the only one—of the few game species that has held its own against the encroachment of growing cities and spreading highways. The fox squirrel, like its smaller cousin, is found over the entire State. It seems to be more numerous in the pine thickets of the central counties and along hills and valleys where pines and hardwoods overlap.

The smaller rodents are represented by the black rat, the eastern wood rat, the harvest mouse, and the common mouse. The cotton rat, a chunky rodent about two thirds as large as the common rat and a fierce fighter, lives along the banks of streams and ditches where it makes its runways and nests of grass under reeds and cane. An animal found in the piney woods is the pocket gopher, a burrowing rodent with small eyes and ears, a broad blunt head, and long digging claws. In color it is cinnamon brown with lighter under-parts. Its external fur-lined cheek pouches are used to carry food to its burrow, though the gopher itself is seldom seen, the mounds of earth it throws out from its tunnels is conspicuous. Common moles are found everywhere in the State.

Several species and subspecies of bats make their homes in Alabama and many more enter the State during migratory flights to and from northern regions. Commonest among these queer flying mammals is the big brown bat. Related species include the Florida bat, the big-eared, and little brown bat.

Smallest of Alabama's mammals is the short-tailed shrew, or mole shrew, a member of the order of insect-eaters. This tiny creature is a bloodthirsty beast of prey, often killing and eating mice larger than itself. Its appetite is enormous; shrews are estimated to eat the weight of their own bodies in 24 hours.

GOLDEN EAGLE AND HAWKS

The largest and perhaps the rarest of Alabama's birds is the great golden eagle, which is seen occasionally in the Appalachian foothills. Bald eagles have almost become extinct, though there are still a few to be found in the timbered hills and the marshy sea coast lands. The coastal area is also the home of the osprey or fishhawk, a skillful and industrious fisherman, furnishing the eagle with many a meal of fresh-caught fish. The eagle itself is a fisherman of sorts, but prefers the easier method of taking fish from the more expert osprey. The osprey, one of the State's most interesting birds, doesn't confine itself to the coastal regions, but will nest anywhere there is a large body of water.

The red-tailed hawk, or "hen hawk" as it is called by farmers, prefers open fields and sparsely wooded areas. Accused of taking poultry and game birds, it also destroys large numbers of mice, rats, and snakes and so merits protection. The Cooper's hawk, called the "blue darter" in Alabama, is a poultry and bird-eating species. These hunter birds breed throughout most of the United States and large numbers winter in Alabama. The marsh hawk also winters in the South. Smallest of Alabama hawks is the swift little sparrow hawk, a true falcon, which destroys many injurious insects, beetles, and small rodents. Turkey buzzards, common in all parts of the State, perform useful service as scavengers, but formerly they were killed unmercifully because they were believed to spread hog cholera. Buzzards, starling, English sparrows, and certain kinds of hawks and owls are not protected by game laws.

Largest and fiercest of the owl family in Alabama is the great horned owl that feeds mostly upon small animals, birds, and reptiles but frequently varies its fare with poultry from the barnyard.

Among the more numerous resident birds are the yellow hammer or flicker, the State bird; whip-poor-will, fly-catcher, Bachman sparrow, Carolina wren, and indigo birds. Blue jays and crows are numerous everywhere. Members of the warbler family that breed in Alabama are the black-throated green warbler, the worm-eating warbler, the Maryland yellow-throated green warbler, ovenbird, black and white warbler, northern parula warbler, pine warbler, and hooded warbler. Other warblers enter the State during migratory flights.

Probably the best known of the resident birds are the robin, cardinal, chipping sparrow, tree swallow, cliff swallow, chimney swift, and gold finch. Crow blackbirds and red-winged blackbirds are found in great numbers, particularly in marshy areas.

With the ever increasing number of farm fish ponds throughout Alabama, many kinds of birds are now seen that at one time were quite rare. A good example is the little blue heron. Though the beautiful bird was formerly found around creeks and river sand bars, now they may be seen at almost any fish pond at any time of the year, though more numerous in the summer. Often erroneously called cranes, herons differ from other wading birds in that they fly with their necks bent in an "S" shape with the head folded back toward the shoulder. All the other wading birds fly with the neck extended in the manner of geese. Vanity of women who wanted aigrette plumes in their hats plus greedy commercialism of hat-makers who hired plume hunters, nearly caused extermination some years ago of that beautiful member of the heron family, the Snowy Egret. Though a shy bird, it wanders much and though it nests in communities, only a few Snowy Egret are ever seen together.

Nighthawks, purple martins, wood peewees, wood thrushes, yellow-throated vireos, red-eyed vireos and vesper sparrows are all useful in destroying insect pests.

Mockingbirds and thrashers, both well distributed, are the finest of the songbirds. The commonest species of woodpecker are the red-headed and the downy woodpecker. The tiny ruby-throated humming bird is the smallest species of bird in the State.

During the breeding season the Warrior tableland marks the southern limit of many types of northern birds, including the phoebe, scarlet tanager, worm-eating warbler, and black-throated green warbler. The central prairie belt limits the northward range of the ground dove, Florida redwing, loggerhead shrike, and Florida yellowthroat. In the semitropical Gulf area occur a number of species rarely found above the boundaries of that region, such as the Louisiana clapper rail, purple gallinule, Florida grackle, boat-tailed grackle, painted bunting, Howell seaside sparrow, and Marion marsh wren. The waters of Mobile Bay and the bayous of Mobile delta shelter waterfowl in winter, and the sand islands along the Gulf shores are breeding grounds for thousands of terns and other shorebirds. The term, almost exterminated when it was hunted for its gay plumage, is now increasing in number.

Most abundant of the game birds is the familiar bobwhite or quail, sometimes called partridge in the South. It is non-migratory and breeds in all sections, hatching two or even three broods of young a year. During mating season, its clear call is a familiar sound throughout the State.

WILD TURKEYS MULTIPLYING

Only Texas has more wild turkey than Alabama's 275,000. Alabama is the Number One State in wild turkey harvesting, killing some 25,000 each year. Fine conservation measures on the part of the State and sportsmen, account for the restoration of this fowl that not too many years ago had almost vanished from the State's woods. Wild turkey hens are not killed in Alabama and none is pen-raised and then put out to be shot. Also, good timber management has been a strong contributing factor. The vast forests offer food for the turkey and, by discouraging trespassers, have provided them sanctuary.

Wild turkeys are no longer hunted for food as they were in the days of early settlers. They therefore have become a "sport fowl:" the sport being more in trying to out-wit the sharp, cagey gobbler than in the actual shooting. There are some turkeys all over the State, but the greatest numbers are in Clarke, Marengo, Wilcox and Monroe Counties.

The mourning dove is both a migratory and resident species. Many doves migrate to northern states in the spring to nest and return to the South in the winter. An increasing number remain in Alabama throughout the year and rear their young here.

Woodcocks and snipe are fairly numerous in the lowlands, where they are joined by a migrant woodcock during the winter months and by a migrant snipe in the early fall and spring. Most species of wild ducks and geese that nest in the North are migrants to Alabama. Found in large flocks at feeding and resting grounds along the Warrior-Tombigbee watercourses, they also congregate on the Gulf Coast where waterfowl sanctuaries have been created.

The favored duck with Alabama hunters is the Mallard, which migrates to Alabama from the far North. A few occasionally nest here. The lordly Canvasback, the beautiful wood duck and the Lesser Scaup (Little Blue-bill or Blackjack) are also abundant, and even the American Pintail is to be found sparingly all over the State after the first severe cold spell.

Alligators, Alabama's largest reptiles, are practically extinct. On rare occasions they may be seen in Gulf State Park, where they are protected.

Alabama has most of the land and water turtles found in other Southeastern states, though there are no more of the huge sea turtles in the coastal waters. Prevalent, however, is the snapping turtle that attacks from beneath the surface and drags its prey under water to drown. These average 40 pounds in weight, though the subspecies alligator snapping turtle reaches 140 pounds.

The most common fresh-water fish are bream, shad, cat, carp, crappie, drum, bass, sucker, and gar. Fresh-water trout are found in a few mountain steams in the northern area and sea trout in brackish waters along the Gulf. Bream, crappie, and bass—the fish most sought by sportsmen—are increasing in the big lakes created by recently completed hydro-electric dams. Other fish, such as the sucker, striped bass, and sturgeon, which run upstream from the sea, are diminishing because of barriers raised against their seasonal migration to spawning grounds. Smallmouthed and largemouthed bass, pike, perch, and catfish are found in most streams and lakes, and eel are abundant in the swampy lakes and creeks surrounding Mobile.

Along the Gulf Coast there are seasonal runs of tarpon, pompano, dolphin, mackerel, king mackerel, bluefish, bonita, sturgeon, redfish, and other fish of Atlantic and West Indian waters. Great runs of mullet, an important market fish, are frequent in the spring, and weakfish (speckled trout) are caught throughout the year. (Ling, introduced several years ago from Asiatic waters, are taken so regularly that they are now considered native to Alabama coast waters.

FISHERIES AND THEIR CONSERVATION

Alabama has within its borders 2,820 miles of major rivers, and 6,942 miles of minor rivers and major creeks. The former have a total water surface of 63,038 acres and the latter 27,543 acres. The many small streams and creeks add another 20,000 acres, making a grand total of 111,581 surface acres in rivers and streams.

Alabama also has many large reservoirs constructed for power, navigation, flood control and industrial-domestic water supplies. The four TVA lakes on the Tennessee River have a combined area of 180,000 surface acres; eleven reservoirs constructed by the Alabama Power Company on the Coosa and Tallapoosa Rivers total 141,610 acres; and those on other rivers and creeks (16) add on an area of 145,150 acres, giving a total area in large reservoirs of 466,760 acres. In addition to these waters, a total of 27,226 farm ponds have been constructed, totalling 99,340 acres. The overall total acreage of fresh waters in the state, then, is 677,681.

Total brackish waters in Mobile Bay, Mississippi Sound and adjoining waters in Alabama are 354,503 acres, giving the state a total of 1,032,184 acres of fresh and brackish waters, or one acre of water for each 32 acres of land.

Since 1955, the area in large impoundments has increased by 93.4 per cent and the area in ponds by 98 per cent.

These "new" and old waters give Alabama remarkably some of the best fishing to be found anywhere in the United States and even old-timers have to admit that fishing is now better than "it used to be." The success in sport fishing is due in part to research on how to produce good fishing, part to correct stocking of fish and part to proper management.

Research on the management of impounded waters and on fish populations of rivers, reservoirs, and ponds was begun in Alabama in 1934 by the Agricultural Experiment Station of Alabama Polytecnic Institute, now known as Auburn University. Their research facilities for fisheries occupy a 1300-acre area with a total of 250 experimental ponds. Research was conducted on methods of stocking fish, breeding, fertilization, feeding and population management. The International Center for Aquaculture was established at Auburn University to help development of fisheries in foreign countries under U.S. Aid projects. Within the last five years the U.S. Bureau of Sport Fishing and Wildlife has also operated a research station at Marion for experiments on breeding and feeding fish.

Hatcheries producing fish for stocking newly-impounded waters and for corrective restocking are operated by the Game & Fish Division of the Alabama Department of Conservation at Eastaboga and Spring Hill, with a total of 22 acres of hatchery ponds. The U.S. Bureau of Sport Fishing and Wildlife operates a large hatchery at Marion and a small one at Carbon Hill, totaling approximately 125 acres.

The management of public waters is the responsibility of the Alabama Department of Conservation. For this purpose the state is divided into seven districts, each with a trained fishery biologist and one or more assistants. These men apply known management techniques, develop new techniques, and watch for pollution and other causes of fish kills. In addition, the Department has constructed and operates 20 public fishing lakes, located where good fishing was not available. Its seafood division operates a station for research and management of coastal waters at Dauphin Island, with research on oyster, shrimp, and fish production.

Yet another important program is being conducted at the University of Alabama's Marine Science Institute, dedicated to determing how to gain full use of the rich marine resources of Alabama's estuaries and adjacent continental shelf without impairing future productivity.

Before establishment of the Institute in 1966 at Point aux Pine, south of Mobile and adjacent to Bayou La Batre—center of the shrimp industry—the University of Alabama had provided summer courses in marine biology in cooperation with the State Department of Conservation. It had also provided research services in marine biology for the state at Dauphin Island.

Presently, a two-term summer session of 10 weeks for undergraduate and graduate students is taught by a resident staff and the departments of Biology, Anatomy and Geology. Courses are offered in experimental marine embryology, vertebrate and invertebrate marine ecology, fisheries science, marine geology, marine science and scientific scuba diving.

The Institute is jointly sponsored by the University of Alabama-Tuscaloosa, and University of Alabama-Birmingham.

First Americans

THE DISCOVERY OF RUSSELL CAVE

ARCHEOLOGICAL remains of prehistoric Indians in Alabama range from "rock towns" or cave shelters along the river bluffs to the great earthen pyramids and fortified town sites of the semi-civilized people popularly known as the Mound Builders. Throughout the State, particularly in the large drainage basins, are large habitation sites, shell refuse heaps (or middens), and terraced flat-topped cere-monial mounds which served as foundations for temples or townhouses.

Until discovery of Russell Cave near Bridgeport in 1953, the oldest human remains that had been found in Alabama were those of a Stone Age folk, known as the Shell Mound People, who inhabited the State some 2,000 years ago.

Excavations at Russell Cave and at the Quad Site near Decatur added 8,000 more years to the history of human habitation in Alabama. We now know that dating back to about 10,000 B.C., there were four major periods of occupation by prehistoric Indians in the State: Paleo-Indian, Archaic, Woodland and Mound Builders.

At the Quad site, excavations unearthed a Clovis point, a type of spear point used by the Ice Age hunters to kill big game. Archeologists using Geiger counters to date radio-activity of other excavated materials in that area, now believe Paleo-Indian hunters came into the Tennessee Valley of Alabama as early as 10,000 B.C., in pursuit of such big game as the prehistoric mastadons and hairy elephants.

As large game became scarce, these nomadic hunters were re-placed by a more settled people—the Archaic Man—whose existence in Alabama was established with the discovery of Russell Cave.

This archeological find, considered one of the most important in North America, began when a powerline worker picked up several unusual spear points near Bridgeport in northeast Alabama.

Shortly thereafter, four members of the Tennessee Archeological Society began digging in the cave. As they dug deeper, they realized this was an archeological find that demanded more intensive effort and expertise than they could give it. They told the Smithsonian Institution of their discovery. That institution, in cooperation with the National Geographic Society, conducted three seasons of archeological exploration. In 1961, the National Geographic Society presented to the Interior Department its deed to the 310-acre farm on which the cave is located.

Other excavations were carried out by the National Park Service, which today administers the site as a National Monument.

From the work of the above mentioned organizations has come the present knowledge of the people Russell Cave sheltered for 8,000 years.

The first inhabitants of the cave camped on an irregular floor of rock slabs, 107 feet wide, with walls 27 feet high. The women, instead of throwing out broken utensils and the refuse from meals, covered them with dirt inside the cave. From these monuments to poor house-keeping, protected from the elements within the dry cave, and from charcoal remains of their fires, archeologists using the Carbon-14 method were able to date human arrival between 6,500 and 7,000 B.C.

For these early people, Russell Cave was a fall and winter haven. Water abounded nearby; the forest bore a rich crop of nuts; the mountains and valley yielded game. In spring and summer, in small bands, they abandoned the cave to camp along the Tennessee River a few miles distant.

As the archeologists dug into the cave's piles of dirt, they uncovered fascinating facts about Archaic Man. He had few tools. The meager household goods he needed had to be portable. A short spear, tipped with a stone point and propelled by a throwing stick, or atlatl, was his chief weapon. He chipped the points from chert, which occurs as nodules and veins in the limestone near the cave.

Beside these weapon points, he worked sharp, flinty stone into scrapers and knives. Bones made into awls and needles suggest that he worked in leather. He also fashioned bones into fish hooks, but no ornaments were found in the deposits.

The Indians probably made other articles that the ground has not preserved. Basketry, wood and leather items have long ago disintegrated. One piece of evidence pointing to the existence of perishable materials was the discovery of cane matting impressions on clay deposits.

Archaic Man wasted little of his game. Meat was roasted or stewed by dropping hot rocks into water-filled containers of bark or skin. Hides provided him with clothing and shelter. Occasionally the Indians buried inside the cave family members who died while living there. Remains of children and adults have been found in the Archaic layers, the bodies having been placed in shallow pits scooped out of the cave floor.

There are hints that during the 3,000 years of this Archaic Period, the Indians of the Tennessee Valley relied on the river for their chief sustenance. The cave then may have been less frequently occupied. But in most other respects the Russell Cave Indian's way of life remained unchanged until the end of the period.

Beginning about 500 B.C., the implements of the Russell Cave dwellers underwent a marked change. Pottery appears for the first time and in quantity. Smaller weapon points suggest that bow and arrow had replaced the earlier throwing stick. Bone tools are better finished, and, for the first time, there are evidences of bone and shell ornaments.

These changes, widespread throughout the eastern United States, mark the beginning of the Woodland Period. It was during that time that burial mounds came into use and ceremonialism increased.

The richer and more complex way of life indicates that the Woodland Indian had more time for activities not directly concerned with mere survival. Excavations determined that by the end of the Woodland Period primitive agriculture had taken hold in the Southeast.

The Indians of this period also used Russell Cave only seasonally. They probably joined other groups at summer villages larger than those of the Archaic period. Archeologists found evidences that within this Woodland Period there were advances in the design of pottery and the shape of arrowpoints.

Shortly after 1,000 A.D. the Indians began to make less and less use of the cave. Ocassionally small parties, probably hunters, left scatterings of objects that differed from those of the Woodland Period. By this time, the Indians lived in permanent villages. Rock bottomlands near the river supported their fields of corn and other plants. Because their villages contained large, flat-topped temple mounds, this Mississippian Period has become known popularly as the Mound Builders Period.

Mounds scattered all over the State, but particularly at Moundville, provide Alabama's most visible link with its pre-historic inhabitants. First of these people were the Shell Mound Builders, who dwelled mostly in the big bend of the Tennessee River. Their skeletons are those of muscular, long-headed Indians with strong jaws and good teeth, the latter much worn down by gritty food. They were non-agriculture peoples who, perhaps, had little, if any, pottery, and who depended largely upon fish and game for sustenance.

The Shell Mound people evidently occupied the river basins over a long period. The shell heaps are frequently more than 15 feet deep, and cover several acres. Along with shells are quantities of burned animal bones, ash, charcoal and broken fire-cracked stones. Although the shell middens were principally occupation sites, many burials are found in them. The skeletons are flexed on the side or doubled up in a sitting position in shallow circular pits.

After the people of the true shell mound culture, came tribes who made pottery, had some agriculture and who used the shell middens of the earlier folk as habitation sites.

PREHISTORIC EVIDENCE AT MOUNDVILLE

One of the most fruitful sources of prehistoric Indian culture is Moundville, now the Moundville State Monument, where a museum containing artifacts found on the site is conducted by the State. This great mound group, one of the best-preserved in the country, is on the south bank of the Black Warrior River in Hale and Tuscaloosa counties. The site includes 34 square and oval platform mounds varying in height from 3 to 58 feet. These are arranged in a rough square on a plain back from the bluffs; graded ways lead from the level ground to the mound tops, where the ceremonial houses and chief's lodges were built. Some of the mounds contained graves, but the majority of the burials were in the level land of the townsite.

The people of Moundville carried pottery making, copper working, and stone carving to a high level. Pottery was decorated with incised patterns and sometimes modeled into graceful bird and animal forms. Two stone effigy vessels from this site are considered the finest yet found in the entire mound area. An exquisite effigy bowl of diorite, in the form of a wood duck, is one of the best examples of ancient art. Designs most frequently used by the Moundville people include the sun pattern, the swastika, the human hand, eye, skull, and arm bones, the horned serpent, eagle, heron, and ivory-billed woodpecker.

In common with other mound-building peoples of the Mississippi Valley and its tributaries, the Moundville people used copper breast-plates and ear plugs and ornaments of mica. Among other unusual ornaments and implements taken from the Moundville site are shell drinking cups, shell gorgets, shell pins, copper fishhooks, stone and copper axes, bone awls, flint points, stone pipes, earthenware ornaments, and a human head carved in amethyst.

In northern Alabama, where the Tennessee River swings in a great bow across the State, are mounds and townsites showing evidence of Middle Mississippi culture. The great quadrangular flat-topped mound at Florence, the largest on the Tennessee River, is a typical ceremonial house mound or temple foundation. Along the Tennessee River in the northeastern section of Alabama are stone graves similar to those of Middle Tennessee, perhaps marking the southern boundary of the Stone Grave culture. The Tennessee Valley mounds have yielded the usual effigy ware, copper ornaments, and stone disks common to the area.

Mound Builder remains are numerous in the valley of the Tombigbee River, where the mounds vary in height from one to 30 feet. Burials found in most of these include the "bunched" variety, extended skeletons, flexed skeletons, and urn burials. Along the lower Tombigbee River some of the skeletons found had artificially deformed skulls. Also present are flint points, knives, drills, celts, potteryware, masses of galena (lead ore) and volcanic stones.

Both mounds and shell heaps have been found along Mobile Bay. Shell deposits contain skeletons and pottery with loop handles and various designs including the cross-hatch and check stamp. Frog and duck effigies were found in a shell heap on Simpson Island, and in a huge shell deposit at Blakely a skeleton with an ornament of sheet copper was unearthed. Quantities of mica were taken from a sand mound near Stark's Landing, Baldwin County. On Bottle Creek in the Mobile delta there is an oblong mound 46 feet high, with base dimensions of 300 by 250 feet.

INDIANS IN HISTORIC TIMES

The largest single linguistic stock represented in Alabama was the Muskhogean which included most of the tribes of the Creek group, and also the neighboring Chocktaw and Chickasaw nations. It was called Muskhogean after the dominant tribe of the Creek Confederacy. Beside the Muskogee or Creek proper, this powerful group embraced the kindred tribes of the Alibamu, Kosati, and Hitchiti, all speaking Muskhogean dialects. Their towns were scattered throughout the well-watered central and southeastern portions of the State, and in central Georgia. The name Creek was first applied to Indians of this stock by early South Carolina traders. It was an abbreviation of Ochesee Creek Indians, who were then living along the Ocmulgee River. Remnants of three other linguistic groups—the Yuchi, Natchez, and a small band of Algonquian Shawnee—were taken into the Creek Confederacy in historic times and occupied land within the Creek domain. The Choctaw occupied portions of southwestern Alabama, and the Chickasaw, also a Muskhogean people, ranged throughout the northwestern part of the State, although their stronghold was in northern Mississippi and West Tennessee. Representing an entirely different linguistic group were the Cherokee, a great detached tribe of Iroquoian stock. Late comers, they pushed into northern Alabama as the white settlers crowded them from the lands in the upper Tennessee Valley.

The culture of the tribes of Alabama followed much the same pattern. They were typical agricultural village Indians, living in well-built houses of logs, often clustered inside stockades for protection against attack. They raised large crops of corn, beans, squash, and tobacco in family gardens and community farms. Their culture centered around maize or corn, and the Green Corn Dance or "busk" was a yearly ceremony among all the tribes of the area.

In the early part of the 16th century Spanish explorers came into contact with the coastal Indians. But it was not until 1540, when Hernando de Soto and more than 500 soldiers and craftsmen began their march inland, that the Spanish met the tribes of the vast interior. De Soto came upon the Lower Creek at Cofitachaqui and passed through the palisaded towns of the Upper Creek in the region between the Coosa and Tallapoosa Rivers. The Spaniards found little trace of gold in Alabama but they reaped the hatred of all the tribes along their line of march. Pushing southwestward they found the way barred by the warriors of the Choctaw. De Soto forced his way through with his firearms, but his losses in men and horses were heavy especially in the bloody battle at Mauvila. Indian warriors with bows of seasoned hickory could send a cane arrow through the best Spanish mail.

FRENCH AND ENGLISH RIVALRY

The next Europeans to come into the interior of Alabama were the French. They planned to exploit the Indians and develop the fur trade, and part of their plan was to get control of the river basins. *Coureurs de bois* and fur traders came in touch with the Choctaw, Chickasaw, and Creek tribes. From Mobile, French goods began to trickle into the country of the Muskhogean tribes. But English traders from Virginia and the Carolinas had already found the valley of the Tennessee and the rich fur regions of the interior. The great fur war began.

In 1714 the French built Fort Toulouse up between the Coosa and Tallapoosa rivers in the domain of the Alibamu, hoping to check the penetration of British traders. In 1736 they erected Fort Tombigbee on the Tombigbee River above its confluence with the Black Warrior to dominate the Choctaw and Chickasaw.

The Choctaw became allies of the French but the Chickasaw were won over by English traders.

When the British were victorious in the struggle for the continent, the long fur war ended. The Indian trade was systematized by the British, prices were fixed, traders licensed, and all affairs placed under the control of a superintendent of Indian affairs. English and Scottish traders then pushed into the region. Many of them married Indian women. The British bought land from the Indians in the vicinity of Mobile and a strip reaching far up the Tombigbee River. Settlers, encouraged to enter Alabama territory, began pouring into the region from Georgia and the Carolinas.

The outbreak of the American Revolution caused unrest among the Alabama tribes. War parties of young braves prowled along the frontier, striking isolated settlements, and returning with scalps and captives. But the Muskhogean tribes were too far removed from the main settlements to cause much trouble. Under the peace treaties which recognized the independence of the United States, the northern coast of the Mexican Gulf again became Spanish. Mobile remained the chief trading center, and Spain continued the licenses of traders importing the English goods to which the Indians had become accustomed. Trading caravans still followed the pack trails, and bateaux plied the rivers. Fur still played a part in the development of the interior.

During the latter years of the 18th century a young Scottish half-breed, Alexander McGillivray, rose to a position of power among the Creek. He was the son of Lachlan McGillivray, a trader, who had married a leading woman of the Creek, who had French and Spanish blood. Through her Alexander inherited membership in the Wind Clan. In 1775 at the outbreak of the Revolution, Georgia seized the property of the elder McGillivray, who was a loyalist in his sympathies. He fled to Scotland, but his son returned to the Creek country, and settled among the Indians. Well educated, shrewd and far-sighted, he rose to a position of power among his tribesmen. To retaliate against the Americans he led raids against their settlements. After the war he retained the leadership of the Creek Confederacy.

The Chickasaw ceded land in northern Alabama to the United States in 1805. A few months later the Cherokee relinquished some of their claims and in the same year the Choctaw ceded 5,000,000 acres of tribal land, part of which was in southwestern Alabama. But more than nine-tenths of all land in the present State still remained in the hands of the Muskogee when the Creek War broke out in 1813.

TECUMSEH VISITS THE CREEKS

As early as 1811 Tecumseh, the Shawnee chief and ally of the British, visited the Alabama tribes in an effort to weld all the Indians into a league against the Americans. As Tecumseh's father and mother belonged to a group of Shawnee who had previously lived on the Tallapoosa River, the chief was well received in the Creek villages. Before starting south, he had been informed by British officials at Detroit of the expected appearance at a certain time of Biela's comet, and he made the most of this bit of information in Alabama by predicting the exact day of the comet's arrival. Many of the tribes believed him to be a messenger with supernatural powers. Of the Muskhogean tribes, only the Creek listened to his plan, and even they were not wholeheartedly for war. Big Warrior, chief of Tuckabatchie Town, was the leader of of the peace party, and Tecumseh could not sway him. In a burst of anger the Shawnee leader said: "When I get back to Detroit I will stamp my foot upon the ground and shake down every house in Tuckabatchie." One month later, in December, 1811, the New Madrid earthquake occurred, and the shock of it was felt in northern Alabama. The Indians of Tuckabatchie ran from their lodges, believing Tecumseh had stamped his foot.

Tecumseh's prophet in the Creek country was Josiah Francis, son of a Scotch-Irish trader, and as implacable a foe of the Americans as McGillivray had been. Through Spanish emissaries in Pensacola the Creek obtained British war supplies, and in the spring of 1813 they took the war path. Their leaders were McGillivray's nephew, Red Eagle, better known as William Weatherford; Josiah Francis, Peter McQueen, and High Head Jim.

The Creek won the first skirmish—the Battle of Burnt Corn— and on August 30, 1814 a great war band under Weatherford captured and destroyed Fort Mims, killing more than 500 persons within the stockade. But the Creek victory was shortlived. Andrew Jackson, with Tennessee riflemen and bands of friendly Indians, marched to the upper Coosa and pushed southward. The Creek fought bravely, asking no quarter, but battle after battle went to the lanky red-headed general of militia from Tennessee. By the battles of Talladega and Horseshoe Bend, the power of the Creek Confederacy was broken forever. Jackson dictated the terms of the Treaty of Fort Jackson, August 9, 1814, and the Creek lost all the land west of the Coosa and were restricted to an area in eastern Alabama.

In 1816 the Cherokee ceded all their lands except a small area in the northeast corner of Alabama, and the Chickasaw gave up all their territory save a small tract in the northwest. The Choctaw kept only a narrow strip west of the Tombigbee.

With three-fourths of the State open for settlement, the whites flocked in to take up the rich farm land. Squatters by the hundreds took over Indian lands, defying the owners to dispossess them. In 1830 the Chocktaw gave up in disgust, ceded their land at the Treaty of Dancing Rabbit Creek and moved west of the Mississippi. The Chickasaw gave up their territory also and, like the Choctaw, left peaceably to establish new homes in the West. But the Creek, who still held much of their tribal domain, blocked the way of the incoming settlers from Georgia. They were restless under the restrictions imposed upon them by the Treaty of Fort Jackson and skirmishes occurred. A treaty signed in Washington in 1832 provided for the ceding of all Creek land and the removal of the Indians to the West.

SETTLERS PUSH OUT CREEKS

But trouble came when the white settlers jumped the boundaries of the Creek country before the time fixed by the treaty. Bitter controversy arose between the State and national governments, and United States troops were sent to enforce the terms of the treaty. The matter was finally settled amicably by Francis Scott Key, sent from Washington as the representative of the Federal Government. The Creek, however, were loath to leave their ancient territory, and as more and more settlers pushed into Alabama they became increasingly restless. Brushes between border whites and Indians were continuous, throughout the summer of 1836. Many Creek joined the Seminole in Florida, who, led by Osceola, himself a native of Alabama, were waging a desperate war against the United States. For a time it looked as though the entire Creek Nation would join the Seminole in a general frontier war, and State militia was mobilized near the Creek towns.

Governor Clay, however, attempted to keep the Creek from taking the warpath, and invited their headmen to a parley. Opothleohole and 11 other leading chiefs responded; they agreed to remain peaceful and even to join forces with the whites against their tribesmen if war came. Meawhile, troops had been marching in from all parts of the State, and an army of 3,000 Alabamians, reinforced by 1,600 friendly Indians, marched against a band of some 700 hostile Creek. General Winfield Scott arrived in time to stop the impending fight by sending his deputy, Judge John A. Campbell, to meet the Creek chiefs; Campbell promised the Creek warriors food and clothing, which they needed badly, and thus got them to surrender. Except for those who had gone to Florida, the Creek allowed themselves to be sent West.

In the northeastern part of the State the Cherokee, for the most part prosperous farmers who had adopted white civilization, still occupied many thousands of acres of their ancestral domain. They had been a literate people since 1821 when the tribal leaders adopted the alphabet invented by the half-breed genius, George Gist, or Guess, better known as Sequoyah (*see Tour 3*). With the help of white missionaries, they published their own newspaper, the *Cherokee Phoenix,* the first of its kind in the world. They had large farms and orchards, raised cattle and horses, and owned Negro slaves. But even these peaceful agricultural people were subjected to persecution by the border whites who wanted the Indians' rich land and well-kept farms.

The removal of all Indians to the West was demanded, and President Andrew Jackson refused to enforce the Government's treaties and protect the Indians from white aggression. Unable to secure justice in Washington, a minority of the tribe led by John Ridge signed the Treaty of New Echota in March, 1835. It was quickly ratified by the Senate, and the Cherokee were ordered to vacate their land. Their leader John Ross and the majority protested, but to no avail. Troops marched into the Indian country, and in the summer of 1838 the Great Removal began. By the following year the Indian population of Alabama, except for a few scattered bands, had all moved beyond the Mississippi.

Descendants of the Indians who once occupied Alabama now live in Oklahoma, where they have their own communities with churches, schools, and stores. Many of them still follow agricultural pursuits and are prosperous farmers. Today the Creek, Choctaw, Chickasaw, Seminole, and Cherokee are known as the Five Civilized Tribes.

History: From Hernando De Soto to George Wallace

W HEN Hernando De Soto was appointed Governor of Cuba in 1537, fleets of galleons were still sailing into Spanish ports with plunder from Mexico and Peru. De Soto had been one of Pizarro's lieutenants in Peru; he knew that the day when a few armored cutthroats could seize fantastic fortunes in the Americas would soon be ended unless new treasure cities were found. And Spanish seamen, who had visited the coast of what is now Alabama as early as 1505, had told stories of a country "where the people wear hats of solid gold and life is gay and luxurious." Before the new Governor of Cuba left Spain he had secured a royal patent to "all lands on the north of Florida over which he shall extend the sovereignty of his Catholic Majesty, Charles V."

In Cuba, De Soto gathered men and supplies and on May 18, 1539, sailed for the mainland with a company of nearly 600 men. Landing at the bay of Espiritu Santo, now Tampa Bay, he wandered northward for almost a year and is believed to have reached western North Carolina. The Spaniards found no golden cities but they looted and burned Indian villages along the line of march. In the spring of 1540 De Soto turned south and cut across parts of present-day Tennessee and Georgia. After entering northeastern Alabama, the Spaniards moved slowly down the valley of the Coosa River where they met resistance from the Indians. A series of fierce skirmishes during the autumn of 1540 culminated in a major engagement at Mauvila—a palisaded town near the present Choctaw Bluff, in Clarke County—where the Indians were defeated and their town burned. Chroniclers' accounts of the battle vary; the Spaniards did not go unscathed; 82 were killed, and hundreds, including De Soto, wounded.

Spurred by rumors of gold farther west, the company dragged northward. Further severe fighting occurred in November, when De Soto reached the Black Warrior River and had to fight his way through the Choctaw country. Leaving the Tombigbee basin, he passed from the territory of Alabama into what is now Mississippi and Tennessee. A year later, after crossing the Mississippi, De Soto died and was lowered at some unknown spot into the great mud-brown river he had discovered.

De Soto's expedition was not the first to traverse areas now part of the State of Alabama. Precedence is now given to Alonso de Pineda, who entered Mobile Bay in 1519 and left behind a map. In the *Atlas of Alabama* Dr. Charles Grayson Summersell of the University of Alabama cites a visit to Mobile Bay by Panfilo de Narvaez and Cabeza de Vaca, with 400 men and 80 horses, in 1528; another by Guido de las Bazares to Mobile Bay in 1558, and one by Tristan de Luna y Arellano in 1559. Members of de Luna's expedition are said to have penetrated as far as the Indian village of Coosa on the Coosa River.

The first white colony in Alabama was founded in 1559 by Tristan de Luna, with authority from the Viceroy of Mexico to settle near Mobile Bay. More than 1,000 colonists landed at Mobile Bay, moved on to Pensacola Bay, and doubled back into Alabama, where they took over the Indian town of Nanipacna. For three years they divided their time between fruitless search for gold mines and fighting among themselves. When De Luna abandoned his plans of colonization in 1561 the colonists returned to Mexico.

Spanish sailors continued to put in along the coast of Alabama for water and to trade with the Indians, and the territory was claimed as part of Florida; but no permanent settlement was made. The failure of the Spaniards to take root on Alabama soil left the way open for the English and French.

Nearly a century after De Soto's venture, England declared its interest in the western region of which Alabama was a part. Under the first Carolina grant of 1629, Charles I gave Sir Robert Heath much of the wilderness claimed by Spain as part of the Province of Florida. A second grant by Charles II in 1663 to others repeated the ineffectual gift. Thus both Spain and England assumed title to Alabama, though neither made an effort to fix their claims by settlement.

By 1682 La Salle had explored the Mississippi River to its mouth and France laid claim to all the vast inland country drained by the Mississippi River and its tributaries. In 1699 Louis XIV sent Pierre Le Moyne, Sieur d'Iberville, to establish a settlement on the Gulf Coast. Choosing a site near the present Biloxi, Mississippi, Iberville landed some 200 colonists and built a fortification, Fort Maurepas, near what is now Ocean Springs. Here was established the seat of government for Louisiana, an enormous territory embracing the entire Mississippi drainage basin.

In 1702 Iberville's brother, Jean Baptiste Le Moyne, Sieur de Bienville, was appointed governor. He removed the territorial government to Fort Louis de la Mobile which had been built several months before on the Mobile River at Twenty-Seven-Mile Bluff. Mobile was organized as a canonical parish by the Bishop of Quebec in 1704. In the same year two dozen orphan "Cassette girls"—so called because the government provided each with a *cassette* or trunk and an outfit of clothing—landed at Mobile. All were married within a month except one who was "coy and hard to please." Seven years later the colony was moved to the present site of Mobile, and here Fort Conde de la Mobile was erected and a small town grew up.

The early years of the colony were disappointing. For the most part, the settlers were criminals and vagrants or ruined noblemen with no taste for work. Because they spent their time in gambling and looking for gold, they were dependent on France for most of their supplies. However, a few hardy immigrants from Canada established a brisk fur trade with the Choctaw, Creek, and Cherokee. By 1714 traders from Mobile were operating as far north as present-day Tennessee.

The undeveloped colony proved a burden rather than a source of revenue to the Crown, and in 1712 Louis XIV farmed out Louisiana to Antoine Crozat, Marquis du Chatel, a French banker and merchant. The contract gave Crozat a commercial monopoly for 15 years in exchange for a share of the profits. Antoine de la Mothe Cadillac, who was appointed Governor with Bienville as his second in command, was instructed to encourage agriculture, develop industry, and promote trade with the Indians and Spaniards. Openly despising Louisiana, Cadillac allowed internal affairs of the colony to drift aimlessly, but in 1714 he took advantage of a war between the Creek Indians and the English of Georgia to build Fort Toulouse on the Coosa River in the heart of the Creek Nation.

Under the management of Crozat's agents the colony grew slowly. Fewer than 500 French settlers lived in the Mississippi Valley by 1716. Crozat had been losing great sums of money in "that bottomless hole called Louisiana" and in 1717 he returned the territory to the Crown.

In France the Grand Monarch was dead and the prodigal Duke of Orleans had become Regent. He and the court became involved in a fever of speculation based on the financial juggling of John Law, a Scotch banker and promoter. In 1717 the colony was turned over to Law's Mississippi Company (*la compagnie des Indes Occidentales*), which had been granted a 25-year monopoly of Louisiana's development. From Law's *Banque Générale* a flood of banknotes was issued with stock in the company as security. In 1718, Law persuaded the Regent to charter a national bank, with Law as director-general, and from this *Banque Royale* came other issuances of paper currency. For a time the paper money passed at face value and stock in the Mississippi Company brought as much as 20,000 *livres* a share.

Bienville was again appointed as Governor of Louisiana to succeed Cadillac. Frenchmen scrambled wildly for lands in the Gulf colony, and settlers came by the boatload to Mobile, Biloxi, and the hamlet of New Orleans. After 1719, when the first cargo of slaves arrived at Dauphin Island, large tracts of land were cleared around the three chief towns and indigo and rice plantations multiplied. In 1719 France went to war against England and Spain, and the capital of Louisiana was removed from Mobile to Biloxi, where there would be less danger of attack from Spanish Florida. In 1719-20, during the war between France and Spain, the Mobile French sacked and burned Pensacola but made no effort to retain the conquered area.

A growing source of danger of Louisiana was the penetration of upper Louisiana territory by English traders. English trade goods were of better quality and cheaper than French, and by 1719 traders from Georgia and the Carolinas were firmly established among the Chickasaw. When the Alibamu, Choctaw, and Creek Indians also showed signs of English influence, Bienville succeeded in holding their allegiance by reducing the price of trade goods and showering the headmen with presents at the annual Indian congress at Mobile.

In 1720 the population of Louisiana totaled more than 6,000, and there was a swelling trickle of revenue to France from the fur trade and from rice and indigo plantations. However, growth of the colony had fallen far short of Law's expectations. It was more and more apparent that the speculative prices of the shares of the Mississippi Company could not be supported by actual developments in the colony. To bolster State finances, the Mississippi Company was merged with the national bank in March, 1720, with Law at its head; but in July, 1720, the national bank was compelled to stop payments, and Law fled from France. Frantic investors suddenly dumped their shares; the market plummeted and the Mississippi Company crashed.

The bankrupt motherland forgot Louisiana during the summer of 1720 and supply ships ceased coming to Mobile. The colonists faced starvation. Though the Choctaw gave them enough corn to tide them over, disorder spread and garrisons mutinied. Only Bienville's strong hand prevented general chaos. Late in 1720 supplies again began coming from France, and Louisiana was placed under a royal commission. Remaining as governor, Bienville in 1722 removed the capital to New Orleans, which had become the leading seaport. Two years later he issued ordinances governing the treatment of slaves, forbidding marriage of whites to Negroes, making the Roman Catholic faith obligatory, and banishing Jews from the colony. Though the Mississippi Company had crashed, "thousands of colonists and many slaves had been brought over; agriculture was promoted . . . and trade with the Indians advanced."

Bienville was recalled to France in 1727 to answer charges placed against him by enemies both in the colony and the homeland. By 1733, when he was exonerated and returned, the colony had entered upon a period of healthy growth. Planters and merchants were growing wealthy as increasing quantities of rice, indigo, sugar, and furs were exported. The population had reached 8,000 and "A splendid New France was beginning on the Gulf."

In other respects, things had been going badly during Bienville's absence. There had been a bloody war with the Natchez Indians, and the Alibamu and Creek had become suspicious of the French. The Georgia grant of 1732, made to Oglethorpe and others "in trust for the poor," had repeated England's claim to the part of Alabama north of the thirty-first parallel. In the year of Bienville's return, Governor Oglethorpe called a congress of the lower Creek at Savannah, Georgia, and the tribe placed itself under English protection. Even among the Choctaw a faction hostile to the French had sprung up.

In the spring of 1736 Bienville dispatched an expedition under Pierre d'Artaguette to humble the Chickasaw and to drive English traders out of their country; Bienville himself followed from Mobile with a stronger column. The Chickasaw, aided by Englishmen from Carolina, defeated both forces and drove the French back to Mobile. Ending his long service to the colony in 1743, Bienville retired to France.

In 1756 the decaying government of France was drawn into another war with England. Known as the Seven Years War in Europe and the French and Indian War in this country, the struggle resulted in the loss of all French holdings in America. By the Treaty of Paris in 1763, Canada and the portion of Louisiana east of the Mississippi were ceded to Great Britain. New Orleans and western Louisiana had already been ceded, secretly, by France to Spain. Although hundreds of families returned to France or migrated to Spanish Louisiana, the French residue was strong enough to influence the culture of coastal Alabama. Many British traders and colonists moved into Alabama at this time. Among them was Lachlan McGillivray whose quarterbreed son, Alexander, became the white leader of the Creek Nation and arch-foe of the Americans.

During the Revolutionary War a British garrison held Mobile and the surrounding country until 1780 when Bernardo de Galvez, Governor of Spanish Louisiana, forced it to capitulate.

UNITED STATES AUTHORITY MOVES IN

By the treaty of 1783 Great Britain gave northern Alabama, as a part of Georgia, to the United States and ceded Florida, including Mobile, to Spain. The boundary of West Florida was set at the thirty-first parallel. A treaty made between the United States and the Choctaw Indians on January 3, 1786 gave the United States the land previously ceded to the British by that tribe.

In 1785 Georgia began pushing the claim, contained in its royal charter, to the territory now comprising Alabama and Mississippi. A boundary dispute with Spain ensued, and in 1796 Andrew Ellicott, Surveyor General of the United States, was appointed commissioner to survey the boundary between the United States and West Florida. In 1799, when the line was fixed at 31° north and Spain accepted it, Fort St. Stephens (north of the line) was turned over to American troops. Ellicott's Stone, 26 miles north of Mobile, still marks the survey. Meanwhile, an act of Congress, April 7, 1798 had formed into the Territory of Mississippi the region from the Chattahoochee River to the Mississippi River between 31° north latitude and 32° 28'. Narsworthy Hunter and Thomas M. Greene were appointed territorial delegates to Congress and President Adams commissioned Winthrop Sargent, of Massachusetts, first Governor of the Territory. Natchez, on the Mississippi, was made the seat of government.

Washington, first county to be organized in present Alabama, with McIntosh Bluff as county seat, was formed in 1800 to include all of

the Mississippi Territory between the Pearl River and the Chattahoochee River. According to the Federal census of that year, its population
consisted of 733 white persons 494 Negro slaves, and 23 free Negroes.
Mobile, under Spanish rule, was not enumerated. Ten years later, with
the addition of Madison and Baldwin counties, the whites numbered
6,422 and the blacks 2,624.

In 1800 Congress provided a legislature for the Mississippi Territory and President Jefferson appointed William C. C. Claiborne, of
Tennessee, as Governor. Two years later the first cotton gin in the region was erected by Abraham Mordecai, a Jewish settler, at Coosada
Bluff, near Montgomery.

The Protestant religion got a foothold in Alabama at the turn of the
century when Lorenzo Dow preached his sermons to frontier congregations on the Tombigbee. By 1808 Baptists and Methodists had local
churches in the territory.

The claims of Georgia to the territory west of the Chattahoochee
from 31° north latitude to 35° were purchased by the Federal Government on April 24, 1802, for $1,250,000. Louisiana, ceded back to
France by Spain in 1800, was sold by Napoleon to the United States in
1803 and the United States claimed Mobile as a part of the purchase.
The Spanish, however, protested that Mobile was part of West Florida
and refused to cede it to the United States. For a time the Spanish
claims were allowed to stand, though the United States did not admit
their validity. Congress added the land bought from Georgia to the
Mississippi Territory in 1804, extending that territory north to the
Tennessee Line.

An event of special concern to the nation occurred in Alabama in
1807—the arrest of Aaron Burr for treason. The former Vice President was recognized by a Washington County man, Nicholas Perkins,
and sent under guard to Richmond. The collapse of the Burr Conspiracy
involving many prominent public officials followed.

War with England broke out in 1812 and gave the Americans the
long-awaited pretext for taking West Florida from Spain. Ostensibly
to stop the use of the Spanish Gulf ports by the British fleet, an army
under General Wilkinson took over Mobile "without the effusion of a
drop of blood."

JACKSON CAMPAIGNS AGAINST THE INDIANS

With the outbreak of hostilities, the Indian situation in Alabama
became critical. The Muskhogean tribes, still occupying more than half
of the territory, were restless, for they had already felt the push of
American immigration into their tribal lands. The Creek listened to
"war talk" from the great Shawnee chief, Tecumseh, who saw in the
war between American and the mother country a chance to unite all the
tribes of the Mississippi Valley into an empire to oppose the westward
march of the white settlers. United States agents managed to keep the
Choctaw in line, but the Creek Nation was divided, and the war party

soon got the upper hand. Creek warriors, led by William Weatherford, a mixed-blood chief, attacked and destroyed Fort Mims at the junction of the Alabama and the Tombigbee. Several hundred white men, women, and children were killed, and the remainder were captured. Throughout the territory, settlers left their cabins and rushed for protection to the forts. The whole southern frontier was in a panic.

The Federal Government was too hard pressed in the North to send help to the far frontier, but Andrew Jackson, energetic and hot-tempered general of the Tennessee militia, organized an immediate campaign against the Creek. With "Remember Fort Mims" as their watchword, the militiamen from Georgia, Alabama, and Tennessee struck the Indians on the upper Coosa and marched against their towns. The Creek put up a brave determined struggle, but Jackson fought his way southward, possibly over the old route followed by De Soto. The battles of Talladega and Horseshoe Bend (March 27, 1814) made Jackson famous and broke the power of the Creek Confederacy. The general put Fort Charlotte and Fort Bowyer on Mobile Point in condition for defense and pushed on to further fame at New Orleans (January 8, 1815). On August 9, 1814, the Indians ceded to the United States nearly half of the present State of Alabama, and on September 14, 1816 the Chickasaw Nation relinquished all claim to its territory south of Tennessee.

Land east of the present State of Mississippi was organized as the Territory of Alabama by an act of Congress on March 3, 1817. John Crowell of St. Stephens was the Territory's first delegate to Congress and President Monroe appointed William Wyatt Bibb first Governor (1817). The first session of the Territorial legislature was held at St. Stephens in 1818.

Making use of the red ore rock found in large deposits over much of the State, northwest Alabama pioneers constructed the first iron furnace of the region in 1818 near Russellville.

ALABAMA BECOMES A STATE

On March 2, 1819, Congress authorized Alabama to draft a State constitution. A constitutional convention met at Huntsville from July 5 to August 2, and on October 25 the first Alabama State legislature convened there. On November 9 William W. Bibb was chosen Governor, and in December Congress passed a joint resolution admitting Alabama into the Union as a State. This became effective December 14, 1819, when President Monroe approved the resolution. The first United States Senators from Alabama were John W. Walker and William Rufus King; the first United States Representative was John Crowell. The seat of government was removed from Huntsville to Cahaba in 1820. In that year the Federal census showed 127,901 inhabitants in Alabama. The principal towns were Cahaba, Claiborne, Florence, Huntsville, Mobile, Montgomery, and St. Stephens.

Fiscal, administrative, and educational problems occupied the attention of the new law-makers. In 1820, by an act of the legislature, a

Alabama in History

REPLICA OF FORT JACKSON, AT CONFLUENCE OF THE COOSA AND
TALLAPOOSA RIVERS, WHERE THE BATTLE OF HORSESHOE BEND IS
ENACTED ELECTRONICALLY WITH SOUND.

INSIDE FORT MORGAN, AT THE MOUTH OF MOBILE BAY,
NOW A RECREATION AREA

MAGNOLIA GROVE, GREENSBORO, ALABAMA, A STATE SHRINE, HOME OF RICHMOND PEARSON HOBSON, REAR ADMIRAL USN, WHO SANK THE OBSTACLE SHIP, MERRIMAC, AT THE ENTRANCE OF SANTIAGO HARBOR DURING THE SPANISH-AMERICAN WAR. BELOW: TROPHY ROOM IN THE HOBSON HOUSE.

NONDENOMINATIONAL CHURCH AT ALPINE, NEAR FORT PAYNE, WITH HUGE ROCK AS FOURTH WALL

INDIANS OF PREHISTORIC ALABAMA, AS FOUND AT MOUND STATE MONUMENT, MOUNDSVILLE, ALABAMA.

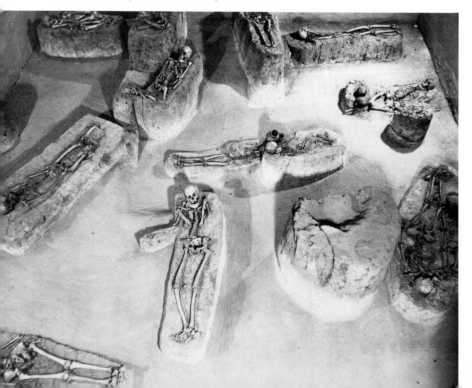

IVY GREEN, BIRTHPLACE OF HELEN KELLER, TUSCUMBIA.

HELEN KELLER CHILDHOOD MEMORABILIA IN IVY GREEN, HER BIRTHPLACE IN TUSCUMBIA.

STATUE OF FATHER RYAN, 1839-1886, POET OF THE CONFEDERATE CAUSE, MOBILE

DEXTER AVENUE, MONTGOMERY, 1851

COURT SQUARE, MONTGOMERY, 1884

Prattville, near Montgomery. The State Bank building at Decatur was completed, its facade adorned with massive stone columns quarried and raised by slaves who, as a reward for their labors, were freed at its dedication. Tuscumbia Railway, chartered in 1830 as the first railroad west of the Allegheny Mountains, was the pioneer transportation system. By the end of 1834 the line had been built 44 miles between Tuscambia and Decatur. Educational opportunities for the youth of Alabama in the decade 1830-40 were improved by the establishment of denominational colleges and by the opening of the University of Alabama under the direction of the State government in April, 1831.

In 1832, the Creek and Chickasaw Indians ceded to the United States all the Indian lands east of the Mississippi. The Indians were not obliged to leave the territory and white immigration was forbidden, pending a Federal survey. White immigrants refused to observe this condition, and settlers already on the Indian land refused to move out. As a result of the dispute Hardeman Owens, a Russell County road commissioner, was killed by Federal soldiers, and settlers in the county brought an indictment against the solders. Ultimately, the intervention of Francis Scott Key, as Federal Commissioner, staved off a State and Federal rupture. A compromise gave the Federal agents the right to remove whites from lands reserved for Indians, but allowed the titles of lands occupied by whites to be purchased from the Indians. The Cherokee ceded their lands to the State of Alabama on December 29, 1835, and agreed to remove beyond the Mississippi within two years, but trouble with their white neighbors during this period resulted in the forcible removal of the tribe from lands given up by treaty. By 1838 the Choctaw were beginning to conform to the Treaty of Dancing Rabbit Creek, signed in 1830, which ceded to the United States all their lands east of the Mississippi.

The anxieties of a financial panic and a yellow fever epidemic were added to the threats of Indian uprisings in 1835-37. The instability of the State Bank, affected by a national depression, brought widespread fear, and yellow fever caused many deaths among slaves. During the period 1837-41 came a long drought and a destructive fire in Mobile. The scene, however, was not wholly gloomy. Social consciousness was reflected in certain penal reforms—the abolition of cropping, branding, flogging, and debt sentences—and the building of a new State prison.

In 1840 the boundary dispute with Georgia was finally settled. Other legislative matters included the removal of the seat of government in 1847 to Montgomery, where a new capitol building was completed. Several levies of troops were organized for the Mexican War, but few saw much active service. In 1847 Reuben Chapman was elected governor and applied himself to the task of relieving the State debt. Revenue laws, including a poll tax and a license tax, were passed by the legislature.

A destructive fire broke out in the State capitol in 1849 and many valuable papers were lost; the capitol was rebuilt in 1851. In the same year resentment against what the South felt was Federal invasion of

States' rights as slaveholders crystallized in the convention of the Southern Rights Party at Montgomery. However, for a time such conservatives as William Rufus King and Henry W. Hilliard were able to keep the extremist elements in check.

The decade before the war was distinguished by advances in education, science, and social welfare. In 1847 the Alabama Medical Association was founded in Mobile, and the Alabama Historical Society at the State University. The State public school system, patterned after that of Mobile, was initiated in 1854; two years later the Methodists opened Southern University at Greensboro. The Institute for the Deaf and Dumb began at Talladega in 1858 and Bryce Hospital for the Insane at Tuscaloosa in 1861.

STATES RIGHTS AND SECESSION

The principle of State sovereignty had formed a bulwark against adverse national policies for the South. But with this principle increasingly threatened, secession sentiment had grown to overwhelming proportions by 1860. Governor Moore accordingly proclaimed an election of delegates to a secession convention, which opened in Montgomery on January 7, 1861. Four days later, an Ordinance of Secession, drawn up by William L. Yancey, was passed by a vote of 61 to 39, making Alabama the fourth State to secede. Alabama members of Congress resigned when Jefferson Davis left the Senate on January 21. The State faced war with a total population of 964,201 (1860 census): 526,431 whites; 435,080 Negro slaves; and 2,690 free Negroes.

On February 4, 1861, at a convention in Montgomery, delegates from Alabama, Georgia, Florida, Louisiana, Mississippi, South Carolina, and Texas created the provisional government of the Confederate States of America. On February 18 Jefferson Davis was inaugurated provisional president in the Alabama capitol; Montgomery continued as the seat of Confederate government until May 21, 1861, when the Confederate Congress adjourned to meet the following July at Richmond, Virginia.

Despite the pervading sentiment of patriotism, anti-slavery feeling was so strong in one section of northern Alabama that formation of a new pro-Union state—to be called Nickajack—was proposed. But most of this factionalism was soon subdued in a common cause. There are no definite figures on Alabama's contributions to the Confederate Army. According to varying estimates, from a population of little more than 500,000 whites, the State gave between 75,000 and 125,000 fighting men. Colonel William Henry Fowler, Superintendent of Army records of Alabama, reported that the loss of men in battle and by disease was heavier than that of any other southern state, but here, too, the estimates vary from 25,000 to 70,000. Alabama furnished to the Confederate Army between 60 and 65 regiments of infantry, from 12 to 15 regiments of cavalry, and at least 20 batteries of artillery. Approximately 2,500 white soldiers and at least 10,000 Negroes went from Alabama to support the Union.

At the outbreak of hostilities State troops seized Fort Morgan and Fort Gaines at the entrance to Mobile Bay and the United States arsenal at Mount Vernon. There was no fighting in Alabama during the first part of the war, but by 1862 Huntsville, Decatur, and Tuscumbia were in the hands of Federal forces. This invasion brought into the Confederate ranks nearly every male Alabamian old enough to carry a rifle. The State's naval hero, Raphael Semmes, first in the *Sumter* and later in the famous *Alabama,* was harassing Union commerce beyond the northern naval blockade.

The task of raising and equipping troops was creditably accomplished by Governor John Gill Shorter (1861-63). The 16 ironworks in the State steadily produced iron for shot, shell, and rifles, and the munitions plants at Selma and Irondale fabricated the products. Alabama supplied most of the iron used by the Confederacy, with an average output running 40,000 tons a year for the four war years.

After the Battle of Mobile Bay, Mobile surrendered in 1865, and the weakened Southern armies laid down their arms. The Emancipation Proclamation gave the Negro full control of his own life and welfare, and also made him the victim of exploiters, many of them from the North, who took advantage of the weakness of the civil governments. Despite the efforts of the Freedmen's Bureau and Northern philanthropists, Negro education was makeshift until the 1880s when a young Negro teacher, Booker T. Washington, was called from Virginia to establish a normal school for Negroes at Tuskegee.

For a number of years after the war, conditions remained in a state of upheaval. Strong anti-Southern feeling and action in the North bound even the hands of President Andrew Johnson. Lewis E. Parsons was appointed provisional governor and served until the election of Robert M. Patton in 1865. In the same year the State constitutional convention ratified the 13th amendment to the constitution abolishing slavery, nullified the ordinance of secession, repudiated the war debt, and provided for the election of State officers.

The Federal Reconstruction Committee had been busy framing a series of laws granting suffrage to Negroes, withholding it from white men who did not take an oath of allegiance to the Union, and denying national representation to States that had seceded. These motions were incorporated into the 14th amendment, which the State legislature refused to ratify. Alabama and other Southern States were immediately placed under military rule and General Wager Swayne was made military commander in Alabama. To force the State to accept the amendment, General Pope in 1867 ordered the registration of voters for the election of delegates to a constitutional convention. Qualifications were broadened so that a Negro man, more than 21 years of age, might vote and hold office; many white men were barred.

The Black Man's Party naturally controlled the convention. When Congress met in 1868, it passed a law to fit the case and declared the State constitution ratified and in effect. The new power of the Negroes attracted hordes of carpetbaggers—adventurers from the North—and scalawags—local office seekers who had formerly been ignored in the South. Exploiting the former slaves and organizing the dominant Negro vote into powerful political machines, these opportunists projected themselves into office and into positions of wealth and power.

Borne on the crest of this wave William Hugh Smith, a scalawag, held the office of governor from 1868 to 1870 with the support of the carpetbaggers and a Negro general assembly. With Federal troops ready to enforce its actions with bayonets, this administration ratified the 14th amendment, and furthered corruption, bribery, and speculation. Politically powerless, Southern white people resisted through secret organizations such as the Ku Klux Klan.

INDUSTRY AND EDUCATION START RISE

In the 1870s, educational and industrial development began anew. Birmingham was founded in 1871 when the South & North Railroad and the Chattanooga & Alabama Railroad crossed at this point. Mining on an extensive scale was started by Daniel Pratt and Henry F. De-Bardeleben in 1872. The University of Alabama reopened in 1869. The State Agricultural and Mechanical College at Auburn opened in the same year. The State Normal College was also established in 1872 at Florence. Normal schools for Negroes were open at Marion in 1874 and at Huntsville in 1875. The latter is now the State Agricultural and Mechanical Institute at Normal.

Governor Houston was inaugurated in 1874. A new constitution was ratified in 1875; the public school system was reorganized in 1876; and salaries of public officials were reduced. Federal troops were finally withdrawn from Alabama. Congress granted 46,080 acres to the State University on April 23, 1884, and further progress was made in education through the opening of normal schools for white teachers in Livingston and Jacksonville.

Montgomery was the scene of two local events of historic significance in 1886; the unveiling of the Confederate Monument on Capitol Hill by Jefferson Davis on April 29, and the replacing of horse-drawn street cars with an electric trolley car system. The legislature began providing assistance to Confederate veterans and their widows, although it was 1889 before the plan was worked out in detail. To supply money for new expenditures, Alabama began leasing convicts to private industry and established the office of examiner of public accounts to help protect the public money.

In 1887 educational opportunities were expanded by the opening of a normal school at Troy, the fourth college of its kind in the State. The Institute for the Deaf and Dumb at Talladega was enlarged, and to it was added the Institute for the Blind.

The first steel from Alabama iron was made in 1888 by the Henderson Manufacturing Company near Bessemer. From that time on, steel manufacture, now a major industry, developed steadily. The national depression of 1893-94 was of short duration, but its effect in Alabama was disastrous. Business was crippled, money was scarce and cotton—the measuring rod of commodity prices—sold at 4¢ a pound.

Oppressed by hard times, the farmers revolted against the old-line Democratic Party, which had been dominant on the issue of white supremacy. During the 1890s they thrice supported Reuben F. Kolb of Eufaula as a candidate for governor against regular Democratic nominees. Kolb had strong organized backing from the Farmers' Alliance and remnants of the Populist and Greenback parties, but the greater efficiency of the Democrats' machine caused his defeat in all three races, though by narrow margins.

After free silver was defeated in the national elections of 1896, bankers gained courage and industry became more active, especially in Birmingham. Alabama iron was shipped in large quantities to foreign ports, and Birmingham rolling mills perfected the open hearth process of converting pig iron into steel. The State was divided into nine Congressional districts. Agricultural schools were founded at Athens and Evergreen, and the Alabama Girl's Industrial School, was opened in 1895 at Montevallo.

When President McKinley, in 1898, issued a call for volunteers to fight in the war against Spain, Alabama mustered two regiments in Mobile. A battalion of Negro troops also answered the call. General Joseph Wheeler, of the Confederate Army, served in the United States Army as commander of the cavalry division at Santiago; from Alabama, too, went Lieutenant Richmond Pearson Hobson, United States Navy, who sank the *Merrimac* at the entrance to Santiago Bay in an effort to bottle up the Spanish fleet.

At the turn of the century a new industrial order was emerging and efforts were being made toward bettering social conditions. By 1900, the population had risen to 1,828,679 and the number of wage earners in industries was 52,711. There were 31 cotton mills producing goods valued at $8,153,136.

From 1901 to 1905 the legislature enacted laws regulating child labor in factories, bettering treatment of convicts, enlarging appropriations for schools and for Confederate veterans, and creating a department of archives and history. The buildings and land at Mount Vernon, granted to the State by Congress, were set aside as a mental hospital for Negroes. A new constitution became effective on November 29, 1901.

COMING OF ELECTRIC POWER

Electric power was first used as a public utility in 1906 when Colonel W. P. Lay organized the Alabama Power Company in Gadsden. The growing demand for electric energy soon so far exceeded the company's original hydroelectric facilities that it began an immense program of expansion. During the next 20 years, the Alabama Power Company supplied electric current in almost every part of Alabama—a development that eventually brought it into conflict with the Tennessee Valley Authority.

In the period immediately preceding World War I, laws were passed permitting the commission form of government in cities, providing for libraries in rural schools, for the safety of miners, for regulation of child labor in mills, and for a constitutional amendment to abolish the fee system in Jefferson County. A highway commission and an oyster commission were created. State-wide prohibition became effective in 1909 but was changed to local option in 1911. State-wide prohibition was again established in 1915, and a law was passed forbidding newspapers to carry whisky advertisements.

The first Alabama soldiers sent to the World War front were those who had been in service on the Mexican border in 1916. Known as the Fighting Fourth regiment, troops of the Alabama National Guard returned to civil life from the hunt for Villa, but within a few weeks were again mustered into Federal service. A few months later, this regiment was officially designated as the 167th United States Infantry, soon becoming an integral part of the celebrated 42nd Rainbow Division. At the time of organization the regiment comprised 3,605 men, exclusive of officers.

Of the 86,916 Alabamians in camps and overseas, there were 6,262 casualties. General Robert Lee Bullard, a native Alabamian, commanded the United States troops at Chateau-Thierry. The first United States sailor to be killed in the war was Seaman Kelly Ingram, of Alabama.

The National Defense Act of 1916 authorized the development of Muscle Shoals for the construction of a plant to "fix" nitrates from the air for use in the manufacture of munitions, and Congress appropriated $20,000,000 for the construction of the power and nitrate plants and Wilson Dam. But the war ended before the project was completed. In 1933 the plant, which had been operated only for experimental purposes, became a unit in the vast Tennessee Valley Authority program. *See Tour 5.*

Not until 1907 was a comparatively adequate child labor law passed. In 1921 legislation included repeal of tax exemption for the Alabama Power Company, creation of a dock commission for the port of Mobile, and abolition of the convict lease system. Public building and highway construction programs were put into effect. The manufacture of several new products was initiated, including copper wire, steel freight cars, paper, pneumatic tires, condensed milk, ribbon, and silk.

The costly effects of the 1929 flood in southern Alabama was added to the disastrous stock market crash, and between 1929 and 1931 a total of 63 banks failed with a loss of more than $16,000,000.

With the State firmly in the grip of a nation-wide depression, B. M. Miller was chosen governor on an economy platform in 1930. Enactment of an income tax law was one of the highlights of his term.

Bibb Graves was elected for a second term in 1934 and State laws were remodeled in line with the aims of the Roosevelt administration. Federal deposit insurance reestablished the banks on a firm basis.

Alabama ratified repeal of the 18th amendment in 1935 but an effort to wipe out the dry law failed to carry in a State-wide election. The dry vote—51.9 percent of the total votes cast—was exactly the same as the percentage of church members in the population—51.9. In 1937, legislative action again changed prohibition to local option and added new forms of taxation.

The Tennessee Valley Authority, authorized by Congress, began operation in Alabama in the summer of 1933, to undertake flood control and conservation work and to provide and sell hydroelectric power on a "yardstick" basis. It soon came into conflict with privately owned utility companies. A series of test cases culminated in the United States Supreme Court opinion, handed down January 30, 1939, upholding the right of the TVA to generate and distribute power.

Local civil service appeared in 1935, when the legislature passed a bill putting city and county employees of Jefferson County under the merit system. This law was fought in the courts and upheld by decision of the State Supreme Court in April, 1936. In May, 1939, State civil service was established, superseding the former spoils system. This was one of the first accomplishments of Governor Frank M. Dixon's administration, which began in January, 1939. A centralized purchasing plan for all State departments and institutions was initiated. Other changes were creation of the Department of Conservation within which the Division of State Parks (formerly the forestry commission) and the Division of Game and Fish carry on conservation work.

ALABAMA AS THE NATION'S ARSENAL

Governor Dixon's administration covered the first part of World War II. While the United States did not enter the conflict until 1941, American defense preparations began much earlier and Alabama was to become one of the nation's largest arsenals.

Old military installations were restored and new ones built. Brookley Field was established as an air depot. Maxwell Air Force Base in Montgomery, now site of the Air University, was greatly expanded. Gunter Field, also in Montgomery, and Craig Air Field near Selma were training sites for airmen and pilots. A new air base, Fort Rucker, was opened at Dothan. Fort McClellan near Anniston became, and is again, the training site for the Women's Army Corps.

Industry throughout the State moved into high gear. Shipyards in Mobile, which stepped up production with introduction of hull welding, built 196 ships and repaired more than 2,000. Along that teeming waterfront, the Alabama State Docks handled millions of tons of shipping.

Shipyards in Decatur on the Tennessee River built troop and supply ships, and in nearby Huntsville the Redstone Arsenal became a center of munitions making and housed the Army Ordnance Guided Missile School.

Birmingham's steel mills ran constantly, turning out plate for warships, and made-in-Birmingham shells burst over the world's battlefields. Farming communities overnight became industrial centers. Childersburg, population 400, boomed into a town when a $70 million powder plant was located there.

World War II took a heavy toll of Alabama's sons. The casualties for Army and Navy totalled 7,626, of which 5,115 were in the Army, 2,511 in the Navy. The Army had 2,736 killed in action, others died of wounds and non-battle causes; the Navy lost 1,114 in combat. Alabama troops were enrolled in the 31st Division, commanded by Major General John C. Persons, Birmingham bank president.

When World War II ended, the number of people working in industries was three times that on farms. Alabama was no longer predominantly agricultural.

Chauncey M. Sparks succeeded Dixon as governor during the period of adjustment to civilian life. Many of the war workers had to be absorbed in other occupations, and the State increased its routine appropriations doubling the one for public education and increasing the responsibilities of the health departments. The State Labor Department, abolished earlier, was reactivated to guide labor relations back to a normal plane. During Sparks' term the Gilbertown Oil Field in Choctaw County was discovered and petroleum production gained a new impetus.

Gordon Persons, Governor, 1951-1955, enjoyed an unusually good relationship with his legislature and was able to put through most of his campaign platform. He reduced cost of automobile license plates, continued to aid education and improved major highways as well as the country roads.

During Persons' administration Alabamians fought in the Korean War. Alabama National Guard units were called into national service as part of the Dixie Division. Fort McClellan was reactiviated as a chemical warfare center, and Maxwell Air Force Base and Brookley Field increased their activities.

James E. Folsom grew up on Coffee County politics to become Alabama's 47th governor and to earn the nickname "Big Jim" because of his size. He ran twice unsuccessfully for Congress and for the governorship before he was elected in 1947. Eight years later he was re-elected. He was the second governor to win two terms under the 1901 State Constitution, which prohibited a governor succeeding himself. Unsuccessful in his bid for a third term in 1962, he entered the Democratic primary again in 1966 and 1974.

Gov. Folsom's administrations were noted for their liberality in building farm-to-market roads and increasing aid to education, veterans and the aged.

THE GREAT SOCIAL READJUSTMENT

When the United States Supreme Court on May 17, 1954, declared that separation by race in the public schools was unconstitutional it opened a period of far-reaching social and political change in Alabama.

It announced that the doctrine of separate but equal, valid since 1896, had no place in public education because separate educational facilities are inherently unequal. Subsequent enactment of civil rights legislation, supported by the Federal courts and enforced by United States marshals, challenged a way of life that had been accepted as just and reasonable ever since the suppression of slave labor.

The initial reaction of officials of the 16 States that had compulsory segregation was dismay, incredulity, and defiance. Some officials called the decision a blow to States' rights, and said it could not be enforced. Governor Folsom condemned it, but when Southern governors at Boca Raton voted to uphold State control of schools, he abstained. It soon developed that sentiment favoring mitigation of separateness had been developing for decades; Negro organizations agitating for changes often had white support, especially among the young. What surprised the officials was the strategy pursued by black leaders to challenge racial discrimination on voting, higher education, rail and bus transportation, employment, dining and all manner of public services, and the financial backing to carry litigation from local courts, which were invariably adverse to change, to higher Federal courts.

The adjustment of Alabama life to enforcement of the civil rights laws took place all through the 1960s and into the 1970-80 decade. As in Northern as well as Southern States, there was opposition and resentment to forcible busing of school children out of their neighborhoods to achieve a dubious racial balance. Protest marches and demonstrations overran the business districts of Montgomery, Birmingham and Mobile. Municipal and private bus lines were served with Federal injunctions to eliminate discrimination in seating. Crowds of black youngsters, intermingled with whites, staged sit-downs in lunch rooms. When Negroes in Montgomery boycotted the buses the circuit court barred their use of car pools. The campaign of Autherine J. Lucy to attend classes at the University of Alabama in Tuscaloosa started a controversy that acquired national news coverage; a student organization supported her efforts. The White Citizens Council organized 60 chapters and enrolled 50,000 to oppose integration. At times there were isolated cases of violence by anonymous partisans: a shotgun blast hit the front door of a house of the Rev. Martin Luther King, Jr., in Montgomery, and a bomb destroyed a house occupied by the Rev. Frank L. Shuttleworth in Birmingham. When a bomb went off at the Sixteenth Street Baptist Church in Birmingham and killed four little girls the revulsion of feeling greatly aided compliance with Federal directives.

After the assassination of Albert Patterson, Attorney General who had fought racketeers, especially in Phenix City, John M. Patterson, his son, was nominated by the Democrats to succeed the father. He carried on a vigorous reform program during his four years in office, and in 1959 was able to defeat George C. Wallace for governor. Governor Patterson was active in improving education and highways.

George Corley Wallace, Patterson's successor, was destined to become the most widely-known governor. In his 1963 inaugural address

Wallace declared his segrationist and state's rights views, which were soon to be challenged by Civil Rights leaders and the Federal Government. He made an unsuccessful attempt to prevent integration of the University of Alabama, but was faced with his greatest confrontation when the Rev. Martin Luther King, Jr., just back from accepting the Nobel Peace Prize, organized and led a march from Selma to the Capital to dramatize black voter registration. Faced with responsibility for law and order, Wallace issued orders forbidding the march. When these were ignored, he called out the State Troopers, who met the marchers as the latter attempted to cross the bridge over the Alabama River. Television cameras were on hand for the confrontation and immediately the event became nation-wide news. Thousands more people flocked into the State. The blacks got a Federal court order allowing the march. President Lyndon Johnson called out the National Guard and the march took place.

Despite hundreds of FBI agents, Federal marshals, plus the Federalized National Guard, violence flared. A white woman from Detroit who was ferrying marchers back and forth between Selma and Montgomery, was killed by shots from a passing car.

President Johnson immediately called a special session of Congress and asked for the Civil Rights Act of 1965, regarded in Alabama as one of the most extreme laws ever passed by Congress. Governor Wallace, encouraged by other proponents of State's Rights, entered preferential presidential primaries in Wisconsin, Indiana and Maryland, receiving as high as 43 percent of the vote.

Unable constitutionally to succeed himself, Governor Wallace was instrumental in having his wife, Lurleen, run for governor in 1966. He was influential in the landslide victory that made her the first woman governor of the State. Until her death in 1968, he served as his wife's advisor. He had announced: "I shall be at her side and shall make the policies and decisions affecting the administration." Mrs. Wallace proved a capable governor. Her efforts to improve mental health programs have had continuing effect.

In this period, thousands of young Alabamians were involved in the unpopular Vietnam war. In Alabama war protests on college campuses never became as bitter as they did in other parts of the country.

Albert P. Brewer, Lieutenant Governor, completed Mrs. Wallace's unexpired term. He did so creditable a job that he almost defeated George Wallace in the primary election for a full-term. The run-off was a bitter one, with Wallace forces rallying for a decisive victory. And so the Wallace era was continued and extended again in 1974, when, due to a permissive constitutional amendment, Wallace was reelected for an unprecedented third term.

Meantime in 1968 Wallace ran for President of the United States and received a surprising 10 million votes after having obtained ballot position in all 50 states.

In 1972, Gov. Wallace tried for nomination, this time within the framework of the Democratic Party. He began his campaign in the

Florida primary, where he carried every county. His active campaigning ended May 15 when he was shot in Maryland and his legs were paralyzed. While still in a Maryland hospital, he learned he had won both the Maryland and Michigan primaries. He also won primaries in Tennessee and North Carolina. At the time he was taken out of the campaign, Wallace had one million more votes than any other candidate in the primaries where all had participated. His dramatic recovery enabled him to appear at the Democratic Convention in Miami and to return to fulltime duties as Governor. At the Miami convention he had 323 delegates against McGovern's 405 and Humphrey's 207.

Wallace's second term in office was marked with progress and economic prosperity. Under his leadership a new four-year medical school was established in Mobile and new two-year residencies were founded at Tuscaloosa and Huntsville. Facilities at the Medical Center in Birmingham were greatly expanded.

A record breaking $1.172 billion Education Appropriation Bill underscored the Governor's continuing interest in education, which was demonstrated during his first term, when he gave the State its network of junior colleges.

George Wallace has been on the Alabama political scene since 1946 when, back from World War II, he became an assistant attorney general. The following year, at the age of 27, he was elected to the State Legislature from Barbour County and in 1953 elected Judge of the Third Judicial Circuit of Alabama. Wallace announced in 1974, while campaigning for Governor of Alabama, that he was also available for the Democratic Presidential nomination in 1976.

To Alabamians goes a large part of the credit for the completion of the Panama Canal. United States Senator John T. Morgan, of Alabama, led the inter-oceanic canal movement in Congress. Dr. William Crawford Gorgas, born in Toulminville near Mobile, served as major general and surgeon general of the U. S. Army, and freed Cuba and the Isthmus of Panama from the scourge of yellow fever. Dr. Gorgas was later director of the International Health Board and active in exterminating yellow fever in Central and South America. General William L. Sibert, born in Etowah County, directed construction of the Gatun locks and dam in the canal, and the excavation of the harbor from Gatun to the Atlantic. In recognition of his services he was made major general by act of Congress in 1917.

Alabamians who have served the Federal Government in Washington include John Archibald Campbell, Justice of the United States Supreme Court, who acted as an informed mediator between commissioners of the Confederacy and those of the Federal Government; William Rufus King, who served as Minister to France before holding office as Vice President of the United States; Hilary A. Herbert, Secretary of the Navy under Cleveland; J. L. M. Curry, Ambassador to Spain, and Senator Oscar W. Underwood, serious contender for the Democratic nomination for President of the United States in 1920.

Senator John H. Bankhead, Sr., father of Senator John H., and

Representative William B. Bankhead, proposed the plan for Federal roads, and US 78 was named the Bankhead Highway in his honor. William B. Bankhead was speaker of the House of Representatives, 1936- 1940. At the 1940 Democratic convention Senator Lister Hill placed in nomination President Roosevelt for his precedent-smashing third term. Hill was co-author of the Hill-Burton Act, supporting hospitals. Senator Hugo Lafayette Black was a Justice of the United States Supreme Court 1937-1971. Sen. John Sparkman was Democratic candidate for vice president on Adlai Stevenson's ticket. Armistead Selden was named ambassador to Ireland. Admiral Thomas H. Moorer became chairman, U. S. Joint Chiefs of Staff after a distinguished career as Commander of the U. S. Pacific fleet, Supreme Allied Commander for the Atlantic; Commander-in-Chief of the U. S. Atlantic Forces, and Commander of the U. S. Atlantic fleet. Admiral Harold Page Smith was Supreme Allied Commander for the Atlantic.

Dr. Luther Terry, U. S. Surgeon General, led the Government campaigns to alert the public to the dangers of cigarette smoking. Both Kenneth Giddings and Edward Barrett became directors of the Voice of America; William Blount was named Postmaster General, Edward Norton became president of the Federal Reserve Board, and Dorothy Vredenburg Bush was secretary of the National Democratic Party.

Alabamians have also made notable contributions in medicine and science. Dr. Robert J. Van de Graaff, of Tuscaloosa, developed the Van de Graaff electrostatic machine that produces electric current of atom-breaking voltage; Dr. Luther L. Hill sutured the human heart; Dr. James Marion Sims founded the Woman's Hospital in New York, and Dr. John Allen Wyeth, who organized the Polyclinical Medical School and Hospital in New York led in graduate medical instruction. John J. Pratt, of Centre, invented a typewriter, called the pterotype, in 1867; he obtained a patent in England and was ready to put the machine on the market when Christopher Latham Sholes patented his typewriter in the Unites States, in 1868. Pratt's machine is now in the British Museum. At Tuskegee, George Washington Carver contributed greatly to the economy of the nation by producing more than 350 useful products from peanuts, sweet potatoes, soybeans, and the like, ranging from oils to synthetic molded articles.

Industry, Commerce, and Labor

ALABAMA'S earliest traders were French and British adventurers. By 1702, the French had pushed inland from their landing place at Dauphin Island to exchange cheap and gaudy trinkets for the Indians' stocks of furs. Even when this trade was broadened in 1711 with the settlement of Mobile, the French had little competition, for the Spaniards were interested in gold rather than furs and there were few British traders.

While traffic was carried on with all four of the Indian tribes, that with the Choctaw in the southwest was most convenient and most abundant. The French were kind to the Choctaw, treating them as equals in all except the ability to bargain.

Strong British competition and subsequent domination were delayed until 1762, when the English gained possession of Mobile by the Treaty of Paris. Almost immediately, traders and trappers began penetrating the Alabama region from Georgia. Trading posts were established throughout the territory, especially among the dominant Creek, and Mobile became a supply base for trading activities in the eastern Mississippi Valley, all of which was controlled by the English.

Although the relations of the British with the tribes were not so friendly as those of the French, the former's trade was more widespread and their exchanges were made on a more equitable basis. They gave the Indians cloth instead of trinkets, firearms instead of pots and pans. By the time of the American Revolution, furs valued at more than $1,000,000 annually were being sent out of the region.

The chief trading posts were in the Alabama-Tombigbee basin, embracing the present counties of Washington, Baldwin, and Clarke. But posts also were established in the vicinity of Muscle Shoals, and a large English post was maintained near the present site of Montgomery. These flourished until 1780, when the English lost control of the Gulf Coast to Spain and their supply base was wiped out.

But this setback was only temporary. In 1776, at the outbreak of the Revolution, several hundred British sympathizers left Georgia to build new homes in the basin of the Alabama and Tombigbee Rivers. By 1798, they had established the first permanent settlements in that territory, and trade was pushed with new vigor. These pioneers had little money and trade was largely a matter of barter. Furs, secured by trade with the Indians and also by hunting and trapping, were given to roaming merchants in exchange for cloth, cooking utensils, and crude implements.

The importance of cotton was recognized early, but its culture was interrupted by the War of 1812. When England, the chief market, was shut off, the growers watched the price of their staple drop. When the war ended the British market was reopened and the price of cotton soared to almost 30¢ a pound in 1815. This was an incentive to other settlers, and they came in a steady flow. By 1820, Alabama's population was 125,000; of this number, 31 percent were slaves. In another ten years, the population increased to 300,000, with slaves comprising 38 percent.

Settlers who had money, or were backed by Easterners, soon claimed most of the land along the rivers and, consequently, the river valley became densely populated by planters and their slaves between 1815 and 1830. The less affluent settlers built homes outside the valleys; many of them tilled their own lands and gathered their own crops, and few had more than two or three slaves.

Alabama's cotton crop of 1816 was 10,000 bales, but primitive ginning methods, despite the use of Whitney's gin, cut deep into the growers' profit. Each farm or plantation was, of necessity, a self-sufficient unit, and both cotton gin and press were home owned. They were crude affairs, run by horse power, and required painstaking care. The removal of seeds and trash was a slow process.

But in the neighboring State of Mississippi, Eleazer Carver was working on a machine to remedy these handicaps. His improved gin was introduced into Alabama in 1822 when James Jackson and General John Coffee installed it in the Tennessee Valley. This gin was a great advance over the old methods, protecting the fiber in the process of removal from the seed, and improving the quality of the staple so that a better market price could be realized.

By 1830 the price of cotton had declined from its high mark to 9¢. Many growers were ruined; but those who were financially able to weather the storm still believed that the "cotton road" was the way to success. Despite financial reverses, they continued sending their staple down the rivers on rafts, barges, and steamboats. The boat trips were slow, requiring two weeks downstream from Montgomery to Mobile, and as many as six weeks returning.

Use of the rivers naturally tended to encourage the building of towns along their banks. As early as 1815, St. Stephens sprang up as an inland port on the Tombigbee. The first State capital, Cahaba, was built at a point where the Cahaba River enters the Alabama, and Selma was founded 12 miles above. Farther east on the Alabama River, Montgomery began to grow.

Commerce did not flourish so readily in the Tennessee Valley area as in the central and southern parts of the State. This was because of the difficulties encountered at Muscle Shoals on the Tennessee River. The shoals were impassable in the dry summer months, and boats traveling upstream were forced to wait until winter, when the river began rising to a high point reached in February. The cotton growers combatted this difficulty by building large warehouses above Muscle Shoals, where they stored their staple to await its transportation downstream.

By 1830 the economy of Alabama was firmly based on agriculture, and northern industry was not affecting it. But some planters who earned little in cotton began to consider other means of livelihood. They turned from the fields to build small water-powered mills for grinding corn and wheat, and sawing logs into lumber. Sawmilling was spurred by a demand for timber resulting from a nationwide pickup in building. As lumber advanced, naval stores—turpentine, tar and resin—also reached an important place in trade. In 1834, distillation had been improved by copper stills and, by 1840, the piney woods of southern Alabama were overrun by turpentine makers.

As early as 1813, Alabama iron had been used to shoe horses in Andrew Jackson's army, and in 1818 Joseph Heslip had built the old Cedar Creek Furnace, near Russellville. Heslip's plant was a crude affair, having a rough stone furnace, Catalan forge, foundry, and a makeshift rolling mill. The forge hammer, weighing 500 pounds, was lifted by water power, and was then allowed to fall by its own weight upon the piece of iron that was being forged. Using charcoal in his furnace, Heslip found the innovation profitable. Farmers in the vicinity allowed him to remove the wine-red surface ore off their lands. He operated for two years, but in 1820 an outbreak of fever among his workers caused him to abandon the plant. Later, the property was acquired by Dr. Robert Napier, a Tennessean, but lack of transport facilities led to its final closing in 1832.

No further venture in iron making was made until 1843, when a furnace was built in Calhoun County. Another was erected in Shelby County five years later, and a third in Cherokee County in 1853. These furnaces, all using charcoal, were the only ones in Alabama before 1856. Their production was confined mostly to pots and pans, nails, and farming equipment.

The mining of coal gained more slowly. In the late 1840s beds were opened in Marshall County and at Tuscaloosa, on the Warrior River. Most of the output was used in blacksmith shops, although some was taken downriver to Mobile. The War between the States disrupted operations.

Alabama had no textile factories until 1832, when a small mill was built on the Flint River, in Madison County. With the opening of markets as a result of improvement in transportation, one plant was opened at Florence and another near Montgomery in 1840. Ten years later, a mill with an annual capacity of 1,200 bales and capitalized at $107,000 was built at Autaugaville, on the Alabama River. By 1860 the State had 14 mills, with 35,700 spindles and 623 looms, representing an investment of $1,316,000.

All of the State's industries were small units, with investments representing only $17 per capita of the free population. Statistics for 1849 showed that 1,000 individuals and firms were engaged in manufacture;

5,000 persons were employed, and products were valued at $4,500,000. Included in the industries were 12 cotton mills, 3 furnaces making pig iron, 10 plants making pig iron castings, and three manufacturers of wrought iron.

By 1860 the manufacture of flour, meal, and cereals held top rank in Alabama, followed by lumber, naval stores, cotton textiles, and iron. But agriculture was still dominant. The State had 55,128 farms, 33,730 slave owners, and 435,000 slaves, with most of the largest planters occupying the rich lands along the lower Tombigbee River. Cotton was the major crop, although more than 1,000,000 bushels of wheat were being raised annually. This grain was grown until the 1880s, when competition from the Midwest made it unprofitable.

During the war, Alabama's industry mobilized to aid the Confederate cause, and for a short period the iron works boomed. But with the overthrow of the South's armies, these operations were brought to a standstill. With Union occupation, the State counted a war loss of 25,000 mean, leaving numberless destitute women and children.

With many of the former slaves refusing to work in the fields, cotton was left to rot for want of picking. The desperate planters attempted to hire white labor, but the supply was undependable and the tax burden so heavy under carpetbag rule that many planters abandoned their homes and left the State. Fertile plantations, once valued at $150,000, now sold for $10,000 and less. Mortgage sales were familiar scenes in every town.

Alabama faced the end of Reconstruction with a huge debt but despite its handicaps industry began a slow revival in the 1870s. At Anniston, the Nobles and Tylers were beginning their venture in iron; the Selma works resumed peacetime activity; iron masters began shaping plans for the development of Jones Valley, which was to become Birmingham; furnaces were built and towns started at Ironaton, Oxmoor, and Talladega, and another furnace was established at Russellville, where Heslip had built his plant half a century before. In 1872, the Louisville & Nashville and the Chattanooga & Alabama railroads were completed, furnishing greatly needed outlets to markets. Flour, meal, and cereals led in production, followed by lumber, iron and steel, and cotton.

START OF THE MAGIC CITY

The most important events in Alabama's industrial history took place in the Birmingham area during the final years of the 19th century and the dawn of the 20th. Coal and iron ore were the ingredients that boomed a little village into the Magic City, magnet for big Northern money and scene of dramatic industrial growth.

For nearly half a century it was coal and iron ore, then steel that became the foundation of the district's economy. They still are—though the Birmingham coal fields in 1971 yielded less than 100,000 tons and Birmingham's mills and furnaces are hauling iron ore from Venezuela and making a better profit than they did when ore came from their own back yards.

Next to Birmingham, Anniston flourished in the coal and iron industry. Bessemer, a few years younger than Anniston and founded by the coal baron Henry F. DeBardeleben, followed with rapid growth. In 1903-04, Gadsden rose to fourth place in iron and steel with the building of five open-hearth furnaces.

It was, however, the Birmingham district that provided the real industrial magic. And while coal and iron ore are inseparable in an industrial sense, it was coal that lured the first money to the area. Twelve-foot veins and eight-foot workings were not uncommon. Coal could be hacked from the great bluffs. It cropped out, broke off and littered forest floors and ridgelines. But there was little use for coal at the start. Homes used firewood. The few iron furnaces used charcoal and railroads burned cordwood.

By the time of Appomatox, railroads began converting to coal, and in the Birmingham area, with practically no railroads, a few men resolved to keep their eyes on the best coal seams and wait out the destitute post Civil War years. One of these men, John F. Milner, in 1871 laid out a model system of town streets on a piece of wrapping paper, called it Birmingham and lured railroads into the district. And with that, a wild, speculative age swung into being.

Four years later, the boom had died and the new town was tottering. The demand for coal was too small and a lot of bad coal was thrown on a weak market. Worried men who had invested everything they had in coal, or because of coal in real estate, sought and eventually found a solution in the industrial marriage of coal and iron ore.

Until 1876, the few furnaces in the area making pig iron used charcoal in their ovens. In February of that year, a remodeled five-oven coke-burning furnace at Oxmoor, rigged for hot air blast instead of cold air, made its first successful run.

The local economy began to climb. Northern capital again began flowing in, and another boom era began, with ironmasters as well as coal barons calling the shots. By 1890 25 blast furnaces were roaring on the Birmingham scene. In the meantime, down from Tennessee came Ironmaster Enoch Ensley with Memphis cotton money in his pocket, ready to buy up the most prosperous furnaces and to open new ones. Close on his heels came an arch competitor, The Tennessee Coal & Iron Company. Power see-sawed between Ensley's group and TCI. The latter eventually swallowed up the big prizes.

TCI in 1895 set another technical milestone when it produced the first local basic pig iron. Before then, Birmingham produced either foundry or mill pig, both of which were comparatively weak. Conversion to basic (Low silicon) pig was imperative, because only basic pig lent itself to steel.

The 1880s thereby began the Iron Decade and Birmingham was firmly established as the Southeast's greatest industrial center. From the stone-broke-charcoal furnaces, the industry had progressed to where Birmingham iron had become a potent factor in the world market.

TCI, with an eye on the future, promptly erected its own steel plant—ironically, in Ensley, the little town named for the man TCI had replaced.

But from the beginning, TCI was handicapped by lack of capital and competition from the Lake Superior district. For years its stock was a football for speculators, with successive owners investing money for expansion and development. During the panic of 1907, the company was taken over by the United States Steel Corporation after President Theodore Roosevelt had approved the sale to stabilize New York banking houses which held stock as collateral. Several millions of dollars were spent for reorganization and a steady advance began, accelerated ten years later by the steel needs during World War II.

Since the first export of local pig began in 1894, Birmingham's iron has been part of world history. The city supplied plate for warships in every conflict since the Civil War. It's works turned out barbed wire for trench fighting in France during World War II and made-in-Birmingham bombs and shells have burst over all the world's battlefields.

In 1971, when Birmingham was celebrating its 100th anniversary, United States Steel operations in the area had become a sophisticated conglomeration ranging from the manufacture of thousands of steel items and coke and coal chemicals to the development of real estate into industrial parks. Whereas in 1937 the company's payroll carried 27,263 names, the introduction of modern technology and curtailment of some of the original activities have reduced the number of employees to around 13,000.

The company's district headquarters on Birmingham's outskirts overlooks its principal operation, the Fairfield plant, which runs for about $2\frac{1}{2}$ miles along Jones Valley. It is in this plant that plate, sheets, rails, bale ties, and industrial strapping and hundreds of other such items are produced. The old Ensley plant has been converted into a service supply depot where steel products are retailed.

TCI no longer mines iron ore, and only one coal mine is in operation. Pig is made only for its own consumption and one dolomite quarry operates to provide flux for its own plants and for sale.

Its Southern Raw Materials Property Division is concerned with protecting the surface lands over the company's mineral properties. There is a realty group developing other land holdings for industrial parks, and at nearby Leeds is located U. S. Steel's Universal Atlas Cement Division.

By 1971, the Birmingham-Anniston district was considered the Cast Iron Pressure Pipe Capital. Here is produced approximately 55% of the cast iron pressure pipe produced in the United States. The five major producers are American Cast Iron Pipe Company; U. S. Pipe & Foundry Company; Clow Corporation; McWane Cast Iron Pipe Company, and Alabama Pipe Company.

Coal mining, first undertaken by blacksmiths in Andrew Jackson's army, has been greatly reduced in recent years. Marble and limestone quarrying remain important industries. Alabama oolitic limestone is especially in demand, being as strong as granite and taking the fine polish of marble. Quarried first near Sylacauga in the 1830s, Alabama marble is noted for its fine texture and luster, which make it valuable for decorative purposes. Among other minerals which have been developed commercially are yellow ocher for paint making, niter, and scatterings of gold.

In 1916 an event of no immediate significance foreshadowed a tremendous industrial growth in northern Alabama—the order of the Federal Government to construct a dam on the Tennessee River and build two plants at Muscle Shoals to produce nitrates for use in the World War. When the plants were not completed in time they remained idle while corporations and Government officials argued over public versus private ownership and operation. In 1933 President Franklin D. Roosevelt started a new era in regional development when he obtained from Congress the authorization for the Tennessee Valley Authority. (*see below*).

Early industrial development of the State was in three fields: primary metals, specifically mining and the production of pig iron; the wood-using industry, primarily lumber; the textile industry, based on the vast cotton crop of the area. By 1971, however, the state had made giant strides toward its great industrial potential, was highly diversified and produced a wide variety of products. There were 4,800 manufacturing facilities representing 22 categories of standard industrial classifications, employing more than 305,000 persons with an annual payroll of a half billion dollars, and producing goods in excess of $3 billion.

The annual capacity of pig iron production in 1970 was 4.4 million tons. Annual steel capacity is even greater. The State's forest industries, including lumber, pulp and paper, use 1,200,000,000 board feet of lumber and almost 5 million cords of pulpwood each year. In total the wood-using industries contribute in excess of $600 million to the State economy annually, and employ over 70,000 people.

The cotton industry continues to be a large factor in Alabama's economy, employing 41,600 people, and the closely related apparel industry employs another 43,400. Among the more important of the otherwide variety of products produced in the State are: converted metal, cements, pulp and paper, building materials, aluminum products, limestone, feeds, wearing apparel, chemicals, fertilizer, marble, tires, rubber products, processed foods, and processing of aluminum ore.

A special chapter in Alabama's industrial growth is linked with rocketry, the rocket which carried the first man to the moon was developed at Huntsville's Redstone Arsenal, which embraces the George C. Marshall Space Flight Center and the Army Missile Command.

Today, banking is one of the most outstanding industries in Alabama, for more and more, banking is not only an institution of financial service and business, but tends to assume leadership in education, development and practices of other industries, economic research and individual counseling.

The relationship between the Alabama Bankers Association and the

State Banking Department is a cordial one. The two cooperate in a variety of ways to disseminate information to bankers throughout the State. The Association helps in areas where the State Banking Department has no direct jurisdiction, such as areas where national law does not necessarily follow state law, and from time to time superintendents are of assistance to governors and legislators.

At the end of 1971, there were 272 banks in Alabama (183 state and 89 national), and 270 branches (77 state and 193 national), with approximate total assets of $6½ billion.

Branch banking is governed by a county option system which requires legislative approval for individual counties. There are no specific state laws governing holding companies. There have been eight or 10 one-bank holding companies in the State for many years, but at present there is only one multi-bank holding company. Many others are anticipated in coming years.

ELECTRICAL ENERGY, GAS, AND OIL

Although the water wheel and wood-burning boiler were adequate for the neighborhood shops and feeble locomotives of ante bellum days, the coming of mechanized manufacturers required new sources of power. These were at first provided by coal-made steam and electricity. At Gadsden, William Lay urged river development for hydroelectric power, and at the opening of the 20th century he began furnishing Gadsden's electricity from a hydroelectric plant on nearby Big Wills Creek. In 1906 he organized the Alabama Power Company. Outside capitalists assumed control of the company in a few years and began carrying its transmission lines to all parts of the State.

The market for electricity grew steadily. By 1970, the company's investment in 56 of the State's 67 counties was $1,203,102,000, and it was selling 20,457,465,000 kilowatts annually to 785,000 customers. At present, to supply the power needs of its customers, Alabama Power operates a highly sophisticated system of five steam electric generating plants, 13 hydroelectric generating plants and one combustion turbine plant with a total installed capacity of 3,907,175 kilowatts. In addition, the company owns one-half the capacity of a one-million-kilowatt steam electric plant operated at Wilsonville, Ala., by Southern Electric Generating Company. Its electric service facilities also include more than 48,666 circuit miles of distribution lines.

Of the 13 hydroelectric projects it operates, Alabama Power built and owns 11, the Federal Government the other two. This system, completed in 1968, represents one of the biggest waterway development programs ever attempted by an investor-owned electric utility.

The company has a long-established policy of encouraging the public to take advantage of the recreational opportunities offered by the 145,000 acres of lake which its hydroelectric projects create. It leases cottage sites to families at reasonable prices. At the start of 1971, more than 2,000 such leases were in effect. At H. Neely Henry Lake work was started on a 60-acre park, the first of several planned by the company. Located near Ragland and Ohatchee, the park was to have 28 camp sites, a swimming area, boat launching ramps, an athletic field, nature trails, and other facilities.

A new recreational area also was being developed on Lay Lake to include picnic areas, parking facilities, boat launching ramps, camping grounds and a beach. Fishing piers were built at Martin Dam and Lewis Smith Dam and plans were being made for a pier at Weiss Dam. The company's development of such recreational facilities is carried out with Federal agencies, the State of Alabama and local and county authorities.

Alabama Power also leased about 230 acres of Martin Lake to the Alabama Society for Crippled Children and Adults, Inc., for development of a camp for recreation and rehabilitation of cripples of all ages.

During 1970, the company also instituted a Recreation and Fishing Newsletter to provide a means of informing the public about its lakes and the manner in which they are operated. This may be obtained by writing to Alabama Power Co., 15 South 20 Street, Birmingham, Ala. 35233.

TENNESSEE VALLEY AUTHORITY

The Tennessee Valley Authority is an agency of the United States Government established by Act of Congress in 1933 to plan for the "proper use, conservation, and development of the natural resources of the Tennessee River drainage basin and its adjoining territory." It has become the largest and most effective public organization for developing a region, exercising flood control and water use through 27 major dams, generating electric power for parts of seven states by means of water power and coal-fired steam plants, making and testing fertilizers on a large scale, restoring eroded land and rebuilding forests, and making navigable 650 miles of the Tennessee River from Knoxville to the Ohio. Its nucleus was a plant built by the Government in 1916 for the manufacture of nitrates to be used in munitions, which was to operate by water power made possible by the Wilson Dam. The act was immediately challenged by privately financed utilities but sustained by the U. S. Supreme Court in 1939.

The immense productivity of TVA is reflected in its report for the fiscal year ended June 30, 1973, which noted that sales of electricity topped 100 billion kilowatt hours. A total of 28.5 million tons of commercial freight moved on the Tennessee waterway in 1972. Steam plants used 37.5 million tons of coal and coal suppliers reclaimed 4,494 acres of retarded strip-mine land. Research in fertilizers supported the Agency's shift from nitrate to sulfur-coated urea as an aid to crops. Advanced fertilizers come from the National Fertilizer Development Center at Muscle Shoals, where "the plant nutrient content of fertilizers has more than doubled, from about 20 percent to 43 percent." The

Annual Report cites the impact of the new processes on agriculture: "Corn acreage is down 85 percent but yields per acre are up 220 percent; cotton acreage is down 85 percent but yields up to 90 percent. Pastures have replaced gullies and the value of livestock products sold in the Valley has increased 1400 percent." Soybeans, which were not grown in the area in TVA's early days, are now the most important crop of the region (18.5 million bushels in 1972); loss from forest fires has been reduced to less than one percent, and nearly 1,200,000 acres have been reforested.

The ability of TVA to exercise flood control was strongly demonstrated in 1973 when rainfall and runoff were the highest in 83 years of record. During March 11.4 inches of rain fell on the Tennessee Valley and numerous reservoirs reached capacity. Flood damage in Chattanooga and Knoxville was materially curtailed by storage in the reservoirs. Development of ports along the Tennessee River has enabled industry to use barges to ship products to foreign countries and to receive loads from distant places. TVA reports that coal, boiler equipment, zinc concentrate, ferrous phosphate ore, and soybean oil were shipped to Europe and Japan. Lumber, molasses, aluminum pigs, and steel were products moved by barges on the Tennessee. Private industry has invested about $1 billion in plants along the waterfront in the last ten years.

For many citizens TVA has opened unexcelled opportunities for recreation within easy driving distance of their homelands. Alabama has expended millions to provide facilities of all kinds at Wheeler State Park, Guntersville State Park, Elk River State Park, and numerous camp sites, woods and beaches along the Tennessee. Fishing, boating, swimming, picnicking, hiking, riding, and living in cabins are possible here. The whole area drained by the Tennessee and its tributaries in Alabama, Tennessee, and Kentucky has two forms of expanding energy —industry and recreation. The number of people using the parks for recreation runs into millions.

In addition to TVA and Alabama Power Company, the State has two other suppliers of electrical energy. Southeastern Power Administration (SEPA) markets electrical power for hydro projects constructed by the U. S. Army Corps of Engineers, such as Miller's Ferry and Walter F. George Dams. These have a combined generating capability of 220,000 kilowatts. Jones' Bluff and West Point each came on line within the next few years, giving a total generating capacity for SEPA in Alabama of approximately 362,000 kilowatts.

The Alabama Electric Cooperative's present generating capability is more than 137,000 kilowatts. Its two thermal plants are Tombigbee at Jackson and McWilliams at Gantt. It also has hydroelectric plants located at Gantt and River Falls. These generating companies have strong interconnecting ties with each other and with utility companies in neighboring states.

In addition to its abundant electrical power, Alabama is traversed by natural gas pipelines of six transmission companies: Southern Natural

Gas Co., Alabama-Tennessee Natural Gas Co., Transcontinental Gas Pipeline Corp., United Gas Pipeline Co., Tennessee Gas Pipeline Co., and Texas Eastern Transmission Corp. Additionally, natural gas is distributed by other private companies, natural gas districts and municipally owned gas systems.

The vast supply of natural resources in Alabama, estimated to be 10 percent of the nation's total, has provided the impetus for the State's industrial growth. Included are 35 commercially valuable minerals. Alabama has the only area in the country where the principal ingredients for making steel—iron ore, coal, and limestone—are found within a 25-mile radius. Reserves of 8 billion tons of iron ore deposits have been proved.

Southeast Alabama recently has had dramatic discoveries of oil. The search began in 1865 when the Watson wells were drilled in Lawrence County. But not until 85 years and 700 dry holes later, was the search successful when the A. R. Jackson No. 1 well at Gilbertown, Choctaw County, came in.

When the Gilbertown Pool was completely developed, it covered an area 40 to 80 acres wide and 13 miles long, and extended almost across Choctaw County. This pool still produces more than 20,000 barrels of oil per month.

In 1950, Alabama's second oil pool, the South Carlton Field, named for the town of Carlton, about eight miles north of the pool, was discovered at the south tip of Clarke County by Humble Oil & Refining Co. This oil pool is in a wilderness swamp straddling the Alabama River, with wells in both Clarke and Baldwin Counties. The oil is the heaviest, thickest and most viscous crude petroleum produced in Alabama. In cold weather it will not flow without being heated. The oil produced from this field is shipped by barge to the Warrior Refinery at Tuscaloosa and is used in the manufacture of asphalt paving materials.

In 1952, Humble discovered the Pollard Oil Pool, a few miles southwest of Brewton in Escambia County. Drilling on the farm of A. W. Moye at a depth of 5,000 feet, "a "gusher-type" of oil with a potential of 1,000 barrels of high grade oil per day was brought in. Twenty years later this pool had produced a total of 1,914,555 barrels.

In 1955, the world's largest oil pool below a depth of 10,000 feet was discovered in Alabama, when, at the north edge of Citronelle in North Mobile County, a wildcat well penetrated oil-bearing formations. Total production in barrels as of Jan. 1, 1971, was 88,583,848

Oil and gas exploration gained considerable momentum during the 1970s as exploration and wildcat drilling became more intense than ever before. The increased exploration activities resulted in the discovery of four new oil fields and one gas/condensate field.

Commercial production of oil in 1971 was located in eight of Alabama's 67 counties in 17 fields. Average daily production from 556 wells during 1970 was 20,027 barrels, or a total production for the year of 7,309,986 barrels.

In 1974 and 1975 speculators and representatives of old-line companies were rushing to lease land around Chunchula, south of Citronelle, site of a new oil pool.

Total employment in important segments of the petroleum industry during 1970 was 14,500 employes who earned $78 million in salaries. Over 450 of these employes are engaged in the exploration and development of oil and gas.

LABOR AND EMPLOYMENT

In 1830 more than two thirds of the population was dependent upon agriculture. In addition there were wheelwrights, blacksmiths, millwrights, and shoemakers who traveled from place to place seeking work. Some of the settlers operated foundries and machine shops in connection with blacksmith shops.

Until this period, none of the small lumber, iron and textile mills employed more than 20 persons; most of them were able to operate with 6 or 8 helpers, and wages were so low that only the most destitute sought jobs. In 1833, however, Daniel Pratt arrived from New Hampshire and established a cotton gin manufacturing plant on Autauga Creek. Soon afterward, he began operating sawmills, blacksmith and tin shops, a carriage factory, and a printing business. By 1834, his ventures were so successful that he employed 347 people. Wages were often less than $1.50 for six sunrise-to-sunset days, but Pratt had struck upon a plan to keep his employees satisfied. He founded the forerunner of the present day company town, building small, fairly comfortable houses for his workers, and providing gardens for growing vegetables. The sale of whisky within the town limits was forbidden.

The ante bellum industries drew upon a plentiful but unskilled supply of white labor from the small, rock-bound mountain farms. In 1850, the 12 cotton factories in the State were employing 736 people, and 10 years later 14 mills employed 1,312 workers. Those who could not find jobs in the cotton factories turned to saw and planing mills, small mines, and furnaces, where they worked for as little as 50¢ for a 12-hour day.

The illiterate whites had a status only slightly above that of slavery. It was not uncommon for them to work in positions inferior to those held by freed Negroes, who had acquired skill in brickmaking, masonry, carpentry, and tinsmithing. In 1860, there were 2,690 Negroes who had bought or been given their freedom. Many of these found semi-skilled work, although their pay was no better than that of the whites.

From 1865 until 1876, the industrial laborer was hard pressed to find any form of employment. But with the lifting of Reconstruction, coal and iron industries revived lumbering operations were renewed and turpentine operators established themselves in southern Alabama. Between 1886 and 1890, coal and iron boomed, but the unskilled laborer did not share in the awakening.

Industry was not slow to adopt plantation paternalism, and in many instances, the lack of training for economic responsibility among farm-reared workers made it a necessity. These people had been accustomed to living in a house owned by the employer, buying supplies from his commissary, and obtaining medical care on his order. In the factory, the mine, and the mill they worked best under a similar arrangement and, partly for this reason, the "company town" came into existence. It was generally successful so long as employees were treated fairly; but it offered many opportunities for exploitation, and some companies were not above taking advantage of them.

Another evil was the convict labor system, which existed throughout the 19th century until organized efforts of women's clubs and reform bodies persuaded the legislature to abolish it. In 1923 an act ordered prisoners out of the mines, but it was July 1, 1928, before the last convict left the mines at Flat Top. Prisoners are employed today on State highways and drainage projects, in the dairy, mill, and shirt factory at Holman prison, and on prison farms.

Exploitation of child labor by early cotton mills and coal mines was ignored by the Legislature, despite vigorous efforts on the part of the clergy, doctors, organized labor and women's clubs, Not until 1907 did the Legislature under pressure from these forces,. led by the Rev. Edgar Gardiner Murphy, then rector of St. John's Episcopal Church in Montgomery, pass a comparatively adequate law.

A succession of amendments has resulted in today's strong and diligently enforced Child Labor Law. Every child or youth under 17 must have a work permit before he goes to work in Alabama. In certain instances, older youngsters may be required to obtain a permit. Neither marriage nor high school graduation exempts them. Children working for their own parents in connection with their own business or trade must have permits, but no permit is required for agricultural or domestic services. These work permits may be obtained at all City and County Boards of Education and at most high schools in the State. However, the issuing officer may refuse to issue a permit, even if the applicant meets basic requirements, if the minor seems to him physically unable to do the work or when, in his opinion, the best interests of the minor would be served by refusal. The issuing officer must refuse a permit to a minor for any employment prohibited by the Alabama Child Labor Law.

Permits are not issued to minors under 14 except that special Summer Employment Certificates may be issued to boys of 12 and 13 for certain occupations. Provisions are also made for issuance of Street Trade permits under special conditions for boys as young as 10 years.

The Alabama law prohibits girls from working in certain occupations and places, but allows the employment of boys in these places. However, with respect to current laws dealing with equal opportunity of the sexes, the Alabama Child Labor Laws are purely protective of young females and do not discriminate against anyone on account of sex.

Alabama does not place a limit on the working hours of men or women, but by Federal law they cannot work more than 40 hours without overtime payment. A liability and compensation law, now known as Alabama Workmen's Compensation Law, passed in 1919, has been updated since then. This law is not compulsory in Alabama, as in many states. If the workmen's compensation is not carried, the employer does not have recourse to the old common law defense of contributory negligence, etc., on the part of the employee. Most plants in the state carry insurance with established insurance companies, while a few carry their own insurance.

Unionization was slow to gain a foothold in Alabama. As early as 1882, the Knights of Labor were attempting to organize unions. But rural-born workers, individualistic in temperament, often joined their employers in opposition. In 1886, when the Knights had become affiliated with the American Federation of Labor, a number of Birmingham coal miners established a local. Other craft unions with minority memberships were organized and a State Federation of Labor was formed in 1901. It remained relatively insignificant under the competition of company unions.

In 1908, a coal miners strike of the United Mine Workers in the Birmingham district was broken by the national guard and union organizers fled the State. When a national coal strike was called in 1922, coal production gained tremendously in Alabama, where miners were unorganized.

Conditions changed somewhat in 1933, with the enactment of the National Industrial Recovery Act (NRA). For the first time in Alabama's history, workers were given the privilege of union membership without fear of company reprisals. New members joined organizations in almost every craft, with unionization chiefly in mines, steel mills and textile factories. Despite this, however, there were strikes in the mining and textile industries for wage increases and better working conditions.

Efforts at unionization were strongly opposed for a number of years in certain plants, but the membership in the Congress of Industrial Organization—composed principally of mine, steel and maritime workers—increased steadily. In 1937, it became dominant in Alabama by obtaining contracts with U. S. Steel's Birmingham plants and other steel companies. Membership in AFL was confined chiefly to the building and printing trades and miscellaneous craft unions. Neither organization had then or since much success with the textile workers. The two powerful organizations merged in Alabama in 1966, a year after national consolidation.

In 1963, the Alabama Legislature passed the Right-to-Work Law, which in substance provides: The right of anyone to work shall not be denied or abridged on account of membership or non-membership in any union; any agreement denying any person employment because of non-membership in a union is illegal; no person shall be required to become or remain a member of any union as a condition of employment or a continuation of employment, nor shall any person be required to abstain or refrain from membership in any union as a condition of employment or continuation of employment; no employer shall require as a condition of employment the payment of any dues etc., to any union; any person who may be denied employment in violation of the Act may recover from such employer and others such damage as he may have sustained.

The Alabama State Employment Service provides a valuable link between employer and employee, often helping new industries to find trained workers, and setting up programs to train workers in the skills needed.

Labor-management conditions are exceptionally good in Alabama. Continuously fewer man hours are lost due to work stoppages than in most other states. There have been no really serious Labor-Management conflicts in a number of years. The largest number of man days lost because of work stoppage was during the last nation-wide steel strike. Productivity is also exceptionally good. Wages in steel and most other industries throughout Alabama are higher than in the textile field. Most textile industries pay the minimum hourly wage under the Federal wage laws.

According to the U. S. Census of 1970, the number of wage-earners in Alabama was 1,339,400—843,822 male, 495,578 female. Of the total, 1,183,600 were in nonagricultural work, 87,700 in agriculture.

By Highways, Waterways, Rails, and Air

THE earliest highways in Alabama followed the paths used by Indian tribes since the distant past. A maze of deeply marked forest trails connected the palisaded Indian towns and villages and formed links in the great foot highways that led to the eastern seaboard and the Ohio River country. The Indians of historic times used the old trails for trade and war. Among the more important were the Southern Trail, or the Great Trading Path, which led from the present site of Augusta, Georgia, west to the Creek towns on the Tallapoosa; and the Pensacola Trading Path, called by the early traders the Wolf Trail, from the Alibamu towns south to Pensacola.

Over these trails French explorers and Jesuit missionaries reached the interior in the early years of the 18th century. French fur traders chose the network of streams that made up the Alabama-Tombigbee system. Many of them were Canadian *voyageurs* whose wandering life in the forests of Louisiana Province was much the same as it had been in the north—except that here were no snow-smothered months and the birchbark canoe was replaced by the *pirogue,* a light serviceable dugout of cypress.

French traders, dissatisfied with the prices paid for furs in Mobile, began crossing the mountains to Charleston. Presently English traders and woods runners were following them westward along Indian trails from Georgia and the Carolinas. By 1720 the English had established posts in the very heart of the region claimed by France and its Creek and Choctaw allies. During the half century that traders and squatters filtered into Alabama from the English colonies, the main trails became horse paths; but not until the close of the 18th century, when immigration began in earnest, were they heavily traveled.

From 1800 to 1805 a series of treaties with the Indians threw open to settlement vast tracts in the valley of the Tennessee River. The need for new routes was imperative. Although flatboats from the headwaters of the river brought many settlers, most of them came overland. From Kentucky and Tennessee they traveled by way of the great Natchez Trace, which the Federal Government purchased in 1801 from the Chickasaw and the Choctaw Indians. This road from Nashville crossed the Tennessee River at Colbert's Landing a few miles below Muscle Shoals, and struck southwest through the wilderness to Natchez, capital of the Mississippi Territory. Ungraded and sown with stumps and mudholes, it was for a decade the only wagon road into the Alabama region.

Settlers from South Carolina and Georgia came over one of the main Creek horse paths through the Tennessee and Alabama River basins. In 1811 this trail became the Federal Road, sometimes called the Three Chopped Way, because the surveyors marked the route with triple blazes on the tree trunks. Entering Alabama near the present site of Columbus, Georgia, it extended to Mims' Ferry on the Alabama River, with branches to Natchez and down the Tombigbee to Fort Stoddert. In 1805 a post route from Knoxville to New Orleans by way of the Alabama-Tombigbee county followed old roads.

At the outset of the Creek War (1813), Andrew Jackson's militiamen opened a third wagon road that led from Columbia, Tennessee, through Fort Deposit on the Tennessee River, about eight miles west of present Guntersville, into the Upper Creek country. First used for the passage of troops and supplies into central Alabama, the road was an important route during the settlement of Indian lands in the Coosa region.

In winter the immigrant roads became either rivers of bottomless mud or systems of ruts and hillocks, iron-hard and highly destructive to wheel and axle. A serious problem encountered by the builders of these and other early roads were numerous streams too deep to be forded. Sizable creeks could be crossed by means of raccoon bridges— tall trees felled to span the stream—or by makeshift rafts. The Tennessee and its larger tributaries required more elaborate devices. As early as 1797 the Chickasaw were poling barges across the river at Colbert's Ferry and by 1820 cable-ferries, powered by horse and windlass, operated regularly at Ditto's Landing and Fort Deposit on the Tennessee, and at Mims' Landing and other points on the Alabama River.

By 1820 farms and plantations along waterways providing flatboat transportation to downriver markets were flourishing, while those 30 or 40 miles from navigable streams stagnated. As the need for good roads grew insistent, private companies secured charters for the construction of turnpikes with tollgates at intervals. There were no toll charges for funeral processions, church-going folk, persons going to vote or to the mill, blacksmiths, doctors, and men on their way to military musters. Regular paying customers, however, had the right of way. County courts were empowered to supervise the repairing of these roads and no tolls were collected when they were in bad repair. This system continued in force, with few changes, until 1901.

The plank road, a refinement of the log corduroy road long used in the East to traverse sloughs, was introduced into Alabama in 1849. Easily built in a region where virgin timber was plentiful, it consisted of parallel rows of squared oak "sleepers" covered with timbers eight feet long and three inches thick. The heavy dust of summer travel and the hub-deep mire of winter were thus avoided. Important among the toll roads were the Central Plank Road, the Greensboro Plank Road, and the Montgomery South Plank Road, capitalized at $50,000 each. Although 24 plank roads were chartered by the Alabama legislature in 1849-50, experience proved them unsatisfactory. Warping in winter and attacks of boring insects and dry rot in summer made expensive repairs constantly necessary.

Three stagecoach lines, carrying passengers and mail, were operating on the Federal Road before 1840: the Mail Line, the Telegraph Line, and the Peoples Line. Relay stations, where horses were changed, were established about 12 miles apart. As roads developed, stagecoach lines increased and were operated on regular schedules.

Little public effort was made to provide good all-weather roads for Alabama until 1911. In that year the State Highway Department was established to supervise building and maintenance. The late Senator John H. Bankhead, Sr., first of the Bankheads to hold office, was a pioneer supporter of highway development. On July 11, 1916, he procured the passage of an act whereby the Federal Government aided the states in the construction of rural post-roads. The annual Federal appropriation of $5,000,000 to Alabama for this purpose was increased after 1921. In recognition of Senator Bankhead's services US 78 was named the Bankhead Highway.

Alabama has more than 20,000 miles in its State Highway System, of which more than 10,000 miles are designated primary, all surfaced. The Federal Interstate Highway System provides Alabama with expressways that bypass the crowded traffic centers and give drivers long stretches of unimpeded routes that bisect the State. Of these the longest is Int. 65, 366 miles, which enters the State at the Tennessee border and moves south via Birmingham and Montgomery to Mobile, short belt routes giving quick access to the metropolitan centers. The Alabama Highway Patrol, established in 1936 to regulate traffic, is the chief factor in keeping the roads safe. Transportation routes traverse Alabama, and general commodity service is provided to all points along these routes by one or more carriers. Special commodity and contract carriers are also available to all points.

Over 600 interstate carriers are certified to operate in Alabama. Approximately 80 percent of all interstate interchange is conducted at Birmingham, Mobile, Montgomery, Dothan, Gadsden and Selma. The abundance of carrier service, the five interstate highways lacing the state, and swift crosstown passage of the super highway system all assure industrial access to the nation.

Greyhound Bus Lines and Continental Trailways operate from border to border. In addition several small companies operate between communities.

From the earliest days of settlement, waterways have played a leading role in Alabama's development. Today the State is fourth in the nation in miles of navigable waterways, with the potential to move into first position. The present 1,000 miles of 9-ft. channel will extend to 1,700 miles within a few years.

The Chattahoochee-Apalachicola system provides navigation from the Gulf Intracoastal Waterway in the Chattahoochee River to Phenix City, Alabama, and Columbus, Georgia.

The Tennessee system is navigable from Northeast Alabama, across the state and Northwest through Tennessee and Kentucky to its confluence with the Ohio and Upper Mississippi Rivers.

The Warrior River drains a basin almost as large as that of the Tennessee and when joined by the Tombigbee and the Alabama Rivers creates a waterway that extends the length of the State to Mobile Bay. Development of a connection between the Tennessee and the Tombigbee, now in the making (1975), will further extend the waterways open to navigation.

To make the Coosa River navigable from Wetumpka to Rome, Georgia, a distance of 275 miles, has been the object of recent engineering plans. The Alabama Power Co. authorized the expenditure of $194,000,000 for building four new dams and raising a fifth on the Coosa, adding 609,900 kw by hydroelectric power. The final objective is a 9-ft. channel from Mobile to Rome.

The Gulf Intracoastal Waterway, with freight service from Panama City, Florida, to Brownsville, Texas, is maintained at a channel depth of 12 ft. and width of 125 ft. It extends for 60 miles along the coast of Alabama. From Carrabelle, Florida, its channel passes through Perdido Bay, inside the outer islands of Baldwin County, and through a cut into Bon Secour Bay, inside the Dixie peninsula, crossing lower Mobile Bay through the Overseas Highway beyond Cedar Point, thence on to Mississippi Sound. The principal tonnages on the waterway are coal, crude oil, petroleum products, and chemicals. At Bayou La Batre the Inland Docks Division has constructed a commercial dock.

Mobile Bay was chosen in 1702 as the site of the first French colony in the territory because of its good harbor and easy access to the interior provided by the Alabama River and its tributaries. Mobile was the capital of Louisiana and the seaport from which indigo and furs were exported to France. After a hurricane had choked the harbor with sand, the capital was removed to Biloxi in 1719. Under subsequent British and Spanish rule Mobile's importance as a port declined.

The dependence on land routes lessened after the first decade of settlement in northern Alabama. Though several freight lines operated trains of Conestoga wagons over the mountains, farmers and especially cotton planters used the rivers more and more to transport their products to market. The Coosa-Alabama river route, extending from the northeastern corner of Alabama to Mobile, was navigable only during high water in late winter and spring. Even then only flatboats could travel over much of its length. Drained by these rivers, the Black Belt was only sparsely settled until the coming of the steamboat. In northern Alabama the rich cotton lands along the great bend of the Tennessee River were rapidly settled and were producing enormous crops by 1820. A lively river traffic sprang up. Imports from the East came downriver in flatboats to Alabama from Tennessee and cotton was shipped north along the river to the Ohio and down the Mississippi to New Orleans.

These first carriers, the flatboats, were built on the upper reaches of the rivers. From 100 to 150 ft. long and 10 to 18 ft. wide, the flatboat was made of rough oak plank, caulked with pitch and crudely decked with pegged boards. The larger ones had space for wagons, teams, and dozens of bales of cotton. Four men were required to manage the steering oar at the stern. These unwieldy craft, loading cotton at Fort Deposit, Triana, at the head of Muscle Shoals, Florence, and Cotton Port, a few miles from the present Decatur, required months to drift to New Orleans. There they were knocked down and sold for timber, and the boatmen returned overland. A development of the flatboat peculiar to Alabama was the cotton box, a huge cumbersome craft whose high sides provided cargo space for hundreds of bales.

The keelboat was smaller than the flatboat and tapered to sharp points at bow and stern. Its heavy oak keel-timbers were proof against the most vicious snags and its deck was well-roofed. Keelboats could be poled upriver as well as down. Where the water was swift, the crews went ashore and "warped" the craft against the current with strong ropes hitched around trees. If low-hanging branches were within reach the crew could stand on deck, grasp them, and pull the boat along. Known as bush-whacking, this method was practiced only on smaller streams. Though Alabama's riverways were superior to land routes, they still left much to be desired. Only the smallest flatboats could navigate the Tennessee during low water. Planters lost heavily because of the delay in getting their cotton to market. As early as 1818 upriver planters, especially handicapped by Muscle Shoals, began promoting a steamboat service. Huntsville and other towns in Alabama and Tennessee joined in the effort. The first steamboat on Alabama waters was the *Alabama*, built at St. Stephens. It steamed down to Mobile in early 1818, but was not able to make its way upstream again. On April 5, 1819 a steamboat company was formed at Huntsville, and in 1821 the *Osage* made its maiden trip from New Orleans to Florence with a cargo of food staples, hardware, pig iron, and woolen cloth. A year later the lightdraft steamers *Rocket, Courier,* and *Velocipede* began a regular schedule between New Orleans and Florence.

For several years steamboat passage over Muscle Shoals was not attempted, and planters above the shoals were forced to dispatch their cotton downriver by flatboat to Florence.

In 1827 the *Atlas,* a steamboat with an extremely light draft, was specially built to pass the shoals. During the high water of February, 1828, this craft managed to ascend the river from Florence to Knoxville, Tennessee, in a little less than 30 days.

There was fairly regular service between Florence and upriver towns; the shoals, however, prevented passage during low water. Engineers suggested connecting the Tennessee by canal with waterways leading to the Gulf, but the idea was abandoned in favor of a canal around the worst section of the shoals. In 1828 Congress authorized the sale of 400,000 acres of public lands in the Huntsville district to finance the undertaking. Excavation started in 1831 and the canal was opened to traffic in 1836. It proved a failure because its terminal approaches could be used only during high water. Funds were not available to correct the defects, and the canal was abandoned the next year. In 1873 and 1877 new Federal surveys were made. Actual work was begun in 1882 and the canal was reopened by U. S. Army Engineers in 1890. *See Tour 5 for the history of Muscle Shoals and the Tennessee Valley Authority.*

The steamboat opened the Black Belt to settlement. By 1835 freight and packet lines were operating out of Mobile along the Tombigbee, Alabama, and Coosa. Central Alabama became the cotton-producing center of the State, and in the flush times that followed planters grew almost incredibly wealthy.

With the coming of the railroads, river traffic declined on the Tennessee. By 1860 most of the cotton grown in the valley was shipped by rail to Memphis, Charleston, and Mobile.

Between 1910 and 1940 the Federal government spent large sums in deepening and widening channels and removing obstructions in Alabama rivers. Dams and locks were built to make them navigable for river packets and barges. The Warrior-Tombigbee-Mobile system became one of the leading canalized river systems. Since 1934 the Tennessee Valley Authority has built or improved great dams on the Tennessee which provide a 9-ft. low water channel, insuring navigation the year around.

The Tennessee-Tombigbee Waterway is a major engineering project in the states of Alabama and Mississippi. It is intended to give barge traffic on the Tennessee a new route to Mobile Bay and the Gulf. The plans call for a connecting link between the two rivers near Pickwick Lake on the Tennessee in the northwestern corner of Alabama. Thence the channel moves down the eastern part of Mississippi until the Tombigbee enters Alabama near Pickensville on State 14 in Pickens County. The Black Warrior joins the Tombigbee near Demopolis and meets the Alabama River in Washington County, where both become the Mobile River, which flows into the Bay of Mobile.

The Warrior and Tombigbee Rivers were utilized by the early planters, who sent flatboats with farm products down the Warrior to Tuscaloosa and other ports. After the boats were unloaded they were knocked down and sold for lumber. Paddle-wheel steamboats were built from 1818 onwards, but progress upstream was hazardous; it took two or three weeks to move from Mobile to Demopolis, a distance of 220 miles. Usually the boats stopped just below Tuscaloosa. When the railroads extended their network during mid-century the steamboat traffic declined. The return to water shipment came with the arrival of the towboat and eventually Diesel power to propel steel barges. For heavy freight water rates were cheaper than any other form of shipping, and producers began calling for a usable channel at a permanent depth, free from floods and drought. Construction of a 6 ft. channel began with Federal help in 1888; this was increased to 8 ft. and eventually, in the 1930s, to 9 ft., at which the depth is maintained by the Corps of Engineers, USA. To create the channel 17 locks and dams were built on the Waterway. By 1924 it moved 1,000,000 tons of shipping; by 1954 3,000,000 tons. By this time the locks and dams proved both too small and too dangerous. Efforts to rebuild the locks and dams were begun by the Warrior-Tombigbee Development Association, and the 17 were reduced to six larger and more efficient dams, and the round trip from Mobile to Birmingham was reduced from 125 hours to 6 or 8. In 1971 more than 12,000,000 tons of freight were moved on the Waterway.

The Federal Government, the State of Alabama and City of Mobile have cooperated in improving Mobile Harbor, modernizing its docks and other port facilities. The Port is served by more than 100 steamship lines, with connections to the major ports of the world. *See Port of Mobile.*

The channel is 36½ miles long from the outer bar to Chickasaw Creek, with a depth of 40 ft. Minimum width in the river section is 500 to 1,000 ft. In the Bay channel, minimum width is 400 ft. The channel over the outer bar is 42 by 600 ft.

Docks are owned by the State of Alabama and operated as the Alabama State Docks Department. Situated on the west side of Mobile River, fronting on the city's main business district, the docks system is responsible for much of Mobile's prosperity.

The State Docks are equipped with more than three miles of concrete wharves, where as many as 25 ocean-going vessels can be accommodated at one time. Covered warehouse space exceeds 2,250,000 square ft. The Inland Docks Division of the Alabama State Docks has constructed terminals along the waterways. These serve as industrial sites for plants requiring water for manufacture and transportation. The State also has constructed terminals near Mobile on the Gulf Intracoastal Canal.

Alabama was a leader in pioneer railroad building ventures. When steamboat transportation over Muscle Shoals proved too hazardous, Tennessee planters organized the Tuscumbia Railway, connecting Tuscumbia and Tennessee River ports. This first railway west of the Appalachians and south of the Ohio River, chartered in 1830, was only 2.2 miles long, but five years later it was 44 miles around the Shoals to Decatur. Rails were of strap iron laid on wooden stringers.

Financed with planters' money, the road, renamed the Tuscumbia, Courtland & Decatur Railway, eliminated the dangers of Muscle Shoals in transporting cotton to New Orleans. On Dec. 15, 1834, the first run was made between Tuscumbia and Decatur by a wood-burning locomotive towing a few cars. Later, mule teams were sometimes the motive power, with relay stations every few miles. In 1847, after several years of uncertain operation, the road was reorganized as the Tennessee Valley Railroad. After the War Between the States, it became part of the Memphis & Charleston Railroad, which later became a unit of the present Southern Railway System.

The excessive rates charged by steamboat lines for hauling cotton and other products during the 1830s stimulated interest in railroads.

More than 25 charters were granted to promoters during the decade, but most of the plans were dropped during the depression following the panic of 1837.

By this time the railroad was accepted as the successor to canal and stagecoach, as a means for linking Alabama with the Gulf Coast. Three or four of the proposed railroads were built, either completely or in part. By 1850, there were 150 miles of track in the state. Chartered on February 3, 1848, the Mobile & Ohio was one of the first land-grant railroads in the United States. In addition to its right-of-way, in 1850 the road was deeded 419,528 acres of public lands in Mississippi and Alabama which were sold to raise funds for construction and rolling stock. The Louisville & Nashville entered Alabama in 1871 by purchase of several small lines, and in 1872 completed its line from Montgomery to Decatur. In the same year the Alabama Great Southern was completed across the State from Chattanooga to Meridian, Mississippi. These two lines crossed at Birmingham, the new town laid out in 1871, in anticipation of their meeting. By absorbing several smaller lines in 1886, the East Tennessee, Virginia & Georgia Railway became Alabama's largest system; later it merged with the Southern Railway.

Birmingham, with vast actual and potential freight tonnage from its rich mineral region, was early accepted as the logical railroad center. All of the leading lines were routed through Birmingham or Mobile and, with the exceptions of the Atlantic Coast Line, Mobile & Ohio, and the Western of Alabama, passed through the mineral belt. Somewhat later the Mobile & Ohio built a branch line from Artesia, Mississippi, by way of Columbus through the Warrior and Cahaba coal fields to Montgomery.

The Illinois Central Railroad entered Alabama in 1899, the Seaboard Airline in 1900, the St. Louis & San Francisco in 1901, the Alabama, Tennessee, & Northern in 1906, and the Atlanta, Birmingham & Coast in 1907.

Today Alabama has 5,000 miles of railways. None of the seven systems operating main line service entered the state under their present names. Those operating now are: Central of Georgia; Illinois Central Gulf, which absorbed the Gulf, Mobile & Ohio; Louisville & Nashville; St. Louis-San Francisco; Seaboard Coast Line, and the Southern Railway. In addition, there are two short line railroads; the Tennessee, Alabama & Georgia, with service from Gadsden to Chattanooga; and Western Railway, with service from Selma and Montgomery to West Point, Georgia.

Birmingham is on two of the Amtrak routes. The terminal cities are New York-New Orleans and Chicago-Miami.

Air transportation began in the state in 1928 when the St. Tammany and Gulf Airlines opened up a route from New Orleans to Mobile, Birmingham and Atlanta. This line, at first for mail service only, is now a part of Delta Airlines.

Alabama today has a balanced, coordinated statewide airport system, with 118 airports available for general use. Major centers are served by daily schedules of five commercial airlines.

Huntsville and Madison County's new Skycenter encompasses 3,000 acres and has unlimited capacity for future modes of aircraft. Nearly 1,000 acres with taxiway access are reserved for cargo and warehouse facilities. Also, the Skycenter is a self-contained city, offering complete accommodations and executive services. The City of Birmingham is enlarging its airport facilities to accommodate all sizes of passenger and cargo aircraft. The new $14 million facility includes a new terminal building, extended runways and 1,200-car parking deck.

Education, Research, Libraries

Four-year higher education is offered at 28 campuses in Alabama, of which 13 are state supported. All are co-educational, with the exception of the Baptist-supported Judson College for women at Marion. Sixteen offer graduate work. There are three branch campuses of four-year institutions: Fort Rucker Branch of Troy State College, Maxwell-Gunter Branch of Troy State College, and Gadsden Center of the University of Alabama. For the school year 1969-70, there were 116,851 full-time students enrolled in state institutions; 15,989 in private ones.

There are 23 two-year institutions, of which 17 state-supported schools are a result of acts passed by the 1963 State Legislature establishing the Junior College and Trade School Program.

The State Board of Education is composed of the Governor, ex-officio, and one member from each Congressional District. A member serves a term of four years, half being elected each two years for overlapping terms.

Alabama's rapidly changing economy and the drastically changed social structure has imposed many new demands on the State Department of Education. Revolutionary changes in agricultural practices have released a substantial number of agricultural workers. At the same time, industry, having found Alabama a good place in which to prosper and expand, has created enough jobs to absorb many of these former agricultural workers. To meet this challenge the State of Alabama is investing some $18 million per year in vocational and technical training. Twenty-six vocational schools turn out approximately 6,000 graduates each year in courses ranging from six months to two years. These institutions, requiring a high school diploma or equivalent for admission, offer training in 45 subjects.

In addition to the vocational technical schools, many of the State's accredited secondary schools provide trade and industrial education. Further, the State universities have established branches where college trained employees can up-grade themselves in their professions. For advancement beyond the scope of academic training, the universities maintain research centers where projects involving multiple sciences can be carried on.

Alabama's public schools are made up of grades one through 12. Instruction in the lower grades consists of the usual subject matter, with some experimental studies in science and languages. Most high schools are accredited by the Southern Association of Colleges and Secondary Schools, with others accredited under State authorization.

At the end of the first month of the school year 1971-72, there were 806,315 pupils enrolled and 33,541 classroom teachers in Alabama's public schools. During 1969-70, there were 285 private and parochial elementary and secondary schools known to the State Department of Education. The total State appropriation for all education in Alabama in 1970-71 was $378,143,924.

JUNIOR COLLEGES AND TRADE SCHOOLS

Alabama began State support of the junior college system on September 8, 1961, when the Legislature authorized formation of a governing body and gave it instructions to open a public junior college. As a result the Northwest Alabama State Junior College opened at Phil Campbell in 1963 with 49 students. On July 16, 1962, the Legislature authorized any county with a population of not less than 65,000 and more than 95,000 to established a junior college, and in 1963 provided a bond issue of $15,000,000 to start construction. The Alabama Trade School and Junior College Authority was formed to control construction and equipment, its members being the Governor, the Director of Finance, and the State Superintendent of Education. Schools were to be built only on sites donated by the community, not more than $1.5 million to be spent on any one school, and the State Board of Education was given complete supervision.

Three existing colleges were brought into the junior college system. They were Southern Union College at Wadley, founded in 1923 as a private institution; the Mobile branch of Alabama State College, opened in 1936, and Snead College of Boaz, founded as a mission school in a private dwelling late in the 1t9h century and chartered by the State in 1935.

During the 1960s the junior college and trade school program opened opportunities for students at low cost, easily accessible to graduates of accredited high schools. Costs are estimated as low as $300 and $400 a year and financial aids are available in the form of loans and grants; there also are opportunities for part-time work, scholarships, and the Federal Work-Study program. Loans up to $1,000 are provided for students in full-time nursing courses. Students are expected to live off campus and commute to college, the State transporting them free in buses.

GROWTH OF PUBLIC EDUCATION

In the early days of French settlement in Alabama no provisions were made for education. Most of the colonists hoped to win fortunes quickly and return to France, and few, if any of them, brought wives or families. Parish priests may have held classes for children, but if they did, they left no records. The first definite effort toward providing instruction for the colonists was made on March 26, 1742, when Governor Bienville asked the French king to organize a college in the Province of Louisiana. The petition was refused on the ground that the settlement was too small to warrant one.

There were no regular schools in Alabama during British and Spanish occupations, though Spanish priests gave some religious instruction to the Indians, and British authorities allotted 25 pounds a year for a schoolmaster. The first Alabama school of record was founded in 1799 at the Boat Yard on Lake Tensaw by John Pierce, a New Englander. Pierce, who operated a gin and traded in cotton, taught in a rude log cabin with puncheon floors and rough log benches. Most of his pupils were children of wealthy families: the McGillivrays, Taits, Weatherfords, Durants, Linders, and Mims. From the affluent patrons of this "blab" school, taught by word of mouth, Pierce made a tidy profit.

In 1811 the General Assembly of the Mississippi Territory chartered Washington Academy at St. Stephens and in 1812 Green Academy at Huntsville. Both schools were granted freedom from taxation and the privilege of raising money by lottery.

Eight years later when Alabama was admitted to the Union, Governor Bibb stressed education in his first message to the legislature, and the State made its first attempt to establish an educational system. Washington Academy, rechartered as St. Stephens Academy, was granted $500 from the treasury. Funds from the sale of the sixteenth section of land in each township were set aside for the support of schools, and two townships were reserved for "the use of a seminary of learning." During the next decade several additional acts were passed concerning the sale and rental of school land and the establishment of a system of control.

In addition to the section funds, the State's part of the national surplus revenue, amounting to $669,086.78, was placed in the State Bank to the credit of the public school fund. When the bank failed in 1843, the funds were lost; many schools were abandoned and others remained open only through private subscriptions.

In 1848 Alabama petitioned Congress for the right to sell all public lands within its boundaries in order to support public education, because the sixteenth section plan had "utterly failed in its noble object." In addition, Congress was asked to appropriate for public schools 100,000 acres of land set aside in 1841 for internal improvement. Both requests were granted. But even funds provided from these sources failed to meet the operating expenses of public schools.

Meanwhile, in 1852, the people of Mobile had founded their own system of primary, grammar, and high school grades. Boys and girls were segregated, a small tuition fee was charged, and taxes were imposed.

The first of these schools was Barton Academy, built in 1835-36 and taken over by the city in November, 1852. In February, 1853, the enrollment was 854. By 1858 enrollment in Mobile proper and the county had reached 6,509.

The success of the Mobile system had great weight. In 1854 the legislature provided a centralized State system for which it appropriated $100,000. Each county was given the power to tax real estate and personal property for its common schools.

While the public school system gained favor among the poor and middle class families, the planters and wealthy merchants held it in contempt. They hired tutors for their sons and daughters or established private schools. Between 1820 and 1840 more than 200 of these academies were founded. Many of them were operated on a subscription basis.

Education of girls was given much attention by leading citizens who founded "female" academies out of their own funds. Towns, churches, and fraternal groups organized colleges and academies for girls. The Tuscaloosa Female Association and the Selma Ladies' Education Society were outstanding.

The gradual acceptance of public schools, even among the planters, is shown by a steady decline in the number of academies between 1840 and 1860. Many were forced to close during the War between the States. After Reconstruction, with cotton wealth swept away, many were absorbed in colleges and the public high school system.

Until 1830, the education of Alabama Negroes was decided solely by the master. Slaves who showed special aptitude were taught to read, write, and do simple arithmetic. Some even attained positions of stewardship, the duties of which included keeping field accounts. But as abolition sentiment gained headway in the North, with a subsequent inflow of Northern literature, these meager advantages were taken away by law. At the outbreak of war, there were 437,000 slaves and 2,690 free Negroes in Alabama, and the planters feared that learning would cause revolt. All printed matter was denied the slaves. However, Negroes continued to learn skilled trades, such as harness making, tanning, blacksmithing, carpentry, and masonry.

Soon after Alabama was admitted to the Union, the legislature passed an act for the incorporation of a state university. The Government had granted 46,080 acres for this purpose, and funds from the sale of lands had been placed in the State Bank. Tuscaloosa was chosen as the site for the school, and construction began in 1827. The university opened in 1831. In 1936 it opened an extension center in Birmingham; in 1950 it started academic programs in Huntsville. These have developed into the three campuses of the university system, with the College of General Studies in Birmingham (8,097 students); the first undergraduate degrees at Huntsville in 1968 (2,687 students), while Tuscaloosa enrolled 13,487 in 1973. The system dates from June, 1969, and the three campuses are autonomous. The School of Medicine was moved to Birmingham in 1945, when the new Medical Center was established.

During the late 1820s, the churches began to support education. In 1830, French Jesuits founded St. Joseph's or Spring Hill College at Mobile and the Methodists founded LaGrange College at LaGrange.

Other Methodist institutions were Athens Female College (1840), Tuskegee Female College, and Southern University (1856). The Baptists established Judson College for Women at Marion in 1839, Howard College at Marion in 1841, and the Alabama Central Female College at Montgomery in 1857. The institution now called Auburn University was founded by Methodists in 1856 as a school for men.

Meantime, a State-wide dearth of competent physicians turned attention to education in medicine. The Medical College of Alabama opened at Mobile in 1859 as a department of the University of Alabama. It had a State endowment of $50,000, and public subscription doubled that amount. From 1865 to 1868 buildings of the school were used by the Federal Government as a school for Negroes.

Teachers' training began in the Normal Institute at Montgomery in 1854. By 1860 395 libraries were operating. There were 61,751 pupils enrolled in 1,903 public schools, and 10,778 students in the 206 academies and private schools. The total enrollment of the 17 colleges was 2,120.

Secession brought a virtual halt to all educational activities. Students and teachers alike deserted the academies and colleges to join the Confederate Army. Then, near the close of the war, invading Union troops burned the State university and other colleges. Some school buildings were used as barracks for troops and as refuges for Negroes who straggled off the plantations to be housed and fed by the Government.

In education, as in every other field, the Reconstruction years between 1865 and 1874 were difficult. Added to the 98,000 white children of school age were thousands of children of former slaves, none of whom had ever seen a textbook. In 1865, the Freedmen's Bureau began functioning under General Wager Swayne, a fair-minded man who tried to give both white and black children educational advantages. In 1867 there were 157 Negro schools with 150 teachers, of whom 126 were white and 24 black.

Matters became worse in 1869 when the Bureau broke down under the pressure of carpetbaggers and scalawags. Serious crop failures from 1865 to 1868 helped turn the public mind away from education. By 1870 only 27 of the Negro schools remained, with ill-equipped teachers and 2,100 pupils compared with the 9,799 pupils of 1867. The status of white education was in turmoil. Thousands kept their children at home, and the inability to read or write was common among those who grew up after the surrender. Schools operated only when children were not needed in the fields.

Efforts to reorganize higher learning were led by the churches, which concentrated on rural communities and centers of Negro population. One of the Baptist schools was the Alabama Baptist Colored Normal and Theological School, which survives today as the coeducational Selma University. Both Southern Baptists and Methodists established schools for needy white children in rural communities. Led by their example, the Northern Methodists founded Snead Seminary at

Boaz in 1899, the Universalists opened the Southern Industrial Institute at Camp Hill, 1898, and the Congregationalists founded Thorsby Institute at Thorsby in 1901.

To better conditions through teacher training a normal school for white teachers was established at Florence in 1872 and similar institutions for Negroes were opened at Marion in 1874 and at Huntsville in 1875. In the 1880s schools for white teachers were founded at Troy, Livingston, and Jacksonville.

Attempts at providing adequate education for the Negro in Alabama started in 1881 with the founding of Tuskegee Normal and Industrial Institute. Lewis Adams, a former slave, was largely responsible for gaining the financial support of Northern and Southern whites. On July 4, 1881, Dr. Booker T. Washington became president, opening classes with 30 students housed in a dilapidated frame building. From that humble beginning came the present Institute of 3,300 students and 1,000 teachers (1973).

Permanent steps toward providing industrial education for whites were taken in 1872 when the State Agricultural and Mechanical College was established at Auburn. Despite bitter criticism by those who favored purely classical instruction, the college employed professors of engineering and agriculture, and offered degrees in both courses. During the 1880s, the State donated $12,500 for a departure of mechanic arts; this has developed into a school of engineering. In 1887 an experiment station was added, and in 1899 the name of the college was changed to Alabama Polytechnic Institute, named Auburn in 1960. It is the oldest co-educational institution in Alabama, having admitted women since 1892. It enrolls 15,300.

Julia S. Tutwiler, president of Livingston Normal School, was the leader of the movement to provide technical training for girls and, as a result of her efforts, the Girls' Industrial School was opened at Montevallo in 1895. It is now the University of Montevallo enrolling 2,700.

Between 1889 and 1895 nine district agricultural schools were established for whites, and a branch agricultural experiment station was established for Negroes attending Tuskegee Institute and Montgomery Normal School. Several private and denominational schools for Negroes gave instruction in trades.

Most of the important colleges of the ante bellum period had been reopened by 1895. In addition the Catholic Church founded the junior St. Bernard College at Cullman. Leading denominational schools at the turn of the century were Southern University and Athens College (Methodist), Judson and Howard Colleges (Baptist), and Spring Hill College (Catholic). All these institutes still hold important places in the State's educational system. In 1918 Southern University became Birmingham-Southern College.

In 1867, the University of Alabama began rebuilding some of the structures destroyed during the war and classes reopened in 1869. The Federal Government donated 46,080 acres of land in restitution for buildings and equipment destroyed during the war and other funds have come from the leasing of coal lands, legislative action, and popular subscription. Women were given the same privileges as men by 1898.

With the Smith-Hughes act in 1917, vocational courses were added to most of the public schools. A division of vocational education was added to the State Department of Education with three branches—agriculture, trades and industries, and home economics—each under a trained supervisor. Secondary schools also added vocational training to their courses of study. Special day and night schools are now conducted for boys, girls, and adults unable to attend day school. Evening classes are held for mill women and foremen in industrial plants.

RESEARCH

Undergirding much of Alabama's greatly expanded and diversified industrial growth, its sociological uplift and preservation of health have been the development of impressive research facilities and programs.

Chief among these facilities is the Southern Research Institute in Birmingham. Organized under the laws of Alabama in 1941, operations were delayed by World War II until 1945. An independent, nonprofit organization, governed by a board of trustees, its financial needs are met from a capital fund of $5.9 million and from charges to sponsors for research services. The institute's physical plant has 26,000 sq. ft. of floor space in buildings covering more than a city block, and its full-time employees number around 500.

The institute, inspired by the late Thomas Wesley Martin, then president of Alabama Power Co., in a recent year carried out $5.7 million in research on 228 separate projects. Sponsors of these projects ranged from small companies with no research capabilities of their own, to some of the country's largest corporations and various government departments and agencies.

Institute scientists have made vital contributions to the nation's defense and space programs combatting air pollution. Equally important have been the contributions in such socio-economic fields as housing, transportation, and better use of government funds for health.

The institute's work for industrial sponsors varies from technical trouble-shooting involving a few hours' or a few days' work, to long-term product development that may continue for several years. It is efficacious in such fields as alloys, metallurgical processes, machine design, polymer synthesis, radiation chemistry, virus chemotherapy, coatings, membrane separation processes, market studies and economic evaluations.

In the programs of the University of Alabama, Auburn University and the University of South Alabama, research is financed by public funds as well as by grants and contracts from private foundations, business and industry, the State of Alabama and the Federal Government.

At Auburn University all academic schools and departments are engaged in research. Its Agricultural Experiment Station, with a network of substations throughout the State, conducts both basic and applied research in agriculture and the Life Sciences. The Engineering Experiment Station assists industries to improve manufacturing processes and to study methods by which resources may be converted into marketable products.

The Auburn Water Resources Research Institute's activities are conducted in cooperation with the Office of Water Resources and Research of the U. S. Department of the Interior and the Geological Survey of Alabama. The Center for Urban and Regional Planning is concerned with promoting orderly socio-economic growth.

In Auburn's Nuclear Science Center with its massive array of equipment, including a 3 Mev accelerator, a 10,000-curie cobalt-60 source, a cobalt-60 therapy unit, and a NMR spectrometer, all phases of basic and applied nuclear science can be researched, including radiation effects on biological and physical materials, radioisotope trace techniques, neutron activation analysis, and basic nuclear physics.

The Auburn University Computer Center is equipped to provide the computing capability and capacity needed for the complex research conducted by the University faculty and students.

On its three campuses at Tuscaloosa, Birmingham and Huntsville, the University of Alabama is also engaged in research in all of its academic departments and divisions. On the Tuscaloosa campus, in-depth work is being done in education, law, social work, engineering, economics, business administration, home economics, natural resources, mining, and public administration.

To implement basic and applied research, extensive graduate programs are offered. A library with over 1,000,000 volumes in general and specialized fields is available. Data banks have been established in relevant areas and University of Alabama has modern data processing equipment, including large soft and hardware computer capacity.

The Research Institute of the University of Alabama in Huntsville is adjacent to the Research Park and near Redstone Arsenal with its Marshall Space Flight Center of NASA and the U.S. Army Missile Command. Though present programs here are strongly oriented toward the aero-space sciences, research for other industries will continue to increase as the Institute grows.

At the University of Alabama's Medical Center in Birmingham, almost every aspect of human health is the subject of intensive research, ranging from cellular mechanisms to mental diseases. University of Alabama-Birmingham also operates the Rust Research Center which conducts extensive research in computing and biophysical sciences.

Since it was established in 1964, the University of South Alabama in Mobile has moved steadily forward in its research programs. Fields of major interest here are marine biology, plant location, long- and short-range economic planning, inventories of human and natural resources, income and marketing surveys, manpower analysis, personnel and labor relations and analysis of the business environment. Its programs, too, are supported by computer programming, and an expanding library.

While the aforementioned centers are the largest and best equipped in the State, there are numerous private laboratories and others in smaller colleges and universities where research is taking place.

GROWTH OF ALABAMA LIBRARIES

There were two notable events in 1819 that found a place in history: Alabama was admitted to the Union as the 22nd State, and Huntsville was selling shares in a projected public library. By 1823 the Huntsville Library Corporation received its charter, and in 1828 the State Legislature authorized the Library Society of Bench and Bar in the capital, Tuscaloosa, for the use especially of the Supreme Bench. In 1830 it appropriated $500 for this library. Here were precedents for the care and nurture of libraries: private capital and public money.

Most of the 19th century book collections were private affairs, their circulation limited to informal associations and served by volunteers. Historians trace the organizing impetus to women's clubs, and especially to the Alabama Federation of Women's Clubs, which in 1897 urged support of traveling libraries. In 1886 Birmingham's superintendent of schools initiated a library for the use of teachers and students, which became the Birmingham Public Library in 1891. An association of women started the Hellen Keller Library in Tuscumbia in 1893; Montgomery Library Assn. was formed in 1898. In 1901 the State established its Dept. of Archives and History. In 1904 the Alabama Library Assn. was formed. By 1907 the State Legislature made library extension part of the duties of the Dept. of Archives & History. One of its devices was to send a lending library of 25 to 30 books to schools and rural communities that applied for it.

Thirty-eight years after Archives & History began functioning the State Legislature established its Public Library Division and appropriated $10,000 for starting book collections. Alabama had three county libraries, 15 municipal libraries and one regional system organized by the Tennessee Valley Authority in Madison, Jackson and Marshall Counties, but there were 58 counties without free public library service. The situation improved when the Federal Government finally voted to support libraries with substantial grants. In 1956 President Eisenhower signed the Library Service Act, which was aimed at extending library services to rural areas, rural including towns of up to 10,000 population.

The first Federal funds, $40,000, arrived March 1, 1957, and started numerous new projects in Alabama. Expenditures under the act rose from 34¢ per capita to 68¢ per capita; the State Agency became a separate department; 10 bookmobiles were added to serve remote areas; 24 counties participated in establishment grants, and 63 independent libraries flourished. In 1959 the State Legislature created the Alabama Public Library Service as a separate agency. On February 11, 1964, substantial support for constructing new buildings came as part of the Library Service & Construction Act signed by President Johnson. Even with this help many buildings remained inadequate, but with an awakened public consciousness local governments took up the task and in five years 26 libraries had new quarters. As the Alabama Historical Assn. reported: "Out of the planning for the building itself many citizens for the first time recognized that a library building was different from a fire station or a city hall; that it was a particular building to give a special quality of services."

As of 1970 Alabama had 18 systems embracing 34 counties, which had 68 libraries, and 67 independent libraries. Under the State Plan libraries had extended their usefulness in many fields of education and civic improvement, providing for adults, dropouts, the blind and handicapped, and persons in prisons and industrial schools. The Alabama Public Library Service supported courses in library science, organized workshops, sent representatives to White House conferences on youth and aging, and published numerous tracts and manuals for professional use and public information. It established the first Regional Public Library Service for the Blind and Physically Handicapped at Talladega in 1965. *See Talladega.*

The number of volumes in public libraries is only a fraction of the large collections in Alabama. The first big group is in the schools, colleges, and universities. In recent years there has been a proliferation of special libraries, chiefly technical. Alabama's collections of books about aviation and the space age is believed to be second only to Washington, D. C. The USAF Historical Division at the Aerospace Studies Institute at Maxwell Air Force Base lists 1,500,000 books and documents. The U. S. Air University there has a library of 50,000 volumes. The Scientific Information Center at Redstone Arsenal has more than 200,000 volumes and 1,200,000 technical reports, while the Missile & Munitions Center and School has more than 35,000 volumes. Other collections are at Fort Rucker, Fort McClellan, Craig Air Force Base, and Gunter Air Force Base, where Extension Course Institute, the correspondence school of the Air Force, is located.

The Alabama Library Assn. in 1970 reported that "expansion of Alabama's industry has nurtured spectacular growth of special libraries —medical, law, military, business, and technical. There are presently over 70 special libraries in the State with over 1,500,000 volumes and many thousands of documents, technical reports, maps." Huntsville alone is a major center for such libraries, with collections by Boeing, IBM, Lockheed Missile & Space Corp. Here even the University of Alabama has a special section devoted to military aeronautics.

Agriculture

THE early history of agriculture in Alabama was largely the story of cotton. Cotton brought the major influx of settlers to the State and set the pattern of its social and economic system. Cotton built railroads, steamboats, and fine mansions. Cotton stratified society, enabling the wealthier planters to live with grace and leisure, but keeping the small farmers in poverty and ignorance. Even today, when crop diversification, manufacturing, and mining are making powerful inroads on its old supremacy, cotton is still important in Alabama's agriculture.

Early explorers of Alabama found the Indians living in stockaded villages surrounded by fields and garden patches, crudely tilled with sharpened sticks for plows and hoes made from the shoulderblades of bison. Nevertheless, soil and climate were so favorable that the tribes lived in plenty. Maize was the principal crop, but watermelons, pumpkins, squash, and beans were raised in abundance.

When the first French settled on Dauphin Island in 1702, they borrowed corn from the Indians of the mainland. The crop sprouted poorly in the sandy soil and then withered in the semitropical heat. Corn was also planted at the head of Mobile Bay, and an attempt was made to raise beans. In 1712 only 12 of the white colonists were attempting to till the soil, though 40 or 50 Indian slaves worked sporadically at gardening. For at least 20 years most of the food consumed in the colony was imported from France, and three times during this period only the charity of the Indians prevented the settlers from starving.

Beginning in 1719, Guinea Negroes were imported from San Domingo to replace the Indian slaves, who had worked unwillingly and rebelliously for the French and who had proved highly susceptible to their masters' diseases. With this plentiful supply of hardy labor the French cleared large tracts of land along the lower reaches of the Alabama and Tombigbee Rivers, where the hot climate and marshiness of the country were ideally suited to indigo, greatly in demand in European markets, and to rice, which provided the main food of the slaves. On the higher ground, corn and sugar cane were grown.

The colony had become almost self-sustaining by 1730, and the plantation system was firmly established. Beans and tobacco were added to indigo as profitable exports, and oranges, figs, peaches, tobacco, grapes, and olives were grown on the coastal meadows. Although the French government made repeated efforts to develop a self-sustaining citizenry of small farmers, only a dozen or so one-family farms were operating in Alabama when the colony was taken over by Great Britain in 1763.

Tobacco, indigo, and rice continued to be the chief exports while Alabama was part of British West Florida. In 1780 the colony was annexed by Spain. To discourage the raising of rice and indigo in competition with Spanish Cuba and Central America, a subsidy was offered for tobacco. Most indigo and rice planters took advantage of the subsidy, but Virginia, producing better tobacco in greater volume, held the market against encroachment. In 1792 the subsidy was abandoned and the settlers turned to cotton and sugar cane raising.

During the American Revolution several hundred Georgia Tories came into the hill country of central Alabama and established small farms where they raised corn, cotton, and tobacco in sufficient quantities for their own consumption. During the next 30 years the Tennessee Valley and the Tombigbee region of southwest Alabama received thousands of settlers from Georgia, the Carolinas, and Virginia, who supported themselves by farming.

Before the dawn of the 19th century the textile industry of Britain had been revolutionized by Hargreaves' and Arkwright's greatly improved spinning and weaving machinery, and by Watt's steam engine. New England began building its own textile mills along its swift-running rivers. Whitney's gin arrived to solve the problem of cleaning raw cotton by machine. Thereafter, cotton rapidly became a crop of world-wide importance.

SPREAD OF COTTON PRODUCTION

After 1800, a fever of cotton planting spread through the South. Cotton became the most important single crop of the planters in southern Alabama. The level fertile Tennessee Valley of northern Alabama, where for years corn, wheat, and cattle had been raised successfully, was found to be excellent cotton country. By 1816 the valley of the Tennessee River had become one vast patchwork of cotton plantations.

Cotton grown at this time was the "blackseed," or naked type, with small bolls containing a low percentage of lint. Mexican-type cotton, introduced in 1820, was a decided improvement on the blackseed variety. The yield per acre was greater and the spreading of the ripe boll made it easier to harvest, enabling a good picker to gather as much as 200 pounds a day.

Wholesale production of cotton naturally brought lower prices for the now plentiful fiber. Where the average price was 30¢ a pound in 1816, cotton brought only 9¢ a pound in 1829. The larger and wealthier landowners were able to survive this sharp drop in price, but smaller growers saw their life's savings swept away. Dispossessed small farmers were among the first settlers in the lowland Black Belt, named for the black soil. When it was discovered that Black Belt cotton grew to great size and fruitfulness, wealthy planters began moving in from the Gulf Coast. So much land was planted to cotton that corn, other staple farm products, and work animals had to be imported.

By the time the Black Belt was settled, erosion had become a serious problem in other parts of the State, particularly in the hill county. Even river-bottom lands began to wear out under years of steady one-crop farming and winter leaching. The Tennessee Valley, the Coosa Valley, and much of the hill country were badly leached by 1850. Emigration, generally westward, became noticeable in the 1850s, as large tracts of gullied land were abandoned to scrub and sedge, and smaller farmers lost out to the big plantations.

By 1860 the agricultural pattern for Alabama was established. To the north, in the Tennessee and Coosa Valleys, much cotton was still grown, though corn and garden crops were now also raised extensively. Hill farmers of the northeast continued in the subsistence garden-patch stage. The central hilly region was turning to mining, the iron industry and cotton textiles. Wealthiest farm region in the State was the central Black Belt. The Gulf Coast had truck farming and citrus fruit. In the wiregrass region, hay and grain crops and cattle were raised for export to the Black Belt.

Of the 565,000 white people in Alabama at the beginning of the 1860s, 33,730 were slave-owners. The large slaveholder was a rarity. Most of the 435,000 slaves were held in small groups of 5 or 6 to an owner and only 34 planters in the State owned more than 200 each.

At the outbreak of the war, cotton was grown in every county, and in most counties occupied more land than any other crop. In 1860, 33,226,000 bushels of corn were raised—an increase of 4,472,000 bushels over 1850. Other crops which had shown increased production were peas and beans, white potatoes, wheat, and tobacco. Dairly products and wool had gained; rice, oats, and sweet potatoes had declined. The number of farms had increased from the 1850 total of 41,964 to 55,128, and the average acreage had risen from 289 to 346. In 1935, by way of contrast, the State's 273,455 farms averaged only 72 acres in size.

Cotton production dropped rapidly during even the first year of the war, when the New England market was lost. As the Federal blockade tightened and the English market was shut off, cotton growing as an industry was completely ruined. Thereafter, only enough cotton was grown for home use and the fields were turned to food crops. The fact that the southern coastal region could produce two and three crops of garden stuff a year goes far toward explaining the prolonged resistance of the Confederacy.

War's end found huge investments in slaves, livestock, and farm machinery swept away. The land itself, practically the only tangible asset left, had depreciated to a fraction of its former value. The landowner found it almost impossible to borrow money on his depreciated property and was often forced to sell part of his holdings to raise money for operating expenses. However, the planter who had managed to remain solvent could expand at the expense of the small farmer. In many instances these small landowners had to sacrifice everything to escape starvation.

It was in this post-war period that the sharecrop system of tenancy was widely developed. Though small farmers who had lost their land and the freed Negroes were willing to work, there were no local business enterprises capable of absorbing such a mass of unskilled labor. At the same time the planters, badly in need of labor to farm their property, had no money for wages. The needs of both sides were met when Negroes and dispossessed whites agreed to work the land for a share of the crops produced.

Another phase of the period was the emphasis on one-crop farming. When New England and British markets were open again, cotton regained its position as the surest cash crop. Because merchants or bankers who made crop loans insisted on cotton as security, most farmers planted it almost exclusively. Only a few kept plots for corn and subsistence crops. The north central hill country, continuing its wartime mining and manufacturing industries, was not as heavily penalized as the rest of the State by one-crop farming and the sharecrop system.

At the turn of the century immense tracts of once fertile land were worn badly and less cotton per acre was harvested each year. By 1910, when the Mexican boll weevil entered Alabama, progressive farmers were already turning to other crops to supplement cotton. A major problem in the development of agriculture was the lack of adequate research information. Land grant colleges and universities had been authorized with the passage of the Morrill Act by the Congress in 1862. Alabama, like other Southern states, had little money to match Federal funds for agricultural research and crop and livestock production and then only at a high rate of interest.

The Pittsburgh Plus system of freight rates caused shipments to northern states to cost more than equal shipments from the North to the South. The Southern farmer had to pay more for his household goods and farm equipment because of this unfair freight rate system. The lack of capital, unfair freight rates, and insufficient agricultural research combined to delay agricultural progress in the South.

During the early part of the 19th century, Alabama farmers literally began to lift themselves by their bootstraps. They gradually became able to obtain more capital and were beginning to take advantage of the little agricultural information available. Peanuts became an important crop in southeast Alabama. They were either marketed through hogs or sold as a cash crop. They were planted where the warm and humid climate had caused excessive boll weevil damage to cotton.

Farmers in central Alabama's Black Belt counties gradually changed from cotton to livestock after the coming of the boll weevil. Beef and dairy cattle, along with some sheep and hogs, began replacing cotton as a source of income. The lime soil of this area furnished good pasture for livestock.

Farmers in southwest Alabama replaced cotton with vegetables, livestock, and timber. The soil, climate, and rainfall combine to make a large portion of this area ideally suited to pine trees. Large acreages of potatoes were planted in Mobile, Baldwin, and Escambia counties.

Markets for these potatoes were found in cities of the northern and eastern states.

The fertile soil of the Tennessee Valley, with a colder climate and the destruction of boll weevils in the winter months, enabled farmers in this section to continue growing on a competitive basis.

World War I brought significant changes in Alabama's agriculture. Farmers responded to the need for more foodstuff by increasing vegetable production and feed for livestock. This change was also accelerated by boll weevil damage to cotton, which became worse each year.

FEDERAL HELP FOR FARMERS

The Extension Service of Alabama's Land Grant College at Auburn began to play an important role in agriculture during and after World War I. Congress had passed the Hatch Act in 1887, which added research in agriculture to Auburn's teaching program. The Smith Lever Act of 1914 enabled the Extension Service to carry research information to rural people through its county agency system.

Alabama farmers continued to increase their efficiency in production until 1929, when the price of farm products dropped below production cost. The Depression spread to all parts of the economy. Large numbers of industrial workers lost their jobs and began subsistence farming. Farmers tried to meet low prices for farm products with increased acreages planted to cash crops. World markets became glutted with an oversupply of American cotton.

Congress passed the Agricultural Adjustment Act in 1933 in an attempt to better farm conditions. This legislation provided production controls with payments for reducing acreages.

Alabama agricultural leaders played a major role in shaping national agricultural policy for many years, beginning with the passage of the first of many farm bills. Dr. L. N. Duncan, Director of Alabama's Agricultural Extension Service and later President of Alabama Polytechnic Institute, exerted strong leadership on farm policy and production. His close friend, Edward A. O'Neal, president of the Alabama Farm Bureau Federation, and later president of the American Farm Bureau, worked with Dr. Duncan and Senator John H. Bankhead on farm legislation. Senator Bankhead was the author and sponsor of most of the farm legislation enacted during this period.

Alabama farmers began planting large acreages to legumes, or soil building crops, on land not used for cash crops. Crop yields increased as better seed varieties became available and higher analysis fertilizers were produced. A more diversified agriculture that included livestock production replaced the old one-crop system of cotton farming. Loans from the Farmers Home Administration helped tenant farmers become farm owners. Soil Conservation Service workers assisted farmers in soil building.

Cash income from the sale of livestock and livestock products amounted to $27,496,000.00 in 1940 as compared with $65,323,000.00

from sales of cash crops. This meant Alabama farmers had increased their total income and that approximately 30 percent of cash farm income was from the sale of livestock and livestock products. The 1940 farm income of $117,325,000.00 from all sources showed farmers were gradually recovering from the depression era.

The 1960 farm income figures in Alabama indicated real progress in a developing and changing agriculture. Cash farm income in 1960 from the sale of livestock and livestock products amounted to $301,771,-000.00 or approximately 57 percent of the total cash income of $528,-826,000.00 obtained from livestock, livestock products, and cash crops.

Further increases in farm income in Alabama were noted in 1969 when the total from all sources amounted to $804,586,000.00. The cash income from the sale of livestock and livestock products amounting to $526,859,000.00 then accounted for more than 72 percent of the combined cash income from livestock, livestock products, and cash crops.

SOYBEANS THIRD LARGEST CROP

The big change in agriculture since the end of World War II has been in the cultivation of soybeans, which now hold third place in value, following cotton, and peanuts. Both cotton and corn acreage have decreased considerably, but soybeans have taken a lead in the Tennessee River Valley and the Black Belt, and are an important factor in the Mobile Bay farming areas. The *Atlas of Alabama* (1973) calls soybeans the glamour crop of Alabama, its acreage having increased by almost five times in the 1960-70 decade, reaching 650,000 acres, and notes that much pasture land in the Black Belt has been plowed up for soybean production. Soybeans are important to livestock as feed.

Poultry and poultry products accounted for 39.1 percent of the receipts from farm marketing in Alabama in 1969; cattle and calves were next with 17.9 percent, with the sale of hogs amounting to 8.8 percent of the total.

Alabama ranked third in broiler production in 1969, fourth in peanuts, and sixth in income from eggs and cotton. Alabama also ranked nineteenth in the United States in cattle and calf production and seventeenth in beef cattle numbers.

Farm production expenses increased from $370.2 million in 1959 to $576 million in 1969. Realized net income per farm increased from $1,911 per farm in 1959 to $3,558 in 1969, the highest net income per farm on record. The total farm income from all sources in 1970 was $918,300,000.

Changes in farm population in Alabama and other southern states now more nearly correspond with that of other parts of the nation. During and after the Reconstruction period, Alabama had a long era of subsistence farming. In 1925 more than 60 percent of Alabama's 237,631 farmers were tenants. The number of tenants increased beginning with the depression of 1929. In 1950, 41 percent of 211,512 farms in Alabama were still farmed by tenants.

The keen competition between farmers after World War II for home and foreign markets made it necessary for those remaining on farms to use all known methods to reduce production costs. This highly competitive period in agricultural production reduced the number of farms to 92,530 in 1964, only 21 percent of this number being farmed by tenants. Farms have increased in size while their number has been reduced. The 1970 figures show a further reduction in the number of farms and a further gain in the size of farms. Both crop and livestock farmers adjusted size and acreage to meet the needs of modern equipment and technology.

The number of Grade A dairies in Alabama had decreased to 726 in May, 1970, or less than one-third the number twenty-five years ago. These dairies produced considerably more milk than at any previous period. Dairy farms which remain have adjusted their size to low cost production.

The importance of agriculture in Alabama as related to the total economy of the State can be illustrated by quoting from some figures contained in the publication, *Agribusiness in Alabama*. This publication was sponsored by members of the Alabama Resource Development Committee. The data obtained by county and state agricultural workers summarize farm productions and firms doing agribusiness.

The volume of agribusiness in Alabama was estimated at $1,790,-897,000 for the business year 1966-67. The 3,538 firms engaged in agribusiness employed 95,827 people and had a capital investment of $1,279,252,000. This is about one-fifth of the volume of all retail, wholesale, and manufacturing firms reported in the 1963 Census of Business, U. S. Department of Agriculture.

The capital investment in Alabama's 83,000 farms is approximately $3 billion. They contain one-half of the state's total land area of about 32,650,000 acres.

The migration of rural people to metropolitan areas has decreased in recent years. Many small industries have located in rural areas during the past decade. Good roads have enabled rural people to commute to jobs in industry. Families in urban areas are now purchasing small tracts of land in rural areas, and commuting to work in industrial plants. This trend of movement away from larger cities to small plots of land in the country is reversing past movements in population.

Religion

Early in the present century Southern and Northern branches of the Christian evangelical denominations disrupted by the war between the States, 1861-65, began to move toward reconciliation. This evolved into a steady progression away from sectionalism toward more national and international involvement and reaction. During this interim, many Alabama churches became identified with the National and World Councils of Churches.

The 1954 Supreme Court ruling on desegregation was followed by a period of profound soul searching as pulpits and congregations grappled with the social problems the decision produced.

Just as the Southern Baptist Convention—not restricted in membership to the South—is the largest single congregation in the nation, 12,297,346 out of 27,588, 478 Baptists, 1975, so are Baptists numerically the largest religious group in Alabama.

Harmony exists between the leadership of the Alabama Baptist Convention and the Alabama section of the (black) National Baptist Convention. They work together on many major social problems, but each still "runs its own ship."

Although the Methodists, second largest group in the State, formally ended their North-South schism in 1939, the Southeastern jurisdiction continued to exercise its prerogatives quite fully until 1968. At a Dallas meeting in that year, the United Methodist Church came into being. In 1972, the (black) Central Conference of Alabama merged with the (white) North Alabama and Alabama-West Florida Conferences.

Since the Synod of Alabama of the Presbyterian Church, U. S., was created in 1835, there have been many churches in the number of presbyteries, in their names and their boundaries within the Synod. The most significant change in recent times was the inclusion in 1952 of the Central Alabama Presbytery, a black presbytery geographically co-extensive with the established bounds of the Synod itself and also including churches within the Presbytery of Florida.

Organizations of Presbyterians in the State include the Presbyterian Church in the U. S. (Southern); the United Presbyterian Church in the U.S.A.; the Cumberland Presbyterian, and the National Presbyterian. The latter group, a Southern conservative coalition of some 259 congregations "free of creeping liberalism in theology, with emphasis on conversion," was formally organized in Birmingham during 1974.

Some religious observers see in this latest Presbyterian "secession" a reflection in extreme of a tendency to return to sectionalism and fundamentalism. Some of this tendency is attributed to a disenchantment with the World Council of Churches and the need for more home mission work.

Within the Roman Catholic and Episcopal Churches, any significant recent unrest is internal. Liturgical changes, actual and proposed, have disturbed congregations of both churches.

In addition to the aforementioned Christian denominations, religions of all kinds are practiced in Alabama today. This is particularly true in Birmingham, the most cosmopolitan city in the State. There the mammoth Medical Center and the Southern Research Institute have attracted many internationals who have brought their own religions.

Alabama's Jewish community is relatively small. The largest concentration is in Birmingham, where there are both Orthodox and Reformed Synagogues.

Only a handful of French soldiers, adventurers and Indians heard Father Davion preach in the rude log church on Dauphin Island nearly three centuries ago. Today, thousands of pastors preach to hundreds of thousands of worshippers for Alabamians, steeped in the precepts of the Bible Belt are church-going folk. These worshippers gather in edifices that range from tiny, one-room wooden country churches, beautiful centuries-old buildings constructed of hand-made bricks, to giant complexes of modern architecture.

Just as there was an upsurge in church building after World War II, so has there been a growing network of Protestant church-owned and church-operated hospitals, nursing homes and schools.

Some of the earlier church colleges have been abandoned or have been merged with larger institutions. The Baptists still operate Judson College (founded in 1839) at Marion as the only female institution of higher learning in the State. The former Howard College was abandoned and a whole new campus created in another section of Birmingham to become Samford University. Cumberland Law School was transferred from Tennessee to the Samford campus in the 1960s. The liberal arts Mobile College is also operated by the Baptists.

A summer camp for youth and adults is operated by the Baptists at Shocco Springs near Talladega, with an average attendance of 12,000.

The Baptist Medical Center in Birmingham, with major hospitals on the eastern and western sides of the city, a school of nursing and full medical training program, is a gigantic operation.

The Methodist Church in Alabama owns and operates three senior colleges. These are Athens College at Athens; Birmingham-Southern College, Birmingham, and Huntingdon College, Montgomery.

The Methodist Children's Home at Selma cares for an annual average of 300 children that come from broken homes or are orphans. There are two retirement homes—Fair Haven in Birmingham, and Wesley Manor in Dothan, with 280 residents of retirement age cared for. There is also a chain of Superannuate Homes where retired ministers or their widows are cared for.

The Carraway Methodist Hospital in Birmingham is a constantly growing medical compound where an average of 14,000 patients are cared for each year.

The two Methodist camps for church activities—Camp Sumatanga near Gallant and Blue Lake near Andalusia, serve some 11,000 campers each year.

St. Vincent's Hospital, a Roman Catholic facility in Birmingham has, in recent years, enlarged its properties and services to become one of the largest in the State.

On the other hand, there has been a decrease in the number of Catholic-operated day schools, but an increase in those operated by Protestant groups. Also, some of the smaller denominations have gone into the retirement home field.

In early church history, we find a number of powerful ministers in every denomination who were outspoken on secular as well as spiritual matters. Such a one was the Rev. Edgar Gardner Murphy, rector of St. John's Episcopal Church, Montgomery, who rallied all denominations against child labor. Although Alabama in 1887 had pioneered in restrictive child labor legislation, it was not fully enforced until 1901, when the Murphy-marshalled forces pressured the State Legislature.

Today the "pulpit's stand" on social issues is usually voiced by inter-denominational ministerial associations, which have worked diligently for over-all harmony in the State.

Twelve priests and four Dominican friars entered Alabama with De Soto in the spring of 1540. Along the line of march the priests made efforts to convert the Indians; they failed because De Soto's cruelty had aroused in the tribes an intense hatred of all things Spanish.

In 1702, when the French established Fort Louis de la Mobile (Twenty-seven Mile Bluff), Father Davion and Father Douay built the first church in the region that is now Alabama. In addition to parochial duties, the two priests worked among the Choctaw of the coastal region, and within a few years hundreds of Indians had been converted. It was largely due to the success of these and other Roman Catholic priests, kindly and devoted men, that the Indians of lower Alabama were consistently friendly toward the French. In 1703, Bishop Saint-Vallier of Quebec established the Mobile district as a canonical parish and placed Father Davion in charge until a curé could be sent.

This first curé, Henri Roulleaux de la Vente, arrived in 1704 on the ship *Pelican*. With him came Father Alexander Huvé, who joined Father Davion and Father Douay in preaching to the Indians of northern Florida and central Alabama.

A church was established on Dauphin Island, and missions at Forts Toulouse, Tombigbee, and Chickasawhay. Missionaries found their efforts hampered by the *coureurs-de-bois,* Canadian wood rangers who wandered through the interior, trapping, trading, and living with the

Indians. Masterly, hard-drinking men with no respect for law and order and scarcely more for religion, they often followed priests into Indian villages, ridiculing their teachings and leaving the natives bewildered.

Not until 1763, when the English occupied Mobile, did Protestants become interested in the region. An Anglican priest, the Reverend Nathaniel Nash, who accompanied the first English governor to Mobile, was called "an ungodly man" by early historians, who charged that even the roughest settlers were awed by his wild carouses. In 1764 he was succeeded by the Reverend Samuel Hart, a missionary from South Carolina. Before the year was out Hart also left, declaring that "the people are hopelessly ungodly; missionary effort among them would be a waste of time."

After the Spaniards captured Mobile in 1780, Roman Catholicism again became the official religion, though no restrictions were placed on the large Protestant element of the colony. Two Irish priests gained many converts among the Protestants. Only an occasional Protestant missionary came into Alabama territory during the following three decades. The first determined attempt to evangelize the frontier came in 1803 when Lorenzo Dow began preaching in the Tombigbee and Tensaw settlements. Astride a pony, with his wife Peggy mounted behind, Dow a former Methodist circuit rider, traveled up and down the western frontier from the Ohio country to the Gulf. Making no effort to organize churches in Alabama, he preached in forest clearings to assemblies of squatters and halfbreeds, whom he described as "sheep without a shepherd."

The Methodists were the first to send an official missionary, the Reverend Matthew P. Sturdivant, to Alabama. He came from South Carolina in 1808 to work in the Territory, and was soon joined by the Reverend Michael Burge, of Georgia. There were less than 100 Methodists in the region at that time, scattered from northern Alabama to the Gulf. However, in 1809 the Reverend Burge had secured enough followers to found a church, Old Zion, in the Tombigbee district.

The Baptists entered Alabama simultaneously with the Methodists. In 1808 Madison County's Flint River Church was organized by the Reverend John Nicholson with 12 members. A year later Enon Church, now the First Baptist Church of Huntsville, was founded. Reverend James Courtney, who began preaching in southern Alabama in 1808, organized Bassett's Creek Church in present Clarke County in 1810.

The Protestants, however, concentrated their early efforts on the Indians in the northern and central sections of the Territory, believing that here work would be more fruitful than on the coast where Catholic domination was strong. But the Indians did not respond to religious instruction and were openly hostile at times.

After the defeat of the Creek in 1814, home seekers in large numbers pushed into the Territory from Georgia, Tennessee, and the Carolinas. With them came the camp meeting, a part of the Great Revival that was sweeping over Kentucky, Tennessee, and Georgia. Begun in Kentucky by James McGready, a Presbyterian, it spread rapidly over the southwest, meeting with great enthusiasm everywhere.

After the meetings had reached their peak in 1811-12, dissension between the denominations grew rapidly. Baptist preachers assailed the Methodists, and the Methodists replied as heatedly. Then the denominations began quarreling within their own ranks. The Presbyterians differed on revivalism and the amount of training a minister should have. The Cumberland Presbytery, centered in Tennessee, became strong in northern Alabama after being voted out of the main body in 1809. The Baptists split into two branches, and eventually into the Missionary Baptists, Church of Christ Baptists, Free Baptists, Free Will Baptists, Primitive Baptists, Seventh Day Baptists, and Two-Seeds-in-the-Spirit Predestinarian Baptists. Three groups of Methodists developed in the State: the Methodist Episcopal and the Methodist Protestant, which began establishing churches in 1827, and the Congregational Methodist, which was organized in 1852 and claimed the right to call its own pastors.

Until the 1820's the Roman Catholic—confined largely to the southern part of the State—the Methodist and the Baptist were the only organized churches in Alabama. The Presbyterian church came with Scotch-Irish settlers from the Carolinas. In 1817 a missionary was sent to the Territory, and a year later a church was built at Huntsville.

The Episcopal faith was brought to Alabama in the eighteenth century by the Reverend Samuel Hart, who made a brief stay in Mobile in 1764, but it was 1825 before the first non-Catholic church was built in Mobile. The membership of the early Episcopal churches included some planters who, "feeling spiritual responsibility for slaves," built chapels on their plantations.

The Disciples of Christ founded a church at Moulton in 1826. Members of the Jewish faith built their first synagogue at Mobile in 1844. They were among the first settlers in the State, but in early days they held services in private homes.

At the beginning of the War Between the States, purely missionary efforts of the churches were slowly dying, and interest in higher education was taking their place. The Southern churches followed the Confederacy almost unanimously. Some Alabama ministers became chaplains and officers in the Army. In 1845, the slavery issue had caused a split in the Methodist church and the southern body had withdrawn to form the Methodist Episcopal Church, South. In the same year the Southern Baptists had withdrawn from the general body and formed the Southern Baptist Convention.

Bitter differences developed in the Episcopal denomination over secession, and Bishop Nicholas Hammer Cobbs voiced the wish that he might die before Alabama left the Union. This wish was fulfilled on January 11, 1861, just as the Secession Convention passed the ordinance of withdrawal. He was succeeded by Bishop Richard H. Wilmer, an ardent secessionist, who soon closed the rift among the Southern Episcopalians. Bishop Wilmer ordered the Episcopal clergy to omit from their prayers a petition for divine blessing upon the President of the United States and to pray instead for the President of the Confederacy. This resulted in all Alabama Episcopalian churches being closed by Federal authorities until the original prayers were resumed.

Like other Southern States, Alabama was invaded during the Reconstruction period by an army of "carpetbag preachers" who caused great unrest among the newly freed Negroes. One carpetbagger went about the country proclaiming that anyone baptized in slavery would not enter heaven; he then charged the blacks a dollar each for a second baptism. Southern ministers who had supported the Confederacy were arrested in large numbers, particularly in Mobile, Montgomery, and Selma, cities called "hotbeds of rebel sympathizers."

Soon after the war, the Negroes, who had been members of white churches, began establishing their own congregations. They had no funds with which to build and found that sites for churches were difficult to obtain. For a time they were forced to meet in any available building, but eventually leading white citizens came to their assistance. They began erecting a few churches, one of the first of which was Little Zion Methodist Church, built in 1867 at Mobile. Its first regular pastor was the Reverend Ferdinand Smith, one of the first Negro ministers ordained in Alabama.

During Reconstruction, the majority of Negroes became Baptist communicants, with the Methodists in second place and the Presbyterians and Episcopalians following in the order named. The Baptists had been strong among the Negroes of northern Alabama as early as 1821, when the Huntsville African Baptist congregation, probably the first Negro church in the State, was admitted to the Flint River Association. At the time of the war this church had a membership of nearly 300, several of whom had bought their freedom from slavery.

The churches broadened their sphere of social service after the Reconstruction period to include orphan asylums, hospitals, institutions for the blind, recreational centers, and other charities. New denominations sprang up, including Christians, Congregationalists, Universalists, and Christian Scientists.

In the rural sections, also, new sects developed. Among these was the Church of God, which reached Alabama in 1900, and whose members believed in healing by faith and speaking in unknown tongues. This sect has since penetrated some of the larger cities, and its meetings hark back to frontier revivalism. The Church of God is theologically premillenarian and morally Puritan.

Communications

T HE FIRST so-called journal to be issued regularly in the territory of Alabama was the Mobile *Centinel*, which appeared May 23, 1811. It was short-lived, as was the second newspaper, the *Madison Gazette* of Huntsville, issued in 1812. It did not survive long, but the Huntsville *Advocate* of 1815 was published for 78 years, stopping in 1893. The Mobile *Gazette*, founded in 1816, became the Mobile *Register*, and is the oldest newspaper in Alabama. In 1828 the *Planter's Gazette* was founded in Montgomery and after six years became the Montgomery *Advertiser*, which became an influential political journal after the capital of the State was moved from Tuscaloosa to Montgomery.

At about this time William Lowndes Yancey was a leading political figure who edited the Wetumpka *Argus*. He deplored the imminence of "the inevitable conflict", and a few other newspapers questioned the right of the South to hold Negroes in bondage. The war knocked out many provincial newspapers but those in the larger cities held on, even though they opposed Federal regulation and had difficulty adjusting to Reconstruction. Publishing did not pay for a long time, but by 1890 there were 179 newspapers, 16 of them dailies, while churches and colleges supported 21 others. Small papers used patent-insides, and eventually wire reports from Washington, and after the turn of the century grew with the increasing prosperity of the country.

Iron and steel industries have contributed an important chapter to the story of Alabama journalism. The rapid rise of Birmingham, with its booms and scarcity of newspapers, attracted publishers from all parts of the South. Most of these pioneer newspapers failed for want of capital, but the *Iron Age*, established in 1874, was successful from the start. It became the *Age-Herald* in 1888, when its rival, the *Birmingham News* was founded by Gen. Rufus N. Rhodes.

The *News*, in 1920, under Victor Hanson and Frank P. Glass, merged with the *Ledger,* and in 1927 took over the *Age-Herald.* This put the *News* into the morning, afternoon and Sunday fields and made it the largest newspaper in the State, which it continues to be.

In 1921 the Scripps-Howard newspapers came into Birmingham by establishing the *Birmingham Post.* Twenty-nine years later, in 1950, the *Age-Herald* merged with the *Post* to become a morning paper, the *Post-Herald.*

S. I. Newhouse of New York bought the *Birmingham News* and its subsidiary properties in 1955, including the *Huntsville Times.*

Although the *Birmingham News* (evening and Sunday) and the *Post-Herald* (morning) are published in the same building and the *News* acts as business agent for the *Post-Herald,* they are editorially independent. The latter remains a part of the Scripps-Howard group.

A general move toward money-saving centralized printing, as illustrated by the Birmingham arrangement, has been largely responsible for Alabama remaining one of the few states with a growing, economically healthy newspaper population rather than a declining one.

In 1973, Alabama had 24 daily papers—17 publishing evenings, seven mornings, and 17 of these had Sunday publications. There were 94 weeklies, 9 semi-weeklies, one tri-weekly, and one six times a year.

Though many of these papers have passed the century mark in continuous publication, few are still home-owned. Of the largest papers, in addition to those of Birmingham, the influential *Montgomery Journal* (evening) and *Advertiser* (morning) are owned by Multi-Media Inc. The newspapers publish jointly on Sunday.

S. I. Newhouse acquired his second Huntsville paper, the *News,* in 1968. He also owns papers in Selma, Dothan and in Mississippi.

There have been vast technological changes as smaller papers have converted from letterpress (hot type) to offset printing and larger ones have gone to a more sophisticated cold type process than offset.

Changes are evident also in the political flavor of Alabama newspapers as more recognize and support the Republican element in this historically Democratic State.

The majority of the newspapers belong to the Alabama Press Association, founded in 1871. APA has been an effective force in the economic, political and social fabric of the State.

There is a total of 71 other type periodicals published in Alabama. Forty-two are monthlies; nine are weeklies and the remainder are published quarterly or on other timetables. Of these, the two largest are the jointly-owned *Progressive Farmer* and *Southern Living.*

Progressive Farmer, a monthly with 1,106,573 circulation (1973), prints editions for thirteen states. *Southern Living,* established in 1966, is a "slick" monthly magazine, with a circulation of 875,200 (1973), devoted to gardening, home making and travel. Both are published in Birmingham by the Oxmoor Press.

The largest black-owned and published newspaper in the State is the *Birmingham World,* founded in 1930, with a circulation of around 13,000.

An important step in the study of communication media was the establishment in 1974 of a School of Communications at the University of Alabama-Tuscaloosa.

RADIO AND TELEVISION

Mobile was the cradle of radio activity in Alabama. On the Gulf of Mexico, it was a natural site for the State's first radio-telegraphy station for communication between ship and shore. From this early

Land and Water

NOCCALULA FALLS, GADSDEN, ALABAMA

Azalea Trail Maidens, WHO HELP WELCOME VISITORS DURING THE AZALEA BLOOMING PERIOD, IN MOBILE COUNTY.

THE BELLINGRATH HOUSE, BUILT 1935 FOR THE OWNERS OF THE FAMOUS BELLINGRATH GARDENS, SOUTH OF MOBILE

ANNUAL BLESSING OF THE SHRIMP FLEET ON THE GULF AT BAYOU
LA BATRE

CATFISH HARVEST IN SEVEN-ACRE FARM POND AT KOENTEN, NEAR
MILLRY, WASHINGTON COUNTY, ALABAMA, DIRECTED BY SOIL
CONSERVATION SERVICE, US DEPT. OF AGRICULTURE.

PLANTING OF FOOD FOR WILDLIFE AND COVER CROP BY SOIL
CONSERVATION SERVICE, US DEPARTMENT OF AGRICULTURE.

FARMS NEAR ANNISTON, CLEBURNE COUNTY, RAISING COTTON,
CORN, BEEF CATTLE, TIMBER, WITH WATERSHED IMPROVED BY
SOIL CONSERVATION SERVICE, US DEPARTMENT OF AGRICULTURE.

MONUMENT TO AN INSECT, THE BOLL WEEVIL, AT ENTERPRISE, ALABAMA. IT COMMEMORATES THE TURN TO DIVERSIFIED FARMING, MADE NECESSARY WHEN THE BOLL WEEVIL DESTROYED THE COTTON CROPS.

ENTRANCE TO RUSSELL CAVE, A NATIONAL MONUMENT NEAR BRIDGEPORT, ALABAMA, WHERE 8,000 YEARS OF HUMAN LIVING HAVE BEEN TRACED.

STALAGTITES IN CATHEDRAL CAVERNS, NEAR GRANT, ALABAMA.

ENTRANCE TO CATHEDRAL CAVERNS AT GRANT, ALABAMA

SEQUOYAH CAVERNS AT VALLEY HEAD, ALABAMA

NEW RECREATION CENTER ON THE BANKS OF THE TENNESSEE

WATERSHED ON TERRAPIN CREEK, BY THE US DEPARTMENT OF AGRICULTURE

point-to-point broadcasting, begun at the turn of the century, interest grew among amateurs to such an extent that by 1922 commercial voice radios were in existence. Also, by this time, the center of radio activity had moved from Mobile to Birmingham.

The first radio broadcasting license was granted to the Montgomery Light & Power Co. in 1922, and the first radio station, WBRC in Birmingham, was licensed on May 18, 1925. Of the first five stations exsting in the State, one was the property of the Montgomery Light & Power Co., (WGH); others were the Mobile Radio Co. (WEAP); the Alabama Power Co. in Birmingham (WSY); Alabama Polytechnic Institute at Auburn (WMAV), and the fifth was owned by John M. Wilder (WOAY).

Today, there are 137 AM radio broadcasting stations in Alabama. Since 1947 when the first frequency modulation (FM) station went on the air, the number has grown to 57. Country and Western music are the most popular radio programs.

The story of Station WAPI illustrates the local and State government support given to development of the electronic media in Alabama. This station began regular broadcasting in September, 1922, under the call letters WMAV (We Make A Voice), at Auburn as a 550-watt station owned by the Alabama Polytechnic Institute, a land grant institution. The station was established to extend the services of the school to the people of Alabama.

In 1925, Station WSY, which had operated in Birmingham, was donated to API, and moved to Auburn to operate with WMAV.

A new one-kilowatt station was built and began operation in 1926 as WAPI. In pursuance of its mission of education, the station, operated for the next two years by the API Extension Division, gave special attention to rural subjects. Market reports, weather forecasts, news broadcasts and athletic contests supplemented the educational features.

In 1928, at the insistence of Gov. Bibb Graves, steps were authorized to enlarge service of the station, particularly in the broadcasting of market reports to farmers. Negotiations were entered into with the City of Birmingham looking to the establishment of a 5-kilowatt station in Birmingham. The operation cost was to be shared jointly with the Birmingham Park & Recreation Board.

The station was installed on a share-time basis with KVOOTulsa and the first program broadcast in December, 1928. A telephone circuit was leased between studios in Birmingham and Montgomery, and between Montgomery and Auburn for the purpose of broadcasting information from a leased wire of the U.S. Department of Agriculture, running from Washington to Montgomery. In 1929, though still partially subsidized by the City of Birmingham, it became jointly owned by Auburn Polytechnic Institute, University of Alabama and Alabama College at Montevallo, with sub-stations at each school. Also in that year the station became affiliated with National Broadcasting.

In 1930, due to increasingly burdensome costs to the colleges and to Birmingham, Station WAPI was authorized to accept local commercial programs for the first time, and the City withdrew its support. In 1937 the station was purchased by a private company, the Voice of Alabama, Inc.

A license was granted for a commercial FM station in 1946 with call letters WAFM. Programming was entirely separate from WAPI. WAFM-TV went on the air July 1, 1949, as Alabama's first television station. In 1974, there were 17 TV stations in Alabama.

The successful role of the early WAPI as an educational force in Alabama made state officials readily amenable to the idea of statewide educational television. Thus it is that Alabama can boast the first state-wide educational television in the nation.

Today, a state-owned-and-operated micro-wave system of relay channels links nine stations and three translator-transmitters for simul-casting statewide educational and public television.

The Alabama Educational Television Commission, created by the Legislature in 1953, controls the network, with some of the state universities, city boards of education and the State Department of Education. Five Commissioners are appointed by the Governor and approved by the State Senate. The Program Board is composed of a general manager, appointed by the Commission, and heads of the sponsoring agencies.

The Alabama Broadcasters Association is the radio and television fraternity, with a large and effective membership.

Sports and Recreation

N ATURE HAS given Alabama many playgrounds that are being developed and used extensively by the inhabitants and thousands of tourists. The great plateau of Lookout Mountain, which extends the Appalachian Range deeply into the State from the northeast, is a scenic wonderland. Canoeing and motorboating on the mountain streams and on the numerous natural and man-made lakes, and exploring trails and caves known to the Indians are popular diversions. Colonies of summer homes are scattered over the peaks and on the slopes; and boys' and girls' recreation clubs have camps where young people swim, boat, fish and learn nature lore and woodcraft in a pioneer setting through the long summer.

There are four National Forests in the State, covering approximately 631,000 acres. In the northwest is the Bankhead Forest, with its Black Warrior Division; the two divisions of the Talladega Forest, Oakmulgee and Shoal Creek, are in the eastern and central sections, the Tuskegee Forest is in the southeastern section, and just north of the Florida line is the Conecuh Forest.

Hydroelectric development dams have impounded the waters of rivers into large lakes, and along their shores are hundreds of both vacation and permanent homes. More and more, Eastern universities are using these magnificent lakes for their rowing teams' spring training headquarters. Dartmouth has established permanent quarters at Kowaliga Beach on Lake Martin, and several others have been attracted to Guntersville Lake, where the crew of the University of Alabama-Huntsville trains. The annual Spring Regatta at Kowaliga attracts thousands of spectators.

More than 150 miles of white beaches mark the coastal boundary of the State. Here warm sunshine and mellow breezes from the Gulf enhance the pleasure of surf bathing, water skiing, sailing, and other seacoast activities. Both summer and permanent homes are numerous on Dolphin Island, across from Mobile, at Gulf Shores and other gulf and bayside resorts. Grand Hotel on Grand Isle, also out from Mobile, is favored by water, tennis and golf enthusiasts. There are numerous Yacht clubs throughout the State, at both coastal and inland water resorts, and regattas and races are held throughout the summer.

All State parks and recreation areas are under the direction of the Parks Division of the State Department of Conservation and Natural Resources. Since 1967 the State Legislature has appropriated $51 million for expansion and improvement of park facilities. Thousands of out-of-state visitors use the parks each year, in addition to the several million Alabamians who enjoy these facilities the year around.

There are 13 major State parks (1975) with two additional ones under construction, and six minor parks, with one more being established. Land has been acquired for a seventh.

Joe Wheeler State Park, in the northwestern part of the State, has 2,550 acres divided into three separate areas. Area A is the Wheeler Dam section on State 101 in Lawrence County, which has boating and fishing and vacation cottages. Next is the Fish Creek Area, in Lauderdale County, off US 72 two miles west of Rogersville, which has an 18-hole golf course, a marina with 134 berths, a resort inn and lodge-convention complex. The third area is in Limestone County, off US 72, 15 miles west of Athens, which has a fishing lodge and facilities for fishing, boating and picnics. Extensive new facilities have been installed in Lake Guntersville State Park, six miles from Guntersville, 5,559 acres overlooking the great Guntersville Reservoir, with restaurant, convention, cottage and golf facilities and a new resort inn. At nearby De Soto in the northeastern section a new lodge and a motel have been added. A new lodge, motel and camp grounds have been installed at Cheaha, 2,719 acres, and additional day use areas, camp grounds and a recreation center have been developed at Oak Mountain Park, 9,940 acres, both of these in the Talladega National Forest.

A new facility, the Albert P. Brewer Park, is located on Lake Eufaula in the Southeastern section; also new is the Gulf State Park in Baldwin County on the Gulf of Mexico. Camden State Park on the Alabama River provides a golf course, camp grounds, beach and cabins. A new activity center and camp grounds have been added at Lake Lurleen in Tuscaloosa County. Information about other parks and reservations may be obtained from the Parks Division, State Department of Conservation and Resources, Montgomery, Alabama.

Small game, including quail, doves, rabbits, squirrels, opossums, raccoons are plentiful in all parts of the State, and abundant in some central and southern sections. Alabama has more wild turkeys per acre than any other state, with an annual harvest of 25,000.

The coming of the crisp, clear days of late November is the signal for thousands of quail hunters to go afield with their dogs. Each season, the National Free for All professional field trial at 9,000-acre "Sedgefield," near Alberta, and the Amateur National Shooting Dog Championship at the 14,000-acre Maytag preserve near Union Springs, attract the best bird dogs in North America. Wrap Up, the 1971 National Quail Dog Champion was owned by Alabamians J. Truett Payne and James Tinton.

When Hernando De Soto crossed the country that is now Alabama, he is said to have found the Indians keeping penned turkey flocks numbering thousands. The Indians had trapped the birds in poulthood and raised them in captivity because of their extreme wariness. The average hunter today cannot successfully match wits against a wily old gobbler who next to the crow is the cageiest of all fowls. The high-pitched challenging call of the wild gobbler rings through the still dawn air of the timber lands and swamp areas of the State, particularly in southwestern Alabama. Turkeys are no longer penned in the State and then released for shooting, and shooting hens is unlawful.

In addition to the large shooting preserves, there are a number of smaller private ones. Also, there are 29 game areas under the management of the State Department of Conservation and Natural Resources, from which information regarding permits to use them may be obtained.

Fish are so plentiful that thousands of anglers flock to the lakes and streams daily during the warmer months, and many enthusiasts fish all winter. Even the most popular spots are seldom crowded, because of the great number of fishing places in the waters of the Alabama, Chattahoochee, Coosa, Tallapoosa and Tennessee river systems. Bass, crappie and bream are the favorites of the fresh-water anglers. Pole and line fishermen catch large numbers of crappie, sometimes called calico bass or white perch. Catfish weighing 30 pounds or more are sometimes caught. The cat is not considered a game fish, but this does not diminish the thrill of landing one of these giants. Raising catfish has become "big business" in the State since these fish have become almost as popular as the hamburger and hot dog.

Seasonal runs of tarpon, bonita, kingfish and numerous other nomad species visit the Gulf Coast during the summer, inviting the skill of deep sea fishermen. Fishing tournaments or "rodeos" are held on the coast, usually in July and August, and numerous other fresh-water rodeos are held throughout the State. The most notable ones are held by the Eufaula Chamber of Commerce and on Lake Demopolis. The Alabama Deep Sea Rodeo, held at Fort Gaines on Dauphin Island, excites keen interest also.

Numerous clubs are affiliated with the Alabama Skeet Shooters, Alabama Trap Shooters Association and the National Rifle Association. This form of sport is popular with both men and women. The late T. K. Lee of Birmingham was one of the great all-time, all-round marksmen in shooting history. Irvine Porter, also of Birmingham, is a former president of the National Rifle Association and Tom Jones of Birmingham was on the All-America Skeet Team several times.

Baseball in recent years has been on the wane, with only two professional Southern League AA teams in the State (1971), Birmingham and Montgomery. Alabama, however, has produced such baseball greats as Willie Mays, Virgil Trucks, Al Worthington, Carlos and Lee May.

All-America football players are one of the State's most abundant products, headed by Auburn University's Pat Sullivan, winner of the 1971 Heisman Trophy. Since Bully Van de Graff was named the first All-America from the University of Alabama in 1925, the roster recently has included such famous names as Joe Namath, Don Hutson,

Harry Gilmer, Ed Salem, Fred Sington, and Dixie Howell. Auburn's list of 21 includes Jimmy Hitchcock, Walter Gilbert, Monk Gafford, Tex Warrington, Travis Tidwell, Jim Ryburn, and Joe Childress.

Joe Lewis (Barrow) world heavyweight boxing champion was an Alabamian, as was Jessie Owen, running and jumping marvel who took four gold medals in the 1936 Olympics.

Since opening of the Alabama International Motor Speedway at Talladega automobile and motorcycle racing have increased in popularity. Minor League racing is also held at Fair Park in Birmingham. Dog racing was legalized in Mobile in 1971.

Several small rodeos, where cowboys and cowgirls display their prowess with horse and rope, are regularly held, and horse shows are staged in several southern areas. Fox hunting has about vanished, though the Birmingham Branchwater Club does still hold hunts annually.

Indoor recreation ranges from championship bridge and checker tournaments to the old-time square dancing conventions.

Because Alabama is still primarily agricultural, most sections hold fairs annually in September and October. Midway attractions supplement the competitive agricultural, educational and industrial exhibits. The largest of the fairs is held in Birmingham in early October.

Other events characteristic of the State are flower shows and garden pilgrimages in several cities. Of these the Mobile Azalea Trail is the best known. Birmingham has the world's largest camellia show in February each year. Dog and cat shows are regular events in the larger cities. There are a number of other events of significance, principal ones being the Festival of Arts in Birmingham, the Peanut Festival in Dothan, Fall Fashion Time in Birmingham, the National Junior Miss competition in Mobile, and the Blue-Gray football game in Montgomery on the last Saturday in December. Mardi Gras, first held in 1711 at Mobile, is always a national attraction.

Folklore and Folkways

FOLKLORE THRIVES best in rural regions before contacts with communal living rub off the awe and wonder that attend primitive beliefs. Farm people are especially amenable to legends and sayings, for they depend on the vagaries of the weather and blame unseen agents for a break in their expectations. Rural Alabama, especially the areas where the black population dominates, is sometimes described as the place where such lore originates, yet it has come down through the generations from the earliest colonists, the European migrations, and the blacks of Africa.

This lore, particularly as it concerns crop planting, the weather, fishing, hog killing and wood cutting, was until relatively recent years widely circulated. Some of it still persists in rural areas, but the old signs and sayings, many of which grew out of observing repeated occurrences under certain climatic conditions, actually have been scientifically established as fact.

Teaching and demonstration programs taken into the rural districts by such organizations as the Auburn University Cooperative Extension Service, 4-H Clubs, and the Tennessee Valley Authority, have replaced superstition with reason. Nor does the farmer have to depend any longer on Nature to signal weather conditions to him. Early morning radio and television programs, beamed especially to the farmer, keep him informed on the weather, planting and harvesting.

Despite these modern aids an almanac with far-reaching forecasts and dream book can still be found in most farm kitchens. Some hill farmers still forecast the coming year by the "Twelve days between the Christmases," with December 26 representing January, and so on. They still accept "Old Christmas," January 7, as the actual date of Christ's birth; and they solemnly affirm that pokeweed puts forth sprouts and all the farm animals kneel with their heads toward Jerusalem at "first daybreak" of that day. This takes place, they say, about an hour before the usual daybreak, and reaches almost the brightness of sunrise. Then darkness returns, the poke sprouts wither, the animals rise, and ordinary daybreak comes. They insist also, that a start on the year's work must be made between the Christmases. It need only be a few briars cut on a dutchbank, or a few furrows plowed in the field, but some farm task must be done to assure good luck.

Moon signs, which abounded in the old folklore, are now dignified with an authoritative lunar calendar. Farmers know that it's best to plant seed crops when the moon is bright, not because of any effect it will have on the seeds, but because predators prowl on moonlight nights, birds take to cover and therefore do not disturb the seeds.

Refrigeration and processing plants scattered throughout the farm sections have dispelled lots of the old myths about times for certain farm activities. But there are many who, though engaged in scientific farming, still assert that root crops do better when planted in the dark of the moon; for bulk and plenty of leafy growth, plants should be planted on the growing of the moon and that such crops as corn, peas, beans and sweet potatoes should be seeded during the waning of the moon. Meat cures and keeps best when hogs are killed on a decreasing moon, but it is best to kill them on the growing moon for fresh pork sales, as the meat will weigh more.

Fishing the creeks, lakes and rivers that abound in Alabama is still one of the farmer's favorite diversions. He sets his crop and labor worries aside when he picks up his fishing rod for he knows "the fish won't bite if you are mad," and he keeps in mind the old verse:

> Wind in the north blows the bait off;
> Wind from the east makes the fish bite least;
> Wind in the south puts the bait in his mouth,
> Wind in the west, fish bite the best.

Fishing or working, the farmer watches the wild birds and the skies with a well-trained "weather eye." When the birds become silent, a storm is brewing. A circle around the sun indicates dry weather, while a circle around the moon shows exactly, by the number of stars within it, the number of days before the next rain.

Automobiles and good farm roads throughout the State make it easier for neighbors and friends to keep in closer touch, so there are not as many of the old time all-day "camp meetings and dinner on the ground" as there used to be. Those that occur now are usually family reunions. There are still periodic religious revivals in all the churches, urban and rural, for Alabama is in the Bible Belt. Only in the very rural areas do baptisms take place in creeks as they once did.

Every Sunday, in groups of 100 or more, young and old gather for Sacred Harp "classes" or sings. This, perhaps the oldest form of folk music in the country, has always had large devotees in Alabama for two of its greatest teachers, the brothers Thomas J. and Seaborn Denson, were Alabamians.

The Denson revision (1936) of the Sacred Harp songs, is the most widely used throughout the South. It differs from the others—all descendants of the original one assembled by William Billings, pioneer music composer—in that special parts are written for the alto section. A monument to the Denson brothers stands on the courthouse square in Winston County.

The sings are still all-day affairs with dinner-on-the-ground. The leader, called either Teacher or Key, still uses the tuning fork, though the better ones with perfect pitch have no need for it. There is no instrumental accompaniment.

One of the larger and most interesting of the "conventions" is the Denson Memorial held each fall at Addison in Winston County. Fa-sol-la singers come from all over the country for this occasion.

An out-growth of the Sacred Harp are the more modern Gospel Singers. These groups are big business today all over the world. Three or four times a year Birmingham's Municipal Auditorium is filled to its 5,500 capacity with fans who sit from early evening until early morning listening while five and six groups perform.

Alabama's most popular group of Gospel Singers are the Birmingham-based Thraser Brothers, who tour internationally, have made numerous recordings and are heard on national television.

While Western, rock and hill-billy music have become increasingly popular with younger people, the Tennessee Valley Old Time Fiddlers Convention, held the first Saturday in October at Athens College, draws hundreds of performers and thousands of spectators for the contests in which the Tennessee Valley Fiddle King is chosen.

On the Athens campus, against a background of stately antebellum academic halls, early American music transmitted through generations lives again. The skirl of the old time fiddle has a peculiar fascination for people from all walks of life, luring scholars, farmers, mechanics, and business executives into the membership of the Tennessee Valley Fiddlers Association.

All day long, the fiddlers regale their listeners with such tunes as Cricket on the Hearth, Soldier's Joy, Billy in the Low Ground, The Old Crow Died in the Forks of the Branch—all tunes without words.

While the fiddling contests headline the event, competitions are also held in banjo, guitar, dulcimer, harmonica, mandolin, old time string bands, and buck dancing. Also, there are exhibits of antique rural American folk music instruments.

The big political rallies that used to bring rural people into town for all-day fun, have faded from the rural scene. However, candidates still tour the state with small bands and combos to lure listeners into the town square for speeches.

The most famous of the sun-to-sun gatherings in Alabama now is First Monday at Scottsboro, where swapping and bartering of every imaginable item takes place.

Though television and radio have made inroads on rural "socializing," swapping tall tales and ghost stories are still favorites when groups get together. The farmer is usually a good storyteller and has a store of personal anecdotes about fishing and hunting that he sprinkles in with recollections about unusual and historical characters. The men who still draw most attention are John Murrell and Rube Barrow.

Murrell was active in the 1830s, and many traditional tales are still current regarding his exploits. His gang included a "preacher," the "Reverend" Sorrell, and his daughter, a song leader. In some stories Murrell is the preacher. The gang would go into a community and start a camp meeting. The fiery eloquence of Sorrell, and the songs of the girl, would bring great throngs to the arbor. Many rode or drove fine horses. While Sorrell was rousing the congregation to an emotional frenzy, part of the gang would pick out the best of the horses and depart unnoticed. The Alabama headquarters of Murrell and his gang were said to be in Dallas County, between Selma and Carlowville.

Toward the close of the century Rube Barrow terrorized Alabama and Mississippi with daring train robberies and murders. In rural communities his exploits are recalled in ballads with many verses and he has become the sort of folk hero who robbed the rich to help the poor. Steve Renfroe, the Outlaw Sheriff, is another big figure in the western part of the Black belt, who was notorious for his many escapes from jail. He was hanged by a Livingston mob. Bob Sims, a Confederate veteran, became famous when he openly defied the "revenooers" by advertising the products of his still and fighting the law until overpowered. Big Sam Dale became a legendary hero of the Creek war of 1813-14, who despatched Indians in hand-to-hand battles. Jean Lafitte, the pirate, and his hidden treasure, is as big a character around Mobile Bay as along the Louisiana shoreline, and some of his mariners are said to have settled down and married Indian women in Alabama. Morris Slater, "Railroad Bill," is a legendary black bad man, whose exploits as a train robber are embellished by his feats of black magic. Folk tales, temporarily ignored by teen-agers addicted to rock and roll, have attained new vitality with the spreading popularity of folk balladry, which is having wide circulation in the South.

Signs, portents and omens still attach to even the simplest activities of some of the blacks and among some of the white people with whom they have been closely associated. They will likely laugh in the telling, but one is cautioned that it is bad luck to sweep out trash or carry out ashes after sunset. It is bad luck to sweep under anyone's feet. If anyone sweeps under the bed of an invalid, or a new mother and baby, he will die. At table, if he drops a knife or fork, someone is coming for a visit, a saying of many nationalities. If his chair falls over when he rises from it, he will not get married during the year.

Even in urban areas and among the more modern groups, blacks seldom bury their dead as quickly as do whites, and most black funeral services usually end in frenzied vocal and physical demonstrations.

The Negroes still contribute much that is charming to Southern speech. They express themselves in picturesque and graphic terms. For instance, they call welfare stipends "pennies." When they make a mistake, they will say, "I'll put salt on that greasy log the next time I cross it." "Going 'round the mountain" means getting older. And while songs from the kitchens are a thing of the past, spirituals can be sung properly only by Negroes. Their sense of rhythm is matched by their sense of humor.

Alabama has many ghosts. Stop in almost any town in the State and the chances are that you will be shown a dilapidated structure known as a haunted house, directed to a crumbling cemetery or overgrown site where some spirit stalks its offenders. Kathryn Tucker Windham and Margaret Gillis Figh rounded up 13 of the State's most distinguished spirits and put them into a hauntingly delightful book that is popular throughout the State.

Three Old World folk customs still survive: the Russian celebration of Christmas on January 6-7 at Brookside, a week-long Norse-type fair among the Swedes of Silvershill, and Rosemary Day of the Germans in Elberta. And, if Mardi Gras can be considered a folk festival, then it should be pointed out that the first of these galas imported from France took place in Mobile, then appeared later in New Orleans.

In the mines and industrial belts, there is lore of a kind among the workers, but here as on the farms, much that gave charm and often eerie fascination to the "old days" has been sacrificed to technology.

Books, Arts and Crafts

MORE THAN 100 years ago an Alabama woman was writing romantic novels that were becoming extremely popular with women readers, especially in the South. She was Augusta Evans Wilson, who had come to Mobile at the age of 11 with her parents, and whose first story, *Inez, A Tale of the Alamo* appeared in 1855. Her most popular novel, *St. Elmo*, was to be published in 1885; by that time she had written *Macaria, or Altars of Sacrifice, Vashti* and *Infelice*. But it was *St. Elmo* that was to carry her reputation into the 20th century; numerous houses were named St. Elmo, and there is a village of that name on US 90 in Mobile County.

Mrs. Evans was not the only popular writer in Alabama; she merely became the best known. Jeremiah Clemens wrote historical novels: *Bernard Lyle* (1856) based on the Texas Revolution; *The Rivals*, set in the time of Aaron Burr; *Tobias Wilson*, dealing with the War Between the States. With the defeat of the Confederacy sentimental novels and humorous essays lost popularity; war stories, biographies of war heroes, and stories of plantation life began to multiply. Sidney Lanier, who came to Montgomery from Georgia at the close of the war and taught in Prattville Academy, published his only novel, *Tiger Lilies,* in 1867. Among biographies of leaders were *Life and Times of William Lowndes Yancey* (1892) by John Witherspoon Dubose and *Life of General Bedford Forrest* (1899) by John Allen Wyeth.

Alabama air was most beneficial to poets, who found their subjects in legends and rural life. The one whose songs struck a common chord throughout the South was Father Abram J. Ryan of Mobile, whose pride in the courage of the Confederate soldier and lament for the Lost Cause, were widely echoed in Dixieland. He was pastor of St. Mary's in Mobile, where his statue stands today. Other Alabama poets whose writings were published around the turn of the century were Samuel Minturn Peck of Tuscaloosa, Martha Young of Greensboro and John Trotwood Moore of Marion, who was editor and novelist as well. Booker T. Washington's personal story, *Up from Slavery,* appeared in 1901 and has been reprinted many times; it is a classic of Negro writings. His *Story of the Negro* (1909) is another milestone. Robert R. Moton, who succeeded Dr. Washington at Tuskegee Institute, contributed *What the Negro Thinks* in 1929. Monroe N. Work, also of the Tuskegee faculty, founded the *Negre Year Book*.

Alabama settings are visible in the writings of Frances Nimmo

Greene (*The Rights of the Strongest*, 1913) James Saxon Childers (*Hilltop in the Rain*, 1928) and Emma Gelders Sterne (*Calico Ball*, 1934). Jack Bethea, Birmingham editor, used novels to emphasize needed penological reforms and in *Cotton* (1928) attacked abuses of tenant farming. T. S. Stribling built a trilogy of novels *The Forge*, (1930), *The Store* (1932) and *Unfinished Cathedral* (1934) on the Tennessee Valley, using Florence and Huntsville as settings. A native of Tennessee, he attended the University of Alabama and State Teachers College in Florence.

Mary Johnston, a Viginian who lived at one time in Alabama, became nationally famous for *To Have and to Hold*, which she wrote in Birmingham. This dealt with the earliest brides coming to Virginia, but *The Long Roll* (1911) and *Cease Firing* (1912) dealt with the War Between the States.

There are a number of instances of authors from outside the State discovering subjects for stories, poems, and novels during a stay in Alabama. The man who gave currency to the phrase *Stars fell on Alabama* was Carl Carmer, who taught English for six years at the University of Alabama and made that his title for a book of folklore. Truman Capote is widely known in Alabama; he is a native of New Orleans and draws on that locale for some of his stories (*The Grass Harp, Breakfast at Tiffany's*). Harper Lee, who won national acclaim for *To Kill a Mockingbird*, is an Alabamian.

William Bradford Huie was born in Hartselle and gives that as his address today. He is an alumnus of the University of Alabama. His books are historical and polemical; he has written *Can Do, the Story of the Seabees, The Hero of Iwo Jima, From Omaha to Okinawa, The Execution of Private Slovik*, books with themes and a drive in the telling. Among other writers who are building reputations are Borden and Babs Deal, Joe Ed Brown, Charles Gaines, Elise Sanguinetti, and John Craig Stewart. Dr. Arnold Powell, director of the Birmingham-Southern College Theater, is a dramatist.

A number of the successful writers are products of the creative writing program of the University of Alabama-Tuscaloosa, directed for many years by the travel writer and biographer of Jefferson Davis, Hudson Strode. Since Dr. Strode's retirement, Thomas Rountree, poet, short story writer and author of critical works on Wordsworth, James Fenimore Cooper and Jane Austen, has continued to develop literary talents through this program.

Three literary magazines of note are published in the State, the oldest being *Folio*, a journal of poetry, graphics and short fiction, published in Birmingham. It appears three times yearly and is edited by Adele Sophie de la Barre. Manuscripts are received from all parts of the United States and foreign countries. It is distributed through a list of subscribers, local bookstores and art galleries.

Southern Humanities Review is issued by Auburn University, from which its principal financial support derives. A presentation of original poetry and prose reflecting interest in the humanities, it appears quarterly.

The Huntsville Literary Association with almost 800 members has an ambitious program including public readings, creative writing, technical writing and seminars. Its organ is *Poem*.

There is also in Alabama an active branch of the National League of Penwomen and the Alabama Writers Conclave holds annual workshops.

One of the highlights of the Birmingham Festival of Arts is an annual Books and Authors Luncheon, featuring talks by authors of works prominent on the national scene. Creative writing awards are included in the Festival competitions, with more than 1,000 manuscripts submitted in 1974 from 49 states.

There are numerous literary study clubs in the state and the Alabama Federation of Women's Clubs gives writing awards each year to its members.

Many scholarly studies, especially in science and history, originate in the numerous universities and colleges that make Alabama an educational proving ground. A recent addition to expository writing is *Atlas of Alabama,* the result of a project of which Neal G. Lineback, of the Department of Geology and Geography of the University of Alabama, was director and editor and 50 other members of the faculties of Alabama educational institutions were contributors. The uniform treatment of graphs, and the concise presentation of every subject by an authority, make this *Atlas* especially attuned to modern use of information.

Two highly useful and influential agencies keep Alabamians alerted to new publications by Alabama authors and nonresidents writing about Alabama. They are the Alabama Library Association, and the Alabama Public Librry Service of the State, both with headquarters in Montgomery. The ALA has an awards and citations committee which annually weighs the merits of fiction and nonfiction and honors the authors at its annual convention. Since 1970 the awards have gone to the following:

1970. Mildred Lee, *The Skating Rink,* fiction; Sara Mayfield, *The Constant Circle,* non-fiction.

1971. Sheldon Hackney, *Populism to Progressivism in Alabama.*

1972. Anne Nall Stallworth, *This Time Next Year,* fiction; Virginia Hamilton, *Hugo Black,* nonfiction.

1973. Joe David Brown, *Addie Pray,* fiction; Dr. John B. Walters, *Merchant of Terror,* nonfiction.

1974. Albert Murray, *Train Whistle Guitar,* fiction; Sara Newton Carroll, *The Search, a Biography of Leo Tolstoy,* nonfiction. Blanche E. Dean, Amy Mason and Joab L. Thomas, *Wildflowers of Alabama and Adjoining States,* special award.

ARTS AND CRAFTS

More than 600 Alabama organizations are producing or sponsoring some type of art expression, according to the 1974 directory of the Alabama Council on the Arts and Humanities.

This current Golden Age of art productivity and patronage in the State was sparked by four major events: 1) Rebirth of the Birmingham Symphony Orchestra in 1946; 2) founding of the Birmingham Festival of Arts in 1951; 3) opening of the multi-million dollar Birmingham Museum of (Fine) Arts in 1957, and 4) creation by the State Legislature in 1967 of the Alabama Council on the Arts and Humanities.

The first three events indicate that impetus for Alabama's art renaissance began in its largest city. In the same sense, creation of the State Arts Council spread the art movement into Alabama's smallest communities, as well as strengthening activities in metropolitan centers.

The late Ann Smolian Jacobson of Birmingham planted the Arts Council idea with the then Governor, George C. Wallace, who, in turn, created the organization by executive order in 1966.

The following year, 1967, Gov. Lurleen Wallace, equally as strong an art sponsor as her husband, signed the enabling legislation which replaced the executive order and put the State of Alabama in the official position of recognizing, encouraging and supporting the growth of the arts. This legislation also enabled Alabama to enter into partnership with the National Foundation on the Arts and Humanities and to participate in the grants-in-aid program of the National Endowment of the Arts.

Just as the Council expanded its services, so the Alabama Legislature increased its appropriations to $125,000 for fiscal years 1970-1972. With this money ACOAH assisted projects throughout the state, including touring productions, traveling exhibitions, technical assistance, an artists-in-schools program and numerous other activities in all of the art disciplines.

The State Council, headquartered in Montgomery with a full-time staff, is parent to a statewide network of city and county arts councils. A lay volunteer board, appointed by the Governor, determines Council policy.

A fifth event deserves to be listed among the art renaissance stimuli: establishment of the Alabama High School of Fine Arts. This significant act was also instigated by the late Ann Smolian Jacobson and activated by Gov. George Wallace.

Founded in 1968 at Birmingham as a pilot project, the school was largely supported by private donations until 1971. In that year the State Legislature made the school an official part of the State's educational system and appropriated monies for its operation. Thus Alabama joined North Carolina as the only states to have such a school entirely supported by state funding.

The school at present rents classrooms, studios and some dormitory space at Birmingham-Southern College in Birmingham. Until the fall of 1974, when enrollment was opened to ninth graders, the school accepted only senior high school students. Also in that year, the name was changed to the School of Fine Arts. And whereas students had previously attended Birmingham high schools during the morning for academic work, in 1974 the whole program was consolidated on the Birmingham-Southern campus.

The number of students is limited to 78, selected by audition and interview. Tuition is free and board is provided for those who live outside Birmingham.

A lay Board of Directors oversees a full-time administrative staff and faculty, the latter supplemented by some part-time teachers in some disciplines. The arts curriculum has four divisions: music, visual arts, dance and drama.

The foregoing is not to say that concern for the arts is a new phenomenen in Alabama. The contrary is true, for the story of art in Alabama had its genesis in the artifacts left behind by the pre-historic Indians who inhabited the State as far back as 10,000 B.C.

The first white settlers were, of course, too busy with mere survival to permit any flowering of formal art. But even in those perilous days women wove baskets and mats, made quilts and other items from whatever materials were handy to "pretty up" their crude frontier cabins.

As more "cultivated" settlers began to replace the soldier-frontiersman, they brought with them more refined possessions and a desire for more cultural expression. By the time cotton affluence had developed the plantation system, books, music, painting, and drama became important in the life style of the wealthy planters and their families. Young ladies were taught water-color and china painting, copying religious and historical works, and even attempted portraits of family and servants.

Planters began to "go abroad" for suitable furniture, paintings and sculptures for the handsome homes they were building. They and their families often traveled long distances to sit for such noted painters as Hart, Earl, Cooper, Poindexter and Rembrandt Peale. Many of these art works are still to be found in Alabama's antebellum homes and museums.

Itinerant artists and art teachers, attracted by the wealth and gracious plantation living, contributed to the artistic life of early Alabama. The most prominent teacher was Edward Troye, a Swiss who came to Mobile from Philadelphia in 1849 to join the Spring Hill College faculty. At the Judson Female Institute in Marion, Nicola Marschall, a Russian, divided his time between teaching art and the violin and painting portraits of his wealthy planter friends. He is best remembered, however, as designer of the Confederate uniform and flag. Many portraits in the Tennessee Valley were painted by William Frye.

Daniel Pratt, master builder, architect and industrialist, provided a studio and added a gallery to his home in Prattville where George Cook could paint and display his work. The Birmingham Museum of Art recently acquired a landscape by Horace W. Robbins, a Mobilian, who had notable success at home and abroad during the 1800's.

However, what native art was being developed was stunted by the War Between the States and its devastating aftermath when again, survival took precedence over aesthetics.

As the 20th Century moved along, the arts again had two short-lived flowerings, only to be retarded first by the great Depression of the 1930s and then by World War II.

There were, however, some Alabama painters whose work received national and international recognition during those years. Among them were Frederick Arthur Bridgeman of Tuskegee, who is represented in many major European collections, at the Art Institute of Chicago, the Washington Corcoran Gallery, the Brooklyn Museum and elsewhere. Lucille Douglas, also of Tuskegee, was commissioned by the French government to make etchings of the ruins of Angkor Wat in Indo-China. Ann Goldthwaite of Montgomery has etchings in the New York Metropolitan Museum.

Art was saved from complete demise during the Depression by special Federally funded projects. The Works Progress Administration Art Project not only urged artists to paint Alabama subjects, but revived interest in such folk crafts as quilting, basket and rug weaving and ornamental needlework.

There were few sculptors in early Alabama. This probably accounts for the scarcity of crude statues of local heroes. Guiseppe Moretti, of Carrara, Italy, was the first sculptor of any note. A resident of Talladega in the latter part of the 19th century, Moretti is best known for a huge cast iron statue of Vulcan, a difficult work surprisingly modern in conception, that stands on the crest of Red Mountain overlooking Birmingham. A kneeling figure of "Brother Bryan," beloved, long-time chaplain of Birmingham, by Georges Bridges, also overlooks the city.

The Confederate Memorial on the capitol grounds at Montgomery, designed by Gorda Chapman Doud of Montgomery and executed by Alexander Doyle of Ohio, is outstanding for its dignity and delicate carving. The best of Alabama's early artists did their work outside the State. Today, most of the scores of fine native painters and sculptors choose to work in the State because of the abundant local and regional "showcases" for their work, and a good market. There is at this time no directory of Alabama painters and sculptors. It would, therefore, be hazardous to attempt to name any of them.

In Alabama the visual arts are developed and served in four principal ways. These are: 1) museums and galleries in the larger cities; 2) art departments and galleries in public and private secondary schools, colleges and universities, 3) community art associations and 4) arts festivals.

Companion to the great groundswell of art productivity in Alabama has been the building of new museums and art centers. There are now more than 40 museums and art galleries in the State, a number of them being the hub of art centers, including auditoriums for the performing arts. These are to be found in cities as municipal enterprises and on university campuses. These art depositories range from museums and galleries of fine art arts, natural history museums, restored ante-bellum homes, to the USS *Alabama,* docked in Mobile Bay.

In addition to these, Alabama has a growing number of commercial galleries. Businesses, particularly banks, are developing excellent art collections for display within their buildings, and hospitals are enriching patient environment with art displays. Private clubs are also collecting art, notably the Birmingham Downtown Club, which recently installed $100,000 worth of 19th century American painting.

The two leading fine arts museums in Alabama are in Birmingham and Montgomery. Of these, the Birmingham Museum is the larger and more significant. Opened to the public in 1951 on the second floor of the City Hall, it then owned nothing and its first year's budget was $16,000. During that summer, however, negotiations were initiated with the Samuel H. Kress Foundation which resulted in the exhibition of 25 fine Italian Renaissance paintings. Later added to and presented to the Museum, these still form an important nucleus of the museum's collection.

The present handsome structure in the heart of the city was dedicated in 1959. It was made possible by a bequest from the estate of a Birmingham financier, Oscar Wells. Built of Italian travertine and dark green Vermont marble, the museum has had three additions. The most recent, the William Spencer wing, adding some 32,000 square feet for a total of 90,000 square feet, was dedicated in 1974. The art of many of the important civilizations of man is illustrated by the more than 10,000 items valued at more than $20 million now recorded by the museum.

One of the galleries was designed and especially equipped for the display of part of the collection of Wedgwood pottery formed by Dwight and Lucille Beeson of Birmingham. The collection, concentrating on works from the earlier periods of Wedgwood and Wedgwood & Bentley and probably the largest of its kind in private hands, is on "revolving loan." In addition to exhibition galleries, the museum's basement houses classrooms, storage vaults, store rooms, loading docks, and a packing and shipping room.

The Birmingham Museum is a municipally owned institution controlled by the Museum Board of Birmingham. Its major support comes from a city appropriation, but some operating and most acquisition monies are derived from private gifts, memberships and special events. Among these events is the annual Sidewalk Art Show sponsored by the Birmingham Art Association. This show, inaugurated in 1948 and held in the Botanical Gardens, draws around 50,000 artists, craftsmen and spectators. By arrangement, all participating artists contribute a percentage of their sales and some give a work to be auctioned for the museum fund.

The museum also benefits from two other elaborate social events, a Mardi Gras type ball and a gala dinner party. The latter is held in the great hall of the museum which has been the scene of many other Birmingham festivities and small concerts.

In addition to its regular series of exhibits and special shows, the Birmingham Museum sponsors a lecture series and a film series. Its Art Education Council conducts an intensive and comprehensive program, staffed by an art education coordinator, professional art teachers, part-time assistants and volunteers.

An annual average of 14,000 Birmingham and Jefferson County school children take part in museum lecture tours. In addition, the museum uses an artmobile to take exhibits to the city's public schools, under a grant made available through Title III, Public Law 89-10.

While not as large as the Birmingham Museum, the Montgomery facility conducts much the same type program on a smaller scale. It is distinguished as sponsor of the Dixie Annual Show, one of the major regional exhibitions, inaugurated in 1959. Open to artists living in 13 states from North Carolina to Texas and from Kentucky to Florida, the Dixie Annual attracts hundreds of entries, restricted to drawings, watercolors, prints and gouaches. Purchase awards have enhanced the extent and quality of the Montgomery Museum's collection.

There are several excellent art-history museums in the state. Significant is the George Washington Carver Museum of Tuskegee Institute. It houses Dr. Carver's former workshop and the only two of his paintings which survived a museum fire.

Ante-bellum homes which combine art and history are Arlington in Birmingham, Sturdivant Hall at Selma, and Oakleigh in Mobile. Old Tavern in Tuscaloosa can also be included in this category. Confederate memorabilia is on display in the home of Jefferson Davis in Montgomery.

Important also are the exhibits of Indian artifacts at Moundville State Park and at the University of Alabama. The latter has, with funding assistance from the Alabama Council on the Arts and Humanities, mounted a traveling exhibit of Indian relics for schools and interested organizations.

The Alabama Department of Archives and History in Montgomery, first of the kind to be supported by a State, is a treasure trove of important visual arts, as well as historical documents.

Art festivals have become another potent feature in the cultural development of Alabama. These vary considerably in quality and the range of exhibits and activities. Most impressive is the Birmingham Festival, which pre-dates the Paris Congress for Cultural Freedom and the Boston Arts Festival.

Staged during a two to three-week period each Spring since 1951, it is designed to promote international understanding through the arts. This is done in two ways. First, the cultural achievements of a particular country are saluted in a series of art exhibitions, musical, dance and theater performances by local artists and others from the honored country. These are arranged in cooperation with the honored country and the U.S. Department of State. The ambassador from that country to the United States is always an honored guest at some of the events. The 1974 festival saluted the Federal Republic of Germany and Brazil was the honored country in 1975. Secondly, a mammoth International Fair held a week during the festival brings together local ethnic groups, cultural and business representatives of other countries to display and perform art products of their native lands. Educational and entertaining in concept, the Fair attracts hundreds of thousands of people each year, including droves of school children.

A voluntary, non-commercial endeavor, the Birmingham Festival is financed by contributions from Birmingham businesses and individuals, and by admission fees to some of the events.

All of the institutions of higher education in the state have art departments and many have galleries. Auburn University, the University of Alabama-Tuscaloosa, the University of Alabama, Samford University and Birmingham-Southern College, all in Birmingham, provide special exhibits by national and international artists as well as works by students and faculty. These are open to the public and thereby are, in a sense, municipal galleries.

State and regional fairs provide more "showcases" for artists. Largest of these is the Alabama State Fair whose Fine Arts Division is under direction of the Birmingham Art Association. Many thousands of entries are received each year, including works by school children as well as by professionals.

Patronage of the arts has paralleled production in Alabama. This is particularly apparent in the number of art associations throughout the state which effectively promote and encourage art interest, production and sales. Some of these associations own or rent exhibition space, sponsor art classes, lectures and gallery tours.

One of the oldest of these organizations is the Alabama Art League. Founded in 1930, its membership is limited to Alabama artists. There are two exhibitions each year, one juried and the other open to all of its members. The juried show becomes a traveling exhibit for the whole state.

Another important group is the Alabama Watercolor Society, composed of 300 members drawn from all fifty states. Membership requirement is acceptance into the annual juried exhibition of the society held at the Birmingham Museum of Art. From this show the society makes up a traveling exhibit which is circulated throughout the Southeast.

CRAFTS

There has been a strong upsurge of interest in, and creation of crafts, evidenced by the increased number of crafts fairs that dot the Alabama landscape in the spring and early autumn. Also, there is a growth of commercial crafts shops.

Work is being done in all kinds of crafts, provincial and contemporary, but the greatest output here is in pottery and anything related to fibers.

Crafts are being taught in most public schools and strong crafts programs are developing in universities' art departments. Most active of the state's groups are the Alabama Designer Craftsmen in Birmingham and the Centrala Craftsmen in the Troy-Dothan area. These groups hold monthly meetings and sponsor at least two public fairs a year. They are affiliated with the Alabama Crafts Council, which is a member of the American Council.

The Performing Arts in Alabama

THEATER

SIXTY-EIGHT THEATER GROUPS are listed with the Alabama Council on the Arts and Humanities. Most of these are community theaters, while the others are located on college and university campuses.

An impressive number of the groups have their own auditoriums and professional directors, though not all of these are full-time salaried personnel. Some of the fledgling groups change volunteer directors with every show.

The community theaters generally concentrate upon plays of popular appeal. Only occasionally do they produce a classic or a new play. Recent Broadway successes are their main fare, with musicals the most popular productions. Relying largely on public support, more adventurous production schedules are not practical.

College and university theatrical productions usually are open to the public. Their seasons are somewhat more varied, reflecting their greater independence of the box office. Outstanding among campus theaters are those at the University of Alabama in Tuscaloosa, Birmingham-Southern College, Florence State University and the Town and Gown Theater in residence as a branch of the University of Alabama-Birmingham.

Children's Theaters are in operation in Birmingham, Mobile, Huntsville and Tuscaloosa. Mobile's Pixie Players has its own building. Fantasy Playhouse in Huntsville has workshop and performance space in the new Huntsville Civic Arts Center. Birmingham Children's Theater has space provided by the city's Park and Recreation Board and gives Saturday performances in school auditoriums in different parts of the city. Tuscaloosa Junior Theater leases a theater building from the University of Alabama. The University of South Alabama has a working relationship with the Pixie Playhouse in Mobile, sharing materials and personnel.

Important in the development of children's theater are the nine district theater festivals conducted throughout the state each year by the Alabama Speech and Theater Association in cooperation with the State Department of Education. Also creative drama is being used as a teaching aid in all the public elementary schools.

An important aspect of theater in Alabama is religious drama.

Principal leadership in this field is given by the youth department of the North Alabama Conference of the Methodist Church and Samford University. Many churches in the state regularly produce religious plays, while Town and Gown Theater gives occasional presentations in area churches. A Passion Play is presented every year at Moundville State Park.

That few traveling theater companies come to the State accounts in great measure for the large number of amateur groups. A lack of suitable auditorium facilities is partly responsible for the scarcity of professional touring groups. Exceptions to this situation are Mobile, with its excellent new Municipal Theater and Auditorium, and Birmingham's new theater in its Civic Center.

Alabama has made a number of stellar contributions to the professional theater and to the movies. Among these are Tallulah Bankhead, Lois Wilson, Henry B. Walthall, Jim Nabors, Gail Patrick, Helen Clair, Fannie Flagg, Mary Badham, May Allison, Harry Townes, John Baragrey, William Rogers and Christina Callahan. Many of the younger of these stars received their training in Town and Gown Theater productions. The most significant community theater in the state, it has brought scores of professional performers and directors to work with local performers and has been the try-out setting for a number of new plays.

MUSIC

When the Spaniards came to what is now Alabama in the sixteenth century, they found the Creek, Choctaw and Cherokee Indians using reed flutes, earthenware drums and gourd rattles as musical accompaniment for their ceremonial dances. Records telling about these instruments and archeological investigation, indicating that the tribes who lived here in prehistoric times used shell rattles, are all that is known about the earliest Alabama music.

The French and Spanish settlers on the Gulf coast brought with them the formal hymns and chants of the Roman Catholic service and the songs of their native lands. Some of the Creole chansons have been handed down from one generation to another and survive with little change. When the State was opened to general settlement in the early 19th century, Anglo-Saxon music from the Eastern seaboard was introduced. The pioneers sang the hymns of the Protestant sects and old English and Scotch folk ballads such as "Hangman Slack on that Line," "The Elfin Knight," and "Barbara Allen." Children, then as now, went to sleep to the sound of "Froggie Went A-Courting."

Spirituals, "discovered" by the musical world in the first decades of the present century, were beginning to develop in plantation cabins and mountain farmhouses. Their origin, whether white or Negro, is an academic consideration; their transmutation into the spirituals as they are known today undoubtedly was contributed by the Negro, whose simple fervor and natural feeling for rhythm found expression in song.

Mobile, more advanced culturally than the rest of Alabama until well into the third quarter of the 19th century, was the chief center for music other than folk songs and tunes. Up to the War Between the States the story of formal music is laid there. The first recorded compositions were the work of a Mobile woman, Josephine Huett Pillichody, who gave a pianoforte concert in New York in 1847 when she was 12 years of age. The best known of her works, which were of the light romantic type, are "Mazurka," "Valse," "Impromptu," and "Romance Sans Paroles."

The guitar was the rage in the 1850s, and no young lady was considered "accomplished" unless she could play "The Spanish Fandango" and one or two other pieces. Judson College, at Marion, met the popular demand by announcing that "piano and guitar music is taught to young ladies who desire it for $25 per term." The spinet, harp, and violin appeared in the plantation big-houses and slave musicians were trained to play the minuet and pavan for dances.

At Spring Hill College, in Mobile, music had been taught since shortly after its founding in 1830, but in this Jesuit institution it was at first largely liturgical. In 1847, Joseph Bloch, one of a group of musically trained Germans who settled in Mobile, joined the faculty and as head of the music department and teacher of piano, violin and flute, profoundly influenced Mobile's musical life.

Bloch founded and conducted the Mobile Music Association, which converted an old church into Alabama's first concert hall. He conducted the singing section of the Turn Verein, was concert master of the city's orchestra, established a music shop and a small-scale music publishing business.

The Bloch shop became the rendezvous of Mobile musicians, professional and amateur, who met there to play newest importations from New York and abroad, as well as to try out their own compositions. One of this group was Sigmund Slesinger, who later achieved a permanent place in the religious musical field by his musical settings for Reformed Jewish services. These compositions, including solos, anthems and canticles, are still used by Reform congregations throughout the nation. Slesinger served as organist and choir director of the Mobile Gates of Heaven Temple for 40 years.

The New Orleans Opera Company had a season each year and for the week of its stay all of Mobile turned out. Jenny Lind, brought to Mobile in 1851 by P. T. Barnum, was a sensational hit.

Musical activity was disrupted by the War Between the States and war songs replaced opera and concerts. "Dixie" was, of course, the most popular song of the war years. It was written by Dan Emmett, a native of Ohio, as a "walk around" for Bryant's Minstrels. First sung, according to tradition, in a burlesque show in New Orleans in the Spring of 1861, the tune and words caught the public fancy. The first New Orleans military company under the newly organized Confederate

Government marched out of the city to the song. Herman F. Arnold of Montgomery wrote the band score for "Dixie," and it was played for the inaugural parade of President Jefferson Davis. Another song popular with Southern soldiers was "Listen to the Mockingbird."

As in other fields, there was a gradual revival of musical initiative after Reconstruction. As early as 1872-73, orchestral concerts were given at Frascati, down the bay from Mobile, and the Fidelia Society, forerunner of present-day music clubs, was organized in Mobile in 1874. By 1889, Fort Payne, in North Alabama, had an opera house where concerts and other performances were given. The building has been renovated recently and is one of the city's showplaces.

The Sacred Harp hymn, popular with the mountain people since the state was settled, gained further favor in 1873 followng a convention in Jasper. In the early "all day sings" the fa-so-la hymn books were used, in which four differently shaped symbols printed in black and white, and easily understood, took the place of conventional music notation. The leader, who presumably had perfect pitch, set the key. In the 1880s the remaining three notes in the music scale, do-re-mi, were added, and a tuning fork was used to "take the sound."

The first Shape Note songbook, put together in 1844 by Benjamin Franklin White, was revised in the 1960s by Alabamians Thomas J. and Seaborn Denson. Alabama Sacred Harp Singers, black and white, were a hit at the Smithsonian Institution's 1970 Festival of American Folklife, in Washington, D.C. (*See "Folklore" for more about Sacred Harp, gospel singers and fiddlers' conventions*).

Spirituals, stemming undoubtedly from both white and black sources, were developed by the Negro's capacity for emotional expression in music. However, there has been a sharp decline in this beautiful *genre* of music since the Negro's socio-economy has shifted from field and kitchen to a broader-based one. Fortunately many of the spirituals that had become popular with choruses and soloists were written down and published. But equally as many lovely ones that were passed from mother to child, are being lost to the rock music more favored by today's younger generation.

Alabama's present widespread interest in music is a flowering of those early activities that ranged from musicals in plantation parlors to the concerts by European artists who came to Mobile in the early half of the 18th century. The Clara Schumann Club organized in Mobile in 1894 still exists. Among the earliest followers was the Birmingham Music Club, which since its founding in 1906, has brought the world's greatest concert stars into the State through its subscription series.

There are now more than 50 senior and junior music clubs throughout the state, banded together in the Alabama Federation of Music Clubs. This organization, nationally affiliated and dedicated to the development of music talent through a scholarship program, was founded in 1916 by Weenonah White Hanson of Uniontown and Birmingham.

In addition to Birmingham, other cities which have concert series are Montgomery, Huntsville, Selma, Dothan, Anniston, Cullman, Sylacauga, Andalusia, Tallassee and the Muscle Shoals area.

In addition to these community-sponsored music events—none of them without at least one event of serious caliber—all of the State's public and private colleges and universities have concert-lecture series, supported by student fees and by sale of subscriptions.

All college and university music departments, as part of their regular academic programs, give solo, chamber and ensemble performances which are open to the public as well as to students. These include both student and faculty performances. The college orchestra also serves as the community orchestra in some college towns.

The Birmingham Symphony Orchestra, founded in 1933 and reconstituted in 1946, is the State's only totally professional orchestra. Under the baton of Amerigo Mareno, 71 full-time musicians play nine subscription concerts each season, ten Youth Concerts for school children of Jefferson County and five "Second Season" concerts of lighter music. The orchestra annually averages twenty-one tour performances throughout the state.

In addition, the Birmingham Symphony plays three programs during the annual Thanksgiving Festival of Sacred Music, sponsored by The Birmingham News; accompanies performances by The Birmingham Civic Opera and The Birmingham-Southern College Opera, and The University of Alabama-Birmingham's Ballet Company. Its annual audiences average 125,000.

Also from its membership comes most of the personnel for the Summer Pops Concerts, given on the campus of Samford University, and for two chamber music groups, The Birmingham Chamber Music Society and The Connoisseur Concert Ensemble.

Huntsville has an admirable symphony orchestra, composed of 75 players, of which 10 per cent are professionals. Everyone in the orchestra receives a small stipend for rehearsals and concerts. Under the baton of Max Pales, fifteen concerts are given during the year. The orchestra doesn't tour, but does repeat its home concerts upon request in towns within a 75-mile radius. Three Young People's Concerts, for grades five and six, are also given each year and there are summer "Pop" concerts in the park. The orchestra is funded by ticket sales, individual and corporate contributions and funds raised by the Women's Guild.

The University of Alabama's Orchestra is composed of students and faculty from its campuses in Tuscaloosa, Birmingham and Huntsville.

Among Alabama composers whose serious music works have been nationally and internationally published are William Levi Dawson, retired director of the School of Music at Tuskegee; Frederic Goossen, Paul Hedwall and Harry Garrett Phillips, University of Alabama-Tuscaloosa; Carl Vollrath, Troy State University; Robert Burroughs, Samford University; and Dr. Jeannie Shaeffer, Judson College, Marion.

In the musical comedy field, Hugh Martin of Birmingham has had a number of Broadway hits. Florence, Alabama, was the birthplace of the pioneer jazz composer William C. Handy. Other composers of popular type music who achieved national publication are Maurice Sigler, Creighton Allen, Mildred White Wallace and Bill Nappi.

Alabama has also contributed a number of notable musical performers to the national scene. Alice Chalifoux was for many years first harpist with the Cleveland Symphony Orchestra and on the faculty of the Curtis Institute of Music.

Nell Rankin of Montgomery and Irene Jordan, Birmingham, are on the Metropolitan Opera roster, the former also having had a distinguished European career. Mary Fabian of Birmingham was a star of the Chicago Opera Company. Rachel Mathes, Steven Kimbrough and Robert Brewster, all of Birmingham, are, at this writing, enjoying distinguished careers in European Opera.

Delores Hodgens and her husband, Sam Howard, of Birmingham, concertize nationally as a two-piano team. Richard Deas, Birmingham, and David Allen Gibson, pianists, had New York Town Hall debuts and are now on the faculties of Furman University and the University of North Carolina, Wilmington, respectively. Mary Anthony Cox, Montgomery, after being graduated from the Paris Conservatory of Music and other European study, has the unique distinction of serving on the faculties of both the Julliard School of Music in New York and the Curtis Institute of Music, Philadelphia.

Other than opera workshops at several colleges and universities, Birmingham and Mobile are the only cities that support civic opera. Both cities import some guest soloists and state directors.

Alabama has several splendid choruses, notably the Huntsville Community Chorus, and the Birmingham Civic Chorus. A Glee Club, composed of students at the Indian Springs School for Boys, near Birmingham, has had successful tours of this country and Europe.

Regular functioning chamber music societies are in Mobile, Montgomery, Huntsville and Auburn, as well as the two aforementioned Birmingham ensembles. Some of these, in addition to programs by their own members, present visiting ensembles.

Music is a part of the public elementary and secondary schools' curricula throughout the state. The extent of emphasis depends upon supplementary fees from individual instruction and community support. This latter revenue is usually given for instruments and instruction for the marching bands which are a major attraction at all high school and college football games.

DANCE

Of all the arts, dance, especially ballet, has had the most dramatic growth in Alabama in recent years. There are at present eight ballet organizations in the state, three of them located in Birmingham.

These three, the Alabama State Ballet, the Birmingham Civic Ballet and the University of Alabama-Birmingham Ballet have the most ambitious programs. All present splendid public performances, some tour the state, and one group has appeared in Europe and South America.

An important project of the Birmingham Civic Ballet is the provision of a grant for a dance artist-in-residence at Birmingham-Southern College. Intent of the grant is to develop a performing ensemble at the college and to stimulate the establishment of an accredited department of the dance. The University Ballet is an integral part of the curriculum of the Birmingham University College.

There are two other active dance organizations in Birmingham. One is the Creative Dance Group, founded and directed by Laura Toffel. It gives annual performances in Birmingham and does some touring. It also sponsores a Creative Arts Fair each year in Birmingham. The other is the Black Fire Creative Dance Group. Associated with Miles College, it is receiving wide acclaim.

Other Alabama cities sponsoring ballet companies are Montgomery, Mobile, Huntsville (two) and Dothan. All have professional artistic directors and each gives two and three performances every year.

An important contribution of the community ballet is the sponsoring of visiting ballet companies in local performances. Occasionally a major ballet company will be included on the concert-lecture series of one of the colleges or universities, or on the community concert series of a major city.

There are also folk dance groups and other types in the State. All of the groups assist local community theaters by providing dancers for their musical productions.

Many of the four-year colleges of the state have courses in dance, but most of them are taught as part of the physical education program, and concentrate on modern dance rather than ballet. Some have special classes in stage movement taught in connection with the schools' theater department.

On many campuses, students enrolled in dance courses have formed groups that give concerts. In most instances they must be considered as demonstrations of work done rather than examples of creative contributions to the art of the dance.

The Alabama Dance Council has undertaken to coordinate activities among the State's dance organizations. It has used a grant from the National Endowment for the Arts and the State Arts Council to conduct area workshops.

CINEMATICS

Film making as an art expression is being encouraged in Alabama by the Council on the Arts and Humanities, and by an annual Educational Film Festival sponsored by Alabama Power Company, the Alabama Education Association and the University of Alabama-Birmingham.

Several notable productions have been accomplished by Spring Hill College, under the direction of the Rev. Robert McCown S.J.

"Once Upon a Rainbow," a semi-animated ecologolical film commissioned by the Birmingham Beautification Board, for use in elementary schools, was written, drawn, scored and filmed by a group of young Birmingham artists.

The Film Festival is an outgrowth of Alabama Power Company's program of providing teaching aids to the state's schools. It is a search for available quality educational films and to encourage production of others.

More than 400 entries were received in the 1974 competition. These came from professional and amateur individuals, large and small film companies, and from eight foreign countries. They are judged by national authorities in the field of cinematics and education.

Cabins, Columns, and Civic Centers

THE EARLIEST BUILDING style to take root in Alabama was French and followed the arrival of Bienville at Mobile in 1702. This French influence remained dominant for more than a century, even during the intervals of Spanish and British rule. Houses were built of brick, one story tall, with courtyards on three sides and the principal apartments facing the street. Here were the original French Colonial houses whose features have become traditional in southern Alabama. Here too was born the "raised cottage" type, originating from necessity rather than artistic considerations, and developed as a means of escaping inundation from seasonal floods. These houses were raised on brick or wooden piers, sometimes as high as ten feet. The space beneath was either left open or enclosed as a none-too-trustworthy basement. The houses were originally built flush with the property lines. The roof, sloping toward the front, extended to small supporting columns forming a full-length gallery across the facade.

Ornamental ironwork was introduced in the 1780s and by the turn of the century it had gained wide use. In the early days the iron was imported from France, but occasionally some of the best examples were wrought by local craftsmen, usually slaves. Later, most of the ironwork came from Philadelphia, the American center of the craft.

The simplest form of the log cabin was generally the same throughout early America. But the double cabin, known in Alabama as the "dog-trot" or "breezeway" house, was a distinctive innovation in the Mid-South. To enlarge his home the pioneer often followed the easy expedient of building a second cabin near the first and joining the two with a porch, either open or roofed. Often the family dogs retreated from the sun to the shade of the roofed space—hence the name.

The coming of the sawmill changed the log cabin into a board structure but otherwise there was little deviation from the original model. Dog-trot houses in their simplest form have been reproduced with board-and-batten in place of heavy logs and may be termed Alabama's folk architecture.

Following General Jackson's victories, which resulted in clearing out the Indians, the first of the big planters came into the fertile valleys of north Alabama. These emigrants from Georgia, Tennessee, Virginia, and the Carolinas constructed their homes in the traditional architectural manner of their native states. Many builders chose the Georgian mode, best exemplified in the structures of the Colonial tidewater region. Others favored the Roman classicism which had been revived and popularized by Thomas Jefferson.

Most of the large houses were built on a simple symmetrical plan, and were plain, four-square, two-story structures of ample dimensions. The rooms averaged 20 feet square with ceilings 14 feet high and higher. Wide central halls on both floors, extending from front to back, were linked by the stair well. Though some of the houses were brick, most were of frame construction. The simple pitched gable roof predominated, though hip and gambrel roofs were occasionally used. Materials for the house came from the owner's estate; his slaves hewed the beams, sawed the lumber, burned the lime, and fired the bricks in the plantation's brick ovens.

During the early Republican period, Roman classicism expressed itself in arched doorways and classic entrance features. After the first quarter of the 19th century, Classical Revival and Georgian Colonial patterns prevailed in northern Alabama. The southern part of the State continued under the traditional influence of French Colonial design. The middle country, the Black Belt, was wilderness as late as 1820.

The three decades 1830-1860, with the exception of a short panic in 1837, was the era of the great cotton boom in Alabama. River packets, plying between plantation and Gulf ports, brought wealth in exchange for cotton. Both large plantation owners and urban Alabamians invested in magnificent homes. Greek Revival architecture, introduced to America by Benjamin Latrobe and developed by William Strickland and other eastern architects, became greatly favored. Itinerant carpenters included *The Modern Builders Guide* (1833) by Minard Lafever among their architectural books. Occasionally architects were induced to come from the seaboard.

These Greek Revival houses were designed with classic details and monumental proportions, but there were modifications of the strict arrangement of the temple form. Few structures were strictly Greek. One of the common variants was the omission of the pediment, generally on houses wider than deep; a contributing influence in this omission was a dislike of visible roofs. Other variants were portico-sheltered galleries, entrance fanlights, and decorative wrought iron grilles. Both square and round columns were used; fluted columns with Ionic capitals were favored. The central portico gave way to the generous colonnade across the entire front.

During the prosperous ante bellum years many of the large, plain, well-built houses of a previous decade were given Greek embellishments. One noted home, built in 1819 by James Jackson and called Forks of Cypress because of its location at the junction of the Big and Little Cypress Creeks, was originally a spacious frame house of Georgian Colonial mode. Jackson, president of the Cypress Land Company, surrounded his house with a broad peristyle of 20 huge Ionic columns resting on a terrace, or stylobate, and supporting a heavily-corniced extending roof. The column shafts were built of brick, then coated with a plaster made of sand mixed with molasses.

The President's House on the grounds of the University of Alabama, completed in 1840, is considered one of the best examples of Greek Revival architecture in the State. Here the two-story colonnaded temple rests upon a high basement, which actually makes the structure three stories in all. The colonnade is reached by a double curving stairway with wrought-iron railings repeated between the columns of the colonnade and in the sheltered balcony of the top floor.

Probably the most famous of Alabama's plantation homes of the Greek Revival period is Gaineswood, near Demopolis. This house was built 1842-1869 by General Nathan Bryan Whitfield, who made his own plans and supervised his slaves in building the structure. He planned the interior as well as the exterior and brought expert artisans from Philadelphia. Three orders of Greek architecture are represented in the house.

In 1847, one year after Montgomery became the State capital, a State House was built from the plans of Stephen D. Button. This building, destroyed by fire two years later, was replaced by the present State capitol, designed by George Nichols, in 1851. Button supervised the construction. The main facade is graced by a Greek portico with six Corinthian columns supporting the entablature. One of the principal features of the interior is gracefully curved twin stairways, semicircular in plan and easy of ascent.

The Greek influence in ante bellum ecclesiastical architecture is best exemplified in the Cathedral of the Immaculate Conception at Mobile, designed by an unnamed French architect. Construction was begun in 1830, but the Cathedral was not completed until 1850. Its twin towers, cupola crowned, were added a quarter of a century later. Of the same type are Mobile's First Presbyterian Church and Christ Church, both designed by Thomas S. James.

Gothic Revival architecture, with its pointed arches, steep pitched roofs, and buttressed walls is represented in the ante bellum period by several churches. A noted example is St. John's Episcopal Church in Montgomery, designed by Wills & Dudley, of New York, and completed in 1855. It is a substantial brick structure of English Gothic design. The steeple is a square tower with octagonal belfry and slender spire.

The war and its aftermath halted progress in building and many existing structures fell into disrepair. In many instances, plantation houses were lost through foreclosure or destroyed, and the ruined planters were forced to live in the quarters of their former slaves. However, Alabama suffered less, architecturally, than most Southern States for the mineral belt was only slightly developed before 1860. But within a decade after the war, iron furnaces were built, coal mines opened, and new industrial cities sprang up. Chief among the new cities born of the great industrial boom were Birmingham, Anniston, Gadsden, and Bessemer.

At the time, the exaggerations of the Queen Anne, Victorian and General Grant styles flourished in the mining towns. Some of the structures built in the 1880s and 1890s remain, with their multi-spindled porch exits and orantely-turned columns, their doorways paneled with heavy beveled glass and interiors decorated with intricate lath work and heavy, yellow oak stairs.

Public buildings erected since the turn of the century vary in style from neo-classic to ultra modern. One of the best examples of the early 20th century renaissance is found in units of the capitol group at Montgomery. By Warren, Knight & Davis of Birmingham, they are neo-classic in design to harmonize with the Capitol.

Also fine examples of neo-classic architecture executed in the traditional southern manner are the Mobile Public Library, designed by George B. Rogers, and the Birmingham Public Library, by Miller, Martin & Lewis.

There has been, in the last decade, a spate of municipal civic centers in major cities of the State. These are of three types: 1) wholly government buildings, 2) art centers, and 3) a combination of the two. The most significant of these are at Huntsville, Mobile, and Birmingham.

The Huntsville center is a combination of art and government structures, with the handsome Madison County Court House as its hub. The Mobile complex reflects the area's French and Spanish heritage. Cities in Spain have sent Mobile gifts of statuary and fountains for the Spanish Plaza, a feature of the Center.

The Birmingham City Hall, Jefferson County Court House, Birmingham Board of Education Building, Municipal Auditorium, Birmingham Public Library, and Birmingham Museum of Art, all built since 1931, and grouped around Woodrow Wilson Park, create a Municipal Plaza.

This plaza has been extended, via a Commemorative GardenWalk to another four-building complex currently known as the Civic Center, but which, in fact, is a performing arts and exhibition center. Composed of an exhibition hall, coliseum, theater and concert hall, the design for this $50 million compound was chosen through a national contest, won by George Quarles of the Philadelphia architecture firm, Geddes, Brecker, Quarles & Cunningham.

Both Birmingham Green and the GardenWalk were achieved with city, Federal and private monies. Cobb, Adams & Benton were architects for both projects. A similar major downtown rejuvenation was accomplished by Montgomery and several other towns have done smaller-scale programs.

Shopping malls and medical centers are also part of the current group-structure trend. None of the malls is of any unique architectural significance. Of the medical centers, the Baptist operation and the tremendous collection of buildings surrounding the Medical College of Alabama, both in Birmingham, are of interest. The Montclair branch of the Baptist Hospitals, with Davis, Speake & Associates as architects, has received architectural commendation, and the landscaping of the Princeton branch is meritorious.

The best turn-of-the-century educational architecture was designed by Miller, Martin & Lewis at the University of Alabama, Tuscaloosa, and at Birmingham-Southern College. George B. Rogers' Murphy High School in Mobile, done in Spanish *motif,* is another fine example.

Unfortunately, some of the group of temple-like buildings of Greek influence that made the Tuscaloosa campus outstandingly handsome, have been replaced by unimaginative modern structures.

Architectural hodge-podge is typical of most of the older campuses. At Auburn University the most impressive of many new buildings is the mammoth Haley Student Center. It was designed for multiple uses by Davis, Speake & Associates of Birmingham and Pearson, Humphries & Jones of Montgomery.

Most dramatic of architectural feats was the construction of the entirely new Baptist-owned Howard College in Birmingham. The school was moved across town in 1957 and the name changed to Samford University. Designed by the architectural firm of Davis, Speake & Associates, the 16 Georgian Colonial academic and dormitory buildings occupy 100 of the 365 acres in Shades Valley owned by the school. In addition to these buildings, there are four fraternity lodges and some faculty apartments. An imposing Fine Arts Center is the latest addition to the campus.

Of the statewide network of junior colleges that has come into existence in the last decade, Jefferson State's Birmingham campus is the most significant. Built in 1965 by McCauley Associates, its present nine contemporary buildings are located on 240 acres of hilltop land.

Of the early 20th century commercial buildings, one of the most beautiful is the Alabama Power Building in Birmingham, designed by Warren, Knight & Davis. An example of the set-back style, the structure of limestone and face-brick has vertical lines accentuated by the use of black glass in the spandrels between windows. A delicate golden statue of Electra tops the building. A recent annex to the building, unfortunately is considered a detraction.

Suburban development during the present century has left its mark upon the residential areas of all of the State's major cities. The City of Birmingham has not been as badly infested with huge apartment complexes as have its surrounding suburbs. Many of these are crowded on too small acreage and are badly designed, a situation that is nationwide. Single-family neighborhoods have developed no distinctive structural patterns, but are pleasing as a whole. Builders have favored Greek Revival prototypes, modified Mediterranean, English Tudor, and California and Florida mission types. The value of proper landscaping is particularly evident in Birmingham, where the irregular terrain presents problems that challenge the ingenuity of both architect and landscape designer.

Alabamians are contributing millions of dollars in restoring and preserving worthy architectural as well as historical landmarks. Most of this work has been done through the Alabama Historical Commission. Mobile has paced the State, followed by Huntsville. Montgomery, in addition to undertaking a number of private projects, has seen the Governor's Mansion rehabilitated, funds appropriated for renovation of the State Capitol and the First White House of the Confederacy, and restoration of the 1850 Rice-Semple-Haardt House as offices for the Historical Commission.

Other cities engaging in considerable restoration are Birmingham, Eufaula, Selma, Florence and Tuscaloosa.

The Alabama Council of the American Institute of Architects, composed of individual and corporate members, has chapters in Birmingham, Mobile, Montgomery and North Alabama. It publishes a bimonthly magazine, the *Alabama Architect*.

PART II

Cities

Anniston

Air Services: Southern Airways, Anniston Municipal Airport. Available also are Reilly Field at Fort McClellan, Talladega Municipal Airport, and Weaver Airport (private).

Bus Lines: Continental Trailways, Greyhound Bus Lines, Ingram Bus Lines, Anniston Transit Co.

Highways: US 78, east-west via Oxford; US 431, north-south; State 21, north-south; Int. 20.

Railroads: Louisville & Nashville, Southern Railway, Seaboard Coast Line.

Information and Accommodations: Anniston Chamber of Commerce; Alabama Motorists Assn.; *Anniston Star,* evening and Sunday, 216 W. 10th St.; *Fort McClellan News,* weekly; *Oxford Sun,* weekly. Four radio stations, one television. Hotels and motels, 13.

Amusements: 5 movie theaters; Anniston Little Theatre, Fort McClellan Playhouse; Municipal Tennis Courts; Municipal Golf Course; Swimming at Tyler Pool, Ezell Pool, Noble Street Pool, Anniston YMCA, Carver Pool; Bowling; Auditoriums for civic and art presentations at Anniston City Auditorium, Liles Memorial Library, Anniston High School.

Banks: 3, with resources of $117,602,322.60 and deposits of $11,728,702.45 (1971).

Churches: 132, representing over 15 denominations.

Clubs: 3 private (Anniston Country Club, Indian Oaks C.C., Pine Hill C.C.) and numerous civic clubs, both national and local.

Education: 15 public schools, including 2 senior high and 1 junior high. Number of pupils, 8,589; teachers, 340.

Hospitals: Anniston Memorial, Stringfellow Memorial, Noble Army Hospital.

Libraries: Public Library of Anniston and Calhoun County, 120,000 volumes in main library, one branch and four member libraries.

Parks: 10, with a total of 116.58 acres.

Annual Events: Calhoun County Fair, Civitan Horse Show, Knox Concert, Kiwanis Travelogues, Friends of the Public Library Paint Daubers art show, Friends of the Public Library book sale.

ANNISTON (710-1,200 alt., 31,533 pop. 1970; 33,657, 1960), seat of Calhoun County, is an industrial city in the foothills of the Appalachian Mountains. The picturesque peaks of the Choccolocco Ridge and Coldwater Mountain tower over the city on east and west and Blue Mountain rises in the north. Anniston has been called the Model

City because its streets were symmetrically laid out by the founders of its industry ten years before it was incorporated as a town in 1883. They had built charcoal furnaces and iron furnaces to smelt the ore found in the forests. This developed into the production of cast iron pipes and fittings that became one of the largest in the country. Today Anniston has more than 110 diversified industries and is a big textile center. Among national corporations represented here are Imperial Reading Company, Monsanto Chemical Co. and National Gypsum Co.

Anniston was governed by a mayor and city council until 1939, when the commission form of government was established. The city-manager pattern was the first in the State. The Municipal Airport was completed with the aid of WPA funds.

The population of Calhoun County increased by 7.5% from 1960 to 1970, a total of 103,092. Most of the towns are small, the largest next to Anniston being Jacksonville with 7,715.

One of the nation's largest permanent ordnance and reclamation depots, ANNISTON ARMY DEPOT, is located about 10 miles west on US 78. FORT McCLELLAN, five miles north on State 21, is the permanent headquarters of the Chemical Corps Training Command as well as the national headquarters for the Women's Army Corps (WACS). The Fort has operated almost continuously since 1917 as a military reservation, training large numbers of men during both World Wars.

Noble Street, named for one of the city's founders, is the main shopping area downtown. Traversing the downtown section north and south, this broad, straight street divides the mills and factories on the west from the principal residential section on the east. Parallel to Noble Street on the east are Wilmer Avenue, named for Bishop R. H. Wilmer; Quintard Avenue, with its broad central landscaped plots serving as the chief north-south traffic route, named for Bishop Charles Todd Quintard; Leighton, Christine and Woodstock Avenues. These chiefly residential (except Quintard Avenue) thoroughfares are arched by water oaks planted by Samuel Noble in the city's early days. Modern residential sections, characterized by spacious gardens and luxurious homes, edge up the eastern slopes and spill over into the verdant countryside beyond, typified by such fanciful names as Glenwood Terrace, Diana Hills, and Sunset Drive.

The upper branch of the Creek Confederacy occupied this region until its removal in 1833-37 under terms of a treaty made with the United States in 1832. At that time there were only a few white settlers. Even after the Creek were removed, migration was so slow that the valley was still sparsely settled as late as 1860, and cotton was planted on the ground where Anniston now stands.

In 1862 the Alabama & Tennessee River Railroad was built to the foot of Blue Mountain, near the present village of Blue Mountain, and a Confederate camp and supply base were established there. A few miles south of the railhead a blast furnace, the Oxford Iron Works, was erected in 1863 to manufacture Confederate war materials. This furnace and stores of cotton were destroyed in 1865, when a division of

General James H. Wilson's forces, under General Croxton, swept through the valley. After these set-backs, the settlers again took up farming.

Samuel Noble, who had been head of the Noble Iron Works in Rome, Georgia, visited the site of the old Oxford works in 1869 and decided there was sufficient iron ore available for new industry. He interested General Daniel Tyler of Connecticut and his sons, Alfred Leigh Tyler and Edmund Leighton Tyler, and in 1872 they formed the Woodstock Iron Co., with Alfred Tyler president and Samuel Noble general manager. They bought the Oxford property, built two furnaces, and laid out a town. Stanford White was one of the architects consulted; he was responsible for the Anniston Inn and two cottages for Noble. The town was to be called Woodstock, but since there was another Woodstock in Alabama it was called Anniston (Annie's town) for Mrs. Annie Scott Tyler, wife of Alfred Tyler.

The Hot Blast, Anniston's first newpaper, was named by Henry W. Grady, editor of the Atlanta *Constitution,* at that time owned by Samuel Noble, as an appropriate masthead for this furnace town's paper. It was first published in 1883 and is still in existence as the Anniston *Star.* One of its early editors was Major James Ryder Randall, author of the song *Maryland, My Maryland.*

A textile mill to give employment to the women of the village was established in 1880, and a pig iron furnace was built in 1882. To tap a richer and broader source of raw materials, the Nobles and Tylers built the Alabama Mineral Railroad, now part of the Louisville & Nashville system, 50 miles south of Sylacauga. A short time later they extended the road north to Gadsden and Attalla.

Increasing demand for outside participation became so insistent that, in October, 1883, the town—a private corporation up to this time— was chartered as a municipality. At a celebration marking the opening of the town to the public, Henry W. Grady, the principal speaker, handed the keys of the city to the newly-elected Mayor, Dr. Richard P. Huger.

Anniston's population increased from 942 in 1880 to 9,998 in 1890. Then came the panic of 1893-95, which retarded industrial progress here as elsewhere. Near the end of the century economic activity was renewed. In 1898 Anniston became the county seat in place of near-by Jacksonville, which had been the county seat since 1833. Three large textile mills were established in 1900 and 1901, and a fourth in 1911.

Fully integrated schools produce a Negro citizen who finds work in factories and public institutions. Anniston Negroes were among the first in the State to enjoy the privileges of integrated restaurants and movie theaters. A Community Improvement Board brings blacks and whites together in harmonious interaction on civic matters.

Among Anniston citizens who have received national recognition are General Robert E. Noble, John B. Knox, Governor Thomas E. Kilby, Charles Erwin, Ruth Elder, Douglas Leigh, Mary Fabian, Kathleen Sutton, Sara Henderson Hay, Thomas C. Turner, Elise A. Sanguinetti and John B. Lagarde.

Anniston's water supply comes from Coldwater Springs (27 separate units), nine miles from the city. It has a flow of 30,000,000 gallons per day, or sufficient to take care of a city of 300,000 persons. Its temperature approximates 62° to 65° F. It owes its enormous volume to the convergence at one point of several great fractures that drain the main part of the mountain pass. Steel and concrete enclosed water reservoirs are located in various high sections of the city, assuring excellent pressure. No filtration is required, but as a precautionary measure, it is chlorinated. This water supplies Fort McClellan with a dual line, for protective measures, and U. S. Army requirements. The water works system is owned and operated by the City of Anniston. There are numerous deep-water wells in the vicinity available for industrial purposes, capable of supplying up to 1,750,000 gallons per day. In addition, Cane Creek, Coldwater Creek, Choccolocco Creek, Oxford Lake and a number of large springs are located in the immediate vicinity. Eighteen miles west of Anniston is Coosa River, with an unlimited supply of water. Logan-Martin Dam, a part of the Alabama-Coosa River Development project, has been completed, giving the community a new area for recreation.

POINTS OF INTEREST

REGAR MUSEUM OF NATURAL HISTORY. 1411 Gurney Ave., ranks high in excellence in the U. S., a gift of H. Severn Regar in 1930. It contains the Regar-Werner Collection of Natural History. In the historical Werner Habitat Bird Groups are 900 specimens of birds and 1,000 bird eggs, including eleven birds now extinct. Each of the exhibits in beautiful glass cases include the natural habitat in which the birds have lived. In addition, there are wild animals, twenty Riker mounts, coral displays, shells, minerals, Egyptian mummies, fish, grasses, sponges, reptiles, relics of the first World War, swords and pistols, old Bibles, old coins, Western Indian relics, Alaskan Indian curios, and native taxidermy and historical displays. A lecture room and projection room also are available. *Open Tues.-Fri. 10-5:30; Sat. 10-5; Sun. 2-5; free.*

LILES MEMORIAL LIBRARY, 10th St. and Wilmer Ave., the public library of Anniston and Calhoun County, was completed in 1966 on the site of the former Carnegie Library. It was named for Luther B. Liles. It is the central library for the city-county system of six libraries and a bookmobile, and has more than 130,000 volumes. One branch is located in Anniston; member libraries are located in Hobson City, Jacksonville, Oxford and Piedmont; the bookmobile stops at over 80 stations throughout the county. In addition, an omnibus is used to place deposits of books in certain schools. Use of a microfiche-to-Xerox cataloging system has enabled the library to expand its services to four libraries in two other counties, Talladega and Cherokee. As the first library in Alabama to use this system, Anniston has served as a proving ground for others. Unusual services offered are: half hour television broadcast each week by the Story Princess, continuous exhibits (in the Harry M. Ayers Auditorium) of art by local artists, Alabama Room, history and genealogy collection, Anniston Room, gallery of photographs and paintings of early Anniston and its people; complete repository of talking books for the blind and physically handicapped; circulating collection of silent movies; circulating collection of framed prints of famous art; extensive collection of classical music on records.

The CHURCH OF SAINT MICHAEL AND ALL ANGELS, at 17th and 18th Sts. and Cobb Ave., is considered one of the showplaces of America. It was built by John W. Noble as a gift to his employees. The group of buildings, church, rectory, 90-foot tower, parish house and chapel are of Norman Gothic architecture. The belfry contains a chime of 12 bells, each in commemoration of a member of the founder's family. The cornerstone of the church was laid in 1888, and the buildings were consecrated on the Feast of St. Michael and All Angels, Sept. 29, 1890. The structures are of native stone. Six windows of stained glass depict scenes from the life of Christ. The altar is made of Carrara marble, and the raredos is of alabaster and granite. The figures of St. Michael, St. Gabriel and St. Raphael and seven angels adorn the altar.

CHEAHA STATE PARK. One of Alabama's State parks, Cheaha stands out as the State's highest recreational playground, 2,407 feet above sea level, 50 feet higher than Lookout Mountain. Located in the counties of Clay, Talladega and Cleburne, 22 miles from Anniston, it comprises 2,679 acres, contains 11 cabins; picnic facilities; a stone observation tower on the crest of Cheaha Mountain; a 14-room lodge and hotel on Bald Knob; Lake Cheaha, for fishing and swimming, and bath house of stone; a reservoir with a storage of 300,000 gallons, fed by several mountain springs at an elevation of 2,225 feet. Pulpit Rock, about which there are many beautiful Indian legends, adjoins the tower by footpaths. The rugged area, with its mountain laurel, flaming azaleas and other wild flowers, make the location not only picturesque, but romantic. An additional tourist attraction is the control room and tower for Educational Television, WBIQ-TV (Channel 10). Reservations can be made by writing Caretaker, Cheaha State Park, Lineville, Alabama. Proceed on State 21, Anniston and Talladega, and at Munford turn left, follow signs.

The ALABAMA INTERNATIONAL MOTOR SPEEDWAY is located about 20 miles southwest. This $6,000,000 speedway is 2.66 miles of five-lane, high-banked asphalt with a grandstand seating more than 150,000. Chargin' Charlie Glotzbach posted a world record speed here of 199.466 miles per hour. A new 6,200-foot Talladega jetport is within walking distance of the north turn, while the track, itself, is less than two miles from Int. 20, which goes west to Birmingham and east to Atlanta.

Anniston is the seat of the HARRY M. AYERS STATE TRADE SCHOOL.

Birmingham

Air Services: Birmingham Municipal Airport, 7 m. ne of Downtown. Delta, Eastern, United, and Southern Air Lines. Passengers enplaned, 1970, 493,486; air freight 3114.1 tons, 1970. Daily flights average 112. The airport in 1973 received new facilities costing $30 million.

Highways: Principal north-south route is I-65, paralleled in large part by US 31; northeast-southwest is I-59 and US 11; others, I-20, US 41, US 78, State 77, 75, 79, 269.

Inter-city Buses: Greyhound, 624 19th St. N.; Continental Trailways, 2324 5th Ave. N. Scheduled buses daily, 168.

Railroads: Major systems, 7; belt and connecting lines, 2; daily passenger trains, 8; daily freight trains, 140. Two stations—Louisville & Nashville, 1821 Morris Ave., also serves for AMTRACK; Terminal Station, 2617 7th Ave., N. for all other lines.

Water Transportation: Birmingham is connected to the Warrior-Tombigbee Waterway via facilities at Port Birmingham, 17 miles west of the city. Barge and tow lines, 5; terminals, 13 private and 1 common carrier.

Motor Freight: Terminals, 100; Birmingham based freight lines, 25; average daily truck movements out of local terminals, 1,996.

Accommodations: 54 motels and hotels in metropolitan Birmingham. Six per cent occupany tax charge.

Information: Birmingham Area Chamber of Commerce, 1914 Sixth Ave., N. 35203; Greater Birmingham Convention & Visitors Bureau, 1909 Seventh Ave., N. 35203; Birmingham Planning Department, City Hall, 35203; Operation New Birmingham, City Hall, 35203; Alabama Motorist Assn. (AAA), 2305 Fifth Ave., N. 35203.

Communications: 2 daily newspapers, the *Birmingham News* (Newhouse Chain) and the *Birmingham Post-Herald* (Scripps-Howard); weekly newspapers, 7; local telephone network, 416,402 phones; 3 Commercial TV stations—WAPI-TV (NBC), WBRC-TV (ABC), WBMG-TV (CBS); Public Television WCIQ and WBIQ, part of statewide network; 12 AM radio stations, 6 FM stations; South Central Bell serves its customers in five states from Birmingham headquarters.

Educational facilities: Colleges and Universities (Jefferson County) 9; 20,531 students and 1,396 faculty. Business and Technical schools: 14. Birmingham Public schools, 89; elementary, 11 high, 3 vocational, with total enrollment of 61,691. Private and Parochial schools: 18 elementary, 7 high.

Religious and Medical: Churches, 2,700; hospitals, 23.

Large Parks: Avondale, 5th Ave. and 41st St., S.; Kelley Ingram, between 17th and 18th Streets and Sixth and Seventh Avenues, N.; Magnolia Park, 21st St., Magnolia Ave., S.; East Lake, 1st Ave., N., 81-84th Sts.; Highland Park, junction of Highland and Clairmont Aves., S.

Municipal Parks: 77, covering 2,381 acres; 3 18-hole and 1 9-hole golf courses; 65 tennis courts; 14 Recreation Centers; 14 swimming pools; 45 Vest Pocket playgrounds, baseball and football fields.

Stadia and Malls: Rickwood Field, 18,000 capacity; Legion Field, 70,000; Oporto Stadium, 10,000; Fair Park Grandstand, 9,500; Civic Center Exhibition Hall, 100,000 sq. ft. exhibition and meeting space; Civilc Center Theater, 800 seats proscenium style, 1,000 seats semi-arena; Civic Center Concert Hall, 3,000 seats; Civic Center Coloseum, 16,500 permanent seats, and up to 20,000 movable seats; Municipal Auditorium, 5,090 capacity.

Cultural Activities and Entertainment: Three community theaters; 29 movie houses and drive-ins within area; 168 night clubs and 68 lounges; Birmingham Symphony Orchestra concerts; wrestling and boxing; Municipal Auditorium; Chamber Music; three ballet companies; regular winter concert series; "Football Capital of the South;" Birmingham Art Museum, open daily; lakes and rivers for fishing and aquatic sports; Alabama International Speedway, longest and fastest Nascar track, 30 minutes away at Talladega; Birmingham A's, Class AA Southern Association, Rickwood Field; Birmingham Americans, WFL Team, Legion Field.

BIRMINGHAM (382-602 alt., 300,910 pop. 1970; 340,887, 1960, dec. 11.7%) seat of Jefferson County (644,991 pop. 1970, 634,864, 1960, inc. 1.6%) is the largest city in Alabama and the major iron and steel producing center in the South. The city with its suburbs occupies 80.02 square miles and has a population density of 3,760.4 per square mile. The Standard Metropolitan Statistical Area takes in 2,727 sq. mi., more than twice the area of Jefferson County, and 739,274 people, almost 100,000 more than the population of the County.

Birmingham observed its centennial year in 1971, and although not incorporated until 1871 it had been smelting iron ore since the early 1860s. In 1880 the first blast furnace was blown in, and in 1888 the first steel was rolled. The proximity of hematitic iron ore, coal, and lime brought Birmingham a great period of industrial growth and prosperity, and although this was halted temporarily by economic depression and labor strife, the city remained one of the principal steel centers of the nation.

By 1974 the furnaces were bigger and fewer. Birmingham's beloved red earth still has abundant iron ore, but it never really was of very high grade. It has become more economical to import South America's high quality ore than mine it here.

In 1974 only McWane Cast Iron & Pipe Co., and the American Cast Iron & Pipe Co., were locally owned. The latter, largest pipe manufacturer in the world, is owned by its employees. The other major companies are United States Steel; Woodward, owned by the Meade

Corp., and U. S. Pipe Company, owned by Jim Walter Corp. United States Steel, with Southern headquarters in Birmingham has consolidated its numerous furnaces, mills, mines and other holdings as the Fairfield Steel Works. All of these operations are converting from the open-hearth process to Q-BOP (basic oxygen process). This program is expected to free Birmingham and surrounding area of smog, the smoke-fog combination that has be-deviled the city since the first furnace went into operation.

A reborn prosperity is resulting from a coal mining boom since the 1974 fuel crisis. Twenty-seven companies are operating at full capacity, including such giants as Alabama By-Products, DeBardeleben, Peabody, Black Diamond, Pratt, and Brookside. Abandoned shafts have been re-opened and new ones built. Many of these are going as deep as 700 feet after the black gold of the great Warrior Coal Field. Strip mining is rampant under stringent rehabilitation laws. Warrior coal is in great demand because of low sulphur and high heat content.

Birmingham's economy is also expected to benefit from the discovery of a significant pocket of natural gas 40 miles north in adjacent Walker County. The find was developed by Shenandoah Oil Corp. which has been doing exploratory drilling in the Black Warrior Basin area since 1970. The new well was named No. 1 First National Bank of Birmingham, in honor of a major mineral rights holder in the drilling consortium. Shenandoah and its partners own 683,000 gross lease-hold acres in a 15-county area of north Alabama, with 161,700 acres of the total in Walker County.

One of the big advantages enjoyed by industry in the Birmingham-Fairfield-Bessemer area is water transportation, which is considerably cheaper and easier to handle than other forms of getting products to market. This was gained by the development of the PORT OF BIRMINGHAM, 17 to 20 miles west of the city on the Locust Fork of the Warrior River, which gives Birmingham access to the Warrior-Tombigbee River System that ends at Mobile. Products are shipped on barges propelled by towboats. A single towboat of 6,000 horsepower can push as much as 50,000 tons. Iron and steel products, cast iron pipe, structural steel, are moved from Birmingham by water to domestic and foreign markets, while products needed in Central Alabama—asphalt, lubricating oil, crude petroleum and gasoline—are unloaded there and distributed. Storage tanks, loading cranes, rail and truck facilities expedite the work of the Port.

BIRMINGHAM MUNICIPAL AIRPORT opened entirely new facilities in 1973 at a cost of $17,201,146. It was built with funds from a $50,000,000 bond issue voted in 1968, and is expected to become self-sustaining in the new few years. An operating fund uses all revenues collected on the airport to pay all of 3,281 personnel. Its four carriers—Delta, Eastern, Southern, and United, had 1,176,382 passengers in 1973-74.

A look at physical Birmingham shows that retail trade, financial institutions and government buildings extend west from 26th St. to 17th

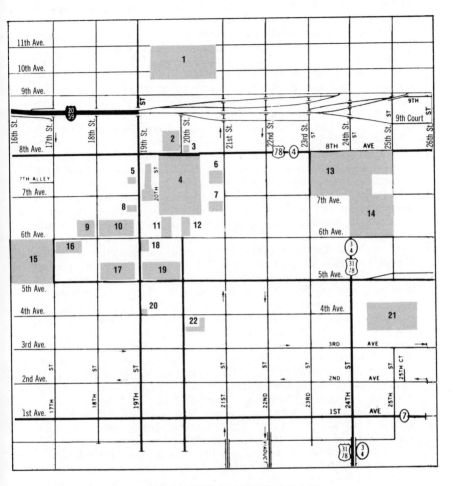

DOWNTOWN BIRMINGHAM

1 Civic Center	10 South Central Bell Bldg.	17 Federal Bldg.
2 Municipal Auditorium	11 Chamber of Commerce	18 Masonic Temple
3 Art Museum	12 Board of Education	19 First National-Southern Natural Gas Bldg.
4 Woodrow Wilson Park	13 Phillips Technical High School	20 Trailways Bus Station
5 City Hall	14 Marconi Park	21 Main Postoffice
6 Court House	15 Ingram Park	22 Exchange Security Bank
7 Public Library	16 South Central Bell Bldg.	
8 Greyhound Bus Station		
9 Alabama Power Co.		

St., between Morris and 8th Avenues, N. The University of Alabama-Birmingham dominates the south side of the core city.

After a 20-year dearth of downtown building, Birmingham's skyline has been markedly changed by a number of new skyscrapers. Three of particular interest are contemporary in design. The 30-storied South Central Bell headquarters building, made of black and white marble, occupies a half city block. Special interior attractions are a 70-foot mosaic wall by Richard Kirk, in a glass-enclosed corridor along a courtyard, and a large, handsome mobile, by Lin Emery of New Orleans, in the lobby. The building was occupied in 1972. Warren, Knight & Davis of Birmingham and Kahn & Jacobs of New York were architects.

Also occupied in 1972, the 30-storied First National Bank-Southern Natural Gas Building is an interesting meld of architecture and landscaping. A below-street restaurant looks out on a lovely garden, and wings of the building are divided by a tree-planted courtyard. Fountains border the set-back approach to the main entrance. Walter Beckett & Associates of Houston designed the building of black reflective glass and marble.

The late Lawrence Whitten designed the graceful 20-storied Daniel Building, occupied in 1970. Of pre-cast concrete, its vertical motif with splayed columns at the base, demonstrates that design is as important an ingredient in a building as is the choice of materials. A play of fountains at the entrance further enhances its visual appeal.

Other notable structures are the Alabama Power Bldg., 7th Ave. and 18th St., and the Bank for Savings, Morris Ave. at 20th St., now owned by the Birmingham Trust National Bank. On the southern outskirts of Birmingham, the Progressive Farmer-Southern Living Building is notable architecturally and for accommodating the building to the terrain with preservation of original trees. Made of Cor-ten steel, the structure was designed by Jova, Daniels & Busby of Atlanta.

Expenditures for new construction increased from $58 million in 1968 to $110 million in 1971. Thirty new enterprises entered Birmingham with headquarters offices or branches. The Social Security Administration located its regional headquarters in a ten-story building.

Of the many residential sections, the best known are Forest Park, Roebuck, Crestwood, Huffman, Woodlawn, East Lake, and Ensley. Most of these have their own business and shopping centers, which, in many instances, have replaced former residences.

As the city pushed from Jones Valley up the slope of Red Mountain, it spilled over into Shades Valley and climbed up Shades Mountain to become the suburbs of Mountain Brook, (19,474 pop. 1970; 12,680, 1960, inc. 22%); Vestavia Hills (8,511 pop. 1970; 4,926, 1960, inc. 106%); Hoover (1,363, pop., 1970), and half a dozen others. Also the contiguous city of Bessemer, which had 33,428 pop. in 1970. Mountain Brook is known for its fine dwellings, set on magnificent grounds. In the spring that whole section becomes a fairyland of azaleas, pink and white dogwood and other flowering trees and shrubs.

A constant battle goes on between developers and conservationists as they seek to halt the rash of high-rise apartments that has spread through the valleys and up the mountainsides.

PIONEER LEADERS OF INDUSTRY

When the city was incorporated in 1871 James R. Powell of the Eylton Land Company named it Birmingham after England's steel center. In 1873, when the city became the county seat in an election, Birmingham experienced the financial panic that swept the country. When it recovered the iron and steel industries climbed to major size in the nation. One of the leaders of this period was Henry F. De-Bardeleben, whose motto was "Life is just a big game of poker." In 1886 he organized the DeBardeleben Coal & Iron Company, which was capitalized at the then stupendous figure of $13,000,000. The population of Birmingham rose from 3,086 in 1880 to 26,178 in 1890; prices rocketed to as much as $1,000 a front foot. Many of the giants of early industry arrived in Alabama. Among them were T. T. Hillman and Enoch T. Ensley, of Tennessee, and Erskine Ramsay, of Pennsylvania. Ensley founded the town of Ensley (now within the city limits) and named it for himself; Hillman was one of the leaders in persuading the Tennessee Coal, Iron & Railroad Company to build in the valley.

Strikes have been numerous in Birmingham history, often with physical clashes, bloodshed, and death; State militia has been called out several times. National guardsmen first went on strike patrol in the coal miners' walkout of 1894. In 1908 a strike called by the United Mine Workers was broken swiftly by military rule set up by Governor B. B. Comer, but in 1919 a strike by coal miners lasted for months, and curtailed Alabama's coal production for the year by 15 percent. The iron ore miners' strike, 1935-36, lasted through months of bitterness between locals of the United Mine Workers and the mine operators. The five-week coal mining "holiday" during the spring of 1939 was a model of tranquility after these bitter periods.

Jones Valley was named for John Jones, one of a group of four soldiers of the Indian wars who settled in the vicinity. They built crude Fort Jonesborough about 1813 on the site of Bessemer. When Jefferson County was formed in 1819, a village called Carrollsville grew up on the site of the present West End. A forge and a school were established and a log courthouse served as the first county seat. About this time William Ely, surveyor-agent for a New England deaf and dumb asylum, arrived to dispose of land given the asylum by the Federal Government. He promptly began promoting development of a town two miles east of Carrollsville, and within less than two years the new town, named Elyton (for himself) became the county seat.

Within a few years Elyton grew into a typical trade town on the main stagecoach line from Huntsville to Tuscaloosa. Generous houses were built in the traditional plantation pattern; magnolias and other evergreens were planted on the grounds, and the inhabitants devoted a generation to growing cotton.

Baylis E. Grace was the first to use Red Mountain iron ore for commercial purposes. In 1860, his workers scooped up a wagon load of the red rock at Grace's Gap, just west of present Ishkooka, and hauled it to the smelter of Newton Smith, in Bibb County, where it was smelted and the iron sold. When the Confederate Government was faced with an acute shortage of munitions in the second year of the war, wagon trains took the ore to Selma for manufacture into cannon and shot. In 1863 small furnaces and ironworks were built at Elyton, Oxmoor, and Irondale to supplement the output of the Selma munitions plants, and Irondale produced rifles as well as cannon balls. All of these plants were destroyed by General James H. Wilson during the Union invasion of Alabama in March and April, 1865.

Having proved its industrial worth, the "paint rock" of Red Mountain served in 1870 to bring two railroads, the South & North, now the Louisville & Nashville, and the Alabama & Chattanooga, now the Alabama Great Southern. Their junction, two miles east of Elyton, determined the site of the village that was to become Birmingham. In January, 1871, speculators organized the Elyton Land Company, with holdings of 4,150 acres of land purchased at $25 an acre. Lots around the railroad junction were sold at public auction.

Birmingham experienced its biggest test for viability during the great Depression of the 1930s, when the steel mills closed and its vast work force, deprived of regular earnings, faced a fight for survival. The experience proved that no great city could exist on a single industry, and that a dominant political organization must be held responsible for the wellbeing of its citizens. A concerted effort by business and industrial leaders brought new enterprise to Birmingham, and the city revived. But the social difficulties did not yield quickly; the black population, which had suffered most in the 1930s, continued to agitate for more opportunities for employment and equal treatment in public accommodations—restuarants, buses, schools, and housing. The city government, still in conservative hands, refused to make concessions and was often blamed for repressive measures used by the police. Birmingham continued to prosper but the underlying grievances were handicaps, and the relations of the races remained tense in the 1940s and early 1950s.

CRISIS IN PUBLIC EDUCATION

The showdown came for Birmingham when the United States Supreme Court began its civil rights decisions in 1954. The order terminating racial segregation in the public schools, and the subsequent directions to local authorities to enforce integration hit directly at municipal practices. Birmingham had segregated the races in the schools, but also had provided liberally for the blacks. The A. H. Parker High School, founded as a vocational school by a Negro educator with the aid of Dr. J. H. Phillips, city superintendent, had become known for the accomplishments of its black enrollment. Civil rights leaders of both races cooperated to follow Federal instructions but met with considerable opposition from the commissioners who were backed by the strong conservative following that wanted to keep the *status quo*. After bitter campaigning the voters in 1962 voted to change from government by commission to the mayor and city council form of civic control, with officials elected by popular franchise. The commissioners tried to invalidate the election in the courts, but their efforts failed. The change in government took place April 15, 1963.

In the 1960s agitations for civil rights turned into street demonstrations that resulted in vandalism and rioting. The Rev. Martin Luther King, Jr., led crowds of blacks through the business district. At first the response was orderly but within weeks thousands of youths without aim swarmed through downtown, and in the resulting disorder the police dispersed them with fire hoses and dogs. Civic leaders realized that peace was imperative and a compromise was effected by a bi-racial committee. But its plan was denounced by the die-hard conservatives and there was new rioting and some bombing of black and white targets. President Kennedy ordered the National Guard to stand ready in local armories. At the same time the Civil Rights Act of 1964 put Federal force behind court decisions.

The culminating agony came on September 15, when bombs hit the Sixteenth Street Baptist Church and killed four little girls who were attending Sunday school. This senseless crime shocked the city and consolidated the workers for civic peace. A Community Affairs Committee of blacks and whites become active. A larger organization called Operation New Birmingham enlisted all groups and sections on a permanent basis, including the Birmingham Area Chamber of Commerce, the Birmingham Development Board, the Downtown Action Committee, and other influential bodies, financed by private and municipal funds and the University of Alabama-Birmingham. The abolition of racial discrimination in public facilities and integration of schools became official policy in Birmingham.

The City Council makes an issue of communicating direct with the citizens and the various departments are accessible to complaints and suggestions for betterment. The city cultivates open meetings and lectures, and mails questionnaires. In fiscal 1974 the City Council appropriated more than $552,000 to the Board of Education, which has 11 community schools in the system. To help keep business flourishing downtown the city added two new parking decks accommodating 2,900 cars. A Cable Television Commission was established to oversee television for training minorities and aiding communities.

The city attempts to expand its boundaries by taking in contiguous communities but has had some opposition. A recent drive added one mile square and 6,000 population. In order to relieve the central city of some of its burdens Birmingham levied an occupational tax on suburban residents who work in the city but live outside its limits.

Conversion of Morris Avenue into an attractive mall has been effected with an appropriation of $300,000, stimulating business and inviting patrons into a romantically decorated environment.

The Birmingham Beautification Board, a quasi-official city agency of 50 volunteer women, promotes a continuing land use, anti-litter and landscaping program. After 23 industrial plants were closed for a period because of bad air pollution, the big steel companies introduced expensive pollution abatement methods. New city parks have been created and old ones rehabilitated. Among the latter is Kelly Ingram Park, scene of most of the 1963 racial demonstrations.

The arts are increasingly lively in Birmingham. A new wing was added in 1974 to the Museum of Arts. The concert hall in the new Civic Center is now the home of the Birmingham Symphony Orchestra. Three community theaters are flourishing.

Every Spring, for two weeks, a Festival of Arts is held in Birmingham. Each festival salutes the arts of a particular country through visual and performing arts and literature. The Ambassador to the United States from the honored country comes to open an International Fair that is part of the festival.

Sports have taken on a new life in a city already passionately addicted to football and baseball. Its major stadium, Legion Field, has been enlarged to 70,000 capacity and is sold out every Saturday. In 1974 the World Football League established Birmingham's first professional team, the Birmingham Americans. Capacity crowds attend the Birmingham Invitational Indoor Tennis Tournament, sponsored by the Junior League, and since 1972 Birmingham's Green Valley Country Club has been on the circuit of the Ladies Professional Golf Assn.

UNIVERSITIES, COLLEGES, AND HOSPITALS

The UNIVERSITY OF ALABAMA IN BIRMINGHAM (UAB) was designated an autonomous unit in the State University System in 1966, comprising the College of General Studies, formed on the base of the University of Alabama Extension Center that had been operating in Birmingham since 1936, and the university's Medical Center, established here in 1945. The new institution began in a 15-square block in the heart of town, which expanded rapidly as urban renewal cleared areas to enlarge the campus by 45 blocks.

The major Medical Center increased by four additional schools over 1966-1969: the School of Health Services Administration was established in 1966 and incorporated into the School of Community and Allied Health Resources in 1970; the School of Nursing moved from Tuscaloosa to this campus in 1967; the School of Optometry was initiated in 1969; and the School of Community and Allied Health Resources was authorized in 1970.

In June, 1969, the administrative structure of the University of Alabama system was changed. The three campuses in Tuscaloosa, Birmingham, and Huntsville became autonomous units, each with its

own president as chief executive officer. The three presidents now comprise the Council of Presidents.

A major physical expansion has been under way at the Medical Center. The new $16 million Basic Science building was to provide sufficient classroom and laboratory space to enable the School of Medicine to increase its size to 640, representing a doubling in enrollment, and the School of Dentistry to increase by 25 percent to 288 students. The new School of Nursing building would provide for an eventual enrollment of 1,000, twice its present size. Enrollment in the School of Community and Allied Health Resources, the Medical Center's newest unit, was expected to grow from 200 students to 1,000. A building for the Regional Technical Institute for Health Occupations was completed in 1970; RTI is one of the first such schools in the United States and offers training in the health science fields at the sub-baccalaureate level. The four-story $1.4 million Medical Center Library, consolidates the library's 105,000-volume collection and has space for 250,000 additional volumes. A new ten-story addition to the Lyons-Harrison Research building was designed to house the Medical Center's programs in cardiovascular research and training, the Institute of Dental Research, and other departments.

A new hospital complex, University Hospital Number Two, with specialty towers for treatment of heart disease, cancer, and diabetes, as well as a pre-admission-convalescent self-care facility, was planned for the mid 1970s. This complex of 440 beds is expected to cost approximately $50 million.

At present the principal hospital facilities include the University of Alabama Hospitals and Clinics, with 700 beds, serving 100,000 patients annually. Closely affiliated are the Veterans Administration Hospital, 479 beds, and the Children's Hospital, 176 beds. The Eye Foundation Hospital, private, is located within the Medical Center.

The new county-owned Mercy Hospital also has been included in the complex. Then there are the Smolian Psychiatric and the Diabetes Hospitals.

UAB in 1974 enrolled 9,552 students and had 1,074 in the faculty. The parent university at Tuscaloosa (University, Ala.) enrolled 14,938 with 732 in the faculty. In 1974 it operated on a budget of $96,642,757.

SAMFORD UNIVERSITY is a coeducational institution of learning operated by the Alabama Baptist State Convention to provide preparation for life in a Christian environment. It was founded in 1841 at Marion and removed to Birmingham in 1887, and was known as Howard College until Nov. 9, 1965, when it was named Samford University in honor of Frank Park Samford, its principal benefactor. It occupied an entirely new campus on the outskirts of Homewood in 1957 and in 1961 added the Cumberland School of Law, formerly located at Lebanon, Tennessee. Samford's organization includes the Howard College of Arts and Sciences, which has a department of journalism in the division of the humanities; Schools of Graduate Studies, Business, Education, and Pharmacy, in addition to Cumberland School of Law. It conducts a summer term.

Students and faculty of the physics department built a cyclotron for experimental use by Samford and the University of Alabama, and for producing isotopes for the Medical College of Alabama. The principal Davis Library at Samford has approx. 245,000 vols. with large collections on Alabama, Baptist history, Tennyson, Ruskin, and other Victorians. The Law Library stocks upwards of 56,000 vols. In 1974 Samford enrolled 3,220 and had a faculty of 175. Cost of tuition, board and room is estimated at under $1,000, subject to price changes.

An attraction at Samford is the Rushton Memorial Carillon in the steeple of Reid Chapel. This is a 49 bell, four chromatic octave carillon; the largest bell weighs 1,521 lbs., the smallest 26 lbs. Each bell bears a Biblical or Latin inscription. The carillon was made in the Netherlands.

MILES COLLEGE, chartered in 1908 by the Colored Methodist Episcopal Church, is under the direction today of the Christian Methodist Episcopal Church, with an interracial board of trustees. Throughout its existence it has had the financial and advisory aid of the Methodist Episcopal Church, South. For most of its years of service, Miles has been the principal four-year college serving black students in the Birmingham area. About half the black teachers in Birmingham schools are Miles graduates. It participates in student exchange programs with the University of Alabama-Birmingham, as well as Wooster College in Ohio, Tuskegee Institute and Alabama A. & M. College. The W. A. Bell Library at Miles College, founded in 1905, has more than 56,000 books. It has collections of black literature and Afro-American materials. Miles has a faculty of 105 and enrolls 1,100.

DANIEL PAYNE COLLEGE chartered in 1889 in Selma, then moved to Birmingham in 1930, occupied a new 150-acre campus in 1974. Among the state's oldest predominantly black colleges, with a student body of 300 in 1973, the school is supported by the African Methodist Episcopal Church. The college grants bachelor of science degrees in elementary education, public school music and social studies.

BIRMINGHAM-SOUTHERN COLLEGE, 8th Ave. at 8th St., is a coeducational institution of the Methodist Church, which occupies a 250-acre campus of rolling woodland overlooking the Jones Valley, three miles west of downtown Birmingham. When the first college building was erected on the present campus in 1898 the area was in the rural community of Owenton, which later became a part of Birmingham. The college is a 1918 consolidation of Birmingham College and Southern Methodist University and in 1974 enrolled 872 students with a faculty of 65. Its library has more than 100,000 vols., including many on Methodism. Among the buildings are a fine small modern theater and a planetarium. The campus is also the home of the Alabama High School of the Fine Arts, a state-subsidized project. It is likely the property will be purchased by Miles College and that Birmingham-Southern will be rebuilt in adjacent Shelby County.

JEFFERSON STATE JUNIOR COLLEGE, opened in 1925, is one of the 18 junior colleges established in Alabama beginning in the 1960s. Built in 1965 by McCauley Associates, its present nine contemporary buildings are located on 234 acres of hilltop land overlooking Pinson Valley. The James B. Allen Library of more than 35,000 vols. is strong in history and the social sciences.

LAWSON STATE JUNIOR COLLEGE offers both technical training and two years of college preparatory work for its 800 students on campus and provides adult education and community service programs off campus. The institution began as a trade school in 1963 but in 1966 moved into four new buildings on Wilson Road, and in 1970 its name was changed to honor its president, Dr. Theodore Alfred Lawson. It was the first time an institution of higher education in Alabama was named for a living president and the first time in Alabama that such an institution was named for a black citizen. Its library has more than 30,000 books, among which is a collection named for Dr. Martin Luther King, Jr.

SOUTHEASTERN BIBLE COLLEGE has the Rowe Memorial Library, 1401 S. 25th St., formed in 1945. It stocks 16,000 vols.

SOUTHERN RESEARCH INSTITUTE, 2000 9th Ave., is the only private research facility to serve industry and government in the Southeast. It has 315,000 sq. ft. of laboratory space in twelve buildings and a technical staff of nearly 500. Though not an educational facility, Southern has attracted scientists of a wide variety of fields whose work has had national and international importance.

COMMUNITY SCHOOLS, a program begun in 1973, is pointed toward keeping Birmingham's Public Schools open day and night, the year around, for special courses and general adult education. In 1975 there were 11 community schools.

Other important institutions include two under Baptist control: PRINCETON CENTER in West End, and MONTCLAIR CEN-

TER on the Southside. They comprise general hospitals, clinic, and school of nursing. The Clyde L. Sibley Library has been established at 800 Montclair Road and 701 Princeton Ave., and the Ida V. Moffett Library of the School of Nursing at 800 Montclair Road.

The continuously growing CARRAWAY METHODIST MEDICAL CENTER covers two city blocks, has 417 beds, 1,047 employees and wide-ranging health education (1973). The Methodists recently acquired nearby Bessemer General Hospital.

Additional large hospitals include St. Vincent's, of the Roman Catholic diocese, and South Highland Infirmary, privately owned; Lloyd Noland Hospital, established by U. S. Steel and later given to the city of Fairfield; Hill Crest, for short-term psychiatric treatment. All of these have completed or have underway massive expansion programs. Brookwood Hospital in the Mountain Brook Area opened in 1973.

POINTS OF INTEREST

The BIRMINGHAM-JEFFERSON CIVIC CENTER is a four-unit complex between 19th and 20th Sts., and 9th and 11th Aves., at the northern line of the central business district. It is the newest and most costly addition to the public facilities of Birmingham. It provides the latest technical equipment and arrangements for conventions, large exhibitions, major sporting events, concerts and festivals. The complex comprises an Exhibit Hall with 100,000 sq. ft. of open space and 12 adjustable meeting rooms; a Concert Hall seating 3,000; a Theater with 800 to 1,000 seats, and the Coliseum, with adjustable sections that can hold 16,000 for hockey games and 17,500 for basketball. It will house the Alabama Sports Hall of Fame.

The Alabama Legislature created the Civic Center Authority with a six-man board, and authority to levy a tax on cigarettes and hotel-motel lodgings, and provision for a national architectural competition for a suitable design. The design was won by George W. Qualls, Philadelphia architect who is also professor of architecture at the University of Pennsylvania. A site north of the present Municipal Auditorium was chosen and four sets of railroad tracks were moved from 9th and 10th Aves. to protect the halls from noise. The land was bought with the help of urban renewal aid from the Federal Government. Construction was begun with the proceeds of a bond issue by the Authority for $23,-700,000, and the Exhibit Hall was opened December 19, 1971. The Coliseum was begun after another bond issue of $10,500,000 had been sold; the contract went to Pearce, DeMoss & Co. for $18,771,631. The Concert Hall-Theater building cost $18,320,000 and the Concert Hall was opened October 3, 1974. Its initial program included the Birmingham Symphony Orchestra, conducted by Amerigo Marino, performing compositions by Samuel Barber, Morton Gould, and Charles Ives, and Van Cliburn in the Tschaikovsky piano concerto.

The JEFFERSON COUNTY COURTHOUSE, between 7th and 8th Aves., on 21st St., N., faces Woodrow Wilson Park. A nine-story structure, built in 1931, it received an addition in 1968. It is of Indiana limestone, trimmed at the base with gray Minnesota granite. Stone spandrels above the sixth floor windows of the original building, and other special stone carvings, modeled by Leo Friedlander of New York, suggest the various nations that have held sovereignty over Alabama. Another group is symbolic of Justice, Mercy, Power, Strength and Equity. Murals by the late John Norton on walls of the first floor lobby portray the Old South and its industrialization. An accurately executed map of the county, constructed of vari-colored terrazzo and mosaic tile, is inlaid on the floor of the county commissioners' reception rooms, north wing, second floor. The Jefferson County Board of Education has headquarters in the building, which also has court rooms, offices, a law library and, on the top floors, the County Jail.

THE FEDERAL BUILDING, at 5th Ave. and 19th St., N., was formerly the Post Office. It is a four-story structure of white granite, with Alabama marble inside.

BIRMINGHAM CITY HALL, between 19th and 20th Sts. and 7th and 8th Aves., N., facing Woodrow Wilson Park, covers half a city block. The 10-story structure of limestone with black granite trim, designed by Charles McCauley & Associates, was opened in 1948.

The MUNICIPAL AUDITORIUM, at 8th Ave. and 20th St., N., is a large red brick building, suitable for everything from rodeos to concerts. It has 6,000 permanent seats.

The BIRMINGHAM PUBLIC AND JEFFERSON COUNTY FREE LIBRARY, 2020 7th Ave., was established in 1902. Its main building is a four-story structure of Indiana limestone designed by Miller & Martin and completed in 1927. In the main room on the first floor and in the children's room are murals by Ezra Winter. It has approx. 840,000 vols., and 28,700 bound periodicals, and circulates more than 3,380,000 annually. Among its special collections are the Grace Hardin children's, and a comprehensive one on southern history. The library operates four bookmobiles and has 16 branches, among which East Lake, 5 S. 77th St., has more than 32,000 vols.; Avondale has over 30,000, and Central Park more than 28,000.

Seven early churches of the city of Birmingham owe their location to the donation of land by the Eylton Land Company. Seven congregations of Protestants, Catholics and Jews occupied new buildings by 1880. Fine permanent structures were completed by the century's turn and it is by five of these, within easy walking distance of each other, that Birmingham's earliest days are commemorated. They are FIRST BAPTIST CHURCH, Sixth Ave. at 22nd St. This church of 1902 cherishes the Good Shepherd Window (West side), one of its many beautiful stained glass windows. ST. PAUL'S CO-CATHEDRAL, Third Ave. at 22nd St. This soaring Gothic church of 1893 dominated the Birmingham skyline for a decade. Particularly lovely are the altars of Italian marble. FIRST PRESBYTERIAN CHURCH, Fourth Ave. at 21st St. was the first church erected in the city (1888). From the carillon intricate compositions ring out over the city. EPISCOPAL

CHURCH OF THE ADVENT, 20th St. at 6th Ave. (1893) is noted for cloistered gardens, beautiful windows and an impressive altar that was imported from Italy. FIRST METHODIST CHURCH, 519 North 19th St., Early Romanesque (1891) has 142 finely crafted stained glass windows.

The ALABAMA POWER COMPANY, 600 N. 18th St., is one of the nation's great public utilities. The major component of the Southern Company, it was incorporated in 1927 to produce electric power for street railways and plants, electric light, and gas. In 1973 the system was serving electricity to 639 communities, including all in Alabama except the northern segment served by the Tennessee Valley Authority; power to 15 municipalities including Anniston, Birmingham, Gadsden, Mobile, Montgomery, Phenix City, Selma, Talladega, and Tuscaloosa, an area of 44,500 sq. mi., holding 2,769,100 people. It had 849,223 customers, 742,270 residential, 106,320 industrial and commercial, produced 4,855,835 kw, of which 1,342,225 kw came from hydroelectric installations, the rest from fossil fuel. Its transmission lines covered 8,067 circuit miles, 37,342 pole miles of distribution lines, and it had 1,053 substations.

Large appropriations of money have been used to build locks and dams with power houses on Alabama rivers, and have resulted in dams on the Coosa up to Rome, Georgia; others on the Warrior, Tallapoosa, and Alabama Rivers. The company has been building new steam plants, using Alabama coal. For several years construction has been continuing at Unit No. 1 of the Joseph M. Farley Nuclear plant near the Chattahoochee River in Houston County, which was planned to have a capacity of 860,000 kw and be in operation by 1976. Unit No. 2 with the same capacity was to be ready a year later. A second nuclear electric generating complex to have four units and a capacity of 1,-200,000 kilowatts is planned for sites in Chilton and Elmore Counties near Clanton, an investment of possibly $2.9 billion, to be in operation in the early 1980s.

ARLINGTON, 331 Cotton Ave. SW, is a Georgian Colonial house built in 1842 and associated with the gay social life of the ante bellum years. It is owned and maintained by the municipality and contains furnishings of its early period. During the spring of 1865 Union General James H. Wilson used the house as headquarters and from here issued the orders to the so-called Wilson's Raiders to attack the Cadet Training School at Tuscaloosa and the arsenal and shipyard at Selma. The house is a half-timber structure and contains relics of the war, a section on great Alabama women, and an Eylton Room with memorabilia of the old town. All that remains of Eylton are this house, the courthouse bell of 1821 in its garden, and two old cemeteries. *Arlington is open 9-5 weekdays, 1-6 Sundays, closed holidays; adults, $1, children, 25¢.*

BIRMINGHAM GREEN, a six-block rehabilitation and beautification project on 19th and 20th Streets, main downtown arteries, was accomplished with funds from City, Federal Government and pri-

vate sector. It is maintained by the Park & Recreation Board's horticulture section. Twentieth Street, principal downtown artery, now
freed of buses, has been transformed into a boulevard of decorative brick
sidewalks, striking light fixtures, and medians of trees, shrubs and
flowering plants, ending at Woodrow Wilson Park.

WOODROW WILSON PARK, is a four-acre park around
which are located Jefferson County Courthouse, Birmingham City Hall,
Central Public Library, Birmingham Board of Education, Art Museum
and Municipal Auditorium. Parallel concrete walks are divided by
reflecting pools. Beyond the last pool facing City Hall a flower garden
is centered with a changing motif saluting special dates and events.
At the main south entrance is a monument to soldiers and sailors of
the Confederacy.

The COMMEMORATIVE GARDEN WALK, on 20th Street,
N., across from Woodrow Wilson Park, between the art museum and
the Municipal Auditorium, is a pedestrian plaza of flowers, shrubs and
water cascade. A travertine pavillion is inscribed with names of donors
and honorees. Sponsored by the Birmingham Beautification Board,
financed with city, private and Federal funds, the Garden walk is a
beautiful approach to the new Civic Center. It is maintained by Birmingham Park & Recreation Board's horticulture section.

BIRMINGHAM MUSEUM OF ART. On the northern side
of Woodrow Wilson Park, Eighth Ave. N., the museum is composed
of the Oscar Wells Memorial Building and the recently added William
E. Spencer Wing. The facades are faced with travertine and inserted
are large panels of dark green terraverde marble. Constantly growing
collections include a Samuel H. Kress Collection of 35 Italian paintings,
furniture and stained glass; English, French, Dutch paintings; American Indian art and artifacts from Alabama, the Plains, the Northwest
Coast; an exceptional collection of Remington bronzes; Near and Far
Eastern art; European silver, porcelain, glass; American contemporary
paintings and watercolors, and the Beeson Collection of Wedgwood,
one of the largest in existence. Constantly changing temporary exhibitions cover all facets of the visual arts. *Open weekdays 10-5, and until
9 p.m. on Thursday, Sundays, 2-6, free.*

VULCAN PARK, a landscaped 4-acre park atop Red Mountain
is home of the mammoth iron statue of Vulcan, god of the forge and
symbol of the City of Birmingham. Weighing 60 tons, 50 ft. in
height, the statue stands on a tower 120 ft. high and is visible from
a wide area. Second in size to the Statue of Liberty, the monument
was executed by Guiseppi Moretti for Birmingham's display at the St.
Louis Exposition in 1904. A geological museum is in the base of the
tower and an observation balcony provides a spectacular panorama of
Birmingham and its surroundings. A torch in the figure's hand burns
red when there has been a fatal traffic accident. The park is also site
of a kneeling statue of the Rev. "Brother" J. A. Bryan by Georges
Bridges, Birmingham sculptor. For many years the city's official chaplain, Brother Bryan's life and works are still an inspiration to Birmingham residents.

JIMMY MORGAN ZOO. On the southern border of the city and across the highway from the Botanical and Japanese Gardens, the municipally owned and operated zoo is the largest in a nine-state area of the Southeast. The Children's Zoo and a mini-train are two special attractions. An international exchange of animals has provided a varied population. Picnic shelters and out-door ovens are provided. *Open daily 9:30-8, small fee.*

BIRMINGHAM BOTANICAL GARDENS. Between Montclair and Montevallo Roads, the Gardens occupy 67 acres, including a large conservatory, the Garden Club Center, a Wild Flower Garden, Touch and See Garden for the blind, and a 26-foot floral clock.

The JAPANESE GARDEN. Adjacent to Botanical Gardens, this display was designed by a Japanese landscape architect especially for Birmingham. The Government of Japan contributed an authentic tea house, originally at the New York World's Fair. Oriental bridges, linked by pebbled pathways, cross the garden's lakes and brooks.

LEGION FIELD, at Graymont Ave. and 4th St., is a municipal stadium with seating capacity of 70,000. Important college, high school and Football League games are held here. At the front entrance is a monument by William Grant honoring Alabama soldiers who served in World War I.

JEWISH COMMUNITY CENTER. 3960 Montclair Road. A spread of buildings including a 500-seat auditorium, handball court, large gymnasium, meeting rooms, facilities for kindergarten and nursery school, lounges, indoor and outdoor swimming pools, and four tennis courts. Open membership for use of facilities.

CLARK MEMORIAL THEATER, 1116 S. 26 St. Originally built for the Birmingham Little Theater, it is currently owned by the University of Alabama and is the home of the university's community theater, Town & Gown. In the gardens are sculpted heads of famous playwrights done by Jamie Howard of Birmingham.

SLOSS FURNACE, First Ave. and 32nd St., N. This was one of the first furnaces constructed in the city. No longer in operation, the property was given to Birmingham by the John Walter Co., to become an industrial museum.

MISS LIBERTY TOUR. Miss Liberty atop the 10-story Liberty National Life Insurance Building in downtown Birmingham, is the country's largest replica of the Statue of Liberty. Weighing more than 20,000 lbs. and standing 31 ft. high, the statue may be viewed from two roof-top observation platforms. *A 40-minute tour Monday through Friday, 10-2.*

Decatur

Airports: Carl T. Jones Jetport, 15 min. from downtown, also serves Huntsville. Runway 5,100 ft. n-s, Daily flights by Eastern, United and Southern Airlines. Pryor Field, adjacent to John C. Calhoun Junior College, hq and training station for one wing of Alabama Civil Air Patrol; used by industries for executive planes and by private planes.

Highways: US 51, north-south; US 72 alternate connecting with Int. 65; State 24,67.

Buses: Greyhound Lines, Continental Trailways.

Railroads: Louisville & Nashville, Southern.

Motor Freight: 15 carrier lines.

Waterways: 25 barge lines on the Tennessee River.

Information and Accommodations: Decatur Chamber of Commerce; Decatur *Daily,* evening and Sunday.

Churches: 70, all major denominations.

Libraries: Decatur Public Library (Headquarters, Wheeler Basin Regional Library), 207 Church Street; I bookmobile operating in Morgan & Limestone Counties to schools and communities; 1 bookmobile in Decatur and Westgate Shopping Centers on alternate weeks. Region branches: Hartselle Public, Sherrill St., Hartsell; Youth Branch, Second Ave., Decatur; Sterrs, Cherry Street, Decatur; Athens, South St., Athens.

Recreation: Three outdoor-indoor centers; swimming, water skiing and competitive Sports on the Tennessee River; 5 municipal golf courses; 2 private country clubs. Special events: Civic Theater, Youth Symphony orchestra; Junior Service League plays for children; art shows. Chief attraction is Point Mallard Park, a 750-acre playground on the banks of the Tennessee. In it a five-acre Aquatic Center has a swimming pool with mechanically produced three-foot waves, an Olympic swimming pool with a 10-meter diving tower, a marine playground for children. There are also an 18-hole golf course, picnic areas, bridle paths, botanical garden and a full-service marina. This park is adjacent to Wheeler National Wildlife Refuge where 100,000 ducks and geese retreat for the winter.

DECATUR (573 alt., 38,044 pop. 1970; 29,217, 1960, inc. 30%), seat of Morgan County, is situated on a high plateau on the south bank of the Tennessee River which, at this point, reached a width of two miles after completion of Wheeler Dam of the Tennessee Valley Authority, 30 miles to the west.

A nine-foot channel makes possible a lively barge traffic on the river, conducted by 25 companies, serviced by private and state-owned dock facilities. The industrial waterfront is a seven-mile stretch along the Decatur bank of the Tennessee, site of 43 industries representing nearly a $1 billion investment. Some of the larger installations that may be visited are:

INGALLS SHIPBUILDING PLANT, 601 Market St., NW, built Liberty ships during World War II and later cargo ships for the Netherlands government. The firm builds and repairs barges and tow boats.

GOODYEAR DECATUR MILLS, 500 19th Ave., manufactures fabric for the tire plants of Goodyear Tire & Rubber Co.

WOLVERINE, 2100 Market St., NE, tube division of Universal Oil Products Co., manufactures copper and copper alloy, seamless tubing, aluminium seamless tubing and extruded aluminium shapes.

MONSANTO TEXTILE CO., on Courtland Highway, is a unit of Monsanto Co., first called the Chemstrand Corp. It has been expanded many times since it first located on a 700-acre tract in 1951. It manufactures acrilan acrylic fiber, blue "C" polyester staples and tire fibers, blue "C" nylon intermediates chemicals and chemcoke. Here was originated Astroturf, marvel of the sports world. Monsanto has 45 plants located principally in Mid-America, and others abroad. In the 1970s the company began an expansion of the Decatur plant with the object of increasing its capacity from 70,000,000 lbs. of fiber a year to 330,000,000 lbs.

MINNESOTA MINING & MANUFACTURING CO., State Docks Road, operates two divisions here. The Chemical Division makes textile treating compounds, plastic and elastomers; the Film Allied Division makes plastic film.

FRUEHAUF CORPORATION, Highway 20, W, makes aluminum sheets and extrusions used in its manufacture of truck and house trailers.

CLIMATROL INDUSTRIES (FEDDERS), 8th St., SE, located in Decatur in 1953 on a 165-acre tract, has, after numerous expansions, become one of the city's largest industries, employing more than 1,000 in the manufacture of air conditioners.

Down the river a few miles is TVA's Brown Ferry plant, a major nuclear power facility.

While this impressive industrial activity was stimulated by TVA programs which provide cheap hydroelectric power, flood control, soil conservation and rehabilitation, Decatur's civic and business leaders parlayed Federal assistance, with private enterprise and vigorous municipal efforts, into a New-Old-South city where gleaming new buildings stand beside mellow ante bellum structures.

In the middle of the business section stands a stately old building that houses the first State Bank, built by slave labor in 1832.

While in South Alabama Mobile flowered with trade and culture, only a few white traders penetrated the wild and verdant Tennessee valley. The large Cherokee nation occupied this valley as far west as Muscle Shoals. Beyond treacherous cataracts lay Chickasaw country. The most fierce, insolent, haughty and cruel of Alabama's Indians, the Chickasaws attacked De Soto, routed the French under Bienville, fought constantly with other tribes, and continually attacked boats of French *voyageurs* on the Mississippi and Tennessee Rivers.

By 1780, however, this lovely and fertile region had been fairly well populated by settlers who, floating down the Tennessee from the east, survived the harrowing trip through hostile Indian settlements and the cataracts at Muscle Shoals. For decades these determined folk suffered murder and plunder at the hands of the Chickasaw and Cherokee, hostilities growing progressively worse at the instigation of Chief Tecumseh.

Yet a culture was born in this remote valley, isolated by wilderness from the cosmopolitan civilization of Alabama's Gulf Coast. With Andrew Jackson's decisive battles against the Creek nation at Talladega and Horseshoe Bend and the coming of peace, the floodgates of the Eastern Seaboard opened and immigrants poured into Alabama.

By 1820 the Classical Revival in building had reached America. Mansions rose in a wilderness only partially cleared of Indians. Faced with primitive conditions settlers made their own brick, felled and sawed their own timber and utilized native limestone and sandstone.

Through 40 years Alabama built, embellishing the classical with innovations—spacious rooms, wide verandahs, winding staircases, hand-carved ornaments, reflecting the growing earnings of the land. Many of these reminders are still to be found in Decatur and its environs.

The present city, including the three municipalities of Decatur, Albany and Austinville, had its beginning as Rhodes Ferry.

In 1820, President Monroe directed the Surveyor General of the United States to reserve a site for a town near a great river to be named for Commodore Stephen Decatur, hero of the Barbary Coast and the War of 1812, who had died following a duel. The site chosen was at an old Cherokee crossing of the Tennessee River where Dr. Henry Rhodes, a pioneer of the region, had located a ferry. The village, then known as Rhodes Ferry, was turned over to the Decatur Land Company for development and chartered as Decatur by the Alabama Legislature on Dec. 8, 1826.

In 1832 the Tuscumbia Railroad, the first railroad west of the Alleghenies, was completed to Decatur, connecting the town with Tuscumbia and permitting shipments down the Tennessee to the Gulf by avoiding the treacherous Muscle Shoals.

The Methodists built the town's first church in 1835; the first business structures, Hines' store and warehouse, were erected in 1836. Two years later a cotton factory was established.

The town was caught between "the upper millstone of invasion and the nether millstone of resistance" during the War Between the

States. It was taken and retaken by both armies. At the close of hostilities only five buildings remained intact.

The Reconstruction period brought rebuilding, and the population, which was only 671 in 1870, almost doubled by 1878. A scourge of yellow fever reduced this number to a scant 300, but growth began anew, and by 1900 the population had increased to 3,114. A period of steady growth followed, interrupted only by the Great Depression, so that in 1970 the city's population had multiplied more than ten times.

In 1927 Decatur combined with the neighboring city of Albany, which had been founded in 1886 under the name of New Decatur, by Major E. C. Gordon as a real estate development around the new Louisville & Nashville Railroad shops and a large tannery. Stimulated by these enterprises, Albany had grown rapidly, and at the time of the consolidation had nearly twice the population of Decatur. There was considerable rivalry between the two towns but finally the citizens got together and named their consolidated city Decatur because of that town's seniority.

Creation of TVA in 1933 dramatically changed the fortunes of Decatur. There was, however, a prior milestone: erection of the Keller Memorial Bridge. Until its completion in 1928, transportation across the Tennessee was entirely by ferry, except for a bridge used by the L. & N. and Southern railroads.

While the bridge was under construction, the area had its last serious flood. This ever-present danger ended with the advent of TVA. Coming at the height of the great depression (1933), the many-faceted TVA program provided the foundation for a new relationship between man, the land, and the river, with man the master.

For Decatur, particularly by erection of Wheeler Dam, TVA provided the stimulus to move from a once-a-year income from the harvesting of one crop, cotton, toward a diversified agriculture and new industrial potentials.

Effects of World War II lifted Decatur from the status and outlook of a small town to a level of a city in the making. In addition to the Army Induction Center, where Company B of the 151st Combat Engineers was quartered, there were two Air Force Pilot Training Centers nearby, one at Courtland and the other at Pryor Field just across the river from Decatur.

The town was flooded with servicemen and their families and workers drawn from over the country, many of whom stayed after the conflict ended. So, too, did many of the war-instigated industries. By 1940 there were 61 manufacturing firms employing 2,834 people with an annual payroll of $3,159,000. By 1944 the number of industries was 68, employing 6,908 people with an annual payroll of $12,927,000. By 1948, the number of manufacturers had reached 87 and employment, off from the wartime peak, was 5,204, but the payroll was $12,605,000.

All of this progress was linked with the development at Tennessee Valley Authority which had been solidly established by the time the war came.

Metropolis

VULCAN, THE IRON MAN OF BIRMINGHAM, 55 FEET TALL, STANDS
ON A 124-FT. PEDESTAL IN VULCAN PARK

DOWNTOWN BIRMINGHAM AS SEEN FROM VULCAN PARK.

ENTRANCE TO BIRMINGHAM ON EXPRESSWAY CUT THROUGH RED MOUNTAIN

AERIAL VIEW OF BIRMINGHAM BUSINESS AREA

CONCERT HALL, CIVIC CENTER, BIRMINGHAM, JANUARY, 1975

ARCHITECTS' AERIAL PLAN FOR CIVIC CENTER: RIGHT, THEATER;
TOP RIGHT, EXHIBITION HALL; LEFT, COLISEUM

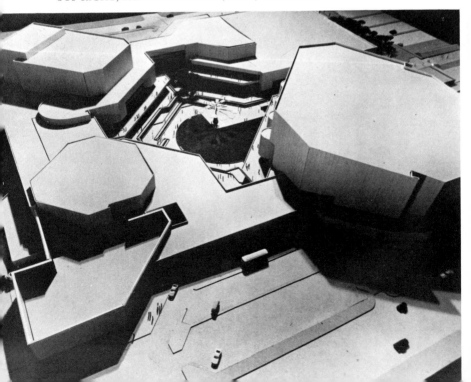

AFTERNOON AUDIENCE IN NEW CONCERT HALL, HOME OF
BIRMINGHAM SYMPHONY ORCHESTRA

ARLINGTON, CONFEDERATE SHRINE IN BIRMINGHAM, BUILT 1841,
NOW A MUSEUM

River, a high-rise apartment for elderly persons, was named for former Mayor H. R. Summer and designed by Gadsden architect Hugh E. Willis. The 101 low-rent housing units occupy all but the lower floor, where are located a library, recreation and craft center. The building occupies a city block. All of the units have outside balconies.

AQUADOME SWIMMING POOL, 1203 5th Ave., SW, one of the largest dome-covered swimming pools in the United States, is open the year around. *Hours in the winter, 7-9 Monday through Saturday; in the summer, 1-5 and 7-9 (fee).*

DELANO PARK, Prospect Drive and U.S. Highway 31, is a 27-acre park including picnic facilities, playground, athletic fields, swimming pool, lighted tennis courts *(fee for swimming).*

DECATUR BOAT HARBOR, adjacent to Wheeler Memorial Bridge, provides docking, boating and picnicking facilities.

McENTIRE HOUSE, 120 Sycamore St. Oldest Morgan County records show that Jesse Whorton of Davidson County, Tennessee, was an early owner and probably the builder in 1824 of this mansion set high on a bluff overlooking the Tennessee River. Completely restored by Mr. and Mrs. LeRoy McEntire, its present owners, the structure is Jeffersonian classic in design. Tall, square columns support the portico roof, and the interior woodwork is hand-carved. The original iron fence, the brick walk and fine boxwood plants are still intact. During the War Between the States the house was owned by the A. A. Burlesons, Mrs. Burleson having received it in 1850 from her parents, the Alexander Pattersons, Sr. It was used as headquarters and hospital by both the Union and Confederate armies. Around its dining room table Gen. Albert Sidney Johnston and his Confederate staff are said to have planned the campaign that led to the Battle of Shiloh on April 14, 1862. In 1869 the Burlesons sold the property to Jerome Hinds. A twenty square-foot plot of land reserved as a cemetery by the Burlesons is on the property. When the Hinds left the home it was used for a boarding house until 1895 when R. P. McEntire purchased the property. It has been in his family ever since.

AMERICAN LEGION AND AUXILIARY HOME (Old State Bank Bldg.), Bank St. and Wilson Ave. *(open by appointment),* was erected in 1832 under President Andrew Jackson's State Bank program. Classical Revival in design, it resembles the original Federal Hall in New York, where George Washington took oath as President of the United States. An innovation is the Gothic window treatment in the pediment. Five massive stone columns from Trinity Mountain quarries eight miles away line the portico. The double entrance doors are eight-paneled and are surmounted by a circle-head transom. In the rotunda a mural painted by Eleanor Bridges Massey of Birmingham, depicts the freeing of the slaves who carried the 100-ton columns from the quarry to the site. President Van Buren attended the dedication of the building. The building was used as a hospital during the War Between the States, became a bank and was later bought by Dr. R. J. Cantwell. He willed it to his niece, Mrs. W. B. Edmundson, who deeded it to the city in 1936. After restoration with WPA funds in 1936, it was named Leila Cantwell Seaton Hall in her honor, and for a number of years was a museum and gathering place for civic and social clubs. It is now owned by the American Legion.

The JOHN C. CALHOUN STATE JUNIOR COLLEGE AND TECHNICAL SCHOOL is located 4 m. north of Decatur. It opened in 1965 with 420 students and in the fall, 1974, enrolled 1,501 and had a faculty of 58.

The WHEELER NATIONAL WILDLIFE REFUGE, two miles southeast of Decatur in Morgan and Madison Counties, with headquarters on State 67, covers 34,988 acres and provides shelter for a vast grouping of wildlife, principally ducks and geese. Hunting is available as regulated by the State and there is plenty of fishing, while the gentler sports, such as bird-watching and picnics, are practiced to great satisfaction. Camping is limited to daylight hours, unless special arrangements are made for youth groups and supervised parties; no guns may be carried in unless a public hunt is on, and no dogs are allowed entrance. The refuge is being improved with a visitors center on Flint Creek Island, which is to include exhibits, an auditorium for lectures, and films that can be activated by the spectator. *Office open Mon.-Fri. 7:30-4:30, except holidays.*

Florence

Air Services: Southern Airways, Muscle Shoals Airport.

Highways: Florence is served by US 43, which comes from Tennessee and is joined by US 72 from Athens before reaching Florence; by Ala 17 and Ala 20. US 72 Alt, has a junction with US 43 6 *m.* s. of Florence. Athens, 44 *m.* east, is on Interstate 65, major route to Birmingham, Montgomery and Mobile.

Bus Lines: Continental Trailways, 311 South Court St.; Greyhound Lines, depot (Joiner's Transit, Inc.) 121 East Alabama St.

Railroads: Louisville & Nashville and Southern Railway, freight stations in East Florence.

Information and Accommodations: Florence Times and *Tri-Cities Daily,* eve. and Sunday, 219 W. Tennessee St. *Florence Herald,* weekly, and *Picture,* weekly. Florence Chamber of Commerce, 104 Pine St. Motels downtown and in suburbs.

Recreation: City swimming and facilities for games in parks; municipal golf course. Commercial boat docks for fishing and boating. Private clubs: Turtle Point Yacht & Country, Florence Golf & Country, Skylark Golf, Sailing.

Annual Events: North Alabama State Fair, Fairgrounds, late September; Lions Club Antique Show, Coliseum, early November.

FLORENCE (429-563 alt. 34,031 pop. 1970; 31,649, 1960, inc. 7.5%) the seat of Lauderdale County, is the largest of the Tri-cities, which include Sheffield (13,115, pop. 1970), and Tuscumbia (8,828 pop. 1970) The district also includes the town of Muscle Shoals, (6,907 pop.) Florence occupies a rolling slope of valley land on the northern bank of the Tennessee River. The downtown section has new Courthouse and municipal buildings, a Postoffice and Federal Courthouse building, modern business and professionnal establishments, schools and churches, and the Florence State University.

Florence is largely a residential city. Older residential areas near downtown contain impressive ante bellum homes as well as homes of a later vintage. These have been augmented by the construction of many new subdivisions, causing a substantial expansion in the city's growth in area as well as in population. As residential areas have extended outward from the heart of the city, several new shopping centers have sprung up. In addition to older industries along the river bank, a number of light industries have been established in a new industrial park to the north of the city. The great WILSON LOCK AND DAM on the Tennessee River touch the city's eastern section, with the lock accommodating substantial barge traffic on the river. Across the river in neighboring Colbert County are located the National Fertilizer Development Center of the Tennessee Valley Authority and large metallurgical and chemical industries.

The Cherokee and Chickasaw Indians disputed possession of the land on which the present city stands long before the first white settlers came. Abundant fish and game, productive land, and vantage points for signal fires on nearby high hills made the section valuable. The tortuous rapids of the shoals offered a challenge to boating skills that delighted the Indians.

About 1779 the first white rivermen paddled into the region and established a trading post here. They named the rapids Muscle, or Mussel Shoals, suggested either by the abundant shell-fish or the strong arm muscles required to paddle a boat through the rapids. In 1892 the United States Geographic Board selected Muscle Shoals as the official name for Government use.

Richard Rapier, river traders, chose this place as a base for his fleet of flatboats; other settlers followed and by 1818 the hamlet showed some promise. General John Coffee, surveyor-general of Alabama Territory and hero of the Battle of New Orleans, John McKinley, later a justice of the United States Supreme Court, and James Jackson, wealthy turfman, were attracted by the industrial possibilities of the site. Together with nine associates they formed the Cypress Land Company and in 1818 bought from the Government the property on which the present city stands. The town was laid out in one-half acre lots, and among those buying the first lots were General Andrew Jackson and President James Monroe.

The town was planned by Ferdinand Sannoner, young Italian surveyor, born in Leghorn, near Florence. In recognition of his competent work, the company asked him to name the development and he chose Florence, in honor of the Italian city.

The Indians had been pushed back from the river, land was cheap, and crop prices were high. Settlers came in increasing numbers, for Florence, at the crossing of the Tennessee River and the Military Road, was in the path of many homeseekers. Finding the land here excellent for producing cotton, and river transportation available for outbound staples and inbound supplies, the shrewder immigrants remained and established homes and plantations. The valley flourished and Florence grew. The East Tennessee Steam Boat Company was organized in 1819 with Leroy Pope, president, and John Coffee and James Jackson, directors. According to contemporary accounts there were, in 1820, a hundred homes, brick warehouses, two taverns, and a weekly newspaper.

To impress prospective settlers and investors, the Cypress Land Company built a tavern at a cost of $30,000, an extravagant expenditure for a hostelry in a small frontier town.

By 1824 river traffic had become so important that President Monroe recommended that Congress authorize a survey of the shoals with a view to improving navigation. As a result of this survey the Federal Government released for sale 400,000 acres of land to finance a canal around the shoals. The canal was completed in 1836, but it did not prove practicable and was closed in 1837. The initial survey marked the beginning of a long series of Government-sponsored development projects, climaxed by the present Tennessee Valley Authority. The original canal was improved in 1840 and expanded in 1876-1890, but it was not a complete success.

A bridge across the Tennessee had been proposed by the Cypress Land Company before Florence was incorporated in 1826; it was not, however, built until 1840 and was later destroyed. A railroad bridge, built in 1858, was wrecked during the War between the States, but was rebuilt after the Reconstruction period. The city was invaded by Federal troops at various times between 1862 and 1865, but its houses escaped complete destruction.

During the decade before the war, several schools had been founded, making the town an educational center. The Florence Synodical College maintained by the Presbyterian Synod of Alabama, was chartered in 1855, and in the same year Wesleyan University was established by the Methodists. These institutions are no longer in existence. Florence Wesleyan University was the successor to the noted La Grange College. In 1872 its property was deeded to Alabama for the establishment of the State Normal School, the first state supported teacher training institution south of the Ohio River. The school developed into the present Florence State University. Florence has a progressive public school system with a number of modern facilities scattered throughout the city.

In the post-Reconstruction decades industries were few and small, and trade was not sufficient to induce rapid growth. Forward looking citizens renewed agitation for Government aid in developing the potentialities of the river. Their first success came in 1916, when President Wilson signed the National Defense Act, a bill providing for the construction of a gigantic hydroelectric dam and two nitrate plants for the manufacture of war supplies at Muscle Shoals. From that beginning has grown the extensive program of the Tennessee Valley Authority (see Tour 4).

Water power is only one of the natural resources that bring prosperity to the region. Lauderdale County is important in the raising of cotton and other agricultural products. Florence's industries include textile mills, fertilizer factory, stove foundry, floor tile factory, and mobile home factory.

Four Alabama governors, Hugh McVay, Robert M. Patton, Edward A. O'Neal, and his son Emmet O'Neal, lived in or near Florence. William C. Handy, famed internationally as the "father of the blues," was born in Florence.

POINTS OF INTEREST

FLORENCE STATE UNIVERSITY, located on 80 acres in the tree-shaded residential part of Florence, is in direct line from the little LaGrange College that the Methodists started in 1830. They soon transfered their activities to Florence and in 1855 the college became Wesleyan University. The venerable Wesleyan Hall on the present campus of contemporary architecture recalls that pioneering period. By 1872 the Methodists donated their college to the State in exchange for support, and it became the State Normal School. In 1874 it was made coeducational; in 1929 it became the State Teachers College with a four-year course in elementary education. When the Graduate Division was organized in 1957 the institution was named Florence State College, and in 1968 its extensive programs justified the change to University. It has a faculty of 164 and enrolled 3,226 in the 1969 fall semester.

In the 1960 decade new construction added materially to the facilities of the University. Buildings erected since 1960 include the Student Union, Lafayette Hall, LaGrange Hall, and the Towers, comprising Rice and Rivers Halls and a cafeteria; the Science Bldg., Kilby Laboratory School, Observatory and Planetarium, Collier Library addition, University Infirmary and 50 apartments for married students. The Lureen Burns Wallace Fine Arts Center, a group of three buildings erected in 1969, has an auditorium seating 1,726. The Health & Physical Education Bldg.-Gymnasium was a recent project.

Among new programs and courses are those in the social sciences on geography, political science, sociology and law enforcement. A new major in sociology prepares for employment in the public welfare services. A master's degree in reading specialization has been added to graduate work in education. In 1969 the Department of Science, in cooperation with the Tennessee Valley Authority established the Institute for Fresh-water Biology, especially to study ways of protecting the valley from pollution and misuse.

The University Administration says: "Probably no aspect of university life has undergone more dramatic change during the past decade than the program of financial aids for needy and worthy students. The institution gives reasonable assurances that no student who has the academic ability and record and the determination to continue college will need to withdraw or fail to enter because of financial barriers."

The University estimates a full-time student's expenses at $611 to $621 for tuition, board and room per semester, not including laboratory fees. Nonresidents of the State are charged $90 in addition. There are two semesters.

The CONFEDERATE MONUMENT, Courthouse Lawn, Court St. is a memorial to Southern men who lost their lives in the War of 1861-65. The gray stone figure of an infantryman in marching equipment was executed in Italy and dedicated April 25, 1903.

COURTVIEW, also known as Rogers Hall, at the north end of

Court St., is a Greek Revival mansion built in 1855 by George Washington Foster. The house is distinguished by four white Ionic columns. The house later became the home of Emmet O'Neal, one of Alabama's governors. The state of Alabama acquired the property from the Rogers family, and it is used by Florence State University for social functions and to house the guests of the university.

The FLORENCE CURB MARKET, corner of South Seminary and East Alabama Sts., is a scene of activity when farmers in motley array set up stalls and sell fresh vegetables, poultry, eggs, and other produce.

The FIRST PRESBYTERIAN CHURCH, corner of East Mobile St. and North Wood Ave., was erected in 1824. In the early days a special section was set aside in the gallery for slaves. The children of the congregation sat on benches facing their parents in pews that were complete with doors. Many other religious groups used the Presbyterian Meeting House during the frontier days. Through the years the church has undergone extensive alterations, but, essentially, has maintained its original form.

POPE'S TAVERN, 203 Hermitage Drive, was in existence as early as the 1840s, possibly earlier. It was a mail stop and tavern in stagecoach days. During the Civil War it was used as a hospital. The Susan K. Vaughn Museum is housed in the tavern. Now owned by the City of Florence, the tavern is operated by the Florence Historical Board. There is a small admission charge.

The IRVINE PLACE, 459 North Court St., was built in 1843 by John Simpson. It was bought in 1870 by James Bennington Irvine. This distinguished home of classical design is surrounded by spacious grounds with giant trees, boxwood hedges, and other old-fashioned shrubs. General Thomas Jackson and his staff, Chief Colbert of the Chickasaw tribe, and Confederate officers Forrest, Stuart, Beauregard, and Hood were entertained here. The house contains old furniture and historic documents.

MONUMENTAL PARK, S. Chestnut St. and Parkway, was built on the site of breastworks used by the Confederates in their stand against Colonel A. D. Streight, and is now the location of the Florence-Lauderdale Coliseum.

INDIAN MOUND AND MUSEUM are located on the south end of Court St. on the Tennessee River. The mound is 43 feet high and is the largest domiciliary mound in the Tennessee Valley. The museum contains a remarkably complete display of Indian artifacts, supplemented by an audio-visual presentation, arranged especially to show the development of Indian culture. The museum and mound are operated by the Florence Historical Board of the City of Florence. There is a small admission charge.

MAPLETON, 420 South Pine St., is a beautiful two-story frame house overlooking the Tennessee River. It was built in 1820 by George Coulter, early settler. The most distinctive feature is the wood-carving around the doors, mantels, and partitions, which shows the influence of Samuel McIntire, the Salem architect.

W. C. HANDY HOME AND MUSEUM are located on West College St. The log-cabin birthplace of William C. Handy, "father of the blues," has been moved to this site. The adjacent museum contains musical instruments and other mementoes of the composer of the *St. Louis Blues,* presented by his family. The home and museum are operated by the Florence Historical Board of the City of Florence. *Tues-Sat., 9-12, 1-4. Admission is charged.*

THIMBLETON, 221 West Tuscaloosa St., was built about 1830. In later years it became the home of Edward A. O'Neal III, president of the American Farm Bureau Federation during the administration of Franklin D. Roosevelt.

WAKEFIELD, 456 North Court St., was built by James Sample in the 1820s. For many years it was the home of Dr. W. H. Mitchell, minister of the First Presbyterian Church, who was arrested and sent north during the Civil War for praying for President Jefferson Davis and success of Confederate arms. Dr. Mitchell served as president of the Synodical Female College.

GOVERNOR EDWARD ASBURY O'NEAL HOME (*commercial*), 468 North Court St., was built in the 1840s and later acquired by Edward A. O'Neal. O'Neal was afterward commissioned general of the Confederate States of America and in the 1880s served as governor of Alabama. As his son Emmet O'Neal also lived in this house and was also governor of the state, it is sometimes known as the home of the father-son governors.

EARLY FEDERAL HOUSE, 303 North Pine St., is an example of early Federal architecture, and is considered rare for this area. It is listed on the National Register of Historic Places. Recently restored by the Florence Housing Authority it is used by this agency as a business office and reception room. This is an excellent example of how historic buildings can be adapted to modern business uses.

SWEETWATER PLANTATION, intersection of Sweetwater Ave. and Florence Boulevard, is one of the outstanding ante-bellum homes. General John Brahan started the house in 1828. Later it was the home of Robert M. Patton, governor of Alabama (1865-1868), who married Brahan's daughter.

Gadsden

Air Services: Southern Airways, 6 flights daily, at Municipal Airport, 6*m.* from downtown. Airport has two runways, each 150 ft. by 4,800 ft, with medium intensity lighting, 36-inch rotating green and white beacon and lighted tetrahedron. Twenty-four hour service is available for major aircraft and engine repair.

Buses: Greyhound and Continental Trailways, with downtown stations, operate regular schedules for intra- and inter-state travel.

Highways: Gadsden is intersected by an Interstate highway, four US highways and one State Road. When fully completed, Interstate 59 will be a direct link between New England and New Orleans. US 11 parallels Interstate 59; US 278 is the East-West route from Atlanta to Memphis; US 431 is the north-south fast route between Chicago and Florida; US 411 is a short cut between Middle Tennessee and Birmingham; State 77 connects many surrounding communities with Gadsden.

Railroads: Louisville & Nashville; Southern Railway System; Tennessee, Alabama & Georgia.

Information and Accommodations: The Gadsden *Times,* daily and Sunday; four radio stations; City of Gadsden Planning and Engineering Dept.; Gadsden Chamber of Commerce. Two hotels have 224 rooms; 14 motels have 450 rooms.

Schools: There are 20 elementary schools; 7 junior and 3 senior high schools; 3 parochial elementary schools; University of Alabama-Gadsden Extension Center; Gadsden State Junior College; Alabama School of Trades; Gadsden Technical School.

Recreation: Twenty-two playgrounds have supervised programs 2-6 daily from June 19 to Aug. 11, offering badminton, croquet, shuffle board, softball teams for girls, Little League and other ball teams for boys, swimming and other activities. There are four recreation center buildings where classes in arts and crafts, gymnastics, and dramatics are conducted for all ages. Each center has kitchen facilities and auditorium. A coliseum is available for basketball games, cattle and dog shows, small circuses. A Little Theater season, art exhibitions and concerts are staged throughout the year. Noccalula Falls and Park are nearby, including a botanical garden, a pioneer community, camping and picnic facilities. Nearby state and national forests are open to nature lovers and campers.

Annual Events: Gadsden Art Association stages two art shows at Noccalula Falls: "Art on the Rocks" in May; and "Art in the Falling Leaves," second Sunday in October.

GADSDEN, seat of Etowah County (550-1100 alt., 53,928 pop. 1970; 58,088, 1960) is located on the upper reaches of the Coosa River on a high broad plain in the foothills of the Appalachian Mountains. It is served by the principal Federal highway, Interstate 59, between Chattanooga, Tennessee, and Birmingham, and by U.S. 471, connecting it with Huntsville and Anniston. Its area includes the old Central City, Alabama City, East Gadsden, and two newer sections, Lookout Mountain Area and Clubview. Gadsden is best described as a modern metropolis in an Old South setting, with many types of architecture represented in its residential areas. It is the second largest steel center in the South and has what is sometimes called the largest tire and tube plant in the world. There is careful municipal structural planning and considerable economic hustle, creating a sense of well-being.

Two large springs in the vicinity gave to the original settlement, a pioneer farm village, the name Double Springs. A post office was established in 1836, with William Walker as the first postmaster. The first settlers moved in among the Creek Indians and lived side by side with them without friction. In 1840, Gabriel Hughes and his brother Joseph, originally from Lincoln County, North Carolina, and John S. Morgan, of Charleston, South Carolina, seeing the beauty of the country and its economic possibilities, planned to build a city here. They bought land around Double Springs and had it platted by W. S. Brown, engineer of the Tennessee & Coosa Railroad. At about this time General James Gadsden, who had negotiated the Gadsden Purchase from Mexico in 1853, visited the area and praised the undertaking. Grateful for his encouragement, the promoters renamed the village Gadsden.

In 1857, when Colonel Robert B. Kyle came to the town, it had about 100 inhabitants and 3 stores. Kyle used his capital to infuse life into the slow, sleepy town—opening a bank, setting up a mercantile business, and organizing a steamboat company to operate on the Coosa and its tributaries. Within a few years 6 stage coach lines had headquarters in Gadsden; river trade boomed and it was not unusual to find as many as 10 steamboats moored at the wharves.

The War between the States halted growth, but it did not actually reach Gadsden until 1863. In that year Federal cavalry under Colonel A. D. Streight raided northeast Alabama, closely pursued by General Nathan Bedford Forrest and his "critter company." The Yankees sacked Gadsden and rode on, following the banks of the Coosa. Captain John H. Wisdom, a Confederate mail contractor, deduced that they were heading for Rome, Georgia, where an important Confederate munitions base was located. With so much at stake, Wisdom made his epic "night ride" of 67 miles from Gadsden to Rome to sound the alarm. He left Gadsden at 3:30 in the afternoon, rode rough, unfamiliar roads, and before midnight was warning the people of Rome.

Meanwhile, General Forrest entered Gadsden as Colonel Streight left. To stop pursuit the Federals burned the bridge over Black Creek, near the town. Emma Sansom, a girl of 15, volunteered to guide Forrest to a ford in the creek. When a bullet ripped close to her, she shouted, "They've only wounded my dress!" She jerked her sunbonnet from her head and waved it at the Federals; her bravery called forth cheers from both sides and firing ceased until she was safe.

Realizing that capture was inevitable, Colonel Streight sent an advance party under Captain M. M. Russell to seize and hold the bridge at Rome. Wisdom, however, was ahead of them, and when Russell saw that Rome, forewarned, was defending the bridge he turned back. This checkmate so discouraged Streight's men that they surrendered next day to Forrest.

Gadsden, in a part of the State where there were few slaves, was not greatly affected by the liberation of the Negroes, though the Reconstruction period was difficult. The Gadsden *Times,* first newspaper of the town, was established in 1867. The 1866 legislature had created Baine County with Gadsden as the seat; two years later the county's name was changed to Etowah, and in 1870 the Etowah County Courthouse was built in Gadsden. In 1871 the town was incorporated and began to develop industrially. As first Mayor, Colonel Kyle again assumed leadership and brought about the organization of several corporations, including a lumber company, a furnace manufactory, and a pipe and foundry plant. By 1872 the population had increased to 1,500.

In 1874, William P. Lay, then a youth of 21, came to Gadsden. His father and grandfather had been riverboat men on the winding Coosa, and young Lay knew the river and saw its possibilities. He dreamed of improving navigation and developing water-borne commerce. With crude maps of his own making, he outlined the industrial prospects and sold his company to investors from New England, Canada, and Great Britain. He built the first electric plant in Gadsden in 1887. It remained in use until 1902, when he built a hydroelectric plant on Big Wills Creek to replace it. Electricity, Lay saw, offered an opportunity to utilize the water resources of the Coosa-Alabama river system, and to carry out his plans he organized and incorporated the Alabama Power Company in 1906. Captain Lay died in Gadsden in 1940. Lay Dam, on the Coosa in Central Alabama, is named for him.

John Jonathan Pratt, a native of Centre, Ala., who in 1873 became editor of the *Gadsden Times,* invented an original typewriter in 1860. It was called the Pterotype at that time. Unable to get financial backing in this country, Pratt went to London where he received a British patent Dec. 1, 1866. It was not, however, until 1921 that he was given full credit for the invention. In that year, the Alabama Business & Professional Women's Clubs at their annual convention in Gadsden, presented documents proving Pratt to have been the inventor. These documents were later uesd for the Remington Typewriter patent. It is believed that Pratt wrote some of his *Times* editorials on his machine and that the *Times* was probably the first newspaper to print from typewritten manuscript.

The natural resources of the region are the basis of its economic stability. Iron, manganese, coal, and limestone—the essential minerals for making manganese steel—are within easy reach of the city's mills and furnaces. Manganese deposits near Gadsden are the largest yet found in Alabama. Other minerals, such as bauxite, sandstone of 99 percent silica, moulding sand, and marble, are in the vicinity. Near-by forests contain yellow pine, oak, ash, gum, poplar, hickory, cedar, and other timber. These readily available raw materials have encouraged the establishment of a variety of manufacturing enterprises.

World War II had significant economic impact on the city. Whereas in the past, cotton growing had been the chief source of income, farmers began diversifying crops, and the abundant and untapped natural resources were exploited.

Camp Seibert, a $30 million chemical warfare center, was named for William Luther Seibert, a Gadsden native who played significant roles in the building of the Panama Canal and in developing chemical warfare. It was located on the rim of the city. An Air Force Supply Depot, a $23,000,000 shell plant, a large Federal contract with the existing Agricola Furnace Co., enlarged activities at the Goodyear Rubber Co., and Republic Steel, and enactment of the Rivers and Harbors Bill containing authorization of $60,000,000 expenditures to develop the Coosa-Alabama rivers, all contributed to swelling the Gadsden economy.

In the same period, several nearby communities were annexed to the city. This added population and the influx of defense personnel earned Gadsden in 1940 the distinction of being "the fastest growing city of its class in the nation."

At war's end the Federal Government transferred to the city, without cost, the Air Force Depot property, the Camp Seibert lands, including that on which the Municipal Airport stands, along with the temporary and wartime housing projects that were turned over to the Greater Gadsden Housing Authority.

A number of new industries were attracted to the city during the early post-war years. The City Commission and far-seeing citizens took advantage of the economic situation to give the city better public facilities, including its Civic Center. Lands were designated and plans made for other municipal structures. Noccalula Falls and 169 adjoining acres of land were purchased for a public park, to which 80 more acres have been added in recent years.

The boom bubble burst in 1958, when the Air Force closed its depot, Republic Steel and Goodyear Rubber Co. curtailed operations, pipe shops and cotton mills shut down. By 1971, however, the city had recovered from the temporary economic jolt and was again forging ahead with diversified industries, augmented by farm products, principally cotton, corn, truck crops, dairy products and poultry. Republic Steel in 1975 adopted plans to increase its raw steel capacity by nearly 1 million tons by 1978, at a cost of $350 million.

Gadsden also has become the regional center of an eight-county area for specialized medical care, served by two general hospitals, one tuberculosis sanitarium, and a health center. A new $1,400,000 mental health center is on the planning boards.

The anticipated potential of Noccalula Falls as a tourist attraction has paid off in impressive revenues. Additions of a handsome botanical garden and an authentic transplanted pioneer settlement, complete with dwellings, craft shops and a covered bridge, have been added by the city, garden clubs and other citizen groups.

Historical sentiment as well as economic foresight influenced the Noccalula purchase. Children learn early the colorful stories of the Choctaw and Cherokee Indians who lived in the present Etowah County area, and among whom the white newcomers found a friendly welcome. From the Indians came many local words and names. The Coosa River, which has played an important role in Gadsden economy and pleasure, derives its name from the Choctaw word, koosha meaning cane or reed. Etowah is from the Cherokee words, ette for tree, and wah for good.

A most beloved story is the typical Indian legend concerning Princess Noccalula, who threw herself over the Falls rather than marry the warrior her father had chosen for her, but whom she did not love.

Since 1931, the city has been administered by a Mayor and Commissioners.

The *Gadsden Times,* published daily and Sunday, is a successor of the city's first paper, founded in 1867. There are four radio stations and all major television networks are received from nearby cities.

POINTS OF INTEREST

The CIVIC CENTER, Bay and First Sts., extending east to the Coosa River, is the seat of the municipal govenment. It is a complex of modern structures and houses administrative offices, including the CITY HALL, the MUNICIPAL COURT, the HEADQUARTERS OF THE POLICE DEPARTMENT, the CONVENTION HALL, AMPHITHEATER, and the BROAD STREET RECREATION CENTER. Architects were Hofferbert-Ellis & Associates. The Convention Hall can seat 2,300 and is equipped for handling large meetings and smaller conferences with committee work. The Amphitheater was begun in 1934 as a work relief project and completed by the WPA in 1936. Constructed entirely of native sandstone from Lookout Mountain, the work was done by unskilled laborers who were trained on the job as stonemasons. This structure follows the plan of the ancient Greek theater of Dionysius and has a seating capacity of 1,700.

The FEDERAL BUILDING, sw. corner Broad and Sixth Sts., erected in 1909, is Italian Renaissance in design, with an exterior of Georgia marble and an interior finished with marble from Gantt's Quarry near Sylacauga, Ala. In the Federal Court Room (*open by request*) is a mural, "Nemesis, Meting Out Justice," by T. Gilbert White.

GADSDEN PUBLIC LIBRARY, between South Seventh and College Sts., facing College, is a handsome contemporary structure (Hofferbert-Ellis & Associates, architects) housing some 87,000 volumes and 700 periodicals, with space for additional collections. It has three branches and a bookmobile.

GADSDEN STATE JUNIOR COLLEGE, opened in 1965, is one of the largest junior schools in the state system. In the fall of 1970 it enrolled 1,964, with a faculty of 180. Contemporary styled structures house administrative offices, the library, science, engineering and mathematics departments, a field house with a 3,600-seat gymnasium and Olympic-size swimming pool, and a Fine Arts Center. Thirty-two fields of study are offered, including 23 professional programs for transfer students and nine two-year technical programs.

GADSDEN STATE TECHNICAL TRADE SCHOOL, opened in 1960, is one of the largest such programs in the state, offering training in 11 vocational skills.

ALABAMA SCHOOL OF TRADES, sw. corner of Broad St. E. and Padenreich Ave., established in 1925, was the first of a network of 26 such coeducational schools in the State. From a beginning four-course curriculum, it has been expanded and adapted to meet needs of business and industry. As at the other State trade schools, tuition is $15 per month, with free transportation.

The CHAPEL at Forrest Cemetery is located inside the main gate, on the west side of 15th St., between Walnut and Chestnut Sts., it is modeled after an English parish church, constructed by unskilled labor as a WPA project. The doors and interior appointments are handmade and the roof's sandstone shingles were cut to size by hand. The cemetery dates back to 1872. The first person to be buried in it was the infant daughter of Capt. A. L. Woodliff, who had selected the site and negotiated the purchase.

The COUNTY CURB MARKET, w. side of 8th St., between Forrest Ave. and Chestnut St., (*open Tues., Thurs., Sat.*), is the second largest produce market in the State. (The largest is in Montgomery). It is operated as a non-profit organization.

HOLY NAME OF JESUS HOSPITAL, se. corner of First and Third Sts., is a white-painted brick building, designed by Schmidt, Garden & Erickson of Chicago in 1931, and enlarged since. It has 177 beds and, along with a nursing school, is operated by the Missionary Servants of the Most Blessed Trinity.

The EMMA SANSOM MONUMENT, center of Broad and First Sts., erected in 1907 by the United Daughters of the Confederacy, honors the city's 15-year-old heroine of the Black Creek incident. The monument, which stands in a miniature park, is 20 ft. high and consists of a life-size marble figure of Emma Sansom on a granite base. A bas-relief shows Emma seated behind General Forrest on his horse, pointing out a ford on Black Creek.

The HUGHES HOUSE (private), nw. corner of Third St. and Tuscaloosa Ave., built in 1835 by a half-breed Cherokee known as John Riley, was the first home erected in the original hamlet of Double Springs. It was purchased in the following year by Gabriel Hughes. Originally made of logs fastened together with wooden pegs, the structure was afterward weather-boarded and ceiled. Subsequent remodeling has converted it into a two-story house with a one-story porch supported by square columns. The house in times past has been an inn, a postoffice, and a community gathering place.

GOODYEAR TIRE & RUBBER CO., 1.8 miles from downtown. On June 13, 1929, an electric impulse on the desk of President Herbert Hoover started the plant in operation and the first tire rolled off the assembly line. Today, the plant is a huge single tire producing facility, employing approx. 3,500.

GULF DIVISION PLANT OF REPUBLIC STEEL, 6th St. s. of Norris Ave., is one of the South's largest steel mills. This unit, Republic's largest in the South, employs approx. 4,508 workers and manufactures a large variety of steel and iron products. (*Guided tours weekdays by permission.*)

NOCCALULA PARK, open the year around, admission free, is a magnificent 250-acre woodland with dramatic falls cascading over 90 feet into a gorge below. It has been enhanced by addition of a splendid outdoor botanical garden and a re-created pioneer settlement. Camp sites and picnic grounds are available, as well as a children's playground. The split-log buildings of the pioneers were brought from their original site near Lawrenceburg, Tenn., and are said to have been built around 1777. The park is municipally operated.

Huntsville

Air Services: Huntsville-Madison County Jetport, also known as Carl T. Jones Jetport, serves Huntsville and Decatur. Located 11 miles from downtown on James Record Blvd., occupies 3,401 acres of land. The Skycenter is the location of all terminal facilities, a restaurant, office services, swimming pool, car service, 152-room hotel and a 600-space parking area. Within the area three major airlines, United, Eastern and Southern operate some 50 daily flights. There are two lighted parallel runways, one 8,000 feet, the other 5,400 feet and both running north and south, capable of handling all types of aircraft. Ground facilities include a U.S. Weather Bureau station, fire-crash station, and 100-foot tower operated by FAA. Passengers enplaned 214,062, deplaned 210,483 (1970).

Highways: Five major four-lane highways—US 431, 231, 72, 72 Alt., 43 and I-65 are main arteries into and out of city.

Buses: Greyhound Lines and Continental Trailways provide interstate service; Huntsville Transit serves metropolitan area.

Railroads: Southern Railway System and Louisville & Nashville Railroad provide freight and limited passenger service.

Schools: There are 28 elementary, 9 junior and 4 senior high schools; University of Alabama-Huntsville, Alabama A & M University, Oakwood College, two state vocational technical schools.

Churches: All denominations are represented in 125 churches.

Accommodations: 2,500 rooms in 42 motels and 1 downtown hotel.

Communications: Two daily newspapers, *Huntsville Times* and *Huntsville News,* two weeklies, three local TV stations, one educational, 4 AM and 2 FM radio stations.

Recreation and Entertainment: Tennessee River and two large TVA lakes provide swimming, boating, water skiing, sailing and year-round fishing. Monte Sano State Park, covering 1,900 acres, offers picnicking, horseback riding, nature trails, shelters and rental cottages. There are three private golf courses and four 18-hole public courses. Supervised year-round programs by city on 280 acres of playgrounds and parks. Football, basketball and baseball, from Little Leagues up; two country clubs; five movie theaters and four drive-ins.

Annual Events: Four Civic Symphony concerts; Community Concert Association concert series; Broadway Theater League's series of four touring plays; four concerts by Civic Chorus; Fantasy Playhouse series of children's plays.

HUNTSVILLE (610-636 alt., 137,802 pop. 1970; 72,365, 1960, inc. 90.4%) is the seat of Madison County and third largest city in Alabama. Traditionally a cotton distributing center, it has attained distinction since 1950 as the country's major site for the design and production of military missiles, rockets and equipment for space exploration. This huge enterprise and the movement of new industries into Huntsville brought the city a 90 percent expansion in population since 1960 and the county a rise of 59 percent—from 117,348 to 186,540—during the same term. The expenditure locally of nearly $2 billion annually for the needs of the Arsenal, and the employment there of more than 17,000 civilians, have had a stimulating effect on the economy of city and county.

Picturesquely located in a valley beside mountain ranges, Huntsville is directly west of Monte Sano, 1,650 ft., and profits by the Monte Sano State Park, 2,140 acres devoted to recreation, and the mountain lakes and fishing areas of the Tennessee River. It is served by all the Interstate, United States and Alabama highways that connect northern Alabama with the deep South and shares with Decatur, only 26 miles away, the water facilities brought to the northern areas by the Tennessee Valley Authority.

John Hunt, a Virginian and veteran of the American Revolution, built a cabin in 1805 near the Big Spring. When the governor of Mississippi Territory opened the land for sale by auction in 1808 Leroy Pope, a planter brought a large area surrounding Big Spring for $23.50 an acre. The settlement was chosen seat of Madison County and at Pope's request was named Twickenham after the home of his favorite poet, Alexander Pope, in England. Growing animosity toward England caused the legislature to change the name to Huntsville on November 25, 1811. In that year the public land office was moved from Nashville to Huntsville, and in 1812 the *Madison Gazette* was founded. Andrew Jackson visited the area during his Indian campaigns and bought land in the vicinity.

On July 5, 1819, a constitutional convention met here and on Aug. 2, 1819 adopted a constitution for Alabama. The first Legislature met in Huntsville three months later. Although Huntsville agitated to become the capital the Legislators thought Cahaba better suited because it was centrally located. CAHABA was shipping cotton on the Black Warrior River in Dallas County, and was the county seat. But the river inundated it seasonally, and the State legislators moved to Tuscaloosa in 1826. Today Cahaba is on the map solely as a ruin off State 22.

In 1820, Huntsville became a terminus on one of Alabama's early stagecoach lines, and from that time until the 1860s, the city's transportation and textile enterprises developed rapidly. A cotton spinning mill on Flint River in 1818 evolved into the first incorporated cotton cloth factory in 1832. Cotton was the money crop, and leading citizens encouraged the building of textile mills and gins to prepare the staple for market. In 1851 the Memphis division of the Memphis & Charleston Railway, financed by Huntsville capital, connected the city with the Decatur-Tuscumbia line.

In April, 1862, Federal troops captured Huntsville and burned its railroad shops and warehouses filled with cotton, and disrupted its

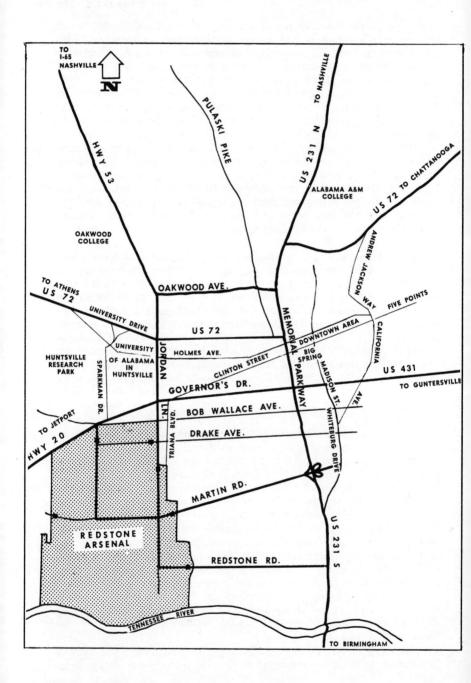

business and social life. After Reconstruction northern capital returned to exploit its possibilities and soon Huntsville was reestablished as a textile manufacturing center. Industry suffered during the depression of the 1930s, but cotton again became its principal trading commodity until the production of munitions during World War II started the city on a new road to prosperity.

During the 1960 to 1965 period, almost all the key economic indicators doubled in Huntsville. The population grew by 90 percent, and employment by 95 percent, both basically due to increased appropriations and expenditures by NASA.

With the build-up in Vietnam from 1965 to 1968 and the de-emphasizing of space exploration goals, NASA expenditures dropped, resulting in a downward trend in Huntsville's economy. However, with the coming of non-space related manufacturing plants into the area and stabilization of space oriented expenditures, the Huntsville economy resumed a sound growth.

A significant and lasting by-product of Huntsville's cosmopolitan population during the NASA peak period, was the development of a wealth of cultural activities. An Arts Council coordinates 49 member organizations and administers a Civic Arts Center in a former school building. The Huntsville Civic Symphony Orchestra presents four concerts featuring national and international soloists with two performances of each concert. One community and two professional theaters provide about 50 performances during the year. Fantasy Playhouse offers three performances for children. There are three ballet groups, a Broadway Theater League which brings touring companies, a Community Chorus and a Civic Opera Company.

In March, 1975, the VON BRAUN CIVIC CENTER, 700 Monroe St., SW, was added to the convention and entertainment facilities of Huntsville. With the newest of accommodations for meetings, exhibits, plays and concerts the complex included an arena seating nearly 9,000, a concert hall with 2,200 seats, an exhibit hall with 20,000 sq. ft. of space available, a 500-seat playhouse for productions in the round, 11 meetings rooms, and banquet facilities. Cost was $15,000,000.

Of the hospitals in Huntsville two are publicly owned and two are private. A military base hospital for active and retired military personnel is located at Redstone Arsenal. The Rehabilitation Center for the Crippled is a comprehensive out-patient facility.

U. S. MILITARY FACILITIES

REDSTONE ARSENAL is described in official publications as "the nerve center of the U. S. Army's missile and rocket programs" and "one of the chief bulwarks in the nation's defense." It comprises an area of 38,881 acres about five miles west of Huntsville. Here are located the U. S. Army Missile Command, the U. S. Army Missile and Munitions Center and School, the George C. Marshall Space Fight Center of the National Aeronautics & Space Administration, and the

Huntsville division of Thiokol Chemical Corp., which is Government-owned and contractor-operated. Off post are the U. S. Army Safeguard System Command and the U. S. Army Engineer Division, Huntsville.

Up to 5,000 military personnel are assigned to the Arsenal, and more than 17,000 civilians work there for the Army or for private contractors, while 10,000 soldiers are trained annually at the missile school. About 3,000 to 5,000 military dependents live at the Arsenal and their children attend school in Huntsville. The civilian employees live all over Madison County and the annual payroll exceeds $150,-000,000. The Army spends up to $1.9 billion a year with the bulk going to American industry missile and space research, development and production.

In 1941 Huntsville Arsenal was formed to make and load chemical mortar and howitzer shells and Redstone Ordnance plant was formed to assemble explosives for the shells. In February, 1943, the Redstone plant was named Redstone Arsenal. During World War II 20,000 were employed here. In 1948 Redstone was chosen as the center of research and development for rockets and related weapons, and Huntsville Arsenal was transfered to Redstone. In April, 1950, the rocket experts who had been working at Fort Bliss, Texas, under Dr. Wernher von Braun were brought to Redstone and the great missile program was in full operation. The post has more than 2,000 buildings, 94 miles of railroads, 330 miles of roads, an airfield for jets and cargo docks on the Tennessee River.

The GEORGE C. MARSHALL SPACE FLIGHT CENTER was formed on July 1, 1960, and dedicated by President Dwight D. Eisenhower. It occupies 1,800 acres at Redstone Arsenal, has 5,500 permanent civil service employees with about 400 located at production and testing facilities operated by contractor firms throughout the country. Hundreds of contractor employees also work at the Center. Executive offices are in a nine-story building; two six-story buildings also are part of headquarters, and there are huge laboratories and test stands at the Center. The Center directs all contractors in private industry that manufacture elements of the space programs. Two huge out-of-state installations are the Michoud Assembly facility in New Orleans, where one single-floor building covers 40 acres, and the Mississippi Test Facility in Hancock County, Miss. Most of the work of Marshall Center is done for the Office of Manned Space Flight of NASA. Saturn rockets were developed here for moon launching, and for earth-orbital projects.

The Army Missile and Munitions Center and School trains from 6,000 to 10,000 students a year. It has a faculty of 800 military and civilian instructors and courses that comprise all forms of explosives used by the Army.

The Arsenal provides quarters and furnishings for the military, including medical services, dental care, retail goods at the Post Exchange, a commissary, clubs for commissioned and non-commissioned officers and their families, religious services, film programs, and veterinary treatment for pets.

Two U. S. Army commands are located in Huntsville but are related to the work of the Safeguard System Command, organized at the Arsenal in 1967 to manage production and deployment of the ballistic missile defense system. The U. S. Army Engineer Division, Huntsville, is responsible for design and production of facilities of the Safeguard System. The U. S. Army Safeguard Logistics Command was organized in 1968 to supervise transportation and maintenance of material used by the System.

The ALABAMA SPACE AND ROCKET CENTER, on State 20, 5 m. west of Huntsville, is a State-supported science exhibit that has the largest display of missile and space devices in the country. Built with an appropriation of $2 million, it presents the products of the U. S. Army Missile Command, the NASA, and corporations actively engaged on space equipment for the national programs. A collection of missiles standing free at the entrance are an arresting sight. *Open weekdays 9-5, September through May; 9-6, June through August. Adults $1.75, children under 12, 75¢; students in groups, 60¢.*

A 70-ft. Army rocket from Redstone stands like a monument near the Methodist Church in Warren, New Hampshire, a village of 631 pop. It was obtained from Redstone Arsenal by Theodore Asselin, innkeeper, former sergeant first class, USA, who was stationed at the Arsenal when the display rocket was about to be discarded. He asked headquarters for the rocket and persuaded his fellow townsmen of Warren to arrange for its installation there. He transported it across the country on a tractor and trailer and it was dedicated at Warren by the governor of New Hampshire on July 4, 1971.

POINTS OF INTEREST

ALABAMA AGRICULTURAL AND MECHANICAL UNIVERSITY is located at Normal, within the city limits of Huntsville, and reached by US 231 and US 431. It was organized by the State Legislature in 1873 through the efforts of its first principal and president, William Hooper Councill, a former slave. It opened in 1875 as the Huntsville Normal School with an appropriation of $1,000 a year, 61 pupils and two teachers. In 1891 it became a land grant institution, received a new location at Normal, and was named the State Agricultural and Mechanical College for Negroes. It became a junior college in 1919, a senior college giving baccalaureate degrees in 1939, and on June 26, 1969, the State Board of Education voted to name it the Alabama Agricultural and Mechanical University. For the 1974 school year it enrolled 3,397 students and had a faculty of 362.

The university has seven undergraduate schools and a School of Graduate Studies that offers the master degree. The schools are those of Agricultural and Environmental Science, Arts and Sciences, Business, Education, Home Economics, Library Media, and Technology. The School of Technology offers courses in the industrial arts, civil engineering, computer sciences, electronics engineering, printing production and management, electromechanical engineering and allied processes. The university offers students in some of the technological and business courses opportunities to take part in cooperative education, by which students are given work assignments that will give them experience in industry alternating with study, and permitting them to earn some of their expenses. There are also some evening classes.

Among new buildings at the university are the centrally located Joseph F. Drake Memorial Library, which has room for 300,000 books; the University Center, expanded in 1971; the Robert B. Prentice Hall for dining, and the George W. Carver Multi-Purpose Complex of classrooms and laboratories. A number of new residential halls was built in the 1960s. There are 46 buildings and 850 scenic acres of campus.

The J. F. DRAKE STATE TECHNICAL TRADE SCHOOL is located in Huntsville.

OAKWOOD COLLEGE is a four-year institution conducted under denominational auspices founded in 1896. In 1974 it enrolled 988 students and had a faculty of 55. The Green Memorial Library stocks more than 47,000 volumes.

The UNIVERSITY OF ALABAMA, HUNTSVILLE, is a full-time four-year institution that has developed from a branch established here in 1951. In 1974 it enrolled 3,059 students and had a faculty of 175. The parent university at Tuscaloosa (P. O. University) in 1974 enrolled 14,938 and had a faculty of 732. Its library of more than 73,000 vols. specializes in space travel and rocketry.

The Huntsville PUBLIC LIBRARY recently reported a stock of 149,978 vols. and circulation of 619,555. There also are technical libraries maintained by the Boeing Company, the International Business Machines, and Lockheed Missiles & Space Co.

The FIRST NATIONAL BANK BUILDING, corner Bank and Canal Sts., opposite Courthouse Square, the oldest business building in Madison County, is a Greek Revival structure with a six-columned Ionic portico and high entablature. It was designed by the architect, George Steele, and erected in 1835-6. The foundation walls, resting on solid limestone, are built of stone slabs from near-by quarries. The column bases, capitals, and shafts are said to have been brought from Baltimore to the Tennessee by oxcart, floated down the river to Triana, and brought from there by canal to Huntsville. The brick walls, two feet thick, are covered with stucco. The entrance doors are approximately 15 feet high; the wide, tall windows have double-hinged shutters folding into compartments. The building originally served both as business house and residence for bank officials. A semidetached structure at the rear contained living quarters for minor officials and detention cells for slaves impounded for their masters' debts.

CHURCH OF THE NATIVITY (Episcopal), Eustis and Greene Sts., built in 1858-9 on the site of an earlier church building, is notable for the beauty of its English Gothic design. It was erected in April, 1859. The nave, including altar and chancel, is 56 by 112 feet; the tower is 20 feet square and 160 feet in height. The adjacent Gothic chapel, built of dark brown brick with red trim to match the older building, was erected in 1883 by Mrs. W. C. Bibb in memory of her husband. The parish house, south of the church, harmonizes with it architecturally and was built at about the same time. The inscription on the church, "Reverence My Sanctuary," saved the building from being occupied by Federal troops during the 1860s. It was the only place of worship not confiscated for Union use as a stable, living quarters, or hospital.

The FIRST METHODIST CHURCH, Randolph and Green Sts., is a large gray concrete structure completed in 1867. The original church, built in 1821, was destroyed by Federal troops in 1862, after they had used it as a stable. The congregation received compensation from the Federal Government in 1916 for the damage.

The HOWARD WEEDEN HOUSE, Green and Gates Sts., was the birthplace of Miss Howard Weeden, Southern writer and artist. The structure is reputed to have been begun in 1819 by Dr. Henry H. Chambers, surgeon in Andrew Jackson's army during the Indian wars, and later United States Senator from Alabama. In 1832 it was purchased by William Weeden who finished construction. It was occupied by Federal troops. Jeffersonian in design, it is built of brick and painted white, and has large many-paned windows. A graceful curving stairway ascends to a balcony that encircles the rear of the hall.

The POPE-SPRAGGINS HOUSE, at Adams Ave. and McClung St., on Echols' Hill, was built about 1815 by Colonel Leroy Pope, who named the pioneer town Twickenham. It was later the home of Leroy Pope Walker who, as Confederate Secretary of War, gave the order to fire on Fort Sumter. The house is a two-story white brick building with red roof, supported by six massive columns.

The FIRST PRESBYTERIAN CHURCH, Gates and Lincoln Sts., houses one of the oldest Presbyterian congregations in Alabama, organized in 1818. The present building was dedicated in 1860. Richly tinted memorial windows are outlined with terra cotta.

The BIBB HOUSE, Williams St., opposite intersection of Green St., was built in 1837 by Governor Thomas Bibb at an estimated cost of $32,000. Of Greek Revival design, it is a massive red brick structure with four large white Doric columns.

The WATSON-MOORE-GRAYSON HOUSE, 421 Adams Ave., was built around 1850 and occupied by Federal General John A. Logan during the war. In 1893 it was owned by Samuel H. Moore, whose Jersey cow, Lily Flag, won first prize as a milk producer at the Columbian World's Fair in Chicago. Moore invited the foremost breeders of the country to pay tribute to Lily Flag at a reception in this house. He placed the cow under a bower of roses in his ballroom, where the guests toasted her.

The FEARN-GARTH HOUSE, east side of Franklin St., is a Greek Revival structure of brick, painted white; the portico with six columns is at one side of the building. It was built about 1820 by Dr. Thomas Fearn.

The NEAL HOUSE, 558 Franklin St., is a 14-room red brick

structure, said to have been built in 1821. It stands on a terrace of gray native stone. In design it suggests a New England dwelling rather than the usual Southern home. The large double entrance doors, set in an alcove, are flanked by small white columns. A half-spiral stairway, gracefully carved, rises from the room at the right of the reception hall. Slave quarters are still intact. On the site was the birthplace of John Hunt Morgan, the Confederate raider.

The LEVERT HOUSE, 517 Adams Ave., built about 1830, is a large square brick mansion, painted white, surrounded by fine old box-wood and tall trees. Known locally as the Chase Home, it has a small portico and six slender white columns. The interior retains the white marble mantels and much of the original ornamental plaster in the formal reception rooms. This house was once headquarters for General Ormsby M. Mitchell of the Federal Army.

The site of the First Constitutional Convention and the First Alabama State Legislature, nw. corner of Franklin and Gates Sts., is marked by a gray stone boulder placed by the Twickenham Chapter of the D.A.R. in 1901. In 1819, President Monroe was entertained at an elaborate banquet in the convention building, since torn down.

ST. BARTLEY PRIMITIVE BAPTIST CHURCH, Oak Ave., built in 1872, is a gray concrete building with Gothic windows of ornamental glass. The original congregation was the Huntsville African Baptist Church, organized about 1820. It is recorded as enter-ing into the Flint River Association in 1821 with 76 members. Later the congregation joined the Primitive group when the denomination divided. It is probably the oldest Negro church in Alabama.

The STEELE-FOWLER HOUSE, McCullough Ave., built about 1840 by the architect, George Steele, is a tall Colonial structure, painted yellow. A portico of white limestone at the center of the front façade is supported by massive Doric columns. Square plastered columns 30 feet high ornament the south end of the building. An elliptical stair-way, with cherry handrail and balustrades, ascends to the upper floor. The large formal rooms have been used for many gay social functions, including the celebration of James K. Polk's successful Presidential campaign. It is said that Steele selected from his herd a splendid ox to be prepared for an elaborate feast in anticipation of the election of Martin Van Buren. When Van Buren was defeated, the celebration was called off, but Steele kept the ox on a fattening diet. When Polk was inaugurated four years later in March, 1845, the feast was held.

CARL T. JONES FIELD, the Huntsville-Madison Jetport is lo-cated on James Record Boulevard on 3,401 acres of land. The Sky-center has all terminal service facilities, a restaurant, office services, swimming pool, auto service, a 152-room hotel, and a 600 space parking area. The terminal area is on the first floor of the Skycenter.

Mobile

Air Services: Available are scheduled flights at Mobile Airport by Delta Airlines, Eastern Airlines, Southern Airways, National Airlines, and United Airlines. Runways are 5,000 and 6,800 ft. long. Total passengers enplaned exceed 200,000 annually. A Coast Guard base with 430 naval personnel aids in search and rescue activities. Private planes may use Fairhope Airport.

Highways: US 90 (extending from the Pacific to the Atlantic); US 31, 43, 98 and 45 (extending from Gulf of Mexico to the Great Lakes); State Highways 5, 12, 16, 42 and 163; Interstate 10 (Florida to California), and Interstate 65 (Alabama to Canada). Parts of Interstate highways under construction.

Railroads: Terminal Station, Beauregard and St. Joseph Sts., for Southern Ry.; 11 Government St. for Frisco and Terminal Railways; S. Royal and Charleston Sts. for the former Gulf, Mobile & Ohio, now Illinois Central Gulf.

Buses: Greyhound, Continental Trailways, and a few local companies, operate 57 schedules daily.

Information and Accommodations: Mobile Area Chamber of Commerce, 401 Roberts Building; Mobile *Press Register* (morning, evening and Sunday), P.O. Box 2488, Mobile; State Department of Publicity and Information, Montgomery, Ala. There are 650 rooms in three hotels; 2,500 modern motel rooms in the Mobile area; resort accommodations on the Eastern Shore or Mobile Bay at Point Clear, south on Dauphin Island and at Gulf Shores. Twenty-four nations have consulates in Mobile. There are three major TV networks, ETV, and nine radio stations.

Climate: Mean annual temperature, 67.4° Fahrenheit; average annual rainfall, 63.1 inches.

Recreation: Tennis courts, golf courses, swimming pools, playgrounds, picnic facilities are abundant. Planned year-round programs are conducted by the City Recreation Department. Located on Mobile Bay and near the Gulf of Mexico, residents and visitors enjoy every type water sport, yachting, sailing, and excellent fresh and salt water fishing. Almost every month of the year some type game is available to the hunter, from duck to deer to turkey.

Entertainment: Mobile Municipal Auditorium is site for performances of symphony orchestras, ballets and musical concerts, art exhibitions, children and adult theater, professional seminars and other types of gatherings, many bringing celebrities in various fields. The Allied Arts Council, 401 Auditorium Drive, maintains listings of all forthcoming events. City of Mobile Museum has fine permanent and loan collections; Mobile Art Gallery displays paintings, sculpture, handicrafts; Fort Morgan and Fort Gaines are Civil War strongholds. Numerous restaurants serve seafood and Creole menus. Water skiing, sailing and regattas are year-round attractions. University of Alabama, Auburn University and other colleges and high schools have football games. *USS Alabama* and *USS Drum,* renowned World War II battleship and submarine, respectively, are moored in Battleship Park.

Greyhound racing at Mobile Greyhound Park, reached from Interstate 10 at Theodore Dawes exit and Old Pascagoula Road. Post time 8 p.m. nightly except Sunday; Wednesday and Saturday matinees, 1:30 p.m.

Tours: Conducted tours are operated by Velma Croom Guide Service, 1001 Augusta St., Washington Square, and Gray Line Tours, 3 North Royal St.

Annual Events: January—Senior Bowl Football Game; Camellia Club of Mobile Show. February-March—Mardi Gras; Azalea Trail Festival. March—Metropolitan Mobile Allied Arts Festival; Mobile Jazz Festival; Fairhope Arts and Crafts Tour; Annual Boat, Sport and Vacation Show. March-April—Dogwood Trail; Historic Open Homes Tour. April—Annual Juried Gulf Coast Art Exhibition; Dauphin Island Regatta. May—America's Junior Miss Pageant. July—(Last Sunday) Blessing of the Shrimp Fleet; (Third weekend) Alabama Deep Sea Fishing Rodeo. September-November—Full schedule of college and high school football at Ladd Stadium. October—Greater Gulf State Fair. December—Senior Bowl Basketball Tournament.

MOBILE (8.57 alt., 190,026 pop. 1970; 194,856, 1960) seat of Mobile County is the second largest city and the only seaport in Alabama. It is the economic capital of what is sometimes called the Greater Gulf State, comprised of Southeast Mississippi, Northwest Florida, and South Alabama. It lies on the upper west shore of Mobile Bay, 31 miles from the Gulf of Mexico and at the foot of a range of low mountains that slope gently westward to Spring Hill (350 alt.), a favored residential district just outside the city limits.

The U. S. Bureau of the Census disclosed after the 1970 count that in both Mobile and Mobile County women exceeded men in number. This was true of both whites and blacks. The city, with 190,026 population had 122,237 whites, 67,356 blacks, and 433 of other races; there were 61,448 white males, 71,938 white females; 19,968 black males, and 24,643 black females. Mobile County had a total of 317,308 people, of whom 214,070 whites included 152,231 males and 165,077 females, and 102,363 blacks, with 43,039 males and 54,344 females. A similar disparity was also found in other Alabama cities, including Birmingham and Montgomery.

The drop in population from 1960 to 1970 in the city of Mobile and the rise in the County are attributed to the fine facilities in roads and housing that enable workers to enjoy suburban advantages and drive daily to employment in the city.

Mobile's history and development may be read in its streets and architecture, with their fascinating blend of the old and new. While alterations and re-routing of traffic have taken place in recent years, many streets still bear names given while the city was under Spanish, French and English rule. These older streets give way to broad avenues and an occasional small park as the city has spread toward the hills.

The four-lane Interstate 65 highway originates in Mobile. Bankhead Tunnel carries automobile traffic between downtown Mobile and the Eastern Bay shore. Beside the Bankhead Tunnel is the George C. Wallace Tunnel, which was opened to traffic in February, 1973. This tunnel and the Cochrane Bridge serve Int. 10 and US 31, 90, and 98.

Mobile has many structures and areas that stir nostalgia for the past, but actually it is one of the busiest cities in the South, with trade, traffic and industry that will profit by new bridges, tunnels and roads, an enlarged port, and a rejuvenated downtown. A new traffic loop, completed at a cost of $10,000,000, enables trucks to bypass the crowded business streets. The Federal Building, which employs 900 and cost $8,500,000 to build, adds to the new skyline, as does the 16-story Sheraton Hotel on Government Street, a block up from the famous Admiral Semmes Hotel and its subsidiary, the Admiral Semmes Motor Hotel across the street. To enable downtown to compete with outlying shopping centers, streets and houses have been restructured; thus Dauphin Street, the heart of Mobile, has been given wider sidewalks, a canopy over part of the street, freedom from trucks, buses, and parking, and Japanese magnolias decorating the walks. A Spanish Plaza gives a fresh approach to the Municipal Auditorium.

Of the 362,000 acres of salt water within Alabama, Mobile Bay covers 252,000 acres. The Port of Mobile is the 12th largest port in the United States. In 1972 it handled more than 27,000,000 tons. Its modern storage and moving equipment comprises about two and one-half miles of piers and warehouses, berths for 25 to 30 ocean-going vessels, rail, truck and barge connections, a grain elevator, a cold storage plant, and bulk handling facilities. The ship channel has a depth of 40 ft., to be deepened presently to 42 ft.

The shipping interests of the Port are served by the INTERNATIONAL TRADE CENTER, where trade representatives from all over the world have offices.

The Port is the outlet for industrial and agricultural products of Alabama, and to some extent of contiguous areas in upper Georgia, Tennessee, and Kentucky that do not use the Ohio and Mississippi River systems. This tonnage comes to Mobile Bay by way of the Warrior-Tombigbee River System. The Warrior flows into the Tombigbee and the Alabama River joins the Tombigbee to form the Mobile River, which flows into Mobile Bay. The Mobile area includes Mississippi Sound, Oyster Bay, and Weeks Bay. The drainage area of the Mobile Basin embraces 2,059 sq. mi. and has 142 miles of rivers, including the Bon Secour, Dog, Fish, Fowl, Magnolia, Middle, Mobile, Raft, Spanish, and Tensaw, and numerous creeks. The area along the Warrior-Tombigbee immediately north of Mobile is the site of Alabama's expanding chemical industry. Here also is based the refining of petroleum. The Mobile area has major paper manufacturing, lumber, alumina refining, and cement, iron, dry dock and ship repair operations.

About 10,000,000 tons of bauxite from Latin America are unloaded annually at the Port of Mobile. Other materials entering the Port for use of basic industry in Alabama include high-grade iron ore from Africa, Labrador, Venezuela, Chile, and Peru. The ore is unloaded from ocean-going vessels at a modern bulk handling plant at Mobile and then transferred to barges for moving up the Warrior-Tombigbee Waterway to plants in Jefferson County and other locations on the rivers. These supplies are carried on barges with capacities of from 550 to 2,000 tons. The small barge for dry bulk cargoes is 140 ft. long and 25 ft. wide; it becomes part of a tow of 7 to 11 units propelled by a towboat of 1,100 to 1,300 hp. The jumbo barge is 215 ft. long and 50 ft. wide. Towboats in the Port, Bay, and river channels are screw propeller diesels moving deep draft steel barges.

Many products that reach the Port of Mobile from inland are transferred to ocean-going vessels. Tinplate comes to Mobile on the Warrior-Tombigbee Waterway for export to fruit and food canning plants as far away as Hawaii. Tinplate also goes by Intracoastal Waterway to domestic concerns for packaging. Outbound iron and steel consist of cast iron pipe, structural steel for bridges and buildings, steel plate for shipbuilding, and steel sheets.

A large increase in waterway tonnage is expected when the Warrior-Tombigbee System is tied up with the Tennessee River System.

Mobile has two daily newspapers, The 'Mobile *Register* and the Mobile *Press,* which combine on Sunday as the Mobile *Press Register,* and five weeklies. There are 9 radio stations, two commercial TVS, ETV and a Pensacola, Fla. TV station is received in Mobile.

While the city's industrial developments may seem out of keeping with its romantic past, there are phases of Mobile life that have survived from French and Spanish days. The Mardi Gras carnival, celebrated annually for about 10 days ending on Shrove Tuesday, was instituted by Bienville on August 24, 1704, as the Masque de la St. Louis. In 1711 the masque was celebrated in the new settlement at Fort Conde de la Mobile, and renamed Boeuf Gras. In 1830 a big papier-mâché bull head was brought over from France and each year for the next decade the mighty *boeuf* headed the parade preceding the ball. It was then replaced by horse-drawn floats, and was finally used as wadding for Confederate cannon. Mardi Gras was held annually until 1861, when it was suspended because of the war. It was revived in 1867, and officially reinstated as an annual celebration in 1869.

Mardi Gras today is a holiday. Emperor Felix enters the city on a warship on the Monday preceding the carnival, is greeted by the mayor, and presented with a three-foot gilded key to the city. The festivities open with the Krewe of Columbus Parade on Friday night, followed by the masked Krewe of Columbus Ball. On Saturday afternoon the floral parade is held. Other mystic societies—the Order of Myth, Comic Cow Boys, and the Infant Mystics—hold masked balls and parades, while the Knights of Revelry have a parade and dance. The celebration culminates with the parade of Mardi Gras day proper, Shrove Tuesday. Throngs of Mobilians and visitors line Government Street to watch the floats and take part in the merrymaking. In 1939 Mobile Negroes

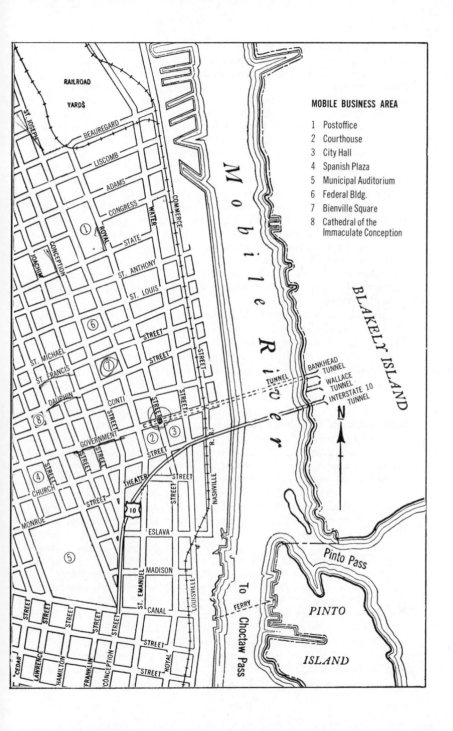

MOBILE BUSINESS AREA

1 Postoffice
2 Courthouse
3 City Hall
4 Spanish Plaza
5 Municipal Auditorium
6 Federal Bldg.
7 Bienville Square
8 Cathedral of the Immaculate Conception

for the first time held their own carnival and parade on Davis Avenue, and this addition has become an annual event.

Second only to Mardi Gras in popularity is the Azalea Trail, a flower festival held annually in mid-February or early March when the azaleas are in bloom. It was organized in 1929 as a joint project of the Garden Clubs, the Chamber of Commerce, and the city government, under sponsorship of the Junior Chamber of Commerce. Opening of the 37-mile trail is celebrated with elaborate ceremonies during which an Azalea Queen is crowned and, with a 50-member court, traverses the route. The azaleas range in color from white through pink and cerise to deep purple, and in size from centuries-old plants 30 feet high to dwarf Japanese varieties. During the weeks of the festival gardens along the route are open to visitors. The trail begins at the Quigley House on Government Street, which has been restored by the Jaycees as Azalea Trail Headquarters and the Tourist Information Center, and is marked by a continuous line of paint down the center of the right hand lane. The line, of course, is azalea pink.

Out of Azalea Trail festivities grew America's Junior Miss Pageant, also sponsored by the Jaycees and carried out by girls from across the nation.

Azaleas were brought to Mobile from France in 1754 and flourished in Alabama soil. Camellias and crepe myrtle also bloom profusely. Roses cloak old walls and picket fences, and in late summer the Mexican *antigny* vine gives brilliant colors to arbors and porches.

Davis Avenue, named for Jefferson Davis, begins at the intersection of St. Anthony and Claiborne Sts., and for a mile and a half runs diagonally across the city to Three Mile Creek. It is noteworthy for the fact that many of its business houses are owned by Negroes and have been built up by black patronage.

While Negro residences are scattered throughout the city, the largest concentration of black homes is still on Davis Avenue. Since the 1940 completion of Orange Groves Homes, a slum clearance project, a number of other housing developments for low-income families have been erected, sponsored by the Mobile Housing Board.

The Waldseemueller Map, drawn in 1505, shows the outline of Mobile Bay, though records do not disclose what navigator first saw it. When Pineda returned from his visit along the shores of the Gulf of Mexico in 1519, his sketches showed Rio del Espiritu Sancto (Mobile Bay and River) and he drew it on his map in 1520. The first written record of Mobile Bay was that of de Narvaez, Spanish explorer, who landed on its shores in 1528. Not until 1559, however, was any attempt made to colonize the area. In that year Tristan De Luna, sent by the Viceroy of Mexico, established a Spanish settlement here, but it was abandoned two years later and the colonists returned to Mexico.

Almost a century and a half passed before settlers came again to the shores of Mobile Bay. Pierre Le Moyne, Sieur d'Iberville, was sent by Louis XIV to establish a colony on the Gulf in 1699. Though Iberville discovered Massacre, now Dauphin Island, 25 miles south of with profits from the year's crop in their wallets, arrived for a row of festivities and spent their money freely. But destructive fires threa ened the life of the growing city in 1827 and again in 1839. Yellow fever also spread suffering. The most disastrous epidemic was in 1853, when 764 persons perished, and in 1839, the year of the second fire, another epidemic raged. Until 1897 the dreaded "yellow jack" was a continuous threat. All who could, left town. Embattled citizens of near-by towns searched every train to see that no one came from the plague-ridden area, for at that time yellow fever was thought to be contagious.

Mobile during the War between the States suffered dislocation of its commercial life, but was less harassed by the Federals than New Orleans. Its shipping of cotton was greatly hampered by the Federal blockade, but Mobile Bay was so thoroughly mined and fortified by land and water batteries that no entrance was attempted before August, 1864. Fort Morgan at Mobile Point and Fort Gaines on Dauphin Island stood guard at the entrance and Fort Powell at Grant Pass, all well armed. Closer to the city were three lines of defense: an outer ring of 15 redoubts, an inner ring of 16 enclosed forts, and a middle ring of 19 bastioned forts and eight redoubts. Ten batteries commanded the channel below Mobile. When Commander David G. Farragut forced the entrance with 18 warships on August 5, 1864, he had to run close to Fort Morgan to avoid the obstructions, and his order "Damn the torpedoes, full speed ahead!" indicated the difficulties. After he had passed the forts with one vessel, the ironclad *Tecumseh,* sunk and his flagship, *Hartford,* and others struck numerous times the Confederate ironclad *Tennessee,* commanded by Admiral Franklin Buchanan, made a spectacular attack on the wooden ships of the Federal squadron, firing at point-blank range until subdued. Although Farragut established his position in the Bay the city did not fall and Fort Morgan held out until August 22, when siege guns had been brought from New Orleans and a full-scale bombardment of 24 hours finally reduced the fort.

The defenses of Mobile were manned by troops under General David H. Maury and were not threatened until March, 1865, when Union General E. S. R. Canby invested Spanish Fort, seven miles east of Mobile, and General Frederick Steele attacked Fort Blakeley. General Maury evacuated Mobile April 12, 1865.

An effort to recover the wreck of the *Tecumseh* in Mobile Bay has been made by Smithsonian Institution.

When the lumber trade declined because of the depletion of forests, naval stores took its place as an export. In the 1940s turpentine, resin, and gum barrels were stowed in the hulls of more than one-third of the freighters clearing Mobile. Lumber shipments increased with the general use of the tupelo and gum trees for veneer and plywood.

During World War II and for some years afterward BROOK-LEY AIR FORCE BASE gave strong support to the economy of Mobile. It was closed in 1968. Its terrain is now used by the Municipal Airport and the University of South Alabama.

Mobile, the expedition continued to the flat beaches of Bilo. a stockade and cabins were built. A colony was also establi Dauphin Island, and three years later, Pierre's brother, Jean Le Moyne, Sieur de Bienville, was appointed governor. He mo government to Fort Louis de la Mobile, which had been built at T Seven Mile Bluff on Mobile River.

The first year was beset with hardships. Weakened by illnes settlers did little more than build a fort and cabins; they depende storeships from France for their food. The colony, however, g by immigration and the arrival of supplies, at first undependable, bec; more regular. The *Pelican,* arriving from Canada in 1704, brou; not only messengers of the King, soldiers, prelates, missionaries, a nuns, but also 24 girls chosen by the Bishop of Quebec to become wiv of the colonists. In a month all but one had husbands and before year had passed the first native child, Jean François LeCan was born ir Mobile.

For the next six years Bienville struggled with Indians and settlers, persuading the latter to become self sustaining through farming and trapping. In 1710, floods caused the removal of the colony to the present site of Mobile, where Bienville erected Fort Conde, later called Fort Charlotte by the British. This was his last achievement before he was removed as governor of Louisiana and replaced by Antoine de la Mothe Cadillac. Cadillac's regime was inept and toward its end he set up an almost feudal court on Dauphin Island, where none except officers and noblemen might wear swords in his presence.

As capital of Louisiana, Mobile prospered during the following years. Its agricultural future was assured when the ships *Africaine* and *Le Duc de Maine* arrived in 1721, bringing more than 600 slaves to Mobile. The town was almost wiped out in 1733 by a hurricane and an epidemic. The capital of Louisiana had been moved to New Orleans and only the hardiest of the early pioneers continued their fight against nature, the Indians, and occasional forays from the Spanish colony at Pensacola. As part of French holdings in America, Mobile was ceded to the British by the Treaty of Paris in 1763 and was able to trade peacefully with the English colonies on the Atlantic Seaboard.

In 1780 Bernardo De Galvez brought the Spanish fleet into the harbor, forced the surrender of Fort Charlotte, and occupied the town. For the following 33 years the flag of Spain waved above Mobile, for although Alabama, as part of the Mississippi Territory, was ceded to the United States in 1799, Mobile remained in Spanish hands. But in 1813, U. S. General Wilkinson, using the War of 1812 as a pretext, ousted the Spanish commandant, Perez, and seized the town for the United States.

Mobile prospered under American rule. It was granted a town charter in 1814 and a city charter in 1819, shortly after Alabama was admitted to the Union. Sole outlet for the rich agricultural lands of the State, Mobile now enjoyed halcyon days. River steamers brought cotton down the Tombigbee and the Alabama to the port. Planters,

Major industries located in the area are shipbuilding, cement, manufacturing of wood pulp and paper products, steel fabricating, foundries, alumina, rayon fibers, naval stores, oil refining, clothing manufacturing, crackers and other bakers' products, furniture manufacturing, pumps, batteries, paints and chemicals.

A West German chemical corporation, Degussa, chose the Mobile area for a chemical plant costing $200 million to build, and the Dow Badische Company, based at Williamsburg, Virginia, arranged to build a $100 million plant for making carpet fiber.

Interest in education has persisted since the city established the State's first public school system in 1852. Mobile today has 88 schools in the Mobile County School System. In addition to these, there are two high schools and 18 elementary parochial schools and a number of private day schools. The larger of the latter are University Military School and, for girls, the Julius T. Wright School.

Colleges, universities and trade schools in the Mobile area include Carver Technical Trade School, Mobile College, Southwest State Technical Institute, Spring Hill College and the University of South Alabama.

POINTS OF INTEREST

BUSINESS SECTION

BIENVILLE SQUARE, bounded by Dauphin, St. Joseph, St. Francis, and Conception Sts., is a public park named in honor of the founder of Mobile. The square, shaded with live oaks and planted with azaleas, was set aside for public purposes by the Alabama legislature more than 100 years ago. In the center is a large fountain honoring Dr. George Ketchum, Mobile physician, for his efforts to provide the city with plentiful and pure drinking water. A granite cross dedicated to Bienville was placed on the south side of the park near Dauphin Street by the Colonial Dames of Alabama. French cannon from old Fort Conde and British cannon from Fort Charlotte, one bearing the initials G.R. (*Georgius Rex*), are mounted in opposite corners of the square. A bronze plaque honoring Pierre Le Moyne, Bienville's brother, is set in a large boulder on the northwest corner of the square. It was presented to the city by a delegation from France in 1937.

Bienville Square is the quiet, green plaza about which Mobile has chosen to build its skyscrapers. The Merchants National Bank, Roberts Building, and the 34-story First National Bank rise above the square.

MOBILE COUNTY COURTHOUSE, sw. corner of Royal and Government Sts., constructed in 1959 on the site of the former County Courthouse, is a modern structure built of tan and brown brick, three stories plus a basement, and designed by Cooper Van Antwerp. The distinguishing feature of the building is a mosaic, 36 feet wide and 7 feet high over the Government St. entrance. The mosaic was created by Conrad A. Albrizio of Bon Secour, Ala., and the mosaic glass was cut and assembled in Venice, Italy, under Albrizio's supervision. Very colorful, it depicts Justice, Good and Evil, and their consequences. Albrizio's work is also found in the lobby of the Municipal Auditorium, and in the lobby of Mobile General Hospital. The theme of various mosaics in the Auditorium is entertainment; the hospital mosaic tells the history of medicine.

The CITY HALL, ne. corner Royal and Church Sts., erected in 1855, is a two-story white building occupying half a city block. Arched openings with wrought ironwork, decorated brackets under the wide eaves, and a cupola show Spanish influences. It was originally used as a market and is still often called the Southern Market. The ground floor, where live fish in cypress tanks, meat, and vegetables were sold, was served by two driveways extending from Royal to Waters Street. The second floor was used as an armory and as headquarters for the local State militia until the completion of the Fort Whiting Armory in 1939. A Confederate soup kitchen was established here during the war to feed thousands of soldiers' dependents. The building was renovated with Federal funds in 1937-8 but the original style was carefully preserved; it is now occupied by municipal offices.

The MOBILE MUNICIPAL AUDITORIUM is the hub of an expanding complex of structures that include the Exposition Hall, and the Show Facility. This is located in the Church Street Square District. The Auditorium seats 10,620 and has auxiliary facilities for conventions, such as 16 individual meeting rooms. The adjoining Theatre has a stage 88 ft. wide and 17 ft. deep, and seats for 1,950. The Exposition Hall can accommodate up to 4,000 and have basketball, wrestling, dances, and shows. The arena has ice shows, midget auto races, track meets, and circuses. The pageant of America's Junior Miss is staged here. For a large horse show 1,200 cubic yards of earth was spread on the floor. The Auditorium can seat and serve 2,500 persons at dinner.

ADMIRAL SEMMES MONUMENT, at Royal and Government Sts., is a bronze figure of Rear Admiral Raphael Semmes in uniform, mounted on a granite base. In bas-relief is the steam cruiser, C.S.S. *Alabama,* which he commanded when it was sunk by the *U.S.S. Kearsarge* off Cherbourg, France, on June 19, 1864.

FORTE CONDE-CHARLOTTE HOUSE, 104 Theater St., operated by the Colonial Dames of America as a historic house-museum, is on the lot next to the site of Mobile's first American theater, which was also a part of the French Fort Conde. Across the front is a porch with large Tuscan columns; four additional columns support the roof. The house was Mobile's first courthouse and jail. It was bought by Jonathan Kirkbridge and converted into an imposing residence in 1885.

The BANKHEAD TUNNEL, beginning at St. Emanuel and Government Sts., passes beneath Government St. to and under the Mobile River; on the east side of the river, at the south end of Blakely Island, it connects with US 90. The route via the tunnel is 7.5 miles shorter than that over Cochrane Bridge. The tunnel, 3,400 feet long with a roadbed 21 feet from curb to curb, was built in 1940 by the city with the aid of Federal funds. It is the "trench type" of construction, having seven sections of fabricated steel tube. In the walls are niches for fire alarm boxes, telephones, carbon monoxide detectors, and other safety devices. At the east entrance are storm gates that can be closed, when necessary, within five minutes.

The FRENCH TYPE DOUBLE HOUSE, 56-58 S. Conception St., built about 1824, is the only remaining example in Mobile of this type of building except the House of Two Cities. It is a two-story brick house of French Colonial design, with a driveway dividing the ground floor into two houses from front to back. A porch across the front has eight slender cast-iron columns supporting the second story balcony. Ornamental cast-iron balustrades on the porch and balcony are characteristic of the period in which the house was built.

CHRIST EPISCOPAL CHURCH, nw. corner St. Emanuel and Church Sts., begun in 1828 and completed in 1840, is Greek Doric is design, with a broad recessed porch and two massive Doric columns. A wrought-iron fence on a stone curbing extends along the sidewalk on both streets. On the St. Emanuel Street side is a solid eight-foot wall separating the church grounds from the adjacent lot. On the right of the entrance steps is the church's old bell, with the inscription West Troy, N. Y. 24th Aug. 1847. It fell from the belfry during the hurricane of 1906, and now is fastened to the masonry stoop, sufficiently raised to permit its use. Before the erection of this building, a church used by all Protestant denominations, stood on the site.

GOVERNMENT STREET PRESBYTERIAN CHURCH, nw. corner Government and Jackson Sts., built in 1837, was designed by Thomas F. James. It is built of brick and shows Greek Revival influence in its design. At the head of a flight of stone steps is a recessed vestibule with two massive Ionic columns. The Burgett Memorial Church School at the rear of the church, erected in 1904, harmonizes in design.

The CATHEDRAL RECTORY nw. corner Government and Franklin Sts., formerly the Major Ketchum House, is a three-story structure with two-story wings on each side and a rear ell. It is a red-brick building with white stone window and door trim, showing French Colonial influence in its design. The porch, extending across the front and Franklin Street sides, is supported by 26 slender cast-iron columns. Ornamental cast-iron work trims the porch and encloses the front yard. Originally the home of Major William H. Ketchum, it is now owned by the Catholic Diocese.

The CATHEDRAL OF THE IMMACULATE CONCEPTION, Claiborne St., between Conti and Dauphin Sts., is an imposing structure showing Roman influence in its design. Across the front façade are eight fluted Doric columns. The exterior is of red brick with limestone and granite base, portico, and cornice. The foundation stone was blessed by Bishop Michael Portier, the first bishop of the diocese of Mobile, on January 29, 1836, and the cathedral was dedicated

14 years later, on December 8, 1850, by the Right Reverend Ignatius Reynolds. The present portico was added after the War between the States, and in 1885 the twin towers were built. The grounds, studded with shade trees, are enclosed by a lace-work iron fence, the work of Bishop Quinlan's cousin, Daniel Geary, who installed it a few weeks before the outbreak of war in 1861.

The Cathedral stands on a part of the burial ground used by the Spaniards during their occupation of Mobile. Fifise Langlois, who introduced the azalea to Mobile in 1754, is buried here.

The GOLDSBY HOUSE, 452 Government St., is a large two-story structure with an iron fence and brick walls across the back and on either side. The wrought-iron gate was brought to Mobile from Europe early in the 19th century. The house is modified Gothic in design, with high gables and steep roof. In the spring of 1865 the building was occupied by Federal naval officers, and Mobile women walked down the middle of the street in order not to come too close to the Union flag draped over the entrance.

BARTON ACADEMY, Government St. between Cedar and Lawrence Sts., the oldest public school in Alabama, is a three-story structure of white stucco over brick. Thomas S. James was architect and builder. In the center of the front façade are six massive columns; behind them, on the second floor, is a small balcony. A column-supported dome surmounts the building. Barton Academy was erected in 1835-6 and was originally used for private and denominational schools. In 1852 the first public school session opened there. By February, 1853, 854 pupils were enrolled.

In the great yellow fever scourge of 1853 the building was the headquarters of the Can't-Get-Away-Club, composed of Mobilians who refused to flee as did nine-tenths of the population when the plague struck, and remained to nurse the fever victims. During the War between the States a soup kitchen was established here for the thousands impoverished by the war. Barton Academy, which celebrated its centennial on May 7, 1936, now houses offices of the Mobile County Board of School Commissioners.

BATTLESHIP ALABAMA MEMORIAL PARK is east of the city on Battleship Parkway, in which is moored the USS *Alabama*. When it was announced that the Navy would scrap the great ship that had earned nine battle stars in far-ranging Pacific raids during World War II, and led the victory fleet into Tokyo Bay, Alabamians contributed $1,000,000 to bring it 5,600 miles from Seattle to Mobile. It is now a state shrine to the Alabamians who served in World War II and the Far East. Alongside is moored the USS *Drum,* a World War II submarine. *Open daily 8 a.m. to sunset.*

RESIDENTIAL SECTION

THE MOBILE PUBLIC LIBRARY, 701 Government St., a two-story brick building covered with stucco, was erected in 1928. Designed by George Rogers, it has a slightly recessed central portion flanked by large wings. In the west wing is the Beatrice B. Bernheim

Auditorium. There are 10 branch libraries and several bookmobiles that serve Mobile County. *Library open Monday through Thursday, 9-9, Friday and Saturday, 9-6.*

The ADMIRAL RAPHAEL SEMMES HOUSE, 802 Government St., is a two-story brick structure, built in 1858 by Peter Horta. The porch and balcony have ornamental iron balustrades and overhead trim of matched design. Admiral Semmes, Confederate naval hero, for whom the house was bought by popular subscription, lived there from 1871 until his death in 1877. Prior to the War between the States, Admiral Semmes was commandant of the U. S. Navy Yard at Pensacola, but when Alabama seceded, he resigned his commission and entered the Confederate service. His book *Service Afloat,* recounts the activities of the Confederate Navy. He is buried in the Catholic Cemetery, and there is a monument to his memory in Confederate Rest, Magnolia Cemetery. The house is owned by the First Baptist Church and used as a chapel.

The FATHER RYAN STATUE, junction of Spring Hill Ave., Scott, and Saint Francis Sts., is a life-sized bronze statue of the priest, poet and patriot of the Confederacy. It stands in a park planted with many azaleas.

SIXTH DISTRICT TUBERCULOSIS HOSPITAL, formerly called U. S. Marine Hospital, 800 Saint Anthony St., occupying an entire block, was erected in 1842 and enlarged to its present capacity in 1932. It is owned and operated by the U. S. Public Health Service, and has 150 beds. Seamen from American ships, employees of the U. S. Coast Guard and others who become ill in the line of duty are cared for here.

OLD CITY HOSPITAL, St. Anthony and Broad Sts., now occupied by a Community Action group, is a two-story-and-basement brick and stucco structure of Greek Revival design built in 1825. Fourteen Doric columns across the front facade support the roof; the balconies are enclosed by green-painted balustrades. The Sisters of Charity, who formerly operated the hospital, turned it over to Mobile County in 1925. Its name was changed to mobile General when it was moved into new quarters at 2451 Fillingim St. It is now under the administration of the University of South Alabama and part of its medical education program.

ST. MARY'S CHURCH, sw. corner Lafayette St. and Old Shell Road, is built on the site of old St. Mary's Church, where Father Ryan served for a time. It was here that he wrote several of his poems. The present church, built in 1927 in Mission style, is a large yellow stucco structure with red-tiled roof and high square tower.

MAGNOLIA CEMETERY, head of George St., contains the graves of Joseph Jefferson, the elder; Charles Anderson, father of the actress, Mary Anderson; William Petrie, actor; Peter Joseph Hamilton, author of *Colonial Mobile;* and Confederate General Braxton Bragg. In the southeast corner of the cemetery is Confederate Rest, memorial to the Southern dead; here are buried approximately 1,200 soldiers. National Cemetery, in the southwest corner, is the burial place of Union soldiers who fell at Fort Blakely.

MEMORIAL PARK, intersection of Government and Houston Sts., is a triangular memorial park to the men who were killed in World War I. In front of Memorial Arch is a small reflecting pool. The park, with its hundreds of azalea bushes, is a show-place of the Azalea Trail.

The BRAGG HOUSE, 1906 Springhill Ave., is a white two-story frame house, with green blinds. Sixteen slender octagonal columns are set around the front porch. The house was built by John Bragg and later willed to his brother, General Braxton Bragg, who won distinction at the Battle of Chickamauga.

OAKLEIGH, at the head of Savannah St., is Mobile's official antebellum mansion and headquarters of the Historic Mobile Preservation Society. Deriving its name from the many giant oaks surrounding it, Oakleigh was designed and built with help of slave labor by James W. Roper. Begun in 1833, it was still under construction as late as 1852. Hand-hewn lumber and handmade brick went into its building, and the original silver plated door knobs remain on the huge doors of the two parlors. In 1935 the Historic American Survey selected Oakleigh as one of the nation's buildings of historic value. The house has been furnished by the Historic Society with period pieces dating prior to 1850. Furniture and accessories are of Early Victorian, Empire and Regency periods. One of its most unusual collections is memorabilia of Mobile's Mardi Gras. A meeting room and dining room are available for club meetings and social affairs. *Open daily 10-4; Sunday, 2-4.*

GEORGIA COTTAGE, 2564 Springhill Avenue, open during the spring Iron Lace and Classic Columns Tour, was erected in 1840 in the Creole style with Greek Revival influence. It was the home of Augusta Evans Wilson, author of *St. Elmo*. It rests in a Deep South setting of towering magnolias and oaks, and is now the home of Dr. and Mrs. E. S. Sledge (1971).

The WARING TEXAS HOUSE, 110 S. Claiborne St., open during the spring Iron Lace and Classic Columns Tour, has been restored and serves as headquarters for Mobile's oldest mystic society, the Strikers. The house was built in 1858 as bachelor quarters for the sons of Moses Waring. Waring had constructed one of the finest Government Street mansions of the day, and built the lodge for the young men of the family. Since it stood apart from the main dwelling as the State of Texas was apart from the United States—it received this title. This structure is the only one of its kind remaining in Mobile. It was sold to the Strikers by descendents of Moses Waring.

PALMETTO HALL, 55 S. McGregor Ave., is the home of the Jay P. Altmayer family, who bought it in 1959 and spent three years restoring it to its original state. They remodelled the interior and added wings to the central block to accommodate modern living. John Cortez Dawson of Charleston built the house in 1846-47 on the lines of his old home near the Battery. He brought many of the shrubs for its garden from Charleston. The Greek Revival style is carried out on the first level in brick covered with cement and above that in pine clapboards. The provincial colonial Doric columns on the first level and classic fluted columns above are all original as are the pine floors throughout the house.

The MOBILE ART GALLERY is located on the lake in Langan (Municipal) Park. There are 700 acres of azaleas, flowering trees, tall pines, with an 18-hole golf course, tennis courts, picnic areas and children's playground. The gallery houses permanent collections and presents a number of individual and group exhibitions throughout the year. The park was named for former City Commissioner and Mayor, Joseph N. Langan, who worked for its creation.

LONG GARDENS, on Tuthill Lane in Spring Hill, 10 acres of knolls and ravines planted with thousands of camellias and azaleas, has been called one of the most beautiful private gardens known. It is open during the Azalea Trail Festival.

PHOENIX FIRE MUSEUM, Claiborne and Monroe Sts., is the official fire museum of the City of Mobile. It occupies the home station house of Phoenix Steam Fire Station No. 6, organized in 1838. Erected in 1859, it was completely restored in 1964. Operated by the Museum Board of the City of Mobile, it houses collections pertaining to the history of firefighting in Mobile since 1819, when its first volunteer companies were organized. *Open daily except Mondays, 10-5, no admission charge.*

PATIO GALLERY, 303 Auditorium Dr., formerly known as the Myers House, was one of Mobile's first telegraph stations in use after 1847, when telegraph wires were strung in the city. Capt. Abrams Lock Myers used the first floor as his office and the second as living quarters when not at sea. Operation of Patio Gallery by the Art Patrons League is in cooperation with the historical development efforts of the City and the National Historic Preservation Program. It serves as sales outlet for local artists and handles articles indigenous to the area. *Open Monday through Friday, 10-4, no charge.*

CARLEN HOUSE, on High School Dr., an important representation of the Creole Cottage as it evolved from the French colonial form, is the only one of its kind publicly preserved and maintained in Mobile. Erected in 1842 on an 1804 Spanish land grant, its threatened destruction spurred the Junior Historical Society of Murphy High School and Historical Mobile Preservation Society to raise funds for its restoration. Furnishings came from the city museums and memorial gifts, all typical of a house of the period. It was opened in October, 1970, and is operated by the Mobile Museum Board. *Open Tuesday through Saturday, 10-5; Sunday 1-5.*

S. D. BISHOP STATE JUNIOR COLLEGE was organized in 1965 as one of the new junior colleges authorized by the State. It is an extension of the Mobile branch of the Alabama State College, which gave a two-year college course and extension courses for teachers in service for 28 years. In the 1973-74 year it enrolled approximately 1,100 students. It has a cooperative arrangement with SOUTHWEST STATE TECHNICAL COLLEGE and CARVER STATE TECHNICAL INSTITUTE, whereby students of the latter two may add to their vocational technical courses by taking studies at Bishop State. Their work is facilitated by free bus connections between the colleges.

SPRING HILL COLLEGE, on Old Shell Road, in the same general area as the University of South Alabama, is venerable when compared with its neighbor. It was founded in 1830 by the first Roman Catholic bishop of Mobile, Michael Portier, who had gone to France for teachers and funds. It had 30 students in its first class. It was chartered by the Alabama legislature in 1836 and turned over to the Society of Jesus in 1847. It continued during the War between the States and lost its principal building by fire in 1869. It offers baccalaureate degrees in the arts and science and preparatory-courses in law, medicine, dentistry, and engineering.

The college occupies a wooded area of 600 acres. Stewartfield, a plantation house of 1845, now houses the Fine Arts department. St. Joseph's Chapel, of 1910, follows a Gothic design, and the little frame Sodality Chapel is a link with the early years. The Thomas Byrne Memorial Library, built in 1931, has more than 126,000 volumes, and is colonial in design. Among new buildings are two residence halls for men and two for women, three science buildings, and the Campus Center. In the 1974 school year Spring Hill College enrolled 900 students and had a faculty of 96.

The UNIVERSITY OF SOUTH ALABAMA, the largest of institutions of higher learning in Mobile, was established in 1963 and opened in June, 1964. It has two locations, the main campus at 307 Gaillard Drive on Spring Hill in West Mobile, entered by the Michigan Ave. gate from Interstate 10, and the so-called Brookley campus, which occupies 327 acres of the former Brookley Air Force Base on Mobile Bay. The university offers courses in 19 departments of the College of Arts and Sciences, the College of Education, and the College of Business and Management Studies. Four modern residence halls, in a quadrangle, are located in the northeast section of the main campus. They can accommodate more than 500 students, with two halls for men and two for women. Residents of each hall elect their own government. Walks are camellia-bordered and the entire campus uses gaslight.

After Brookley AFB was terminated its buildings were acquired by the University of South Alabama and occupied by its Educational, Research and Development Center. The Bay Front Drive moves along the eastern limits of the campus and a golf course projects into the Bay east of that. The Center includes 165 single family units, three dormitories, a large cafeteria, a conference center, and various units from the former base, which were adapted for use of seminars, workshops, and special purposes. The campus has a golf course, bowling alley, tennis courts, and two swimming pools. The former Brookley Manor is preserved.

In the 1974 school year the university enrolled 5,760 students and had a faculty of 259.

MOBILE COLLEGE, a four-year institution, was established in 1961. Its J. L. Bledsoe Library has approximately 40,000 volumes. In 1973 it enrolled 629 students and had a faculty of 40.

Montgomery

Air Services: Two carriers, Southern Airways and Eastern Airlines, have scheduled flights that connect with other lines in nearby Birmingham and Atlanta. Dannelly Municipal Airport is about six miles from the heart of Montgomery, US 80.

Buses: Greyhound and Continental Trailways provide interstate service. Montgomery City Lines connects the downtown with residential sections (fare is 30 cents, transfers 5 cents). Greyhound station is at 210 South Court St.; Continental Trailways is at 235 Lee St.

Highways: US 31, 231, 331, 80 and 82 are routed through Montgomery, and Interstate 65 and 85 provide routes to Atlanta and Washington, New Orleans and the Gulf coast region, and to major mid-western cities. The Alabama River is navigable to Mobile.

Railroads: Central of Georgia; Illinois Central Gulf; Louisville & Nashville; Seaboard Coastline; Southern Railway, and Western Railway of Alabama provide freight and limited passenger services.

Information: Montgomery Area Chamber of Commerce, 41 Commerce St., Montgomery, 36101; State Department of Publicity and Information, The Capitol, Montgomery; Morning, afternoon and Sunday newspapers published by the *Advertiser-Journal*, P.O. Box 950, Montgomery, 36102. *Montgomery Independent, Prattville Progress, Prattville Sun,* and *Wetumpka Herald* are area weeklies.

Radio and Television: Three major television networks, educational TV, and 13 radio stations serve the area.

Accommodations: There are four hotels with a total of 707 rooms, and more than 2,000 modern motel rooms in the area with others in the building stage. Numerous restaurants provide excellent southern and seafood specialties.

Climate: Average annual temperature, 65°. Yearly average, 8 hours sunshine per day; the growing season, 253 days; average rainfall, 50.7 in.; average snowfall, .3 in.

Recreation: City Recreation Department through its 22 parks, 21 playgrounds and 12 community centers provides a variety of supervised activities including Little League, Pony and Babe Ruth League baseball, youth football and basketball, and arts and crafts. The YMCA through its downtown center and four branches provides complete athetic facilities. Seven private golf courses, two public courses and tennis courts are available for year-round use. Crampton Bowl is home of the annual Blue-Gray Football Game played in December between collegiate stars from northern and southern teams. Patterson Field is home of Montgomery Rebels Baseball Team. Within a 70-mile radius are 80,000 acres for public hunting of deer, turkey, squirrel, quail, rabbit, dove and other game. There are some 5,000 fishing ponds and 11 lakes of various sizes, and deep sea fishing in the Gulf of Mexico is only three hours driving time from Montgomery. Camping facilities are available in the area.

Tours: Guided tours of Montgomery and Environs may be arranged through Public Relations Department, Montgomery Area Chamber of Commerce, 41 Commerce St., P.O. Box 79, Montgomery, Alabama 36101.

Annual Events: January—Southern Regional Angus Cattle Show and Sale, Garrett Coliseum. *February*—Indoor Track Relay Meet, Garrett Coliseum; Montgomery Art Guild Jury Show, Museum of Fine Arts. *March*—Southeastern Livestock Exposition and Rodeo, Garrett Coliseum; Dixie Annual Art Show, Museum of Fine Arts. *April*—Spring Arts Craft and Hobby Fair at Camp Grandview; Colonial Acres Invitational Men's Golf Tournament, Colonial Country Club; Home and Garden Tour (may be in May), contact Museum of Fine Arts. *May*—Montgomery Kennel Club Show, Garrett Coliseum; Alabama League Non-Jury Art Show, Museum of Fine Arts; High School Art Jury Show at Museum; May Day Festival, Huntingdon College; Montgomery Art Guild's Carnival of Arts, Normandale Arcade. *June*—Montgomery Country Club Men's Invitational Golf Tournament; Arrowhead Country Club Men's Invitational Golf Tournament. *July*—Independence Day Celebration, Cramton Bowl. *August*—Montgomery 200, Montgomery International Speedway, Old Selma Road; Woodley Country Club Men's Invitational Golf Tournament. *September*—Montgomery Area Square Dance Association, Garrett Coliseum; Junior League Annual Rummage Sale, City Hall; Montgomery Art Guild's First National Bank Show. *October*—South Alabama Fair, Garrett Coliseum; Montgomery Art Guild's South Alabama Show, Coliseum. *November*—Southern Championship Charity Horse Show, Coliseum; Alabama Art League Jury Show, Museum of Fine Arts; Woman's Medical Society Auxiliary's Countywide Antique Show, Fort Dixie Graves Armory. *December*—Holiday House Tour, Federation of Garden Clubs; Blue-Gray Football Classic, Cramton Bowl; Jaycee Christmas Pageant, Coliseum; Christmas Trees around the World Exhibit, Museum of Fine Arts; Christmas Program for Children, Montgomery Civic Ballet, at Sidney Lanier Auditorium.

MONTGOMERY (160-303 alt., 133,386 pop. 1970; 134,393, 1960) is the capital of Alabama and seat of Montgomery County (167,790 pop.). It was incorporated in 1819 and is the fourth largest city in the State. Considered typically southern in its appearance, Montgomery has a special place in southern memories of the Confederacy, for it was here that the provisional government of the Confederate States of America was formed by seven seceding states on February 4, 1861; Jefferson Davis was inaugurated provisional president, and the government met until its removal to Richmond (*see History*).

Montgomery is built on several hills that slope gradually toward the business section. The principal streets radiate from Court Square, which has been undergoing extensive reconstruction, but, with the McMonnies foundation erected in 1885 and fed from an artesian well, still the hub around which traffic will move. The wide, tawny Alabama River, which has shaped the character, business and interests of Montgomery, flows along the northwestern edge and is but a stone's throw from the heart of the business district.

Still the key to Montgomery's economic growth, the Alabama-Coosa River Development is one of the largest river systems in southeastern United States. It has a watershed of 22,500 square miles and extends from the Blue Ridge Mountains in northern Georgia and Tennessee southward and southwesterly until it forms the Mobile River, 45 miles from the Port of Mobile.

The initial and comprehensive development of this great river system for navigation, hydro-electric power, flood control, recreation and other benefits was authorized by Congress in 1945. Improvement of the Alabama River has been accomplished by construction of three large dams consisting of one navigation lock and dam and two multiple-purpose dams which contain navigation locks and power plants.

When construction of navigation locks through six privately-owned electric power dams on the Coosa River is completed, Montgomery, the largest urban center on the Alabama-Coosa System, is destined for impressive economic growth. In addition to increased commercial river traffic between Montgomery, New Orleans, Chicago, St. Paul, Pittsburgh, and other cities throughout the eastern region, the basins of the rivers contain a variety of minerals and other natural resources that will be utilized for economic benefit.

Rimming the business section and the Capitol complex, are a number of beautifully developed suburban areas, with well-tended spacious lawns and flowering gardens surrounding handsome houses.

The political aspect of the city is as kaleidoscopic as the State's geography and people. The white-domed Capitol on Goat Hill is open every day, whether the legislature is in session or not. When the lawmakers are there, its corridors are thronged. Lobbyists from every corner of Alabama congregate in the marble rotunda. Below the circular stairs those who are merely curious congregate. The Governor's anteroom is open from early morning until late at night. Secretaries welcome every visitor, whether he is a small farmer in some bleak section who wants a stretch of road built to his farm, or an industrialist trying to head off a proposed raw material tax. The scene is as informal as that outside a country church on prayer meeting night.

Montgomery's municipal affairs are directed by three City Commissioners. The President of the Commission serves as Mayor. They are elected for a term of four years. County affairs are handled by a Commission of five members who are also elected for four-year terms.

Montgomery is built on the site of the Indian towns, Ikanatchati and Towasa, on a high red bluff known to the Alibamu Indians as Chunnanuga Chatty. That the territory was thickly settled is indicated by the numerous mounds and burial sites in the surrounding countryside. Hernando De Soto and his gold-hungry Spaniards, who passed near here in the autumn of 1540, were the first Europeans to visit the region. The first white man to live in the vicinity was James McQueen, a Scotch trader, who came in 1716. When the Alabama lands were offered for sale in 1817, two groups of speculators made their initial payments. One group, a company of Georgians led by General John Scott, first built the town of Alabama, but when the second group, a company of almost penniless New Englanders and

Eastern adventurers, founded the town of Philadelphia, the Georgians abandoned Alabama, and built the town of East Alabama in competition.

A bitter rivalry between the two groups was terminated when the two towns were merged under the name of Montgomery. Incorporated on December 3, 1819, eleven days before Alabama was admitted to the Union, Montgomery was named in honor of Major General Richard Montgomery of Revolutionary fame, who lost his life in the Arnold expedition against Quebec. Montgomery County had been named three years earlier in honor of Major Lemuel P. Montgomery, who was killed in the Battle of Horseshoe Bend while serving with Andrew Jackson in the Creek War.

In 1821 the first steamboats to reach Montgomery arrived from Mobile, a stage line was established to the East, and Jonathan Batelle began publishing a newspaper, the Montgomery *Republican*.

One of the highlights in the town's early history was the visit of Lafayette in 1825. A guard of honor, 300 strong, journeyed eastward to the banks of the Chattahoochee and escorted Lafayette the remainder of the way. Some of the pomp of the triumphal entry was spoiled by the presence of curious Indians, now bereft of their ancestral lands. Lafayette's secretary thought them "very pitiable creatures." The Marquis reached Montgomery on April 2 and marched from the river bank up Goat Hill, where the Capitol now stands, while the band played Hail to the Chief. Governor Israel Pickens waited with a welcoming speech, but in the presence of this august guest his voice failed him. Lafayette had the use of John Edmundson's fine home; on the second night of his visit, festivities rose to a climax with a grand ball at Freney's Tavern.

A branch of the State Bank, organized in 1832 with John Gindrat as president, stimulated business and several real estate companies became active. In 1834 the Montgomery Railroad Company was chartered by the legislature with a capital of $1,000,000, to build a road to West Point, Georgia. Ground was broken on February 2, 1836. The road, completed in the spring of 1851, became an important link in the trunk line between New York and New Orleans.

From the first days of settlement, cotton production had been the chief economic interest. The first commercial gin in the State was installed by Abram Mordecai, a Pennsylvania veteran of the Revolution, on the eastern river bluff below the junction of the Tallapoosa and the Coosa, in 1802.

On January 30, 1846 the legislature had voted to remove the State capital from Tuscaloosa to Montgomery after a stubborn fight of many years. The first legislative session convened in the new capital December 6, 1847. George Nichols, a Philadelphia architect, designed the Capitol, which stood at the head of Market Street (now Dexter Avenue). The Capitol burned two years later but was rebuilt in 1851 according to the original plans.

Nowhere in the South was the hostility to Northern abolitionists felt more keenly than in this capital of agrarian Alabama. The secession movement gained momentum rapidly and the Secession Convention convened in Montgomery January 6, 1861. On February 4, representatives of six seceding States assembled in Montgomery and chose that city as provisional capital of the Confederate States of America. On February 9, Jefferson Davis by a unanimous vote was elected President of the Confederacy. Nine days later he arrived for his inauguration, and was introduced by William Lowndes Yancey from the balcony of the Exchange Hotel, with the words, "The man and the hour have met." That night a torchlight parade moved down Market Street. On March 4, the Stars and Bars were raised above the Capitol by Letitia Tyler, granddaughter of former President Tyler. The flag was designed by Nicola Marschall, of Marion, Alabama.

Montgomery did not long remain the capital of the Confederacy. In order to shorten the line of communication between armies in the field and military headquarters, the resolution terminating the first session of the Provisional Congress directed that it should reassemble in two months in Richmond, Virginia.

Devotion to the Confederate cause remained steadfast in Montgomery even after disaster had swept over the Southern Army. General James Wilson's Federal raiders entered the city on April 12, 1865. The public records of the State had been taken by wagon train to Eufaula, and more than 100,000 bales of Confederate cotton had been burned lest they fall to the invader. This costly bonfire was Alabama's last gesture of defiance in the waning moments of war. The Union troops burned the small arms factories, rolling stock of the railroads, and five steamboats.

The Reconstruction period was difficult. The city's accumulated wealth had been swept away, articles of common use were scarce, stores were empty, and farms and homes were devastated. Means of transportation by steamer and by rail had been destroyed.

Recovery was slow and painful, but in the 1880s railroad expansion throughout the country improved conditions in Montgomery. Its geographic location and the fact that it was the State capital made it an important center, and highways as well as railrods soon connected the city with other sections. Nearness to the most productive agricultural regions of the State also contributed to its rapid growth. In 1885 an electric trolley car system was installed. The first large lumber mill was established in 1890, and by 1900 textile and garment factories, cotton processing plants, and fertilizer factories were built. Montgomery is still an economic focal point for cotton farmers, though in recent years livestock and dairying interests have taken first place. In addition, Montgomery is a center for packing plants, furniture, chemicals, food processing, and building materials. Manufactured products include lumber, concrete, brick, art stone and tile, and proprietary medicines.

Just as the Alabama River has influenced the character and economy of Montgomery, so has the presence of Maxwell Air Force Base and Gunter Air Force Base had impressive effects on the city. This began in 1910 when Wilbur Wright established the Wright Flying

School with only two aviation students, a mechanic and one airplane. He closed his school in the summer of that year and returned to Ohio, but eight years later the United States Govenment acquired the land. The area, operated as a repair depot, consisted of some 300 acres and 52 buildings, a sharp contrast to Maxwell AFB today, which has 650 buildings on 2,423 acres.

In 1920, the Aviation Repair Depot was redesignated Montgomery Air Intermediate Depot, and in 1922 it was renamed Maxwell Field in honor of 2nd Lt. William C. Maxwell of Atmore, Ala., who died in an airplane accident in the Philippines.

The Air Corps Tactical School was transferred to Maxwell in the spring of 1931 and troops arrived at the field in the summer of that year. It was at this school that Lt. Gen. Claire L. Chenault developed and taught his pursuit tactics and Gen. Lawrence S. Kuter pioneered bombardment aviation.

The Southeastern Air Corps Training Center took over the TAC school facilities in 1940 for training Air Corps cadets assigned to bases in the southeastern part of the country. Also, in that year, Gunter Field, named for Montgomery Mayor William Gunter, longtime aviation supporter, was activated as a basic flying school for American aviators and cadets from Britain, France and other allied countries.

In 1945, the facility became the Air University, with three major schools: Air Command and Staff College, Squadron Officer School, and Air War College. Among other educational and research organizations under Air University are: Aerospace Studies Institute, Air Force Chaplain School, Academic Instructor and Allied Officer School, Air Force ROTC, the Extension Course Institute at Gunter, and the Air Force Institute of Technology at Wright-Patterson AFB, Ohio. Headquarters, Civil Air Patrol, also is based at Maxwell.

The 3800th Air Base Wing supports logistically the activities located at Maxwell and Gunter and operates the two bases.

The Air Force Data Systems Design Center was transferred from the Washington, D.C. area to Gunter AFB during 1971. It employs approximately 900 military and civilian personnel. Established on Oct. 26, 1967, as a separate operating agency of the U. S. Air Force, the Design Center has the responsibility for designing standard automated data systems assigned by the USAF Headquarters and combines data systems design activities formerly assigned to various Air Staff agencies. A new addition to the General Muir S. Fairchild Library, the Air University library, will house the USAF Historical Archives, now located in an old building at Maxwell. The more than 1,000,000 documents that make up the archives are mostly histories of U. S. Air Force units from all over the world and span the history of the Air arm from 1907 to the Space Age of today.

POINTS OF INTEREST

COURT SQUARE FOUNTAIN, by Frederick MacMonnies, erected in 1885 in the heart of the downtown business section, remains the hub of Court Square, despite the complete renovation of the area in 1971 as the Court Square Mall. The fountain is near the site of the first County Courthouse (1822), which gave the square its name. Its 25 jets, surrounding a bronze life-size female figure, are fed by an artesian spring around which an Indian tribe made its village long before whites settled here. The tribe's prophetess, Chiscoo Telenen (Yellow Bird), according to legend, reported a vision in these words, "I saw a strange people. They are many and strong. Their strength reaches to the very heavens and the source of their strength lies in a stream of clear water flowing from the sun." The fact that Court Square is still the gathering spot for the community, where business transactions take place, campaign speeches are made and celebrations begin, keeps alive the old legend that binds the city's prosperity to the perpetuation of water via the fountain at this spot.

The CAPITOL, on Goat Hill at the east end of Dexter Ave., was designed by George Nichols, Philadelphia architect. The building, constructed of brick covered with stucco and patterned after the National Capitol, ranks among the most beautiful of the Greek Revival capitols built during ante bellum days. Its 97-foot dome, glistening in the sunlight, is visible from many points in the city. The building was originally square, but it has been extended on three sides to accommodate the expanding executive branch of the government and new departments. The rear, or east, wing, was built in 1885; the south wing was added in 1907 and the north wing in 1912. These additions conform to the original design.

The trees and plants of the Capitol grounds bear plates giving their botanical names and historical associations. A garden in the rear of the building has such a variety of roses that there are some in bloom every month of the year. On the north lawn is the Confederate Monument, the cornerstone of which was laid by Jefferson Davis, April 26, 1886. The completed monument, unveiled December 7, 1898, was designed by Gorda C. Doud, a Montgomery artist, and executed by Alexander Doyle. On the south lawn is a bronze statute of Allen Wyeth, noted surgeon and founder of the New York Polyclinic Medical School, by Gutzon Borglum, and a bronze statue of James Marion Sims, the celebrated Montgomery physician, by Biagio Paul Melorangno, of Boston. The Sims statue was placed there by the Alabama Medical Association in 1939. Near by is a boulder commemorating the 100th anniversary of General Lafayette's visit to Montgomery in 1825, and a flagpole made from the mast of a Spanish cruiser sunk at the battle of Santiago in 1898. The flagpole was presented to the State through the efforts of Rear Admiral Richmond Pearson Hobson, of Greensboro, Alabama, naval hero of the Spanish-American War. On the terrace to the left of the capitol steps is a monument of Jefferson Davis, erected by the United Daughters of the Confederacy.

Across from the south portico is Memorial Circle, where flags from all 50 states were placed in 1969.

A portico, with six Corinthian columns and entablature, adorns the main façade of the Capitol. The large timepiece above the entrance, was Montgomery's town clock until 1852. Three flights of steps give access to the entrance portal. On the main (west) portico is the brass, six-pointed Davis Star, unveiled May 20, 1897, marking the spot where Jefferson Davis stood while Howell Cobb of Georgia administered the presidential oath.

The Rotunda is the outstanding interior feature. At each side a spiral cantilever stairway, without visible means of support, winds up two flights. The House and Senate chambers are situated on the second floor. A tablet bears an inscription telling of the origin of the first flag of the Confederacy, known as the Stars and Bars. The upper part of the rotunda is decorated with eight murals by the late Roderick Mac-kenzie, Mobile artist, depicting outstanding events in Alabama history.

In the first floor lobby is a bronze bust of General William Craw-ford Gorgas, Alabama physician who won international fame for his fight against yellow fever. Executed by P. Bryant Baker, New York sculptor, the bust was placed by the State and by the Medical Associa-tion of Alabama on April 20, 1937.

The chamber of the House of Representatives is on the second floor on the right of the hall, and the Senate Chamber is on the left. Voices of many notables have resounded in these rooms, among them Sam Houston, Robert Toombs and William Lowndes Yancey. Portraits of Alabama Governors line the walls of the corridors. (*Open seven days a week, 8-5, except Dec. 24 and 25.*)

The ALABAMA DEPARTMENT OF ARCHIVES AND HISTORY, Adams, Washington and Bainbridge Sts., was completed in 1940 with the aid of WPA funds. It is a three-story structure of steel and concrete, Greek Revival in design, and is one of the group of State buildings designed by Warren, Knight, and Davis, of Birming-ham. Six massive columns on the front façade reach to the second floor. The lobby columns and interior trim are of cream-colored marble. The Department was established in 1901. It has Indian relics, a Military Section, a Music Room, with the score of *Dixie,* played at the inaugura-tion of President Jefferson Davis; the William Rufus King Room, with objects owned by a former U. S. vice president; the French Room, where mementoes of the Vine and Olive Colony are preserved. In the Hall of Fame are enrolled outstanding Alabamians, among them Dr. William Crawford Gorgas, who conquered yellow fever; Julia Strudwick Tut-wiler, educator and social reformer; Dr. Booker T. Washington, founder of Tuskegee Institute; Dr. J. Marion Sims, surgeon and founder of the Women's Hospital in New York; Oscar W. Underwood, statesman. *Open 5 days a week 8-4:30; half days Sat.-Sun.*

The FIRST WHITE HOUSE OF THE CONFEDERACY, 625 Washington St., was the Montgomery home of Jefferson Davis and his family during their brief stay in 1861. This two-story, white frame house with green shutters was built about 1825 by William

Sayre; A. M. Bradley was the architect. It was formerly located on the southwest corner of Bibb and Lee Sts., and moved to its present location in 1921.

The building now houses war relics, including General Lee's compass, President Davis' sword, and the round table on which Davis wrote *The Rise and Fall of the Confederate Government.* Here are some of Davis' personal belongings from his home at Beauvoir, Mississippi; a bedspread made for him by a group of Southern women, each crocheting one shell, and oil paintings of Mrs. Napoleon Lockett who inspired the Confederate flag, Nicola Marschall who designed it, Mrs. Jefferson Davis, and Winnie Davis, daughter of the president. *Open weekdays, 9-4:30; half days Sat.-Sun.*

The STATE HIGHWAY BUILDING, sw. corner Bainbridge St. and Dexter Ave., is a three-story modified V-shaped building of modern design, derived from the Greek Revival, erected with the aid of WPA funds. The exterior is of monolithic concrete and sandstone with poured concrete construction throughout. Completed in 1937, the structure was designed by Warren, Knight and Davis, of Birmingham. *Open weekdays 8:30-4:30, Sat. 8:30-12.*

The STATE JUDICIAL BUILDING, 415 Dexter Ave., designed by Hyman W. Whitcover, Georgia architect, as the Scottish Rite Temple, was completed in 1926. It is a three-story building of reinforced concrete, brick, and Indiana limestone, originally designed in the modern mode with Egyptian mosque motif, since changed to the classical. In 1932 the temple was sold to the State, and in 1938 it was converted into a building to house the Supreme Court and Appellate Court of Alabama, the attorney general's office, and a law library. The new façade is of Alabama limestone. *Open Mon.-Fri., 8:30-4:30; Sat. 8:30-12.*

The WINTER BUILDING, on Court Square Mall, was erected in 1841 by John Gindrat, an early Montgomery settler. Though remodeled and modernized in 1939, much of the original remains. It was an early Victorian frame structure with several porches supported by slender posts. These were removed and the building was painted white, but the deep overhanding eaves and corniced windows are much as they were in 1861, when the offices of the Southern Telegraph Company were located here. From a corner room on the second floor, Leroy Pope Walker, Confederate Secretary of War, sent his famous message to General Beauregard, giving his discretionary power to open fire on Fort Sumter. The building houses shops and offices. *Open weekdays, 8:30-6.*

The HILL BUILDING, 21 S. Perry St., was formerly the infirmary of Dr. J. Marion Sims. The Montgomery County Medical Association has placed a marker commemorating Dr. Sims near the entrance. The building later housed the offices of Dr. L. L. Hill, who attained renown as the first surgeon to operate successfully on the human heart. His son, Lister Hill, represented Alabama 46 years in the U. S. Congress, first as Representative and then for five terms as Senator. A former Alabama Governor, John Patterson, located his law offices in the building.

The LOMAX HOUSE, 235 S. Court St., is a three-story Greek Revival structure of brick, painted cream color, with white columns across the front, and green shutters. The house was built about 1848 by James J. Gilmer, brother of George R. Gilmer, former Governor of Georgia, and of Mrs. Sophia Bibb, remembered for her ardent work for the Confederacy. Gilmer deeded the property to Reuben C. Shorter, Jr., brother of John Gill Shorter, war-time Governor of Alabama. In 1867 the widow of Reuben C. Shorter married Tennant Lomax and the mansion became known as the Lomax residence. Now the offices of an insurance company, it is listed in the Historic American Buildings Survey.

The PICKETT HOUSE, 2 Clayton St., was built in the late 1830's by slave labor under direction of John P. Figh. A porch and balustrade have been added, and the structure now has white trim and green blinds. The dining room floor is made of stone blocks from the first capitol at Montgomery, salvaged after the destruction of the building by fire in 1849. The property was purchased in 1958 by the historian, Albert J. Pickett. It was later owned and occupied by the Barnes School for Boys, but is now a paint shop.

The SEIBELS HOUSE, now the Scottish Rite Temple, 405 Adams St., was built in 1845. Colonel John J. Seibels, a South Carolinian, was appointed United States Minister to Belgium in 1855. The house, resembling old Charleston houses in design, stands about 60 feet back from the street.

The TEAGUE HOUSE, 468 S. Perry St., now the Alabama State Chamber of Commerce, a two-story Greek Revival mansion built in 1848, has a columned portico and second floor balcony, and slave quarters in the rear of the brick-walled courtyard. General J. H. Wilson, who brought his raiders to Montgomery in the spring of 1865, was quartered here with his staff, and from the porch read President Lincoln's Emancipation Proclamation to a throng of Negroes. *Open 8:30-4:45, weekdays; free.*

The EVANS HOUSE, 535 S. Hull St., is a gray painted, simple cottage built in 1853 by John M. Nowell. In the front room a model was cut out for the first State flag of Alabama, designed by J. W. A. Samford, III, and adopted by legislative act of February 16, 1895.

The GOVERNOR'S MANSION, 1142 South Perry St., built by Gen. Robert F. Ligon Jr., in 1907, was sold by his heirs to the State of Alabama in 1950. It is Greek Revival design, with four towering Corinthian columns across the front. A second-story balcony with ornate balustrade, a handsome porte-cochere, arched windows and window balconies add to its impressiveness. Inside, a handsome staircase, parquet floors, Greek style medallions and cornices are attractive features. Splendid chandeliers are over the staircase and in the dining room. The furniture is Victorian and was designed by a Montgomery cabinet maker.

The MUSEUM OF FINE ARTS, 440 South McDonough St., adjoining the Public Library, is the oldest fine arts museum in Alabama. Originating in a condemned school building in 1930, it moved to its present site in 1959. All the galleries are on one floor of the H-shaped structure. Its permanent collections are supplemented by traveling exhibitions, special group and individual shows. Lectures, films and concerts are offered throughout the year. *Open Tuesday through Saturday, 10-5, Sunday 2:30-5.*

The MURPHY HOUSE, Bibb and Coosa Sts., an impressive Greek Revival mansion was restored in 1970 to its original condition. Erected by John H. Murphy, its interior is rich in detail, with many of the original furnishings. Both Jefferson Davis and William L. Yancey were frequent visitors. When the Union Army came into Montgomery, the house was taken as headquarters. Many Confederate officers surrendered their troops and petitioned for pardon here.

The CODY HOUSE, 504 South Perry St., one of three antebellum homes at the intersection of High and Perry Streets, stands on the southwest corner. Built before 1830, its architecture is a meld of Federal and Greek Revival styles, with an Adamesque front door frame. Although built as a small town house for a planter, a magnificent dining room, 42 feet in length with a 25-foot-high ceiling, was added later. Descendants of Michael Cody, who bought the house in 1899, still live there.

The WASHBURN HOUSE, 505 South Perry St., built in 1836, was a wedding gift to Mary Ann Stubbs by her father, Beytop Stubbs, when she became the bride of Elliot Cromwell Hannon. Of Dutch Colonial design, this home was the center of much social activity. The Teasley family was also one of the owners. A circular staircase and fine antiques are special attractions.

The TYSON HOUSE, 423 Mildred St., was built in the 1830s on a three-acre lot by the McBryde family. Listed in the Historic American Buildings Survey, this fine example of southern architecture has four square columns across the front, small upper balcony, front, side and back porches. One of its owners was Maj. William Wallace Screws, southern editor. In 1889 it was purchased by John Tyson and has been in his family since.

The DICKERSON-ARNOLD-GREIL HOUSE, 305 South Lawrence St., headquarters of the Junior League of Montgomery, Inc., was built 1854-1856 by John P. Dickerson and was occupied by Gov. John G. Shorter, 1861-63. David S. Arnold bought the house in 1865 and 13 years later it was sold at public auction to Mrs. Mena Greil. The original exterior was of Italianate design, with later additions showing Greek and Roman influences. Consoles supporting the lintels of the windows and doors are carved cast iron with an acanthus leaf pattern. Double parlors have Italian marble mantels. Painted paneling in the dining room and Victorian gingerbread carving on the stairway are other interesting features.

The THOMAS HOUSE, 3175 Thomas Ave., called Edgewood, is Montgomery's oldest residence. Built in 1821 by Zachariah T. Watkins on Woodley St., it was dismantled in 1832, timber by timber, and moved to its present site, a 300-acre land grant from President Andrew Jackson. It has been occupied by descendants of John Gregory Thomas since he inherited it in 1861. It is neo-classical Greek Revival architecture.

The FALCONER HOUSE, 428 South Lawrence St., was formerly located on South Perry St., in what was known as New Philadelphia. Constructed 1840-1845 by John Falconer, Montgomery's first postmaster, it is now occupied by the Young Women's Organization. *Open weekdays, 9-4:30.*

BLUE MOON INN, 1816 Goode St., a five-room, L-shaped frame cottage of Early American design, was accidentally purchased by John Dowe in 1869. As he passed the fountain in Court Square, he waved a greeting to a friend who was conducting a property auction. Later in the day, the friend told Dowe that his bid was the high one. Although three wings have been added since Miss Leila Dowe converted it into one of Alabama's favorite resaurants, the original house with hand-hewn timbers joined with wooden pegs, has been preserved in its original state.

The DOWE HOUSE, 334 Washington Ave., of Greek Revival architecture, has undergone several alterations since its erection in 1862. A large two-story structure of wood and brick, it was the first house of its size in Montgomery to have an inside kitchen and the first to have a bathroom. It has been continually occupied by the same family.

The W. A. GAYLE PLANETARIUM, 1010 Forrest Ave., in the Oak Park section of Montgomery, was opened in 1958. It has a Space Transit instrument built by the Spitz Laboratories, a 50-ft. inner dome, and seats for 236. It is able to reproduce all the star phenomena of times past, present, and future, and in accordance with knowledge gained in recent years it reproduces the earth as seen from outer space, and with auxiliary projectors simulates the sensations associated with travel on a space craft, and moon walks. One-hour programs are given regularly. The Planetarium is operated jointly by Troy State University in Montgomery and the City of Montgomery.

HUNTINGDON COLLEGE, 1500 East Fairview Ave., was founded in 1854 as the Tuskegee Female College. It was moved to its present location in the heart of one of the most attractive residential areas of Montgomery in 1909. When it became a coeducational school, the name was changed to Huntingdon, in honor of the Countess of Huntingdon, an active member in the Wesleyan movement. It is a Methodist operated college.

ALABAMA STATE UNIVERSITY, 915 South Jackson St., founded in 1874, is the oldest predominantly Negro institution of higher education in the State of Alabama. In the 1973 school year it enrolled 3,272 students and had a faculty of 127.

AUBURN UNIVERSITY AT MONTGOMERY, Bell Road and Int. 85, was established by the Alabama Legislature in 1967. First buildings on the new 500-acre campus were opened in 1971.

The CRAMPTON BOWL, 1022 Madison Ave., built in 1922, is one of Alabama's largest stadias. Built of solid steel and concrete, its sunken-bowl athletic field is used for major collegiate football games. It was named in honor of Fred Crampton, donor of the site.

ST. JOHN'S EPISCOPAL CHURCH, ne. corner Madison Ave. and N. Perry St., built in 1855, is a brick and stucco structure of English Gothic design with limestone trim. President Davis worshiped here and a bronze tablet marks his pew. In the nave are 15 memorial windows, 6 of them in the chancel. The great chimes consist of 9 bells, the largest weighing 1,045 pounds. Bishop Nicholas Hamner Cobbs, previously rector of St. Paul's Church, Cincinnati, served as rector until he died just before the opening of the War between the States. When Federal troops entered Montgomery the commanding officer remembered Bishop Cobbs as his former minister in Cincinnati and ordered a special guard placed about this church. Bishop Wilmer, Bishop Cobbs' successor, advised his parishioners to pray for the President of the Confederacy instead of the President of the United States. Federal troops closed the church but services continued in private homes.

ALABAMA CHRISTIAN COLLEGE, one-half mile from intersection of Eastern Bypass on the Atlanta Highway, was established in 1942 as an independent liberal arts junior college. The E.L. Cullom Rotunda houses offices, 13 large classrooms, two conference rooms and an auditorium. A master plan calls for increasing the present seven buildings to 16 on the 92-acre campus. In 1973 it enrolled 232 students.

ST. PETER'S ROMAN CATHOLIC CHURCH, 219 Adams Ave., was erected in 1852 on the site of a church, dedicated in 1834. Of Spanish architecture, its stained glass windows portray stories and scenes from the Old and New Testaments. In keeping with recommendations of the Vatican Council, an Altar of Sacrifice has been placed in front of the old altar that depicts the Holy Family, so that the priest may face the congregation.

The CURB MARKET, 1004 Madison Ave., begun in 1927 on another site, was moved to its present indoor location in 1946. Booths are laden with fresh or home canned fruits and vegetables, many dairy products, flowers, plants and some arts and crafts. *Open Tuesday, Thursday, Saturday, 5-5.*

The ALABAMA PUBLIC LIBRARY SERVICE, 64 N Union St., reported a stock of 3,682,154 vols. and a circulation of 15,550,777 in 1974. MONTGOMERY PUBLIC LIBRARY, 445 S. Lawrence

St., with a branch at 1275 Cleveland Ave., offers paintings and records as well as books for its borrowers. Special services include a bookmobile, inter-library loans, and a summer reading program for children. The MONTGOMERY COUNTY LIBRARY is located at 142 Washington Ave.

The OLD MONTGOMERY THEATER (Webber Company Department Store), 39 North Perry St., erected in 1860, was site of many famous productions as Montgomery was on the direct route from Washington to New Orleans. On its walls, Herman Frank Arnold, a Montgomery musician, wrote in charcoal the notes to "Dixie" as its composer, Daniel D. Emmett, an Ohio minstrel man, hummed it.

GARRETT COLISEUM, Federal Drive and Highway 31, North, rises from the ground like a huge turtle. Completed in 1953, it was built as an educational and promotional aid for agriculture, with a seating capacity of 13,500. In addition to the main building, there are cattle and livestock barns and a show and sale barn.

JUNIUS BRAGG SMITH THEATER, 432 South Goldthwaite St., is an excellent example of Carpenters' Gothic architecture. Begun in the 1860s and completed in 1888, it was the Episcopal Church of the Holy Comforter until 1958. At that time it was bought by the Montgomery Little Theater, Inc. This self-supporting group presents five or more plays a year, and a summer musical runs from mid-July into August.

The ORDEMAN-SHAW HOUSE, at Hull St. and Jefferson Ave., is the structure in the HULL STREET HISTORIC DISTRICT, which occupies the 200 block of North Hull St., and is a restoration of the 1850-55 period, when Montgomery was a boom town. It was restored by the Landmarks Foundation, which administers the property as a museum for the city of Montgomery. Unlike the many pillared houses of the South this is a product of a turn to Italianate in domestic architecture and the only survivor in Montgomery of numerous houses of that style built in the 1850s. It was built in 1848 by Charles C. Ordemann, a German immigrant who prospered as city surveyor, architect and engineer, and who introduced the city's first gas lights. Authentic furnishings have been installed. The courtyard has a group of service buildings, including a kitchen and scullery, and slave quarters built in 1852. Diagonally from the house is the DeWOLF-COOPER COTTAGE, (1856), 309 N. Hull St., where admission tickets to the Ordeman-Shaw House may be purchased (*Adults, $1.25; students, 6-18, 50¢; children under 6 free.*) The Tourist Information Center is in the CAMPBELL-HOLTZCLAW HOUSE (1852) 210 N. Hull St., where a film, *A Visit to 1850,* is shown and tour information may be obtained. (*Tours daily except Monday*).

The VETERANS ADMINISTRATION has its Alabama headquarters in the Regional Office, 474 South Court St., which handles benefits for 421,000 Alabama veterans and their dependents. Alabama veterans include some 375,000 of the Vietnam period. Disability compensation is paid to 37,271, and pensions go to 20,896 others of insufficient income. In 1974 the Regional Office granted loans to 6,573, while 56,000 held G. I. insurance policies with a face value of $465,095,000. Under the G. I. Bill 39,501 veterans and servicemen received training in 1974.

The VETERANS ADMINISTRATION HOSPITAL, is located on a 57-acre wooded reservation at 215 Perry Hill Road, five miles east of Downtown Montgomery. It has 15 permanent buildings begun in 1940. About 4,000 patients are admitted annually and 50,000 veterans receive out-patient service. There are 365 professional and service employees. The hospital is affiliated with St. Margaret's School of Nursing; with the University of Alabama and Huntingdon College for social work trainees, and with the School of Pharmacy of Auburn University. This is one of four Veterans Administration hospitals in Alabama, the others being in Tuscaloosa, Birmingham, and Tuskegee.

Selma

Airport: Selfield, municipally owned airport, has three paved runways, one 5,800 feet, which is lighted, and two 4,400 feet. There is no commercial service available at Selfield, but Dannelly Field, 40 miles east of the city on US 80, sw of Montgomery, has regularly scheduled flights by Delta; Southern, and Eastern Airlines. Selfield Flying Service provides transit service and maintenance to private aircraft. Charter service is available.

Highways: US 80, State 8, 14, 22 and 41 and a network of hard-surfaced farm-to-market roads radiate in all directions.

Railroads: Southern Railway System; Louisville & Nashville R.R. Co., and Western Railway of Alabama provide freight and limited passenger service.

Buses: Southeastern Greyhound and Capital Trailways operate scheduled runs.

Waterways: The Alabama River, adjacent to the south corporate limits of Selma provides a water route from Selma to the Gulf of Mexico via the Tombigbee and Mobile Rivers. Miller Ferry Lock operates eight hours per day seven days a week, 7 a.m. to 3 p.m. The river is open to navigation from Selma to Mobile, with a permanent 9-foot channel for inland waterway traffic. A 400,000 bushel grain elevator is leased by Alabama State Inland Docks to the Bunge Corp.

Motor Freight: Six major motor truck lines along with REA and UPS serve Selma on a direct basis. Five moving and storage companies operate in the city.

Accommodations: Nine motels have 325 rooms.

Information: Selma Chamber of Commerce; Selma *Time-Journal,* daily except Saturday; four radio stations, including one FM; Cablevision Service.

Health Services: Three hospitals with 307 beds; three nursing homes, with 147 beds.

Schools: Eleven public schools, including two junior and one senior high schools; 4 parochial schools; Selma University, Lutheran Academy, John T. Morgan Academy, the George C. Wallace State Junior College, and Technical Institute.

Library: Carneige Library has 25,575 volumes.

Recreation: Dallas County Public Lake and Recreation Park 15 miles south on State 41; Valley Creek State Park and Lake and Camp Grist, 17 miles north; Memorial Stadium, capacity 9,822 plus 6,000 temporary bleacher seats; two movie theaters and two drive-ins; baseball park, bowling lanes; two country clubs; public golf course; YMCA and Health Club; Municipal swimming pool; 4 municipal fishing ponds; year-around hunting nearby; 15 tennis courts; a Senior Citizens' Center; Teenage Recreation Center; a marina nearby on Alabama River.

Government: Mayor and Council.

Annual Events: Columbia Concert Series during the winter; Marching Band Festival and Christmas Parade, both sponsored by the Chamber of Commerce; Horse Show usually in the Spring at Bloch Park.

SELMA (147 alt., 27,379 pop. 1970; 28,385, 1960; dec. 3.5%), the seat of Dallas County, occupies a high bluff on the north bank of the Alabama River. Modern as are some of its aspects, an ante bellum atmosphere that the march of progress has not destroyed is still evident. Ante bellum homes and old buildings erected not long after Lafayette visited the town in 1825, stand side by side with more recently built houses. In the downtown district are new business structures, sprawling cotton warehouses, and churches singularly beautiful in design.

Selma's central location in the state and excellent transportation facilities have made it an important distribution center. Its wholesale trade is a significant business activity, and its more than 50 industries, large and small, help create its prosperity.

The Selma and Dallas County Chamber of Commerce has established a 154-acre industrial park within the city limits and adjacent to rail and truck terminals. Another 285 acres of land has been set aside by the City of Selma and Dallas County for a second of these industrial compounds.

Selma, like so many of Alabama's cities, is a fascinating meld of the new and the old. Its site was first known to white in 1540, when Hernando De Soto spent about 20 days in the vicinity. In 1702 the Sieur de Bienville, founder of Mobile, ventured upriver and repulsed a band of Indians here, but the site was not recorded on the map until 1732, when D'Anville designated it as Ecor Bienville, or Bienville Bluff.

No area recalls the Old South more forcefully than this Black Belt region where cotton was absolute monarch and great plantations reached out toward the horizon. Cradled in the rich fields lies Selma, once the industrial center of Alabama and a critical holding in the War Between the States.

Here were the Confederate navy yard, naval foundry, rolling mills, arsenal, powder works and magazine. It is estimated that half the cannon and two-thirds the fixed ammunition used by Confederates in the last two years of the War were made in Selma foundries and factories. In the shipyard naval vessels of sturdy construction took shape—including the armored ram *Tennessee,* which withstood the shot and shell of Farragut's fleet in the Battle of Mobile Bay. Government establishments alone covered 5 acres and employed 6,000 men.

Selma was Gen. J. H. Wilson's prime target, when with 13,500 Federal troops he set out from north Alabama. Splitting forces at Elyton (now in Birmingham), Wilson dispatched Croxton and his division to Tuscaloosa, while he led 9,000 troops to Selma. In earthworks about the city he encountered Gen. Nathan Redford Forrest with

3,000 soldiers, home guards and civilians. The city fell by nightfall. Forrest escaped with 200-300 men and the Federal pillaged the town.

Wilson's men got drunk on barrels of government whisky, which the Confederates did not have time to destroy. Ignoring their general's orders against plundering, Federals robbed, burned, killed mules and horses, intimidated and murdered. Personal property went the way of legitimate war booty and Selma was left in ruins.

Two granite monuments commemorate the site of the Confederate Arsenal, Water Avenue at Church Street. Stone taken from the Arsenal's ruins built in 1869 the Gothic church, Our Lady of the Assumption, 413 Washington Street. The Naval Foundry Monument marks the site where the rams *Tennessee, Gaines, Morgan* and *Selma* were built. Their guns were also cast here.

The city was slow to recover from the devastation of war. The resources of the planters were destroyed. At the close of the Reconstruction some of the planters turned again to cotton growing, but they never recaptured their pre-war afluence. When the cotton market plummeted at the end of the century, they turned to diversified agriculture. Today's top crops are livestock products, cotton, and soybeans, which along with timber sales produce for Dallas County an average annual income of $17,000,000.

Dallas County farmers own and operate an efficient commercial fertilizer cooperative and a complete seed-cleaning plant equipped to process clovers, legumes and grass seed. There is a farmers' feed cooperative at Marion Junction, 15 miles from Selma on US 80. A vast forest acreage in the county is producing pine and hardwood.

CRAIG AIR FORCE BASE, located about 4½ miles northeast from downtown Selma, adds much to the city's economy. The base has grown from 12 army tents in a cotton field into one of the key installations of the United States Air Force's Air Training Command. When first activated as Selma Army Air Base on Aug. 4, 1940, it was assiged the mission of providing advanced flying training for Army Corps cadets. Craig is still charged with the mission of producing pilots.

The first contingent of 120 army personnel, under the command of Col. Vincent B. Dixon, arrived on Aug. 5, 1940. Shortly thereafter the name was changed to Craig Field, in honor of Lt. Bruce K. Craig, a Selmian killed while serving as a flight test engineer at San Diego, Calif.

By the end of World War II more than 9,000 pilots had been graduated from Craig. In June, 1946, Craig Field was assigned to conduct the Special Staff School as part of the university developed by the USAF; its function was to train squadron and group staff officers. During the Korean War more than 4,000 instructors were graduated and 700 American and Allied airmen received their wings at Craig. By 1955 the school was fully jet-equipped. In March, 1961, the Undergraduate Pilot Training Program was begun. Today, both American and foreign students have 48 weeks in which to complete their training. The program includes instruction in the propellor-driven T-41 aircraft, at Selfield Municipal Airport by civilian instructors; and in the jet-powered T-37, and T-38 aircraft, both at Craig. This training leads to the silver wings of a pilot, and reassignment into operational units of the Air Force.

Educational facilities have been greatly expanded in recent years. There are 11 public schools, including two junior and one senior high schools; four parochial and three private schools. SELMA UNIVER- SITY, established in 1878 by the Alabama Baptist Colored Convention but now supported by the Alabama State Baptist Convention, has courses for teachers and manual training, and gives a bachelor of theology degree. In 1974 it enrolled 321 and had a faculty of 23. The Lutheran Academy offers instruction from first grade through junior college, and the John T. Morgan Academy has courses from kindergarten through the tenth grade.

After a State junior college was built in 1970-71 on the same campus with the William A. King State Technical Institute, the name was changed to The George C. Wallace State Junior College and Technical Institute. The same president and governing body have charge of operating the two facilities. Students are transported by buses from a six-county area to the Institute at an average cost of $15 monthly, including tuition and transportation. Basic liberal arts preparatory courses are offered at the two-year Junior College, with credits transferable to a four-year college. The Junior College also conducts night classes for adults at Craig Air Force Base.

In addition to these educational institutions, there are within a radius of 100 miles, 11 colleges and universities, including the Baptist-supported Judson College at Marion, the State's only college exclusively for women.

POINTS OF INTEREST

LAFAYETTE'S DISEMBARKATION SITE, 1200 Water Ave., is memorialized by a bronze marker on a pillar at the end of the Water Avenue Bridge, near the spot where the general came ashore on his visit to Selma on April 5, 1825.

ST. JAMES HOTEL BUILDING, 1200 Water Ave., for many years the town's most fashionable hostelery, was erected in 1837 and used for a time as a prison for Federal soldiers. Across the front and on one side are balconies ornamented with iron filigree in morning glory design with iron pillars to match, decorations reminiscent of the French influence in New Orleans and Mobile. In 1893 it discontinued operation as a hotel and since then has been used for a variety of purposes, presently as a tire re-capping station.

The NAVAL FOUNDRY MONUMENT, Water Ave. and Sylvan St., marks the site of the Confederate navy yard where the rams, *Tennessee, Gaines, Morgan,* and *Selma* were built. Their guns were also cast here. These vessels without their iron plates were taken down the Alabama River to Mobile; there the iron sheathing was put on and they engaged Farragut's fleet in the Battle of Mobile Bay, August 5, 1864.

The ECOR BIENVILLE BOULDER, Water Ave. and Lauderdale St., marks the site where Bienville met a band of Alibamu Indians in a minor engagement in 1702. An oak, presented to the city on April 23, 1919, by the French government, was planted beside the boulder.

ARSENAL PLACE, intersection of Water Ave. and Church St., is the site of the Confederate arsenal that covered three square blocks extending to Union Street and employed 10,000 workmen. The names of officers in charge are inscribed on monuments.

The BURNS-BENNETT-BELL HOUSE, 412 Lauderdale St., built in the 1840s, is a frame structure with a two-story portico and four square pillars supporting the roof. The entrance transom is decorated with fanlights, and carved wood work in intricate design surrounds door and window facings. Rising from the entrance hall is an unsupported spiral stairway with wide steps and railing of walnut.

The OLD VAUGHAN MEMORIAL HOSPITAL, Alabama Ave. and Union St., built in 1842 as a Masonic School, is a red brick Greek Revival structure, with four plastered iron columns, painted white, supporting the portico. The door and window trim is white marble. The building served as a hospital during the War Between the States, became the Dallas County Courthouse in 1866, and was later used as a school by the Presbyterians. In 1911, it was remodeled as a hospital, and was operated as such until a new Vaughan Memorial Hospital was opened in 1960. Since then the building has been restored by the City. It has a museum, meeting hall, offices for the Boy Scouts and United Appeal, and meeting rooms for civic clubs and patriotic and cultural organizations.

LIVE OAK CEMETERY, on Valley Creek between Dallas and Selma Aves., the oldest burial ground in the city, contains the graves of William Rufus King, General William Hardee, C.S.A., Senator John Tyler Morgan, U. S. Senator Edmund W. Pettus, and Captain Catesby ap R. Jones, C. S. N., hero of the *Merrimac*. Here, also, lies William Murphy, famed in Alabama for his oratory. His powerful plea for a friendless young Frenchman, unjustly accused of crime, elicited the thanks of the King of France. On the grave stone is the tribute: "The blaze of wit, the flash of bright intelligence, the beam of social eloquence sank with his sun."

The JOHN TYLER MORGAN HOUSE, 719 Tremont St., built in the 1850s, is a square white frame house, with six square columns across the front and wide verandas at each floor. In a second story room, General Morgan was fired upon by carpetbaggers. He was an active leader in restoring order after Reconstruction, and served as U. S. Senator from 1877 until his death in 1907.

The DAWSON-VAUGHN HOUSE, 704 Tremont St., was the home of Colonel N. H. R. Dawson, whose wife, Elodie Breck Dawson, was a half-sister of Mrs. Abraham Lincoln. It is a frame building, with two winding staircases and marble mantels.

Pillars and Porches

HISTORIC CENTRAL SECTION OF STATE CAPITOL, MONTGOMERY, BUILT 1851. UNDER MAIN PORTICO JEFFERSON DAVIS WAS SWORN IN AS PRESIDENT OF THE CONFEDERATE STATES OF AMERICA.

GREAT SEAL

TEAGUE HOUSE, MONTGOMERY, BUILT 1848. OFFICES OF ALABAMA STATE CHAMBER OF COMMERCE.

GOVERNOR'S MANSION, MONTGOMERY, BUILT IN 1900.

FIRST WHITE HOUSE OF THE CONFEDERACY, OPPOSITE THE
CAPITOL, NOW A STATE SHRINE.

MODERN COLUMNS OF MONTGOMERY, THE STATE DEPARTMENT
OF ARCHIVES AND HISTORY

BURRITT MUSEUM, NEAR HUNTSVILLE, OLD MANSION IN THE
FORM OF A MALTESE CROSS.

SLIM PILLARS OF TODAY: BIBB GRAVES HALL AT LIVINGSTON
UNIVERSITY

WHITE COLUMNS, NEAR CAMDEN, ALABAMA, BUILT 1860,
COLLECTIONS OPEN TO VISITORS

GAINESWOOD, DEMOPOLIS, COMPLETED 1860 BY GENERAL NATHAN
B. WHITFIELD.

Tuscaloosa

Air Services: Southern Airways, scheduled, and Dixie Air, charter service. Tuscaloosa Municipal Airport, Van DeGraaff Field, has 6,500 ft. lighted jet runway. Major airline terminals are easily accessible in Birmingham, Huntsville, Decatur, Montgomery and Mobile.

Buses: Continental Trailways and Greyhound Bus Lines operate interstate and intrastate schedules.

Highways: Interstate 59 and 20 pass through Tuscaloosa and will ultimately link the area with New Orleans to the southwest and the west, and with other interstate highways leading to all of the major cities of the north, northeast, east and south. Other highways are US 11, 43, and 82, and State routes 13, 69, 76 and 171.

Railroads: The New York-Birmingham-New Orleans main line of the Southern Railway System goes through Tuscaloosa and provides overnight sleeper service to Washington, Baltimore, Philadelphia and New York. Gulf, Mobile & Ohio and Louisville & Nashville provide additional freight service.

Waterways: The Black Warrior River provides a 9-ft. channel, 400-mile waterway from Port Birmingham to Mobile. This is accomplished by a system of locks and dams. In addition to the commercial movement of more than 9,000,000 tons of freight annually, it links Tuscaloosa's pleasure craft with the Gulf of Mexico.

Information and Accommodations: The *Tuscaloosa News,* afternoon and Sunday; The *Graphic,* weekly; Tuscaloosa Area Chamber of Commerce Information Bureau, P.O. Box 430, Tuscaloosa, Ala. 35403; one hotel, The Stafford, 150 rooms; 22 motels, 913 rooms.

Radio and Television: Seven radio stations; one television station; one ETV station operated by the University of Alabama.

Climate: 64°, mean average; 58.8°, Fall and Winter; 76.2°, Spring-Summer average; average annual rainfall, 56.46 inches; 25.5 inches fall and winter; 27.01 spring & summer; growing season, 209 days.

Recreation: Fifteen parks and squares (337 acres) available for city supervised and private programs and events. The upper Warrior River above the Holt dam and lock near Tuscaloosa, and Lake Bankhead, the impounded waters of the Warrior above the final lock and dam, offer many miles of waterways for boating, water skiing and fishing. Many public and private lakes surround the area, which, with the lower reaches of the Warrior River, provide excellent hunting and fishing. A few miles west of the city, Lake Lurleen State Park is being developed for recreation and camping. There are four private golf courses. Tuscaloosa YMCA provides numerous programs, and there are many Little League baseball and football teams.

Entertainment: Tuscaloosa residents share with University of Alabama students numerous musical concerts, plays, ballett, as well as sports contest, particularly football games of the famed University of Alabama's Crimson Tide. (See Education. University of Alabama, Tuscaloosa).

Annual Events: Camellia Show, last weekend in January; Easter Sunrise Service, in Historical Mound State Park, 19 miles southeast of Tuscaloosa, on Highway 69; Heritage Week, including pilgrimage to historical sites and homes, sponsored by Tuscaloosa County Preservation Society, Mid-April; JWA Horse Show, southwide display of thoroughbreds, third week in June; West Alabama Fair, sponsored by Tuscaloosa Jaycees, Inc., last week in September.

TUSCALOOSA (113-230 alt., 65,773 pop. 1970; 63,370, 1960, inc. 3.8%) the seat of Tuscaloosa County (116,029 pop.), once the State capital, occupies a high level plateau at the fall line of the Black Warrior River. It is the urban center of West Alabama, shopping center for the region, medical center and home of the University of Alabama. The University campus is located just east of the center of the city.

Because of the university, the social fiber of the city is youthful. Shops keep the tastes and needs of the young in mind. Town and gown team up to enjoy the cultural offerings and activities centered at the university. Sports, and football in particular, has long been a favorite of all ages, encouraging a healthy, robust kind of life.

University Boulevard and Greensboro Avenue are the two main arteries of the central city. Extending east and south along these broad avenues is a variety of department stores and fashionable shops. Modern shopping plazas ring the inter city, one such center being conveniently located to every residential area.

In the Choctaw Indian language, Tuscaloosa is compounded of two words—*tusko,* meaning warrior, and *loosa,* meaning black. The history of the city dates back to 1809 when a Creek chief, Occechemolta, obtained permission from the government to establish a settlement at the falls of the Warrior River. Known as Black Warrior Town, the settlement prospered as a trading post under the guidance of George S. Gaines, U. S. Agent in the Creek territory. But when the Indians revolted against the whites in 1813, American troops under General John Coffee captured and burned the town. Davy Crockett, frontier scout, was with Coffee and wrote in his autobiography (1834), that the town was "wiped from the face of the earth."

The Creeks were defeated and their leaders surrendered by treaty their claims to lands lying between Alabama and the Black Warrior Rivers. This opened the way to white settlers, who began using a site about two miles north of the destroyed trading post as a camping ground. They called the place Tuskaloosa, and in 1816 Thomas York built a cabin and brought his family from Blount County. By the following year, other houses had been built by settlers who came with their families from Georgia, the Carolinas, and Tennessee. A few of these were professional men and merchants, but the majority were planters of moderate wealth whose slaves cleared the canebrakes from river lowlands, laid out plantations, and planted corn and cotton. In another three years modest frame churches were built by the Baptists and Methodists, a school was opened, and a newspaper, the *American Mirror,* was established.

At this time Judge William R. Smith, Dr. James Gould, John S. Bealle, and other leading citizens predicted that the town was destined to become the State's largest city. It was strategically located in a fertile farming section on a river large enough to afford transportation of cotton, and along the much-traveled trade route that extended from Southern Alabama to Huntsville. When the State capital was established at Cahaba in 1819, Tuscaloosa protested strongly; and in 1825, when floods at Cahaba forced removal of the capital, the town was so determined in its bidding that it won the seat of State government with little opposition.

Almost immediately, new business structures and plantation houses were erected, steamboats began making regular trips to Mobile, and a second newspaper, the *Alabama Sentinel,* was founded. Tuscaloosa now sought to become the educational center of Alabama. In 1829 a school was opened by William Price, and the Sims Female Academy was organized. In 1831 came the establishment of the Tuscaloosa Female Academy, and the University of Alabama. The churches also were active during this period.

During Tuscaloosa's years as State capital (1826-46) a cultured society developed. The planters continued to build huge, columned mansions, for cotton was bringing in enormous profits. Under the guidance of Thomas Maxwell, an Englishman who had come to Tuscaloosa in 1826, rows of water oaks were planted along the streets, and Tuscaloosa was called the City of Oaks, and the Druid City.

Its growth was halted abruptly in 1846 when the State capital was removed to Montgomery. Many business and professional men moved away. It was still, however, a center for the surrounding agricultural region and the home of the State university.

The War between the States exacted a heavy toll. On April 4, 1865, about 1,500 Federal troops under General Croxton seized the bridge on the Black Warrior, and after a brief skirmish with a handful of university cadets, captured the city. Despite the pleas of leading citizens the university buildings were burned. In addition, hundreds of cotton bales were destroyed, and all supplies of possible military value were confiscated.

The city was placed under strict military supervision during Reconstruction. The planters were ruined; many of the manor houses were sold at auction, and some of the larger plantations were broken up. When the Federal blockade was lifted from Mobile Bay, the way for cotton commerce was reopened, but little of the staple passed down the Warrior. Crop failures added to the distress in 1867 and 1868.

Tuscaloosa slowy began to recover in the 1870s. The cotton market became more steady, and the Alabama Great Southern Railroad extended its line into the city. But despite some commercial progress, Tuscaloosa remained agrarian and educational. Until the turn of the century, the city was dependent on agriculture for its economic life. After the Mobile & Ohio Railroad was built in 1898, some attention was given to the development of mineral resources. At the town of Holt, six miles to the north, large-scale coal mining was begun, and within a few years coal mines and iron works were opened near Tuscaloosa.

Over the years the city has enjoyed steady growth and today it has 105 manufacturing establishments employing more than 10,500. The Black Warrior River continues to play an important role in commerce. River development and locks enable barge lines to navigate from the Gulf to Birmingport.

The Tuscaloosa area is served by both city and county school systems. Each of the school systems is governed by a five-man board of education and administered by superintendents appointed by the boards. Each of the senior high schools is fully accredited by the Southern Association of colleges and schools. A well-planned long-range building program has provided the area with excellent school buildings.

Tuscaloosa is a city of churches, with more than 135 within the city limits, representing most denominations.

Tuscaloosa offers a wide variety of outdoor recreation. The upper Warrior River above the Holt Lock and Dam near Tuscaloosa, and Lake Bankhead, the impounded waters of the Warrior above the final lock and dam, offer many miles of excellent waterways for boating, water skiing and fishing. Many lakes surround the area, both public and private, which, together with the lower reaches of the Warrior River, provide excellent hunting and fishing. Lake Lurleen State Park, 12 miles northwest, is one of the new areas for recreation.

Young people find many useful programs, such as those of the Tuscaloosa YMCA, which sponsors a variety of supervised sports. There are many Little League baseball teams and some football teams, which are extremely popular with teenage groups.

THE UNIVERSITY OF ALABAMA

The UNIVERSITY OF ALABAMA, the capstone of the public educational system of the State, is located on an extensive, landscaped campus near the Warrior River, where approx. 160 administrative and functional buildings, athletic centers, and residential halls serve a community of more than 12,000 students, 900 faculty members, and hundreds of employees. University Boulevard, the principal highway from downtown Tuscaloosa, leads to the central axis of the campus, where the Denny Chimes, a brick campanile rising 115 ft., faces the white colonial President's Mansion to the south and the Main Library to the north. The postal address is University, Alabama.

On April 12, 1831, the University opened its doors to 52 male students with a faculty of four. Gorgas House, built in 1829 for a dining hall, is the only relic of the original campus still standing; it is a memorial to General Josiah Gorgas, Confederate Chief of Ordnance, who lived here in 1874 when president of the University. He was the father of General William C. Gorgas. On April 4, 1865, Union troops under Gen. J. T. Croxton burned most of the buildings, sparring the President's Mansion after energetic pleas by the president's wife, Mrs. Lansom C. Garland. The Mansion, built in 1840, is a fine example of colonial design, with six ionic columns, a double winding stair leading to the elevated entrance, and an overhanging iron balcony on the second floor. The University resumed sessions in 1871 and became coeducational in 1892. Racial integration was effected on June 11, 1963. The first Negro graduate, a woman, received a degree in May, 1965.

The University has five colleges: Arts and Sciences, Commerce and Business Administration, Education, Engineering, and the New College. It has five schools: Graduate, Home Economics, Law, Mines, and Social Work. There is a Division of Continuing Education. The New College was added in 1970 and as stated officially "is patterned on the most innovative educational ideas, stressing independent study, individual counselling, and word-study encounters off-campus."

The University has been able to widen its usefulness in recent decades by increasing its physical plant in Tuscaloosa and developing branch campuses in Birmingham and Huntsville. The main library, built in 1940 on the edge of the Central Campus at Captone Drive, received a 1970 addition that doubled the seating capacity of its reading rooms. It is the core of the libraries, which have more than 1,200,000 volumes, 42,000 maps, 3,000,000 manuscripts, and receive 8,000 periodicals. The Education Library Bldg. serves the College of Education and has room for 100,000 volumes. It is adjacent to Graves Hall, which houses that college.

The new Rose Administration Bldg. contains the offices of the President and principal officials. Gordon Palmer Hall, 1968, contains the Departments of Mathematics and Psychology, and the Computer Center. Gallalee Hall has the Departments of Physics and Astronomy. One wing has the Astronomical Observatory with a new 10-inch refracting telescope. The Music and Speech Bldg. (1955) has soundproof teaching studios, a debate workshop, and the University Theatre. The Natatorium (1959) has eight lanes of seven feet each and is suitable for intercollegiate competition. Denny Stadium, recently enlarged, now seats 56,000. It is the home field of the Crimson Tide, the University football team.

The University has greatly improved its facilities for residence. Julia Tutweiler Hall, a women's hall completed in 1968, rises 13 stories on Tenth St. and has a library, study quarters, and a bookstore. The Martha Parham Hall complex, (1963) houses 564 women in two halls; Mary Burke Hall West provides similar facilities. Among the men's residential halls is Mary Burke Hall East, for 282 men.

The Arboretum, 60 acres, is located 3 miles east of the campus and was acquired from the Federal Government in 1958. By gift the University received from Sidney A. Mitchell and his father the Ann Jordan Farm of 5,000 acres in Tallapoosa County for use by faculty members on vacation.

The UNIVERSITY OF ALABAMA PRESS publishes up to 21 scholarly works (hardbound) annually as well as three periodicals and various paperbacks.

Alumni of the University are interested in the restoration of Woods Hall, erected in 1868 as the first new building to rise on the ruins of the university, destroyed by Union troops in 1865. This three-story brick building was planned to contain the classrooms and living quarters for 180 military cadets. For 16 years Woods Hall was truly the university. Journalism and art are now studied in its walls and a coffee shop attracts lively talk along its colonnade.

Across the street from Gorgas House, behind the library is Little Round House, second of the four buildings which survived Federal flames. Ironically the Round House was the only building on campus used for military purposes, being utilized as a guard post. Another of the original buildings is the Old Observatory. The low flat mound in front of the library is the earth-covered rubble of Washington Hall, a domed edifice burned by the Federal Army. Across the grounds stand the Denny Chimes, symbol of the University.

Of special interest to the public is the Museum of Natural History in Smith Hall, which became a part of the University in 1961. Three floors are filled with exhibits. The Museum also supervises the Mound State Monument, at Moundsville, 17 miles south of Tuscaloosa.

Branch campuses of the University are the Medical College of Alabama at Birmingham, opened in 1945, and the University of Alabama at Huntsville. Birmingham has the School of Dentistry (1948), the College of General Studies (1966), the School of Nursing (1967), and a Division of Health Services. At Huntsville the Research Institute of the University is busy with the physical sciences and engineering related to space and missile subjects.

In 1974 the University reported an enrollment of 14,938 students and a faculty of 732 at Tuscaloosa; 9,552 students and 1,074 faculty at Birmingham, and 3,059 students and 175 faculty at Huntsville.

POINTS OF INTEREST

STILLMAN COLLEGE occupies 105 acres at 15th St., between 36th and 38th Sts. It is a four-year coeducational college that gives baccalaureate degrees in the arts and sciences, and has 14 major buildings and 21 residences. The institution is controlled by the United Presbyterian Church in the U.S. It was founded in 1874 by a group of Presbyterians headed by the Rev. Charles Allen Stillman, a Tuscaloosa minister, as a training school for Negro ministers and was opened in 1876 as Tuscaloosa Institute. Dr. Stillman served as its head until 1893 and the school was re-named in his honor. The college was opened to non-ministerial students and later to women. For some years the college also operated a nurses' training school and hospital, but discontinued these in 1947. It became a four-year college in 1949. In the fall, 1973, Stillman had 610 students and had a faculty of 46.

A number of new buildings enlarged the facilities of the college in the 1960s. They included the Myrtle Williamson Memorial Prayer Chapel, which has the sphere as the basic element in its design; the Samuel Burney Hay College Center; the Alexander Batchelor Administration and Classroom Building, and the Martin Luther King, Jr., Hall, a residence for men. A new mathematics-science building designed by Davis, Speake & Associates is one of its latest achievements.

The OLD TAVERN, 2512 5th St., is a two-storied brick structure with hanging balcony. It was built about 1826 for use as an inn. In design it suggests the French houses of Mobile and New Orleans. The original wide-planked pine floors are in good condition. Believed to be the site of the first legislative session in Tuscaloosa after it became the State capital, it has recently been restored by the Tuscaloosa County Preservation Society as a public museum. *Open Tuesday through Sunday, 2-5.*

CAPITAL PARK, bounded by 5th and 6th Sts., and by 28th and 29th Aves., is the site of the old capitol building. When the capital was removed to Montgomery, the structure housed the Central College, a Baptist institution. It was destroyed by fire in 1923, and only an entrance stairway of stone remains. A boulder in the southeast corner of the park, almost hidden by shrubbery, marks the capitol site.

TUSCALOOSA COUNTY COURTHOUSE, Greensboro Ave. and 7th St., is a three-story structure of gray brick (basement included), built in 1907. Stone steps, 30 feet wide, lead to the front entrance. At the front of the building is a granite monolith erected in memory of the Indian Chief Tuskaloosa, who led his poorly equipped warriors against De Soto's Spaniards at Mauvila.

The FRIEDMAN LIBRARY, 1305 Greensboro Avenue, formerly the Jemison House, was built 1860-1862 in Italian Villa style by Robert Jemison, legislator, merchant, and member of the secession convention, 1861. Two-storied masonry, it has slender pillars, thin square colonettes and arched openings between each group of posts.

The SWAIM HOUSE, 2111 14th Street, built 1835-36, is two-storied solid brick construction. Sixteen Ionic columns around three sides support a hipped roof with plain pediment and pilasters in Greek Revival architecture. The front entrance has double doors with side lights, a square transom, original wide board floors and large beams put together with pegs and black marble mantles.

The GOVERNOR'S MANSION, (University Club), 421 18th Avenue, a two-storied brick structure of classic Revival design, was built in 1834 by James H. Dearing, Tuscaloosa merchant. It has the low hip roof, paneled doors, Adam fanlight and Ionic column. A broad veranda extends the full width of the house. In 1833, when

John Gayle was Governor of Alabama, Francis Scott Key was a visitor in the house while negotiating a settlement of Indian claims over lands ceded to the State. Mrs. Gayle wrote of him in her diary, "Mr. Key, the agent of the Government here, interests me greatly. He is a man of much intelligence, a lawyer of high standing, a man of honor, a poet and Christian. He wrote in my daughter's album today. The piece was beautiful."

CHRIST EPISCOPAL CHURCH, Sixth St. and 25th Ave., is a two-story structure of stucco-covered brick, built in 1830. The large, Gothic type windows have memorial panels. The church was organized on January 7, 1828, and is the second oldest congregation of the Episcopal faith in Alabama; Christ Church, at Mobile, was founded a few years earlier.

ST. JOHN'S CATHOLIC CHURCH, 25th Ave. and 8th St., is a brick structure built in 1845 and the first Catholic church in the Tuscaloosa District.

The DRISH BUILDING, 23rd & 18th Street, now used by the Southside Baptist Church, is a two-storied wood structure of Greek Revival style, built before the War between the States. Federal troops captured at the battle of Shiloh were interned here briefly as prisoners of war.

The FRIEDMAN HOUSE, 1010 Greensboro Ave., is a two-storied brick with six square columns and a colonial doorway with two wooden doors and narrow side-lights of cut crystal. The interior ceilings have elaborate frescos. It was built in 1835 by Alfred Battle, purchased by the Friedman family in 1875, and was once home of the Alabama poet, Robert Loveman. *Open Sundays.*

COLLIER-OVERBY HOUSE, 9th Street & 21st Ave., a two-storied wooden Greek Revival structure, was built in the 1820s. It has six square pillars across the front veranda. It was the home of Henry W. Collier as Governor (1849-1853) Chief Justice. Virginia Tunstall, author of *Belle of the Fifties* married Senator Clement Clay here. The first organized charity group in Tuscaloosa started in this house.

GAINESVILLE BANK, North River Hunt Club, the State's oldest bank building, is a one-story frame building, originally built in Gainesville in 1835. Inside is the king of desks, a patent secretary, built by W. S. Wooten in 1874. One of just three made like it, it has one known counterpart, which is in the Smithsonian Institution in Washington. Also inside the old bank is the vault from the old Shelby Iron Works, where office and commissary funds were handled. The building was moved from Gainesville to the North River Hunt Club and restored by the Tuscaloosa County Preservation Society. The old bank and an old church, "sometimes Methodist, sometimes Baptist," are among buildings opening their doors for annual Heritage Week in Tuscaloosa.

The BROWN-JAMES HOUSE, 907 17th Ave., was built in 1835 by Marmaduke Williams, a candidate in the first gubernatorial race in Alabama. It is a two-storied wood frame house, home of Henry Bacon Foster, Tuscaloosa County Judge and home of Admiral Charles R. Brown, Commander-in-Chief of Allied Forces in Europe 1958-62.

The ORMOND-LITTLE HOUSE, 325 Queen City Ave., built in 1835 of pink brick from England, used as ballast in boats, it is of Georgian style. The floors and beams are of hand-hewn pine with marble mantles and silver door knobs.

The JEMISON-BRANDON HOUSE, 1005 17th Ave., a two-storied wooden house with French Gothic gables, built in the 1850's, was the home of Confederate General Wood, later the home of William W. Brandon, Probate Judge of Tuscaloosa County and Governor of Alabama.

The MURPHEE-CAPLES HOUSE, 815 17th Ave., built about 1838 as a wedding gift for Laura Owen, who married James T. Murphee. Murphee was elected president of Howard College in Marion before the college was moved to Birmingham.

BRYCE HOSPITAL, near the University of Alabama, one of the earliest psychiatric hospitals in the nation, was established in 1860. A drive through the landscaped grounds takes the visitors past the old imposing administration building with its white dome, and the tomb of Dr. Peter Bryce, foresighted scientist who pioneered the theories of humane care and work therapy.

The VETERANS ADMINISTRATION HOSPITAL of Tuscaloosa is located on a 212-acre tract adjoining the golf course of the University of Alabama. It has 834 professional and service employees and a full-time out-patient and research program. Its affiliation with the University of Alabama gives it access to training programs for psychologists, social workers, recreation therapists, manual arts therapists, and accountants. Special courses are available for courses in management and psychiatry.

The FOSTER MOORE HOUSE, outside the city limits, is a two-storied Georgian house dating from the 1820s, now completely restored. It was the home of Wade Foster, one of the founders of Sigma Alpha Epsilon fraternity, who is buried nearby.

CHRISTAN HOME, Northport, on State 69, dates from the 1830s. It is a brick colonial cottage with much original material extant.

The WILLIAM BACON OLIVER LOCK AND DAM on the Warrior River below Tuscaloosa was opened in 1940 and considered adequate for navigation at that time, but plans to replace it have been drawn by the Warrior-Tombigbee Waterway Development Assn. The lock chamber, 95 ft. wide and 460 ft. long is to be increased to the standard dimension of 110 ft. by 600 ft. Six miles upstream from Tuscaloosa is one of the newest of the structures on the river, the HOLT LOCK AND DAM, which replaced Locks and Dams Nos. 13, 14, and 15, in 1968. It has a lift of 63.6 ft. and lockage can be accomplished in approximately 30 minutes. It has a gravity spillway controlled by 14 individually operated gates across the channel. The powerhouse of the Alabama Power Co. is located on the right bank.

PART III

Tours

Tour 1

DOWN THE CENTER OF ALABAMA
FROM ATHENS TO MOBILE

Ardmore — Athens —Decatur — Hartselle — Cullman —Hanceville — Warrior —Birmingham — Montevallo —Clanton — Montgomery — Greenville — Brewton — Atmore— Bay Minette — Mobile.

431 *m*. US 31, Int. 65

US 31 bisects Alabama from the Tennessee line to Mobile Bay. It crosses the Tennessee Valley, climbs the western part of the Sand Mountain plateau and traverses the more rugged region of the mineral belt through Birmingham to Calera. From there it runs through the fruit growing area of central Alabama, the fertile Black Belt, and the subtropical lowlands and pine forests in Baldwin County and enters Mobile from the east.

Interstate 65 comes down from Nashville and for two-thirds of the route runs parallel with US 31, bypassing Decatur but not Birmingham or Montgomery, and following a more direct line between Montgomery and Mobile, enters Mobile from the north parallel with US 43.

Section a. TENNESSEE LINE to BIRMINGHAM; 122.1 m.

Crossing the broadest section of the Tennessee Valley, which at this point forms a gentle, undulating plain, the route traverses one of the finest cotton-growing regions in the State. In early summer the fields are a sea of dark green, spotted with the red and white blooms of cotton. The only breaks are occasional clumps of tall timber and scrubby wood lots which supply fuel for the plantation tenants. As fall comes on fields shed their mantle of green and emerge in fleecy white, remaining thus until cotton pickers swarm through with their trailing gunny sacks to lift the blanket.

A few wandering French trappers, coming down from the Ohio, entered northern Alabama in the early part of the eighteenth century and English traders, pushing westward from the Carolinas and Georgia to trade with the Chickasaw, followed the Tennessee River through the region. Then came settlers, who passed down the Tennessee on flatboats on their way to the west. Actual settlement of the area, however, did not begin until after the Indian wars of the early 1800's. Then land-hungry pioneers poured in from the surrounding States in a mad scramble for the former Indian farms. The plantation system developed and flourished until 1861.

US 31, the Bee Line Highway, crosses the Tennessee Line 0 *m.* in ARDMORE (756 alt., 761 pop. 1970; 439, 1960), at a point 16 miles southeast of Pulaski, Tennessee. The town, which is half in Tennessee and half in Alabama, is a trading place for farmers or northeastern Limestone County.

The Cedars, 16.5 *m.*, sits back from the highway on rolling wooded lawns. Built in 1846 by Colonel James Malone, a wealthy Tennessee Valley planter, it is a fine example of an ante-bellum manor. Pattie Malone, a black girl whose contralto voice received international acclaim, was born a slave on the Cedars plantation in the spring of 1858. When Pattie was about 8 years old the Malones sent her to a school for Negroes that had been opened at Athens by Miss Araminta W. Wells, a Northerner. From there she went to Fisk University, Nashville, Tennessee, where she studied piano and voice. As a member of the original Jubilee Singers, she toured Europe with the famous chorus. Returning from Europe in 1896, Pattie was seriously injured aboard ship during a storm. Close upon this accident came word of her fiancé's death, and this blow, coupled with her physically weakened state, caused her death. She was buried in Athens.

ATHENS COLLEGE, 17.2 *m.*, is dominated by a group of stately old buildings standing on a level campus shaded by ancient oaks. The main building is massive Founders Hall, whose four Ionic columns accentuate the Greek Revival design and were erected in 1843-44. The walls, now covered with ivy, are of brick made by slave labor from local clay.

First called the Tennessee Conference Female Institute, then in succession the Athens Female Institute and Athens College for Young Women, it became Athens College and coeducational in 1931. It has been operated since its charter was granted in 1843 by the Methodist Episcopal Church, South. It remains affiliated with the North Alabama Conference of the United Methodist Church. In 1974 it enrolled 802 students and had a faculty of 57.

At 17.5 *m.*, is the northern junction with US 72 (*see Tour 5*), which unites briefly southward with US 31.

ATHENS, 18.7 *m.*, (695 alt., 14,360 pop. 1970; 9,930, 1960) founded in 1816 as Athenson, has a number of well-preserved antebellum houses, the family homes of the prewar planter aristocracy. It is a quiet town, with oak and elm lined streets radiating from the court square.

Athens, in 1934, was the first Alabama city to buy its electrical current from TVA. Energized by the TVA development, the city increased 50 percent in population during 1960-70.

Limestone County was the first of Alabama's counties to be invaded by Union troops during the War between the States; and Athens, as county seat, was the first important town to be occupied in 1862. During much of the war Athens was under the control of Russian-born brigadier-general Ivan Vasilivitch Turchinov, who subjected the towns-people to many indignities. He burned homes on the slightest pretext, and refused to discipline the rowdy element among his troops. Protests from the citizens only made matters worse, and an abiding dislike for Yankees was inculcated in Athenians at the time.

The Pryor House, North Jefferson St., two blocks north of the court square, is the former home of Luke Pryor, who served in the State legislature 1855-6, as U. S. Senator 1879-80, and as Representative 1883-5. The large square house is Greek Revival in design, with square box columns and a second-floor balcony extending across the whole width of a fine arched portico. Brackets of cast iron are used in the corners of the column bases. There is a cast-iron balcony on the right side of the mansion and a cast-iron porch on the left. On top of the mansion is a glass-enclosed cupola the size of a small room that Pryor was said to have used for a watch tower. Here he sat with a telescope, watching his slaves as they worked in distant fields. The thought that the master was in the cupola with his spy-glass kept the men from idling even when they knew he was in Montgomery or Washington.

Houston House, Houston St., two blocks west of the court square, was the home of George S. Houston, Governor of Alabama from 1874 to 1876. He is remembered in the State for his careful administration after the excesses of Reconstruction. This property was given to the city in 1937 by George Houston, Jr., son of the former Governor. Houston, member of Congress 1841-49 and 1851-61, never wavered in his opposition to secession, but kept the respect of neighbors and friends.

St. Timothy's Episcopal Church, Washington St., is a small brick ivy-covered chapel where the early valley planters attended services. The nearby-by churchyard is one of north Alabama's oldest burial grounds. Many of the markers bear dates of the period before Alabama became a State. On these oldest graves are the family names of many men active in the business life of Athens today.

The gray brick, three-storied Mason House, 211 South Beaty St., was designed with pioneer simplicity as a school house, but was used as a home. The brass knocker bears the inscription: "Robert Beaty 1826, John R. Mason 1845." The house was used to care for the wounded and as officers' quarters by Federal troops during the War between the States. The old carriage shed and slave kitchen of split logs are still standing. The house has been refurbished to serve as the residence of the president of Athens College.

On near-by Coleman Hill, southwest of the court square, is Trinity School, which the Congregational church built for educating Negroes. Here General Nathan Bedford Forrest's cavalry dislodged a heavily entrenched Union force under Colonel Campbell in 1864. To give the impression of a much larger force than he actually had, the Confederate leader marched his men before the enemy, first as cavalry and then as infantry, the first horsemen dismounting and falling in on foot behind their own rear guard. Convinced that he was outnumbered, Campbell surrendered, handing his sword to General Forrest just east of the court square.

At 30 *m.* US 31 is joined by US Alt. 72 to cross the Tennessee River. At 31.7 the route uses the southbound Keller Memorial Bridge to the foot of Alabama St., Decatur. The bridge was built in 1928 and named for William Simpson Keller, first chief engineer of the Alabama Highway Dept. and brother of Helen Keller.

DECATUR, 32 *m.* (38,044 pop. 1970). *See Decatur.* Junctions with US Alt. 72 east-west, State 24, 67.

South of Decatur US 31 crosses the bottom lands of the Tennessee Valley, rising gradually over a series of terraces to the coves and hills of Sand Mountain. Corn grows tall in the river bottoms, cotton and hay flourish on the red and brown soils of the first elevation. As the route climbs the higher ridges, fruits and vegetables take the place of corn, and the wooded hills are checkered with small pastures. Farther south, as the soil changes to sand loam, strawberries are an important crop, and in April and May, hordes of pickers work here. Back from the highway stand a few old plantation houses, but newer, smaller houses indicate the general rehabilitation.

On State 67 12 *m.* se of Decatur is SOMERVILLE, settled in 1819. It was named for Lieut. Robt. Somerville of Tennessee, who was killed at the battle of Horseshoe Bend. This was the seat of Morgan County until 1891, when Decatur was chosen. Samuel D. Weakley, once Justice of the Alabama Supreme Court, and Malcom R. Patterson, Governor of Tennessee, 1907-11, were born here, and Major General James Longstreet CSA, spent his boyhood here.

While the village of Somerville had only 185 residents in 1970, the Somerville Division of Morgan County had 4,318 in 1970 and 3,618 in 1960, a gain of 19%.

From Somerville a county road connects with State 36 and VAL-HERMOSO SPRINGS and LACEYS SPRING, in an area known for mineral waters and widely patronized in the early 19th century. The Laceys Spring Division of Morgan County had 5,383 pop. in 1970, 4,376 in 1960, a rise of 23%. Valhermoso was at the peak of its popularity as a health resort in the 1830s. Known as the Vale of Beauty, it is dominated by the Valhermoso Knob, covered with cedar, pine, and hardwood. In the 1820s and 1830s the Cedar Hotel here was known for its balls and festivities; it lasted for more than a century and ended its days as a dwelling. The mineral springs have white sulphur, black sulphur, and chalybeate waters.

Back to US 31, FLINT CITY is hardly 3 *m.* south of the limits of Decatur. Named for flint stone found plentifully in the area, it had 404 pop. in 1970, having suffered a loss of 28 since 1960. It has the Morgan County Tuberculosis Sanitarium, built in 1934 with CWA funds.

HARTSELLE, 45 *m.* (672 alt., 7,355 pop. 1970; 5,000, 1960, inc. 47%) in Morgan County, is at a junction with State 36 east-west.

Originally founded north of its present site in 1870, it moved to the area of the depot of the railroad that later became the Louisville & Nashville. It was incorporated March 1, 1875. It ships lumber and cotton. The Morgan County High School, originally the Male and Female Academy, has separate buildings for manual training (male) and domestic science (female).

Int. 65, which ran parallel to US 31 and to the east, moved west of US 31 near the Cullman County line.

CULLMAN, 68 m. (802 alt. 12,601 pop. 1970; 10,883, 1960, inc. 15%) was settled by German immigrants from the Rhineland, led by John Cullman, who bought a tract of land for colonizing in 1872. The town was platted in 1873. In 1878 the Legislature established the County of Cullman with Cullman as its seat. The town is located on Brindley Mountain, part of the Cumberland plateau, and a short distance northeast of Lewis Smith Lake. It became a shipping center for coal, which is found in the Sano Mountain area, and for timber, and today makes electrical equipment and processes poultry. There is an estimated work force of 15,000 in Cullman County.

Sacred Heart College, a two-year college for women established in 1940 by the Benedictine Sisters, became CULLMAN COLLEGE in 1970 and reorganized as a public service institution. While the Benedictines continued to sponsor the college laymen were introduced on the governing board. It turned coeducational and admitted male students, who are assigned to Benet Hall, formerly Gertrude Hall. In 1974 it had 250 students and 19 teachers.

Left from Cullman on US 278 1.5 m. to another road, 2 m. to ST. BERNARD COLLEGE, a Roman Catholic school founded 1892 and chartered the following year. In 1974 it had 469 students and a faculty of 33. Across the road is the famous AVE MARIA GROTTO, a rocky woodland glade, ornamented with Talladega marble, slag, crystal, and other rock formations. Stone steps descend from the iron entrance gate to a clearing in the oak and pine woods. Here are 40 miniature reproductions of shrine ruins, mosques, temples, monasteries, churches, statues, and scenes in the Holy Land. Left of the main unit are Vatican miniatures. The grounds are landscaped with small rock plants, little lagoons, fountains and streams.

South of Cullman, US 31 passes the low rolling foothills of the Arkadelphia Mountains.

HANCEVILLE, 77 m. (541 alt. 2,027 pop. 1970; 1,174, 1960, inc. 72%) is an agricultural shipping point and a trading center for the surrounding countryside. Founded in 1876, the village was first called Gilmer, and was in Blount County until the legislature added it to Cullman County in 1899, and designated the Mulberry River as the county boundary line.

Left from Hanceville on State 91 to BLOUNTSVILLE, 13 m. (426 alt., 1,254 pop. 1970; 672, 1960, inc. 66%), a farm trading center. It was opened to settlement after the Creek War, 1813-14, and was the seat of Blount County from 1820 until 1899. In that year the seat was removed to Oneonta.

Caleb Friley, the first settler, moved here soon after 1815 and occupied the deserted cabin of a Creek chief. Blountsville's first religious service, conducted by Reverend Ebenezer Hearn, a Methodist frontier preacher, was held in Friley's cabin. Indian mounds in the vicinity of Blountsville have yielded many relics, such as chipped implements, copper artifacts, bark matting, and pottery. On May 2, 1863, Colonel A. D. Streight and his Union Cavalry passed through here with Forrest's "critter company" close behind. In Blountsville Streight set fire to his supply wagons and abandoned them, but the Confederates arrived in time to put out the fire and save the supplies.

US 31 crosses the Mulberry Fork of the Black Warrior River, 83 *m.*, winding through low densely wooded mountains and following small streams overhung by maples, beeches, and undergrowth. The highway here is laid on the old roadbed of the Louisville & Nashville Railroad. It leads through deep cuts between walls of solid rock, where in summer overhanging limbs of oak, elm, beech, and hickory trees form a shady corridor. Here GARDEN CITY (745 pop. 1970) connects with County Road 26.

Until 1914, when the railroad was re-routed, BLOUNT SPRINGS, 88.1 *m.* was a popular health and summer resort. Many Birmingham residents had summer homes here and visitors from other sections came to drink the sulphur and arsenic waters. The vicinity offers excellent quail, rabbit, and squirrel hunting.

WARRIOR, 99 *m.* in Jefferson County (2,621 pop. 1970; 2,448, 1960), a coal mining community, the highway is bordered with great oak and elm trees whose limbs often meet to form a shady arch. There are attractive homes in the environs. The route between Warrior and Birmingham is US 31, crosses the Locust Fork of the Black Warrior River, 101 *m.*, in the coal country, where Kimberly is a town of 847 pop. (1970) and MORRIS, 3 *m.* farther on, has 519.

GARDENDALE, 112 *m.* (6,502 pop. 1970; 8,712, 1960) profits by the expansion of Birmingham. During the Depression of the 1930s the Federal Government began a subsistence homestead project 3 *m.* west called Mt. Olive Homesteads, at which the Resettlement Administration experimented with houses of rammed earth construction, with walls formed by a mixture of clay, sand and a coarse aggregate, packed hard.

FULTONDALE, 114 *m.* (6,502 pop. 1970; 4,712, 1960) is an incorporated city in the environs of Birmingham.

BIRMINGHAM, 122 *m.* (300,910 pop. 1970). Excellent highways connect with all cities and sections of the State. Int. 59 comes from the northeast, parallel with US 11, and proceeds to Tuscaloosa. Int. 20 enters from the east. US 78 comes from the northwest. US 280 combined with US 231 comes from the southeast. State 269 has gathered a number of northwest roads, including State 195, which traverses the heart of the William B. Bankhead National Forest. State 75 and 79 bring traffic from the northeast. *See Birmingham.*

Section b. BIRMINGHAM *to* MONTGOMERY; *101.4 m.*

South of Birmingham the route passes through the southern part of the mineral belt. It crosses rough timbered ridges and winds through deep cuts where ore-bearing rock is visible. Near Calera this rugged region gives way to gently rolling land which becomes almost level as US 31 nears Montgomery.

Leaving BIRMINGHAM, 0 *m.,* the highway crosses the wooded ridge of Red Mountain, 2.4 *m.* (800 alt.), a residential section at the southern limits of the city; it passes through a wide gap that cuts a great vein of the red iron ore, easily distinguishable in its course through the bordering shale.

Immediately above the gap, on the brow is the great iron Statue of Vulcan. From Vulcan Park there is a splendid view of Birmingham spread out along the tree-covered slope of Red Mountain and across the valley below. At night the scene is illuminated by electric lights and myriads of flashing, colored neon signs, while along the distant edges of the city the glow from the iron furnaces flares against the sky.

HOMEWOOD, 3.2 *m.* (800 alt., 21,245 pop. 1970; 20,289, 1960) is an incorporated city that is really a close-in suburb of Birmingham. Its main growth took place after World War II, and in the 1960-70 decade recorded an increase of only 4%. The highway ascends the northern slope of Shades Mountain. One of the projects carried out by the WPA in the 1940s was to plant climbing rose on the slope, which is wooded with pines, redbud and dogwood.

On the crest of the mountain, 6.2 *m.* (1,000 alt.), is a junction with the Shades Crest Road. Left on this road to VESTAVIA HILLS, now an incorporated town of 8,311 (1970) up from 4,029 (1960) or 106%. It was named for the house built by the late George B. Ward, former mayor of Birmingham, and described as follows: "Vestavia is a copy of the temple of Vesta in Rome, and the little observatory across the road directly in front of the main entrance is a miniature of the temple of Sibyl in Tivoli. The circular red sandstone house, is 60 feet in diameter. A 14-foot pillared portico surrounds it. In early summer red roses climb over the tall metal supports that enclose the 25-acre grounds; later there are roses of other varieties and peonies and chrysanthemums. From this vantage point a panorama of rugged hills and green-clad valleys stretches away to the distant horizon."

HOOVER, 8 *m.* (1,393 pop. 1970) had 1,846 when annexed to Birmingham. It lies directly beyond Vestavia Hills.

PELHAM, 16 *m.* reported 931 pop. in 1970. A special census, Jan. 8, 1973, returned 3,047, a gain of 2,116 or 227.3%.

At 19 *m.,* left on County Road 43 to OAK MOUNTAIN STATE PARK, 6 *m.;* here a spacious stone lodge and cabins provide facilities for picnic parties. Oak Mountain rears its stony, scrub-covered head nearly 1,000 feet to overlook a panorama of rugged, timbered valleys. Within the park's 9,940 acres are footpaths that wind among points of scenic beauty. One of the loveliest is Peavine Falls, a "wet weather branch" dropping over a 40-foot wall; only a trickle in dry season, rainy weather swells it to a small cataract.

Activities in the park include camping, picnicking, tennis, golf, riding, roller skating, bicycling, swimming, boating, fishing, and hiking. There gift shops, cottages, a riding stable, and a mountain top restaurant. A demonstration farm is stocked with animals and a huge red barn has practical demonstrations of farm practices. It is classified as a day-use park, especially popular with Birmingham residents.

US 31 now traverses the lime areas of Shelby County, where lime kilns were established in colonial times.

ALABASTER, 23 *m.* (432 alt., 2,642 pop. 1970; 1,623 1960, inc. 62%) ships lime and farm products. SAGINAW, 25.5 *m.,* with a population not visible to the Census Bureau, has been similarly employed.

CALERA, 34.3 *m.* (502 alt., 1,625 pop. 1970; 1,928, 1960, dec. 14%) which bears the Spanish word for lime, was named by John R. Gamble, first settler and a veteran of the Creek War. Some of the ancient lime kilns were worked by the Spaniards.

Right from Calera on State 25 to MONTEVALLO, 7 *m.,* (3,719 pop. 1970; 2,755, 1960; inc. 35%) a town in the extreme southwest corner of Shelby County. It was settled in 1815 by James Wilson, veteran of General Jackson's campaigns, who first called the place Wilson's Hill. It is the seat of the UNIVERSITY OF MONTE-VALLO, a coeducational liberal arts college, established in 1896 as Alabama College, a girls' school. The college admitted male students in 1956. The university has three colleges, granting baccalaureate degrees in arts, music, music education, and science, and graduate degrees of master of arts in teaching and master of education.

Montevallo has 106 acres and buildings both historic and modern. In 1974 it reported enrollment of 3,600, with a faculty of 150, charged tuition of $180 a semester, $360 a session, and estimated total costs, with room and board, to be $552 a semester, $1,104 a session.

Among the newer buildings, Farmer Hall, the student union, was opened in 1965. The new building of the Carmichael Library, named for the fourth president, Oliver Cromwell Carmichael, was opened in 1968. The library has approximately 110,000 volumes. Harman Hall, containing laboratories and classrooms for biology, chemistry, mathematics and physics, was opened in 1968. The Tower, traditional landmark, was renovated in 1963 for the Schulmerich Carillon. The university recently added a new music building and a speech and hearing clinic building.

The King House on the campus was built in 1823 by Edmund King and was the first brick house erected in central Alabama. The original structure is a two-story rectangular building with two large rooms, a central hall, and chimneys on both ends. The bricks were made from clay on the banks of a near-by creek. When the house was built, settlers came from miles around to see the small-paned glass windows first in the backwoods country.

Reynolds Hall, built on land donated by King, was erected in

1851 to house students of the Montevallo Male Institute. Lack of funds caused the Institute to be closed after the War between the States. After serving some 20 years as the one building of a school for women, Reynolds Hall was finally turned over to Alabama College. During the extensive building program, made possible by grants from the Public Works Administration in 1939, the college converted "Old Reynolds" into a College Union Building, housing offices of student organizations and publications, a tearoom, a men's lounge, and an experimental workshop for the college theater. Among other buildings are Comer Hall, a classroom and radio building, named for the first governor to show an active interest in public education; Tutwiler Hall, named for Julia Stanwick Tutwiler, whose pioneering in the field of education for women made possible the founding of Alabama College.

In the center of a recreational field near by is the burying plot of the Kings and Shortridges. One of the stone markers commemorates Frank Forrester Shortridge, killed in battle, Atlanta, Ga., Aug. 24, 1864.

At the end of Main Street on the eastern edge of the town once stood Hangman's Tree, where public executions were held. Old residents insist that Montevallo never had a lynching, but admit that the people did sometimes "anticipate the sheriff in his duties."

South of Calera US 31 passes over gently rolling sandy land, the beginning of the open farming country that characterizes the route between this point and Montgomery. Large crops of watermelons are grown and, in season, long lines of trucks roll along the highway loaded with melons for larger markets.

At 46.7 m. is a junction with a dirt road. Left on this road to a junction with another road 4 m.; right on this second road across a small creek where gold is sometimes panned. At the fording place occasional tiny flakes of gold may be seen in the creek bottom. The Jim Cobb House, 4.5 m., is a three-room, frame structure built in the early 1800s. The original whipsawed boards are still in place in the inner walls. When the War between the States began, Jim Cobb and his brother organized a group of men to kill deserters from the Confederate Army. The families of some of the men that were killed retaliated by organizing a group of their own. They attacked the Cobb house and after a three-day battle, broke into the barricaded room, took Cobb and hanged him to a crab-apple tree. The tree is not standing, but the bullet roles are still visible in the walls of the house. In the rear of the structure is the old Cobb family burying ground with the red brick vault, where Jim Cobb is buried.

At 46.7 m. is a junction with a dirt road.

JEMISON, 47 m. (710 alt., 1,423 pop. 1970; 977, 1960, inc. 45%) has some lumbering activities.

THORSBY, 50.6 m. (944 pop. 1970; 468, 1960) settled mainly by Scandinavians, is a well-groomed farming community where peaches, strawberries, and watermelons share the cash crop market with cotton.

Small roadside stands sell these products and figs, pecans, and tomatoes to passing motorists.

At 50.7 *m.* is THORSBY INSTITUTE, a vocational and secondary school sponsored by the Education Society of the Congregational Church. Founded in 1906, this coeducational school gives practical and theoretical training and helps indigent students earn part of their expenses.

CLANTON, 58.3 *m.* (571 alt., 5,808 pop. 1970; 5,683, 1960) a city and the county seat of Chilton County, was incorporated in 1873 and named for the Confederate general, James H. Clanton. Originally lumbering and turpentining were the principal occupations, but as the lands were cleared, cotton and other crops and poultry raising developed. The community is a farming center with a cotton gin, sawmills, and a graphite plant. The Chilton County *News* is published weekly.

Clanton has a junction with State 22 which combines with US 31 for about 8 *m.*, then turns west. County Road 55, 2 *m.* ne of Clanton, goes to Lay Dam on the Coosa River, where the Alabama Power Co. has one of its large hydroelectric generating plants. The dam produces Lay Lake. There is a ferry on the river.

In 1969 the Alabama Power Co. announced plans to utilize nuclear fuel for the generation of electricity at installations near Clanton, of which the first unit was planned for 1975. It would produce 860,000 kw. Additional units were planned for the later 1970s, and eventually nuclear power was to be used in new plants in the 1980s, in expectation of a huge rise in demand for electricity.

County Road 28 moves east from Clanton to Mitchell Dam on the Coosa River and Mitchell Lake. At 66.6 *m.* State 22 leaves US 31. It crosses the Coosa and goes northeast of Lake Martin in Tallapoosa County and north of Horseshoe Bend National Military Park (*see Tour 8*).

VERBENA, 68 *m.*, on US 31, was founded by settlers from Montgomery who came here to escape the recurring epidemics of yellow fever in the 1860s. The town was first called Summerfield, but since there was a village near Selma by that name, it was renamed for the abundant wild verbena that grew in the vicinity. Right from Verbena on a footpath along Chestnut Creek to the site of Sidney Lanier's Camp, 0.5 *m.* Here Sidney Lanier, the Georgia poet, lived in a tent in the grove of pine trees for almost a year, seeking to regain his health.

Three miles south of Verbena is MOUNTAIN CREST, a hamlet, where US 11 has a junction with State 145, which goes south, 10 *m.*, to DEATSVILLE, a division in Elmore County (3,003 pop. 1970; 3,327, 1960). East of this village are located major units of the Board of Corrections of the State of Alabama.

DRAPER CORRECTIONAL CENTER, named for Hamp Draper, a former warden for the system, was completed in 1939 and operates with a staff of 128 employees. It is a minimum, medium and maximum security facility, located on a 3,200 acre reservation 25 miles north of Montgomery. Built for 600 inmates Draper accommodates in excess of 900, mostly younger offenders with an average age of 23. The buildings are located within a compound protected by an 18-foot chain-link fence. This reformatory type of institution applies the main rehabilitative programs of the system. It has classes in basic education, vocational training shops for automotive service, barbering, welding and meat cutting. The inmates are also taken to the J. F. Ingram Trade State Vocational School for additional vocational training. Draper has a full-scale two-year college program, making Alabama one of a dozen states that offer on-site college training to eligible inmates. It is provided through Alexander City State Junior College, and extends also to Tutwiler Women's Center and Frank Lee Youth Center from Draper. Draper provides four classrooms, library space, faculty and student lounges, college offices, etc., for the part and full-time college staff of 13.

The J. F. INGRAM STATE VOCATIONAL SCHOOL, located a few miles west of Draper, near Deatsville, was opened in 1966. Since then some 1,026 men have graduated in trade training, and 516 have been awarded a high school certificate. Trades being taught at the school include auto body repair, auto mechanics, brick masonry, small gasoline engine repair, upholstery, cabinet making and welding.

Adjacent to the Ingram School is the FRANK LEE YOUTH CENTER for youthful offenders. The Center, named for former Commissioner A. Frank Lee, was designed to accommodate 102 inmates, but has undergone remodeling and can accommodate approximately 200 inmates. These inmates have an opportunity to attend classes in education as well as the Trade School.

At 90.1 m., is a junction with State 14, which leads 2 m. west to PRATTVILLE, 1.4 m. (162 alt., 13,116 pop. 1970; 6,616, 1960, inc. 98%), seat of Autauga County, first settled in 1816. It is known for the fine artesian wells within the city limits.

The Cotton Ginning Machinery Plant was the outgrowth of a factory founded in 1833 by Daniel Pratt, for whom the town is named. Pratt was born July 20, 1799, at Temple, New Hampshire, and worked with Samuel Griswold, a gin builder at Clinton, Georgia, in the 1830's. While the ginning machinery business was in its infancy, Pratt invented many improvements in methods of delinting cotton seeds, cleaning cotton, and handling the product in the ginhouse. The business grew and he became the leading industrialist of Alabama. In his later years he associated himself with the group that developed the Birmingham district's minerals. His work was recognized in 1847 by the University of Alabama with an honorary degree of Master of Mechanical and Useful Arts, and by a similar degree in 1867 from the University of Georgia.

The Prathoma Park Deer Ranch (*open by permission*), was started by Judge C. E. Thomas as a hobby. Its 15 acres of hills and park-like meadows, where the deer graze, are enclosed by a high wire fence. The herds include two European species—the fallow deer and red deer—and the common American variety, the Virginia or white-tail deer. They are sold chiefly to parks and zoos. The Thomas home,

PRATHOMA, a two-story concrete structure with a turreted roof garden and a broad gallery, is on top of a hill (R) overlooking the park. It is surrounded by live oaks, pines and sycamores.

Here the State Department of Conservation has established a game farm and the State Forest Nursery as a part of its program for the restoration of wild-life resources.

MAXWELL AIR FORCE BASE, 94.8 *m.*, an important unit of the USAF, occupied 2,423 acres with landing field and 650 buildings. It is described in the article on Montgomery.

A large white stone, 96 *m.*, bears the dates, 1540-1814, and the inscription: "This stone Marks the Site of the Indian Town, Tawasa, visited by De Soto September 13, 1540; also by Bienville, 1715." The marker was erected in 1930 by the National Society of Colonial Dames in Alabama.

MONTGOMERY, 101 *m.* (133,386 pop. 1970) *See article on Montgomery.*

In Montgomery are junctions with US 80, US 82, US 231, US 331, Int. 85.

Section c. *MONTGOMERY to MOBILE; 207.6 m.*

The route south of MONTGOMERY, 0 *m.,* passes through the undulating Black Belt country, a region once devoted almost exclusively to cotton and corn, but now turning to large-scale dairying, stock raising, and diversified farming.

Early spring brings a thick carpet of primroses to the fields and roadsides. Their blossoms change the green acres to an expanse of pale pink that appears to roll in waves before the wind. In haying time, the air is filled with the sweet perfume of melilotus, a plant that yields honey of a peculiar and delicious flavor. Bee keeping is carried on to a considerable extent, especially in Montgomery County.

HOPE HULL, 3 *m.* is the core of Hope Hull Division (6,265 pop. 1970; 4,071, 1960, inc. 53%).

At 6.2 is the southern junction with US 31. FORT DEPOSIT, 39 *m.* (445 alt., 1,438 pop. 1970; 1,466, 1960) a town in Lowndes County, was established as a fort and supply base by General Jackson during the Indian wars. Settlers gathered here for protection, and gradually the fort developed into a town. Farming and pecan growing are the principal activities. The town is 3 *m.* west of Int. 65, 5 *m.* west of US 31.

The seat of Butler County, GREENVILLE, 51.9 *m.* (423 alt., 8,033 pop. 1970; 6,894, 1960, inc. 16.5 %) was settled in 1819 by a party from Greenville, South Carolina and incorporated in 1820 and given the name of Buttsville in honor of a Georgia Indian fighter in the Creek War. The name was changed shortly thereafter to Greenville, to commemorate the home settlement of most of the early inhabitants. The town is a trading center for a widespread cotton growing area and a shipping point for pecans excellent variety. Like most old Alabama towns, it has broad oak-lined streets and many stately homes whose deep shady lawns are studded with magnolias, japonicas, and other plants in keeping with their old-fashioned elegance. Greenville was the home of Hilary A. Herbert, Secretary of the Navy under Cleveland.

The LOMAX-HANNON STATE JUNIOR COLLEGE was founded in Greenville under the terms of the Junior College Act in the 1960s. Greenville is the hub of numerous roads. Besides Int. 65 and US 31 there are State 10, State 185 combined with State 263 and County roads.

John Shepherd, who came from Georgia in 1824, was the first settler in GEORGIANA, 67.5 m. (264 alt., 2,148 pop. 1970; 2,003, 1960) a town in Butler County. Following him came Pitt S. Milner, a Baptist minister, also from Georgia; the town was named in honor of his little daughter, Anna, and his home state. It is a progressive and prosperous country town with many modern facilities. Local industries serve cotton and lumber production. The red soil is fertile and the town is a trucking center for strawberries and beans.

Noted for its strawberries, McKENZIE, 75.1 m. (491 pop. 1970; 588, 1960) also specializes in beans and cucumbers, shipments of which are made by the truckload.

At 88 m. US 31 has a junction with US 84, which joins it for 9m.

The widespread custom of using sprigs of green for decorations brings EVERGREEN, 94.9 m. (258 alt., 3,928 pop. 1970; 3,703, 1960), a large portion of its income. The commercial exploitation of evergreen shrubs began, so the story goes, when an unemployed man wandered into a St. Louis florist's shop looking for a job. The florist was telling a customer about the cost of evergreens and the difficulty of obtaining them. The customer remarked that she had seen these evergreens growing in great abundance near Evergreen, Alabama. The unemployed man made his way to Evergreen where he started a business of shipping smilax, holly and mistletoe in large quantities.

Evergreen is the seat of Conecuh County. In frontier days it was called Cosey's Old Field because it had been a part of the farm cleared by John Cosey, a Revolutionary soldier, who settled here about 1820. Upon becoming a small town, the settlement was given its present name because of the nature of the surrounding lowlands.

William Barrett Travis, whose family had a plantation nearby attended school here. In the turbulent days of the Texas Rebellion, Travis then a young lawyer, turned soldier of fortune, casting his lot with Sam Houston, Davy Crockett, and other Texas leaders. He lost his life at the battle of the Alamo.

One of the largest strawberry growing areas in the State ships from CASTLEBERRY, 106.3 m. (174 alt. 666 pop. 1970; 669, 1960). When the harvest is at its height, trucks, piled high with crates of scarlet berries, rush for the big markets.

From Castleberry the tourist who seeks historic sites may make an excursion over country roads to the spot on the Conecuh River where Sparta was once a busy frontier town. Its promise was cut short in the early decades of the 19th century by yellow fever and the destructive raids of the Federal Army during the 1860s. Nothing remains of the town.

While Int. 65 swings westward in a curved line toward Mobile, US 31 moves more directly south toward the Florida border.

BREWTON, 121.3 m. (6.747 pop. 1970; 6,309, 1960) is the seat of Escambia County. When Brewton became a prosperous lumber center it managed to get the county seat away from the village of Pollard. Local tradition says that the men of Pollard, in retaliation, gathered up a great number of cats and let them loose in Brewton.

This is the seat of the JEFFERSON DAVIS STATE JUNIOR COLLEGE, established in 1965. It enrolled 1,452 students and had a faculty of 51 in 1974.

In 1852 an oil gusher on a farm a few miles southwest of Brewton suddenly galvanized activity in this area. It arrived at a depth of 5,000 ft. drilled by the Humble Oil & Refining Co., and established the location of Pollard Oil Pool. The well was described as having daily a potential of 1,000 bbl. of high grade oil.

EAST BREWTON (2336 pop. 1970; 2,511, 1960) is located across the creek from Brewton. Here on a high bluff the Federal Government built Fort Crawford in 1818 as an outpost against hostile Indians. It had five structures of hewn logs and weatherboards on Three Notch Road, the post road from Fort Mitchell on the Chattahoochee to Fort Mims.

US 29, coming from Andalusia to East Brewton, crosses the creek to a junction with US 31 at Brewton.

Murder Creek winds along the foot of the bluff at Fort Crawford, so named because early traders were slain on its banks by Indians. After the Fort Sims massacre soldiers of General Andrew Jackson's army discovered that they were being trailed by Creek warriors. A detachment under Lieut. Crawford made camp, prepared dummies out of brush and clothing and placed them around the campfire to simulate sleeping soldiers, while his men hid to await an attack. When the Indians charged the camp they were cut down by the hidden soldiers. US 31 proceeds southwest toward the Florida border. At FLOMATON 136.9 m. (1,584 pop. 1970; 1,454, 1960) it comes within 2 m. of Florida, then turns west.

The route traverses land that flattens out gradually from rolling hills to the nearly level country of the coastal plain, laced with a network of deep, clear streams, well stocked with largemouthed bass and other freshwater game fish. In many of the lower valleys are great wooded swamps which still afford shelter for black bear, white-tail deer, wildcats, and many smaller animals. The high ground is good cover for quail, doves, and rabbits. Hunters, however, should beware of cottonmouth moccasins and rattlesnakes when tramping through the wooded regions.

ATMORE, 151.4 m. (281 alt., 8,293 pop. 1970; 8,173, 1960),

is a shipping center for a wide truck farming area. Products include large crops of potatoes, cabbage, green beans, and other vegetables.

At Atmore is a junction with State 21, a heavily traveled road in Central Alabama, which continues south into Florida. HOLMAN PRISON, the State's maximum security prison, is located 9 *m.* east of Atmore. It was named for William E. Holman, former warden at Kilby Prison, and first occupied in November, 1969. It has 7½ acres, a staff of 110 employees and is surrounded by a double chain link fence. The complex consists of four dormitories and four cell blocks. The former death row is located in a wing at one end of a building and has 20 cells. It has not been used since 1965. This area is now used for a segregated administrative unit. Holman was designed for 600 inmates and has for several years housed in excess of 700.

The tag plant which produces all vehicle license plates for the State is located within the compound and operated under maximum security. The inmates at Holman are mostly disciplinary problems, escapees who have been recaptured and all inmates there are classified as maximum security.

The FOUNTAIN CORRECTIONAL CENTER, formerly named Atmore Prison Farm, was completed in 1949, and is located 10 miles north of Atmore. Designed for approximately 800 inmates it for several years has housed 1,100 or more. Operating with a staff of 130 employees, some 4,500 of the sprawling 8,000 acres of the property are used in farming. The farming operation produces cotton, soybeans, cucumbers, corn, and sugar cane; 33,500 gallons of cane syrup were produced in Fountain's own syrup mill from their 1973 sugar cane crop. The rest is timber and pasture land.

LITTLE RIVER STATE PARK, 17.4 *m.* (*Cabins, fishing, boating*), is a 2,120-acre tract on Little River; the area was once thickly settled by Indians, as is evidenced by the remains of their village sites.

BAY MINETTE, 171.6 *m.* (278 alt., 6,727 pop. 1970; 5,197, 1960, inc. 29%), is the seat of Baldwin County. In 1900 the courthouse was at Daphne, a village on the shore of Mobile Bay in western Baldwin County. Because of its central location, Bay Minette was regarded as the logical county seat by its citizens; the plan of changing the seat was presented to the people of Daphne, who rejected it. After two years of argument between the two towns, the State Supreme Court ruled in favor of Bay Minette.

Daphne refused to release the court records and move the prisoners from the jail. A second decision of the courts upheld Bay Minette's cause, but still Daphne refused to yield. This was too much for Bay Minette. An army of citizens proceeded to Daphne to bring the judge as well as the court records to Bay Minette. To conceal the real purpose of the visit, they brought along a prisoner, presumably for lodgement in the Daphne jail; but once inside they overpowered the sheriff, took the county records and the judge home with them. Bay Minette has been the county seat of Baldwin County ever since.

Like other Alabama cities of French and Spanish origin, Bay

Minette follows a tranquil way of living. Many of the houses, gray with age, reflect the architectural taste of early French builders and contain fine specimens of old furniture. Huge live oaks draped with Spanish moss shade the narrow white streets of crushed shell, and broad lawns are colorful with radiant japonicas, azaleas, and other semitropical flowers.

The JAMES H. FAULKNER STATE JUNIOR COLLEGE was founded in 1963 as the William L. Yancey College. The State Board of Education in 1970 authorized changing the name to honor Faulkner, who was instrumental in locating the college in Bay Minette. In addition to its classroom and administrative buildings it has erected two modern dormitories that can accommodate 116 women and 148 men. There are evening courses for occupational and cultural improvement open to the community, and certificates of completion are available to individuals who attend. In 1974 Faulkner enrolled 1,923 students and had a faculty of 78.

Bay Minette is a busy industrial center, Kaiser Aluminum Co. has invested $2,500,000 in a plant making cables for electric utility lines; the International Paper Co. makes corrugated containers; Bay Slacks, Inc. produces 4,000 slacks a day; Baldwin Pole & Piling Co. makes creosote poles; Tenneco Chemicals and Standard Furniture are other large plants.

West of Bay Minette in the Mobile Delta region are the Tensaw Swamp and the Tensaw River, an area with good hunting and fishing. Bear, deer, and wild turkey roam the semitropical jungles, which are criss-crossed by creeks, bayous, and arms of rivers. Veteran swamp men, familiar with the region, may be procured as guides (*apply at hotels at Bay Minette*).

There are numerous large aboriginal Indian mounds on the islands and higher ground of the Mobile Delta, left by long vanished tribes. Earthworks have yielded many relics.

Right from Bay Minette on State 59 to Tensaw, 22.6 *m.*, a hamlet, where John Pierce taught a small group of pupils in 1799, the first school in Alabama. This area east of the Tensaw River is Creek Indian country. About 10 *m.* nw is the site of the FORT MIMS MASSACRE of August 30, 1813. Fort Mims was a stockade built around the log house of Sam Mims. It was said that 200 militiamen under Major Beasley were inside, as well as some settlers and Indians who had defected from the war-making faction of the Creeks. Although warned that an attack was imminent Major Beasley was not prepared when the hostile Creek rushed the gates of the stockade, gained entrance and killed the inmates. The massacre increased the bitterness of the settlers toward the Creeks and led to their eventual defeat by General Andrew Jackson.

A monument erected by the United Daughters of the Confederacy marks the approximate site of Fort Mims.

This area along the Tensaw River is also the site of old FORT BLAKELY and the defeat of its Confederate defenders in the final days of the war. At 2 *m.* south of Bay Minette State 138, right, connects with State 225; proceed south on the latter 7 *m.* to a graded road, right, thence 2 *m.* to the site of OLD BLAKELY and Blakely Cemetery. Blakely was incorporated in 1815. For a number of years it grew in population and prospered but after a yellow fever epidemic and financial crises the survivors moved to Mobile in the 1830s. The fort, which had been built in pioneer days to protect the settlers, was manned by the Confederates as a defense of Mobile, and attacked in March, 1865, by 15,000 Federal troops after the latter had taken Spanish Fort, a short distance southwest.

The old Cemetery is a forlorn relic of the days when Blakely was a busy place. Going farther back in time are the shell mounds, heaped up by Indians who ate shellfish here for generations.

At Stapleton, 182 *m.,* a hamlet, US 31 turns sharply west to join several other highways to cross Cochrane Bridge and the 10 *m.* stretch of filled-in roadway and bridges that spans the upper reaches of Mobile Bay. Here are junctions with roads that come west through Baldwin County from Florida, including Int. 10, US 90, and US 98.

The shimmering waters of the bay spread southward to the Gulf of Mexico, reflecting the yellow bluffs of the eastern shore with their dark green fringe of moss-festooned live oaks silhouetted against the sky. The western shore is a low, dark streak along the horizon, broken by the skyline of Mobile, and fading into a soft haze to the south. The air is tangy with brine from the Gulf and the salt marshes that spread in a green expanse to the north. Terns, gulls, and other shorebirds continually circle overhead, making shrill noises.

At Mobile US 31 completes the long tour that began at the Tennessee line, 207 *m.* to the north. Int. 65 had moved far west from US 31 after Evergreen and entered Mobile from the north. Mobile is the terminal for US 45, US 43, US 98, State 217 and State 225. From Mobile State 163 goes out to Fort Gaines and connections with Dauphin Island.

Tour 2

FROM MOBILE TO THE RECREATION AREAS
ALONG THE SHORE ROADS

I. Junction with US 90—Daphne—Fairhope—Point Clear—Foley—
Bon Secour—Gulf Shores—Fort Morgan. US 98, State 59, State 180.
II. Clarke Gardens—Bellingrath Gardens—Mon Louis Island—
Cedar Point—Dauphin Island—Fort Gaines—Coden—Bayou La Batre
—Grand Bay. State 163, State 188.

Section a. The Eastern Shore

Most of the fine, hardsurfaced roads that run down the western
half of Alabama from the north to the Gulf meet at Mobile. This is
the hub whence tourists, sportsmen, and vacationers fan out into the
Gulf Shores, the concentrated area where hunting is good, fishing is
better, the woods are ideal for camping and the salt spray greets the
swimmers on miles of beaches.

Those who have reached Mobile Bay on US 11 or Int. 65, and
US 90, have an opportunity to travel with ease to the recreation areas
along the Gulf in the only two counties of Alabama that touch salt
water, Mobile and Baldwin. The Eastern Shore Roads turn south from
US 90, 15.4 *m.* east of Mobile and proceeds down the east coast of
Mobile Bay. On the highway map it is US 98.

Baldwin County is a prosperous truck farming area, especially in
the western half. It grows the largest crops of potatoes, including sweet
potatoes, in the State, has a large income from soy beans and cabbage,
and gets up to 75 bu. of corn per acre. Watermelon and cantaloupe
thrive in the sandy soil. At the beginning of 1970 Baldwin County had
1,432 farms that produced farm products worth $13,245,000 and live-
stock valued at $6,918,000. About 5,000 Mexican migrants are em-
ployed during the truck harvest.

There are stands of pine in the eastern half and some lumber is
cut. The planting of pecan trees began after the boll weevil scare and
has proved profitable. In the northern part pines are treated with
creosote for poles and piling.

The Eastern Shore has proved a popular residential area for retired
persons, as well as for those with weekday occupations in Mobile. The
spectacular Dogwood Trail runs through several towns of the Eastern
Shore. Climatic conditions have been so favorable that trees often rise
more than 50 ft.

At the junction of US 90 and US 96 is the Greek Orthodox Church and the Mablis Plantation. In 1906 Jason Mablis, a priest of the Greek Orthodox communion, chose this area as "a full land" on which to settle numbers of immigrants from Greece and start them in truck farming. The settlement prospered and became self-sustaining. In 1965 it completed the church, which is of modified Byzantine architecture. It is embellished with white and colored marble, murals, and brilliant stained glass.

At 2.2 *m.* is a stand of ancient live oaks, which identify the site as an encampment of General Andrew Jackson's troops on their march to Pensacola in the winter of 1814. At a council here General Jackson is said to have reacted violently when soldiers asked for leave to work on their farms. There have been French and Spanish settlers in this area and in 1743 a brickyard and pottery plant were built and bricks for Fort Bowyer, now Fort Morgan, were made here.

DAPHNE, 3.9 *m.* (2,382 pop. 1970; 1,527, 1960, a village looking out over Mobile Bay from a high bluff, was for many years the landing point for steam ferryboats. This steamboat traffic ceased when the Cochrane bridge was built.

In 1888 Alessandro Mastro-Valerio established an Italian colony for agrarian immigrants. Originally they planned to cultivate extensive vineyards, but with the coming of prohibtion they took up truck gardening and citrus fruits. Valerio's contribution to the welfare of his fellow countrymen won recognition from the Italian government.

The clays that form the high bluff at Daphne once furnished material for manufacturing brick and pottery.

At 7.9 *m.* is a junction with a graded road to SILVERHILL, 8.2 *m.* (552 pop. 1970; 417, 1960) *See Tour 2A.*

FAIRHOPE, 9.6 *m.* (5,720 pop. 1970; 4,858, 1960), was settled by a small group from Des Moines, Iowa, who banded together in the winter of 1893-4 to put the teachings of Henry George into practice; they selected Fairhope as the site for a single-tax colony. Today their holdings are about 15% of the city's terrain. The streets are bordered with attractive cottages and gardens of semitropical flowers. The bluff slopes sharply to the water's edge, and a municipal park bordering the water is available for picnic parties. Fishing craft and pleasure boats dock at a long modern pier. There are swimming facilities for children and adults.

Fairhope is considered by some to be the site of Tristan de Luna's settlement on Mobile Bay. In 1559 Luna landed with 1,500 Spanish settlers and soldiers at Mobile Point and moved inland to start a cattle ranch. After many hardships, the colonists re-embarked for Mexico.

In Knoll Park is one of the numerous Indian mounds that testify to prolonged Indian living in this locality.

Fairhope is the seat of the Marietta Johnson School of Organic Education, which carries children from kindergarten through high school along progressive lines. It was established in 1907. An experimental station of Auburn University also has been located here. The

Percy H. Whiting Art Center has a permanent gallery, a studio, and periodical shows.

Fairhope Airport has a runway of 5,200 ft. and is available for private planes.

BATTLES WHARF, 12.7 *m.,* has developed as a summer resort for the Catholic orphans of Mobile and the priests of Spring Hill College. The region between Battles Wharf and Point Clear is haunted, so the natives say. A man was hanged for stealing a horse, and the execution was accomplished by placing the prisoner astride the horse, binding his feet together, and tying the hangman's rope to a large limb overhead. When the noose was fixed around his neck the horse was struck a smart blow and dashed away. The man was decapitated and the story goes that his ghost has been riding the woods ever since seeking his lost head.

POINT CLEAR, 14.7 *m.* is half way down the bay, and almost hidden among moss-draped live oaks and pines. This resort was settled in 1820 by a small group of immigrants from Massachusetts. It had its greatest period of popularity shortly after the War between the States when wealthy people from all parts of the South came here. Planters from all over the South met in the Texas bar of the original Point Clear Hotel, which served as an emergency hospital in 1870 when a boiler explosion destroyed the *Ocean Wave,* an excursion steamer plying between Mobile and Point Clear. The explosion occurred at the pier; more than 100 were killed. The hotel was demolished in 1940.

The present Grand Hotel is the third of the name and is located in 500 wooded acres. It is open the year around, but its peak seasons are Mar. 1-May 31, and Oct. 15-Nov. 15. It operates the Lakewood Golf Club, which has 27 holes. Water skiing, sailing, deep-sea and bill fishing, freshwater fishing for speckled trout and bass, and quail hunting are among the available activities.

Gunnison House, a white frame two-story house was used to care for wounded Confederate soldiers, more than 150 of whom are buried in the Point Clear Cemetery. When Point Clear was bombarded by Admiral Farragut's fleet in 1864 a ball hit Gunnison House, and a brass plate bearing the inscription "Compliments of Admiral Farragut, 1865" now covers the hole made by the shot. After the war Gunnison House became a casino, where money, cotton crops, and sometimes entire plantations changed hands at the gambling tables.

The Public Library is next to the Point Clear post office. It is a one-story structure with only 80 square feet of floor space.

At Point Clear the route turns left over McKenzie's Ferry Road and winds through flat piney woods country with little settlements of rough board shanties marking the camps of the turpentiners. The pines, though old, are small compared to those farther north, but their slow growth makes them so hard that they are used for piling and framing. The trees are also tapped for turpentine and marks of tapping knives have left white scars on their trunks. The soft resinous sap from these scars is periodically scraped off and hauled away to the turpentine stills.

There are small settlements of Italians, Greeks, Scandinavians, Poles, French, Croatians, and Russians scattered through the region, where the older members still cling to their religious and folk customs.

McKENZIE'S FERRY, 24.1 *m.,* crosses Fish River just north of where that stream flows into Weeks Bay. In addition to fresh-water fish, salt-water trout (weakfish), red fish (red drum), and sheephead run up the rest of the river from its mouth a short distance below the ferry. Ducks are plentiful during the hunting season.

At 28.3 *m.,* the route passes through the outskirts of MAGNOLIA SPRINGS, a resort with excellent fishing.

FOLEY, 33.6 *m.,* (3,360 pop. 1970; 2,889, 1960) is a truck and citrus growing center and the terminus of a branch of the Louisville & Nashville Railroad. It also has light industry, making textile fibers for carpets, processing soybeans for oil and feed, making fertilizer, and fishing equipment. One plant, the Vulcan Signs and Stamping corporation makes metal street signs for cities often remote from Alabama. Here satsuma oranges and vegetables are loaded on trucks. Its modern hotel is a meeting place for sportsmen, principally those engaged in deep-sea fishing.

At Foley is a junction with State 59, which goes south to the Gulf. US 98 continues east to Perdido Bay, passing through Elberta, a hamlet of 365 people, 5 *m.* beyond Foley. It continues 9 *m.* farther to LILLIAN, where a toll bridge crosses Perdido Bay into Florida. The Bay Shore is fringed with dense swamps of magnolia and bay trees, yaupon thickets and tangled masses of evergreen vines. Now and then patches of yucca raise their panicles of bell-shaped flowers like snow-white spires. To this tropical-like jungle with its lurking alligators, moccasins and rattlesnakes came the Spanish sea captain de Narvaez in 1528 seeking gold, but finding only hardship. Bass fishing above the bridge is particularly good, and boats and guides are available.

To reach Gulf Shores and the seashore the traveler turns right at Foley, leaving US 98 for State 59, which has come south from Stapleton, where US 31 turned southwest to Mobile. On the way south in Baldwin County State 59 passes through ROBERTSDALE (2,078 pop. 1970; 1,474, 1960), and SUMMERDALE (550 pop.). At Robertsdale Vanity Fair Mills makes nationally-advertised lingerie.

South of Foley the route passes through flat country where patches of pine and clumps of marsh grass are the only vegetation. At 36.6 *m.* is a junction with a graded road. Right on this road to BON SECOUR, 3.8 *m.,* fish and oyster center. *Boats to Dauphin Island; no scheduled service.* In this fishing village descendants of early settlers hold land grants dating back to 1700. Here women may be seen washing Bon Secour oysters.

There is an ancient cemetery behind St. Peter's Episcopal Church. There are remains of a fascinating "tabby" structure, a deserted ruin even in 1798. Recent archaeological digs at the Old Fort have yielded ancient French and Spanish artifacts. It is privately owned but shown by request.

At 43.3 *m.* on State 59, is the entrance to GULF STATE PARK. Here the State has appropriated 6,000 acres with 2½ miles of beach front for the purposes of recreation in the tangy air of the Gulf shores, where, according to the sponsors "sea gulls and sea shells, the surging surf and the sun-kissed sand" are setting the scene. As thousands of visitors move into this tropical area the park provides lodge, restaurant and convention facilities, a beach pavilion and an 825-ft. fishing pier. Slightly off the beach and secluded beneath moss-draped oaks and tall pines are 468 improved camping sites, cottages, 144 resort inn units, picnic area, tennis courts, and farther out, an 18-hole golf course with club house. The proximity to the Gulf does not inhibit fishing a large fresh-water lake, where boating, skiing and swimming are also available. The park was developed by the State Department of Conservation, Division of State Parks, under the supervision of the National Park Service. The Civilian Conservation Corps converted the sand dune area into a recreation spot.

Administration of the park is at Gulf Shores. *For reservations address Gulf Shores Park, 36542; phone (205) 968-4662.*

All the area east of the highway is the Gulf State Park, as State 59 moves toward the sea. Two roads run along the Gulf: State 180, which becomes the DIXIE GRAVES PARKWAY on the long spit of land that runs all the way into Mobile Bay to Fort Morgan. The other road is State 182, which carries the traveler to GULF SHORES and then moves east, crosses Perdido Bay and joins Florida roads at Pensacola.

The first route follows the long, narrow peninsula which separates Bon Secour Bay from the Gulf of Mexico. There are amazingly abrupt changes in the profuse vegetation, which includes scrub blackjack oak, pine, myrtle, small palmettoes, magnolias and holly. The sandy soil becomes dazzlingly white near Fort Morgan; trees give way to grass and scrub palmettoes, and bay and gulf can be seen from the highway.

There are several scattered shell and sand mounds that have long held the interest of archeologists. Excavations have revealed pottery, knives, tokens used in gambling games, and remains of house structures left by generations of primitive shore tribes. Some of them probably still occupied this site when Narvaez sailed into the cove in 1528.

At 50.6 *m.,* is an aboriginal mound covered by trees and underbrush. On the top of the mound is an iron-fenced grave marked with the name Captain William H. Wallace.

The road ends at historic FORT MORGAN on Mobile Point. Seven flags of seven eras fly above its entrance court.

On Mobile Point old Fort Bowyer was fortified during the War of 1812. The garrison defeated a British fleet on September 15, 1814; the British returned and captured the fort the following February, but withdrew in April. The fort was unoccupied until 1837 when it was regarrisoned and named Fort Morgan in honor of General John H. Morgan, hero of the Mexican War. The American flag flew over it until the War between the States, when Governor Moore of Alabama ordered the fortification seized for the Confederacy. The old fort's guns roared again in 1864 during the battle of Mobile Bay, when Admiral Farragut worked his way through the mined waters and shelled the Confederate stronghold.

The defense of Fort Morgan against the concentrated fire of Farragut's ships became a famous chapter in military-naval annals. The fort had 4 ft. 8 inches of solid brickwork reinforced by huge piles of sandbags, and mounted 32 smoothbore guns and 8 rifles in three tiers. The commander was Brig. General Richard L. Page, CSA. Due to the condition of the channel the Federal ships had to pass the fort at close range, and during the hour of action the fort fired 401 shots, about 8 to a minute. To reduce the fort the Federal Navy had to make use of land troops under General Gordon Granger, and it took more than 3,000 shells from ships and army during 12 hours to reduce Fort Morgan, the last defense of Mobile Bay to surrender, 17 days after the naval battle.

The fort was neglected until the outbreak of the Spanish-American War in 1898. When rumors of an attack by the Spanish fleet reached Mobile, new guns were mounted, and sentries kept a sharp watch seaward. No attack was made however, and the fort was again abandoned, until it was garrisoned at the opening of World War I. It is not now used as a fortification, but is a popular picnic ground. It contains an excellent museum and has a launching ramp, beach, and picnic tables. *Open 8-6 the year around.*

Section b. Down the West Shore of Mobile Bay

Here US 90 again serves as the starting point for a journey down the shoreline of Mobile Bay, this time beginning at the junction with State 163, which runs down the west coast and after meeting some county roads reaches recreation spots in Mobile County.

As State 163 moves closer to the Bay it passes west of the former Brookley Air Force Base, which occupied 4,000 acres on Mobile Bay during and after World War II. When this was terminated in 1968 327 acres were acquired by the University of South Alabama as a second campus, and this is now occupied by its Educational, Research and Development Center. Buildings that had been used as officers quarters and for administration were adapted to the needs of the university. There are 165 single dwelling units, three dormitories, and a large cafeteria. The campus extends along the Bay Front Drive for about $1\frac{1}{2}$ miles, and includes a golf course, bowling alley, tennis courts, and two swimming pools. The principal acreage of the former Air Force Base is occupied by Mobile Airport.

At 7 *m.* CLARKE GARDENS lies to the right. This is a high point on the famous Azalea Trail. Nearby is the Mobile Yacht Club, one of the oldest in the nation. Just beyond, the road crosses the Dog River, historic site of Indian villages through the ages. There is some evidence that the first white settlers located here. This is the Mobile municipal boundary line.

South of the river is Hollingers Island, chiefly industrial. West of the route is the Theodore Industrial Park and the freight terminal of the Louisville & Nashville Railroad. Theodore is a site on US 90 and THEODORE DIVISION (17,473 pop. 1970; 10,068, 1960) takes in a wide area. At 24 m. State 163 crosses the Fowl River, which drains a swamp area of Mobile County.

The pirates Pierre and Jean Lafitte are said to have used the mouth of the river as a place to hide from the British constabulary. Its distinction today rests on the proximity of the great BELLINGRATH GARDENS, at the River and State 59, which comes down from Theodore on US 90. Gardens and House were designed in 1918 as the country estate of Mr. and Mrs. Walter D. Bellingrath, of Mobile. It includes one of the most remarkable collections of rare azaleas and japonicas in the United States and is a colorful spot along the famed Azalea Trail. Set on a bluff overlooking three clear, green-colored streams, the gardens are planted with thousands of boxwood, azalea, and other flowering shrubs. Paths cross rustic bridges over clear lakes and pass through aisles of moss-draped trees.

A winding trail, flanked by ferns and blooming flowers, leads from the entrance to the fountain plaza, in the center of the garden. Here amid ancient moss-hung, ivy-wrapped live oaks is the Bellingrath House, its delicately wrought iron railings and iron lace patio in dark relief against sunbathed walls. Wide flower-flanked steps ascend to the terrace, which fronts the river, and down to a boathouse where there is a deck with inviting chairs and tables. Further along the trail is Belle-camp, a lodge remodeled by the Bellingraths soon after they purchased the estate in 1918. In the immense living room, which has a beamed ceiling treated and weathered to suggest age, is a huge open fireplace. Adjoining this room is a screened and glassed porch, large enough for a refectory table seating 24 persons.

South of the main garden is a rose garden enclosed by a chain fence with climbing roses intertwined in its links. Here are the conservatories, filled with palms, ferns, and tropical plants; in the open, thousands of roses are planted about two large pools and beds of yellow lilies surround benches placed beneath rose-hung trellises.

The gardens have an almost continuous succession of color. The camellia blooms from January to March, and long before this display is ended, azaleas blossom in variegated colors. They flaunt their gorgeous tints until mountain laurel brightens the woods with delicate pink and white, and sweet olive fills the spring air with heavy fragrance. In May the gardens are respendent with hydrangea and gardenia, followed by crape myrtle, oleander, brilliant hibiscus and Allamanda. These and numberless other gay flowers and red berries make an entrancing summer scene in a setting of old oaks decked in long strands of Spanish moss that swing lazily in the breeze.

Originally jungle land, this garden was developed by George B. Rogers, Mobile architect of grounds and house, who directed 100 laborers. Under his supervision, the rock gardens, grottoes, ravines, cascades, and fountains were placed, and more than 20,000 azalea bushes, including 75 varieties ranging in age from 1 to 100 years, were planted.

The property is administered by the Bellingrath-Morse Foundation. *The gardens are open 7 a.m. to sunset; adults $2, children, $1. The house is open 8-5; adults and children, $2.50.*

The Fowl River follows an erratic course, giving part of the county the appearance of an island called MON LOUIS ISLAND, and outlining an area inhabited by gay and hospitable folk that are descended from French, Spanish, and Indian forebears and speak English with accents similar to those of the Cajuns. South of the river is Faustinas Beach.

The OLDE FORT ALABAMA RELIC MUSEUM has collections of Indian artifacts, pottery, stone tools, and beads, as well as canon balls, guns, and other reminders of military campaigns. Also on exhibit are some personal belongings of the Apache leader Geronimo. *Open 8 till sunset; admission charge.*

From CEDAR POINT, the last bit of Mobile County that frames HERON BAY, State 163 takes the Gordon Persons Overseas Highway, *3m.* long, to Dauphin Island.

DAUPHIN ISLAND, visible across the channel from Fort Morgan, was called Massacre Island when Iberville established a base here for the colonization of Louisiana in 1699. When the Frenchmen landed on the island they found human bones bleaching on the sands, but undisturbed by these gruesome relics they proceed to build barracks, a warehouse, and a powder magazine. Settlers from Fort Louis de la Louisiane, on the Mobile River, joined the Island colony in 1708 and it was renamed Dauphine in honor of Marie Adelaide of Savoy, wife of Dauphin Louis, Duke of Burgundy. The settlement prospered until 1711 when a raid by English privateers almost ruined the colony. Under Governor L'Épinay, who arrived in 1712, development continued but the hurricanes that swept up from the Mexican Gulf were a continued menace. One of these storms in 1717 raised a sand bar that closed the port on the south and washed away half of the island. In 1740 another great hurricane struck, flattened buildings, and swept away more than 300 head of cattle. The island became a Spanish possession in 1762 when France, by a secret treaty, ceded all her Louisiana territory east of the Mississippi River to Spain. In 1763, by the Treaty of Paris, the island was ceded to England and the few remaining inhabitants remained British subjects until it was returned to Spain 20 years later.

The United States claimed the island in 1803 as part of the Louisiana Purchase, but Spain held it until General James Wilkinson, U.S.A., seized it in April, 1813, because the British were using it as a base.

Dauphin Island is today a non-profit development of the Mobile Area Chamber of Commerce. There is a year-round colony of residents, as well as a large summer population, some occupying their own vacation homes and others using motels. All types of water sports are available, as well as golf and fishing. The Alabama Deep Sea Fishing Rodeo is held here annually.

On the eastern point of Dauphin Island stands FORT GAINES. It was begun in 1822, during the administration of President Monroe and named for General Edmund Pendleton Gaines, the officer who arrested Aaron Burr when the latter was accused of conspiring against the United States government. The principal works were constructed in the 1850s under the supervision of Jefferson Davis, Secretary of War.

On the eve of the Civil War, January 5, 1861, Alabama militia seized the fort, as well as Fort Morgan, to insure control of Mobile Bay. The Confederates held the forts until August 8, 1864, when Rear Admiral David G. Farragut fought the battle of Mobile Bay and took Mobile. The huge anchor and chain from Farragut's flagship, the *USS Hartford,* are an exhibit at the entrance of the fort. *Open daily, 8-5.*

After leaving Dauphin Island and returning north State 163 has a junction 1 *m.* above Cedar Point with State 188, which runs west along the coast 8 *m.* to CODEN, a small resort and fishing village on a bayou. Tarpon fishing is excellent in summer, and kingfish, mackerel, bluefish, weakfish, and pompano are also caught. Capable boatmen operate charter craft at reasonable rates. The quaint white-painted Catholic church and the ramshackle oyster houses stand beside the bayou where the boats discharge their daily catch.

About 2 *m.* farther is the town of BAYOU LA BATRE (2,664 pop. 1970; 2,572, 1960) on the bayou of the same name. Here is a commercial dock of the Inland Docks Division. This is a community of winding streets and cottages set in gardens of roses, poppies, geraniums, larkspur and golden glow. The road curves down to a waterfront littered with piles of oyster shells, dumped by the canning factories, where many of the townfolk work. Smelly oyster and shrimp boats, their scarred hulls salt-stained and drab, crowd the shoreline while discharging cargoes. For many years the town was a port for steamers plying between Mobile and New Orleans. In recent years the town has gained popularity as a resort. Its settlement goes back as far as 1796. Its principal event is the annual blessing of the shrimp boats, which calls out a display of colorful decorations, bright pennants, flowers cast as memorials on the waters, a water parade and prayers for the fishermen.

After Bayou La Batre State 188 turns northwest to GRAND BAY, 10 *m.,* an inland farm village at a junction with US 90. Grand Bay Division, which takes in much more ground, had 9,685 pop. 1970; 6,164, 1960. The return to Mobile is made on US 90. *See Tour 3.*

Tour 3

TWO HIGHWAYS ACROSS THE SOUTHERNMOST
COUNTIES

(Florida line)—Styx River—Robertsdale—Loxley—Cochrane Bridge
—Mobile—Theodore—Irvington—St. Elmo—Grand Bay—(Mississippi Line)

US 90. Int. 10. 77 *m.*

These two highways, following the shore lines of Florida, Alabama,
Mississippi, and Louisiana, provide quick transit for traffic on Interstate
10 and a more leisurely drive with numerous stops in the recreational
counties of Baldwin and Mobile. Part of the route follows the Old
Spanish Trail, by means of which the early explorers managed a passage
through the tropical jungle on their way toward and around Mobile Bay.

A large part of the area is devoted to farming; the sandy soil and
abundant water helping plant growth. Trees are mainly scrub pines and
palmettoes; swampy jungle-like forests fringe the water courses. Truck
farms, tobacco fields, pecan and satsuma orange groves abound. The
streams are filled with black bass and bream; the woods and fields have
flocks of quail and doves. Foxes and bobcats are numerous, and black
bears are seen occasionally in the densely wooded swamps.

US 90 crosses the Florida Line, 0 *m.,* on a bridge over the Perdido
River, 16 miles northwest of Pensacola, Florida. The river was once
the boundary between French Louisiana and Spanish Florida.

For a century before the bridge was erected in 1919, Nunez Ferry
was situated here. It was put into operation in 1815 by Henry Allen
Nunez, who helped build a road between Pensacola and Blakely over
which a stagecoach line operated. There was considerable travel despite
the bad road and cumbersome coaches, and Nunez's tolls grew to a
fortune that rumor said he kept buried near his house.

During the War between the States stories of this buried gold
reached Federal troops garrisoned at Pensacola, and a band of raiding
Yankees came to investigate. When Nunez refused to talk, the soldiers
strung him up by the thumbs from a large live oak in his yard. He still
was grimly silent, and his wife was brought from the house to witness his
agony. He ordered her not to speak, but she revealed the hiding place
of a considerable number of silver coins. The raiders lowered Nunez
to the ground, divided the money and departed. But they soon returned,
saying, "We didn't know about the silver, but we do know about your

gold, and we've come for it!" Again, Nunez refused to speak and was suspended by his neck in an open well, the raiders threatening to cut the rope strand by strand until he dropped to the bottom. Finally his wife revealed the cache of gold, and Nunez was hauled up. He never recovered from his ordeal and died less than two years later.

The STYX RIVER, 1 *m.*, a tributary of the Perdido, was given its name by a Virginia schoolmaster. He came to the region early in the 19th century to teach the settlers' children in a pine pole cabin, and was so overwhelmed by the stillness of the forest and the dark waters of the river that he named it after the mythological river of Hades.

At 5.9 *m.* is a turpentine settlement, a group of unpainted shacks on both sides of the road.

ROBERTSDALE, 16.3 *m.* (2,078 pop. 1970; 1,474, 1960), is the trading and shipping point for a wide farming section. The main exports are vegetables and satsuma oranges. There are many pecan groves here. Robertsdale Division had 8,275 pop. 1970; 7,847, 1960. It has a junction with State 59, which joins it going north for 7 *m.*, and State 104, going west to the Bay Shore Road. At 3 *m.* on State 104 is SILVERHILL, (552 pop. 1970, 417, 1960) agricultural village founded by immigrant families from Europe. In 1897 Oscar Johnson and two friends, of Chicago, bought 1,500 acres of land in Baldwin County and promoted an all-Scandinavian settlement. The soil was responsive and the climate favorable, so Swedish settlers came from many points to establish permanent homes and farms. Thirteen Bohemian families joined the community in 1909, other Swedes and Bohemians followed, and the section began to prosper. Oscar Johnson cast his lot fully with his project and was elected the first mayor when Silverhill was incorporated in 1926.

LOXLEY, 22.1 *m.* (859, pop. 1970; 831, 1960), is in a potato growing district. Nearly 20,000 acres are planted in potatoes and many truckloads are shipped from the town annually.

At 32.7 *m.* is the junction with the Bay Shore Road.

Breastworks of the old SPANISH FORT (*see Tour 1*) are visible, 33.4 *m.*, a few yards from the highway.

Between the eastern end of COCHRANE BRIDGE, 34.2 *m.*, and Mobile, the route is over this 10-mile causeway across Mobile Bay, used also by Int. 10, US 31 and US 98. The outskirts of the city begin at the western end of the bridge, 44.4 *m.*, where docks, warehouses, and railroad yards cover a wide area.

MOBILE, 48.1 *m. See Mobile.*

Southwest of Mobile, US 90 traverses the red ridge country. Int. 10 moves parallel and west of US 90. Dark green expanses of satsuma orange groves, interspersed with flourishing truck gardens and poultry farms, stretch over rolling hills and valleys. At intervals there are clusters of ancient gnarled live oaks. The route dips gradually into low, marshy land carpeted with tough green grass. Clumps of palmettos spread sharply pointed fans as a background for dull-hued blossoms of the orchid family.

SPANISH FORT, 9 *m.* east on US 90, is the site of a Confederate last stand in defense of Mobile. After the fall of Fort Morgan Federal General E. R. S. Canby led 32,000 Union troops against Spanish Fort. The Confederate force held out 12 days. Earthworks of both forces remain, and military relics are found from time to time. After Spanish Fort had been taken, General Canby led his troops against Blakely on the Tensaw River, which he took the following day.

The villages on US 90 are few, but there is a substantial farming population in the Divisions. THEODORE, 62.4 *m.* (50 alt.) has a junction with County Road 59, which goes down the middle of the county and has connections with the West Shore Road. While the village has only a nominal population, the Theodore Division had 17,473 pop. in 1970, 10,068 in 1960, an increase of 73.5%.

Theodore is designated in various guidebooks as the spot from which to start for the Belligrath Gardens and House. However, the Gardens are 17 miles from Theodore, and are easier to reach via State 163 out of Mobile to the Fowl River, where the Gardens occupy a bluff overlooking the river (*see Tour 2*).

IRVINGTON, 66.9 *m.* has been a busy shipping center for the pecan crops of the area, but the exploitation of tung trees for tung oil has diminished. While trees are still cultivated, the groves have been reduced by heavy frosts in recent years. Left from Irvington a country road runs to Bayou La Batre (*see Tour 2*).

At 68.2 *m.* is SAINT ELMO, named for the hero of Augusta Evans Wilson's novel, *Saint Elmo.* In addition to the customary truck farming products of the vicinity, considerable pulpwood is cut for shipment to paper mills, and pecan orchards are cultivated.

GRAND BAY, 73.7 *m.* is the center of a diversified truck farming district. Watermelons and sweet potatoes are the leading crops, and many fine turkeys are raised here for shipment to markets throughout the country. Grand Bay Division had 9,685 pop., 1970; 6,174, 1960, inc. 56%. From Grand Bay State 188 goes to Bayou La Batre and connects with the Shore Road to Dauphin Island and Fort Gaines. *See Tour 2.*

US 90 crosses the Mississippi Line, 77.4 *m.*, at a point 12 miles east of Moss Point, Mississippi.

~~~~~~

Tour 4

ACROSS THE STATE THROUGH THE BLACK BELT

(Columbus, Ga.)—Phenix City—Tuskegee—Montgomery—Selma—
Marion — Greensboro — Uniontown — Demopolis — Livingston —
(Meridian, Miss.). US 80

Georgia Line to Mississippi Line 227.5 *m.*

US 80, which runs in a direct line from Georgia to Mississippi
across the center of Alabama, follows one of the old roads that the
settlers used when they came in their Conestoga wagons to seek new
acreage. Here, too, came the stage coaches, all traffic floundering
through the thick mud of the Black Belt during the rainy season. The
land was good for cotton and when cotton was king the route passed
large plantation houses and numerous cabins of the tenant farmers.
Much of that prosperity has diminished, and the mechanization of the
farms has deprived many of the black farmers of their traditional
occupation.

The first telegraph line across the State was stretched along
present US 80.

Section a. *GEORGIA LINE to MONTGOMERY; 82.8 m.*

The eastern section of US 80 crosses an area of flat and rolling
farm land. Here are the gray sand hills of the Chattahoochee watershed, a region which, according to local tradition, was occupied first
by the Kawita Indians. West of Tuskegee the highway is through
the rich Black Belt. Wide fields, mostly cotton and corn, spread far
on both sides of the highway. Along the streams the monotony of the
level land is broken by tall woods of bay, sweet gum, and oak, the bay
remaining green in winter and giving color to the otherwise drab landscape.

US 80 crosses the Georgia Line, 0 *m.,* at the west end of the
Chattahoochee River Bridge, between Phenix City, Alabama and
Columbus, Georgia.

PHENIX CITY, 0.1 *m.* (263 alt., 25,281 pop. 1970.) (*see
Tour 5*), is at a junction with US 241, which unites with US 80 for
1.5 miles.

CRAWFORD, 11.7 *m.* (234 alt., 2,347 pop. 1970 in Crawford
Division), is a farming village, founded in 1814. Early settlers called
it Crockettsville in honor of Davy Crockett, the Tennessee scout who
helped Andrew Jackson defeat the Creek Indians at the Battle of Horse-

shoe Bend (*see Tour 5*). Under that name it became the first permanent seat of Russell County, and retained this office until 1868. In
1843, a group of Georgians changed the town's name to Crawford,
honoring Joel Crawford, a native of their state who had also distinguished himself during the Creek War. In 1846, the town was visited
by Sir Charles Lyell, noted British geologist, who wrote in his journal
of a small log hotel, where he dined on "roast turkey, venison steak,
partridge pie, and a jug of milk." After Seale succeeded it as county
seat, many of the inhabitants moved away, and Crawford shrank to
village size.

SOCIETY HILL, 26 *m.*, a hamlet in Macon County, has a
junction with County 43. The Little Texas-Society Hill Division had
1,724 pop. in 1970, a loss of 18% from 2,104 in 1960.

At 35.7 *m.* is a junction with US 29 (*see Tour 10*), which unites
with US 80 for 7.6 *m.* to Tuskegee. South of US 80 in Macon County
is the TUSKEGEE NATIONAL FOREST, also reached by County
22 and 26 from Society Hill.

TUSKEGEE, 43.3 *m.* (459 alt., 11,028 pop. 1970; 7,240, 1960;
inc. 52%), is the seat of Macon County, and the home of Alabama's
noted Negro college, Tuskegee Institute. The first white men to settle
in the region were French traders. When France surrendered the territory to England in 1763, British troops marched in and garrisoned the
blockhouse. In 1813, Andrew Jackson's soldiers occupied the old fort,
an outpost in the territory of the Creek Confederacy. The name
Tuskegee is a version of Taskigi, a near-by Indian village where Sehoy,
mother of Alexander McGillivray, was born (*see First Americans*).

The artist, Lucille Douglass, was a native of Tuskegee and received
her early art training here. Frederick Arthur Bridgeman, artist, lived
here until he was about 18.

Wide, shaded streets that reach into the residential sections radiate
from Monument Square, the business hub of the town. A Confederate
monument stands partly hidden by thick elms and magnolias.

The Varner-Alexander House, Montgomery St., was built in 1840
by William Varner. Its soft tan brick deepened by time, the house
has colonnaded verandas on two sides, and a cupola built along mansard
lines surmounting the roof. President Theodore Roosevelt was entertained here in 1905 when he visited Tuskegee Institute at the invitation
of Dr. Booker T. Washington, famous director of the school. During
the War between the States, Federal troops were about to destroy the
house when their commander recognized Varner as a classmate at
Harvard. He apologized and saved the house.

The Woodward House, Main St., was built about 1830 by General T. S. Woodward, Indian fighter who also was prominent in the
founding of Tuskegee. The rear rooms of the white frame house, since
remodeled, were the scene of Macon County's first court session, held in
1833 before a courthouse was built.

Surrounded by beds of bright flowers, the Cobb House, Main St.,
was built in the 1840's. A second-story balcony shades a wide doorway,

and pilasters at the edge of the porch conform with the Ionic fluted columns.

The G. C. Thompson House, 303 Main St., is an excellent example of Greek Revival design. An iron balcony subjoining the second floor has a lyre for motif. On December 16, 1898, when President William McKinley addressed citizens of Tuskegee from a platform made of cotton bales, he was a guest of Representative Charles W. Thompson, owner of the house.

The Drakeford-Curtwright House, 511 N. Main St., (1838) has six fluted pillars extending from the ground floor balcony, encircled by a simple balustrade. In the interior are hand-carved stairways, and mantels with delicately finished woodwork.

TUSKEGEE INSTITUTE, 1 *m.* northwest of the city of Tuskegee on US 80, and 3 *m.* south of Interstate 85, is a coeducational, privately controlled, nonsectarian, professional, scientific, and technical institution opened July 4, 1881, by Booker T. Washington (1858-1915), educator. Authorized by the Alabama legislature, it began with an annual appropriation of $2,000 for salaries for the first normal school for the training of Negro teachers. From a humble beginning in a one-room shanty the institute has grown to more than 60 buildings on a campus of 1,800 acres (out of 5,189 acres owned), and six major areas of instruction: the College of Arts & Sciences, and the Schools of Applied Sciences, Education, Engineering, Nursing, and Veterinary Medicine. In the 1974 school year it enrolled 3,171 students and had a teaching staff of 375.

Among the notable structures on campus are the Chapel, the Hollis Burke Frissell Library, and the George Washington Carver Museum. Associated is the John A. Andrew Memorial Hospital, which has 160 beds and serves not only the institute but the surrounding area. A notable monument is a statue of Booker T. Washington in the symbolic act of lifting a veil from a Negro laborer to aid his rise by education and industry.

The institute offers a rounded education in the arts and sciences. Its courses on black studies, social and cultural changes in Africa, and the black experience on the American continent have a logical place in the sections on sociology, history and political science. In its Department of Aerospace Studies and Military Science it offers courses in the Reserve Officers Training Corps (ROTC) of the Air Force and the U. S. Army, which are mandatory for first-year male students and voluntary for the three succeeding years. In 1952 the hq of the Air Force ROTC was placed under the Air University at Maxwell AFB, Alabama. In 1964 a revitalizing program was adopted.

Tuskegee Institute has two semesters and a summer session. Tuition for full-time study is $500 a semester and this is the charge for all non-residents of the State; for others agriculture alone has a fee of $225, and home economics $255 per semester. Lodging and meals are $350 to $400, subject to revision. There is space for 2,000 students in dormitories on campus.

In 1896, Booker T. Washington brought a young Negro teacher, George Washington Carver, to Tuskegee to take charge of the Agricultural Department. Carver, born a slave, had worked his way through high school and Iowa State College at Ames, Iowa, where he received a master's degree in agriculture. While attending college, Carver made a thorough study of plant life, doing laboratory work in systematic bacteriology. In his spare time he studied music and art.

At Tuskegee, Carver, after a general survey of the school farms, laid out the great program that became his life work. He made much of his own laboratory equipment from material brought to him by students. He proved to the inhabitants of Macon County that scientific farming was a profitable business; from all parts of the county, white and Negro farmers came to him for advice.

His pioneering developed new uses for the peanut, the pecan nut, and the sweet potato, and he made paint from the local clays. His work is commemorated in the George Washington Carver Museum, which was dedicated by Henry Ford in 1941. It houses the materials for study collected by Dr. Carver, including plants, minerals, and birds, and the records of his achievements. In 1947 a fire seriously damaged the museum; Dr. Carver's records were saved but many of his 100 paintings were damaged. In 1951 the building was enlarged to house collections of African art and books and photographs about Negro activities. The George Washington Carver Research Foundation supports the museum as well as research in behavioral science and other disciplines. The Art Gallery has become part of the Carver Museum.

The VETERANS ADMINISTRATION HOSPITAL, Tuskegee, is a general medical and surgical hospital occupying 94 buildings on a tract of 290 acres, $1\frac{1}{2}$ miles from Tuskegee Institute. When opened June 15, 1923, it was planned to accommodate Negro veterans of World War I living in the South. In 1930 it became part of the Veterans Administration, its name was changed to the present one, and integration of the races was begun. However, the hospital was not fully integrated until the 1958-62 period. It consists of 1,103 beds and a 112-bed nursing home care unit (1974). The hospital is equipped with modern facilities throughout. There are specialized clinics, surgical units, intensive care units, a clinical laboratory, a blind rehabilitation clinic, physical medicine and rehabilitation clinics, and a well-stocked medical library. Residency training and teaching programs are devised by a Medical Advisory Committee from the principal southern medical colleges. The staff of 1,252 comprises professionals as well as volunteer workers, and employees have full housekeeping and recreational facilities.

The route between Tuskegee and Montgomery is paralleled at an average distance of five miles by the Tallapoosa River. Here begins the fertile Black Belt region, with its typical sluggish, lowland streams and dark swamps shaded by bay trees; cypress, gums, and magnolias. On higher knolls, old manor houses, partly hidden by groves of oaks, overlook broad, often neglected acres on which stand weathered tenant shacks.

Fifty years ago this was crop country, with corn and cotton the mainstays of agriculture, together with hay and dairy products. In recent years cotton has diminished in quantity and livestock has been increasing, and some parts have been turned into timber land.

US 80 passes through the old hunting grounds of the Creek Confederacy. Their towns formed an almost unbroken chain along the banks of the Coosa and Tallapoosa Rivers, and British traders used this route in their commerce with the Indians. In 1714, the French established a fort and trading post at the confluence of the Coosa and Tallapoosa, cutting deeply into the trading district of the English. Until the end of the French and Indian War there was strong rivalry between the two nations for control of the Indian trade.

Union Church, 50.5 *m.*, is a white frame building serving a scattered rural congregation. Near here a large Creek war band ambushed a force of 1,300 Georgia militia and friendly Indians under General John Floyd during the Creek War. On a cautious march from Fort Hull to Tukabatchee, General Floyd had encamped for the night of January 26, 1814, near Calabee Creek. Just before dawn the next morning, the Creek, led by High Head Jim, their half-breed chief, attacked the camp. The Americans were saved from utter rout by the cool action of Captain Jett Thomas' artillery, assisted by a supporting rifle company, under Captain William E. Adams. This gave two Georgia battalions time to reorganize. They counter-attacked and drove the Indians back. The Indians' losses were greater than the whites', but the battle ended in a technical victory for the Creek. Floyd ordered a retreat to Fort Hull that day, and did not move his army from its walls again during the war. Weatherford, the half-white Creek chief, is said to have planned the attack and moved the Indians into position. His idea was to wait and strike while the American force was crossing the stream, but he was overruled by High Head Jim, the other leader, who refused to wait.

At 55.5 *m.*, in front of the little white frame LaPlace Methodist Church, is a monument to Matthew Parham Sturdivant, the first minister sent by the Methodist Episcopal Church into the Alabama territory. He preached among the Indians and the scattered white settlers in 1808-09.

POLE CAT SPRINGS, 57.4 *m.*, a farming hamlet, is on the site of a United States Indian agency where, as early as 1805, the young government at Washington was trying simultaneously to protect the Indians from land-hungry settlers and to restrain the tribesmen in their disputes with the squatters. Eleven years after the agency was founded, Walker's Tavern was built here. The site is marked by a shaft placed by the Alabama Anthropological Society.

At 60.6 *m.* is a junction with a graded dirt road.

Right on this road 3 *m.* to another graded road; L. on the second road 3.9 *m.* to a third graded road. L. here to a path 4.2 *m.; L.* on this path to OLD FORT DECATUR, 4.7 *m.* in the great bend of the Tallapoosa River. Built early in 1814 by Colonel Homer V. Milton of the 3rd U. S. Infantry, the earthwork was named for Commodore Stephen Decatur. The following year General "Nolichucky Jack" Sevier, hero of Kings Mountain and thrice Governor of Tennessee, who died while serving as commissioner to fix the boundary line between the Mississippi Territory and the Indian lands, was buried in the ramparts of the fort. In 1888 his remains were carried back to Tennessee and re-buried in Knoxville. Although grown over by timber, the earthwork is in a fine state of preservation and retains its original contour. The redoubts and trenches form a square with sally ports of the north, south, and west. Local history has it that the fort was built on an ancient Indian mound. Around a small marker placed on the site by the Alabama Anthropological Society in 1931 is the old iron fence that enclosed Sevier's grave. Osceola, the Seminole war chief, was born near Fort Decatur. Near here, also, was the home of John McQueen, the Creek half-breed who is credited with having lived to be 128 years old.

A small log house in WAUGH, 66.5 *m.,* once was Lucas Tavern, where in April, 1825, General Lafayette spent the night while en route to Montgomery. The event is commemorated by a marker on the highway.

At the foot of a hill is the site of Abram Mordecai's Trading Post, established in 1783. Mordecai, a Pennsylvania Dutch Jew who fought in the Revolution, was the first white man to settle in what is now Montgomery County, where he erected the first cotton gin in Alabama.

MOUNT MEIGS, 70 *m.* a village, is the center of the Mount Meigs Division of Montgomery County (2,318 pop. 1970; 2,707, 1960, loss 14%). Ten miles east on the Wares Ferry Road is located the MOUNT MEIGS MEDICAL AND DIAGNOSTIC CENTER, newest of the facilities of the Board of Corrections, opened in 1970. The M & D Center, as it is called, has minimum, medium, and maximum security and receives all prisoners from the courts. It can accommodate 503 inmates and is always near capacity because it is the receiving center for the system of corrections. At times there is a backlog of as many as 400 inmates in county jails, who already have been sentenced but have not yet been received by the State. There is a permanent staff of 118. Approximately 125 inmates are assigned as permanent party to the center and have clerical, kitchen, and janitorial duties; the rest are kept for a few weeks while being classified for assignment to other institutions. This process involves evaluation, age, education, background, type of felony committed, medical and dental examination, and any previous FBI record. A fully equipped hospital and separate tuberculosis ward, all with maximum security, serve the entire correctional system.

A five-member Board of Corrections was established by the State Legislature in 1952 and superseded the former Dept. of Corrections & Institutions. The members are appointed by the governor to 10-year terms, with one member appointed every two years, subject to Senate confirmation. No two members may reside in the same Congressional District. In 1974 there were 4,170 inmates in the major institutions, work release centers, eight highway road camps and the cattle ranch, of whom 170 were women. The work release program has special responsibilities and rewards. Only carefully chosen inmates are allowed to join the program. To be eligible a candidate must have a favorable work and conduct record, be in minimum custody for 60 days and have not more than 18 months left before his release date. He resumes support of his family and his own expenses.

MONTGOMERY, 82 *m.* (133,386 pop. 1970). *See article on Montgomery.*

In Montgomery are junctions with US 31, US 231, US 82, US 331, Int. 65 and Int. 85.

Section b. MONTGOMERY to MISSISSIPPI LINE; 144.7 m.

West of MONTGOMERY, 0 *m.,* the route traverses the center of the rich Black Belt, a gently rolling, open country similar to the Midwestern prairies. This strip of rich black loam, of which Alabama has the largest share, stretches across three Southeastern States, and is identified with cotton. Under the brilliant redbud trees in many pastures are large herds of fine cattle, fattening on Johnson grass, and great Poland China hogs rooting through deep stands of cover crops— crimson clover, vetch, and lespedeza. Big, rambling mansions along the road are the visible reminders of the region's historic and romantic past.

At 6.2 *m.* is the southern junction with US 31 (*see Tour 1*).

Here is DANNELLY MUNICIPAL AIRPORT, also accessible from US 31 and Int. 65, which has scheduled flights by Delta, Southern and Eastern Airlines.

The highway crosses Pintlalle Creek, which runs north into the Alabama River.

The highway runs along the southern edge of LOWNDESBORO, 22.2 *m.* (198 alt., 219 pop. 1970), settled about 1818. Lowndesboro has always been the home of planters, and has a number of ante bellum mansions comfortably separated by wide lawns, landscaped with boxwood, japonica, and crape myrtle. Many of the old houses are occupied by descendants of the builders.

The Squire George Thomas House (*private*), Main St., across from the Junior high school, is a large two-story building with 13 fluted columns rising to a bracketed roof. The front and side balconies are balustraded with hand-wrought iron. Woodwork on the interior is carved, and black marble mantels ornament the fireplaces.

Old Homestead (*private*), Main St. was the home of Dixon H. Lewis, Alabama senator who weighed 500 pounds. His bulk required an especially built seat in Congress. A witticism among other senators of his time was that Alabama had the largest representation of any State. The carriage in which he traveled was specially sprung to accommodate his weight. A stone marker before the house bears the date 1823.

On the Negro Methodist Church here is the dome of Alabama's first Capitol. It was brought to Lowndesboro from Cahaba by white people, who built and first used the church.

For many years the densest Negro population in the State was found in his section. But tractor farming and cattle raising have removed half of the Negroes from the plantations where, as tenants and sharecroppers, they grew corn and cotton on the same acres that their ancestors tilled as slaves.

BENTON, 35.3 *m.* (129 alt., 115 pop. 1970), which is located a few miles south of a major bend in the Alabama River, is in the heart of an area, southeast of Selma, which has many reminders of the historic past. The area was the site of Indian villages for many centuries and is full of archaeological remains. Here the advancing whites fought to dislodge the Indians and routed them, and when the land prospered white owners built substantial plantation houses that survive. East of the bend on the Alabama River is Jones Bluff Lock and Dam. South in Dallas County is the Tyson Plantation, site of a Creek ceremonial place. The Creek were defeated here in December, 1813, by General Claiborne and a mixed army of white troops, renegade Creek and Choctaw warriors. The Indians had been told by Josiah Francis, their prophet, that no force could defeat them on this ground; but in a short, bloody engagement, their ranks were shattered. The main body of warriors fled to the river, and was able to cross while a rear guard fought off the attacking whites and Choctaws. In the confusion of retreat, however, the half-breed Creek leader, Bill Weatherford, was surrounded by a group of Americans and almost captured. But he fought his way out of the trap and then raced his horse toward the river. Tradition says that he jumped the horse off a bluff to elude his pursuers. The river bank at this point is frequently spoken of as Weatherford's Bluff.

At 37.2 *m.* is a junction with County Road 7. Left on this road to PLEASANT HILL, 11.5 *m.* named for a slave dealer who built one of the first houses in the settlement. Later, it became the haunt of so many disreputable characters that it was called Fort Rascal. The worst of these eventually left the region and the original name was resumed.

Right from Pleasant Hill on a graded road to Belvoir (*private*) 16.9 *m.,* the ante bellum home of Reuben Saffold, Chief Justice of Alabama. Built in 1825, the two-storied neoclassic frame house has six massive columns supporting the portico. A balcony overhangs a paneled front entrance, which is flanked by sidelights and has a paneled fanlight. Judge Saffold was born in Georgia, where he studied law. After moving to Jackson, in present Clarke County and fighting in the Creek War (1813-14), he built and occupied Belvoir and resumed his law practice; when the system of State courts was inaugurated, he was appointed judge of the second judicial district and ex officio a member of the State supreme court. He retired from the bench in 1836.

About halfway from Benton to Selma on US 80 is CRAIG AIR FORCE BASE, where the Undergraduate Pilot Training Program is turning out pilots.

SELMA, 50.3 *m.* (127-147 alt., 27,379 pop. 1970). *See article on Selma.*

In Selma US 80 has a junction with State 22, a north-south highway. South on State 80 to a junction with a graded road 4.9 *m.;* L. on this road, 9.8 *m.,* to the site of CAHABA, the capital of Alabama from 1819 to 1826. Built where the old French trading post stood at the confluence of the Alabama and Cahaba Rivers, the first capital was at one time the center of Alabama culture and industry. But it was doomed from the beginning. In spring and autumn the two rivers overflowed their banks, flooding large areas and bringing epidemics of fevers in their wakes. In the spring, 1825 the town greeted Lafayette, who arrived by river boat. Later there was a great flood while the legislature was in session, causing a part of the capitol to crumble. The legislators immediately voted to remove the seat of government to Tuscaloosa. Many of the leading citizens moved away, tearing down their mansions to rebuild them at Selma and Mobile. Cahaba clung subbornly to the faint traces of affluence that remained, for it was still the seat of Dallas County. Then another flood came in 1833, and more folk moved away. But a few loyal citizens continued to transact business there and gradually Cahaba revived. Between 1840 and 1860 it regained importance. But the War between the States and the dark years that followed, again swept its wealth away. Another exodus was begun, reaching a climax in 1866 when the county seat was removed to Selma.

In recent years efforts have been made to mark streets and houses among the ruins and the old cemeteries have been cleared of wild growth. A picnic area overlooks the river.

West and northwest of Selma US 80 taps the rich agricultural county of the Black Belt, reaching up to the Oakmulgee Division of the TALLADEGA NATIONAL FOREST, which covers sections of Tuscaloosa, Bibb, Hale, Perry, and Chilton Counties and a small segment of Autauga. In the 99-mile stretch between Selma and Demopolis US 80 has junctions with a number of State roads. The principal towns in this area are Marion and Greensboro.

One of these roads is County Road 37, which goes north from Selma 6.3 *m.* to SUMMERFIELD, where Centenary College, founded in 1839, once held high rank as a school for the daughters of planters. A favorite bit of folksay concerns a great drouth that occurred here years ago. Crops were scorched and ruined, livestock suffered, and wells dried up. Assembling in the community church, the alarmed people called upon A. H. Mitchell, Methodist minister, and Dr. Drury Fair, local physician, to lead the prayers. Preacher Mitchell, a large man with a powerful voice, pleaded for a great downpour; but Dr. Fair, small and quiet-spoken, asked for soft showers. As they prayed, rain began falling. It fell in torrential sheets near the Mitchell home, where trees and chimneys were blown down, but some persons asserted there was only a gentle shower at Dr. Fair's.

County Road 37 continues north to VALLEY CREEK STATE PARK, a recreational area of 700 acres, southeast of the Talladega National Forest.

At BROWNS, 17 *m*. west of Selma, US 80 has a junction with State 5, which proceeds north 14 *m*. to MARION (263 alt., 4,289 pop. 1970; 3,807, 1960, inc. 12.7%), seat of Perry County (15,388 pop. 1970; 17,358, 1960, dec. 11%).

Marion, built about the courthouse square, was known first as Muckle Ridge, because Michael Muckle had a cabin near by in 1817. The name was changed to honor Francis Marion, the Swamp Fox of the Revolution. Broad streets are shaded by giant oaks, and large lawns front many mansions built in the ante bellum period. The atmosphere of serenity is dispelled only on Saturdays, when farmers throng into town for "socializing" and trading.

Perry County Courthouse is a brick structure with marble flagged corridors; six white columns reach almost to the big clock over the main entrance. A monument to Nicola Marschall, Prussian artist and music teacher who designed the Confederate flag, stands just off the main entrance walk. In the deeply shaded Lea House, 318 Green St., occurred the marriage in 1840, of Margaret Lea and Sam Houston, former Governor of Tennessee (1827-9), and President of the Texas Republic.

Captain Porter King House (*private*), Main St., was the home of the Confederate officer to whom General Bee, at the first Battle of Manassas, made the remark about General Thomas J. Jackson "standing like a stone wall." From this time on Jackson was known to his troops as Stonewall Jackson.

JUDSON COLLEGE is a senior liberal arts college for women that was founded in 1838 as the Judson Female Institute and since 1843 has been maintained by the Alabama Baptist State Convention. It is dedicated to the education of young women in a Christian atmosphere and grants the degrees of bachelor of arts, of science, and of science in music education. It has the distinction of having continued instruction since its founding, even remaining active during the Civil War, when so many other institutions had to close.

Milo P. Jewett served as president for 16½ years, after which he went to New York to become organizer and first president of Vassar College.

Judson has fourteen major buildings on a campus of 100 acres, of which Jewett Hall, the administrative building, was designed by Warren, Knight & Davis of Birmingham and built in 1950. Its east wing contains the Erskine Ramsay Memorial Chapel. Among buildings of recent construction Julia Tarrant Barron Residence Hall (1962) can accommodate 104 students; Anna Elizabeth Kirkland Hall (1969) holds 88. The Robert Bowling Memorial Library, opened in 1963, was designed by Pearson, Humphries & Jones of Montgomery. It has more than 40,000 volumes, microfilms and other materials. These architects also designed the Judson Union and the Kirtley and Barron Residence Halls. The King Science Hall is named for the King family that has been closely associated with the college of four generations.

The annual fee for instruction at Judson is $900. With room and meals added the cost runs from $1,800 to $2,190, depending on semesters and rooms selected. In the fall of 1974 Judson reported enrollment of 421 students and a faculty of 40.

Elmcrest, the ancestral home and birthplace of the poet John Trotwood Moore was built in 1851 and rebuilt in 1949 to provide living quarters for faculty and staff.

MARION INSTITUTE is a college preparatory school on junior college and secondary levels located on 120 acres in the residential part of Marion. It was founded in 1842 as a college for young men and when the Baptist denomination opened another college in Birmingham in 1887, the Institute was taken over by a resident group as a non-profit college with a military base, free of State and church control. There are four academic divisions: the Preparatory School; the Junior College with the humanities, sciences and pre-professional courses; the Preparation for Military, Naval, Air Force, and Coast Guard academies, and the Reserve Officers Training Corps. Originally for men, the Institute now offers the girls of Judson College the privilege of attending classes and obtaining a reserve commission on the same basis as that of the cadets. Women in grades 10, 11, and 12 are qualified for admission and Judson and Marion are often associated in social affairs.

The Mildred Pope Baer Library, completed in 1966, contains more than 23,000 books and a large audio-visual collection. The Trustees' Hall, a dormitory with classrooms, was completed in 1968; the Chapel and Johnson Hall were refurnished in 1972, and there are a new football field, track and stadium. The all-inclusive charge for boarding students, exclusive of laundry and dry cleaning but including haircuts, is $2,690; tuition for a single semester is $1,605. In 1973 Marion enrolled 374 students and had a faculty of 75.

Right from Marion on State 5 to the Warmwater Fish Cultural Development Center of the Division of Fish Hatcheries of the Fish and Wildlife Service of the U. S. Department of the Interior. Here black bass, bream, and crappie are bred in 52 ponds on a reserve of 600 acres. Immediately east of the Fish Hatchery on the Cahaba River is one of the disputed sites of Chief Tuscaloosa's Indian city mentioned by DeSoto's chroniclers. Here DeSoto is said to have betrayed the confidence of the chief by making him a prisoner, a move that infuriated the Indians and caused them to attack DeSoto at Mauvila.

Here State 14 is the principal northwest route. At 18 *m.* from Marion seven State roads converge at the seat of Hale County.

GREENSBORO (220 alt., 3,371 pop. 1970; 3,081, 1960). Three brothers named Russell are believed to have been the first settlers; by 1816, a few crude log houses had been erected and the place was called Troy. The nucleus of the town was located on the site of what later became Southern University. Incorporated in 1823, the village published a newspaper the following year, and put up 20 kerosene street lamps.

A treasure box of fine old homes, Greensboro came through the

Civil War completely unscathed. On the northern edge of the great Black Belt, the thriving cotton center contained little industry to help the Southern war effort. In the latter stages of the War, Federal troops streamed both to the east and west of Greensboro, which stood intact. The torch was not applied, as it was in so many other towns.

Planters of Greensboro built elaborate town houses to gratify their extravagant whims. Charming cottages with intricate filigree work are equally fascinating. In excellent condition today, many are occupied by descendants of the builders. A drive around town discloses the merits of Magnolia Hall, one of the great mansions of the South; the Japonica Path; the old General Patrick May Place, a picturesque stone house; the Noel-Hurtel House, built by Napoleonic refugees in 1821 and perhaps the oldest house still standing in Alabama between Huntsville and Mobile; and the Gayle-Hobson-Tunstall House, built by John Gayle, sixth Governor of the State. There are scores of others.

MAGNOLIA GROVE, on Main St., is the ancestral home of Rear Admiral Richmond Pearson Hobson, U.S.N. This charming Greek Revival mansion (1838) sits serenely among spreading magnolias. Of particular architectural interest are the simple Doric columns of the front verandah. Columns of the rear verandah are of cast iron, embellished with fluted Corinthian capitals. A cantilevered staircase rises to the second floor from the foyer. Pier mirrors, antique silver, chandeliers, and hand-hammered brass cornices are among the original furnishings. In the museum room are mementoes of Hobson, the handsome, dashing hero of the Spanish-American War, including the nameplate of the *Merrimac,* the collier that he sank at the mouth of Santiago Harbor June 3, 1898, to bottle up the Spanish fleet. This daring exploit under the guns of the Spanish forts did not quite accomplish its object, for the Spanish ships under Cervera were able to emerge and were destroyed by Rear Adm. Sampson and Commodore W. S. Schley on July 4, 1898. Hobson received promotion from lieutenant to rear admiral, the Medal of Honor, and later was elected Representative in Congress.

John Erwin House, Church St., was built in the 1830s by John Erwin, who lived here until his death in 1860. Erwin was one of the founders of Southern University at Greensboro, forerunner of the present Birmingham-Southern College. The two-story house is on a slight elevation surrounded by oaks, hickories, and magnolias, and has wide, handsome double entrance doors. A central hall opens to large, high-ceilinged rooms, and the stairway has a hand-carved mahogany balustrade.

Israel Pickens House, N. Main St., is the former home of Israel Pickens, third governor of Alabama (1821-5). It was built first on the governor's plantation at Greenwood, three miles from Greensboro, but was moved to its present site in 1856 where it became the property of the governor's great nephew. The drawing and dining rooms, which are connected by folding doors, have mantels of black marble. But the interior and exterior of the house are decorated with ornamental woodwork, and large fluted Corinthian columns support the roof of the broad veranda.

The original Southern University Building, University St., was built in 1856. In 1824 the Methodist Episcopal Church incorporated the university, but more than 30 years passed before the first students enrolled. During the ensuing war, many students and faculty members joined the Confederate Army. In 1918 the school was consolidated with Birmingham College, and is now operated under the sponsorship of the Methodist Church as Birmingham-Southern College, at Birmingham. The building is now used by a private school.

Otts Place, Main St., was built in 1856 by D. F. McCrary. Corinthian columns extend along the full width of the front porch to support the pediment above the second floor level. A winding stairway leads to a small balcony with iron supports and rails.

Tunstall House, 11 W. Main St., was built by slave labor under the direction of James L. Tunstall. The house is two-storied, with Corinthian columns rising from a porch that extends across the entire front. Large double doors open into a central hall, with the stairway rising from a cross hall in the rear. The second floor is similar in arrangement.

St. Paul's Episcopal Church (1843), beautiful in its simplicity, saw the election of the first Bishop of Alabama, Nicholas Hamner Cobbs. An interesting feature of the pretty Greensboro Presbyterian Church (1859) is the slave balcony at the rear.

Jay's Caboose is a unique railroad museum, containing countless relics and mementoes of early Alabama railroading, housed in authentic cabooses, painted red.

The Tour now turns back to US 80.

UNIONTOWN, 78.3 m. (284 alt., 2,133 pop. 1970; 1,993, 1960, inc. 7%) in Perry County, occupies the highest point between the Alabama and Tombigbee Rivers, was settled in 1818 and until 1861 was called Woodville. During ante bellum days, cotton was the town's chief staple, but now an extensive grassland helps promote a growing dairying industry. Many thousand pounds of butter are shipped annually.

The Roy Peony Fields, East St., five acres in extent, are devoted to the culture of peonies and iris. In spring and summer these fields are a mass of beautiful color.

Right from Uniontown on the graded old Cahaba Road to Pitts' Folly (private), 1 m., a house built in 1849 by Philip Henry Pitts, who came to Alabama from Virginia in 1833. The house was named by settlers who ridiculed its location in what was then a densely wooded section. It stands far back on broad grounds, surrounded by ancient oaks and boxwood. A wide porch with 14 massive Doric columns runs along the north and east side. Double doors, flanked by lights, stand in a small alcove, which is supported by two Doric columns of walnut.

Right from Uniontown on State 61 to Westwood (private), 0.5 m., the Davidson house. This ante bellum residence is much the same today as in 1840, when it was built with slave labor by Colonel James L. Price. Only a kitchen and servant house have been removed. The two-storied, white-painted mansion has ten large rooms, some of which have adjoining dressing rooms. A spiral stairway rises from the rear vestibule. The gardens, extending broadly on all sides, are bright with flowers throughout the year. In the background are wide fields, surrounded by a vast woodland. A semicircular driveway links the house with the highway.

FAUNSDALE, 83.3 *m.* (202 alt., 227 pop. 1970) in Marengo County, is a farm community, named for the Roman god Faunus. Dr. Thomas A. Harrison, the first settler here, built his home one mile south of present Faunsdale in 1843.

At 90 *m.* US 80 has a junction with State 69, which comes down from Greensboro through the rich prairielands, joins US 80 for 1 *m.,* then turns south. At the junction is PRAIRIEVILLE, a farm village, notable chiefly for ST. ANDREWS OF THE PRAIRIE.

This little red clapboard church played an integral part in the lives of early settlers coming to the Canebrake. Designed by Upjohn, construction of the lovely building was supervised by two slaves, both master carpenters. One is credited with the excellent wood carvings. The interior walls are finished in a rich dark brown achieved by careful staining with tobacco juice. The old cemetery is historically interesting.

At 97.3 *m.* there is a junction with US 43, which unites with US 80 for 2.1 miles (*see Tour 9*).

DEMOPOLIS, 99.4 *m.* (106 alt., 7,651 pop. 1970; 7,377, 1960) occupies a white bluff in Marengo County overlooking the Tombigbee River, is a city that is becoming increasingly important in the paper industry and river navigation. Located in the Warrior basin, with the advantage of a 9-ft. channel to the Port of Mobile, Demopolis has projections for a major spurt in population and industry, in the decades ahead. It is the site of the Gulf States Paper Corporation's big plant, the Demopolis Hickory Mill, the Warrior Box Co., a unit of the Lone Star Cement Co., and plants making fertilizer, chemicals and lumber, as well as a steam plant of the Alabama Power Co., a few miles away. It ships products of the large soybean crops of the County.

Demopolis was a port before the railroads came, but it was hardly a place for rapid shipments. Supplies coming upriver from Mobile by steamboat took 2 to 3 weeks en route, a distance of 220 miles. The steam packets lasted until the railroads became dependable. The last steamboat to dock at Demopolis was the *James T. Staples.* Like many another packet it blew up, with a loss of 26 lives.

Demopolis was settled by a group of French *emigres,* who had been ruined by the downfall of Napoleon and came to Mobile in 1817. Among them were veterans who had served in close contact with the Emperor. Called the Association of French Emigrants for the Cultivation of the Vine and the Olive, they had been granted four townships by the U. S. Government and elected to settle on the Tombigbee. After trying to cultivate the soil in the area they found farming disastrous and either moved on to Mobile and New Orleans or returned to France.

Historic buildings in Demopolis date from ante bellum days. Of interest is the Old Courthouse, built in 1843 as a Presbyterian Church. Doric pilasters reflect the Greek revival influence of this now-altered building, which has served successively as church, war-time courthouse, Federal Headquarters during Reconstruction, and now houses the Fire Department.

Bluff Hall, fortress-like in its strength and severity, was built in 1832 on the white bluffs where the French landed. Purchased by the Marengo County Historical Society, it was restored and is open to the public. Lacking the grace of later Greek Revival structures, Bluff Hall is an interesting example of ambitious early architecture. The massive, stocky columns of the front colonnade are softened by a remarkable doorway. Chief ornaments of the interior are Corinthian columns in the drawing room, plaster medallions in the ceilings and several marble mantles.

Lyon Hall (1853) is a mansion in the grand manner. The Old Railroad Tavern (1860) accommodated thirsty travelers. The Ashe Cottage with its Swiss exterior woodwork has great charm.

The finest example of a planter's mansion in Demopolis is GAINESWOOD, a Greek Revival house built in 1842 by General Nathan Bryan Whitfield. It has a Doric exterior, an Ionic interior, and a Corinthian drawing room. Sunk between pillars in the walls of the ballroom are mirrors that give the effect of endless aisles. In some of the smaller rooms the ceilings are domed. The rotunda once seated musicians for the elaborate parties held here. Exceptional is the plaster in intricate patterns. The interior was not fully completed until 1860.

To the right of the entrance is a venerable oak under which the Choctaw Chief is said to have met General Gaines to sign a treaty on land rights.

DEMOPOLIS LOCK AND DAM is located just below the confluence of the Warrior and Tombigbee Rivers. It was opened in August, 1954, to replace four old locks and dams and was the first modern structure built on the Warrior-Tombigbee Waterway since 1940. It consists of a 600 ft. by 110 ft. lock with a 40 ft. lift, a spillway 1,485 ft. long and an earth dike 4,500 ft. long. Behind the dam LAKE DEMOPOLIS extends for 50 miles and provides new areas for fishing, camping, and recreation along its banks.

US 80 crosses the Tombigbee River on Rooster Bridge 112.2 *m.*, built during World War I with funds from an auction of roosters. Among many famous persons who bought Marengo and Sumter County fowls were President Woodrow Wilson, British Prime Minister David Lloyd George, and French Premier Georges Clemenceau. Helen Keller sent a little blue hen that was sold for $5,000.

At 110 *m.* US 80 has a junction with State 28, which joins it for 7 *m.* and then turns north to Livingston. At 5 *m.* beyond a farm road turns left to BELLAMY, 6.3 *m.*, headquarters of the Allison Game Preserve organized in 1901 by Frank Allison. In a day when other lumbermen were thinking only of cutting trees to serve the booming lumber market, Allison was starting a conservation project that, in 1933, brought him recognition from the Lumber Code Administration. In 1936 the annual cut was 15,000,000 feet of timber from 121,000 acres; this was fully replaced by new growth. Deer and wild turkey within the area had multiplied until their number was conservatively estimated at 5,000 and 3,000 respectively.

As vice president of the State Conservation Commission, Allison was in charge of the Alabama conservation program, and nationally known experts came to Bellamy to study his methods. After his death in 1937, his conservation and reforestation program was carried on by his grandson, Andrew Allison and associates.

Five miles beyond the Bellamy intersection a State Road turns north from US 80 to LIVINGSTON, seat of Sumter County (2,358 pop. 1970; 1,544, 1960, inc. 52%) which is served by US 11 and Int. 59. The town grew from a Black Belt settlement which still provides material for historical fiction. It was named for Edward Livingston, Secretary of State under President Andrew Jackson.

Livingston was a hot bed of strife during Reconstruction. Facts surrounding the ambush slaying of William P. Billings, a New York abolitionist, and of Tom Ivey, Negro political agitator, have been embellished by storytellers. Enlarged, also, are the exploits of one of Alabama's most picturesque figures, Steve Renfroe, who is described as a strong leader of a band of vigilantes who was elected sheriff with great acclaim. Some time later he was accused of horse stealing and other robberies and was hanged by his former associates.

Grampian Hill, a one-story frame house with a pedimented porch, is on the eastern outskirts of Livingston. It served as a gathering place for Southern sympathizers during Reconstruction, and many political agitations started here. Shortly before the War between the States, a "flying machine" was manufactured on the grounds by a Dr. Davidson. The Doctor attempted a flight from a hill, but the machine collapsed and he suffered a broken leg.

LIVINGSTON UNIVERSITY, an institution of higher learning maintained by the State, acquired its present title in 1967, but its roots go back to 1835, when citizens of the town raised a fund for school construction. In 1840 it was incorporated as a female academy and in 1883 was designated a normal school for white girls. It gave its first normal school diploma in 1886. Its development as an outstanding school in this field was largely credited to the energies of Dr. Carlos G. Smith and Miss Julia Tutwiler, both of whom became president. The State assumed control in 1907. The institution became Livingston State College in 1957 and established a graduate division in 1958. The university has four instructional units: the College of Arts & Sciences, Business & Commerce, and Education, and the School of Graduate Studies.

The principal buildings are Bibb Graves Hall, which has the administrative offices and the computer center; Julia Tutwiler Library, Lucille Foust Hall, a classroom building; Pruitt Hall, used by the music department and physical education department; and Lurleen Burnes Wallace Hall, chiefly classrooms and an auditorium. There is a Student Center. New dormitories provide facilities for men and women. Spieth Hall and Selden Hall house 208 women residents each. The Tutwiler Library has more than 60,000 volumes and its Alabama Room holds historical collections. In 1974 Livingston enrolled 1,170 and had a faculty of 74.

At Livingston is a junction with US 11 and Int. 59. US 80 has a junction with State 17, which leads 4 m. north to YORK, (3,044 pop. 1970; 2,932, 1960) a farm products and lumbering shipping locality. Last town in Alabama on US 80 is CUBA (386 pop. 1970), where US 11 joins US 80. Two miles farther US 80 crosses the Mississippi line, 144.7 m. and the combined highways proceed 18 m. to Meridian, Miss.

∞∞

Tour 5

NORTH AND SOUTH OF THE TENNESSEE RIVER

I. (Tennessee Line)—Bridgeport—Scottsboro—Paint Rock—Monte Sano State Park—Huntsville—Athens—Coxey—Rogersville—Wheeler Dam—Wilson Dam—Florence—Sheffield—Muscle Shoals—Jct. US 43. US 72.

II. Huntsville—Madison—Mooresville—Jct. Int. 565—Jct. US 31—Decatur—Wheeler—Town Creek—Jct. US 72. US 72 Alt.

Cross-State mileage on US 72, 170.6 m.

US 72 and US 72 Alternate constitute the key highways to the valley of the Tennessee River in Alabama. In consequence they also are the routes to the dams, reservoirs, and power installations of the Tennesse Valley Authority. US 72, the original Lee Highway, enters the State at its northeast corner and runs parallel with the Tennessee to Scottsboro, where it turns directly west to Huntsville. From Huntsville it runs north of the River to Florence, where combined with US 43 it proceeds south through Muscle Shoals. At Huntsville US 72 Alt. starts southwest to Decatur and then moves south of the Tennessee River until it returns to US 72 at Tuscumbia to move west to Mississippi.

Actually, both routes follow the right-of-way of the Southern Railway, which runs parallel with US 72 to Huntsville and accompanies US 72 Alt. from Decatur west to the border.

Tour 4 is a combination of the two routes, which are described as separate units.

Section a. TENNESSEE LINE TO FLORENCE on US 72

The Cumberland, old and eroded foothills of the Appalachian Chain, pushes its tattered hills into the north Alabama sky. Pocked with caves and huge caverns, split with gaps and canyons, the Cumberland cradles the coursing Tennessee River. Interlocked with the scenic geography of this region is its history, for the caves and cliff shelters, which mean natural beauty to men of this day, meant life itself to man of twilight times. The hunting Nomad of the Stone Age sought shelter, water and safety of seclusion. Such homesites abound in the rugged mountains of north Alabama. Rich archaeological strikes have been made here.

The river shaped the destiny of the area. Its broad and fertile valley supported large Indian farming communities, as culture advanced. This is the Cherokee country. Into it, braving hostiles and rapids, came sturdy pioneers. After Andrew Jackson subdued the warring Creeks, it was the river that spawned the graceful, wealthy ante-bellum civilization that flourished on its banks. The lucrative staple, cotton, thrived in the rich soil and the river carried the bales to market. The prosperity of this era is reflected in the surviving mansions of the valley, those that escaped the Federal torch.

During the War between the States, caves of northern Alabama provided handy hiding places and ammunition caches for Confederates. Union forces made periodic dashes into this area from Tennessee, foraging and burning. And when Major General Abel D. Streight brought his Federal raiders across this region on a mission of cutting Southern Railroad connections, the whole of northern Alabama flared with fiery fighting.

This region was the setting for the legendary exploits of Confederate General Nathan Bedford Forrest. Forrest with his "critter company" of cavalrymen harassed Streight at every step, striking so suddenly and often that Streight misjudged Forrest's strength and surrendered to one-third of his numbers.

Thirty-five miles west of Chattanooga, US 72 crosses the Tennessee Line, 0 *m.*, and swings southwest through Brown's Valley between the Cumberland Plateau and the Tennessee River.

Plantation homes still dot the valley as they did when General Sherman came through on his march to the sea, with the shacks of the field hand families tucked in the poorer spots. In the late 1930s tractors began replacing farmhands and thousands of families were thrown out of work.

BRIDGEPORT, 2.5 *m.* (662 alt., 2,908 pop. 1970; 2,906, 1960), in Jackson County, marked the head of navigation on the Tennessee River until the TVA improved the channel and opened the river to Knoxville.

The first white settlers in Bridgeport were Charles and Delia Smithson, who came from Virginia in 1814. The town was occupied by Union forces under General Sherman in the fall of 1863. He established a supply depot and fortified Battery Hill, and from this base started the "march to the sea" in the spring of 1864. Twenty-five years after the war there was a local land boom (1889-94) engineered by Eastern financiers led by the elder Henry Morgenthau. A hotel and houses, designed by Stanford White, were being built when the panic of 1893 stopped activities. The hotel was dismantled and given to the University of the South, Sewanee, Tennessee, to be rebuilt on the campus.

On an island in the Tennessee River near by is the Site of Long Island Town, one of the Five Lower Towns of the Chickamauga during the Revolution.

A County road left from US 72 at Bridgeport leads 4 m. to RUS-SELL CAVE NATIONAL MONUMENT, site of the oldest human habitation so far discovered in Alabama. An area of 310 acres was presented by the National Geographic Society to the State in 1961, after it had explored the cave in cooperation with the Smithsonian Institution and found evidence of human use reaching back at least 8,000 years. The site is administered by the National Park Service, which continues to make archaeological investigations.

Here in a natural cliff shelter at the mouth of a cave hundreds of prehistoric Americans lived a rigorous life. Primitive nomads, these people had little time for anything but securing food and shelter. The tools, weapons, charcoal from their fires, bones left from meals and camp debris accumulated layer upon layer through thousands of years, finally to lie hidden in Alabama soil. Discovery of this site in 1953 was a most important archaeological strike. The museum exhibits these relics, tells the story of their development and use. Visitors may inspect the excavations, and hear a short description of early cultures. *Open 8-5 daily; free.*

STEVENSON, 11.9 m. (2,300 pop. 1970; 1,456, 1960, inc. 64%) is a town in Jackson County.

The backwaters of the Tennessee River from Guntersville Dam are crossed at 14 m.

SCOTTSBORO, 31.4 m. (9,324 pop., 1970; 6,449, 1960, inc. 44%) seat of Jackson County, is a farm center, which also handles timber and cotton products and makes men's underwear. The Southern Railway provides freight service. Saturday is a busy day for farmers who come to town to shop, but the first Monday of each month is traditionally a day for trading, which originated with horse-and-mule swapping many decades ago.

Scottsboro is an important point of the Tennessee Valley Authority, for here are locations for two nuclear power plants, Bellefonte Unit No. 1, which is to be operative in 1979, and Bellefonte Unit No. 2, to start in 1980. Each will be capable of producing 1,213,000 kw of power.

In 1931 Scottsboro gained national attention in the newspapers

Recreation and Industry on the Tennessee River

AERIAL VIEW OF INDUSTRIAL DECATUR ALONG TENNESSEE RIVER
DEVELOPED BY TVA.

GUNTERSVILLE DAM OF TVA ON THE TENNESSEE RIVER

MOTOR BOAT RACES ON GUNTERSVILLE LAKE DURING BOAT RACE FESTIVAL.

GUNTERSVILLE ON THE TENNESSEE RIVER

WHEELER DAM OF TVA, ON THE TENNESSEE RIVER, 16 MILES ABOVE WILSON DAM AT MUSCLE SHOALS. BEHIND IT WHEELER LAKE IS 74.1 MILES LONG, HAS A SHORELINE OF 1,063 MILES AND COVERS 67,100 ACRES.

WILSON DAM AT MUSCLE SHOALS, ALABAMA, A NATIONAL HISTORICAL MONUMENT, WHERE THE TVA POWERHOUSE HAS 21 UNITS WITH 630,000 KW CAPACITY. A NEW NAVIGATION LOCK WAS COMPLETED IN 1959.

MUSCLE SHOALS DURING LOW WATER BEFORE WILSON DAM WAS BUILT IN 1925

ROCKET VEHICLES DISPLAYED AT SPACE ORIENTATION CENTER, MARSHALL SPACE FLIGHT CENTER, HUNTSVILLE

ARCHITECT'S DRAWING OF COMPLETED NUCLEAR POWER PLANT OF TVA AT BROWN'S FERRY ON WHEELER LAKE

NASA-MARSHALL SPACE FLIGHT CENTER, COMPRISING CENTRAL LABORATORY AND OFFICE BUILDING, PROJECT ENGINEERS' OFFICE BUILDING, AND ENGINEERING AND OFFICE BUILDING.

BUILDING A REACTOR CONTAINER VESSEL FOR TVA NUCLEAR POWER PLANT AT BROWN'S FERRY

MAIN GATE, USA MISSILE COMMAND, REDSTONE ARSENAL

HEADQUARTERS, U. S. ARMY MISSILE COMMAND, REDSTONE ARSENAL

RECREATION ON GUNTERSVILLE LAKE, A TVA INSTALLATION ON
THE TENNESSEE RIVER

when nine Negro boys were convicted of criminal assault against two white women. The case brought charges of discrimination, and the Communist party made political capital out of it. Defense organizations obtained a reversal by the U. S. Supreme Court, which declared in 1932 that the defendants "did not have a fair and impartial trial within the meaning of the due process clause of the 14th amendment." Four of the accused were eventually freed.

The *Sentinel* is the daily evening newspaper.

At 31.9 *m.* is a junction, left, with a graded road. Left on this road to Saltpeter Cave, 8.3 *m.,* one of the many caverns along the Tennessee River in this section. According to local legends, a tribe of Indians once lived there. Saltpeter Cave was the first seat of justice when Jackson County was created in 1819, and court was held here for two years while a courthouse was being built. During the War between the States the Confederates worked the cave extensively for saltpeter. The old wooden rails of the mule-car tramway built at this time and an immense Evaporation Kettle, in which the leached solution was boiled, are still in the cave.

West of Scottsboro US 72 passes among knobby outposts of the Cumberlands, with the higher lands of the plateau showing through the pale blue haze to the north. To the south, Gunter Mountains, along the Tennessee, are occasionally visible in the distance.

WOODVILLE, 46 *m.* is a hamlet at the intersection of County 63. Left on County 63 to CATHEDRAL CAVERNS. This picturesque drive leads first to Kennamer's Cove. This was a favorite hiding place for draft evaders during the Civil War. The valley in the side of Gunter Mountain, locally called cove, was secluded, and its inhabitants were sympathetic.

The hill people, descendants of Revolutionary War soldiers who had pushed through the wilderness to these parts, were generally not in agreement with the Southern cause. Many of them joined the Federals. Through the years these fair-skinned, tow-headed folk maintained their Anglican blood strain. They also held to their primitive way of life, scratching a living from the steep farmlands. Thinly clad and poorly nourished, the children had neither modern medicine nor education.

In 1924 a remarkable school came—the KATE DUNCAN SCHOOL FOR MOUNTAIN CHILDREN. Funded and maintained by the Daughters of the American Revolution, the mountain people contributed time and labor for construction. The original structures were erected in the best old-time barn raising tradition. The growth, success and service of this unusual facility, which stands on the northern edge of Gunter Mountain, reads like a fairy tale. Five miles farther are the Cathedral Caverns, spectacular chambers of great size and extent. *Open 9-5 winter; 8-6 summer. Adults, $2; children 5-12, $1; children under 5, free.*

At 49.4 *m.* the route crosses Paint Rock River Bridge.

PAINT ROCK, 52.3 *m.* (599 alt., 226 pop. 1970), and Paint

Rock River were named for a large rock at the confluence of this river with the Tennessee, used as a navigation marker by boatmen.

West of GURLEY, 56.7 *m.* (647 pop. 1970) in Madison County, is a farm trade center. US 72 follows the northern base of MONTE SANO to the outskirts of Huntsville. On this 1,600-foot mountain is MONTE SANO STATE PARK (*see Tour 5*).

At 67.7 *m.* is a junction with a graded road. Right here to the Chase Nursery, one of the largest in the country. It comprises 535 acres devoted to the production of evergreens, other ornamental plants, and fruit trees. The nursery has its own post office.

HUNTSVILLE, 72.1 *m.* (610-630 alt., 137,802 pop. 1970.) *See Huntsville.*

In Huntsville is the junction with US 231 and US 431. (*see Tour 5*).

West of Huntsville the main route is over a fertile plateau, following a stretch of rugged hills composed largely of crumbling limestone and heavily grown with cedars. Farmers here find supplementary income in cutting and hauling red cedar used in manufacturing pencils, mothproof chests, and furniture. Many of them held such deep-rooted love for their land that they refused to sell flowage rights to the TVA. They stubbornly clung to their property even after court action condemned it, and it was necessary to evict them by threat of force.

At 94.7 *m.* is a junction with US 31 (*see Tour 1*), which unites briefly northward with US 72.

ATHENS, 96.2 *m.* (695 alt., 14,360 pop. 1970). *See Tour 1.*

Section b. *ATHENS to SHEFFIELD*

West of ATHENS, 0 *m.*, the terrain changes to rolling farmlands interspersed with small woodlots.

At 0.8 *m.* is the northern junction with US 31 and Int. 65. *See Tour 1.*

At BROWN'S FERRY, 10 *m.* southwest of Athens the Tennessee Valley Authority has been building what the plans call the world's largest nuclear power plant. The generating capacity is nearly $3\frac{1}{2}$ million kilowatts in three units.

COXEY, 13 *m.*, is a farm village. On a hill is the site of Fort Hampton, a stockade built to protect settlers in the days of Indian raids, and extended later as a Confederate garrison post. At 15 *m.* the road crosses Elk River, a tributary of the Tennessee, on the banks of which is ELK RIVER STATE PARK.

ROGERSVILLE, 19.2 *m.* (950 pop. 1970; 766, 1960) is a farm village in Lauderdale County. A road right leads to ELK RIVER STATE PARK.

At ELGIN, 25.1 *m.* in Lauderdale County, US 72 has a junction with State 101, the Wheeler Dam route. Left on this road to WHEELER DAM.

Wheeler Dam is one of the nine mainstream dams of the TVA. It provides flood control, regulates the channel for navigation, and gives the power that generates electricity. The impounded waters are controlled by a roller gate. The power plant has eleven generating units of the outdoor type with a capacity of 356,400 kilowatts. A bridge carries vehicular traffic over the dam. Construction of the dam began November 21, 1933, and first power was generated November 9, 1936. The original lock was rebuilt and placed in service in April, 1962. A second and larger lock was completed in May, 1963.

WHEELER LAKE is 74.1 miles long, with a 1,063 mile shore-line and a surface area of 67,100 acres. The waters extend upriver to the Gunterville Dam. JOE WHEELER STATE PARK, 2,600 acres, is a popular objective for vacations with cottages and resort inns, fishing and camping.

A bridge 35.6 *m.* crosses an arm of LAKE WILSON which covers 15,930 acres. This is an excellent fishing territory, and tourist camps are numerous.

At 39.5 *m.* is a junction with paved Wilson Dam Road. Left here to WILSON DAM, 14 *m.,* first of the great dams named for President Wilson and a National Historical Monument. Lake Wilson, impounded by the dam, extends to Wheeler Dam, 17 miles up the Tennessee River; it covers 23 square miles, is 97 ft. deep at the dam, and has a normal pool elevation of 505 ft. above sea-level. Wilson is a concrete gravity type dam, 137 ft. high and nearly a mile long.

Each of the 58 spillways permits a flow of 10,000 cubic ft. of water a second at normal lake level, with a total capacity of 4,350,000 gallons per second. The powerhouse has a capacity of 630,000 kilowatts in 21 units. An elevator that descends about 160 ft. to the river bed provides entrance to the powerhouse. Navigation Locks at the north end of the dam operates electrically at a speed that will lift boats and barges from the level of Pickwick Lake, below the dam, to that of Lake Wilson-89 ft.-in less than an hour. A 148-ft. lift bridge across these locks connects the trans-dam highway with the shore. A new navigation lock was completed in 1959.

Nitrate Plant No. 2, on the south bank of the river, was built in 1917-18 at a cost of $75,000,000 as part of the war-time national defense program. It has a capacity of 110,000 tons of ammonium nitrate per year. Equipment includes a steam power generating plant with a capacity of 76,000 horsepower. After the war the plant was not used until the creation of the TVA in 1933.

About 10 *m.* west of Elgin US 43 joins US 72 and continues south with it 14 *m.* through Florence to Tuscumbia.

For 37 miles above Florence stretches the area of MUSCLE SHOALS, originally a mass of jagged rocks where the torrents of spring created dangerous rapids that became pools during the dry season. Cotton growers stored their bales in warehouses above the shoals and sent them on barges across the shoals during high water. In 1828 a steamboat actually managed to get upstream and reach Knoxville, but the handicap of the shoals made free navigation impossible. For years shippers lobbied in legislatures for eradication of the Muscle Shoals barrier and finally, in 1875, the Federal Government appropriated funds for building a new canal. It was completed in 1890, the engineer finally responsible being the young Capt. George W. Goethals, a native of Alabama.

The canal was 14 miles long and the excavated earth formed a tow-path, along which a small locomotive pulled steamboats through the canal. It had nine locks in the main channel and two at Elk River Shoals, and at Shoal Creek it ran through an aqueduct built on a wooden trestle. The canal helped steamboats but did not entirely eliminate their grounding on rocks during low water.

In 1898 Brig. General Joseph Wheeler, USA, introduced a bill in Congress to permit the Alabama Power Co. to operate a hydroelectric power plant at Muscle Shoals. The great principle of land and water conservation for public use was implicit in the act establishing the Inland Waterways Commission in 1907. In 1908 President Theodore Roosevelt, a powerful force for saving the nation's resources, named the National Conservation Commission to initiate a plan for reforestation, combatting soil erosion, and improving river navigation by building locks and dams and producing hydroelectric power, for regional use, to help pay for them.

In 1905 the Government had authorized the Tennessee Electric Power Company to erect a dam at Hales Bar, 33 miles below Chattanooga, for producing power and aiding navigation, the Government retaining ownership and leasing operation to the company. The dam had a lock chamber of 60 by 267 ft. and a lift of 33 ft. It was opened in 1913.

This spurred the Muscle Shoals Hydroelectric Company to urge building three such dams with Government money for private operation. But before it could get approval the European war broke out, and Congress passed the National Defense Act of 1916, which provided that the President select sites for making nitrates, which are used in munitions and formerly came from Chili, and to get power from a Government-owned dam. Senator Oscar Underwood of Alabama and Senator Kenneth D. MacKellar of Tennessee recommended the Muscle Shoals area and President Woodrow Wilson chose Sheffield for the first site. This saved Muscle Shoals for public development.

This first dam on the main river was named Wilson Dam. It was 4,869 ft. long, 137 ft. high, had two lock chambers 60 by 300 ft. and a double lift of 90 ft., with a highway crossing the top. Nearby would be the two nitrate plants, with an auxiliary plant run by steam.

The war ended before the Muscle Shoals project was completed, and when the Republicans elected the next President and a majority of Congress, they took steps to stop further expenditures of money, which already had reached $69,000,000. The Government then offered the incomplete structure at public sale, but there were no immediate takers. Then, in July, 1921, Henry Ford proposed to finish two dams for the

Government at cost and offered $5,000,000 for a 99-year lease of dams and plants for producing fertilizer and possibly other products. This brought competing offers from the Alabama Power Company and other private interests, and a boom started in the Tri-cities, of which Sheffield was the center.

A spirited controversy over public versus private operation was waged in and out of Congress. The House voted to accept Ford's plan, but Senator Norris' Committee on Agriculture and Forestry accused Ford of making a petty offer for huge Government assets that would return him many millions. As a result the Senate refused agreement. Henry Ford withdrew his proposal and the realty boom in the Tricities collapsed.

In the meantime high floods on the Mississippi started studies on how much the great tributaries contributed to its volume, and the Tennessee River was found to drain a huge area in the foothills of the Appalachians. Thus flood control was added to navigation as an objective on the Tennessee. Army Engineers outlined a series of storage dams as a remedy and in 1928 Senator Norris proposed such a dam at Cove Creek on the Clinch River near Knoxville. To this Congress added Government operation of the plants. The bill passed but was not signed by President Coolidge. Two years later a similar bill, providing for private operation, was passed and vetoed by President Hoover.

When Franklin D. Roosevelt was elected President the controversy over public or private development of the Tennessee came to an abrupt end, for Roosevelt was a supporter of Federal development of resources that served a large region. In March, 1933, he signed an act of Congress calling for operation of Wilson Dam and its plants by the Corps of Engineers, USA. On May 18, 1933, the President signed an act establishing the TENNESSEE VALLEY AUTHORITY, the most far-reaching regional enterprise in American history. It was to be responsible for developing navigation, flood control, hydroelectric power, soil replacement, reforestation, and in general plan "for the proper use, conservation, and development of the natural resources of the Tennessee River drainage basin and its adjoining territory." Headquarters were placed in Knoxville, and the agency was to cooperate closely with local communities and other administrations inside its terrain.

TVA began waterway control in 1933. Demand for electricity in the area became so great that in 1940 TVA had to supplement its water power with steam plants that used coal. The situation became crucial when TVA began supplying electric power to the atomic installation at Oak Ridge. Today coal accounts for about 80 percent of the power generated by TVA. In order to offset the high cost of coal and prepare for future demands for electricity TVA decided to turn to nuclear energy. It began construction of two nuclear plants: Sequoyah, north of Chattanooga, and Brown's Ferry, 10 miles southwest of Athens and 33 miles east of Florence, the latter expected to have the largest steam plant ever built.

TVA now generates over 100 billion kilowatt hours a year in an area that used about $1\frac{1}{2}$ billion in 1933. Today 160 local electrical systems buy power from TVA for 2,300,000 customers. The average home uses more than 15,000 kwh a year.

The Tennessee, fifth largest river in the country, carries the waters of numerous brooks and rivers that start as far away as the Great Smokies, where precipitation has reached as high as 84 inches a year. To channel the floods of spring so that the Tennessee will have a normal flow, the TVA operates 32 dams on the river and its tributaries. Six of the dams belong to the Aluminum Company of America, but are part of the TVA system. One of the earliest dams on a tributary waterway is the Norris Dam on the Clinch River near Knoxville, finished in 1936, which is 256 ft. high. The highest dam is at Fontana on the Little Tennessee, in the Great Smokies.

When the flood control made the river navigable through most of its 650 miles not only was a substantial barge industry born, but industries migrated to the Valley to take advantage of lower rates for hauling freight. TVA estimates that private industry has invested about $1.8 billion in waterfront plants and terminals.

When the Federal Government reactivated the Wilson Dam plants that had been built to make nitrates, it began producing fertilizers instead. These products have improved many Alabama acres and opened large areas of damaged soil to cultivation. At Muscle Shoals TVA conducts the National Fertilizer Development Center and makes results available to the industry throughout the country. It also conducts test demonstrations to encourage conservation on about 1,500 farms. Among other activities intended to raise community standards TVA has been experimenting with ways to control air pollution. In 1969 it sponsored a seven-state air pollution control conference to stimulate ways of keeping the air pure in the Valley.

FLORENCE, 43.1 *m.* (429-563 alt., 34,031 pop. 1970; 31,640, 1960, inc. 7.5%) a city in Lauderdale County on the north bank of the Tennessee. *See article on Florence.*

South of Florence, US 72 crosses the Tennessee River and follows its south bank for several miles.

At 44.1 *m.* is a large Indian Mound, said to be the largest earthwork in the Tennessee Valley. Standing on the bottomlands near the river, the mound is now overgrown with trees and brush but is plainly visible from the highway. It is a flat-topped pyramidal mound of the type common in the South and was probably used as a foundation for a ceremonial house or council lodge.

SHEFFIELD, 47.2 *m.* (481 alt., 13,115 pop. 1970; 13,491, 1960), on the high south bank of the Tennessee, is the principal railroad and industrial center in the rich iron and coal area of the northwest section of the State. In the heart of the TVA development, Sheffield along with Florence and Tuscumbia is included in the Tri-Cities area. Important industries are iron manufacturers and production of coke and other by-products of coal.

Beginning as a trading post in 1815, Sheffield for many years was a shipping port for cotton.

Andrew Jackson and his "right hand," John Coffee, started the speculative history of the town in 1816 by buying much of the land. In 1820 General Coffee surveyed and promoted a town called York Bluff. A few houses were built, but the place was soon abandoned in favor of Tuscumbia. The Sheffield Land Development Company started a new town in 1884 in the hope of developing the water power, coal, iron, asbestos, and other natural resources. A banking crisis halted the development, but three years later another promotion was attempted. This eventually obtained a fairly firm foothold, but on a scale much smaller than the promoters planned. A new boom began when Henry Ford offered to develop a great manufacturing center in the area, but stopped when Ford withdrew. Since TVA was established, Florence, Sheffield, and all adjoining places have had substantial growth in business and residential sections.

Section b. HUNTSVILLE to TUSCUMBIA via US 72 alt.

US 72 Alt. proceeds southwest from US 72 in Huntsville and follows the right-of-way of the Southern Railway. From downtown Huntsville to Decatur on the south bank of the Tennessee River, 26 *m.,* MADISON, (3,086 pop. 1970; 1,425, 1960) is to the north of the Carl T. Jones Jet Airport, which serves Huntsville and Decatur. An express highway between the two cities has been termed Int. 565.

At 26 *m.* is MOORESVILLE, a village of 72 in 1970, 93 in 1960, a loss of 22%). It has been called "an enchanted village where life seems suspended in a leisurely rhythm." Incorporated in 1818, before Alabama was a State, it was founded by settlers who wrested a living from wild territory. Under towering oaks, small and sturdy buildings portray these early struggles, while its neo-classic mansions recall the splendor of the ante-bellum South. Visitors stop first at the Postoffice (7-11 a.m., 3-5 p.m.) to inquire for directions and admission to houses. This little building contains the original wooden call boxes, most of them still used by descendants of the first residents who rented them. The Tavern, a two-story frame building with outside stairway, is typical of the stagecoach stops that used to double as taverns. The little red brick Community Church (1817) contains the traditional slave gallery. On the lectern lies U.S. General Garfield's Bible, left there by him more than 100 years ago. Surrounded by a white picket fence is the old Peebles store, now a residence. The house in which President Andrew Johnson lived during his tailoring apprenticeship still stands.

Left from Mooresville 1.2 *m.* to Belle Mina (*no admission*), built in 1826 by Thomas Bibb, Governor of Alabama 1820-2, member of the legislature of 1827 and 1828. The house stands 200 feet from the highway in a grove of large oaks. It is square-built of brick with a projecting roof supported by massive Ionic columns, the centers of which are hewn poplar logs. The broad floor planks are an inch thick.

At 1 *m*. west US 72 Alt. has a junction with Int. 65, north-south, which bypasses Decatur, and 3 *m*. farther a junction with US 31, which proceeds south all the way to Mobile. The latter two highways combine to cross the Tennessee River.

DECATUR, 26 *m*. (38,044 pop. 1970). *See article on Decatur*.

WHEELER, 17 *m*. Left here through a grove of magnificent spreading oaks to the Joe Wheeler House. This is actually two square-built, frame buildings, called the east and west wings. The original east wing was built in 1818; the west wing was added by General Wheeler in the late 1860s. Entrance to the 16-room house is through a wide double door to a spacious hallway in which are old portraits and other paintings, rare books, newspapers, state papers, and other time-stained documents. Glass cases contain the uniforms worn by General Wheeler in two wars.

General Wheeler was a member of Congress, and Lieutenant General in the Confederate Army. He was a Major General of the U. S. Army volunteers in the War with Spain, and later Brigadier General in the United States Army. Services are conducted annually here on the anniversary of General Wheeler's birth.

COURTLAND, 20.1 *m*. (547 pop. 1970) is a business center for farmers. The old brick Presbyterian Church still uses its original bell. When Texas was fighting Mexico for its independence, Dr. Shackelford, a leader in the community, organized a company of 100 young men from Courtland and vicinity to aid the Texans. Every man furnished his equipment and horse. Dr. Shackelford and his Alabama Red Rovers went to the Mexican War, and all except the doctor were killed.

Rocky Hill Castle, 23.5 *m*., at the end of a long entrance drive was built in 1845 by James Saunders, later a colonel in the Confederate Army. Many noted Southern military leaders were entertained in this house, and on one occasion the military court of the Army of Tennessee met here. It is legendary that money, jewels, and silverware, hidden in the tower from plundering Union soldiers, were left in their hiding place for more than 60 years. The tower, standing apart from the residence was built by Hugh Jones, a Welsh carpenter.

TOWN CREEK, 25.9 *m*. (545 alt., 1,203 pop. 1970; 810, 1960) was the scene of a sharp skirmish on April 27, 1863, when Confederate General Philip D. Roddy attempted to block the advance of the Federal force under General Dodge. Forrest's cavalry rushed here to the aid of Roddy, and in the ensuing fight Dodge was beaten back. Meantime, Major General A. D. Streight left the main Federal force in a wild dash to cut the Confederate communication lines and destroy their supply depots at Rome, Georgia. Forrest guessed this plan and pursued with a much smaller force. Six days later the chase ended with Streight's surrender near Center. (*See Tour 13*).

In Town Creek is a junction with Wheeler Dam Road, State 101.

In TUSCUMBIA, 49.3 *m*. (466 alt., 8,898 pop. 1970) is the southern junction with US 43. *See Tour 7*.

From Tuscumbia to the Mississippi Line, the road passes through the gently rolling hills of Colbert County. It is a fertile sweetgrain section, devoted to farming and stock raising.

CHEROKEE, 66 *m.* (514 alt., 1,484 pop. 1970; 1,349, 1960), is an industrial village, dependent on numerous wells of magnesia and sulphur. There are also asphalt mines and marble quarries.

At 69 *m.* the highway crosses the route of the notorious NATCHEZ TRACE, which here entered a corner of Alabama on its way from Tennessee into Mississippi. Part of this is now a parkway.

The Colbert brothers, halfbreed leaders of the Chickasaw tribe, for whom the county was named, operated a ferry and tavern where the Trace crossed the Tennessee River.

During the early days travelers in this lonesome Natchez Trace country were plagued by outlaws. The most notorious of these were the Terrible Harpes, quadroon brothers named Micajah and Wiley, known respectively as Big Harpe and Little Harpe. Roaming the wilderness from Tennessee to the Mississippi, the pair robbed, tortured, and murdered until they came to be known as madmen. Driven from their North Carolina home after repeated crimes, they terrorized the Trace for months, defying efforts to capture them. At last, however, Micajah murdered the wife and baby of a man who had befriended him. The man gathered a posse and, after a chase through the wilderness, shot and captured Micajah. In *The Outlaw Years,* Robert M. Coates writes that while Harpe was still alive and conscious, his one-time friend cut off his head with a butcher knife.

Wiley escaped and joined the band of Samuel Mason, another Trace outlaw for whom authorities had set a considerable reward. Some months later a swarthy, scowling little man turned up in Natchez carrying a head that had been rolled in blue clay. He said the head was that of Mason, and claimed the reward. But the little man was soon identified as Wiley Harpe. He was seized, tried speedily, and hanged.

As the river swings northwest the Pickwick Dam creates PICK-WICK LAKE, 42,800 acres, an arm of which extends south along the Mississippi border as far as the route of US 72. This is the largest of the TVA lakes.

At 74.4 *m.* US 72 crosses the MISSISSIPPI LINE, at a point 13 *m.* east of Iuka and 33 *m.* east of Corinth, Mississippi.

≈≈

Tour 6

TO THE WILLIAM B. BANKHEAD NATIONAL FOREST

Decatur—Moulton—William B. Bankhead National Forest—Houston —Arley.

72 *m*. State 24, State 33, State 195.

This tour is intended to give easy routes into the William B. Bankhead National Forest for visitors from the areas of Huntsville, Decatur, and the Tennessee River Valley. A number of State routes turn south from US 72 Alt. and meet at or near Moulton, in Lawrence County, mileage is figured from Decatur.

DECATUR, 0 *m*. (38,044 pop. 1970). *See Decatur*.

In Decatur US 11 and Int. 75 are the main routes going north-south; US 72 Alt. comes from Huntsville. State 24, State 33, and State 157, move south from US 72 Alt. Most of this area is a high flat tableland, where cotton is the principal crop.

At 14.9 *m.,* on State 14 is a junction with a graded dirt road. Left on this road to OAKVILLE, 2.6 *m*. near which one of the earliest deposits of asphalt in the United States was discovered. A letter by John Prince concerning the deposit was published by State Geologist Michael Tuomey in his *Second Biennial Report on the Geology of Alabama* in 1858. Prince stated that the tar-like substance was used for various ailments by hunters and traders and that they had learned of its healing properties from the Indians. The asphalt outcrop, known as Tar Spring, had been shown to Prince when he bought the property in 1840. The spring ceased to flow years ago.

MOUTON, 22.9 *m*. (2,470 pop. 1970; 1,716, 1960, inc. 43%) is the seat of Lawrence County. It was one of the first towns in the State to be incorporated, and was established by an act of the Territorial legislature February 6, 1818. For many years its population was small for a county seat, but in recent decades it has shown growth. Here is a junction with State 33; State 24 continues west to Mississippi, whereas State 33, which has been known as the Cheatham Highway, continues south and after passing a tiny village called WREN, 3 *m.,* at 1 *m*. farther on enters the WILLIAM B. BANKHEAD NATIONAL FOREST.

This rugged domain of 179,224 acres, supervised by the Forest Service of the U. S. Department of Agriculture, was long known as Black Warrior National Forest. It was renamed to honor Alabama's

Senator Bankhead. The highway enters the forest in the shadow of pine-clad Buzzard Roost Mountain, through a gate of native stone. A large part of the northern half of the forest has rugged hills and cliffs, with numerous creeks threading the valleys and creating the Bee Branch Scenic Area and other natural panorama. On the highway is the Central Lookout Tower. In the center is the Black Warrior Wildlife Management Area. East of State 33 is Brushy Creek and Brushy Lake.

Winding through deep gorges beside clear mountain streams, and traversing steep, tortuous slopes in twisting curves, many miles of graded rock and dirt roads open the forest to visitors and vacationists. For convenience in controlling fires, hundreds of miles of ranger roads have been built into the farthest reaches of the dense woods. These ranger roads are convenient for hikers, but not practical for cars.

Throughout the forest area wild life is abundant. There are squirrels, rabbits, opossums, raccoons, and other small game and all the varieties of birds common to the region. White-tail deer, protected by law, are increasing. Hunting and fishing are permitted in season outside the game refuge.

Along the way are rock-quarries that provide surface material for the numerous roads. Although the highway easily accommodates two-way traffic, it appears to be no more than a lane because the dense growth of oak, hickory, pine, and dogwood crowd so closely upon it from both sides.

In the central section there is no evidence of human occupation aside from the forestry work that has been done, and to all appearances it is an untouched wilderness save for the winding highway. Thick-limbed hemlocks grow side by side with the stately pines, and immense, white-trunked poplars thrust their tops above spreading oaks and gray beeches standing tall and straight.

Spring brings flowers in profusion. Patches of dogwood bloom early, spreading banks of glistening white against the background of lingering winter brown and new spring green. Streams are bordered by pink and white mountain laurel. Azaleas, in shades ranging from pink to white, red sweet Williams and violets cluster about the higher banks.

At 36.6 m. is a junction with Cranal Road. Right on this road to the Sipsey River and Picnic Grounds, in a pine forest a short distance below the confluence of two creeks that form the river. There are 18 picnic facilities. Cranal Road leads to Kinlock Road; right on this road to KINLOCK FALLS, where Hubbard Creek falls over a rock shelf into a deep and narrow gorge. At 19.2 m. on Kinlock Road to a junction with Ridge Road, established in 1819 as Byler Road, the first State highway in Alabama. Right on the Ridge Road to the site of the Jennie Brooks House, home until 1925 of the mother of a family of numerous males who had been ruined by the War Between the States and turned outlaws. All had been killed during brushes with the law and left the mother the lone survivor, who lived to be 98 years of age.

US 278 crosses the park east-west, entering near ADDISON (692 pop. 1970) in Winston County and crossing to DOUBLE SPRINGS (957 pop. 1970), near the western boundary, where there is a junction with State 33 and State 195. Here is the Bankhead Ranger Station, where the District Ranger is available for information. *Address Box 278, Double Springs, Ala., 35553.*

From Double Springs US 278 moves 13 *m.* west to NATURAL BRIDGE, a hamlet at a junction with State 13. Adjoining is the Natural Bridge recreation ground of 20 acres, with six picnic units. The bridge is a sandstone rock formed in an arch by the erosion of lighter materials. It is 80 ft. long, 15 ft. wide, and rises 30 ft. near the head of a gorge that has 70 ft. cliffs on three sides. Numerous shallow caves in the cliffs also are the results of erosion.

More picnic sites have been developed recently at Houston, south of Natural Bridge.

HOUSTON, 51.4 *m.* became the first county seat of Winston County (Hancock then) in 1850. The citizens built a log courthouse and jail in that year; the jail is still standing and has been remodeled as a dwelling. The walls, floors, and ceilings, made by double layers of logs, are from 16 to 20 inches thick. The doors were made of three layers of two-inch whipsawed plank. The interior walls, ceilings, and the inner side of the door were studded with square, handmade nails spaced two or three inches apart, a bristling hindrance against jailbreaks. In remodeling, lighter doors and shutters have replaced the old ones.

West of the Houston area and extending almost up to the middle of the forest are the arms of LEWIS SMITH LAKE, 21,200 acres, made by impounding the water of the Sipsey Fork of the Warrior River by the LEWIS SMITH DAM of the Alabama Power Company. The Warrior watershed has an annual rainfall of about 53 inches, of which about 25% of the runoff drains into the Sipsey. The rest reaches the Warrior by the Mulberry and Locust Forks in Cullman and Blount Counties. The Lewis Smith Dam is 300 ft. high and supplies a power generating plant of 78,750 kilowatts. The lake is extremely popular for recreation.

ARLEY, 60.9 *m.,* near the line of Cullman County, is a village where timber, mostly pine, is processed. The southern boundary of the Bankhead Forest is the Walker County line. Exits from the forest are County 41 from Arley, and State 195, which join State 269 to Birmingham.

Tour 7

DOWN EASTERN ALABAMA FROM TENNESSEE TO FLORIDA

(Tennessee Line)—Huntsville—Monte Sano State Park—New Hope —Guntersville—Albertville—Boaz—Attalla—Gadsden — Jacksonville —Piedmont—Fort McClellan Military Reservation—Anniston—Oxford—Talladega National Forest—Cheaha State Park—Cheaha Mountain—Wedowee—Roanoke—Horseshoe Bend National Military Park—Lafayette—Opelika—Auburn—Phenix City—Seale—Eufala—Clayton —Abbeville—Headland—Dothan. (Florida Line) US 431.

US 431 is the most easterly of the Alabama highways that carry traffic from Tennessee to Florida. When it enters the State it is combined with US 231, but after entering Huntsville US 431, usually called the Florida Short Route, turns southeast and serves most of the important points near the Georgia border, while US 231 proceeds directly south from Huntsville and take a somewhat more erratic course westward of US 431. Both routes eventually meet at Dothan close by the Florida line.

US 431 crosses the Tennessee Line, 0 *m.*, 13 miles south of Fayetteville, Tennessee, and bears directly southward, passing through a level fertile region with timber-clad mountains stretching away toward the east. A large-scale farming area where cotton is the predominating crop, this fertile region was Cherokee land prior to the Great Removal in 1838. Before the Cherokee cleared their farms and built their villages here, earlier tribes of mound-building Indians planted corn and established towns in the area. As US 431 nears the Tennessee River the highway winds through rugged spurs and knobs, thickly timbered with pine, cedar and hardwoods.

HAZEL GREEN, 4.1 *m.,* was an incorporated town in 1821, with several hundred people, chiefly planter families from Virginia, the Carolinas, and Tennessee. Later many found Huntsville more amenable and moved there. Hazel Green is now the name of a Division of Madison County and in 1970 had 3,930 pop. It is memorable for a feud that developed in the 1830-1850 decades when a woman named Elizabeth Dale was accused of disposing of six husbands in succession, as well as plotting the death of a neighbor. The charges were never proved but the ill feeling of the community caused her to leave for Mississippi in 1855. Her house, which bears the name of one of her husbands, Alexander Jeffries, stands on the top of an Indian mound in the environs of the former village.

HUNTSVILLE, 12 *m.* (610-636 alt., 137,802 pop. 1970) is at a junction with US 72, the east-west route, which, with US 72 Alternate, serves the Tennessee River Valley. *See Huntsville.*

NORMAL, 14.5 *m.*, at one time at the northern outskirts of Huntsville, is now part of the city and notable chiefly as the seat of the Alabama Agricultural and Mechanical University. It has an attractive campus of 850 acres and has been located here since 1891. *For description see Huntsville.*

From the eastern limits of Huntsville US 271 climbs the huge ridge of Monte Sano, (1650 ft.) and follows a winding road up the mountainside.

MONTE SANO STATE PARK, 22.5 *m.* on the crest of Monte Sano, 2,140 acres is a prime recreation spot for those who seek heights instead of wildfowl refuges and waterways. It was developed by the joint efforts of the Tennessee Valley Authority, the Civilian Conservation Corps, the National Park Service, the Alabama Forestry Commission, and Madison County. There are picnic sites, cabins, and a community house called the Tavern.

Of special interest is the BURRITT MUSEUM, located on 167 acres at the top of the mountain. It has articles of archaeological and historical significance, documents and paintings. The museum occupies an 11-room house built in the form of a maltese cross in 1936 by William H. Burritt, who willed it to the city of Huntsville with an annuity of $10,000 for maintenance. *Open Tues.-Sun. 1-5, closed Mondays. Donation expected.* The development of a pioneer homestead on the grounds began with assembling of a cabin of cedar logs and erection of a split-rail fence; furniture and tools of the early settlements are being added.

Also on the crest is the Observatory-Planetarium, an 800 sq. ft. structure on a 16-acre plot leased from the State. It shelters a 21-inch reflector telescope built by a local scientist.

US 431 descends the southern slope of Monte Sano in a long winding curve. From the foot of the mountain it crosses a broad section of the Tennessee River basin. The view here is limited by lines of broken cedar-covered knobs that extend along both sides of the highway to the broad Tennessee.

NEW HOPE, 40.4 *m.* (1,300 pop. 1970; 953, 1960), is a shipping and saw-milling village with a large cotton gin and warehouse.

The route crosses Point Rock River at 41.8 *m.*

At 45 *m.* is a junction with a country road. Right on this road 3.8 *m.* to GUNTERSVILLE DAM on the Tennessee River in Marshall County, built by the TVA, 1935-1939. It is a multiple-purpose structure, creating a reservoir for flood regulation, a 76-mile segment of the main river navigation channel, and providing 97,200 kilowatts of installed generating capacity. The dam is 94 feet high, feet long, and impounds a lake 67,900 acres in area. A second lock chamber 110 x 600 feet was opened to traffic in June, 1965. ortheast of Guntersville State 227 moves through LAKE

GUNTERSVILLE STATE PARK, 5,559 acres, with cottages, a resort inn, camp sites, a golf course. South of Guntersville the highway crosses Sand Mountain, the broad sandy plateau south of the Tennessee Valley. It follows the united course of two historic trails, the Great Trade Path and the Cumberland River Trail. Andrew Jackson brought his army of Tennesseans over this same trail in 1813; and along it rode the cavalry of Federal General Rousseau in 1864. In this comparatively treeless country it is easy to see from the highway many examples of the intensive farming that makes Sand Mountain one of the great food producing sections of the State. The population here is almost entirely white, in sharp contrast to some parts of the Black Belt where more than 80 percent of the inhabitants are Negroes.

US 431 crosses the Tennessee River at 57.8 *m.*, affording a view of the valley with its flooded lowlands flanked by distant hills.

GUNTERSVILLE, 59.1 *m.* (592 alt., 6,491 pop. 1970; 6,592, 1960, dec. 1.5%), seat of Marshall County, is a thriving river port and an industrial city. Formerly a land-locked community, Guntersville now rests on a peninsula jutting into Guntersville Lake. A portion of the waterfront is zoned for recreation and other sections are reserved for industry. TVA's Guntersville Dam impounds the lake. TVA, the State of Alabama, and the city joined in developing a land-use plan for the city.

This was the site of a Cherokee village in 1790. From Gunter's Landing, the Cherokees took their canoes up and down the Tennessee; before the coming of steamers in the early 1820s, the landing was known far and wide and flatboats carried products to New Orleans. Steamboats made Gunter's Landing a boom town. Backwoodsmen and Indians lived for "boat day" and crowded the banks when the boat arrived with homeseekers and fortune hunters.

General Winfield Scott was sent here in 1837 to force the removal of the Cherokee to the Indian Territory. Many were sent downriver by boat to new lands in the west. It is said that among the Cherokee sent west from here was a great-grandmother of Will Rogers, cowboy humorist. Rogers, who was proud of his Indian blood, had planned to visit Guntersville in the winter of 1935. Some of the old landmarks had been partly rebuilt in anticipation of his visit, when news arrived of his fatal crash in Alaska.

US 431 leaves Guntersville over the SAM HOUSTON BRIDGE. Right from the bridge is a view of McKEE'S ISLAND, on which Hernando De Soto is said to have rested while collecting supplies and making prisoners of 200 Indians.

ALBERTVILLE, 69.7 *m.* (1,054 alt., 9,963 pop. 1970; 8,250, 1960, inc. 20%), near the top of Sand Mountain's northern slope is surrounded by fertile truck farms and orchards. A cotton mill, cottonseed oil mill, cotton gin, and corn meal mill are the principal industries. Here are junctions with State 75 and 205.

BOAZ, 75.7 *m.* (1,071 alt., 5,621 pop. 1970; 4,654, 1960, inc. 20%), is an agricultural trading center, formerly a camp site on the old

Indian trail later called Jackson Trace. The town was founded in 1878 by 42 Georgians, who migrated here in covered wagons. In 1886 a post office, given the Biblical name Boaz, was established with postal service over Jackson Trace first supplied by horseback riders.

SNEAD STATE JUNIOR COLLEGE was chartered by the State of Alabama in 1935 after it had been growing from a mission school to a college supported by a Methodist denomination. It became part of Alabama's junior college system in 1967. The Norton Library and the Joe Starnes Memorial Chapel are two of its fine buildings and it has erected residence halls and new classroom structures. In 1974 it enrolled 1,512 and had a faculty of 96. It is coeducational and has liberal arts, science and vocational courses.

ATTALLA, 90.8 *m.* (530 alt., 7,510 pop. 1970; 8,257, 1960, dec. 9%), is a city in the Gadsden industrial area of Etowah County. It has pipe plants, coke ovens, and cotton mills; coal, iron ore, and marble are mined and quarried in the vicinity.

In Attalla is the junction with US 11 (*see Tour 14*).

In GADSDEN, 96.1 *m.* (519-621 alt., 53,928 pop. 1970; 58,088, 1960, dec. 7.2%) (*see Gadsden*) is a junction with US 411 and Int. 59.

South of Gadsden the route crosses the Coosa River on Etowah Memorial Bridge.

At DUKE, a village 8 *m.* south of Glencoe, US 431 has a junction with State 204, Left on State 204.

JACKSONVILLE, 9 *m.* (720 alt., 7,715 pop. 1970; 5,678, 1960, inc. 35%) in Calhoun County, is located in the foothills of the Choccolocco range of the Blue Ridge Mountains that form rolling hills and sheltered valleys. Originally cotton formed the basis for trade, but in recent years industry has been diversified and the town is prospering. East of it lies the great TALLADEGA NATIONAL FOREST.

Jacksonville was long the site of one of the four State normal schools. It was organized in 1888, and known as a Teachers' College until the expansion of its schools and departments caused it to be named JACKSONVILLE STATE UNIVERSITY in 1966. Actually it was an outgrowth of the Male and Female Academies established in Jacksonville in 1848. In 1871 they were merged with Calhoun College, a two-year institution that continued in operation until 1883, when it was merged with Jacksonville State Normal School. Classes continued at the Calhoun campus until 1900, when they took over the Calhoun County Courthouse, vacated when the county seat was moved to Anniston. The old Iron Hotel, next door, became the first dormitory. In 1908 the college returned to the enlarged Calhoun campus; in 1929 it became a four-year college as Jacksonville State Teachers College and moved to the present Pelham Road campus. In 1966 it became a university. In recent decades it added the Martin Science Bldg., the Merrill Business Bldg., the Albert Brewer School of Law Enforcement, the Ivo Sparkman dormitory for women, the Student Commons and the Main Library, which rises 12 stories and is called the tallest academic structure in Alabama.

The university has undergraduate courses in the arts, science, education, nursing, and law enforcement, and in basic engineering and pre-professional subjects. It gives the master's degree in these and public administration. There is a division of the ROTC with two-year and four-year programs, in which women may enroll for academic courses without military obligations. Students in the Lurleen B. Wallace School of Nursing who obtain loans, will have up to 50% cancelled when they enter nursing. The university asks students to refrain from unauthorized demonstrations and activities "which might shock the community sense of propriety or reflect discredit on the institution." "Jax State" has two semesters of 16 weeks each and a minisemester of one month; there is also a summer term. Fees for room, meals and tuition are estimated at $625 per semester (1974). In the fall, 1974, it registered 5,220 students and had a faculty of 260.

Jacksonville was settled in 1822 and was first called Drayton. The name later was changed to commemorate General Andrew Jackson who had camped in the neighborhood during his campaign against the Creek. Invading Federal troops did much damage to the town in 1862. During the following year it served as headquarters for Confederate Generals Beauregard, Polk, and "Fighting Joe" Wheeler. In the old cemetery, South Church and May Sts., is the grave of General John H. Forney, professor of mathematics at West Point just before the War between the States, who resigned and returned to Alabama to become aide to the governor. A monument has been placed over his grave by the United Daughters of the Confederacy. A monument of Italian marble, also erected by the U. D. C. marks the grave of the "gallant John Pelham" whose body was brought here from the battlefield for burial. An artillery commander under "Jeb" Stuart, he fought unscathed through 60 engagements. His commission as lieutenant-colonel had been signed and was on its way to him when he was killed by a stray shell at the battle of Kelly's Ford, Virginia, on March 17, 1863.

The C. W. Daugette House, South Pelham Road, was built before the War between the States and long occupied by descendants of General Forney. It is a two-story brick structure of Greek Revival design, with two Ionic and two square columns. Old boxwood hedges border it along north and south sides, and large magnolias grow in the front grounds.

The Rowan House, South Pelham Road, was built in 1857 and later occupied by Major Peyton Rowan. During 1863 it was used as headquarters by General Beauregard. Built of heart pine, it suggests the Italian Renaissance in design and contains 13 rooms and an observatory. Sliding doors, connecting the double parlors, bannisters, mantels, and the three stairways are hand-carved solid walnut. Some of the old furnishings and rare objects date back to 1776.

The First Presbyterian Church, East Clinton and Church Sts., is a red brick structure with high arched windows and a steeple. A marker in the church yard states that the building served as a Confederate hospital during the War between the States. Another pre-war edifice is St. Luke's Episcopal Church.

North of Jacksonville on State 21 to PIEDMONT, 12 *m.* (5,063 pop. 1970; 4,794, 1960) in the northwest corner of Calhoun County. It has a junction with State 9 and one mile away is US 278, which crosses Alabama from Georgia to Mississippi.

Return to US 431.

BLUE MOUNTAIN, 123.4 *m.* (446 pop. 1970, 446, 1960) apparently had the most stable citizens in Alabama, according to the reports of the U. S. Census. Located in the foothills of the Appalachians, it was in the center of an ore mining area before the War Between the States, and the terminus of a local railroad. The Confederates placed a training camp and a supply depot at Blue Mountain; both were destroyed by Federal forces in 1865. In the subsequent decades it had some iron works and after 1900 the American Net & Twine Company built a plant, but competition from Oxford and Anniston cut down its work force. In recent years US 431 has been rerouted to pass along the northern limits of the town to a junction with State 21. Saks School is its principal educational institution.

East of State 21 and US 431 and extending as far as Anniston is the FORT McCLELLAN MILITARY RESERVATION, 46,374 acres, which extends to the Choccolocco Mountains. It has the Army Chemical Center and the Women's Army Corps Center and is headquarters of the Chemical Corps Training Command and the WAC School. Also located here are the Noncommissioned Officer Academy of the 3rd Army, and the Army Combat Chemical, Biological and Radiological Agency. The military forces average 6,000 and civilian employees 1,300.

ANNISTON, 125.7 *m.* (31,533 pop. 1970) seat of Calhoun County. *See article on Anniston.*

In Anniston US 431 has junctions with State 21, which comes down from Jacksonville, 10 *m.* away, and State 202, which goes west 10 *m.* to the ANNISTON ARMY DEPOT.

OXFORD, 2 *m.* south (647 alt., 4,361 pop. 1970; 3,603, 1960, inc. 21%) is at a junction with US 78, which crosses the State from Georgia to Mississippi via Birmingham. Parallel with US 78 is Int. 20. Oxford is contiguous with Anniston, but is separately incorporated.

Oxford was in the heart of iron ore mining when the Alabama & Tennessee River Railroad extended its line to Blue Mountain a few miles west. The Confederates used the railhead as the place for a training camp and supply base. In 1863 a blast furnace, the Oxford Iron Works, was built on the site of the present town to manufacture munitions for the Confederate forces. The enterprise was short-lived, for by 1865 Federal forces had penetrated into the valley and destroyed the blast furnaces round about. In 1868 Samuel Noble, who had headed the former Noble Iron Works in Rome, Georgia, evaluated the ore supply in this region and formed a company with Connecticut investors to build a new plant. He bought the Oxford property and built two blast furnaces. The group, known as the Woodstock Iron Company, also bought farmland to the east and north for a town site and platted it as Anniston, named for the wife of one of the partners.

US 431 combines with US 78 eastward from Oxford for 5 *m.*, then crosses the Talledega National Forest for 9 *m.* to a junction with State 9 at HOLLIS, a village at the eastern rim of the forest.

The TALLEDEGA DIVISION of the TALLADEGA NATIONAL FOREST is the largest of the four forests administered in Alabama by the Forest Service of the U. S. Department of Agriculture. It covers 362,458 acres and has as its backbone the southernmost extension of the Appalachian Mountain chain, running in a northeast-southwest direction from Piedmont to Sylacauga, in the counties of Calhoun, Cleburne, Talladega, and Clay. It is a terrain of long ridges, far views, rock cliffs towering over wooded valleys, filled with scenic drives, well-marked trails and wildlife, with opportunities for hunting and fishing, and studying an abundant bird life. Talladega still supports stands of hardwoods in addition to the pines that grow everywhere.

In the northern sector the Choccolocco mountains reach an elevation of 880 ft. Access roads from Piedmont are State 9, State 21, and US 278. On US 278 a road turns south at Vigo where the heights reach 1,150 ft.; this connects with the Skyway Motorway to Coleman Lake camping grounds, Sweetwater Lake, and a campground at Pine Glen. On the east State 46 comes from Georgia to HEFLIN, (2,872 pop. 1970; 2,400, 1960) in Cleburn County, where the Shoal Creek Ranger Station stands to an entrance to the Forest and a jct. with US 78, which runs to Lake Charles and crosses the Forest. Inside the Forest stands the Bankhead Tower. East of the Forest in Calhoun County is Anniston. Southwest of the city is Cold Water Mountain, 1,667 ft., and north are the Skeleton Mountains, 960 ft. Int. 20 enters the State from Atlanta and crosses the Horseblock Mountain range to Anniston. State 22 gives Anniston direct connection with forest highways State 9 and State 55. IRON CITY on State 9 is another reminder of the days when ore was worked in the mountains.

The largest attraction in the central part of the Forest is the CHEAHA STATE PARK, 2,719 acres, reached via State 42 from the west, connecting with State 21 to Talladega and State 49 from the east. Headquarters are at Lineville on State 49. There are available an observation tower, stone cottages, a lake, hiking trails, a resort inn, chalets, and a restaurant. CHEAHA MOUNTAIN, 2,407 ft., is the tallest in the State.

The Talladega Scenic Drive follows the top of the ridge and the Skyway Motorway runs all the way south. Talladega has direct connections with the southern third of the Forest via State 42 to Ironaton, State 21 and State 77. Lake Chinnabee has camping facilities as has Horn Mountain Tower near Sherman Cliffs in the Talladega Mountain range. Sylacauga is located at the end of the Forest in close proximity to numerous creeks, lakes, heights, and a wildlife management area.

US 431 now moves close to the Georgia border in Randolph and

Chambers Counties, touching farm villages of nominal population. WEDOWEE, which had 842 people in 1970, down from 917 in 1960, is the county seat of Randolph County, where the largest city, ROANOKE, had 5,251 in 1970 and 5,288 in 1960, a loss of 37 in ten years. In 1974 the Alabama Power Co. obtained a license to build a hydroelectric generating plant on the Tallapoosa River near Wedowee. At Wedowee US 431 has a junction with State 48, which connects with State 49 at Lineville (1,984 pop. 1970; 1,612, 1970) in Clay County.

At Roanoke US 431 has a junction with State 22, which goes southwest. At 28 *m.* State 22 has a junction with State 49; left on State 49 5 *m.* to the Tallapoosa River and the HORSESHOE BEND NATIONAL MILITARY PARK, 2,040 acres, site of the battle on May 27, 1814, when General Andrew Jackson routed the Creek Indian confederacy, breaking forever the Indian opposition to white settlement of eastern Alabama. The park was established by the National Park Service Aug. 11, 1959. Park offices are in Dadeville where State 49 meets US 280 (*See also Tour 8*).

In the adjoining Chambers county, the largest city is LAFAYETTE (3,530 pop. 1970; 2,605, 1960). Here is a junction with State 50. Left on this road 13 *m.* to LANETT (6,908 pop. 1970; 7,674, 1960) on the Chattahoochee River near West Point Lock and Dam. Lanett makes textiles and textile machinery and among products shipped are peaches. The Valley Times-News is the newspaper for this area.

Twenty miles south of Lafayette US 431 reaches OPELIKA (19,027 pop. 1970; 15,678, 1960), the seat of Lee County, a busy distribution center for cotton processing, and a retail market for a number of chains. The Opelika-Auburn Parkway, which combines the routes of US 431, US 29 and US 280, has a two-mile long avenue of stores and theaters. In 1973 the Village Mall was opened with 35 stores in operation. Opelika makes plastics, pine products, textiles, and athletic equipment. Dairying is profitable in the countryside. The *News* is its evening newspaper.

Opelika is the seat of OPELIKA STATE VOCATIONAL TECHNICAL INSTITUTE. Int. 85 runs two miles east of the town and provides an expressway to Montgomery. From Opelika US 431 and US 280 are combined for 28 miles to Phenix City.

PHENIX CITY, (263 alt., 25,281 pop. 1970; 27,630, 1960, dec. 8.3%) is located on the west bank of the Chattahooche River, commanding a view of Columbus, Georgia, and of the country to the East for many miles. The city is one of the major textile sites of the eastern cotton counties of Alabama, and specializes also in cloth, carpets, towels and sheets. Most of its important textile firms were organized, or reorganized, in the 1960-1970 decade, but its oldest industry, brick and tile, has been operating since the beginning of the century. Although Russell County has lost population, employment in Phenix City has increased, and among the new products are water skis and modular homes.

The largest employer, Southern Phenix Textiles, has 650 on its payroll; Fieldcrest, which came in 1974, has 400. Other employers of note are Alabama Craft Co., paper board, 358; Opelika Manufacturing Co., cloth, 330; and Bickerstaff Clay Products, 286.

Phenix City has a commission form of government. Its two railroads give it 26 freight trains daily, and its air depot is the airport of Columbus, Georgia, only 5 miles from downtown.

The area of Phenix City was occupied by the Kawita tribe of Indians before the white man came and by the Hichiti afterward; the latter joined the Creek confederacy and suffered its fate. Originally Phenix City was a settlement south of Girard and contiguous with it; Girard became the county seat in 1832. When Lee County was formed in 1866 the boundary line was adjusted to place the whole town in Russell County. When a postoffice was located here in 1890 it was called Phenix City, which became the county seat in 1932.

Farmers have been moving out of Russell County, which has had a loss of 2.1%; similarly Bullock and Barbour Counties, also cotton areas of eastern Alabama, have had losses, but Lee County had an increase of 23% during the 1960-1970 decade. The Ladonia Division of Russell County, directly west of Phenix City, increased its population.

Horace King, who was part Negro and part Catawa Indian, was brought as a slave to Columbus, Georgia, by his owner, John Godwin, a contractor and builder. King was Godwin's labor foreman, who built some of the first houses in Columbus and Girard. He also built the bridges that spanned the Chattahoochee. After Godwin's death King provided for the widow. During Reconstruction he served in the Alabama legislature. Over Godwin's grave in Godwin Cemetery in Phenix City King placed a shaft with an inscription saying it was placed "by Horace King in lasting remembrance of the love and gratitude he felt for his lost friend and former master."

South of Phenix City, 0 *m.*, US 431 passes through hilly country that parallels the Chattahoochee River to the vicinity of Abbeville and then enters the flat Wiregrass section.

At 4.9 *m.* is a junction with a graded road. Left on this road to a junction with another graded road, 3.5 *m.*; left here to the site of Fort Mitchell, 5.9 *m.*, built in 1811 on the Federal Road opened in 1805. The U.S. Government maintained a large garrison and an Indian resident agent here until 1837. The fort entertained Lafayette in 1825 and Francis Scott Key in 1835, when he was sent from Washington as mediator between State and nation in the controversy over the Indian lands. A large magnolia tree beside the road marks the site of John Crowell's Storehouse, built in 1816. Colonel Crowell was the last U.S. Indian Agent (1821-36) and Alabama's first Congressman. In 1739 James Oglethorpe, of Georgia, came here from Savannah and made a treaty with the Indians.

South from Phenix City US 431 moves several miles west from the Georgia border and State 165 runs close to the Chattahoochee River as far as Barbour County, where it joins US 431. The latter crosses an arm of Lake Eufaula at EUFAULA STATE PARK. The lake is impounded by Walter F. George Lock and Dam on the Chattahoochee. Phenix City to Eufaula on US 431 is 39 *m.*

SEALE, 18.3 *m.* is one of the components of the Cottonton-Seale Division of Russell County (4,293 pop. 1970; 5,218, 1960, loss 2.1%). It was made the seat of Russell County in 1868. When the seat was moved to Phenix City, a branch was kept in Seale and the early county records are still here.

EUFAULA, 47.4 *m.* (250 alt., 9,102 pop. 1970; 8,357, 1960) in Barbour County, is located on a bluff above Lake Eufaula, a body of water created by the impoundment of the Chattahoochee River by the Walter F. George Lock and Dam. Here US 431 has a junction with US 82, which runs west to connect with US 231 and Montgomery. Eufaula is 45 miles south of Columbus, Georgia. In a cotton growing area, it has large cotton mills and makes a variety of cotton products, including yarn, cloth, shirts, and children's socks, as well as cottonseed oil. It also makes soft drinks and ships peanuts, pine lumber, and cattle. The *Tribune* is its biweekly newspaper. The Carnegie Public Library, founded 1904, is a member of the Choctawhatchee Regional Library.

A modern city, Eufaula retains memorabilia of ante bellum times in houses of Greek Revival style set on shaded grounds. Veterans of the wars are commemorated by the statue of a doughboy in Jefferson Davis Park.

The Tree That Owns Itself, a huge oak, is near the center of Eufaula. The city, through its mayor, in 1935 recorded a deed that reads in part: "I, H. E. Graves, as mayor of the city of Eufaula, do hereby grant, bargain, sell and convey unto the Post Oak Tree, not as an individual, partnership, nor corporation, but as a creation and gift of the Almighty, standing in our midst, to itself, to have and to hold itself, its branches, limbs, trunk and roots so long as it shall live."

Eufaula was first named Irwinton in honor of one of its early settlers. In 1843 the name was changed because of confusion in the mails with Irwinton, Georgia. Eufaula was the name of a tribe of the Creek Confederacy that had long lived in the region.

Right from Eufaula on State 30 to the Clayton Cemetery, 20 *m.* Here, over the grave of Amos Mullins, is the Whisky Bottle Tombstone. Mullins was a heavy drinker and his wife an ardent teetotaler. In her efforts to lead him away from his bad habit she tried everything—cajolery, nagging, threats. Finally she lost all patience and told him to go ahead and drink himself to death. She threatened to put a whisky bottle tombstone at his grave, and she did. The monument is a replica of a bottle, standing several feet high. A counterpart, even to the stone cork, stands at the foot of the grave.

CLAYTON, 21.1 *m.* (200 alt., 1,626 pop. 1970; 1,313, 1960), seat of Barbour County, is at the headwaters of the Pea and Choctawhatchee Rivers. It was founded in 1833. In 1836, trouble with the Indians led to the erection of a fort in the vicinity, where the settlers sometimes went for protection. On the west side of the town square is the County Courthouse. The center portion was built in 1852; it was remodeled in 1900, and two wings were added in 1924. In a garden of Louisville St., is the old Town Bell, which stood in the center of the square for more than 100 years, and served as official timepiece of the town. It was also used in ante bellum days to call together members of the Slave Patrol, an organization of overseers.

ABBEVILLE, 75.7 *m.* (499 alt., 2,996 pop. 1970; 2,524, 1960), in the red hills of the Wiregrass secton, has been the seat of Henry County since 1833. The origin of the name is thought to be the Creek Yatta Abba, meaning "far distant." Abbeville is one of the oldest farming settlements of the State.

HEADLAND, 94 *m.* (2,545 pop. 1970; 2,630, 1960), has sawmills, fertilizer plant, wagon shop, planing mills, and cotton gins. Situated on a fertile plateau, it is a trade center for much of Henry and Houston Counties. The town was laid out by and named for Dr. J. J. Head in 1817, and was probably incorporated under the general laws when Alabama became a State in 1819.

DOTHAN, 104.5 *m.* (355 alt., 36,733 pop. 1970) (*see Tour 8*).

In Dothan are junctions with US 84 (*see Tour 10*) and US 231 (*see Tour 8*).

~~~~~~

Tour 8

DOWN THE MIDDLE OF THE STATE, HUNTSVILLE TO DOTHAN

Huntsville — Oneonta — Pell City — Childersburg — Talladega — Sylacauga — Alexander City —Dadeville — Horseshoe Bend — Montgomery—Orion—Troy—Ozark—Dothan.

135 *m.* US 231. US 280

US 231 and US 431 are combined when they come into Alabama from Tennessee and enter Huntsville 12 *m.* south of the border. There they part company; US 431 starts on its long run down the eastern counties of Alabama detailed in Tour 5. US 231 moves through Huntsville east of the Redstone Arsenal and finds a new route roughly halfway between US 431 and US 31, running through Morgan, Marshall, Blount, St. Clair, and Talledega Counties.

Most of the settlements on the route are farm villages of nominal population. The largest towns are ARAB, in Marshall County, (4,399 pop. 1970; 2,989, 1960, inc. 47%); ONEONTA, in Blount County

(4,390 pop. 1970; 4,136, 1960), and PELL CITY, in St. Clair County (5,381 pop. 1970; 4,165, 1960, inc. 29%).

At Oneonta US 231 has a junction with State 75, a route that runs from the northeast corner of Alabama to Birmingham. Five miles north of Oneonta off State 75 is the HORTON MILL COVERED BRIDGE, 220 ft. long, crossing a scenic rocky gorge and higher above water than any registered bridge. Alabama has 14 covered bridges carefully preserved from the 19th century.

At Pell City there are junctions with US 78 and Int. 20, which go to Birmingham. Here US 231 now takes two directions. The main route continues south, as follows:

At 2 *m.* from Pell City US 231 reaches LOGAN MARTIN LAKE, impounded by the Logan Martin Dam on the Coosa River, where the Alabama Power Co. has three hydroelectric units producing 128,250 kw. At HARPERSVILLE, 21 *m.* (639 pop. 1970) it turns sharply southeast. Here it is joined by US 280, a major highway out of Birmingham, which continues with US 231 to Sylacauga. Right from Harpersville on State 23 to WILSONVILLE, 8 *m.* (659 pop. 1970), near which town the Alabama Power Co. has been developing its Ernest C. Gaston facility and preparing for a steam electric generating plant to supply 880,000 km. with the use of coal from a new mine in the reserves of the Republic Steel Co. in Tuscaloosa County.

At 28 *m.* on US 231 is CHILDERSBURG (4,831 pop. 1970; 4,884, 1960), seat of the NUNNELLEY STATE VOCATIONAL TECHNICAL INSTITUTE.

Here, left, is a junction with State 76, which leads to the KYMULGA ONYX CAVE. This is the oldest cave known to white men, for Hernando de Soto came here in 1540, and the oldest inscriptions on its walls date from 1723. It always has been distinctive among caves because of the glistening onyx formations. The main cavern, 378 ft. long and 127 ft. high, opens on numerous side chambers. It was used as a shelter and burial site in prehistoric times, and became a hallowed place for the Creek Indians after they reached here from the East around 1500. They ascribed it to supernatural origin and cultivated the legend that they had emerged from the cave as a people. General Andrew Jackson passed it when he was pursuing the warring faction of the Creeks, and Indian refugees took shelter here after the battle of the Horseshoe Bend. During the Civil War saltpeter was mined here and used in making gunpowder; the leaching well and trenches dug at that time are still extant. Excavations by archaeologists determined the age of an Indian burial site as more than 2,000 years. *Open 8-6 daily; adults, $1.50; children 6-12, 75¢, under 6 free.*

Back to Pell City and the junction with US 78 and Int. 20. Take either of these routes to LINCOLN, 13 *m.* (1,127 pop. 1970; 629, 1960, inc. 79%). Here US 231 Alt. turns south. At 8 *m.* it has a junction with State 21, which has come down from Anniston. This is on the southern outskirts of Talladega.

TALLADEGA, (353 alt., 17,662 pop. 1970; 17,742, 1960), seat

of Talladega County, is in the foothills of the Blue Ridge Mountains, where US 231 Alt. joins State 21, 24 miles south of Anniston. As in most county seats, the courthouse is in the town square with store buildings grouped around it. The interlacing foliage of old oaks and elms shades the broad streets that radiate from the central square. Some of the houses, built in pioneer days, are still occupied by descendants of the original owners and furnishings brought through the wilderness by flatboats and ox wagons are still in use.

Talladega is one of the oldest white settlements in the Alabama interior. Pioneers moved here while it was on the boundary line between Creek and Cherokee domains and called the place Border Town. In and around the city are Indian mounds, indicating prehistoric occupation of the region over a long period.

At the beginning of the 19th century the United States Government obtained through treaty with the Creek nation a half-section of land including Big Springs, two blocks west of the present town square. John Bruner, halfbreed Indian, received a grant to this tract as a reward for his services as interpreter and peacemaker between whites and Indians. Bruner built a fort later called Leslie's Station. Andrew Jackson defeated the Creek here on November 9, 1813, in the Battle of Talladega, first in the series of victories by which he destroyed the power of the Creek Confederacy.

The present city of Talladega is an industrial and educational center. There are textile mills, cottonseed oil mills, foundries, and pipe plants. The Skyway Motorway, built along the top of the Talladega Mountain range in Talladega National Forest, passes close by the town.

The Elliott Museum, South St., five blocks west of East St. (*open Wednesday and Sunday afternoons*), occupies a red brick, two-story structure of 10 rooms, containing Colonial, Indian, and Confederate States relics, minerals, and art objects. The collection of fans is unusually varied; the costume display includes a wedding dress in the style of the early 1800's worn by a Talladega County bride. The children's room contains dolls of many nations, with native costumes. In this room also is the cradle of Hugo L. Black, who became a justice of the United States Supreme Court. Prominently displayed is a page from an old newspaper advertising a reward for the capture of Jefferson Davis.

Fort Lashley, now in process of restoration, is located opposite the cemetery. Here 14 Tennessee Volunteers and 125 friendly Creeks took refuge from the hostile Upper Creeks and were so effectively bottled up that not a single warrior could escape to seek help. One night an Indian is said to have draped himself in the skin of a large hog, head and legs attached. He crawled from the fort and through the camps of the hostiles until he reached Jackson's lines. Jackson responded, forded the Coosa, attacked the encircling Creeks, and rescued the beseiged.

The ALABAMA INSTITUTE FOR DEAF AND BLIND is the largest complex of its kind in the United States. Its facilities are located on six different campuses that cover a distance of about four miles from the eastern edge of Talladega to its western edge. It includes divisions for elementary, secondary, and vocational education and serves approximately 1,200 children and adults in a residential setting; it also has supervision over all the services affecting the handicapped throughout Alabama. The elementary and secondary programs are limited to residents of the State, and while the Department of Adult Blind and Deaf serves principally clients from within the State, individuals from other states can be enrolled by special arrangement.

The Institute began in Manning Hall, erected in 1850 for the Masonic East Alabama Female Institute, and acquired in the late 1850s by the State for the education of "deaf-mutes." In 1867 a Department of the Blind was opened, and since then departments for the Adult Blind and Deaf have been added, as well as a Department of Deaf-Blind, where 51 deaf-blind children from 12 states were enrolled in 1974. The budget for the complex is about $8 million per year. Its principal funds come from the Alabama Legislature, with additional funds from the Federal Government.

The first Alabama Regional LIBRARY FOR THE BLIND AND HANDICAPPED was opened in Talladega in 1965. This is a library in which books have no covers, pages, or printed matter; most of its patrons never enter the building, and talking is encouraged. The library distributes talking books on phonograph records, books printed in extra large-size type, braille, and magnetic tape recordings. Most of the material is provided free by the Library of Congress; all of it moves without expense through the mails, and repairs are made free by the Telephone Pioneers, retired employees of the Bell Telephone Co. There is a greater demand for tapes than for braille. The library makes an effort to locate handicapped people in order to alert them to the fine services they can receive without cost.

Talladega College, 25.6 m., on both sides of the highway, was founded in 1867 by two former slaves, William Savory and Thomas Tarrant, in the cabin of another former slave, David White. The original building had been erected in 1852 as a high school for white boys. It is a red brick structure, with six large white pillars in front and delicate wrought-iron balconies front and rear; grouped around it on the 270-acre campus are the other college buildings. Savory Library contains murals painted by Hale Woodruff, Georgia artist. The library is used both by the college and by the city. It has more than 66,000 vols. and specializes in black studies. The institution is co-educational 4-year college sponsored by the American Missionary Association but independently controlled. In 1974 it had 454 students and 57 instructors.

The Jackson Trace Marker, 29.8 m., indicates that the route follows the Indian trail, widened by General Jackson when he led his troops over it to Horseshoe Bend during the Creek War. Near here was the site of the first United States Land Office in this area.

After Sylacauga, US 231 turns south toward Montgomery, from

which it continues its route to the southeastern corner of Alabama and across the border into Florida. US 280 leaves US 231 and moves independently in a southeasterly direction, and after joining US 431 at Opelika continues to the Georgia border at Phenix City. Because it enables the visitor to find easy ways of reaching General Jackson's battlefield in Horseshoe Bend National Military Park the route of US 280 is inserted here.

GOODWATER, 14 m. south of Sylacauga (672 alt., 2,172 pop. 1970; 2,023, 1960) in Coosa County, was first called Adkin's Gap, then changed to Goodwater because the supply of a large spring that is the source of Hatchett Creek and of the town's water supply.

ALEXANDER CITY, 29 m. (727 alt., 12,358 pop. 1970; 13,140, 1960), called Youngville until its incorporation in 1873, was built upon the site of one of the early towns of the Tuckabatchee, a tribe of the Creek Confederacy. Cotton gins and textile mills have been the chief industries.

The principal educational institution is the Alexander City State Junior College, opened in 1965. Its Thomas D. Russell Library had 22,659 books in 1973 and many periodicals. In 1974 the college enrolled 1,633 students and had 80 in the faculty.

Right from Alexander City on State 63 to a junction with an improved road, 19.1 m. Left on this road to LAKE MARTIN, 25.1 m. The lake is formed by Martin Dam, one of the Alabama Power Company's hydroelectric developments on the Tallapoosa River at Cherokee Bluff. It has a shore line of about 750 miles, and its arms reach back along the river's former watercourses into rugged, heavily timbered hills. In spring, azalea, honeysuckle, and dogwood border the cool, shady waters that eventually narrow down to trickling brooks. The lake contains calico, large-mouthed, and small-mouthed bass, and speedy robins, or rose breasted bream. In addition to game fish there are many bottom-feeding species. In season, hunting for rabbits, squirrels, quail and turkeys is good. Land adjacent to the water is owned by the Alabama Power Company, and camping is permitted with the request that caution be taken to prevent forest fires.

DADEVILLE, 44 m. (779 alt., 2,847 pop. 1970; 2,940, 1960), seat of Tallapoosa County, is a prosperous lumbering town. Rich mineral deposits near by include gold, tin, and asbestos. Originally established as an Indian trading post in 1832, Dadeville was named for Major Francis Langhorne Dade, who with his entire command was killed by the Seminole Indians on December 28, 1835, while on a march to Fort King, Florida.

The Dennis Hotel, a two-story frame building one block north of the courthouse square, was erected in 1832 and called the United States Hotel. In the upper rooms, Johnson Jones Hooper wrote *Adventures and Travels of Capt. Simon Suggs,* published in 1846. Dadeville was the home town of Bozeman Bulger, sports and short story writer and of Morgan D. Jones, whose *Nest of the Vipers* (1910), attracted wide attention.

Dadeville is the headquarters town of the Horseshoe Bend Regional Library, which has 124,331 books available and circulates more than 800,000.

From Dadeville State 49 offers a short route (10 *m.*) to HORSE-SHOE BEND NATIONAL MILITARY PARK, 2,040 acres, in the center of which is the site on the Tallapoosa River of the battle of March 27, 1814, in which General Andrew Jackson and his army of frontiersmen destroyed the forces of the Creek Indian Confederacy. A peninsula of about 100 acres was formed by a great bend in the river and fortified by a zigzag wall that stretched across its narrow neck. Within this enclosure about 1,000 Creek fighters were ready for battle. They were led by Monahee, the principal prophet, and Menawa, who had caused a number of massacres of settlers on the frontier. Jackson's Cherokee allies, who opposed the Creek war faction, swam the river and burned huts of the Creeks.

A museum reproduces the battle with figures controlled automatically and sounds of action reproduced. The building is a reproduction of Fort Jackson of 1814, built on the site of Fort Toulouse of the French. *Battle open daily, 8 a.m. to sunset; adults, $1.50; children, 6-12, 75¢; under 6, free. Park open about the same time, except Mondays and Tuesdays; free.*

US 280 continues to Opelika, where it joins US 431 to Phenix City. The main highway, US 231, resumes its route southward from Sylacauga to Montgomery, passing through an agricultural area, where cotton is still a profitable staple. HANOVER, 11 *m.* is a small farm village. ROCKFORD, 19 *m.* (603 pop. 1970; 328, 1960, inc. 63%) in Coosa County has a junction with State 22, which goes to Alexander City, 18 *m.* east.

After entering Elmore County US 231 moves south toward Wetumpka, gradually drawing closer to the Coosa River and LAKE JORDAN, about 15 *m.* north of the town, a body of water impounded by an earthen dam built in the 1960s for the Alabama Power Company. It served electric installations that had a generating capacity of 225 megawatts. On February 10, 1975, the dam suffered a major break that drained the waters of Lake Jordan to such an extent that the plant was put out of action and the generating capacity of the Alabama Power Co. reduced by about 4 percent.

US 231 moves south through Wetumpka and Montgomery. (*See Tour 13.*) It is able to bypass Montgomery or to make junction with US 80, US 82, US 31 and Int. 85.

Upon leaving Montgomery US 231 becomes the principal highway moving in a southeasterly direction to Dothan and thence directly from Houston County to Florida. It is a multilane highway throughout. For 12 miles it is combined with US 82, which crosses the State from Georgia to Mississippi via Montgomery.

Southeast of Montgomery, US 231 passes through a region where hardwood swamps and pine ridges are interspersed with wide flat areas. This was once cotton country, but dairying and cattle raising are now carried on extensively. In spring the pastures and hayfields are carpeted with primroses and other wild flowers; beekeepers place their apiaries in orchards and roadside meadows along the route. Throughout the region are many old unpainted cabins, some of them log with wooden shutters, reminders of ante bellum plantation days. Villages in Montgomery County are quite small. PINE LEVEL DIVISION reported 1,798 pop. 1970; 2,111, 1960.

ORION, 37.2 *m.*, not counted by the U. S. Census, is historic. It was settled in the early 1830s by a group of wealthy planters and named for the constellation. Cotton was the foundation of the region's wealth, and until 1860 Orion was a center of culture and affluence. Known for many years as Prospect Ridge, it was chosen in 1848 as the site of one of Pike County's earliest schools, the Orion Institute. The school was made possible by two planters—Isaac Nall, who donated land, and Solomon Siler, who furnished the building funds—and was an important factor in the development of the town. Following the War between the States Orion began to decline, and weathered buildings of the old planter period are the only remaining signs of its former affluence.

For a brief period in its early history, the town was the rendezvous of gold seekers, drawn there by claims of an aged backwoodsman that he had discovered a rich seam of the precious metal. He appeared with a supply of gold nuggets, and for a time created excitement. But the ardor of residents cooled when it was discovered that the venerable "prospector" possessed a far-reaching imagination and loved practical jokes. The gold nuggets were real enough but he had obtained them far from Orion. Later he used the metal to decorate the heads of walking canes, which he sold to travelers.

The Siler House, built between 1840 and 1850 by Solomon Siler, was erected by skilled slave labor. Stately and white-columned, it was placed back from the street on oak-shaded grounds.

TROY, 49.1 *m.* (581 alt., 11,482 pop. 1970; 10,234, 1960, inc. 12%), the seat of Pike County, is built on a series of radiating ridges, with the courthouse square at their hub. The main business section surrounds the square, with shaded streets branching away to residential sections on lower grounds and adjoining hills. Troy is a busy manufacturing and trading town, and has cottonseed oil mills, food processing, textile and fertilizer factories. Three Notch Street, which the route follows, is a part of the old Three Notch Road, blazed in 1824 as a military highway from Fort Mitchell to Pensacola, Florida.

In Indian days, the site of Troy was a hunting ground called Deer Stand, but the first white settlers called it Zebulon, and later Centreville. They came in 1824. The first log cabin was built by "Granny" Love who, with her two sons, operated a tavern on the southeast corner of the present public square. The name Troy was eventually agreed upon, honoring Alexander Troy, father of Colonel D. S. Troy, of Montgomery.

Troy is a center for farm products in processing food and selling fertilizer. Saturday is the day when farmers come to town with their families, visit the supermarkets and stock up on household supplies. There is a profitable market for cattle and hogs. The Seaboard, Southern, and Central of Georgia provide freight service. The *Messenger* is the morning newspaper.

TROY STATE UNIVERSITY is the third largest institution of higher learning in Alabama. It occupies a campus of nearly 300 acres and most of its 20 buildings are of recent construction. It dates from 1887, when it began as a two-year normal school, became a four-year degree-granting college by 1931 and Troy State College in 1957. On December 14, 1967, when its services had expanded greatly, it was named Troy State University. In the fall, 1974, it reported a total enrollment of 6,010 students and a faculty of 211. Two degree-granting branches are located at Fort Rucker and Maxwell Air Force Base in Montgomery; each has more than 1,000 students annually.

The main divisions of the University are the Colleges of Arts and Sciences, the School of Business and Commerce, the School of Education, the School of Nursing, and the Graduate Division. There are 11 academic departments. Among recent additions to the curricula are courses in Medical Technology and Sanitary Science. A department of Philosophy and Religion also has been established. Teaching, which was the most important study in the normal school period, no longer dominates, but many teachers are trained in the university's courses, which include practice terms in the public schools. About 85 percent of the student body comes from Alabama.

During the 1960s Troy State added many new buildings and facilities, among them Smith Hall, a combination student center, music wing, and auditorium; Sartain Hall, athletic building and gymnasium; the Lurleen Burns Wallace Library; a number of dormitories for single and married men and women; the Alumni Hall, and a new field house. The University enters into all intercollegiate sports and its athletic programs include every phase of activity, with playing fields for all games.

Louise Short Home, on the eastern outskirts of the city, is a Baptist institution for widows and orphans. The institution was formerly in Evergreen, but it grew so rapidly that the Baptist Convention of 1919 recommended its removal to a larger town. Troy secured the institution by offering not less than 50 acres of land, $100,000 in cash, free use of the public schools, free medical services for the children, and other inducements. The home occupies a 207-acre tract of land.

In Troy is a junction with US 29 (*see Tour 12*).

At Hobdy's Bridge, 53.1 *m.*, across Walnut Creek, several hundred Creek Indians, en route from their old homes on the Tallapoosa River to new lands in the West, were massacred by whites in 1836. The Indians were camping near by when some unscrupulous white settlers who were entering Indian lands without legal right accused them of theft and disturbances, and clamored for protection against the "savages." A force of whites under General William Wellborn, a local militia officer, attacked them suddenly and without mercy. For a time, the Indians, led by Chief Enatochopka, fought with reckless bravery; but at last the small band was practically annihilated. Some of those who survived escaped into Florida, others were rounded up and sent West, while still others were kept as prisoners. As late as 1873, an Indian was found in practical slavery near Eufaula.

BRUNDIDGE, 61 *m.* (515 alt., 2,709 pop. 1970; 2,523, 1960), is the trading center of a section that produces peanuts and sugar cane, and is a shipping point for hogs raised in the vicinity. Settled as early as 1810, it was then known as Collier's Store.

At 66.5 *m.* is a water mill with an old wooden dam which backs the water up into a tree-shaded pond. Both mill and dam are in a good state of preservation.

OZARK, 89.5 *m.* (400 alt., 13,555 pop. 1970; 9,534, 1960, inc. 42%), is the seat of Dale County, and was known as Woodshop until the present name was chosen in 1855. It was named by the postmaster, who was reading a history of the Ozark Indians at the time. Once dependent on cotton, local farmers were forced to change their crop pattern radically when the boll weevil swept through here. They found the region especially suitable for hog raising since peanuts and corn, both important crops, could be used to fatten the hogs. Today Ozark ships large numbers of these animals each year. On the southern outskirts of Ozark is the Claybank Methodist Church, a small structure built of split logs in 1830. Annually, on the first Sunday in May, a reunion is held at the old church by descendants of pioneer Dale County families.

The ALABAMA INSTITUTE OF AVIATION TECHNOLOGY is located at Ozark.

Right from Ozark on State 249 to FORT RUCKER, 5 *m.,* site of the U. S. AVIATION CENTER AND SCHOOL, a training center for airmen of the USAF, Army, Navy, and Marine Corps. It occupies 59,000 acres and in 1970 had 14,242 in residence, of whom almost one-half were civilian employees and their families. Fort Rucker is practically equidistant from Ozark and Enterprise, which is 16 *m.* sw of Ozark on State 27. (*See Tour 10*).

The Center is building up strong library facilities. In 1974 it reported the following sections and volumes available: Human Resources Research, 23,997; Special Services Aviation Center, 25,600; Aero-Medical Research, 12,000; Army Aviation School, 30,000.

NEWTON, 99.4 *m.* (216 alt., 1,865 pop. 1970; 958, 1960, inc. 94%), is in a region of sand hills where diversified agriculture is carried on. It is a center for pecans and garden truck.

In 1865 Newton was the scene of the last raid of Joe Sanders' partisan band, guerilla raiders recruited from among non-slave owners who had rebelled against the Confederacy. Sanders had served with the Confederate Army in Virginia, where he had held the rank of captain. But he was not in sympathy with the Southern cause, and returned to his home in Georgia when he learned that some of the planters were hiring soldiers to serve for them at the front. Shortly afterward, conscription was begun and Sanders was ordered to report for further duty. He flatly refused and, when pressed, fled to the wild country near the Alabama-Georgia Line. Here he became the leader of a band of raiders who terrorized the countryside, looting stores and stables and robbing individuals. When peace came, the band dispersed and Sanders returned to his home, but he had made many enemies and a few months after the war he was shot dead by an unknown assassin.

DOTHAN, 117 *m.* (355 alt., 36,733 pop. 1970; 31,440, 1960, inc. 16%) is the seat of Houston County (56,574 pop. 1970) and the metropolis of southeastern Alabama. A busy industrial center, leading with textiles and food processing, especially in meats and peanuts, it has added in recent decades a wide variety of manufactures, including aircraft equipment, cigars, clothing, cottonseed oil, flour, fertilizer, yarns, underwear, toys, latex products, furniture, veneers and plywood. Its location was determined by springs. Its commercial history started with lumber and turpentine because it was in an area of pine forests; when the trees were gone the settlers planted cotton, grains and pecans. It is at the crossroads of routes leading into Florida and Georgia, in close communication with the Gulf. Its daily newspaper is the *Dothan Eagle*.

The name of the city derives from a passage in the Bible, "For I heard them say, 'Let us go to Dothan.'" (Gen. 37:17), chosen by a minister. For years there was debating over whether to spell the name Dothan or Dothen, but the post office chose Dothan and the citizens approved. As a frontier town its early years were turbulent, but there is a tradition that a strong-willed town marshall subdued the lawless element in the 1880s and kept order for 40 years.

In 1973 the Alabama Power Co. announced that between 1975 and 1977 it would place in operation at the Joseph M. Farley plant, 16½ miles east of Dothan, two units fueled by nuclear power, each to produce 860,000 kw. The first unit was to cost $436,000,000 and the second $369,320,000.

In 1965 Dothan citizens made use of the State's Junior College Act to organize the GEORGE C. WALLACE STATE TECHNICAL JUNIOR COLLEGE. In 1974 the college reported an enrollment of 2,239 students and a faculty of 96.

In Dothan are junctions with US 431 (*see Tour 7*) and US 84 (*see Tour 10*).

South of Dothan the route crosses flat land, broken only by occasional red knolls, washed free of the sandy top soil. This is the Wiregrass region, noted for its splendid growth of longleaf pine until, with the advent of railroads, turpentine and sawmill operations made deep inroads on the timber. Agriculture developed slowly here until it was found that commercial fertilizer could be used to advantage on the cutover pine lands. Then settlement became rapid, and the region is now one of the richest agricultural sections of the State. Principal crops are peanuts, cotton, corn, potatoes, and watermelons.

At 133 *m.* is a junction with a graded road. Left on this road,

4.1 *m.*, to a junction with another graded road. Right on this second road, 7.8 *m.*, to a third graded road. Right here to Sealy's Hot Salt Mineral Well, 8.9 *m.*, a health resort famous for its curative water. The well, discovered during drilling for oil and gas, is said to be 4,000 feet deep, and has a flow of approximately 10,500 gallons per hour. The water is infused with natural gas, lime, chloride, sodium oxide, iron, and aluminum oxide, and can be ignited, producing a bluish flame.

US 231 crosses the Florida Line, 135.3 *m.*, at a point 66 miles north of Panama City, Florida.

Tour 9

DOWN THE WEST SIDE OF ALABAMA FROM TENNESSEE TO MOBILE

Tennessee Line — Florence — Sheffield — Tuscumbia — Russellville — Hamilton — Fayette — Northport — Tuscaloosa — Demopolis — Linden—Saraland—Chickasaw—Prichard—Mobile. US 43.

Tennessee to Mobile, 370 *m.*

US 43 is the main route through the western length of the State from Tennessee to Mobile Bay. It crosses the Tennessee River Valley and passes through an upland region where there are panoramic views of dense woodlands and grayish crags. South of the wooded ridges are broad valleys and fertile farm lands. As the route near the coast it passes through flat pine woods country where lumbering and turpentining are the chief industries. The sandy soil is productive and in the region north of Mobile, there are truck farms and groves of tung trees. The road is known as the Jackson Highway.

Section a. TENNESSEE LINE to TUSCALOOSA, 165.2 m.

US 43 crosses the Tennessee Line, 0 *m.*, 20 miles south of Lawrenceburg, Tennessee. It follows parts of the Natchez Trace, one of the earliest of the Federal roads, which later became a part of the Military Road used by General Andrew Jackson's troops on their return from the Battle of New Orleans.

Although the river basin was rich in minerals, its early settlers were attracted chiefly by the fertile soil. Cotton is still the dominant crop, but diversified farming has advanced, and terracing to prevent soil erosion is carried on. Many of the farm houses are modern, but occasional ante bellum mansions stand along the route.

At 13.8 *m.* is a junction with a dirt road. *Left* here to Hickory Hill, once the home of General John Coffee, Indian fighter, surveyor general of the Alabama Territory, and brother-in-law of Andrew Jackson. It is a two-story frame house with large chimneys at each end.

FLORENCE, 18 *m.* (429-563 alt., 34,031 pop. 1970.) *See Florence.*

In Florence is a junction with US 72, which unites southward with US 43 to Tuscumbia.

On the southern outskirts of Florence is the old bridge, 19.9 *m.,* spanning the Tennessee River. As early as 1840, a bridge was built at this spot but it was destroyed by a storm. Another structure, laid on the same supports, was burned by Federal troops during the War between the States. The old bridge was constructed in 1870 but it was so narrow that traffic was handicapped. The present route crosses the river on a bridge completed in 1939, downstream from the old one. It has a center span of 420 feet; nearly 4,000 tons of steel were used in the construction. From the bridge Wilson Dam may be seen, left. At times the air is heavy with mist that rises below the dam.

South of the river the route crosses a narrow strip of the Tennessee Valley, then passes over the ridges of Tuscumbia Mountain.

SHEFFIELD, 22.8 *m.* (481 alt., 13,115 pop. 1970. (*See Tour 5*).

At 24.7 *m.* is a marker giving directions to the birthplace of Helen Keller (*see below*).

TUSCUMBIA, 24.9 *m.* (466 alt., 8,828 pop. 1970; 8,994, 1960), the seat of Colbert County, was platted by General John Coffee, and founded in 1817.

From Tuscumbia the united highway of US 72 and US 72 Alt. proceeds west through Colbert County to Mississippi.

When the first white men arrived there was a Chickasaw town here. It was ransacked and burned in 1787 by a raiding party of Cumberland settlers and Cherokee warriors led by Colonel James Robertson of Nashville. By 1821 settlers had built a frontier town on the site and had named it Big Spring for the near-by big spring and creek. A year later the name was changed to Tuscumbia, an anglicized version of the Indian Tashka Ambi (warrior who kills).

During the 1830s, Tuscumbia was the scene of financial speculation when a canal was built around Muscle Shoals, and the first railway west of the Alleghenies was laid between the town and a boat landing on the Tennessee River. The "railway" was a crude tramway with iron bars laid on wooden stringers; the cars were drawn by mules. However, it solved a transportation problem, and Tuscumbia became an important port for river boats.

Several old houses in Tuscumbia bear the result of skirmishes between Federal invaders and troopers of Forrest's "critter company."

Bullets still remain embedded in the walls and many small shot and Minié balls have been found in the vicinity.

At the northern limits of the town is Belmont, the old home of Governor Robert B. Lindsay, once occupied by Governor Anthony Winston. The red brick mansion was built in 1822. The walls and large white pillars are overgrown with ivy. In the cemetery near by are the graves of Governor Winston, Governor Lindsay, and Captain A. H. Keller, father of Helen Keller.

Near the business district, three blocks off the highway, is Keller Lane, leading to Ivy Green (*open*), the birthplace and old home of Helen Keller. Built on ten acres purchased from the University of Alabama, Ivy Green is an ivy-covered small frame cottage.

Helen Keller was born here and called the place, "The Rose and Honeysuckle Home." When she was three years old she lost her sight, hearing, and power of speech after an attack of scarlet fever. Beneath large oaks and elms in the picket-fence yard is the old Rocked Well, where Helen first learned that objects have names, and where it was noted that she was deeply responsive to nature. Along the paths grow box elders and stately pecan trees, magnolias, jasmines, honeysuckles and roses.

Helen was taken by her father to Baltimore, where doctors advised him to consult Dr. Alexander Graham Bell. The physician-inventor spent considerable time studying the little girl's case, and he was so greatly impressed by her intelligence and willingness to learn that he urged that a teacher be engaged from the Perkins Institute for the Blind, in Boston.

This teacher, Anne Mansfield Sullivan (later Mrs. John A. Macy), guided and tutored her pupil so well that on her tenth birthday Helen was able to "count" the candles on her birthday cake and make signs the family could understand. Within a few years, she had learned so rapidly that she entered Radcliffe College and was graduated four years later. For 49 years, until Mrs. Macy's death in 1936, Helen and her teacher were inseparable, touring Europe several times and appearing before royalty.

When President Franklin D. Roosevelt visited nearby-by Muscle Shoals in 1933, Helen "talked" with him and later described his physical features even to the color of his eyes. William Gibson's play, *The Miracle Worker,* is staged here on Friday nights in the summer.

The First Presbyterian Church, Fourth and Broad Sts., was built in 1824 by slave labor. White-painted box pews with gates are characteristic of the period, as is the old slave gallery along the sides of the church.

Big Spring in Legion Park, foot of North Main St., has a daily flow of 55,000,000 gallons. It forms a lake with an outlet stream which reaches the Tennessee River, two and one-half miles away.

Two skeletons discovered during excavation near Big Spring some years ago revived the story of a mysterious duel that occurred here on New Year's morning, 1824. On Christmas Day, 1823, a tall young man arrived on the northbound stagecoach, registered at the inn, and reserved a second room for "a friend who will arrive later." Two days after Christmas, the "friend" arrived on the southbound coach, and the two men were together constantly. They took long walks, apparently engrossed by the matter they quietly discussed.

On New Year's morning, they invited four men to walk with them to the Big Spring, where they said they intended to practice with their pistols. Arriving at the spot, one of the strangers announced. "This, gentlemen, is an affair of honor; we request your aid as seconds." After a few minutes of parley among the astonished "seconds," the duelists faced each other at ten paces. The order to fire was given, and the two pistols cracked simultaneously. Both men fell, killed instantly. In the coat pocket of each was a note requesting that, in event of death, the writer be buried where he fell. The strangers' identities and the cause of the duel were never learned.

At 30 *m.* is a panoramic view of the Tennessee Valley stretching away to the East and North; beyond the broad fields and farmhouses are heavily wooded hills. The best point of vantage is reached by walking about 200 feet to the edge of the cliff.

The route follows the plateau through a region of small farms, where cotton and poultry production are the main sources of income. In the backyards of farmhouses along the way are huge black kettles for boiling clothes and trying out fat at hog killing time. In some places, old ash hoppers are still used to soak lye from wood ashes and to make soap and hominy, as in pioneer days. The route passes through rugged country timbered with one of the remaining stands of the State's virgin forests. Small game is abundant here and deer find ample cover in the deep woods. Along the banks of streams that tumble over small falls are old grist mills. People in this section believe that the slowly-turning grindstones of water mills do not get hot and burn out the flavor of the meal.

RUSSELLVILLE, 43.1 *m.* (742 alt., 7,814 pop. 1970; 6,628, 1960), the seat of Franklin County, was named for Major William Russell, who commanded a company of Tennessee scouts in the War of 1812. Returning to Tennessee from the Battle of New Orleans, Major Russell and other soldiers were so impressed with the fertility of this region that they came back to form a settlement. Today, Russellville is an agricultural trading center; its industries include grain mills, cotton gins, and a stone quarry. Russellville is at a junction with State 24, east-west highway.

Sevier House, Franklin and Gaines Sts., was the home of Bonnie Kate Sevier, second wife of General John Sevier, hero of the Revolution and first Governor of Tennessee. In 1836 she came to Russellville to live with her son, Dr. Samuel Sevier. She died in October of the same year and was buried in the old town cemetery on North Washington Street; her body was removed to Knoxville and buried beside the grave of her husband in 1922. Near the Sevier house is a monument to the county's Confederate dead.

Memorial Oak, Jackson and Lawrence Sts., was transplanted from the Argonne Forest in France in commemoration of Alabamians who fought in World War I.

ISBELL, 47.3 *m.* (740 alt.), is a small farming community, named for a family that settled here in pioneer days.

Right from Isbell on a dirt road to the ruins of old Cedar Creek Furnace, 2.6 *m.,* where iron was smelted in 1818. Built by Joseph Heslip on property acquired for $2 an acre, limestone slabs for the furnace were quarried in the nearby hills, and clay bricks for its lining were made by hand. The brown ore was strip-mined and hauled in oxcarts to the furnace; charcoal used in smelting was produced in the surrounding forest. The small furnace operated only a few years but was the forerunner of the iron industry developed in this section. This same vein of ore later directed attention of iron and steel companies to the Franklin County deposits.

SPRUCE PINE, 52.8 *m.* (1,024 alt.), is a small farming and lumber community.

PHIL CAMPBELL, 56 *m.* (1,230 pop. 1970; 898, 1960) is another farm town in Franklin County. It has been chosen as the site of the NORTHWEST ALABAMA STATE JUNIOR COLLEGE.

At 57 *m.* County Road 41 turns west. South of this road to Dismal Wonder Gardens at Wonder Gulch, a great jagged cut in the face of the mountain, with sheer rock walls more than 100 feet high. Paths that wind between enormous boulders and beneath overhanging cliffs lead to caves and springs that are ideal picnicking spots. A stream with many small pools flows along the ravine floor. In spring mountain laurel and other wild flowers cover the banks.

HACKLEBURG, 66.1 *m.* (726 pop. 1970), is an agricultural village, settled in the early 1800s. It is situated at a point that was once the intersection of the Russellville Pike and the Allens' Factory and Iuka stagecoach road.

Northwest of Hackleburg are traces of the old Jackson Military Road, which branched from the Natchez Trace at Columbia, Tennessee, and crossed the Tennessee River at Muscle Shoals. Along the Jackson Military Road one of the first telegraph lines in the South was strung in 1848.

US 43 now crosses rugged, rocky country, bare or covered with sparse vegetation and moss. Southward are forested hills and broad lowland fields.

HAMILTON, 80.3 *m.* (3,088 pop. 1970; 1,934, 1960), is the seat of Marion County, on the old Byler Turnpike, a toll road built in 1819. Considerable travel passed over the turnpike after Tuscaloosa became Alabama's capital in 1826; the toll was $1 for a four-wheeled carriage and "one bit" (12½¢) for a horseback rider. Drovers paid a toll on each head of livestock driven over the road, and if a traveler was found using the pike after detouring around the toll gate, he was fined $5 plus the toll.

Hamilton was named for an early settler, Captain Albert Hamilton.

It is in the center of a large farming area, and is the home of NORTH-WEST ALABAMA STATE TECHNICAL INSTITUTE.

In Hamilton is a junction with US 78, which unites southward with US 43 for 20 *m.* to Winfield and then moves southeast to Birmingham. Moving from Hamilton east across the State is US 278, which goes to NATURAL BRIDGE, 24 *m.,* and WILLIAM B. BANKHEAD NATIONAL FOREST, 37*m.* (*see Tour 6*).

This Forest is located in Lawrence and Winston Counties and is a land of rugged bluffs, streams and lakes. Sheer rock walls rise above Lake Lewis Smith, which is formed by a dam on the Sipsey Fork, a tributary of the Black Warrior River. In the northwest the Sipsey flows at times through deep canyons. There is a wildlife management area. Facilities for camping, swimming, and boating have been developed. Five miles west of the Forest on State 195 in Winston County is HALEYVILLE (4,134 pop. 1970; 3,780, 1960), with a Ranger station. Another station is near the entrance of the Forest on US 278.

In Marion County US 43 enters the drainage basin of the Black Warrior River. As it proceeds south it is the only major highway that has contact with the Warrior-Tombigbee-Mobile River Waterway, an important artery for navigation serving the coal mines of the Warrior basin and the industries dependent on coal and water power. Nearly 40% of the State's industries are located in the 16 counties of this basin.

GUIN, 94.1 *m.* (432 alt., 2,220 pop. 1970; 1,462, 1960), is at the head of the Sipsey River Valley, a large drainage area of western Alabama. The town has an unusual municipal water supply system, the source of which is a large spring gushing from a gulch on a mountain top, and yielding 100,000 gallons daily. The water is piped to a tank of 250,000-gallon capacity, and no mechanical devices except pipes are used to carry it to homes and business houses.

In WINFIELD, 100.7 *m.* (469 alt., 3,292 pop. 1970; 2,907, 1960), is the southern junction with US 78 (*see Tour 16*).

FAYETTE, 121.1 *m.* (135 alt., 4,568 pop. 1970; 4,227, 1960), on the Sipsey River, is the seat of Fayette County. It was incorporated in 1821 but for 77 years had no name that pleased a majority of the population. Early names included Frog Level, Latone, Fayette Courthouse, Lafayette, and Fayette Depot town. Finally in 1898, the name Fayette was chosen by popular vote in honor of the French general. Although it is one of the oldest towns in Alabama, Fayette has few buildings to recall its pioneer history. In 1911, fire destroyed many of the old structures and they were rebuilt along modern lines. Fayette once had a gas field, developed at 1,400 feet, which supplied the town and vicinity with natural gas far nine years until it gave out.

In NORTHPORT, 164.2 *m.* (126 alt., 9,435 pop. 1970; 5,245, 1960, inc. 79%), is the western junction with US 82, which unites with US 43 to Tuscaloosa. East of the city is Lake Tuscaloosa on the Black Warrior River. The route crosses the Black Warrior River between Northport and Tuscaloosa. From the bridge there is a comprehensive view embracing Northport, Tuscaloosa, and Oliver Dam, one of the

Government locks that make the river navigable. This dam is located between high cliffs covered with a dense wood growth. Barges are towed upriver as far as Birmingport, in Jefferson County, and downstream to the Gulf.

TUSCALOOSA, 165.2 *m.* (65,773 pop. 1970) *see Tuscaloosa.*

In Tuscaloosa is the eastern junction with US 82 (*see Tour 14*), and the northern junction with US 11 (*see Tour 3*), which unites southward with US 43 to Eutaw (*see Tour 3*). It is also on Int. 59.

Section b. *TUSCALOOSA to MOBILE; 205.7 m.*

South of TUSCALOOSA, 0 *m.,* the combined route, US 43 and US 11, crosses the fertile prairie lands of the Black Belt, a section of immense wealth in ante bellum days. At the beginning of the War between the States, 75 percent of Alabama's slaves were concentrated on the large plantations of this region. An early writer called the Black Belt, "wide, spreading plains of a level, or gently waving land, without timber, clothed in grass, herbage, and flowers, insulated by narrow skirts of rich interval woodland." Wild flowers grow profusely here in spring and summer, filling the air with a sweetly pungent fragrance. Large apiaries are found throughout the section.

Int. 59, which crosses the State parallel with US 11, passes along the southern edge of Tuscaloosa.

MOUND STATE MONUMENT, an important archeological site, is a few miles east of US 43, but is reached best in a side trip of about 17 miles from Tuscaloosa on State 69. Located in a bend of the Warrior River, it is one of the productive archeological sites of Alabama. Here on a 320-acre expanse of grassy meadow rise forty monumental mounds representing a pre-Indian culture which dates before 1200 A.D. The park, which also contains an archeological museum and a research building, is part of the University of Alabama Museum of Natural History and is carefully maintained. There are two in situ burial groups in the museum, and a reproduction of a ceremonial temple has been constructed on top of the tallest mound. There is an increasing assemblage of artifacts relating to Indian culture and history. Outdoor tables and benches are provided on the side of the park that overlooks the river.

Continue on US 43.

EUTAW, 35.4 *m.* (180 alt. 2,805 pop. 1970; 2,784, 1960) a city in Greene County, sees US 43 and US 11 separate, US 43 going straight south, US 11 southwesterly to Meridian, Mississippi, Int. 59 bypasses Eutaw by 2 *m.,* continues parallel with US 11.

Encircling a memorable Town Square, Eutaw rivaled Greensboro as an agricultural center in ante bellum days. Scores of fine old homes line the shady streets: Kirkwood, with soaring Ionic columns lining two sides of the house, beautiful Austrian glass framing the heavy doors; the charming Dunlap House, behind its Chippendale gate; the White-McGifford Home, oldest house in town built by Eutaw's founder, with double-deck porches.

The Presbyterian Church dates from 1851. The neo-classic Court-house of 1870, which occupies the Square, is a duplicate of the original of 1840, which was burned in 1868, presumably by persons interested in destroying indictments made during the rule of the Carpetbaggers.

One of the regulatory structures of the Warrior-Tombigbee Water-way is the WARRIOR LOCK AND DAM, built in 1957 a few miles below Eutaw. It replaced the old locks and dams Nos. 8 and 9. It consists of an earth-fill dam and a concrete spillway controlled by six vertical lift gates, and a cut-off canal, 240 ft. wide, 12 ft. deep, and about one mile long. The canal eliminated about five miles in naviga-tion. The lock is 110 ft. wide, 600 ft. long, and has a lift of 22 ft.

FORKLAND, 50.4 *m.*, is an agricultural village which contains an Indian mound of large size. Here US 43 ascends the high bluff near the confluence of the Tombigbee and Black Warrior Rivers, identi-fied by some historians as the bluff mentioned by the De Soto chroniclers as near Mauvila, scene of the sanguinary Spanish-Indian battle on October 15, 1540. Thousands of acres of forests flank the streams, providing cover for deer, fox, wild turkey, and other game. Fishing is good in the rivers and creeks.

In DEMOPOLIS, 61.8 *m.* (7,651 pop. 1970) is the junction with US 80. *See Tour 3.*

CHICKASAW STATE PARK, 74.8 *m.*, is a 640-acre forested section with motor roads, hiking trails, and picnicking facilities.

LINDEN, 77.6 *m.* (2,697 pop. 1970; 2,516, 1960), the seat of Marengo County, was founded in 1823 by French settlers who came to Alabama after the fall of Napoleon. Its name was originally Hohen-linden, commemorating the French victory over the Austrians in 1800. Marengo also commemorates a Napoleonic battle.

THOMASVILLE, 107.3 *m.* (3,769 pop. 1970; 3,182, 1960) is a lumbering and farm center of Clarke County, founded in 1887. The lumber shipped from here is chiefly yellow pine. An important trade school is the RICHMOND P. HOBSON STATE TECHNICAL INSTITUTE.

GROVE HILL, 121.8 *m.* (1,825 pop. 1970; 1,834, 1960), has been the seat of Clarke County since 1832, when the county's offices were removed here from Clarksville. Built on the original Choctaw Indian boundary, fixed by the British in 1765, it was called Fort White in 1813, when it served as a refuge for early settlers. As the name im-plies, the town is built at the top of a hill where ancient trees shade its sandy streets.

The region surrounding Grove Hill was prosperous in frontier days but its timber land has been depleted and erosion has washed away many once-fertile farms. A public school building, erected in the 1930s, stands on the site of the old Macon Male and Female Academy.

At 122.7 *m.* is the northern junction with US 84, east-west.

JACKSON, 138.7 *m.* (5,957 pop. 1970; 4,959, 1960, inc. 20%), was a trading post in the early settlement days. Built upon a plateau near the southern limits of the Red Hills, its sandy, oak-shaded streets are lined with old Greek Revival mansions and modern houses. Mounted in the town square is a Cannon, once part of the Oven Bluff fortification on the Tombigbee River, to the south. Lumbering and agriculture are the town's principal activities.

South of Jackson are the great swamps of the Tombigbee where white-tail deer and black bear are found, and wild turkey, squirrel, and other game is plentiful.

The route crosses the Tombigbee River, 142.9 *m.*, over a concrete and steel bridge.

LEROY, 145.9 *m.*, was named for LeRoy Bowling, one of the hosts to General Lafayette when he visited the settlement in 1825. The region was settled by the French but later occupied by the Spanish, who in turn surrendered it to the United States in 1799. During pioneer days LeRoy was a social center, drawing its wealth from cotton. Steamers plied the near-by river to Mobile and New Orleans; some of these had bars, dance floors, and gambling rooms. Wealthy planters from this section often made river trips for the express purpose of gaming.

In WAGARVILLE, 151.6 *m.*, is a junction with State 56, westbound.

McINTOSH, 164.2 *m.* is a sawmill hamlet in the Cajan region. Turpentining and small scale lumbering are the principal industries. According to local tradition, Aaron Burr was held here for a short time after his capture.

Right from McIntosh on a dirt road a short distance to a Black Gum Tree, where Aaron Burr, former Vice President of the United States, was arrested by Captain Edmund P. Gaines on a charge of treason in February, 1807. He had been recognized the night before by Nicholas Perkins when he inquired the route to Colonel Hinson's plantation, where he spent the night.

East of Wagarville and McIntosh in the swampy area between the Tombigbee and Alabama Rivers lies a huge oil field that extends south into Baldwin County. The first oil well in this terrain was brought in 8 miles south of the village of CARLTON, by the Humble Oil & Refining Co. in 1950. The oil is heavy crude and is shipped by barge to Tuscaloosa, where it is used in asphalt.

MOUNT VERNON, 176.8 *m.* (29 alt., 1,079 pop. 1970; 553, 1960), was founded in 1811 as a military post. Old four-inch field pieces are sunk at intervals along the boundary of the original Mount Vernon Reservation. These little cast-iron guns are relics of an arsenal that, as early as 1828, was established here by the United States Army.

The Searcy Mental Health Hospital is located here.

Left from Mount Vernon on an unimproved dirt road to site of Fort Stoddert, 2.5 *m.*, fortification of the Indian wars. Aaron Burr was imprisoned at the fort for several days before he was sent to Richmond for trial. In the near-by cemetery is the grave of Ephraim Kirby, who drew up an early temperance pledge and agitated constantly for prohibition laws until his death from yellow fever in 1802.

The first newspaper of the Alabama Territory was published at Fort Stoddert on May 23, 1811. It was a four-page, four-column paper called the *Mobile Centinel,* and its owners, Miller and Hood, asked a subscription price of $4 a year. Growing along what was once an avenue near the fort are several large magnolias, planted by Amelia Gayle, who came to Fort Stoddert in flight from an epidemic of yellow fever. Here she met the young commandant, Lieutenant Josiah Gorgas, whom she married (*see Tour 11*).

In April 1887, the Apache Indian Chief, Geronimo and several hundred of his followers were brought as prisoners to Fort Stoddert. They had been captured in Mexico after their campaign against the United States Army in the Southwest. Geronimo was soon removed to Fort Sill, Oklahoma, where he died, but many of his warriors were kept here for seven years before they also were removed to Oklahoma. While at Mount Vernon, the Indians were provided with a camp outside the arsenal walls and had the range of the country during daylight hours. They were required to be in camp by nightfall, a regulation that was not violated.

ELLICOTT'S STONE, 182.9 *m.,* on a footpath immediately across the railroad, marks the 31st degree North Latitude, designated as the boundary between Spanish territory and the United States in 1799. It was placed by the Quaker surveyor, Andrew Ellicott, who also was the first man to measure Niagara Falls.

About 12 *m.* south of Mount Vernon County Road 84 moves west to the environs of CHUNCHULA, the newest oil strike, where the Union Oil Co. of California began drilling in 1975.

US 43 parallels the Mobile River southward to Mobile. At Twenty-Seven Mile Bluff, on the river, is the site of Fort Louis de la Mobile de la Louisiane, founded by Bienville in 1702. Buried in an unmarked grave near the site of the fort is Henri de Tonti, the Italian soldier-adventurer who was known the length of the Mississippi Valley as Tonti of the Iron Hand. Tonti lost a hand in the Sicilian War with Spain, and the substitution of an iron hook caused the Indians to give him the name. He died at Fort Louis during a yellow fever epidemic in 1704. The old fort, also called Fort Louis de la Louisiane and Fort Louis de la Mobile, was abandoned about May, 1711, in favor of the present site of Mobile (*see Mobile*).

As US 43 enters the environs of Mobile it passes through several contiguous cities that have been incorporated separately but are now part of the Mobile industrial area. Several have lost population by the movement away of part of the work force.

SARALAND, 195 *m.* (7,840 pop. 1970; 4,595 1960, inc. 70%), farthest north of the Mobile industrial suburbs, differs from others in that it has gained population.

CHICKASAW, 199.8 *m.* (8,447 pop. 1970; 10,002, 1960, dec. 15%), a city in Mobile County, on the Chickasaw-Bogue, is noted for its splendid fishing. Steel produced in Birmingham is loaded on freighters here for export. Near the end of the World War I many large freighters were launched at Chickasaw. The shipyard was reestablished in 1940 as a part of the National Defense shipbuilding program.

PRICHARD, 202.8 *m.* (41,528 pop. 1970; 47,371, 1960, dec. 12%), incorporated in 1925, is an industrial town. Its industries include cotton mills, a packing house and a chemical plant. Left from Prichard, 1.5 *m.,* is PLATEAU, an industrial location. At Plateau is Africky Town, a settlement of descendants of the last shipload of slaves brought to the South. Though the importation of slaves had become illegal after 1807, a brisk smuggling trade continued. The War between the States was threatening when the ship *Clothilde* arrived in Mississippi Sound from the Guinea Coast with a cargo of blacks. Under the direction of Captain Tim Meaher, wealthy slave trader, she was run up the Mobile River at night, the Negroes were hidden in the delta marshes, and the ship was burned. But Meaher found it difficult to dispose of his cargo. A few were sent to upriver plantations and some were put to work on the fortifications of Mobile, but the rest were left to shift for themselves. From this group has developed the present community.

The Negroes of Africky Town still have many customs and beliefs brought from Africa. The last of the original slaves, Uncle Cudjo Lewis, died in 1935 when, according to his record, he was 105 years old. For 75 years he lived in a cabin adjoining the Negro Union Baptist Church, of which he was a devout member.

MOBILE, 205.7 *m.* (190,026 pop. 1970). *See article on Mobile.*

Tour 10

SOUTHERN ROUTE, FLORIDA TO MISSISSIPPI

Ashford — Dothan — Enterprise — Elba — Opp — Andalusia — Evergreen — Monroeville — Claiborne — Grove Hill — Coffeeville —(Waynesboro, Mississippi).

US 84. 259 *m.*

This route constitutes the main thoroughfare across the lower coastal plain. Its eastern third is through the Wiregrass section, a flat region dotted with stands of long and shortleaf pine. In the days of early statehood, north Alabamians contemptuously called it the "cow country" because of its tough, stringy grass and apparently poor soil. They considered it worthless as an agricultural area, and only fit for the scrub cattle of the backwoods. Most of the early pioneers passed it by entirely, preferring the richness of the Black Belt. First to settle in the region were sawmill and turpentine operators, who paid scant heed to the soil as they cut and slashed the pine timber. Not until the early 1880s, when the forests had been cleared, did a few venturesome farmers discover that the soils were rich and suited to varied crops. The section's production of cotton became highly valuable. Hay, peanuts, corn, sweet potatoes, sugar cane, and watermelons are also grown, and dairying and hog raising greatly supplement farm incomes. There are still large patches of pine, and turpentining is carried on to a considerable extent.

West of the Wiregrass lies a section of low hills with farms impoverished by single-cropping and erosion. The extreme western part of the route is through the turpentine and timber area of the pine flatwoods.

US 84 crosses the Georgia Line, 0 *m.,* over a bridge that spans the Chattahoochee River, 22 *m.* west of Bainbridge, Georgia. On the border is the town of Gordon (312 pop. 1970) in Houston County, and a County Road goes south 11 *m.* to CHATTAHOOCHEE STATE PARK, a thickly wooded section of 590 acres. A fresh-water lake, bordered with semitropical plants, provides a pleasant site for camping and picnicking (fee, $2).

ASHFORD, 12.1 *m.* (1,980 pop. 1970; 1,511, 1960), is a trading center for the surrounding agricultural district.

In DOTHAN, 22.9 *m.* (36,733 pop. 1970) (*see Tour 5*) are junctions with US 231 and US 431.

West of Dothan the route is through a fertile farming section. Much of the land is terraced and cover crops are usually planted.

The Choctawhatchee River, 40.8 *m.,* provides excellent bass, bream and crappie fishing. Several large Creek villages once stood along the river's banks, but little remains to mark the sites.

ENTERPRISE, 53 *m.* (218 alt., 15,581 pop. 1970; 11,410, 1960, inc. 36%) is the largest trade and shipping center of Coffee County, with its economy based on agriculture, industry, and proximity to Fort Rucker, the U. S. Aviation Training Center and School. Production comprises peanuts, poultry, livestock, timber, vegetables, and cotton, and gross sales in its area approx. $20 million per year. Factory production consists of peanut butter, peanut oil, dress shirts, women's dresses, athletic wear, textiles, steel and aluminum fabrication, electronic equipment, truck bodies, and poultry processing. It profits from the buying power of Fort Rucker, which generally has in residence more than 14,000 persons, military and civilian.

Enterprise is famous in American economic history as the community that successfully introduced diversification in agriculture when much of Alabama was committed to growing cotton. In the summer of 1915 a pest called boll weevil began destroying cotton crops to such an extent that one-third of the crop, usually 35,000 bales, was lost for several years. Enterprise started a campaign to persuade farmers to diversify their crops, and they found that peanuts, corn, potatoes, sugar cane, hay, cattle and hogs brought prosperity back to Coffee County. In 1917 the county harvested more than one million bushels of peanuts.

On December 11, 1918, the citizens erected a fountain with a monument on top of which is a boll weevil. An inscription reads: "In profound appreciation of the boll weevil and what it has done as the herald of prosperity this monument was erected by the citizens of Enterprise, Coffee County, Alabama." As the city explained, the monument is "a beacon pointing ever toward the saneness of diversified farming."

Enterprise has a mayor and five councilmen, chosen for four-year terms. It has Enterprise Hospital and Coffee General Hospital, and the Rescue Squad, fully equipped for emergency work and housed in new quarters. There are five shopping centers.

Enterprise Public Library, 110 East College Ave., circulates more than 100,000 books annually and has a full program of special services. The Recreation Center, with provision for sports for all ages, in cooperation with the YMCA, has a new center built by public subscription and supported by a 1¢ cigarette tax. The ALA-FLI Boy Scout Reservation has 500 acres, which include a 65-acre lake built by the Corps of Engineers of Fort Rucker.

ENTERPRISE STATE JUNIOR COLLEGE was established in 1965 pursuant to the designation of the State Board of Education, which initiated the Junior College and Trade School Program. The site of the college was provided by the community and consists of 100 acres three miles east of Enterprise. It began with 256 students and passed the 1,000 mark in 1969. Besides the courses of the regular curriculum it offers special short courses for citizens who wish to expand their interests, such as modern math for parents, interior decorating, sewing, painting and business letter writing. Courses are also fashioned to meet the needs of veterans from the military services. The association of the city with the elimination of the boll weevil has become a slogan for student activities; the athletic teams are the Boll Weevils and the Boll Weevil Invitational Debate is an intercollegiate contest sponsored by the college. The buildings, attractively placed on hilly ground, were designed by Pearson, Humphries & Jones of Montgomery.

ELBA, 69 *m.* (204 alt., 4,634 pop. 1970; 4,321, 1960), the seat of Coffee County, is an agricultural trading town, named by an early French settler for Napoleon's place of exile. Built on the banks of Pea River, at the site of a ferry established about 1840, the town became the county seat in 1852.

Whitewater Creek flows into the Pea at Elba, making the town a danger point during floods. In 1929, when it was inundated, some of the residents escaped in boats, but many were forced to seek refuge in trees and on housetops. When the flood waters had subsided a levee was built along the river, and Elba became one of the few levee-protected towns in Alabama.

West of Elba the country is more hilly. Farmsteads are older here and the land has been intensively farmed.

OPP, 87.8 *m.* (6,493 pop. 1970; 5,535, 1960), is a trading and shipping point for a large agricultural area that produces corn and cotton. Pine lumbering is the leading industry.

At Opp there is a junction with US 331, a major north-south highway. It continues south 45 *m.* through Covington County to FLORALA (2,701 pop. 1970; 3,011, 1960, dec. 10%). One mile west on State 55 is LOCKHART (698 pop. 1970). US 331 crosses the Florida line 2 *m.* beyond Florala. On the border are Lake Jackson and Florala State Park.

ANDALUSIA, 103.2 *m.* (856 alt., 10,092 pop. 1970; 10,263, 1960). US 84 has a junction with US 29 2 *m.* before the city and with State 55, both of which move south into the CONECUH NATIONAL FOREST, the most southerly of the four national forests in Alabama. This fine recreation area, entirely within Covington and Eascambia Counties on the border of Florida, has tropical vegetation and offers an alluring variation for hunters and campers from the more northern recreation spots. Conecuh is in the flat, sandy coastal plain, where streams meander quietly through semitropical vegetation and run straight and level through the lush pine forests.

The route now turns northwest over a short stretch of red-soiled ridge country, where the forest growth is mainly cutover pines. Farms are small, generally producing peanuts, cotton, corn, and meat sufficient only for home consumption.

McKENZIE, 127.4 *m.* (491 pop. 1970; 558, 1960) in Butler County, is at the junction with US 31, which unites with US 84 for 22.8 miles.

Clear, slow-flowing streams are now crossed frequently, their courses marked by tangled clusters of semitropical growth. In spring and summer, the woods are bright with jasmine and trumpet vine flowers, and the air is scented by magnolias and bay trees. Beekeepers place their apiaries near the bay trees because the blossoms furnish a honey that neither ferments nor crystallizes, and is prized for its exceptional flavor.

EVERGREEN, 147.2 *m.* (258 alt., 3,924 pop. 1970; 3,703, 1960).

At 150.2 *m.* is the southern junction with US 31 and with Int. 65, which provides an expressway from Montgomery to Mobile.

BELLEVILLE, 157 *m.,* is a small rural community where a Baptist church was established in 1820 by Alexander Travis, backwoods minister and uncle of William Barrett Travis, a hero of the Alamo. The present building, a small frame structure, was erected in 1852 and has a gallery for slaves. Travis spent a lifetime in missionary work, preaching among the Indians and settlers from 1810 until his death in 1852. He sometimes walked as many as 35 miles to preach, carrying his clothing in a pack, sleeping in the forests, and swimming the streams.

In a bend of near-by Burnt Corn Creek occurred the first engagement of the Creek War. The battle was begun by a group of militiamen and volunteers under Colonel James Caller, who attacked a Creek party led by Peter McQueen, High-Head Jim, and Josiah Francis on July 27, 1813. The Americans routed the Indians, but when they stopped to gather up guns, they were in turn surprised by a counter-attack. A confused retreat followed, with the Indians scattering the Americans so badly that some of them were lost in the forest for days. Afterward, it was considered a disgrace to have been in this battle, for the Indians accepted it as a test of the Americans' valor. Their loss of respect for the Americans was emphasized a month later when they massacred the garrison and settlers at Fort Mims (see Tour 1).

At Excel, 172.1 m., a lumbering center in a flat pine woods (4,846 pop. 1970; 3,632, 1960), State 21 has a junction with US 84. Five miles north on State 21 to:

MONROEVILLE, 179 m., has been the seat of Monroe County since 1832. Named for James Monroe when he was Secretary of State, the town is a trading center for the fertile farming area of the near-by Alabama River bottom lands. Soon after the Creek War, settlers in these bottom lands were terrified repeatedly by John Haigue, a mixed breed known throughout southern Alabama as Savannah Jack. Leading a band of outlaws, he raided along the frontier, burning homes, and robbing and killing the occupants. His victims were always found scalped. He claimed to be an avenger for the conquered Indians, but the remaining tribesmen disclaimed him and helped American militiamen rout him from his hiding places. He was finally driven into the Florida swamps.

From Monroeville the route turns left almost at right angles. The country is hilly, heavily wooded with large pines, and gashed with deep boulder-strewn gulches. Along the road are a few small farms with old cabins of rough hewn timber.

The James Dellet House, 192 m., is a two-story white frame dwelling, built about 1816. Much of the original rosewood, mahogany and teakwood furniture is still in use, and the library contains rare books and documents. In 1825 General Lafayette was entertained here, and Colonel William Barrett Travis lived here while studying law and teaching school in Claiborne in 1828. He married one of his pupils, Rosanna Cato, and later joined Sam Houston in the Texas war for independence; he was killed in the Battle of the Alamo.

CLAIBORNE, 193 m., is a scattered group of weathered houses shaded by tall, white-trunked sycamores. The town was built on the Old Federal Road upon the high east bank of the Alabama River. At the time of the War between the States, it was the largest inland cotton market in Alabama, with a population of nearly 6,000. But its wealth was lost during Reconstruction, and most of its residents moved away.

In River Bluff Cemetery is the grave of Arthur Bagby, Governor of Alabama, and United States ambassador to Russia. Also buried here are many who died when yellow fever struck Claiborne in 1830, almost wiping out the town's population.

On the river bluff is the site of Fort Claiborne, built in 1813 by General F. L. Claiborne. Nearby are the ruins of a warehouse, where cotton was stored and loaded into river boats during pioneer days. In the river at this point Big Sam Dale's famous canoe battle was fought. Dale, Jeremiah Austill, James Smith, and Caesar, a Negro, were paddling across the stream when they met another dugout containing 11 Creek warriors. A hand to hand fight followed while Caesar held the two dugouts together. Only one of the Creek escaped, leaping into the stream and swimming to shore.

At 193 *m.* is a boulder with a plaque commemorating Piache, an Indian town visited by De Soto in 1540. De Luna made a settlement here, Nanipacna, in 1560. The marker was erected by the Alabama Society of Colonial Dames in March, 1939.

The fossil beds of the Alabama River around Claiborne supplied material for a colossal hoax perpetrated by Albert C. Koch, German geologist, who explored the region in 1844-5. Using the bones of several Zeuglodons, prehistoric whale-like creatures, he reconstructed a skeleton 114 feet long, weighing 7,500 pounds. This he claimed to be a sea serpent, *Hydrargos Stillimanii,* and exhibited it to wondering crowds in the United States and Europe before his trickery was exposed.

In 1965 the citizens of Monroeville took advantage of State support of education and opened PATRICK HENRY STATE JUNIOR COLLEGE, which in 1973 had 500 students and 26 teachers.

The Alabama River is crossed at 193 *m.* over a steel bridge. When General Andrew Jackson brought his Tennessee militiamen down the Alabama to Fort Claiborne in 1814, he disembarked at the landing of John Weatherford's Ferry, where the bridge now stands. John was a brother of William Weatherford, halfbreed war leader of the Creek. Numerous descendants of the Weatherfords live in this section.

WHATLEY, 207 *m.* is a farming and lumbering village on the site of Fort Sinquefield, object of Indian attacks during the Creek War. On August 30, 1813, the day of the Fort Mims massacre, Indians murdered 12 members of two white families on Bassett's Creek, which flows near the fort. The bodies were brought to the stockade, and burial services were arranged for the following day. In the midst of the services, which were being held near the fort, a large band of Creek warriors dashed from the forest and surrounded the settlers. Another massacre appeared imminent, but as the Indians began closing in, Isaac Hayden, who had been hunting stray cattle with a pack of hounds, saw the attack from the edge of the woods. He spurred his horse into the open and set dogs on the Indians. The yelping hounds distracted the warriors' attention and they retreated a few yards from the fort's entrance. The settlers immediately made a rush for the gate, and all escaped with the exception of one woman, who was shot and scalped. After a battle lasting two hours, the Indians retreated, leaving 11 dead.

A mixed-blood named Josiah Francis, known to the Creek as Hillis Hadjo, the Prophet, planned and inspired the Indian attacks in this section. More than 6 feet tall, with dominant personality, he was held in awe by his tribesmen, who believed he possessed supernatural power.

Tecumseh had made Francis the prophet of the Red Sticks, the warring faction of the Creek Confederacy.

General Jackson recognized Francis as more dangerous than other leaders among the Red Sticks and tried to come to grips with him in 1815, but the Prophet was taken to England by Edward Nichols, commander of the British forces in the Creek Nation. While the British heaped honors upon Francis, including the commission and uniform of a brigadier general, Old Hickory bided his time. Finally, in 1817, Francis was captured in Florida, promptly court martialed, and hanged.

At 213 *m.* is a junction with US 43, north-south, which proceeds to Mobile. Formerly US 84 joined US 43 for 28 miles south to Jackson, (*see Tour 9*), but after rerouting it now moves one mile north to GROVE HILL (1,825 pop. 1970; 1,834, 1960) in Clarke County and then proceeds due west.

SIMCO, 219 *m.,* is a small farm village.

COFFEEVILLE, 233 *m.* (441 pop., 1970; 250, 1960) is at a junction with State 69, which proceeds 22 miles south to Jackson.

Two miles west of Coffeeville and 23 miles northwest of Jackson is the JACKSON LOCK AND DAM on the Tombigbee River, part of the Warrior-Tombigbee Waterway that has a 9-ft. channel to Mobile Bay. The installation was completed in 1966 and replaced three old locks and dams. In locating the new lock and dam the old lock and Dam No. 1 was bypassed by a cutoff canal, 4,800 ft. long and 9 ft. deep that saved four miles of river travel. Jackson Lock is 110 ft. by 600 ft., with a lift of 34 ft. The spillway, 536 ft. long, has eight gates.

Five miles beyond Coffeeville a county road goes to the village of BLADON SPRINGS. Three quarters of a mile north is BLADON SPRINGS STATE PARK, with full camping facilities (*fee $2*).

BOLINGER, 250 *m.,* a farm village in Choctaw County is at a junction with State 17, north-south. About 10 *m.* north on State 117 is GILBERTOWN, a village of 207 people, the center of a huge oil pool discovered in 1950. The Jackson No. 1 well here produces 20,000 bbl. of oil per month. The pool extends over an area 40 to 80 acres wide and 13 miles long in Choctaw County.

ISLEY, 259 *m.,* a village, is one mile from the Mississippi line, and 16 miles from Waynesboro, Mississippi.

Tour 11

LAND OF THE ALABAMA CAJUNS

(Waynesboro, Mississippi)—Fruitdale—Citronelle—Suburbs of Mobile.

US 45. Mississippi to Mobile, 55 *m.*

This short route of less than 63 miles is the Alabama extension of US 45, one of the principal highways of Mississippi, which moves all the way down the eastern border of that State to find its terminus in Mobile. It enters only two counties in Alabama—Washington and Mobile.

US 45 crosses the Mississippi Line, 0 *m.*, 21 miles south of Waynesboro, Mississippi, and follows an old Choctaw Indian trail. The rolling expanse of cotton and corn fields along the northern part of the route are interrupted here and there by forests of virgin timber; to the south, satsuma orange and pecan groves alternate with large poultry, dairy, and truck farms.

Large areas of cutover land provide low-grade free pasturage for the sheep and cattle herds that are the principal source of income for hundreds of farm families. Although this half-wild scrub stock brings the lowest market prices, the steady increase in herds, aided by a moderate climate, makes stock raising profitable.

Several game preserves are well stocked with deer and wild turkey, while the unreserved forests abound in quail, squirrel, and other small game.

At YELLOW PINE, 1.9 *m.*, is the former eastern junction with US 84, a service now performed by State 56, which connects with US 43.

The region surrounding FRUITDALE, 7 *m.*, an agricultural village, was once covered with vast stands of virgin pine. Wasteful lumbering practices, however, destroyed the forests. The pioneers' only aim was to convert the forests into lumber and profits as speedily as possible. Having ripped out the choice timber, the sawmills moved on, and roving herds of razorback hogs, nosing out the roots of the few longleaf pine seedlings that remained, prevented natural reforestation.

An attempt to utilize a large part of this area was made by planting orchards, but the scheme collapsed in 1904 when the San José scale ruined the trees. It was from these large orchards of fruit trees that the town received its name.

At 14.4 *m.* is a junction with an unimproved dirt road. Right on this road to Vinegar Bend, a lumbering and turpentine center. A large sawmill once operated here on the Escatawpa (Choctaw) River, with convicts under lease from the State. Bringing liquor to the company's property was strictly forbidden, and smuggling "moonshine" into the lumber camps from the deep swamps became a profitable, though risky, business. Whenever a person was observed carrying a jug or can, its contents was immediately questioned by the guards. So frequently was the claim made that the container held vinegar, that the place became known as Vinegar Bend.

CITRONELLE, 29.2 *m.* (1,935 pop. 1970; 1,918, 1960) in the northern part of Mobile County, has the distinction of being located over the largest oil field in the South. This was found by a wildcat drilling operation in 1952. Production has continued on a profitable basis. Oil underlies a large acreage in Choctaw, Clarke, Escambia, Mobile, and Baldwin Counties. *See report on oil, p. 62.*

Citronelle was named for the citronella grass which thrives in this section. This was one of the first sites selected for the experimental introduction of the tung tree from China in 1906, and has been a center for the tung oil industry ever since. Tung trees line the highway for several miles here. The town also has small sawmills and ships some pine lumber.

In the heavily wooded region around Citronelle are several Cajan settlements, occupied by a people of undetermined racial origin. The name, Cajun, is not applied correctly, for these people are not related to the Cajuns of the Gulf Coast, who are descended from the Acadians of Canada. The Alabama Cajans are believed to be descended from early French, Spanish, and English settlers who married Indian women. Some of them say that their forefathers were buccaneers from Mexico, who made this region a base for their operations.

In 1929 that the Cajans of Washington County sought a court test on the issue of their children being barred from white schools. Testimony was concerned chiefly with the ancestry of one woman. The State attempted to show that she was a Negro, and that during the War between the States she had been sold as a slave at Jackson, Alabama; Cajans contended that she was a fullblood Cherokee, unlawfully placed in slavery. When the case was concluded, tension in the crowded courtroom caused the judge to postpone announcement of a decision. It was never made public, but the Cajans claimed a victory, because the State installed a tri-racial system in Washington, Mobile, and Clarke counties. At one time Cajans were not allowed to attend Alabama colleges, but the laws against racial discrimination eliminated the ancient barriers.

A sharp contrast in types has contributed to the racial confusion. In a single family, where both parents are dark complexioned, one child may have black, coarse hair, swarthy complexion, and jet-black eyes, while another has deep blue eyes, fair complexion, and blond hair. Many Cajan women are pretty, but their good looks are frequently spoiled by stained and sometimes broken teeth. Cajan women love bright colors and often wear scarfs wound about their hair, and glittering cheap jewelry, which makes them resemble gypsies. The olive hued men are darkened by outdoor living.

Cajan houses are much alike, although some are more comfortably equipped than others. There are usually only two rooms; the cooking is done in one and the entire family, sometimes consisting of as many as ten persons, sleeps in the other. Furniture is made up of odds and ends, and most of the beds are homemade. On the board walls are pictures of Biblical scenes, newspapers to guard against winter winds, and broken pieces of mirrors. Believing in conjure, ha'nts, and signs, many of the Cajans wear "tricks" to guard against disease and bad fortune. They believe that every murdered thing, man or animal, has the power to return to life as an avenger.

The churches have for many years tried to improve their condition and to win converts, but progress has been slow. The adult Cajan does not like to congregate except with his own kind. He also like his Sunday leisure and does not sacrifice it easily for church-going. This is especially true if the preacher refers to such subjects as drinking, rowdying, and men and women living together out of wedlock. But despite this independence the Cajan usually has a high sense of honor.

Most of the Cajans depend upon lumbering and turpentining for their livelihood. As the great stands of timber have been cut away, employment in these industries has diminished. They do not complain, however, and most of them continue to live their solitary lives in their own way, accepting aid only when faced with actual starvation.

Choctaw Indians had long been settled in this region of agreeable elevation and pure water when the first Spanish explorers came. Although the Choctaw claimed all the southern part of the present State, most of their towns were west of the Tombigbee River not many miles east of Citronelle. They were a sedentary, agricultural people, who built large villages and raised corn, sweet potatoes, squash, and pumpkins. They warred intermittently with the Creek to the east and the Chickasaw to the north and allied themselves with the French. It was the Choctaw in this section who most bitterly opposed the scheme of the Shawnee war chief, Tecumseh, to ally all Southern Indians on the side of the British in the War of 1812. Pushmataha, their principal chief at the time, rejected Tecumseh's war belts and kept his tribesmen neutral. When the Creek joined Tecumseh's league in 1813, and began to attack the white settlers, the Choctaw joined the American forces under Andrew Jackson, against their ancient enemies.

In earlier editions of the Alabama State Guide WHISTLER, 55.2 m. not only had an identity as a separate community but fame in its own right; since then it has become a suburb of Mobile, although it retained its local postoffice. In 1935 the U. S. Post Office Department issued a commemorative stamp for Mother's Day, which carried a modified reproduction of James McNeill Whistler's portrait of his mother. As a result the place was swamped with letters from collectors who desired the Whistler postmark. According to tradition the town was not named for the artist but for a locomotive engineer who impressed workers with his prolonged whistling when the line was being built.

TOULMINVILLE, 58.2 *m.,* a suburb of Mobile, is part of the metropolitan area of that city and perhaps its oldest suburban center. It was made the headquarters of General Claiborne during the War of 1812.

A greater claim to fame for Toulminville is its native son, William Crawford Gorgas, born here in 1854. General Gorgas is acclaimed as the surgeon general of the U. S. Army who made possible the construction of the Panama Canal by conquering the yellow fever plague. This dread disease was causing so many deaths among the workers that, for a time, abandonment of canal construction was being considered. Under the direction of General Gorgas, however, the area soon became as free from disease as the average city of the temperate zones, and the work was carried to completion.

Gorgas' parents were General Josiah Gorgas, soldier and member of the Confederate cabinet, and Amelia Gayle Gorgas, daughter of John Gayle, once Governor of Alabama. During the War between the States William Gorgas, then a boy, was in Richmond, and when he saw the ragged Confederate troops tramping the streets with bare feet, he refused to wear his shoes and vowed that some day he would become a soldier. Unfavorable conditions following the war kept him from attending West Point, so he studied medicine in order to enter the army through the medical corps. He achieved his objective, and built a memorable career.

Toulminville received its name from General Theophilus Lindsey Toulmin. Toulmin came to the State in 1804, and from 1831 until 1865, served successively as legislator, sheriff of Mobile County, and State senator.

The General's work ended with the defeat of the Confederacy, and he died shortly thereafter. The story has been handed down among blacks that family treasures were buried on the place when Federal troops entered Mobile, and that the General's ghost returns nightly to keep watch. At midnight, seated in a rocker on the porch, a favorite spot in his declining years, he is reported to rock gently to and fro, the creak of his chair plainly audible in the night stillness. So firmly entrenched was the Toulmin legend that it caused frequent midnight searches for buried treasure. It was no unusual event for the occupants of the Toulmin house, for many years after the war, to find evidence of digging that had been done during the night.

In MOBILE (190,026 pop. 1970) are junctions with US 31 (*see Tour 1*), US 43 (*see Tour 7*), US 90 (*see Tour 12*), US 98 (*see Tour 2*), Interstate 10 and Interstate 65.

Tour 12

ROUNDING THE SOUTHEAST CORNER OF ALABAMA

(La Grange, Georgia)—Lanett—Opelika—Auburn—Athens—Tuskegee—Union Springs—Troy—Luverne—Andalusia—Conecuh National
Forest—Brewton—Flomaton.

U. S. 29. Int. 85

Georgia to Florida, 231 *m.*

US 29 appears to be routed through the southeast corner of Alabama in order to give the smaller towns and villages in this cotton growing area an opportunity to connect with main highways. Its rambling
character through Macon, Bullock, Pike, Crenshaw, and Covington
Counties suggests that its usefulness is as a connecting road for the
more direct highways out of Montgomery, such as US 231, US 82,
US 331, and US 80. The largest city in the corner is Dothan, in
Houston County (36,733 pop. 1970). The driver who perseveres on
US 29 for more than 230 miles in Alabama is rewarded by direct access
to Pensacola Bay and its outlying shores.

Eastern Alabama is a region varying from hilly to rolling lands,
long denuded of big timber and presenting in winter a rather bleak
panorama of eroded gullies and scrubby, weed-grown fields. This section
has a number of large cotton mills; there are many model mill towns
with parks and playgrounds and well-spaced, neatly-painted houses.
South of the hilly region the route crosses the level Coastal Plain into
Florida.

US 29 crosses the Georgia Line, 0 *m.,* 17 miles southwest of La
Grange, Georgia. On the west bank of the Chattahoochee is the site
of old Fort Tyler, where on April 16, 1865, one of the concluding engagements of the War between the States occurred. A handful of
wounded and convalescent Confederates made a futile attempt to hold
the bridgehead against General Wilson's 3,000 Union troops, who were
preparing to attack West Point. Only the outline of old earthworks
marks the site.

LANETT, 1.3 *m.* (6,908 pop. 1970; 7,674, 1960) is the principal
cotton mill city in Chambers County. It was known as Bluffton until
in 1893, when it was incorporated and named for a partner in the
Lanett & Barnett cotton mill. Lanett also makes textile machines.
Besides corn and grain it ships peaches. In 1974 Lanett reported its
population had grown to 10,650. It is 75 *m.* northeast of Montgomery

by way of Int. 85. The Valley Times-News is the organ for this area.

FAIRFAX, 6.2 m. (2,772 pop. 1970; 3,107, 1960), is a mill town with many well-kept homes. South of Fairfax cotton and corn are the principal crops.

OPELIKA, 22.9 m. (817 alt., 19,027 pop. 1970; 15,678, 1960), the seat of Lee County, is a busy agricultural and textile manufacturing city. *See Tour 7.*

The first settlers came from Georgia in 1836, and the first building was the Lebanon Methodist Church, about a mile and a half from the present courthouse. In 1840, a postoffice was established, known officially as Opelikan. This was an error, as the name was derived from the Creek word, Opilako, meaning large swamp, but the spelling was not corrected in the records until 1851. During the ante bellum period, the fertile farming lands in this section attracted wealthy planters, who contributed much to the town's early growth. In 1848, when it was reached by the Montgomery & West Point Railroad (later the Western Railway of Alabama), Opelika entered a boom period. It was incorporated in 1854 with a population of 2,000 and, with the exception of Reconstruction, its growth has been steady.

South of Opelika the sharp ridges and hills gradually level out into a rolling landscape marked by occasional swamps along small winding tributaries of the Tallapoosa River. The route here passes through the ancient border-line region between the Upper and Lower Creek tribes. Along the ridge tops are traces of Indian trade paths, centuries old, that led from the Upper Creek country to old Kawita and on to the region around Savannah. This section of Alabama suffered considerable devastation during the War between the States and bore the brunt of carpetbagger rule during Reconstruction days.

At 25.5 m. PEPPERELL is a village originally built to house employees of the Pepperell cloth mills. The houses are well-spaced, each with lawn and garden, and there are two parks with playground equipment, a community building, school, and library.

AUBURN, 29.9 m. (698 alt., 22,767 pop. 1970; 16,261, 1960, inc. 40%) a city in Lee County, is a trading center on the southern edge of the Piedmont Plateau. Many beautiful homes line its shaded streets, but only a few of the very old houses remain and of these, many have been remodeled.

The first settlers were a group of Georgians who erected a number of buildings in 1836 and returned to Georgia to bring their slaves and other property to the new site. A name had not been chosen for the settlement and while the founders were back in Georgia, Tom Harper, son of Judge Harper, mentioned the fact to his sweetheart, Miss Lizzie Taylor. She had been reading Goldsmith's *Deserted Village* and promptly exclaimed, "Name it Auburn, sweet Auburn, loveliest village of the plain!"

AUBURN UNIVERSITY, one of the major public institutions of Alabama, occupies a campus of 1,871 acres in Auburn and 500 acres in Montgomery, where it is developing a new branch. It was founded in 1856 as a college for men by the Methodist Church, which presented it to the State of Alabama in 1872. It became the Alabama Agricultural and Mechanical College, a land grant institution. In 1892 it admitted women as students, and in 1899 became the Alabama Polytechnic Institute. In 1960 it was named Auburn University. In 1967 the university agreed to take over the University of Alabama Extension Center in Montgomery, and when the Legislature voted a $5,000,000 bond issue for a campus there, Auburn University at Montgomery was organized as a new four-year college. In 1973 Auburn reported a total enrollment of 15,339 and a faculty of 897.

Auburn's main campus has 114 buildings, of which the most recent include the Edmund C. Leach Nuclear Science Center and the Ralph Brown Draughon Library, which has more than 650,000 volumes and capacity for 1,000,000 and can accommodate 2,000 students at one time. The Paul Shields Haley Center of classrooms and laboratories was an important addition to the facilities in 1969. It is ten stories tall, contains three auditoriums, and has a fully equipped foreign language laboratory and closed circuit television. It cost a total of $6,-768,306 from State and Federal appropriations.

College buildings of historical significance are Founders Hall, the main administrative building, and the Mason-Beaty House, now the President's home.

Founders Hall was started in 1842 and completed in 1844 with an Athens resident, Col. H. H. Higgins, as architect. This building is a majestic structure that has become the visual trademark of the college. Its facade is graced by four Ionic columns which students have named Matthew, Mark, Luke, and John. Although changed somewhat by later additions, it shows clearly the Greek influence common to early Southern Architecture. The bricks used in the construction were burned on the campus. The mortar is powdered limestone made up and allowed to stand and ripen for months before using. The massive outside walls are solid brick, 15 inches thick.

The Mason-Beaty House, now home of the President, is the oldest house in Athens. It was built in 1826 by Robert Beaty, one of the founders of both the town and Athens Female Academy.

There are 10 schools in the University, the most recently established being the School of Business. The Graduate School dates from 1872. Each school is involved in research programs and faculty and graduate students "are actively at work increasing man's understanding of man and the world in which he lives." The cost of tuition, board, lodging, and personal needs was estimated in 1972 as between $1,600 and $2,000 a year.

The Drake House, Gay St., one block right from US 29, was built in the 1830s. During his student days at Auburn, General Robert Lee Bullard kept a horse in the Drake stables. He left a linen duster hanging in the barn when he went from Auburn to West Point Military Academy, and World War I had ended before he was again a visitor in the Drake Home. He was greeted by Mrs. Drake with the words, "Hello, Bobby Bullard, did you come back for your old linen duster?"

The Thomas Hotel stands on the site of a double log cabin, the first house in Auburn. It was built by Judge John H. Harper, leader of the little band of Georgians that came here to found a settlement in 1836, shortly after the United States Government obtained the land from the Indians.

The Simeon Perry House, E. Drake Ave., is a sturdy ante bellum cottage built by Simeon Perry, a civil engineer who came with Judge Harper to plat the town. Its hewed timber and hand-planed lumber are joined by wooden pegs and hand-forged nails. Soon after arrival in the frontier country, Perry married a widow named Wimberly, who owned numerous slaves and whose acres covered many square miles. Their first house burned and with it a money bag in which Mrs. Perry kept her ready cash. Years later, the couple's grandchildren found coins on the site of the original home. One of the old slave houses stands on the property.

Jones Hotel, College Ave., was called the Stage Inn in the 1840s. Its exterior, with wide porch supported by four large columns, is characteristic of that period. Isaac McElhaney, who bought and enlarged Stage Inn, drove a stagecoach between Georgia and Auburn.

General James H. Lane House, College and Thach Sts., has a bronze tablet affixed by the United Daughters of the Confederacy of Auburn stating that General Lane lived here from 1833 to 1907. He was the youngest brigadier general in the Confederate army and taught at Auburn after the war.

A monument at the railroad station commemorates a review of the Auburn Guards by Jefferson Davis on February 17, 1861. Davis was on his way to Montgomery to be inaugurated President of the Confederate States of America.

The Presbyterian Church, Thach Street, was erected in 1850 and was used by the Confederates to care for wounded soldiers.

Halliday-Cary House, N. College Ave., is a story-and-a-half structure of the raised cottage type with high, narrow windows and wide verandas balustraded with wrought iron. It was a center of the social life during the war. A Confederate Officer, convalescing here, hid in the attic many days after Union soldiers took the town. He eventually escaped to his regiment.

Left from Auburn on a dirt road is CHEWACLA STATE PARK, 4.1 *m.*, comprising 577 acres in one of the most rugged valleys south of the Appalachian Mountains. Within the park are streams, cascades and palisades, bridle paths and hiking trails. It is equipped for all-year use (*fee $2*).

South of Auburn the route enters the upper Coastal Plain. Here the land is rolling and the hills are less knobby than those to the north. The soil is sandy and fertile. Patches of hardwood trees growing along the stream banks, and thick pine forests cover the higher ground.

At 41.6 *m.* is a junction with US 80, which united with US 29 to Tuskegee. *See Tour 3.*

In TUSKEGEE, 48.7 *m.* (11,022 pop. 1970) is the southern junction with US 80.

US 29 swings sharply southward from Tuskegee, passing through wide stretches of flat country sparsely timbered with pines. This part of the Coastal Plain is cultivated extensively and there are many farms along the highway. Cotton, corn, peanuts, and potatoes are the principal crops.

UNION SPRINGS, 70.1 *m.* (284 alt., 4,324 pop. 1970; 3,704, 1960), is the seat of Bullock County. The town was named for the large springs on Chunnennuggee Ridge, which are the source of the Conecuh River and three other streams. Unlike most county courthouses in Alabama which are prominently situated in a town square surrounded by broad lawns, trees, and hitching posts, the Courthouse, Prairie St., is tucked away between business houses quite similar to it in appearance. The World War Memorial Boulder on the courthouse lawn was placed by the American Mothers of National Defenders.

DELLA ROSA, Main St., near the center of town, is a fine example of the Southern plantation manor house. It was the home of Captain Richard Powell, and figures in Augusta Evans Wilson's novel, *At the Mercy of Tiberius.*

The Confederate Monument, Hardaway and N. Prairie Sts., is a white marble shaft erected by the United Daughters of the Confederacy.

US 29 has a junction with US 82, which goes to Montgomery. South of Union Springs US 29 continues through the broken terrain of Chunnennuggee Ridge.

BANKS, 100.6 *m.* is an agricultural village and small trading center for farmers.

Between Banks and Troy the route passes through rolling sandy country, dotted with pines and patches of hardwoods. It follows closely the course of the old Three Notch Road that ran from Fort Mitchell on the Chattahoochee River to Pensacola, Florida. The Three Notch Road, designated by the U. S. War Department as Federal Road No. 6, followed an ancient Indian trail that wound along the ridges from Kawita to the Gulf and was one of the main communication lines of the prehistoric South. It was widened for the use of express riders between the military posts at Fort Mitchell and Pensacola. Aaron Burr was carried, a prisoner, along the Federal road after his arrest near McIntosh, in 1807, and from one of the houses on the route Andrew Jackson dispatched his resignation as Governor of Florida. Like many other trails of the Southern frontier, it was traveled by Lorenzo Dow, the backwoods preacher and his wife, Peggy. In 1825 it was one of the stops in General LaFayette's tour.

Big Sam Dale, Government scout, traveled this route in January 1815, on a heartbreaking ride that excited admiration even in that day of boots and saddles. The War of 1812 was over and a treaty had been signed, but the news had not yet reached the far-flung frontier.

Riding his horse, Paddy, Dale set out from Milledgeville, Georgia, in raw January rain, with orders to carry news of the treaty to General Jackson in New Orleans. Six hundred miles of mud roads and swollen streams lay ahead. Dale put Paddy over the trail at a grueling pace and reached New Orleans within eight days. The battle of New Orleans was at its height when he arrived and he did not reach General Jackson until hours later, during a lull in the fighting. In Dale's memoirs General Jackson is quoted as saying, when he read the dispatch, "Too late! Too late! Washington is always too late!"

In TROY, 110.6 *m.* (581 alt., 11,482 pop. 1970) is a junction with US 231.

LUVERNE, 132.1 *m.* (412 alt., 2,440 pop. 1970; 2,238, 1960), is the seat of Crenshaw County and a farm trading center. It ships livestock, cotton, peanuts, and pecans, and manufactures cottonseed oil, peanut oil, and lumber.

South of Luverne US 29 traverses more level land with occasional swamps, densely grown with bay trees.

BRANTLEY, 141.5 *m.* (1,066 pop. 1970; 1,014, 1960), is a sawmilling and farming town. Most of the lumber used is pine.

Southwest of Brantley the route follows the valley of the Conecuh River, crossing the stream at 161.4 *m.*

ANDALUSIA, 169.2 *m.* (856 alt., 10,092 pop. 1970; 10,263, 1960), on the tableland east of the Conecuh River, is the seat of Covington County. Many of the buildings about the town square are modern and the aspect of the entire town is one of newness despite the fact that the original settlement (called New Site) was established in the 1830s. In Andalusia is a junction with US 84 (*see Tour 8*).

South of Andalusia US 29 tops ridge after ridge, the elevation dropping a little after each rise, and enters a section of the CONECUH NATIONAL FOREST, 180.1 *m.,* in the lowlands east of Conecuh River. The whole forest covers 83,955 acres. Here are groves of virgin pine, magnificent live oaks, bays, magnolias, and a profesion of semi-tropical undergrowth. There are alligators and reptiles in the stream; black bear, deer, wildcat, and great numbers of small game find refuge in the dense swampy forests. West of the Conecuh the route strikes across a succession of ridges, then descends gradually to level country.

In 1821 when flatboat freight lines were operating, the Conecuh River was an important waterway. Commonly called keelboats, the river craft were 60 to 70 ft. long, 8 or 10 ft. wide, and were propelled by the "hook-and-jam" method. Men stood in the bow and reached out with long poles on which were steel hooks that caught in tree trunks, thus pulling the boat forward, while others in the stern used poles to push against the stream bottom and the banks. At one time there were 17 such barges operating between Brooklyn, near Andalusia, and Gull Point, in Escambia Bay, Florida. Freight rates averaged about 37½¢ per hundredweight. It cost 50¢ per cwt. to ship iron, $1.50 per keg for whisky, $1.25 per barrel for flour, and $1.50 per bale for cotton. In August 1845, the first steamer entered the Conecuh, and things looked bad for the flatboatmen. The steamer, *Shaw,* took aboard a cargo of cotton at Brooklyn during high water, and set out for Pensacola. Amid cheers from throngs on the banks the *Shaw* got off but was barely well under way before she struck a snag and sank. For a long time thereafter the hook-and-jam men had the undisputed run of the river.

The route crosses the Conecuh River, 194.8 *m.,* and passes out of the Conecuh National Forest.

Murder Creek (*see Tour 1*), is crossed on a bridge, 214 *m.,* between Brewton and East Brewton. During the days when the hook-and-jam boats were operating on the Conecuh, the thriving frontier town of Sparta was near the east bank of Murder Creek, 15 miles north.

It is said that a scourge of fever drove Sparta's inhabitants away. Some buildings were torn down and rebuilt in other places; others were abandoned and burned down during the years that followed. Weeds and underbrush grew up on the site of the old town and eventually nothing remained but a few ruins.

In BREWTON, 214.8 *m.* (85 alt., 6,747 pop. 1970) (*see Tour 1*), is a junction with US 31 which unites westward with US 29 to Flomaton (*see Tour 1*).

POLLARD, 224.8 *m.* (73 alt.) first seat of Escambia County, is today only a rural trading village, where the Census of 1970 found only 80 people, a drop of 61% from the 1960 figure of 210. It was Confederate post, and the scene of an engagement between Federal raiders and troops stationed here. The town was burned during the subsequent action.

In this region stories are still told of the outlaw Negro, Railroad Bill. In life he was Morris Slater, a worker from the turpentine stills who turned bandit. In death he became endowed with all manner of magic. Railroad Bill came into being when an Escambia County deputy attempted to arrest Slater for carrying a gun. He shot the deputy and escaped on a passing freight car. For several months afterward, he terrorized the country, looting freight cars of valuables which he sold at low prices to farm and lumber workers. At last, both the State and the railroad company offered a reward for his capture or death. When Ed. S. McMillan became sheriff, he determined to capture the outlaw, who had once worked for him. As he was preparing to start on the search, he received a laboriously written note. "Don't come, Mr. Ed." the note read, "I love you." But the sheriff went on the search, encountered the outlaw, and was killed by a bullet in his heart. At once a posse was organized but Railroad Bill evaded them for more than a week. At last he was cornered in a store that he had entered to obtain food, and while he sat on the floor eating, with his rifle at his side, he was slain by shotgun blasts. He became the subject of a folk ballad.

In FLOMATON, 230.4 *m.* (100 alt., 1,584 pop. 1970) is the western junction with US 31 (*see Tour 1*).

US 29 crosses the Florida Line, 231.4 *m.* at a point 43.5 miles north of Pensacola, Florida.

Tour 13

FROM MONTGOMERY TO FORT TOULOUSE AND THE CREEK VILLAGES

Montgomery — Fort Toulouse — Wetumpka — Tallassee — Auburn ; 63.5 *m.*

State 9 and State 14.

State 9 follows the route of an ancient Indian path across the Black Belt prairies and into the low southern ridges of the Appalachians—a path which traversed the heart of the old Creek country. Between Montgomery and the Tallapoosa River the route is through flat lands ; north of the Tallapoosa are wooded hills. The fertility of this region was first mentioned by DeSoto's chroniclers who spoke of the people as the most prosperous they saw in their wanderings. A century and a half later came Englishmen from Charleston and Frenchmen from Mobile to bargain with the Creek for furs, deerskins and buffalo hides, and the footpath became a pack trail. The French succeeded in wresting the bulk of tribal trade from the British a generation later, but the latter won undisputed political and economic control of the region in the French and Indian War, and were aided during the Revolution by the Creek. When the American settlers pushed westward, the pack trail was widened as pioneer supplies were hauled over it. It had become a frontier road by 1804 when Preacher Lorenzo Dow and his wife, Peggy, followed it on their first southwestern missionary tour ; the fiery Lorenzo reputedly called the wayside settlements "the most unholy in the world." During 1840-60, this was one of the most popular roads in the State ; as the Central Plank Road it was a successful example of this type of highway.

In the days when the Creek claimed this region as their domain, their towns were close together along the Tallapoosa and Coosa Rivers ; the sites are identified by bits of pottery, flint arrowheads, and flint chips. Burials frequently yield relics with bones and each site has legends associated with it.

MONTGOMERY, 0 *m.,* (160-222 alt., 133,386 pop. 1970). *See Montgomery.*

State 9 branches northward from US 80 within the city limits of Montgomery.

A bridge, 9.8 *m.,* spans the Tallapoosa River where Judkin's Ferry transported plank road travelers across the stream more than 100 years ago. The Appalachian foothills begin here with the bluff that forms the northern bank of the stream, and steep slopes covered with pine, oak, and hickory replace the level Black Belt lands beside the route.

At 14.4 *m.* a lane leads a short distance to the Bullard-Owen House. Built in 1823 by John Bullard, the house originally contained two rooms downstairs and two upstairs, divided by open central halls. Hand-planed lumber was used in the original structure. Between 1880-5 the halls were enclosed, porches were added on each floor, and the exterior was weatherboarded.

At 15.1 *m.* is a junction was a gravel road. Left on this road to a marker indicating the site of FORT TOULOUSE, 3.3 *m.,* built by the French in 1714 and surrendered to the British in 1763. James Adair, a British trader among the Cherokee and Chickasaw, was imprisoned at the fort for two weeks in 1747. His narrative details a thrilling midnight escape with the French clattering after him on horseback, "and the howling savages pursuing my tracks . . . on a needless pursuit."

Fort Toulouse was built on the site of the Alibamu town of Taskigi. There were some 30 houses in the compact village during British trader days, and the prosperous inhabitants had large herds of cattle ranging in the 3,000 acres of canebrake pasture around the town. Sam MacNac, brother-in-law of William Weatherford, the half-breed chief, lived here and owned 180 calves in 1799. His son, David, was the first West Point cadet from Alabama, graduating in 1822. David became a cotton planter but returned to military service during the Seminole outbreak of 1835 and was killed in the Battle of Wahoo Swamp, November, 1836. The Indians showed their bitter hatred of the mixed bloods who fought against them by the 67 bullets they fired into David's body when they recognized him. The fort was abandoned by the British at the close of the Revolution and remained unoccupied until rebuilt by Andrew Jackson in 1814. Here William Weatherford surrendered to Andrew Jackson shortly after the Battle of Horseshoe Bend.

Fort Toulouse site is a convenient point from which to visit the Indian mounds and townsites along the rivers here. The sites on the left bank of the Coosa can be reached easily on foot or horseback, but those on the right bank are less accessible by land.

On the Alabama River, below the confluence of the Coosa and Tallapoosa, 4.3 *m.,* is Big Eddy Landing. Left here by a swamp 4.8 *m.,* is a 30-acre field of the Baldwin plantation containing an Indian Mound, 13 feet high, which has many aboriginal burials. Three miles below the headwaters of the Alabama is the site of Koassati, a village of the Alibamu. Early traders found its people speaking an impure Alibamu dialect, and claiming to be a different tribe from the Creek. Koassati was the birthplace of William Weatherford.

The site of Oktchayiudshi (Little Oktchayi) is on the right bank of the Coosa just above Taskigi and Fort Toulouse sites. The inhabitants of Little Oktchayi were a branch of the Tallapoosa Oktchayi, one of the seven Okfuski towns.

Odshiapofa (Hickory Ground) extended from about 3 miles north of the confluence of the Tallapoosa and Coosa Rivers, just above Little

The Seats of Learning

THE PILLARS OF LEARNING, BROWN HALL, MILES COLLEGE,
BIRMINGHAM

CHANGING STYLES AT AUBURN UNIVERSITY: ABOVE, THE
ITALIANATE CLOCK TOWER OF WILLIAM J. SAMFORD HALL,
BUILT 1888; BELOW, THE OPEN STAIRCASE OF HALEY CENTER, 10
STORIES TALL, SEATS 8,000 IN CLASSROOMS.

FOUNDERS HALL, ATHENS COLLEGE

SCIENCE BUILDING, FLORENCE STATE UNIVERSITY, BUILT 1962

CAMPUS SCENE AT SAMFORD UNIVERSITY, BIRMINGHAM

THE GEORGE WASHINGTON CARVER MUSEUM AT TUSKEGEE INSTITUTE.

TOMPKINS HALL, STUDENT UNION, TUSKEGEE INSTITUTE.

ACADEMIC PROCESSION, JUDSON COLLEGE, MARION, ALABAMA

Tour 14

FROM THE BLUE RIDGE INTO THE DEEP SOUTH

(Northwest Georgia)—Sulphur Springs—Hammondville—De Soto State Park—Fort Payne—Sequoyah—Collinsville—Attalla—Steele—St. Clair Springs—Crystal Caverns—Trussville—Birmingham—Bessemer—Tuscaloosa—Mound State Monument—Eutaw—Tombigbee River—Livingston. US 11, Int. 59.

US 11 swings through Alabama in a wide arc from the northeast corner where Georgia and Tennessee are almost within hailing distance, to the middle of Mississippi, a highway that expeditiously carries traffic from the Blue Ridge and the western slopes of the Appalachians to the fair cotton fields of the Deep South. Keeping abreast with it at every turn, crossing and recrossing, is Interstate 59, a corridor permitting quick transit for a huge trucking industry. These two highways constitute spokes of the wheel of which Birmingham is the hub, having junctions with practically every route that comes south from the lands of the Cherokees.

Section a. GEORGIA LINE to BIRMINGHAM; 116.1 m.

US 11 crosses the Georgia Line, 0 *m.*, at a point 32.5 miles southwest of Chattanooga, Tennessee, and winds through Wills Valley, which is cradled between the lower slopes of Lookout Mountain (l) and Raccoon Mountain (r), the latter locally called Sand Mountain. Roads branch right and left from the highway and ascend to crests that are approximately 2,000 feet in elevation. The lower mountain slopes are heavily wooded with oaks, tulip trees, and dogwood; the high ridges on the right are covered with thickets of pine, and hardwoods grow on the crests of Lookout Mountain. Mountain laurel, azalea, and rhododendron form a tangle of undergrowth in the valleys.

Deep ravines have been cut by streams, and crowning rock palisades honeycombed by small caves and crevices rise above the thickets. Some historians believe that this is the country called Chiaha by De Soto's chroniclers, and that the route of the Spanish explorers followed the southward course of the present highway. This section attracts thousands of vacationists each year and many of the hill folk operate summer camps. Some of these resorts are along the route, and others are reached by branch roads over the mountains. The most popular camps are at Mentone and Valley Head.

On the tablelands, where the soils are light and fertile, are productive farms. Cotton, corn, and potatoes are the principal crops but strawberry and peanut crops and poultry are increasing. Peaches, apples, and other fruits of excellent quality are also grown, and pecan groves are numerous.

Sulphur Spring, 0.9 *m.* a small village in a narrow part of Wills Valley, has several mineral springs reputed to have medicinal properties. Their curative value was recognized by the Indians; it is said that they first became known to the whites through the experience of a pioneer who was left to die, but recovered after drinking from the springs.

HAMMONDVILLE, 8 *m.*, had an astonishing increase of 64% in population by rising from 134 in 1960 to 221 in 1970. Here US 11 and Int. 59 have junctions with State 117, which is combined at this point with State 40. West of Hammondville near State 117 are the SEQUOYAH CAVERNS, famed for the brilliant color range of their onyx formations, encrusted with fossils from remote ages. Known to have been occupied as early as 500 B. C., the caverns sheltered the Cherokee Indians for centuries before the white man appeared. One of the great stalagmites, known as Chief Tuscaloosa, bears the name of Sam Houston, who lived among the Cherokees and left his mark here in 1830. *Open daily all year, 7-5:30; adults, $1.50; children, 6-12, 75¢, under 6 free.*

At 1 *m.* east of Hammondville on State 117 is VALLEY HEAD, (470 pop. 1970; 424, 1960) a shipping point on the AGS for products of the Wills Valley farms. Here Dr. John S. Gardner, a Methodist minister from North Carolina who invested in more than 3,000 acres of farm land, planted mulberry trees in a vain effort to start a silk culture, a project that had inspired others in the ante bellum South. He also built the Winston House, named after its later owner, Colonel W. O. Winston, delegate to the Secession convention. In 1863 it was the hq of Colonel Jefferson C. Davis, USA, a cousin of the Confederate President who served in the Union army.

Old-timers in the section tell the story of a bearded grandpap who rode his mule down from the hills to see the Union encampment around the spring on the Winston Place. Tethering his critter to one of the mulberry trees, he joined a knot of hillmen who were talking to the sentries. He listened for a while, then quavered, "Sojer boys, who's the bossman around here?"

"Jeff Davis," one of them said.

After a pause the old man poked the sentry with his cane, "Did you say Jeff Davis?"

"That's right, Colonel Jeff Davis."

The old man sat down, to think this over. Finally he hobbled up to a sentry, "I want to see Colonel Jeff Davis," he exclaimed. The sentry told him he couldn't see the Colonel, but he hung around. When the officer made his evening rounds, Grandpap stopped him. He caught Davis' hand and pumped it. "Jeff Davis," he said, "I couldn't be easy till I shaken the hand of the only man with a lick of sense in this war.

And, say, Jeff, which pays you the most? Colonelin' the Bluecoats or Presidentin' the Confederates?"

MENTONE, 4 m. farther on State 117, is located at the crest of one of the highest hills in the area. The town, with only 470 inhabitants (1970) expands during the vacation season and the environs are dotted with camps and cottages. The Valley Head-Mentone Division had 2,342 pop. in 1970, 2,521 in 1960.

From Mentone the green length of Willis Valley, dotted with farmsteads, spreads toward the rampart of Sand Mountain. There are wide-flung panoramas of valleys and ridge chains; bypaths lead to natural rock gardens and the rapids and waterfalls of Little River.

In early May, boat trips down the river from Mentone pass solid masses of magenta rhododendron and mountain laurel, alive with bees and heavily fragrant. Just below the turn is an old covered bridge spanning the quiet water of Little River, sometimes called De Soto River (*bass and bream fishing*).

The Scenic Highway turns right in Mentone and runs along the crest of the mountain ridge.

Sunset Rock, 4.9 m., is a shelf of granite jutting from the top of a high bluff above the valley. On clear days distant ranges in Georgia and Tennessee are visible. When, as often happens, low-hanging clouds conceal the valley, only the taller hogbacks stand out darkly above the misty gulf.

At 6.5 m. is a junction with a graded road. Left here to DE SOTO FALLS, 2 m., where Little River's western fork makes its first great leap in its descent from the high tableland. Between sheer walls of sandstone, to which dwarfed trees and flowering shrubs cling, the water drops 80 feet to explode with a pulsing roar and clouds of spray. A deep cave opens behind the falls.

At 10.1 m. on the Scenic Highway, State 89, is the junction with a graded road. Left on this road to River Park, 9.6 m., a small summer colony on the slope above Little River's western fork. The stream is well stocked with bass and bream, and deep pools among the rapids sometimes yield trout (*fishing best during spring freshets*). Stone houses here have some of the features of Swiss chalets and English cottages, and pinepole houses, patterned after the log cabins of early settlers, are furnished with sturdy furniture built by the mountain people.

Alpine Lodge, once a summer hotel, is part of a summer camp. It was originally built to serve as a dormitory for the Master School founded by Colonel Milford W. Howard as the nucleus for a proposed mountain school system. The school was discontinued when State schools began to serve the hill people. Near Alpine Lodge is the Sally A. Howard Memorial Chapel, erected by Colonel Howard in memory of his wife. The Chapel, a reproduction of the Annie Laurie Chapel in Scotland, is built of sandstone, roughly cut so that veins of pink, green, and brown are shown in the cream of the rock. The wall behind the altar is formed by an enormous granite boulder. Above the altar are two great hand-carved beams bearing Biblical inscriptions.

On the edge of the old campus is the Granny Dollar Cabin built by a Cherokee for his white wife. Granny Dollar, their daughter, refused to leave when the Indians moved from the region in 1838. She lived alone in the woods until the danger of being sent away was past, then took up her residence in this cabin. Until her death at the age of 110, Granny Dollar was a noted herb doctor and midwife, and feared by many as a witch.

Most of the people of this section are descendants of the earliest settlers of the Blue Ridge country. Many old habits and customs survive. Locks are virtually unknown and latch-strings are always out for friend and stranger. A man who showed distrust of his neighbors by locking his smokehouse or corncrib would be ostracized. House raisings, corn shuckings, and quilting bees are still favorite community amusements.

After work is done on such occasions there are wrestling bouts, games, frolics, and break-down dancing where old fiddlers saw away on "Hell's Broke Loose in Georgy," "Sugar Valley," "Rabbit in the Pea Patch," "Sail Away Ladies," and "Turkey Bone Buzzer." Christmas, New Year, and the Fourth of July are the only formally recognized holidays, and Easter celebrations are considered "downright popery." Some of the older people celebrate Old Christmas, which comes on January 6, the date on which the birth of Jesus was celebrated before the adoption of the Gregorian calendar.

In these hills families are almost independent units, growing most of the food needed, even making most of their tools by hand. Sale of surplus products to summer visitors brings in cash for a few luxuries—cosmetics, a bit of ribbon or cloth, and, occasionally, some household article. The speech of the uplander is often puzzling to the outsider. "Anti-godlin," "catawampus," and "whopper-jawed" mean out of alignment. The Old English "holp" for helped, "drug" for dragged, "fotch" for fetched, and "wrop" for wrapped, are part of everyday speech. Still current among the older people are the ballads sung in England before the colonists came to America. "Barbara Allen" and "Lord Randall" are popular and some of the old airs and musical phrases are preserved in more recent songs, describing local happenings. Students of folklore often have visited cabins in northeastern Alabama to transcribe songs of the hill people, many of the ballads having come down during the generations from Scottish and English pioneers.

From Mentone State 89 traverses an area between US 11 and the Georgian border, where the LITTLE RIVER flows through the gorges of DE SOTO STATE PARK. This park of 4,825 acres is exceptional for its wild, natural beauty, where the slopes have remained wooded and the waters of the river move in foaming cascades. The most spectacular part of the rugged scenery is LITTLE RIVER CANYON. This area is crossed, east to west, by State 35, which has a junction with US 11 about 2 m. above Fort Payne. A great ravine from which the Little River emerges is known as May's Gulf. When Federal troops under General May reached this point on their march to Rome, Georgia, they were impressed by its beauty. After the war

General May returned to make a special study of the canyon, which became known locally as May's Gulf. A paved road with picnic tables at vantage points skirts the canyon. In the towering rock walls that enclose the Gulf are remains of rock caverns used by the Indians. Since De Soto entered the Cherokee villages in Northeastern Alabama it is popularly supposed that he knew this area. One series of caverns called De Soto's Caves is below the falls in a massive outcrop of rock, where several large chambers open on a narrow ledge 70 ft. above the falls. In ancient times communicating passages were cut in the rock walls.

State 35 moves southeast to GALESVILLE (160 pop. 1970) a village on an arm of WEISS LAKE, formed by a dam on the Coosa River for hydroelectrical installations of the Alabama Power Co. Return to US 11.

FORT PAYNE, 22.5 m. (873 alt., 8,435 pop. 1970; 7,029, 1960, inc. 20%), seat of De Kalb County, is a trading center for the neighboring mountain people. On Saturdays the sidewalks are crowded with farm folk.

In the vicinity are deposits of clay of varying types, suitable for the manufacture of china, porcelain, earthenware, and firebrick. There are also deposits of coal, iron, and fuller's earth. In the early 1880s, when iron was discovered, a land boom struck the town. Large subdivisions were mapped, lots were sold at public auction, and many new houses and public buildings sprang up almost overnight. The Old Depot, still in service dates from those years. But the vein was not as promising as expected, and Fort Payne settled back to the slower pace of an agricultural center.

Near by is the site of the Cherokee Indian village of Will's Town, where the Indian genius, Sequoyah (Sequoia), inventer of the Cherokee alphabet, lived in the early 1800s. Sequoyah, also known as George Gist or Guess, was born some time between 1760 and 1770 near Chota, the old capital of the Cherokee Nation in what is now East Tennessee, and moved to Will's Town about 1800. Here he conducted his fur trading business, and worked as silversmith and blacksmith, and here he succeeded, after years of patient effort, in devising the Cherokee alphabet —a spectacular achievement.

Sequoyah was the son of a white trader and a Cherokee woman of mixed blood. The identity of his father has never been fully established, but recent historians have identified Nathaniel Gist, son of Christopher Gist, famous frontiersman and friend of George Washington. Sequoyah was crippled in his youth, some say as the result of a hunting accident, but this did not keep him from an active life. He went on hunting expeditions, herded horses and broke the colts for saddle, helped his mother with her fur trading business, and after her death, about 1800, carried on the trade himself. He had some artistic ability and painted pictures on bark, smooth boards, and pieces of tanned deerskin. While still a youth, Sequoyah, who spoke no English, became interested in the "talking leaves" of the white man. About 1809 he began to experiment with an alphabet for his people, making slow progress at first since he tried to devise a sign or symbol for every word. He neglected his farm and his business. His tribesmen, who advised him to "get his reason back" and resume his regular work, ridiculed him and began to shun his little workshop in the woods.

Sequoyah now began to devise symbols for all the basic sounds or syllables in the Cherokee language, rather than the words. After obtaining an old English speller, the work progressed rapidly. He did not understand English sounds but used the letters for symbols along with the marks he had invented.

During a dramatic trial for witchcraft in 1821, he and his six year-old daughter, his first pupil, sent messages to each other by means of his alphabet. This convinced the headmen of the Cherokee Nation that Sequoyah's magic was good—and soon the entire tribe was learning to read and write.

Sequoyah then journeyed to the western band of Cherokee who had moved beyond the Mississippi, and taught them the alphabet. Letters were exchanged between the two groups and national and family ties were strengthened. With the aid of missionaries, a newpaper in Cherokee, called the *Cherokee Phoenix,* was published by the eastern Cherokee, the first of its kind. In commemoration of his great work, Sequoyah was given a silver medal by his people. He was made a member of the Cherokee national council, and later went to Washington with a treaty delegation. For many years after that he visited various Indian tribes on the Great Plains, studying their languages, working on a universal Indian alphabet, and writing an Indian history. He continued his journeys, traveling on horseback and by oxcart until his death in 1843. He died in northern Mexico while on a visit to a detached band of his tribesmen, and his manuscripts were buried with him. His final work was never published, but the memory of this great native American is perpetuated by the giant Sequoia trees of California, which were named in his honor.

Lieutenant John Payne, who had charge of the removal of the Cherokee from this region after the Indians had been forced into ceding their eastern land for new territory west of the Mississippi, had his headquarters here. The Great Removal, as it was called, is one of the dark chapters in American history. Almost before the Indians were on the march, white settlers, eager to take possession of Cherokee farms, rushed into the territory and forcibly drove many Cherokee families from their homes. The Treaty of Removal itself was unfair. The United States Senate had hurriedly ratified an agreement which, although signed by some of the Cherokee headmen, had never been accepted by the majority of the tribe. So harsh was the treatment of the Cherokee at the hands of the Americans, and so bitter were the Indians over the wrongs they had suffered, that they called the westward journey the Trail of Tears.

Six blocks from downtown off US 11 is the MANITOU CAVE, which archaeologists believe was inhabited thousands of years ago, and in historic times used as a shelter by the Cherokee Indians. In the

1890s it was a setting for dances by candlelight, especially effective in the "ballroom" at the most remote part of the marked tour. Today the paths are well-lighted and the multicolored calcite rocks created an imposing impression. Indian artifacts are on display.

West to the junction with State 35. At the Interstate 59 interchange is the Tourist Welcome Center, located in a pioneer cabin, two rooms and dogtrot, reassembled here and supplied with authentic furnishings. This old homestead of 1852 served for many years as the Pea Ridge Postoffice, only one between Albertville, Ala., and Trenton, Ga.

RAINSVILLE, 8 *m.* west on State 35 (2,099 pop. 1970; 568, 1960, inc. 26.9%) is the location of the NORTHEAST ALABAMA STATE JUNIOR COLLEGE, opened in 1963. In 1974 it enrolled 1,034 students and had 51 instructors.

COLLINSVILLE, 37.6 *m.* (726 alt., 1,300 pop. 1970; 1,199, 1960), in a narrow part of the valley, is the trading point for a large area that reaches to the plateaus of Lookout and Sand Mountains. Here an annual Turkey Trot is celebrated on the day before Thanksgiving. The people of town and countryside assemble for the biggest trade day of the year. The climax is reached when choice turkeys and guineas are carried to the roof of the tallest building and set one by one on a gangplank run out from the roof over the heads of the crowd. The fowls must walk the plank and be shooed off by the master of ceremonies. As each one pauses on the end of the plank to make his selection of a place to alight, there is a made scramble among the crowd, the spectators attempting to calculate the fowl's probable landing. Each bird is the prize of the person who captures it. Most of the turkeys are promptly caught, but the alert, keen-witted, strong winged guineas often escape.

Right from Collinsville on State 68, which winds over ridges and up to the crest of Sand Mountain. It crosses Little Wills Creek and runs along ledges overlooking wooded heights and narrow valleys. DAMSON, 4.8 *m.*, on the ridge of Sand Mountain, is a small village 1,700 feet above sea level. This wild country is said to have been the hideout for Jesse James' gang as it crossed back and forth over Sand Mountain in the 1880s.

CROSSVILLE, 8.7 *m.* at a junction with State 75, was the site of an important agricultural experiment station and fish hatchery, directed by Alabama Polytechnic Institute, now Auburn University.

REECE CITY, 58 *m.,* (496 pop. 1970, 470, 1960) is 3 *m.* from NOCCALULA FALLS. Black Creek drops nearly 100 feet into a churning pool that extends behind the water curtain into a large cave. Like other falls on Lookout Mountain, Noccalula is reduced by dry weather to a mere trickle and swollen by spring freshets to a roaring torrent. The falls have the usual lover's leap legend common to most mountain regions. In this instance it was Noccalula, an Indian girl, who plunged to death over the falls rather than accept an unwelcome marriage arranged by her father. After her death her lover saw her spirit in the spray of the falls and gave them her name.

ATTALLA, 58.8 *m.* (7,510 pop. 1970; 8,257, 1960) in Etowah County, is a shipping center and long a junction for four railroads. There are cotton storage warehouses, pipe foundries, and other industries. A mine shaft, reputedly the first in the region, was sunk at Attalia just before the War between the States; the first railroad car of ore was shipped from here over the new Alabama & Chattanooga Railroad in 1871. In 1812 Andrew Jackson's Tennessee militia, on their punitive expedition against the Creek nation, cut the Jackson Trace through the wilderness near Attalla.

In Attalla is the northern junction with US 431 and US 278 (*See Tour 5*). US 11 and Int. 59 pass along the northwest limits of Gadsden.

STEELE, 67.8 *m.,* (798 pop. 1970; 625, 1960) is a lumbering village with sawmill operating at the side of the highway. On the right the gaunt rocky walls of Blount Mountain replace Sand Mountain, and on the left are more distant Beaver Creek Mountains.

At 75 *m.* is a junction with US 231. Left here to ASHVILLE, 4.1 *m.* (680 alt., 986 pop. 1970; 973, 1960), settled about 1820, the northern seat of St. Clair County. When good roads were rare in Alabama, Beaver Creek Mountains divided the county as effectively that two county seats were necessary. Pell City was made the southern seat and Ashville the northern seat. Although good roads now unify the county the old arrangement has remained unchanged. John Ashe, for whom the town was named, was the first settler and served as senator in the first State legislature. Ashville was the birthplace of Rufus Wills Cobb, who, as Governor of Alabama, signed the legislative act (1881) creating Tuskegee Normal and Industrial Institute for Negroes. Oran B. Roberts, who became Governor of Texas, was also born in Ashville.

The Courthouse, a brick building of simple design served as a recruiting station for troops during the War between the States. It was repaired with Federal funds in 1938 without destroying the original design. Records in the courthouse include interesting items dating back to 1821, including transactions with the Creek Indians of Catula Town, near here.

At 85.3 *m.* is a junction with State 23. Left on this road to ST. CLAIR SPRINGS, 1.9 *m.,* once a popular resort. There are five springs here, producing sulphur water, chalybeate, lithia, red sulphur and black sulphur; a sixth produced white sulphur but began flowing with clear water when piped. The springs, all within a radius of a few yards, are shaded with handsome oaks and hickories. Alabama planters came here in ante bellum summers to escape the heat and malaria. In those days there was an excellent hotel with quarters for slaves near the main building, but after the war the popularity of the resort declined. The hotel was destroyed by fire in the early 1930s.

SPRINGVILLE, 87.8 *m.* (717 alt., 1,153 pop. 1970; 622, 1960) in St. Clair County, was named after a large spring that the village converted into a pool.

At 91 *m.* is a junction with a narrow road. Right on this road to Crystal Caverns, 5.9 *m.* The caverns have about a mile of stalagmites and stalactites, which help divide the area into fantastic rooms. The walls are 75 ft. high in places. The caverns are well-lighted, clean and dry. They were discovered in 1840 and were mined for saltpeter by the Confederates.

At 9 *m.* on this road is the State Training School for Girls, moved to this former estate of General Louis V. Clark from Birmingham in 1937. Vocational training is part of the curriculum.

TRUSSVILLE, 101 *m.* on US 11 (2,985 pop. 1970; 2,510, 1960) has one of the original subsistence homestead projects, Cahaba Village, established by the U. S. Government during the Depression.

At 110.4 *m.* is a junction with 75th St. Birmingham. Right on 75th St. 1 *m.* to Birmingham Municipal Airport, a fully equipped major facility with 112 daily flights by Delta, Eastern, United, and Southern Airlines.

BIRMINGHAM, 116 *m.* (300,910 pop. 1970). US 11 proceeds southwest through the city, and Int. 59 follows much the same route, and there are junctions with main highways US 31, US 78, Int. 20, and State roads. *See Birmingham.*

Section b. BIRMINGHAM to LIVINGSTON; 121.5 m.

Southwest from Birmingham the route lies through the mineral belt where the hilly country is covered with second-growth timber. Scattered along the highway are many mining villages. Dogwood is plentiful, with its white blossoms and red berries beautifying the landscape in spring and fall. On the outskirts of BIRMINGHAM, 0 *m.,* the tipples of Ishkooda, Muscoda, and Wenonah red ore mines are visible, left, on the hogback of Red Mountain.

US 11 moves through Downtown Birmingham and thence west and southwest through Owenton and Fairview. On Bessemer Road, 4.6 *m.,* it passes the Alabama State Fairgrounds. Here Ensley Road runs west to a junction with Int. 56. The area west of this is Ensley, named for Colonel Enoch Ensley, who pioneered by buying several small mines and furnaces and combining them with the Tennessee Coal, Iron & Railroad Company (TCI). This company moved to Alabama from the Cumberland hills and had 76,000 acres of coal lands, 460 coke ovens, two blast furnaces and about 13,000 acres of land containing seven and one-half miles of the Red Mountain iron ore seam. Its main production was pig iron.

In 1892 the company acquired the DeBardeleben Coal & Iron Co. In 1899 it decided to make steel, and by 1900 the first commercial steel was being made in the Birmingham area. The plants began to expand in Jones Valley.

In 1907 TCI was the focus of a financial crisis. Unable to meet its obligations, its default threatened the stability of several important banks. To save the company United States Steel Co. was persuaded to buy the major interest. As this implied possible infringement on the anti-monopoly laws President Theodore Roosevelt was enlisted to approve the merger and thereby obviate a panic.

Since that time U. S. Steel has been expanding the enterprise, adding different types of mills. At the Fairfield Steel Works it now produces coke, coal chemicals, iron, steel ingots, semi-finished steel, structural shapes, sheared and universal plates, merchant bars, concrete reinforcing bars, black plate, electrolytic tin plate, hot and cold rolled sheets, hot rolled strip, galvanized, painted and culvert sheets, axiles, rails, wire, wire rods, woven fence, welded fabric, barbed wire, nails and staples, and cotton ties. The Fairfield Works was created to make steel for ships in World War I.

U. S. Steel laid out the town of FAIRFIELD (14,369 pop. 1970; 15,816, 1960, dec. 9%). It financed housing for its employees. In order to abate frequent absences because of illness the corporation established a health department and materially improved the work force. Miles College and Lloyd Noland Hospital are in Fairfield.

The need for water caused U. S. Steel to build the Bayview Dam, 407 ft. long, 106 ft. high, which impounded more than 3.5 million gallons of water on 530 acres.

BESSEMER, 13.7 m. (514 alt., 33,428 pop. 1970; 33,054, 1960; inc. 1.1%), ranks seventh in Alabama cities in population and is the seat of the southwestern section of Jefferson County, locally called the Bessemer Cutoff. Named in honor of Sir Henry Bessemer, the inventor of the Bessemer process of making steel, the city is one of the State's important centers of heavy industry. Pig iron, steel ingots, fabricated steel, cast iron pipe, chemicals, fertilizer, building materials, explosives, and steel railway cars have been among its manufactured products.

Broad shady boulevards with landscaped center plots spread through the residential section of handsome homes on the slope of Red Mountain and extend westward to the compact, smoke-begrimed business section on the level floor of Jones Valley. The industrial area of pipe plants, blast furnaces, and mills lies east of 19th Street and north toward Hueytown, an attractive residential suburb.

In Bessemer US 11 is routed down Bessemer Super Highway, which is also taken by State 5 and State 7. State 150, which winds over Shades Mountain, enters Bessemer on 14th St. and joins the Super Highway and US 11.

Henry F. De Bardeleben built the first steel furnace in the district in 1887, and started the town of Bessemer around it as a rival of Birmingham. Although the Bessemer process was not used here, De-Bardeleben named his town for the English iron master. From 1900, when the population was 6,358, to 1930, the growth was rapid and the population tripled. After a sharp setback during the depression years, Bessemer started growing again.

Roosevelt Park, at the west end of Arlington Ave., is the principal municipal playground. Its walks are bordered by well-kept flower beds, and roses and dahlias bloom near the entrance. There are picnic grounds with barbecue and steak-fry ovens, a brick community house with a fully-equipped kitchen, a swimming pool, a 200-yard cinder track, tennis courts, and a playground for small children. Hall's Creek runs through the park.

BUCKSVILLE, 25.2 m. (475 alt.), is a mining hamlet surrounded by wooded hills.

US 11 winds westward through hills heavily timbered with second-growth pine, oak, and hickory.

BROOKWOOD, 38.8 m. (191 alt.), is a mining and agricultural town, with busy stores.

PETERSON, 48.3 m. (186 alt.), another mining and farming village, also has some lumbering activity.

TUSCALOOSA, 58.2 m. (113-230 alt., 65,773 pop. 1970) (see Tuscaloosa). Here are junctions with State 13, and US 43 (see Tour 7), which unites with US 11 for 35.4 miles.

Left from Tuscaloosa on State 13 to MOUNDVILLE, 16.6 m., (996 pop. 1970; 922, 1960), a progressive trading village serving a wide agricultural area. It has modern stores and homes, and is a shipping point for farm produce.

Right from Moundville to MOUND STATE MONUMENT, 17.5 m. The park covers about 300 acres. Near the center is the museum, an air-conditioned monolithic style building 130 feet long and 40 feet wide, dedicated in 1939. It contains displays of burials and relics uncovered on the site and models of aboriginal houses and earth-works. The Moundville site supported a large population of agricultural Indians who planted corn, made excellent pottery and possessed considerable artistic skill. *Open 9-5, except Christmas. Admission charged. Camping facilities available.*

The mounds themselves are grouped in a rough square on the plain above the bluffs of the Black Warrior River, which forms the northern boundary of the park. There are 34 square and oval mounds in the group, the highest of which is the great pyramid-like structure known as Mound B, 58½ feet high and covering 1¼ acres at its base. Its area on top is ¾ acres and it probably supported a ceremonial building. It has been estimated that if 100 men worked 10 hours a day, they would have needed more than 10 years to build this earthwork. Other mounds vary in height from 3 to 35 feet, and most of them are flat on top, indicating that they served as foundations for structures. Graded ways lead from the level land to the summits of the mounds.

Archaeological investigations at Moundville were begun in 1906 by Dr. Clarence B. Moore of the Philadelphia Academy of Sciences. Since then excavations have revealed graves, midden deposits, and the post-mold patterns of house structures. Thousands of burials have been unearthed; most of them in the level lands. The skeletons are found buried in an extended position, often with the arms crossed. In the burial pits are found hammers and axes of stone, bone awls and needles, copper ear plugs and pendants, beads of shell and bone, water jars and bowls of pottery which once contained food and drink for the deceased. The absence of weapons and evidence of violence seem to indicate that the Moundville people were not warlike. Skeletal material shows that they were round-headed Indians of average height and that head deformation was practiced.

Animals, birds, and human figures furnished motifs for the Moundville potters. Effigy ware includes frog, duck, beaver, eagle, owl, rabbit, and human forms. Designs most frequently found are the human hand, eye, skull, and arm bones; the serpent, which is horned or plumed as in Mexico, the swastika and the sun pattern. The pottery is glazed, plain, or painted in color. Color pots, stone palettes with streaks of paint on them, and mortars and pestles for mixing paints have been found. The frieze on the outside of the museum's central chamber depicts the skull and long bone design used by the craftsmen.

South of Tuscaloosa the route lies through the valley of the Black Warrior River, a fertile farm and grazing country. Beyond the Tombigbee the level Black Belt prairie land is broken by numerous low hills marked by scars of erosion and thick clusters of small cedar trees. Much of the woodland has been damaged by careless sawmilling, and haphazard farming has destroyed the fertility of the once amazingly rich farm land. The river swamps of the Tombigbee and the Black Warrior are good hunting ground for deer, turkey, 'coon, 'possum, and squirrel.

EUTAW, 93.6 *m.* (180 alt., 2,805 pop. 1970; 2,784, 1960), on the northern border of the Black Belt, is a busy trading town for a large farming region. The business section is crowded together on the west side of the public square. Founded in 1818 as Mesopotamia, the town succeeded Erie as county seat when the county decided to select a new site on higher ground. Captain John Nelson made the final choice of the new seat, the move was made, and the name changed to Eutaw in 1838, to commemorate the Battle of Eutaw Springs, South Carolina, in 1781.

The two-story, white cemented brick Courthouse is of Greek Revival design with a handsome iron balcony. It is a reproduction of the original structure, built in 1838 and destroyed by fire in the 1860s. Close by are the town's churches, the oldest of which is St. Stephens Episcopal Church, on Mesopotamia Street, built in 1848.

Eutaw's many old mansions are reminders of ante bellum days when slaves and cotton provided sumptuous living for this community and planters flocked over the virgin black lands after the Choctaw had been pushed westward. Spacious grounds, wide verandas, and high-ceilinged rooms are typical.

Kirkwood, west of the courthouse on Mesopotamia St., is the only Kirksey house. Shrub-bordered footpaths paved with homemake brick lead through the natural woodland park.

The Webb-Alexander House, 309 Main St., has been called the Ruffled Shirt House because of its broad, impressive front and narrow back. It is a white building with green shutters, four Doric columns and an iron-railed balcony above its broad veranda. The Wilson House, one block south of the courthouse on Prairie St., was built in the 1830s. Like many other plantation houses of that period, its timbers are of hewed pine and most of its lumber is hand planed. The outside walls of white plaster are cut by high green-shuttered windows. Inside, a mahogany-railed stairway winds to the half-story above the high, plastered hall. Rooms are furnished with old mahogany and decorated with beveled mirrors and marble mantels. A sword that hangs in the hall was carried through the War between the States by Captain Robert E. Wilson of the 20th Alabama Infantry.

In Eutaw is the southern junction with US 43. At 102.1 *m.* is a junction with a dirt road. Left on this road to Myrtle Hall, 0.8 *m.,* a three-story house of Greek Revival design, built in 1832 of hewed pine and hand-planed cedar and walnut. Four fluted columns extend to the second floor in front and there is a central hallway on each floor with paneled doors opening into the rooms on both sides. The house contains old documents, rare etchings, engravings, and antique furniture.

In BOLIGEE, 104.2 *m.* (114 alt., 225 pop. 1970; 134, 1960, inc. 67%), is a junction with a dirt road. Left on this road to several ante bellum houses. At 0.8 *m.* is a lane which leads to Hill of Howth, the McKee-Gould house planned after the ancestral McKee home in Scotland. It was originally a typical pioneer log structure of the "dog-run" type, used as an Indian trading post. Some of the furniture placed in the house in 1812 by John McKee, United States agent for the Chickasaw Nation in eastern Mississippi Territory, has been preserved.

McKee, a native of Virginia, played an important part in local history within a year after taking up his duties as Indian agent here. His influence had helped to turn the sympathies of the Chickasaw and Choctaw to the side of the whites in the Creek War of 1813, and he led a force of these Indian allies on a foray against the Creek at the falls of the Warrior River (*see Tuscaloosa*). In 1830, however, he was a party to the unfair Treaty of Dancing Rabbit Creek, appropriating for the benefit of greedy whites the remainder of the rich Choctaw lands west of the Tombigbee River. He had previously given up the Indian agency for a place in the Government land office at Tuscaloosa, and had gone from there to Congress in 1823-29. Still a bachelor, he died at Hill of Howth in 1834.

Many of his books and records and much of his correspondence are preserved in the old house. Other relics include the whipsaw used to cut the timber for the building. From McKee, the property passed to the Gould family. A simple gate swung on home-forged hinges opens into the old-fashioned garden thickly set with mimosa, magnolia, and other trees. The house and informal garden form an unexpected glimpse of soft and mellowed loveliness easily overlooked by the casual traveler.

Thornhill, 8.1 *m.,* was built in 1833 by James Innes Thornton and named for the family's ancestral home Thorn-on-the-Hill in England. Fluted Corinthian pillars uphold a balcony with wrought-iron railings over the broad front portico. A mahogany stairway spirals to the second floor.

Among the many treasures gathered here is a field glass presented by George Washington to his cousin, the master of Thornhill, and a brass candlestick that Nellie Custis used. Other Washingtonia include a cup and saucer from a set used at Mount Vernon by Bushrod Washington.

Rosemount (*adm.*), 10.5 *m.*, is a 20-room plantation mansion that required five years, 1830-35, to build. Williamson Allen Glover's slaves hewed the pine timbers from the forests on his land, pinned them in place with wooden pegs, and planed the lumber by hand. Italian marble mantels, glass from Bohemia, and a rosewood parlor suite from France were shipped from Europe by way of Mobile and the Tombigbee River, and made the final overland journey by oxcart from the river. In each of the 20 rooms is a bell pull connected with its distinctively toned bell in the servants' quarters. The staircase and doors are of walnut and the furnishings are rare antiques. The house occupies an eminence commanding the broad acreage of the estate. A winding road among semitropical plants and trees, that were a part of the original forest when the plantation was settled, connects the entrance gate with the house almost a mile away.

The main route crosses the Tombigbee River at 110.7 *m.* over Gorgas Bridge. At the south end of the bridge is Jones Bluff, the site of Fort Tombigbee. Bienville, governor of Louisiana Territory, sent a company of soldiers and artisans under Colonel M. Lussier to erect the fort in 1735 as a supply depot and permanent trading post. In April, 1736, Bienville, himself set out from Mobile on what was planned as a punitive expedition against the Chickasaw. In the fleet of more than 60 boats he brought soldiers, convicts, sailors, Canadian woodsmen, monks, and priests. After a brief stop at Fort Tombigbee the company proceeded to Ackia, in present eastern Mississippi, and was defeated by the aroused Chickasaw with the loss of many men. Bienville retreated to the fort and then returned to Mobile, leaving behind a garrison of 30 French and 20 Swiss soldiers under De Berthel.

In 1752, when the Chickasaw were again giving trouble, the Marquis de Vaudreuil, who had succeeded Bienville as governor, invaded their country and was also defeated. He likewise returned to Mobile by way of Fort Tombigbee, and ordered the post enlarged and strengthened. At the close of the French and Indian Wars, in 1763, the British were given possession of the fort and renamed it Fort York. After 5 years of occupation they removed the garrison and left it undefended for the remaining 15 years of their domination. When the Spaniards took over in 1783, they rebuilt the post and called it Fort Confederation. Later, when the boundary of the Spanish Territory was fixed on parallel 31°, Americans occupied the old defense.

Here, in 1802, was negotiated one of the series of treaties by which the United States absorbed the Choctaw lands. The Colonial Dames of America have placed on the site a marker with the inscription: "Here civilization and savagery met and the wilderness beheld the glory of France." Among the cedars the Choctaw gathered in 1831 for three days of lamentation before they began the long trip westward, away from their ancestral homeland.

At 113.9 *m.* is a junction with State 39. Right on State 39, 2.9 *m.,* to a junction with a graded road. Left on this second road 4.4 *m.,* to SUMTERVILLE, a farming community. Left here on a dirt road to Forked Lightning Ranch, 6.3 *m.,* scene of an annual Fourth of July rodeo and barbecue (*adm.*). This celebration was initiated to encourage beef and cattle ranching.

On State 39 is GAINESVILLE, 11.1 *m.* (240 alt., 255 pop. 1970; 214, 1960), once capital of a cotton principality. For years the town government, supported by business licenses, operated without levying municipal taxes. In ante bellum days Gainesville was noted for its duels. For several years Joseph Baldwin, author of *Flush Times in Alabama* and other books, lived here. It was here that General Nathan B. Forrest surrendered to General Canby of the Federal Army, in 1865. A marker has been placed on the site of Forrest's Surrender.

At LIVINGSTON, 121.5 *m.* (2,358 pop. 1970), US 11 unites with US 80 (*see Tour 3*).

※※※※※※※※※※※※※※※※※※※※※※※※※※※※※※※※※※※※※※

Tour 15

A DIAGONAL ROUTE ACROSS ALABAMA

(Georgia Line)—Eufaula—Union Springs—Montgomery—Prattville—Talladega National Forest—Centerville—Tuscaloosa—Lake Lurleen State Park—Gordo—Reform—(Columbus, Miss.); US 82

US 82 serves a good purpose in providing a highway that runs diagonally across Alabama from lower Georgia to mid-Mississippi. It crosses Lake Eufaula, the body of water created in the Chattahoochee River by Walter F. George Lock and Dam, and has a junction with US 431 (north-south), which keeps the Chattahoochee in view for a score of miles. Then US 82 strikes west in Barbour County and traverses the cotton-growing area of that and Bullock County. The small towns are mostly shipping points on the Central of Georgia. The only town of any importance is the county seat, UNION SPRINGS (4,324 pop. 1970; 3,704, 1960), 40 miles from Eufaula, where US 82 has a junction with US 29, (north-south), described under Tour 12.

Montgomery is another 40 miles away. About 12 miles east US 82 joins US 231 and the two routes are combined to the capital. *See Montgomery.* US 82 leaves Montgomery combined with US 31 and after six miles turns west through Prattville (*see Tour 1*). The highway proceeds through the farmlands of Autauga, Chilton and Bibb Counties.

US 82 reaches MAPLESVILLE, the gateway to the Oakmulgee Division of the Talladega National Forest, 32 *m.* beyond Prattville. Three State roads have junctions at Maplesville, which had 596 pop. 1970, down from 679, 1960. US 82 continues in a northwesterly direction on the northern rim of the forest.

CENTERVILLE, 15 *m.* (2,233 pop. 1970; 1,981, 1960, inc. 12.7%) is the seat of Bibb County and the center of a number of State roads that connect with parts of Talladega National Forest. The principal north-south road, which actually passes 1 *m.* west of Centerville, is State 5, which has a junction with US 11 in the north and US 80 and US 43 south. US 82 proceeds west to Tuscaloosa, after junctions with US 11 and Int. 59.

TUSCALOOSA, 188 *m.* from the border (65,773 pop. 1970). *See Tuscaloosa.*

The jagged hills flanking this route between Tuscaloosa and Mississippi were once covered by huge first-growth pines and magnificent hardwoods, but are now scarred by barren slopes and eroded gullies. Second-growth short leaf pine and scrub oak furnish timber for the little "woodpecker" sawmills scattered throughout the region. Where the land is not badly eroded considerable farming is carried on; cotton, corn, and sweet potatoes are the principal crops.

Before the white man came, this region was used as a hunting ground by both the Creek and Choctaw Indians, each of which claimed ownership. According to legend, the tribes agreed that the winning side in a game of ball should be given full possession, but when the Creek won the Choctaw demanded another contest, this time with knives, war clubs, and tomahawks. The Creek was again victorious and the Choctaw were driven from the field. They refused to admit defeat, however, and the region was still disputed territory when the first white settlers arrived.

Northwest of Tuscaloosa, US 82 and US 43 are united to NORTHPORT, 1 *m.* (126 alt., 9,435 pop. 1970; 5,245, 1960; inc. 70%). US 82 then branches west and crosses the basin of the Warrior River, where brownish-grey soils produce large crops of cotton, corn, oats, and sugar cane. The poorly drained lower areas are not suitable for cultivation and are used as pasture lands. Livestock raising is profitable. Lake Tuscaloosa connects with the Black Warrior River above Northport.

Hargrove Van de Graff Airport, 2.9 *m.,* is Tuscaloosa's municipal field. Sponsored by the city and the University of Alabama, it is used for the university's aviation courses, initiated in 1938 with the aid of the Federal government. Southern Airways has scheduled flights daily.

At 4.4 *m.* is a 3,300-acre farm on which the State raises livestock and agricultural products for use in the State hospital here and at Tuscaloosa.

At 7 *m.* COKER, (3,757 pop. 1970; 3,055, 1960) at a junction with several county roads is a county subdivision in an area of poultry farms.

LAKE LURLEEN STATE PARK, 12 *m.* named for the late Governor Lurleen B. Wallace, is scenically located on the banks of a 250-acre lake, and is equipped with fishing piers, bathhouse, picnic shelters, camp store, and activities building.

ELROD, 15 *m.* west of Tuscaloosa, is now on State 140, a 10-*m.* segment of the former US 82, since relocated. Elrod is part of the Elrod-Echola County Division, which had 1,086 pop. in 1970. It is a processing point for pine timber. In pioneer days, when the thick forests were being cleared, this region was noted for its big log rollings. After the wasteful fashion of the frontier, the timber was completely destroyed; trees and underbrush were cut and burned, though sometimes the largest timber was girdled and left to rot and fall. When an area was to be made into "new ground" the men and women of the neighborhood gathered for the log rolling at the home of the settler whose land was to be cleared. Using smooth, strong sticks called hand spikes, the men in groups of from four to eight, dragged the logs together for a huge bonfire. The host supplied whisky for the occasion and the womenfolk held a quilting party, taking time, however, to prepare a substantial dinner for their men. A square dance, with a fiddler or two furnishing the music, closed the festivities.

GORDO, 23.1 *m.* (246 alt., 1,991 pop. 1970; 1,714, 1960) a sawmill center in Pickens County settled in 1831, lies on the broad plateau of the Sipsey River watershed. Stacks of lumber are piled for many acres along the highway, with high mounds of sawdust in the background. The town's industrial plants include cotton gins, a cottonseed, oil mill, a planing mill, and a bottling plant. Robert Kennon Hargrove, Bishop of the Methodist Episcopal Church, South, was born here. He was a member of the Cape May Commission that tried vainly in 1852 to settle differences between the Southern and Northern branches of his church. Bishop Hargrove became president of the board of trustees of Vanderbilt University, Nashville, Tennessee, in 1889. The area around Gordo is excellent for quail shooting. There are junctions with State 86 and 159.

REFORM, 31.8 *m.* (308 alt., 1,893, pop. 1970; 1,241, 1960) a farm settlement since 1807, when it was settled by pioneers from South Carolina. Lorenzo Dow, itinerant backwoods missionary, preached here and his fiery sermons made many converts. When Dow was asked to give the community a name, he replied, "Call it Reform! Brethren, call it Reform!"

Right from Reform on State 17 to United Grove Church, 8.2 *m.,* where an assembly known as Camp Meeting has met periodically. The meeting, religious in character, is also a homecoming event. Days and evenings are devoted to evangelistic appeals, mass singing, and "dinners and the ground."

Left from Reform on State 17 to CARROLLTON, 10 *m.* (923 pop. 1970, 894, 1960), the seat of Pickens County. The town named for Charles Carroll, of Carrollton, Maryland, one of the signers of the Declaration of Independence, became the county seat in 1834 when the courthouse was moved here from Pickensville. In 1865 Federal troops burned the courthouse and destroyed many records. The present courthouse, erected soon after the war, is a square building of yellow brick, set on a square terrace in the center of the town.

A legend that has persisted for many years is that the outlines of a man's face can be seen in a window of the courthouse garret. It was identified as that of Henry Wells, a black accused of setting fire to the old courthouse. Wells was arrested and escaped, and when recaptured was taken to the local jail. When a crowd gathered the sheriff, fearing for the safety of his prisoner, removed him to the garret of the new courthouse. Here Wells was looking out of the window at the crowd below with agonized features when a thunderstorm erupted with a flash of intensely brilliant lightning. When the sheriff went up to his prisoner next day he found him slumped beneath the window, dead. From the street observers discerned the outlines of Wells' face in the garret window.

For years this was pointed out to visitors. In 1940 the Carrollton Civic Club investigated the phenomenon and reported:

"While Wells was standing at the window, looking upon the mob below, the unusually bright flash of lightning struck. This was a case of lightning photography, for it stamped the prisoner's features indelibly on the window pane."

In front of the Phoenix hotel an oak tree was planted in 1868. When the tree was small, General Nathan Bedford Forrest came to Carrollton to promote a new railroad and hitched a team of spirited horses to the sapling. The horses bolted and almost uprooted the tree; Forrest reset it, but the trunk remained bent ever after. The railroad company represented by Forrest made plans to build the line, and the town, impoverished by war, authorized a bond issue to raise funds. Pickens County expected prosperity, but a national panic swept away the railroad company together with the county's bonds.

The main route, US 82, crosses the Mississippi line, 51.4 *m.,* at a point 15 miles east of Columbus, Mississippi.

Tour 16

VIA THE COAL BELT AND THE WARRIOR-TOMBIGBEE WATERWAY

(Tallapoosa, Ga.)—Heflin—Talladega National Forest—Oxford—
Anniston—Pell City—Leeds—Port Birmingham—Cordova—Jasper—
Carbon Hill—Hamilton—(Tupelo, Miss.) US 78. Int. 20

Georgia Line to Mississippi Line, 213.4 m.

Section a. GEORGIA LINE to BIRMINGHAM 99.8 m.

US 78 was officially named the Bankhead Highway, in honor of Senator John H. Bankhead, Sr., who worked for Federal support of good roads. It crosses the Georgia Line 4 m. west of Tallapoosa, Georgia, then swings westward from the Tallapoosa River valley, and ascends the watershed of the Piedmont Plateau. This high rolling upland county, with its reddish loamy soils, lies among the last spurs of the Appalachian Mountains. It is timbered with second-growth pine, oak, beech, poplar, and hickory, and is a good hunting and fishing region. Wild turkeys, quail, squirrels, and foxes roam the woods that spread in each direction from the highway. Beyond the plateau the route drops into the Coosa Valley and continues through a hilly wooded region to Birmingham.

The uplands were settled in the early 19th century. Careless lumbering and haphazard farming have destroyed the productivity of much fertile land. But enough remains for the profitable growing of corn, cotton, Irish and sweet potatoes, sorghum, peanuts, hay, and ribbon cane. Many square miles of country lying north and south of the highway are now inside Talladega National Forest, where conservation is saving the area from exploitation.

MUSCADINE, 1.1 m. a village, was named for the profusion of muscadine grape vines in the vicinity. Muscadine Creek and the Tallapoosa River are well-stocked with fish.

Where piney woods mark the southern extremity of the Piedmont Plateau is FRUITHURST, 4.7 m. (1,076 alt., 229 pop. 1970; 255, 1960), colonized by a Northern land development company in 1899. Most of the settlers were Scandinavian and Polish immigrants. The promoters felt that the original name of the village, Sidonia, lacked sales appeal and offered a prize for a more suitable name hence Fruithurst. Every man who bought 10 acres of vineyard land was given a lot in the town, its location determined by the type of house he planned to build. Trees were set out along the streets and on both sides of Central Avenue there were wide gardens of roses. Vineyards began to flourish on the hills surrounding the town, and apples, peaches, pears, and plums hung heavily on orchard trees.

But prosperity did not endure. The colonists found that they were selling their grapes to Northern markets at a loss, a lumber mill showed no profit, an excelsior mill and two wineries burned. State prohibition spelled the doom of the wine-making industry. Discouraged by these failures and unable to adapt themselves to changed economic conditions, the people departed.

EDWARDSVILLE, 9.9 m. (945 alt., 146 pop. 1970; 168, 1960), was a boom town during the Alabama gold rush days. Buildings sprang up overnight as newcomers, many of them carrying picks and shovels, arrived from Georgia and western Alabama. Saloons and gambling halls teemed with trade. Men quarreled and fought on the red-mud main street, and more than one fight was climaxed by fatal knife and gun play. But the boom ended abruptly when gold was discovered in California in '48.

Edwardsville was made the seat of Cleburne County in 1867. It had excellent schools, credited to the influence of John W. Abercrombie, later State superintendent of education. One of the first acts of the county court was to provide for a superintendent of education at a salary of $250 a year.

When the price of gold was almost doubled in 1937, many of the 90-year-old workings were reopened and new ones were started. But the ore found today is of a low grade, with samples usually running less than $20 a ton. In addition to gold, this region has deposits of mica, copper, kaolin, pyrites, iron, zinc, and silver.

South of Edwardsville US 78 crosses a corner of the Talladega National Forest on the way to Heflin, south of the Forest.

HEFLIN, 17.3 m. (984 alt., 2,672 pop. 1970; 2,400, 1960) the seat of Cleburne County since 1906, was settled in 1883 and named in honor of Dr. Wilson L. Heflin, pioneer physician and father of Thomas Heflin, U. S. Senator, and incorporated by the legislature on December 10, 1892. Lumbering is the principal industry and sawmills and lumber stacks line both sides of the highway. The town also has gristmills, a planing mill and a cotton warehouse. Its factories make chenille, men's coats, women's uniforms, and mica products.

At 19.4 m. U. S. 78 enters the TALLADEGA NATIONAL FOREST, a tract of rugged mountains, heavily timbered with pine and hardwoods. There are high ridges on both side of the highway; narrow, brawling streams rush by the base of high cliffs and tumble through boulder-strewn gulches. In 1847 this region was the gold-mining center of eastern Alabama. Prospectors scoured the hills, and boom towns sprang up overnight when strikes were made. Trails were widened into roads for supply wagons, bringing merchandise to the new Eldorado. Miners spent their dust freely and trade was conducted on the "pinch" basis. A drink of whisky cost the amount of dust the bartender could pick up and hold between thumb and finger, roughly reckoned as a dollar—bartenders and store clerks with broad fingers were in demand. Then came the California gold rush, and the Alabama region, soon deserted, became a wilderness again.

South of Heflin Int. 20, coming from Georgia, begins to move parallel with US 78, both crossing the Forest to Calhoun County. At 21 m. US 78 leaves the Forest. Here State 9, which joined US 78 for the route through the Forest, turns north to Piedmont and Centre and crosses Weiss Lake.

OXFORD, 32 m. (647 alt., 4,361 pop. 1970; 3,603, 1960) in Calhoun County, is an industrial and farm center, with a history of iron production, described under Tour 7.

In Oxford is a junction with US 241 which unites with US 78 to Anniston. *See Tour 7.*

Adjoining Oxford is HOBSON CITY (1,124 pop. 1970; 770, 1960), incorporated August 1, 1899. A group of progressive Negroes conducted their own successful campaign for incorporation. Hobson City has a mayor and council type of municipal government with clerk, treasurer, and police force.

ANNISTON, 35.6 m. (31,533 pop. 1970). *See Anniston.* At 37.1 m. the Monsanto Chemical Company built one of the largest electro-chemical plants in the United States.

West from Anniston the road descends into the comparatively level lowlands of the Coosa Valley, praised by the chroniclers of the De Soto expedition as the most productive and beautiful section they saw.

At 44.1 m., is a junction with a graded road. Right to the Eastaboga Fish Hatchery, 1 m., one of the important sources for restocking the streams of the State with bass and bream.

US 78 crosses the Coosa River, largest stream of the Alabama River system, at RIVERSIDE, 58.2 m. (351 pop. 1970; 159, 1960). Along the banks of the Coosa were Indian towns which were despoiled by De Soto and his men. Now the stream is a source of hydroelectric power in the central part of the State where it flows through a region rich in mineral deposits.

PELL CITY, 63.9 m. (567 alt., 5,381 pop. 1970; 4,165, 1960), is the southern division county seat of St. Clair County, which was divided effectively by the Beaver Creek Mountains. Ashville, 13 m. north on US 231, is the seat of the northern division. Pell City was incorporated in 1890 by the Pell City Iron & Land Company and named for the company's president, George H. Pell. Sumter Cogswell, of Charleston, South Carolina, sold the land to the company in 1890 for $50,000 and bought it back ten years later for $5,000. Textiles became the principal industry.

West of Pell City, the route crosses the spurs of Beaver Creek Mountains and winds through a hilly region to Birmingham.

Cooks Springs, 69.3 m., was once a popular health resort. It is now attractive chiefly because of numerous cool, shaded spots near the mineral springs. William Prater Cook bought this land in 1836 in order to establish a health resort and by 1861 the place had become a popular spot, with swimming pool, dance pavilion, and a 68-room hotel. After his death it was used chiefly for picnics and church conventions. Visitors may drink the mineral water from the springs without charge.

LEEDS, 82 *m.* (624 alt., 6,991 pop. 1970; 6,162, 1960), was founded in 1881 by Major E. M. Tutwiler, Colonel J. A. Montgomery, John Milner, and his brother, Ross Milner. All were then young engineers brought to the locality to help build the old Georgia Pacific Railroad. The town was named for Leeds, England. It is located in three counties: Jefferson, St. Clair, and Shelby, and as 20 miles east of Birmingham it is closely associated with the latter's civic events. Leeds has industries producing cement, steel wire products, men's clothing, and processing cotton. Local interests are chronicled by the *News*, a weekly.

The cement industry is represented by the huge plant of the Universal Atlas Cement Division of the United States Steel Corporation, which is one of ten plants that produce Atlas White cements, Atlas cement, Atlas Lumnite (calcium-aluminate) cement and Unaflo oil well cement. A wet process is used in order to eliminate dust. A towering stack and 30-ft. high storage bins are landmarks on the horizon.

BIRMINGHAM, 99.8 *m.* (300,910 pop. 1970). *See Birmingham.*

Section b. BIRMINGHAM to MISSISSIPPI LINE, 113.6 m.

US 78 veers sharply northwest from Birmingham, 0 *m.,* through the rugged country of the huge bituminous coal belt. As the route moves toward Jasper it is paralleled in erratic fashion by State 269, which, 17 *m.* beyond reaches the busy PORT OF BIRMINGHAM on the Locust Fork of the Warrior River. This gives Birmingham the needed outlet to the Warrior-Tombigbee Waterway, which carries the products of the west-of-central Alabama areas to Mobile Bay. A network of county roads from all the productive regions brings the shipping of the Birmingham-Fairfield-Bessemer district to the Port.

Around Port Birmingham are storage tank farms, docks and pipes for conveying Bunker C oil, an industrial fuel, from barges. This comes from Louisiana via the Gulf Intracoastal Waterway. Bunker C oil, like some asphalt and heavy petroleum products, must be heated before it can be pumped out of the barges. Heat is applied by circulating steam through coils of pipe built into the bottoms of the barges. About 10,000,000 gallons of bulk lubricating oil from Texas are moved to a plant near Port Birmingham, where the oil is transferred to pipes and drums.

The Warrior-Tombigbee Waterway is the most important channel for moving industrial and agricultural products from the interior of Alabama to the sea. It starts with the waters of the Sipsey, Mulberry, and Locust Forks, which feed the Black Warrior River, which joins the Tombigbee. The Alabama River, coming south from the environs of Montgomery, then joins the Tombigbee to create the Mobile River, which flows into Mobile Bay. The Waterway is the principal artery carrying coal from the Warrior Field, which has reserves of more than five billion tons. The waterway enables the steel mills of the Birmingham-Fairfield section to ship to the Gulf and foreign ports. Principal cargoes downriver are coal, limestone, iron and steel products, pulpwood, logs, and chemicals. Moving upstream is crude petroleum, which goes to conversion plants to produce and distribute gasoline, naphtha, solvents, diesel and tractor fuel, paving and roofing asphalt. Coastal refineries in Texas and Louisiana move millions of gallons of gasoline by barge over the Gulf Intracoastal Waterway and the Warrior-Tombigbee System to storage tank farms and terminals on the rivers.

The water facilities at Port Birmingham are kept to a 9 ft. channel by the JOHN HOLLIS BANKHEAD LOCK AND DAM on the Warrior River below the confluence of Mulberry Fork and Locust Fork. Since 1970 the Corps of Engineers, USA, has been replacing the original structures with more efficient ones. Bankhead had operated for years with two locks, 285 ft. long by 52 ft. wide, so inadequate in size that tows had to be split and moved in two sections. The two locks have been replaced by a single lift, 600 ft. long and 110 ft. wide. Bankhead is the farthest upstream in the Warrior System.

Downstream from the Port is a big strip-mining operation of the Peabody Coal Company, which ships hundreds of thousands of tons of coal via barges. Powerful earth-moving machinery is used to strip the surface, such as a shovel that can move 75 cubic yards of soil in one operation. Another shovel with a capacity of 25 cubic yards can load a 125-ton truck in a matter of minutes.

US 78 continues northwest in Jefferson and Walker Counties.

GRAYSVILLE, 14.5 m. (3,182 pop. 1970; 3,061 1960) originally a mining town, has been attracting a suburban class of residents, and has stores supplying all household wants. On a road right 4 m. is the hamlet of BROOKSIDE (990 pop. 1970; 999,1960) settled about 1902 by immigrants from Russia, who continued their customs and religious services, some of which have survived to this day.

At 27 m. is SUMMITON, in Walker County (2,374 pop. 1970; 1,287, 1960). The Walker County State Trade School is located at Summiton.

Left from Summiton on a country road 2 m. to DORA (1,862 pop. 1970; 1,776, 1960). Thence west 4 m. on County 30 to CORDOVA (2,750 pop. 1970; 3,184, 1960). Here Birmingham Forest Products, Inc., owned by U. S. Steel Corp. and Champion International, has a plywood plant, two sawmills, and a laminated decking facility. Using logs harvested from the surrounding area, the plants produce plywood, which is marketed nationally; wood chip for pulp factories, and tests the findings of research in wood products.

The Cordova-Jasper area of Walker County makes use of the facilities of the Warrior River for shipping. The Inland State Dock has been constructed at Cordova, Jasper, and ports farther south. The

Vulcan Asphalt Co. is located in this area, and the Alabama Power Co. has two steam-generating plants, the Gorgas and the Lewis Smith.

JASPER, 42 m. (307 alt., 10,798 pop. 1970; 10,799, 1960), seat of Walker County (56,246 pop. 1970) has the unique record in the U.S. Census reports of practically unchanged population figures in a decade. Yet Jasper is a city of prosperous industry and trade, where factories profit from the coal mined in the county and the opportunities for land and water shipping. Jasper has the commission form of government with a mayor, city manager, two commissioners; it makes men's shirts, golf bags, carpet yarn, hosiery, metal and concrete pipes, furniture, and lumber, and processes poultry and foods.

WALKER COLLEGE is an independent junior college organized in 1938, which enrolled 721 students in 1974 and had a faculty of 45. There are two hospitals with 172 beds, also clinics and nursing homes. The Carl Elliott Regional Library stocks up to 60,000 volumes. The daily newspaper, the *Mountain Eagle*, was established in 1960; *Walker Eagle Community News* is a weekly.

The Arrow Company, a division of Cluett, Peabody & Co. has plants in Jasper, Carbon Hill, and Albertville; the Jasper plant makes 3,700-dozen dress shirts a week and employes 507. The Burton Manufacturing Co., founded 1909, developed from making horse collars and saddles into the nation's largest maker of professional golf bags—65,000 a year. The Marshall Durbin Company employs 450 and in a 10-hour day ships 138,000 dressed poultry. The Tennessee River Pulp & Paper Co. turns out lumber and chips. A special field for infant supplies has been developed by the Kant-Wet Baby Products Co. Other industries are the Brown Pipe Co., the Jasper Brassiere Co., and the National Mattress Co.

The Walker County Airport is located near Jasper. It has a runway of 3,700 ft.

The Bankhead family has been associated with Jasper and their house, a large frame dwelling on a hill, called Sunset, was the home successively of Senator John Hollis Bankhead, remembered as "the father of good roads"; William B. Bankhead, former Speaker of the U. S. House of Representatives, and the latter's daughter, Tallulah Bankhead, who as a child enjoyed playing theater here.

CARBON HILL, 60.8 m. (1,929 pop. 1970; 1,944, 1960) is another mining town that shows little change in population. It contributes to Alabama's production of coal, which reached a value of $190,000,000 in 1970. The Warrior field is in Walker, Jefferson, and Tuscaloosa Counties.

Two miles beyond Carbon Hill is a town named KANSAS (227 pop. 1970) and 5 miles beyond that is ELDRIDGE, the site of Indian Springs and an ancient Indian village. The Baptist Academy was founded to help farm youths get an education and gives aid to underprivileged students. US 78 has a junction with State 13, north-south route. Twelve miles north on State 13 to a junction with US 278, which crosses the William H. Bankhead National Forest (*see Tour 6*).

This junction is at NATURAL BRIDGE, a formation produced by erosion.

SMITH LAKE is an erratically shaped body of water of 21,200 acres, north of Jasper and southwest of Cullman in Winston, Walker, and Cullman Counties, formed by the LEWIS SMITH LOCK AND DAM on the Sipsey Fork of the Black Warrior River. This impoundment has produced a remarkable recreation area, one-third of it inside the Bankhead National Forest, where innumerable valleys have become filled with water from dozens of creeks that feed them. The whole terrain is filled with marinas, fishing lodges, country stores, bait shops, and fishing supplies, with enough camp sites to accommodate half the State. In Jasper US 78 has junctions with State 69, which goes north to Cullman and has connections with Boldo, Burrows Crossing, Wilburn, Cold Springs, and Bremen along the arms of the lake; State 189 which divides into State 257 and State 195, both of which move into Bankhead National Forest, the first to Arley, the second to Double Springs. The popularity of Smith Lake accounts for the multitude of sporting goods stores, outboard motors, boats and marine supplies in Jasper, Sipsey, Cordova, Cullman and other near localities.

TEXAS, 71.1 *m.,* is another of the mining villages that line 78 throughout the mineral belt. Left from Texas on a foot trail to an Indian Mound, 1 *m.,* beside New River. Pieces of pottery, arrowheads, artifacts, and bones have been uncovered. Unlike most prehistoric earthworks, this mound contains large proportions of sand and gravel buttressed about the base with flat stones.

The Spanish type Pemberton House, 77.2 *m.,* is on a hillside 100 yards from the highway. W. G. Pemberton, Northern artist, began to build it when he moved to Marion County in 1925. The walls, floors and ceilings of the house are embellished with marble, granite, flint, brick and tile. Old coach lamps have been transformed into porch lights and wagon thimbles serve as bases for the wall lights on each side of the exposed stone chimney.

WINFIELD, 80.1 *m.* (469 alt., 3,292 pop. 1970; 2,907, 1960), is a busy agricultural center in both Marion and Fayette Counties. Here is a junction with US 43, which unites westward with US 78 for 20.4 miles. See *Tour 9.*

GUIN, 86.7 *m.* (2,220 pop. 1970; 356, 1960, inc. 155%), a farm town, is on the site of Pikesville, important trading post on the old military road and once seat of Marion County. Some of the early settlers were veterans of Andrew Jackson's campaigns, who returned here after the Battle of New Orleans.

Soon after the first electric power wire was strung through this section, the district was visited by a disastrous drought. Many people believed the wire had caused the drought and bands of men cut down the poles and destroyed many miles of line.

HAMILTON, 100.5 *m.* (3,088 pop. 1970; 1,934, 1960, inc. 59%), is at the western junction with US 43 (*see Tour 9*).

BEXAR, 110.7 *m.* (a Division, 1,609 pop. 1970; 1,690, 1960), settled about 1830, is the oldest existing postoffice in Marion County. It was named for the Alamo de la Bexar. During the Texan War for independence, some Marion County men served in Sam Houston's army, and when news of the San Jacinto victory reached their families here, the latter named their community after the Alamo.

At 113.6 *m.* the route crosses the Mississippi Line at a point 35 miles east of Tupelo, Mississippi.

Chronology

1505   Mobile Bay appears in outline on Waldseemueller Map.

1520   Rio del Espiritu Sancto (probably Mobile Bay and River) appears on map drawn by Pineda, who visited Gulf in 1519.

1528   De Narvaez arrives at Mobile Bay.

1540   July 2. Hernando De Soto leads first white men into Creek areas.

1544   Rio del Espiritu Sancto shown on map by Cabot.

1559   De Luna starts Spanish settlement on Mobile Bay. Ended 1561.

1629   Charles I makes Carolina grant to Sir Robert Heath overlapping Spanish Alabama territory.

1663   Second Carolina grant from Charles II to Carteret and others.

1699   Iberville discovers Massacre, now Dauphin Island.

1702   Bienville builds settlement at Fort Louis de la Mobile.

1711   Fort Louis de la Mobile moved to present site of Mobile.

1714   Fort Toulouse built near site of present Wetumpka.

1719   Ship *Marechal de Villars,* the De Serigny flagship, lands first shipload of slaves on Dauphin Island.

1720   July 1. Ship *Hercules* lands slaves in Mobile.
Name of Fort Louis de la Mobile changed to Fort Condé la Mobile.

1722   New Orleans becomes capital of Louisiana.

1732   Alabama territory included in Georgia grant to Oglethorpe and others "in trust for the poor."

1733   Disastrous hurricane and epidemic sweep Mobile.

1735   Fort Tombecbe (Epes) on (Tombigbee) built by Bienville.

1763   Mobile ceded to Great Britain by Treaty of Paris.

1780   March 4. Galvez captures Mobile. Spain rules city 33 years.

1783   Britain cedes all land east of Mississippi except Florida.

1786   United States-Choctaw treaty gives land grants to Choctaw nation and guarantees protection.

1796   Andrew Ellicott to define southern U. S. boundary with Spain.

1798   April 7. Territory of Mississippi created; Winthrop Sargent governor; Natchez, capital.

1799   Andrew Ellicott completes survey of 31st parallel.
May. Spanish garrison at Fort St. Stephens relieved by U. S.

1800   June. First county (Washington) in Alabama established.

1802   First cotton gin in Alabama erected at Coosada Bluff, present Montgomery County, by Abram Mordecai.
April 24. Georgia cedes to United States all territory between 31st and 35th parallels for $1,250,000.

1804   Ephraim Kirby appointed first judge of Alabama Section.

1806-07   Jefferson College, Autauga County, founded.

1807   St. Stephens platted on site of Spanish fort (built about 1788).
Feb. 19. Aaron Burr, arrested by Captain E. P. Gaines in Washington County, returned to Virginia to be tried for treason.

1808   Madison County organized.
Baptists erect church on Flint River near Huntsville.

1809   Baldwin County organized.

1811   *Mobile Centinel,* Alabama's first newspaper, established.

1812   Madison *Gazette,* second newspaper, established.
Mobile and Clarke Counties organized.

1813   April 15. General James Wilkinson captures Mobile from Spain.
July 27. First Creek battle on Burnt Corn Creek.
Aug. 30. Massacre of 200 troops by Creek at Fort Mims.
Dec. 23. Battle of Holy Ground.

1814   March 27. Gen. Andrew Jackson defeats Creek at Horseshoe Bend.
Aug. 9. Creek Indians cede their land to United States.
Fort Jackson erected on site of Fort Toulouse.
Monroe County organized.

1816   Montgomery County formed from Monroe County.
Sept. 14. Chickasaw relinquish claim to territory south of Tennessee.

1817   Alabama Territory created; William Wyatt Bibb governor; John Crowell, delegate to Congress; capital, St. Stephens.

1818   French Vine and Olive Colony Company, formed by Napoleonic exiles, settled on 92,160 acres of land in Marengo County.
Jan. 19. Territorial general assembly at St. Stephens.
St. Stephens Academy chartered; lottery authorized to raise $4,000 to erect buildings.
St. Stephens Steamboat Company chartered with $100,000 capital; first steamboat, *Alabama,* built; moves to Mobile.
First pig iron made in Territory near Russellville, Franklin County.
Cahaba designated as permanent capital of Alabama.

1819   Aug. 2. State constitution adopted at Huntsville convention.
Oct. 25. First legislative assembly convened in Huntsville.
Dec. 14. Alabama admitted into Union.
Dec. 17. Mobile granted city charter.

1820   First Federal census; population 127,901.
William R. King and John W. Walker, first United States Senators from Alabama; John Crowell, Representative.
April 21. Federal District Court established.
Dec. Univ. of Alabama chartered. State Bank authorized.

1821   Patrol system established to prevent escape of slaves.
March 1. First Alabama Presbytery organized at Cahaba.

1824   Dec. 7. Survey of Muscle Shoals for canal ordered.

1825   Vicarate Apostolic of Alabama created by Roman Catholics.
Protestant Episcopal Church organized in Mobile.
April 3. General Lafayette welcomed at Montgomery.

1826   Seat of government moved to Tuscaloosa.
1827   Disastrous fire sweeps Mobile.
       Stage mail service to New Orleans over Montgomery begins.
1828   Congressional grant of 400,000 acres along Tennessee River to finance canal at Muscle Shoals.
1829   Methodist Protestant church organized.
1830   Population 309,527.
       Sept. 27. Treaty of Dancing Rabbit Creek signed.
       Colleges founded: Spring Hill College at Mobile by Catholics; La Grange College (near Florence) by Methodists.
1831   April 19. University of Alabama opened.
       First Alabama railroad begun.
1832   Creek and Chickasaw Indians cede all land east of Mississippi.
       Bell Factory, first textile mill, incorporated.
1833   First canal in Alabama; Huntsville to Looney's Landing.
       First cotton gin factory in Autauga County.
       Nov. 13. Meteoric shower—when "stars fell on Alabama."
1834   First railroad west of Allegheny Mountains completed 44 miles eastward from Tuscumbia to Decatur.
1835   Dec. 29. Cherokee cede lands in Cherokee, DeKalb, Marshall Counties.
1836   Jan. 9. General assembly abolishes direct taxation; State Bank charged with all governmental expense.
       Creek Indians commit sporadic depredations in East Alabama.
       Transfer of Indians to Western reservations begun.
1837   National panic felt with unusual severity in Alabama. General Assembly called in session for emergency relief measures.
1838   Choctaw cede to Alabama all their lands east of Mississippi.
1839   Jan. 7. Judson College opened.
       Feb. 1. Imprisonment for debt abolished.
1840   Population 590,756.
       August to January. Disastrous drought.
       Yellow fever epidemic, 686 die in Mobile; ruinous fire in Mobile.
1841   Dec. 29. Howard College chartered.
1842   General Assembly restores State taxation.
1843   State Bank fails. Liquidated by 1853.
1845   Legislative sessions changed from annual to biennial.
1846
1847   July 13. First geological exploration of State begun by Michael Tuomey. Published, 1849.
       Dec. 4. Medical Association of Alabama founded in Mobile.
       Dec. 6. Alabama legislature meets in new capital, Montgomery.
1849   Election of judges by popular vote established.
       Dec. 14. Capitol in Montgomery burned.
1850   Population 771,623.
1851   Southern Rights Party convention at Montgomery.
       Present capitol in Montgomery completed.

1852 Feb. 6. Alabama Hospital for the Insane at Tuscaloosa authorized.

1853 Yellow fever epidemic in Mobile; 764 die.

1854 South & North Railroad, now Louisville & Nashville, begun. Juliet Ann (Opie) Hopkins, the Florence Nightingale of the Confederacy, settles in Mobile; begins work that results in establishment of Alabama Hospital.

1856 Alabama Educational Association organized.

1858 Oct. 1. Alabama Institute for Deaf, Dumb and Blind opened at Talladega.

1859 Medical College of Alabama founded in Mobile by Univ. of A.

1860 Population 964,201.
Dec. 24. Delegates elected to secession convention.

1861 Jan. State troops occupy Ft. Gaines, Ft. Morgan, Mt. Vernon. Jan. 7. Secession convention meets at Montgomery. Jan. 11. Alabama votes to secede from Union, 61 to 39.
Feb. 4. Delegates from seven southern states form provisional government of Confederate States of America at Montgomery.
Feb. 18. Jefferson Davis of Mississippi and Alexander H. Stephens, of Georgia, inaugurated at Mongomery as President and Vice President of the Confederate States.
Feb. 19. Alabama legislature appropriates $500,000 for defense; authorizes indebtedness of $3,000,000 for war.
May 21. Confederate government moved from Montgomery to Richmond.

1862 Federal blockade creates salt famine.
Aug. 24. Commander Rafael Semmes, CSN, placed in charge of the newly built *Alabama* and in first month sank 20 Federal merchant vessels on North Atlantic and gunboat *Hatteras*.

1863 Semi-submarine hand-propelled torpedo boat, the *Hundley*, built at Mobile; unsuccessful.
Aug. Legislature sets conscript ages from 16 to 60 and appropriates $1,000,000 for support of soldiers' families for remainder of the year.
Nov. Legislature votes $3,000,000 for support of soldiers' families during 1864; taxes all products 10 per cent; votes $1,500,000 for military defense.

1864 June 19. CNS raider *Alabama,* Commander Semmes, accepts challenge of Capt. Winslow of USN Kearsarge to come out of Cherbourg harbor and fight; *Alabama* sunk after sea battle.
Aug. 6. Federal squadron under Commander David G. Farragut attacks Forts Morgan and Gaines and passes minefield into Mobile Bay with loss of ironclad *Tecumseh;* in pitched battle Admiral Franklin Buchanan CSN in ironclad ram *Tennessee* fights the Federal line at close quarters. Fort Gaines surrenders; Fort Morgan, despite fierce bombardment, holds out until Aug. 22.

1865 April 2-4. Federals take Selma; destroy U. of Ala.
April 12. General Maury, CSA, evacuated Mobile. Montgomery surrenders.
May 4. General Richard Taylor, Dept. of the West, surrenders at Citronelle.
May 4-21. Civil government suspended; martial law declared.
June 21. Lewis E. Parsons appointed provisional governor.
Sept. 12. Constitutional convention; slavery abolished. Ordinance of Secession annulled; election called for November.

1866 Dec. 6. Legislature refuses to ratify 14th amendment to Constitution.

1867 March 27. State placed under military rule.

1868 July 13. Legislature ratifies 14th amendment.

1869 April. University reopens.
Nov. 24. Legislature ratifies 15th amendment.

1870 Population 996,992.

1871 Dec. 19. Birmingham granted charter by legislature.

1872 March 20. Alabama Polytechnic Institute opened at Auburn.
Daniel Pratt and H. F. DeBardeleben begin extensive mining.
Alabama & Chattanooga Ry. completed.
State Normal College opened at Florence.

1873 Cholera in Birmingham. Yellow fever in Mobile.

1874 State Normal School for Negroes opened at Marion.

1875 Nov. 16. New State constitution ratified.

1876 Public school system reorganized.
April 3. Great storm wreaks havoc throughout State.
Federal troops withdraw from Alabama.

1878 Yellow fever epidemic.

1880 Population 1,262,505.
Nov. 23. First furnace in Birmingham, Alice No. 1, goes into blast.

1881 Feb. 10. Tuskegee Normal and Industrial Institute opened by Booker T. Washington July 4.

1882 State Normal School established at Jacksonville.

1883 Feb. 23. State Department of Agriculture established.

1885 First electric street cars in the South operate in Montgomery.

1886-87 Land boom in Birmingham; lots sell at $1,000 per foot.

1888 Savannah & Western, now Central of Georgia Ry., opened to Birmingham.
March 8. First Alabama steel produced at North Birmingham furnaces and rolled in Bessemer.

1889 Feb. 28. Pensions authorized for disabled Confederate veterans.

1890 Population 1,513,017.

1892 Alabama Polytechnic Institute becomes coeducational.

1893 University of Alabama opens some courses to women; becomes coeducational in 1898.
Chair of Electrical Engineering at Auburn; first in South.

1894   Coal miners strike in northern Alabama; 10 killed in Birmingham.
1896   July-Dec. 75,000 tons of iron shipped from Alabama to foreign port, first export of iron from State.
        First hydroelectric power development on Tallapoosa River.
        July 24. First open hearth steel manufactured.
        Legislature enacts safety regulations for coal miners.
1898   Dec. 7. Confederate monument on Capitol Hill, Montgomery.
1899   First rail mill built in Birmingham.
1900   Population 1,828,697.
1901   Nov. 11. New State constitution ratified.
1902   Jan. 22. Two-hundredth anniversary of founding of Fort Louis de la Mobile, celebrated at Mobile and Twenty-Seven Mile Bluff.
1904   University of Alabama establishes first summer school.
1906   Alabama Power Company organized.
1907   United States Steel Corp. buys Tennessee Coal, Iron & R. R. Co.
1908   July 6-Aug. 31. Miner's strike in Birmingham district.
1910   Population 2,138,093.
        Wilbur Wright selects Montgomery for aviation research.
1911   April 5. State Highway Department created.
        Birmingham adopts commission form of government.
1913   Interest rates in State lowered by passage of Federal Reserve Act.
1914   Smith-Lever Act (agricultural extension) passed by Congress; Federal and State work carried on through Alabama Polytechnic Institute.
1915   Bone dry prohibition law adopted.
1916   Federal power and nitrate plant at Muscle Shoals authorized.
1917   Aug. 14. 167th Infantry, United States Army, formed from Fourth Alabama to become part of Rainbow Division in World War.
        Camp Sheridan located at Montgomery as mobilization center.
        Vocational education introduced into schools under Federal Smith-Hughes Act. 15th Amend. to U. S. Constitution (prohibition) in effect.
1918   State Child Welfare Department created.
        Workmen's compensation measure passed by Legislature.
        Maxwell Field, Montgomery, instruction camp for USAC.
1920   Population 2,348,174. Volstead prohibition enforcement act in effect.
1923   State Docks Commission created to develop port of Mobile.
        First of two $25,000,000 bond issues for good roads authorized.
1928   July. Convict lease system abolished.
1929   March. Disastrous flood in southeast Alabama.
1930   Population 2,646,248.
1932   March 21. Tornado kills 315, injuries 3,000 in State.
1933   Tennessee Valley Authority created by Congress. 21st Amend. to U. S. Constitution annuls 15th (prohibition).

1934 Jan. State Planning Commission appointed.
1935 Decision of Federal Judge W. I. Grubb denying Tennessee Valley Authority the right to sell power to cities is overruled. Aug. 28. Civil Service in counties of 200,000 or more (Jefferson) legislated. Dept. of Public Welfare established.
1936 Feb. 19. Tennessee Valley Authority's right to sell surplus power upheld by United States Supreme Court.
April 4. State Supreme Court holds civil service law constitutional.
1937 Feb. State 2 per cent sales tax imposed.
March 10. Cochrane Bridge, Mobile Bay, last to abolish toll.
March 10. Local option goes into effect.
Aug. 12. Hugo Lafayette Black, Senator, appointed justice of the U. S. Supreme Court.
1938 April 24-29. General Methodist Conference in Birmingham votes to reunite three branches separated since 1861.
1939 April. Mobile made site of $10,000,000 Army air base.
May. State civil service established.
Aug. Little Hatch bill, prohibits political activity by State county, and municipal employees and officials.
Dec. First illuminated inter-city highway in State opened between Attalla and Gadsden.
Alabama Department of Docks and Terminals established.
1940 Population 2,832,961.
1941 With the United States at war after the Japanese attack on Pearl Harbor Alabama becomes a huge arsenal, air force training field, munitions industry and center for building troop and supply ships. *Consult History.*
1948 Redstone Arsenal made center for rockets and related weapons.
1950 Population, 3,061,743. Dr. Von Braun's missile program established at Redstone.
1954 May 17. U. S. Supreme Court declared racial segregation of public schools unconstitutional and overturned policy of separate but equal education. National enforcement of civil rights legislation started long period of social and political readjustment with busing of school children, riots, and controversies.
1960 Population, 3,266, 740.
At Democratic National convention delegates from 10 Southern States repudiated majority report on platform as intended to "drive the South out of the Democratic Party." Platform endorsed civil rights legislation, guaranteed Negro voting rights, supported school desegregation.

National Presidential Election Returns Since 1940.

1940 Roosevelt, D, 250,726; Willkie, R, 42,144; Comm. 509; Soc. 190.
1944 Roosevelt, D, 190,518; Dewey, R, 44,540; Prohib. 1095; Soc. 190.

1948 Thurmond, States Rights, 171,443; Dewey, R, 40,930; Wallace, Prog. 1522; Prohib. 1085.
1952 Eisenhower, R, 149,231; Stevenson, D, 275,075.
1956 Stevenson, D, 290,344; Eisenhower, R, 195,694; Ind. 20,323.
1960 Kennedy, D, 324,050; Faubus, States R. 4,367; King, Afro-Amer. 1,485.
1964 Unpledged electors, 209,848; Goldwater, R, 479,085.
1968 Nixon, R, 146,923; Humphrey, 196,579; Wallace, 691,425.
1972 McGovern, D, 256,923; Nixon, 728,701.

Bibliography

A SELECTED LIST OF RECENT BOOKS BY ALABAMIANS
OR ABOUT ALABAMA

Chosen from Alabamiana, a check list compiled by
the Alabama Public Library Service, Montgomery.

Abernathy, Thomas Perkins. *The Formative Period in Alabama, 1815-1828.* New ed. Univ. of Alabama Press, 1965.

Akens, David S. *Historical Origins of the George C. Marshall Space Flight Center.* Huntville, 1960. Also *Rocket City, USA,* Strode, 1959, *Rockets & Rocketry,* a Picture History, Strode, 1966.

Akens, Helen Morgan. *Alabama, Mounds to Missiles.* With Virginia Pounds Brown. Strode, 1966.

Alabama Department of Education. *Alabama Course of Study.* Also *College Scholarships and Loans for High School Graduates.* Montgomery, 1964.

Alabama, University of. *History & Development of Clark Theater.* U. of A. Press, 1965.

Anderson, John Q., comp. *With the Bark On; Popular Humor of the Old South.* Vanderbilt U. Press, 1967.

Azbell, Joe Foreword by Willie Gayle. *The Riotmakers.* Montgomery, 1968.

Bankhead, Tallulah. *Tullulah, My Autobiography.* Harper, 1952.

Bell, Robert E. *The Butterfly Tree.* Lippincott, 1959.

Bellingrath Morse Foundation. *Bellingrath Gardens and the Bellingrath Home.* Mobile, 1958.

Bennett, Lerone, Jr. *What Manner of Man, Martin Luther King.* Chicago, 1964.

Cambron, James W., et al. *Handbook of Alabama Archaeology; Point Types.* Archaeological Research Assn. of Alabama, 1965.

Capote, Truman. *The Thanksgiving Visitor.* Random, 1968.

Carter, Dan T. *Scottsboro: A Tragedy of the American South.* Louisiana State U. Press, 1969.

Cheney, Cora. *The Incredible Deborah.* Scribner, 1967.

Childers, James Saxon, Jr., ed., et al. *Listen to the Leaders in Business,* 1963; *Listen to the Leaders in Engineering,* 1965; *Listen to the Leaders in Science,* 1965.

Daniel, Thomas W., et al. *Rocks and Minerals of Alabama.* University, 1966.

Deal, Babs Hodges. *The Walls Came Tumbling Down,* Doubleday, 1968; *Summer Games,* Doubleday, 1972; *Crystal Mouse,* Doubleday, 1973.

Deal, Borden. *The Tobacco Men,* Holt, 1965; *A Long Way to Go,* Doubleday, 1965; *The Advocate,* Doubleday, 1968.

Dean, Blanche Evans. *Ferns of Alabama and Fern Allies,* Northport, 1964.

Dolan, Edward F., Jr. *William Crawford Gorgas,* Cornwall Press, 1968.

Gaines, Charles. *Stay Hungry.* Doubleday, 1972.

Graff, Stewart, and Polly Anne Graff. *Helen Keller.* Garrard, 1965.

Graham, Mary Ruth. *These Came Back; A Study of Alabama Parolees.* U. of Alabama, 1965.

Graham, Shirley, with George D. Lipscomb. *Dr. George Washington Carver, Scientist.* Messner, 1944.

Green, Asa N. and Robt. T. Daland. *Revenues for Alabama's Cities.* U. of Alabama, 1956.

Griffith, Lucille. *History of Alabama, 1540-1900,* Northport, 1962.

Grove, Frank L. *Library of Alabama Lives.* Hopkinsville, 1961.

Haagen, Victor B. *Alabama: Portrait of a State.* Huntsville, 1968.

Heath, W. L. *Most Valuable Player,* Harcourt, 1973.

Hagedorn, Hermann. *Americans, A Book of Lives.* Includes Booker T. Washington, George Washington Carver, Helen Keller. Day, 1946.

Hammond, Ralph. *Ante Bellum Mansions of Alabama.* New York, 1951.

Hay, Sara Henderson. *A Footing on This Earth.* Doubleday, 1966.

Henley, John C., Jr. *This is Birmingham.* Southern Univ. Press, 1960.

Hoole, William Stanley. *And Still We Conquer, Diary of a Nazi Officer,* 1968.

Huie, William Bradford. *The Klansman.* Delacorte, 1967.

Jones, William Grover. *The Wallace Story.* Northport, 1966.

Kane, Harnett T. *Gone Are the Days.* Dutton, 1960.

King, Martin Luther, Jr. *Stride Toward Freedom: the Montgomery Story.* Harper, 1958. Also *Why We Can't Wait, Where Do We Go From Here,* and *Trumpet of Conscience,* 1964-68.

Lee, Harper. *To Kill a Mockingbird.* Lippincott, 1960.

Lee, Mildred. *The Rock and the Willow.* New York, 1963.

Ley, Willis, and Dr. Wernher von Braun. *Exploration of Mars*. Viking, 1956.

Martin, Thomas Wesley. *The Story of Horseshoe Bend National Military Park*. Southern U. Press, 1959.

Mayfield, Sara. *The Constant Circle: H. L. Mencken and His Friends*. Delacorte, 1968.

Morris, Willie, ed. *The South Today, 100 Years After Appomattox*. Harper, 1965.

Pennell, Anne Gary. *Julia S. Tutweiler and Social Progress in Alabama*. U. of Alabama Press, 1961.

Parks, Edd Winfield. *Sidney Lanier: the Man, the Poet, the Critic*. U. of Georgia, 1968.

Percy, Walker. *The Last Gentleman*. Farrar, Straus, 1966.

Randall, Ruth Painter. *I, Varina, a Biography of the Girl Who Married Jefferson Davis*. Little, 1962.

Rayford, Julian Lee, *Whistlin' Woman and Crowin' Hen, the True Legend of Dauphin Island*. Mobile, 1956.

Sanguinetti, Elise. *The Dowager*. Scribner, 1968. Also *The New Girl*, 1964, and *The Last of the Whitfields*, 1962.

Smith, Lee. *Fancy Strut*. Harper, 1973.

Sterne, Emma Gelders. *They Took Their Stand*. Crowell-Collier, 1968.

Strode, Hudson, ed. *Jefferson Davis' Private Letters, 1823-1889*. Harcourt, 1966.

Summerdell, Charles G. *Journal of George Townley Fullan*. U. of A. Press, 1972.

Van Every, Dale. *Disinherited; the Lost Birthright of the American Indian*, Morrow, 1966.

Van Braun, Wernher. *First Men to the Moon*, Holt , 1960; Also *Exploration of Mars, Space Flight, Space Frontier*.

Wallace, George Corley. *Hear Me Out*. Grosset, 1968.

Walters, John B. *Merchant of Terror*. Bobbs Merrill, 1973.

INDEX TO STATE MAP SECTIONS

Roman numerals indicate sections

Pine Hill	IV	Sheffield	I	Union Springs	VI
Plantersville	V	Springville	II	Uniontown	IV
Prairieville	IV	Sprott	V	Uriah	VII
Prattville	V	Sulligent	I		
		Sylacauga	V	Valley Head	III
Red Bay	I			Vernon	I
Reform	IV	Talladega	III		
Roanoke	VI	Theodore	VII	Walnut Grove	II
Rockford	V	Thomasville	IV	Warrior	II
Russellville	I	Townley	I	Wedowee	VI
		Troy	IX	Wetumpka	V
Safford	IV	Trussville	II	Winfield	I
Samson	VIII	Tuscaloosa	IV		
Scottsboro	II	Tuscumbia	I	Yellow Pine	VII
Seale	VI	Tuskegee	VI	York	IV
Selma	V	Tensaw	VII		

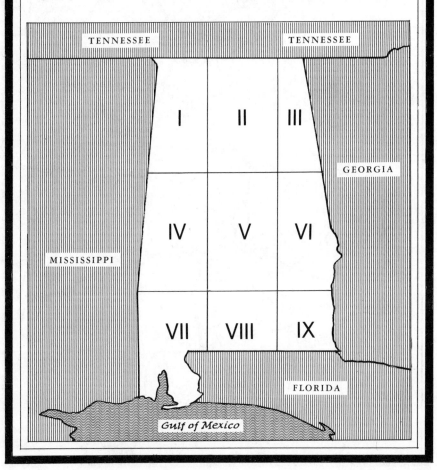

KEY

U.S. HIGHWAYS —⟨411⟩—
INTERSTATE HIGHWAYS =⟨65⟩=
STATE HIGHWAYS —⟨431⟩—

SECTIONAL DIVISION OF STATE MAP

TENNESSEE   TENNESSEE

GEORGIA

I   II   III

IV   V   VI

MISSISSIPPI

VII   VIII   IX

FLORIDA

Gulf of Mexico

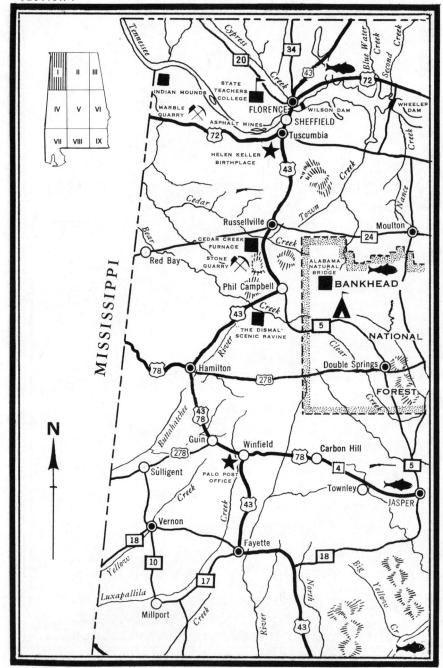

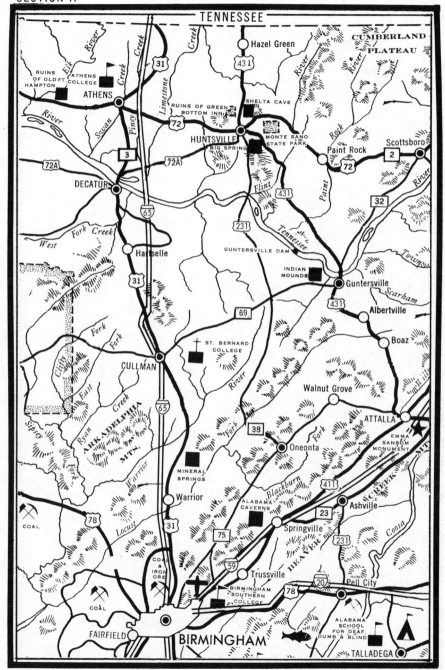

III

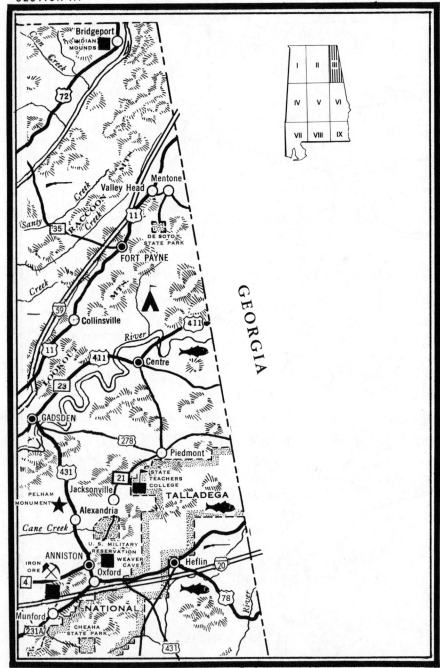

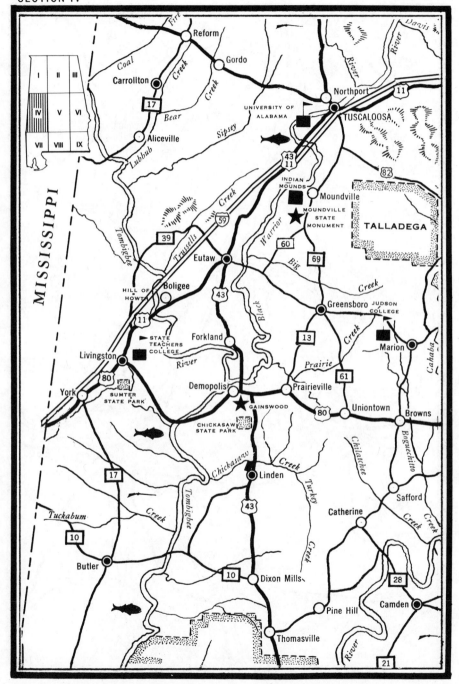

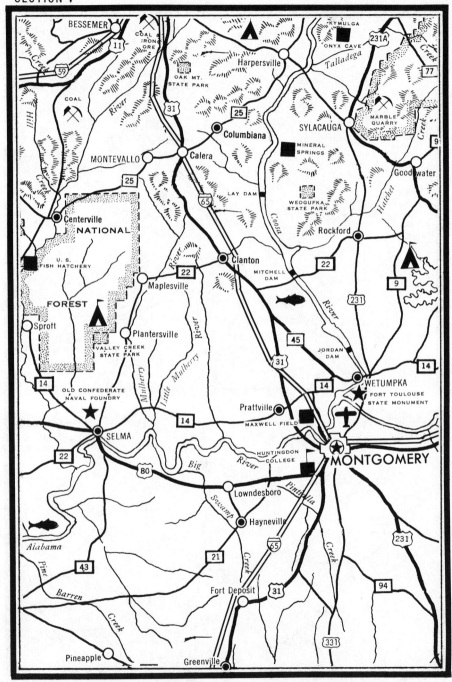

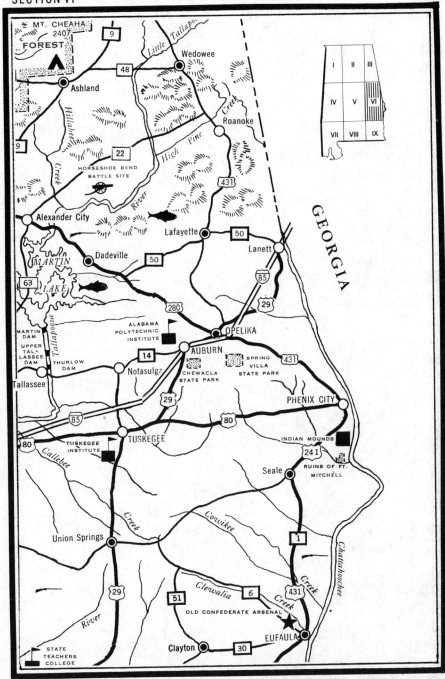

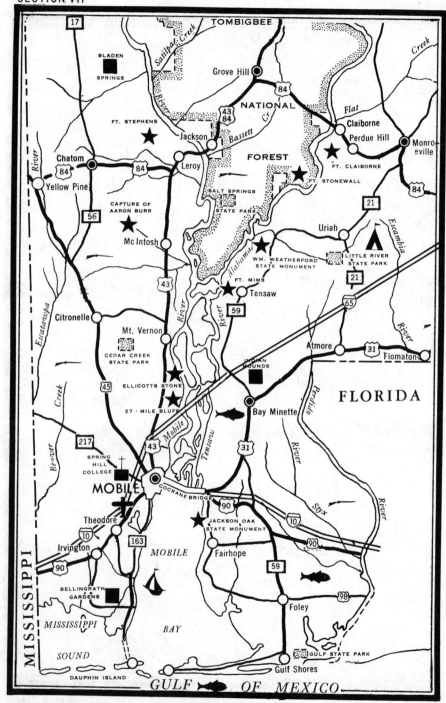

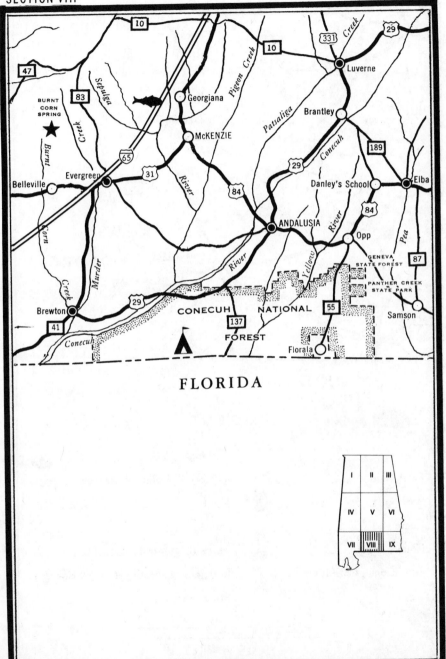

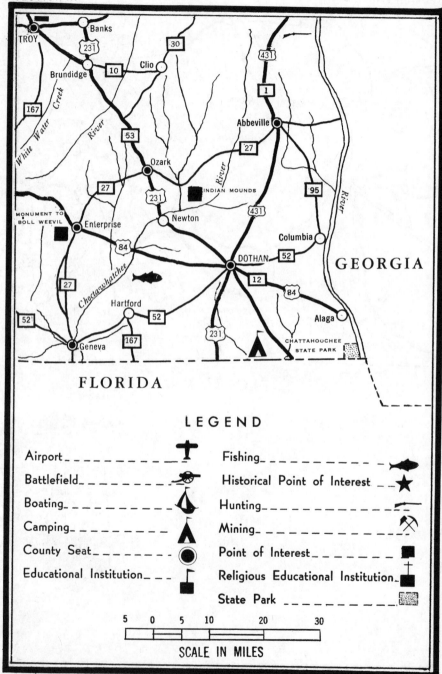

LEGEND

Airport _____ ✈

Battlefield _____ 🔫

Boating _____ ⛵

Camping _____ ▲

County Seat _____ ◉

Educational Institution ___ ⬛

Fishing _____ 🐟

Historical Point of Interest ___ ★

Hunting _____ ➵

Mining _____ ⛏

Point of Interest _____ ■

Religious Educational Institution ⬛

State Park _____ ▦

SCALE IN MILES

Index